THE ROUTLEDGE HANDBOOK OF DEMOCRACY AND SUSTAINABILITY

This handbook provides comprehensive and critical coverage of the dynamic and complex relationship between democracy and sustainability in contemporary theory, discourse and practice. Distinguished scholars from different disciplines, such as political science, sociology, philosophy and international relations, look at the present state of this relationship, asking how it has evolved and where it is likely to go in the future. They examine compatibilities and tensions, continuities and changes, as well as challenges and potentials across theoretical, empirical and practical contexts.

This wide-spanning collection brings together multiple established and emerging viewpoints on the debate between democracy and sustainability which have, until now, been fragmented and diffuse. It comprises diverse theoretical and methodological perspectives discussing democracy's role in, and potential for, coping with sustainability issues from the local to the global scales. This handbook provides a comprehensive overview of arguments, claims, questions and insights that are put forward regarding the relationship between democracy and sustainability. In the process, it not only consolidates and condenses, but also broadens and captures the many nuances of the debate.

By showing how theoretical, empirical and practical accounts are interrelated, focusing on diverse problem areas and spheres of action, it serves as a knowledge source for professionals who seek to develop action strategies that do justice to both sustainability and democracy, as well as providing a valuable reference for academic researchers, lecturers and students.

Basil Bornemann is a senior researcher and lecturer at the Social Research and Methodology Group and the Sustainability Research Group, University of Basel, Switzerland. He has an interdisciplinary study background in environmental sciences and holds a PhD in political science from Leuphana University of Lüneburg, Germany, and a venia legendi in political science and sustainability research from the University of Basel. His research focuses on sustainability-oriented governance transformations and their democratic implications in various areas such as energy and food. At present, he is involved in a research project on "Sustainabilisation of the State" funded by the Swiss National Science Foundation. Basil is further interested in principles and practices of transformative sustainability research.

Henrike Knappe is a post-doc scholar and research group leader at the Institute for Advanced Sustainability Studies (IASS) in Potsdam, Germany. Previously, she was a research associate at the Institute for Advanced Study in the Humanities (KWI) Essen and held guest fellowships at the University of Washington, Seattle and Stockholm University. Her research interests are future representations in global environmental politics, practices of translation, as well as post-colonial and feminist futures.

Patrizia Nanz is a political scientist and expert on democracy, citizen participation and sustainable transformations. Currently, she is Vice President of the Federal Office for the Safety of Nuclear Waste Disposal (BASE), Germany. She is also co-director of the Franco–German Forum for the Future, a dialogue forum for societal transformations. Previously, she has been Scientific Director at the Institute for Advanced Sustainability Studies (IASS), Co-Chair of the Science Platform Sustainability 2030 for the German government and Professor of Transformative Sustainability Science at the University of Potsdam.

THE ROUTLEDGE HANDBOOK OF DEMOCRACY AND SUSTAINABILITY

Edited by
Basil Bornemann, Henrike Knappe and Patrizia Nanz

First published 2022
by Routledge
4 Park Square, Milton Park, Abingdon, Oxon OX14 4RN

and by Routledge
605 Third Avenue, New York, NY 10158

Routledge is an imprint of the Taylor & Francis Group, an informa business

© 2022 selection and editorial matter, Basil Bornemann, Henrike Knappe and Patrizia Nanz; individual chapters, the contributors.

The right of Basil Bornemann, Henrike Knappe and Patrizia Nanz to be identified as the authors of the editorial material, and of the authors for their individual chapters, has been asserted in accordance with sections 77 and 78 of the Copyright, Designs and Patents Act 1988.

All rights reserved. No part of this book may be reprinted or reproduced or utilised in any form or by any electronic, mechanical, or other means, now known or hereafter invented, including photocopying and recording, or in any information storage or retrieval system, without permission in writing from the publishers.

Trademark notice: Product or corporate names may be trademarks or registered trademarks, and are used only for identification and explanation without intent to infringe.

British Library Cataloguing-in-Publication Data
A catalogue record for this book is available from the British Library

Library of Congress Cataloging-in-Publication Data
Names: Bornemann, Basil, editor. | Knappe, Henrike, 1985– editor. | Nanz, Patrizia, editor.
Title: The Routledge handbook of democracy and sustainability / edited by Basil Bornemann, Henrike Knappe and Patrizia Nanz.
Description: New York, NY : Routledge, 2022. | Includes bibliographical references and index.
Identifiers: LCCN 2021038853 (print) | LCCN 2021038854 (ebook) | ISBN 9780367109585 (hardback) | ISBN 9781032194936 (paperback) | ISBN 9780429024085 (ebook)
Subjects: LCSH: Sustainable development. | Democracy.
Classification: LCC HC79.E5 R67468 2022 (print) | LCC HC79.E5 (ebook) | DDC 338.9/27–dc23/eng/20211001
LC record available at https://lccn.loc.gov/2021038853
LC ebook record available at https://lccn.loc.gov/2021038854

ISBN: 978-0-367-10958-5 (hbk)
ISBN: 978-1-032-19493-6 (pbk)
ISBN: 978-0-429-02408-5 (ebk)

DOI: 10.4324/9780429024085

Typeset in Bembo
by Newgen Publishing UK

CONTENTS

List of illustrations ix
List of contributors x

1 General introduction: democracy and sustainability 1
  Basil Bornemann, Henrike Knappe and Patrizia Nanz

PART I
Origins and developments 19

2 Origins and developments of democratic thinking and practice 21
  Felix Heidenreich

3 Sustainable development: between reformist change and radical transformation 35
  Susan Baker

4 Democracy and sustainability: an evolving relationship 51
  Manuel Arias-Maldonado

PART II
Theories and concepts 67

5 Inclusion, participation and future generations 69
  Maija Setälä

6 Political representation and sustainable futures 83
  Henrike Knappe

7 Deliberation and sustainability: from policy instrument to emancipation   96
   Marit Hammond and Graham Smith

8 Temporality and democratic sustainability   107
   Rosine Kelz, Henrike Knappe and Alexander Neupert-Doppler

9 Sustainability, democracy and the value of freedom   121
   Marcel Wissenburg

10 Sustainability, well-being and justice   135
    Paul Burger and Marius Christen

PART III
Structures and dynamics   151

11 Escalating side effects: the transformation of modern society through processes of cosmopolitanization, acceleration and increasing global risks   153
    Ulrich Beck and Hartmut Rosa

12 Capitalism, consumerism and democracy in contemporary societies   163
    Karl-Michael Brunner, Michael Jonas and Beate Littig

13 Power and democracy in the transition to sustainability   178
    Lena Partzsch

14 Postsecularity and sustainable development   189
    Jens Köhrsen

PART IV
Actors and governance contexts   205

15 The modern state and sustainability: challenges to governance   207
    Daniel Fiorino

16 Corporate power and the shaping of sustainability governance   222
    Doris Fuchs and Sophie Dolinga

17 Democracy beyond the state: non-state actors and the legitimacy of climate governance   237
    Jens Marquardt and Karin Bäckstrand

18 Global governance and democracy: aligning procedural and substantive accounts?   254
    Magdalena Bexell

19 Urban sustainability and (post-)democracy: policies, practices and
    movements   267
    Marit Rosol and Vincent Béal

20 Science and democracy: partners for sustainability?   283
    Jennifer S. Bansard and Sandra van der Hel

PART V
Issues and policy areas   **299**

21 Climate change and green democratic transformations   301
    Amanda Machin

22 Biodiversity conservation and the role of democracy   313
    Stefan Ewert and Susanne Stoll-Kleemann

23 Gendered pathways of democracy to sustainability   328
    Philippe Doneys and Bernadette P. Resurrección

24 Migration and mobility: environmental, social and
    political dimensions   339
    Katrin Sontag

25 Food sustainability and food democracy: exploring the links   350
    Basil Bornemann

26 Health and human rights   368
    Markus Sperl, Anna Holzscheiter and Thurid Bahr

PART VI
Innovations and experiments   **385**

27 Behavioral economics and nudging: assessing the democratic quality of
    sustainable behavior change agendas   387
    Tobias Gumbert

28 Collaborative consumption: a mechanism for sustainability
    and democracy?   401
    Anna Davies

29 Socio-environmental movements as democratizing agents   413
    Viviana Asara

PART VII
Challenges and perspectives   **429**

30 Sustainable development and regime type: what can we learn from a comparison of democracies and autocracies?   431
    Stefan Wurster

31 Democratic governance and environmental sustainability: engaging the technocratic challenge deliberatively   447
    Frank Fischer

32 Reframing the Anthropocene: democratic challenges and openings for sustainability   461
    Ayşem Mert and Jens Marquardt

33 Post-democracy and post-sustainability   476
    Ingolfur Blühdorn

34 Structural irresponsibility: politics of an imperfect future   495
    Barbara Adam

Index   507

ILLUSTRATIONS

Figures

10.1	Eudemonic item battery for well-being/quality of life	139
10.2	Nussbaum's capability list (1999)	141
17.1	Research on non-state actor involvement in climate governance	241
30.1	Sustainability Instruments in Democracies	440

Tables

13.1	Power and responsibility for change	179
17.1	Five dimensions of the democratic values approach	240
25.1	Relating dimensions of democratic legitimacy with sustainability dimensions	362

CONTRIBUTORS

Barbara Adam is Emerita Professor at Cardiff University's School of Social Sciences, Wales, and Affiliate Scholar at the Institute for Advanced Sustainability Studies, Potsdam, Germany. The social temporal has been the key intellectual project throughout her academic career, resulting in five research monographs and a large number of articles in which she sought to bring time to the center of socio-ecological analysis. She is founding editor of the journal *Time & Society*.

Manuel Arias-Maldonado is Associate Professor of Political Science at the University of Málaga, Spain. He is the author of *Real Green: Sustainability after the End of Nature* (Routledge 2016) as well as co-editor of *Rethinking the Environment for the Anthropocene* (Routledge 2019, together with Zev Trachtenberg).

Viviana Asara is Assistant Professor (tenure track) at the Department of Human Studies at the University of Ferrara, Italy. She is a social scientist working at the intersection between social, political and environmental issues. Her research interests span democracy and state theories, social movements, grassroots/social innovations and political parties, and degrowth and social-ecological transformation. Her work has appeared in journals such as *Environmental Politics*, *Social Movement Studies*, *Environmental Values*, *Environmental Policy and Governance*, *Democratic Theory*, *Sustainability Science*, *Participation and Conflict*. She is currently editing the *Elgar Handbook of Critical Environmental Politics* together with Prof. Luigi Pellizzoni (University of Pisa) and Dr. Emanuele Leonardi (University of Parma), forthcoming in spring 2022.

Karin Bäckstrand is a professor in Environmental Social Science at the Department of Political Science at Stockholm University, Sweden. Her research revolves around global environmental politics, non-state actors in climate change governance after the Paris Agreement, the negotiation of UN sustainable development and 2030 Agenda, and the democratic legitimacy of global governance. She is a member of the Swedish government's Climate Policy Council. She has been a professor at the Department of Political Science, Lund University (2012–2014), Visiting Professor, Department of Political Science and International Relations, University of Oxford, and Wallenberg Postdoctoral Fellow on Environment and Sustainability, Laboratory for Energy and Environment, Massachusetts Institute of Technology.

List of contributors

Thurid Bahr is a social scientist with five years of empirical research experience in global health. She is a PhD fellow at Freie Universität Berlin, Germany. Thurid previously worked as a research fellow on *Governance for Global Health* (Freie Universität & WZB Berlin Social Science Center). She was a junior visiting fellow at the Graduate Institute's Global Health Centre in Geneva in spring 2018.

Susan Baker is Co-Founder and Co-Director, Sustainable Places Research Institute, Cardiff University, Wales. Her research examines the governance of complex, adaptative social-environment relations in pursuit of sustainable development. She was the first woman to be awarded a Royal Appointment as *King Carl XVI Gustaf Professor in Environmental Science*, Sweden. She received an honorary Doctorate for her contribution to interdisciplinary research from Umeå University Sweden, 2005. She has since been appointed by the UK Government to the Expert Group, United Nations Intergovernmental Science Policy Platform for Biodiversity and Ecosystem Services (IPBES). She has over 200 scientific publications and her work has been translated into several languages.

Jennifer S. Bansard is an environmental governance scholar with a background in international relations. Her research centers on science-policy practices and the role of non-state actors, such as city networks, in the sustainability transformation. In addition to her academic work, Jennifer is a team leader and writer for the Earth Negotiations Bulletin and has extensive experience covering international environmental conferences, such as those of the UN Climate Change Convention.

Vincent Béal is a senior lecturer in Sociology at the University of Strasbourg. He received a PhD from the University of Saint-Etienne, France, and then he has been a lecturer in King's College London. His current research focuses on urban environmental policies and governance, especially in declining and shrinking cities. Theoretically, he has contributed to debates on urban policy and governance, (urban) political ecology, policy mobility, and state and territorial restructuring.

Ulrich Beck is one of the world's most renowned sociologists. His book *Risk Society: Toward a Different Modernity* (1992) made him famous internationally and far beyond academic circles. After studying sociology, philosophy, psychology and political science in Munich, Beck received his doctorate there in 1972. Between 1992 and 2009, he was professor of sociology at Ludwig Maximilian University in Munich. His main research interest were the fundamental changes in modern societies, which he captured, in addition to the concept of risk, with concepts such as reflexive modernization, second modernity, unintended side effects and cosmopolitanism. Beck received several honorary doctorates from European universities and numerous awards, including the Lifetime Achievement Award – For Most Distinguished Contribution to Futures Research from the International Sociological Association at the 2014 World Sociological Congress in Yokohama, Japan. He died on January 1, 2015.

Magdalena Bexell is Associate Professor at the Department of Political Science, Lund University, Sweden. Her research is about legitimacy, accountability and responsibility in global governance, with a focus on the United Nations' 2030 Agenda for Sustainable Development. Her earlier publications concern notions of public and private in human rights protection and transnational public–private partnerships.

List of contributors

Ingolfur Blühdorn holds a Chair in Social Sustainability and is Director of the Institute for Social Change and Sustainability (IGN) at the University of Economics and Business in Vienna, Austria. He is a political sociologist and socio-political theorist. His work explores the legacy of the emancipatory social movements since the early 1970s, their participatory revolution and the transformation of emancipatory and environmental politics over the past five decades.

Basil Bornemann is a senior researcher and lecturer at the Social Research and Methodology Group and the Sustainability Research Group, University of Basel, Switzerland. He has an interdisciplinary study background in environmental sciences and holds a PhD in political science from Leuphana University of Lüneburg, Germany, and a venia legendi in political science and sustainability research from the University of Basel. His research focuses on sustainability-oriented governance transformations and their democratic implications in various areas such as energy and food. At present, he is involved in a research project on "Sustainabilisation of the State" funded by the Swiss National Science Foundation. Basil is further interested in principles and practices of transformative sustainability research.

Karl-Michael Brunner is a sociologist at the institute for sociology and social research at the University of Economics and Business in Vienna. His research focuses on sustainable consumption and production, food and energy studies, energy poverty and socio-ecological transformations.

Paul Burger is Professor and head of the Sustainability Research Group within the Department of Social Sciences, University of Basel, Switzerland. His research focuses on theoretical foundations for sustainable development including particularly its normative basis, on governance of sustainable development and on social-science-based approaches to understanding change of household (energy) consumption. He headed the work package 2 on change of behaviour within the Swiss socio-economic research center SCCER-CREST (2014–2020) and was director of the Upper Rhine Cluster for Sustainability Research (2016–2018). Among others, he is currently a member of the EU-ITN-project SmartBEEjs, looking at energy justice issues in positive energy districts.

Marius Christen studied philosophy and history at the University of Basel, Switzerland, and completed his doctorate with a thesis on the axiological fundament of sustainability. After gaining practical experience in a local Agenda 21, he returned as a lecturer and Postdoctoral Researcher to the Sustainability Research Group at the University of Basel. His research focuses on sustainability governance, especially on the sustainabilization of the state. Additional to his academic studies, he consults public administration and is interested in connecting practical with scientific knowledge.

Anna Davies is Chair of Geography Environment and Society at Trinity College Dublin, Ireland, where she directs the Environmental Governance Research Group. She is a board member of the European Roundtable on Sustainable Consumption and Production and a founding member of the Future Earth Systems of Sustainable Consumption and Production Knowledge Action Network.

Sophie Dolinga is a master's student in political science at the University of Münster, Germany, and works at the chair of Prof. Doris Fuchs. Throughout her studies in Heidelberg,

Paris and Münster, she focused on the nexus between sustainability and participation. At the intersection of sustainability research, political theory and protest research, she is particularly interested in comprehensive social change towards sustainability from a bottom-up perspective.

Philippe Doneys recently joined SEI Asia as lead of the Gender, Environment and Development research cluster. Previously he was Associate Professor in Gender and Development Studies at the Asian Institute of Technology, Thailand. His current research interests focus on the political and human rights dimensions of gender, development and environmental change.

Stefan Ewert is a political scientist and landscape ecologist. He works as a postdoctoral researcher in the Interdisciplinary Centre for Baltic Sea Region Research (IFZO) at the University of Greifswald, Germany. His research fields are agricultural policy, the politics of sustainability and peatland protection.

Daniel Fiorino is Director of the Center for Environmental Policy in the School of Public Affairs at American University, US. Recent books are *A Good Life on a Finite Earth: The Political Economy of Green Growth* (2018); *Can Democracy Handle Climate Change?* (2018); and *Conceptual Innovation in Environmental Policy* (with James Meadowcroft, 2017). He previously worked in the policy office of the U.S. Environmental Protection Agency on a variety of risk, economic and policy issues.

Frank Fischer is Distinguished Professor Emeritus Politics and Global at Rutgers University of USA and Faculty Research Fellow at the University of Kassel, Germany. Included among his numerous books are *Citizens, Experts and the Environment: The Politics of Local Knowledge* (2000) and *Climate Crisis and the Democratic Prospect: Participatory Governance in Sustainable Communities* (2017). He has also received the Harold Lasswell Award from the Policy Studies Organization and the Aaron Wildavsky Award for public policy from the American Political Science Association.

Doris Fuchs is Professor of International Relations and Sustainable Development and Speaker of the Center for Interdisciplinary Sustainability Research at the University of Münster, Germany. A political scientist and economist by training, her research focuses on the political economy of multi-level sustainability governance, and especially the power and influence of actors and structures. She addresses challenges and opportunities for sustainable consumption governance in particular, exploring the role of structural barriers and potential transformative strategies such as the development and implementation of consumption corridors. She is an expert in agrifood, climate, and energy governance.

Tobias Gumbert is currently a postdoctoral researcher/lecturer at the Institute of Political Science and the Center for Interdisciplinary Sustainability Studies in Muenster, Germany. He completed his PhD in political science at the WWU Muenster in 2019 with a study on responsibility in environmental governance where he examined the governance of food waste across scales. He is interested in issues of environmental politics and governance, focusing on the areas of food governance and waste governance, and sustainable consumption policies in particular. Most recently, he has published on freedom and ecological limits, and sustainable behavior change agendas.

List of contributors

Marit Hammond is Lecturer in Politics at Keele University, England, as well as Co-Investigator of the Centre for the Understanding of Sustainable Prosperity (CUSP). Her research interests span environmental political theory, normative democratic theory and critical theory. Recent work includes the book *Power in Deliberative Democracy: Norms, Forums, Systems* (with Nicole Curato and John B. Min, 2019) as well as numerous articles in journals such as *Environmental Politics, Environmental Values, Contemporary Political Theory, Critical Review of International Social and Political Philosophy*, and *Critical Policy Studies*.

Felix Heidenreich is a scientific coordinator at the International Center for Cultural and Technological Research at the University of Stuttgart and an associate researcher at the Center for Political Research, Sciences Po, Paris. He studied political science and philosophy in Heidelberg, Paris and Berlin with a PhD from the University of Heidelberg and a venia legendi in political science from the University of Stuttgart. He has published widely on modern political theory, cultural philosophy and business ethics. He is a member of the Green Academy of the Heinrich Böll Foundation.

Anna Holzscheiter is Professor of International Politics at TU Dresden, Germany. Since April 2015, she has been the Head of the Research Group *Governance for Global Health* at Social Science Research Centre Berlin (WZB), Germany. Previously, she was a John F. Kennedy Memorial Research Fellow at Harvard University (2014–2015), Research Fellow at the London School of Hygiene and Tropical Medicine (2007–2010), Research Associate at the Center for Transnational Relations, Foreign and Security Policy, Freie Universität Berlin (2006–2015) and Assistant Professor of International Relations at FU Berlin (2015–2019). She has published widely on global health governance, non-state actors in international politics, international human rights (particularly those of children and young persons), discourse analytical methods, and the turbulent biographies of norms in international relations.

Michael Jonas is a sociologist. His research comprises topics from economic sociology and sociology of consumption, urban sociology, sustainability studies and socio-ecological transformation research.

Rosine Kelz is a research associate in the group "Politicizing the Future" at the Institute for Advanced Sustainability Studies (IASS) in Potsdam, Germany. Previously, she was an Andrew W. Mellow Fellow in the Bio-Humanities at the Illinois Program for Research in the Humanities at the University of Illinois. She holds a DPhil in Political Theory from the University of Oxford. Her current research focuses on the role of temporality in contemporary political and moral thought. She also works on ethical and ontological questions associated with the use of new biotechnologies.

Henrike Knappe is a post-doc scholar and research group leader at the Institute for Advanced Sustainability Studies (IASS) in Potsdam, Germany. Previously, she was a research associate at the Institute for Advanced Study in the Humanities (KWI) Essen and held guest fellowships at the University of Washington, Seattle and Stockholm University. Her research interests are future representations in global environmental politics, practices of translation, as well as post-colonial and feminist futures.

Jens Köhrsen is an associate professor for "Religion and Society" at the University of Oslo. He conducted his PhD research about the relationship between religion and social inequality in Latin America. In 2013, he received his PhD in sociology for his study about the religious tastes of middle class Pentecostals in Argentina from the University of Bielefeld and the École des Hautes Études en Sciences Sociales (EHESS). From 2013, he has worked at University of Basel's Centre for Religion, Economy and Politics. Currently, Jens Koehrsen is undertaking sociological research about climate change and low carbon transitions as well as the relationship between religion and sustainable development.

Beate Littig is a sociologist and since her retirement in 2021 fellow at the Institute of Advanced Studies in Vienna. Her work focusses on the socio-ecological transformation of work(ing) societies from a feminist perspective.

Amanda Machin is currently a research fellow at the department of Philosophy, Politics and Economics and a member of the PPE Institute for Social and Institutional Change (ISIC) at the University of Witten/Herdecke in Germany. Her research focuses upon radical democratic politics and the political dynamics, identifications and discourses of socio-ecological transformation. Her books include *Society and Climate: Transformations and Challenges* (2019, co-authored with Nico Stehr) and *Negotiating Climate Change: Radical Democracy and the Illusion of Consensus* (2013) and her most recent book *Bodies of Democracy: Modes of Embodied Politics* will be published in 2022. Together with Marcel Wissenburg, she is currently editing a collection on Green Political Theory with Edward Elgar and she is a member of editorial review board, the Global Epistemics book series at Rowman & Littlefield International.

Jens Marquardt is Research Associate at the Department of Political Science at the Technical University of Darmstadt, Germany. He has previously worked on non-state climate action at the Department of Political Science at Stockholm University and the relation between climate science and politics at Harvard University's Program on Science, Technology and Society. With a background in political science and science and technology studies (STS), his research interests revolve around environmental governance, climate politics, and development. Jens is currently committed to a joint research project on the institutionalization of climate change mitigation efforts in the Global South.

Ayşem Mert is Associate Professor at the Political Science Department of Stockholm University and a member of Shadow Places and Earth System Governance networks. She uses post-structural discourse theory, critical fantasy studies and other critical approaches to study discourses of democracy and environment in the Anthropocene, public–private cooperation in sustainability governance, and the post-corona world order. She is the editor of *Earth System Governance Working Papers*, and the author of *Environmental Governance through Partnerships A Discourse Theoretical Study* (2015).

Patrizia Nanz is a political scientist and expert on democracy, citizen participation and sustainable transformations. Currently, she is Vice President of the Federal Office for the Safety of Nuclear Waste Disposal (BASE), Germany. She is also co-director of the Franco-German Forum for the Future, a dialogue forum for societal transformations. Previously, she has been Scientific Director at the Institute for Advanced Sustainability Studies (IASS), Co-Chair of the Science Platform Sustainability 2030 for the German government and Professor of Transformative Sustainability Science at the University of Potsdam.

List of contributors

Alexander Neupert-Doppler is a professor for social philosophy at Düsseldorf University of Applied Sciences in 2021/2022. Before that he was a research associate at the IASS Potsdam in 2019/2020. He holds a PhD in Political Theory/Philosophy from the University of Osnabrück, Germany. His main areas of research include state and democracy theory, utopia research, critical theory and the philosophy of history.

Lena Partzsch is Chair of Environmental Governance at the Technische Universität Berlin, since April 2021. Before, she was interim Chair of Development Politics at the University of Passau (winter 2020–2021) and Chair of Comparative Government at the University of Erfurt (winter 2019–2020, and summer 2020). Since 2018, she was an extraordinary Professor at the University of Freiburg, Germany. The University of Muenster awarded her the Habilitation (postdoctoral qualification) in 2014 and she received her PhD from Freie Universitaet Berlin in 2007. Her research deals with sustainability transitions in the Global North and South.

Bernadette P. Resurreción is currently Associate Professor and Queen's National Scholar at the Department of Global Development Studies, Queen's University, Ontario, Canada. Her research is on various dimensions of gender, environment and development in Southeast Asia.

Hartmut Rosa is Director of the Max Weber Center for Advanced Cultural and Social Studies at University of Erfurt and Chair of Sociology and Social Theory at Friedrich Schiller University, Jena, Germany. He received his PhD from Humboldt University, Berlin, in 1997 and has been a visiting professor at the New School for Social Research in New York, 2001–2006. He received numerous awards, among them the Tractatus Award and the Paul Watzlawick Ehrenring (Austria), the Erich Fromm Preis (Germany) and the Annual Rob Rhoads Global Citizenship Education Award 2020 (UCLA). His papers and books have been translated into more than 25 languages. Among his most important publications are *Alienation and Acceleration* (2007), *Social Acceleration: A New Theory of Modernity* (2013), *Resonance: A Sociology of Our Relationship to the World* (2019) and *The Uncontrollability of the World* (2020).

Marit Rosol is Canada Research Chair in Global Urban Studies and Associate Professor in the Department of Geography at the University of Calgary, Canada. She received her PhD from Humboldt-Universität zu Berlin, Germany. Her current research focuses on alternative food systems and urban-based food movements. Besides critical (urban) food studies, she also specializes in – and published widely on –housing, participation, urban gardening and governance. Theoretically, she has contributed to debates on governmentality, political economy, (urban) political ecology and hegemony.

Maija Setälä is a professor in Political Science at the University of Turku, Finland. Setälä received her PhD at the London School of Economics in 1997. Setälä specializes in democratic theory, especially theories of deliberative democracy, direct democracy and democratic innovations. She has published a number of books and articles on these topics. Currently, she leads a project entitled "Participation in Long-Term Decision-Making", funded by the Strategic Research Council of the Academy of Finland.

Katrin Sontag is a PostDoc researcher and lecturer at the University of Basel, Switzerland, in Cultural Anthropology and a fellow at the nccr – on the move in Switzerland. Her research focuses on migration and mobility, for example, in the field of migration of the highly skilled, transnational entrepreneurship, forced migration, access to higher education, negotiations of citizenship, political participation, undocumented migration, and social and political civil society initiatives.

Graham Smith is Professor of Politics and Director of the Centre for the Study of Democracy at the University of Westminster, England. He is a specialist in democratic theory and practice, with particular expertise in democratic innovations – new forms of public participation in political decision making. His publications include *Democratic Innovations: Designing Institutions for Citizen Participation* (2009) and *Can Democracy Safeguard the Future?* (2021). He is Chair of the Foundation for Democracy and Sustainable Development and Chair of the Knowledge Network on Climate Assemblies funded by the European Climate Foundation.

Markus Sperl studied Political Science and Sociology in Munich, Berlin and Copenhagen. His research interests range from Global Health to Critical Security Studies and International Political Sociology. By the time of writing the contribution, he was research assistant in Anna Holzscheiter's WZB research group *Governance for Global Health*.

Susanne Stoll-Kleemann is a geographer and political scientist. She is Professor for Sustainability Sciences and Applied Geography at the University of Greifswald, Germany. Her research fields are the psychology of sustainability and behaviour change, the management of protected areas and food consumption.

Sandra van der Hel is a research fellow and lecturer with the Copernicus Institute of Sustainable Development at Utrecht University. In her PhD research, Sandra focused on the role of science in sustainability governance. Currently, she studies the potential of creative practices for sustainability transformations as part of the H2020 CreaTures project.

Marcel Wissenburg is Professor of Political Theory at the Department of Political Science, Radboud University, and formerly Professor of Humanist Philosophy at Wageningen University, both in the Netherlands. Over the past 30 years, he has published or (co-)edited well over a hundred books and articles on green or environmental political theory, particularly from liberal and libertarian perspectives. In recent years, he focused on linking environmental and animal political theory. A monograph developing a liberal perspective on the Anthropocene has moved beyond the embryonic into an infant stage.

Stefan Wurster is Professor for Policy Analysis at the TUM School of Governance, Germany. He conducts research on policy analysis in areas closely linked to sustainability such as education, research, innovation, environmental policy and energy policy. His specific research interests include the comparison of democracies and autocracies as well as different instruments of policy regulation.

1
GENERAL INTRODUCTION
Democracy and sustainability

Basil Bornemann, Henrike Knappe and Patrizia Nanz

Relating democracy and sustainability

Democracy and sustainability are political ideas that have shaped the course of human history and continue to do so today. On a very general level, these ideas have multiple commonalities. Both have strong, universal normative implications (Dobson 1998; Sen 1999). They develop an image of the good society and, thus, also critically refer to a negatively evaluated other. The concept of democracy is oriented toward an equal and free society in which collective problems and conflicts are resolved by a demos consisting of equals in an ordered process of interest articulation and decision-making; it is the counter-model to highly asymmetrical authoritarian forms of rule, in which the suppression of freedom and autonomy of many members of society prevails (Dahl 2000; Saward 2007). Sustainability, on the other hand, refers to the negative consequences of the "unsustainable" (predominantly Western) model of development for the environment and equity of societies around the world (Christen and Schmidt 2012; Dryzek 2013). A sustainable society is imagined as one in which all present and future people have equal opportunities to satisfy their needs or even a good life in the long term (WCED 1987; Jackson 2017). The prerequisite for this is shaping human development in such a way that it remains within planetary boundaries, i.e., below tipping points for potentially sudden and severe environmental change (Meadowcroft 2012; Steffen et al. 2015). Another commonality is that democracy and sustainability are both fundamentally contested and dynamic concepts. This means that they have two levels of meaning: a relatively stable and universal first-level meaning, below which controversial debates about their respective meanings unfold on a second level (Jacobs 1999). Thus, there is general agreement that democracy means rule by the people and that sustainability requires compliance with ecosystem boundaries. However, how exactly the rule of the people and the compliance with ecosystem boundaries are to be realized and organized in concrete terms is subject to an ongoing debate. The empirical implication of this is that both democracy and sustainability do not exist in any kind of pure form but in manifold discursive, institutional, and practical manifestations that are subject to ongoing change (Hopwood, Mellor, and O'Brien 2005; Saward 2007).

Notwithstanding these basic commonalities, democracy and sustainability overall form relatively independent discourses, so that large parts of the political and scientific talk about democracy and sustainability are disconnected. Both discourses mainly move in their own ways and revolve around their own questions. Nevertheless, there is an area where the two discourses intersect and relate to each other. At the center of this interdiscourse are theoretical and empirical questions about the democratic compatibility of sustainability and, conversely, the sustainability compatibility of democracy (Lafferty and Meadowcroft 1997; Meadowcroft, Langhelle, and Rudd 2012; with a focus on climate change, see Burnell 2012). These questions are now part of the classical repertoire of green political theory and corresponding empirical research (Eckersley 2020). With some simplification, two basic positions regarding the relationship between democracy and sustainability can be identified.

First, there is the pessimistic position that assumes fundamental incompatibility between democracy and sustainability, claiming that sustainability and democracy are mutually exclusive. Both cannot be realized at the same time; democracy thrives at the expense of sustainability and vice versa. This strand of thinking goes back to the ideas according to which democratic states simply do not have the capacity to solve highly complex and urgent environmental problems (Ophuls 1977; for an overview, see Doherty and de Geus 1996). Contradictions and tensions arise, for example, between the goal orientation of sustainability and the process character of democracy. Democracy is a process that is necessarily open and not predetermined regarding its results. It aims at achieving a fair balance of different voices, opinions, and interests – a type of decision-making that can lead to the shifting of costs to non-involved future generations and, accordingly, to short-sighted decisions. In contrast, sustainability is about realizing certain objectively given and science-based functions, such as social-ecological resilience (Berkes, Colding, and Folke 2006) or a safe operating space for humanity (Rockström et al. 2009), or long-term goals that span different election cycles, such as the United Nations Sustainable Development Goals (SDGs). Moreover, while sustainability concepts stem from the recognition of the need to limit resource use and other forms of industrial production and extraction, (liberal) democracies are seen to be trapped in impasse of economic growth and environmental exploitation (Lafferty 2012; Pichler, Brand, and Görg 2020).

Apart from these functional tensions, sustainability is also seen to be at odds with the normative logic of the majority rule characteristic for democratic governance. To keep human development within the carrying capacities of the earth and achieve the just distributions of resources and ability to satisfy basic needs, far-reaching and very impactful decisions will have to be made, ones that will be against the preferences of a generally myopic majority. Therefore, sustainability governance will need to rely on modes of governance that overcome the rule of the errant majority to enforce environmental protections and social justice. For sustainability issues such as the fight against climate change, the democratic process must be suspended, at least temporarily, and the relevant decisions must be handed over to nonelected but well-intended scientific experts and political elites who can make good decisions and implement them in an effective manner (Shearman and Smith 2007).

The second position is much more optimistic because it assumes a basically productive relationship between democracy and sustainability (Mason 1999). Sustainability depends on a functioning democracy; democracy provides fertile grounds for attaining a sustainable society. From this vantage point, democracy is not the only legitimate form of organizing political life. Democracy is also the only promising route for dealing with the complexity of sustainability issues in an adequate way. Only democracy can ensure that sustainability problems are sufficiently identified, articulated, and debated in such a way that the plurality of perspectives, knowledge, and values in society can be considered (Dryzek 2000; Eckersley 2000; Smith 2003). Compared with autocracies, democracies are more responsive to the articulation of environmental concerns. The current failure of the democratic process to deal with sustainability problems is not an expression of too much democracy, but of too little. Therefore, the answer to the sustainability crisis lies in the continued democratization of democracy. This conviction has given rise to claims for the democratization of modern democracies in light of environmental and sustainability issues. Rather than abolishing democracy, political systems must reinvent and deepen their democratic structures to deal with the sustainability challenge (Eckersley 2004).

Recent transformations of democracy and sustainability

Although pessimistic and optimistic positions are still important reference points in the debate, we believe that there are good reasons to begin discussions on the relationship between democracy and sustainability from a more open middle position, one that emphasizes contingency and ambivalence in the relationship. This means that questions regarding the relationship between sustainability and democracy can hardly be answered in a definite and unequivocal way (Burnell 2012). Rather, sustainability and democracy interact differently in different contexts, which makes open and context-specific clarification and analysis necessary. This position is not only supported by empirical research that points to mixed and sometimes contested evidence regarding the sustainability performance of democracies (Scruggs 2003; Saretzki 2007; Wurster 2013). It also reflects the fact that there have been important changes in both the democracy and sustainability discourses in recent years, which also affect the relationship between democracy and sustainability. The terms and their relationship have become more significant and "visible" in political life, and there are also developments in the ways of thinking about democracy and sustainability that make it necessary to take a fresh look at the relationship between the two.

Transformations of democracy

Regarding *democracy*, we can observe both declining and reviving tendencies. Antidemocratic right-wing politicians and political agendas have emerged in all parts of the globe, and almost simultaneously, many prodemocratic and emancipatory movements have mobilized large parts of populations. Both tendencies can be linked to a growing politicization, which is understood as the opening of issues to public scrutiny and contestation (Zürn et al. 2012) that were formerly treated as purely administrative or technical issues. Sustainability issues are one area in which politicization went in both directions – the strengthening of democratic culture through vivid and controversial public debate, popular protests making visible groups and voices unheard before, and a growing awareness of the political interests and social implications behind seemingly "neutral" or technical sustainability politics. On the other hand, the politicization of sustainability issues has also led to the erosion of democratic practice and democratic systems through, for example, the use of climate change denial as a tool for authoritarian politics, the distortion and closing down of public discourse areas through disinformation campaigns, and the growing violations of environmental activists' citizen rights through threats by corporate, private, and state actors across the globe.

With these current developments and in the broader context of a globalizing world, democratic theorists and democracy scholars have proposed new concepts and tools to think about democracy by reinventing institutions or by shifting toward a more practice-oriented approach in democracy studies.

When we look back at the most recent history of democracy, we can see the decline and revival of democracy in different places and materialized as different phenomena. In Europe, for example, the governments in Poland and Hungary are actively dismantling democratic principles, such as the balance of power or citizen rights. The authoritarian populism of

Donald Trump not only eroded democratic attitudes in the US (Wodak and Krzyżanowski 2017), but also mobilized a right-wing and right extremist movement that led to devastating demonstrations around and inside the Capitol in January 2021. Political leaders such as Trump, Bolsonaro, or Putin were and are explicitly questioning democratic values, in their political communication and practice. The rise of right-wing populism and disinformation campaigns in many countries around the world even reached a new level of coalition building and extremism during the COVID-19 pandemic. Countries such as Brazil, the UK, or the US suffered from high infection rates, their citizens were kept from appropriate access to health care because their political leaders initially or partly denied the danger of the virus. Similar forms of science scepticism can also be observed with regard to the climate crisis.

At the same time, democratic values have been fought for by many social movements that were partly initiated as a reaction to those antidemocratic developments. Three emancipatory movements may serve as examples here: the women's rights movement in South America, the global climate justice movement, and the Black Lives Matter movement in the US and Europe. Mobilizing against femicides and gender-based violence, many women first gathered in Argentina in 2015 after a young girl was murdered. Under the slogans "Ni una menos" (Not one [woman] less) and "Vivas nos queremos" (We want us alive), they organized mass demonstrations that quickly spread into other countries of the region, such as Chile, Peru, Bolivia, Uruguay, Guatemala, and Mexico. The Women's March in Washington in January 2017, which occurred after the election of Donald Trump, was inspired by the Argentinian Ni Una Menos movement. In 2020, Argentina legalized first trimester abortion, which signaled success in the fight for women's rights. The global climate justice movement is a second example of how democratic values are revitalized. Since 2018, when Greta Thunberg started her school strikes, there has been a growing Fridays for Future movement that not only managed to mobilize mass demonstrations worldwide in 2019, but also managed to put the climate crisis center stage in UN negotiations, EU elections, the World Economic Forum, and many more arenas of high politics decision making. Fridays for Future activists and other young activists also challenge elected governments with climate litigation cases. By (partly successfully) suing governments to stick to the Paris Agreement goals they have signed, they fight for the democratic rights of future citizens. The Black Lives Matter movement mobilized mass protests in a momentum of rage and fear after George Floyd was murdered by a police officer in May 2020. This movement symbolizes the growing awareness of the tremendous violations of the citizen rights of black people in the US and beyond. Like the other movements, we can see the Black Lives Matter movement in the US as an emancipatory movement, here in the context of the Trump presidency and the growing violence against minority groups, as well as a discursive shift toward racist and antidemocratic narratives.

Recently, there has been growing activism and scholarship connecting the dots between different movements and highlighting their intersectionality (Irvine et al. 2019). In the three movements described above, we can observe how they all connect to struggles of north–south justice and/or racial justice. With this global approach, they attempt to highlight intersectionality as the simultaneity of multiple kinds of oppression (Crenshaw 1989). Such intersectional approaches also shed light on the multiple struggles in environmental initiatives that now increasingly combine the struggles of climate, antiracist, and antiausterity politics (Kenis 2021). Indeed, environmental justice scholars have pointed to the disproportional affectedness of marginalized groups by environmental hazards and climate change (Schlosberg and Collins 2014). At the same time, these are the groups (e.g., Global Southern actors) that are mostly excluded from decision making in environmental politics (Biermann and Möller 2019; Gereke and Brühl 2019). The different intersections of inclusion and exclusion between people in different regions of the world, people with different resources and backgrounds, and people living in the future pose challenges for democratic practice in sustainability politics. Although having eyes on the future, sustainability politics must not forget the different exclusions on a global level in the here and now (Lafferty and Meadowcroft 1997; Lawrence 2019). As Christoff and Eckersley (2013) argue, global sustainability politics face the double democratic challenge of transnationality and transtemporality: political representatives can be held accountable neither by a clear-cut geographical community, such as a nation-state, nor by a clearly defined temporal community because the impacts of their political decisions stretch into the lives of future generations. Transtemporal and transnational distances between decision makers and "affected environments" (Christoff and Eckersley 2013, 168) render even standard forms of democratic representation almost impossible.

The rethinking of democratic norms in light of a transnational sphere that is characterized by dynamic, borderless, and informal relations is a research area of international relations (IR) and democratic theory that is quite well established (Little and Macdonald 2013; Mulieri 2013; Näsström 2015; Knappe 2017). In recent years, this scholarship has been accompanied in IR by a turn to practice theory (Gadinger 2016; Holthaus 2020); this analytical shift from static democratic institutions to dynamic practices and performative claims (Saward 2010; Severs 2010; Montanaro 2018) opened up research that would analyze and evaluate democracy in and of nonstate actors in a more fine-grained manner. The focus on nonstate actors in global democracy studies is not new. Since the 1990s, an increased emphasis on nonstate actors has led scholars to investigate the role and specific practices of nonstate actors in democratizing global politics or pushing for human rights adoption (Keck and Sikkink 1998). However, the way democratic practices are studied as dynamic and evolving is a more recent field of scholarship. Kuyper and Bäckstrand (2016), for example, study the accountability practices of UN major groups and developed a detailed catalog of different practices that show how the UN major groups represent their constituencies and engage in participation and dialogue practices. In this regard, newer approaches to studying democratic practice can help to better understand the evolving and concrete interpretation of the democratic norms under circumstances of transnational and transtemporal distances in global sustainability politics.

Transformations of sustainability

When it comes to sustainability, we can observe similar politicization tendencies in terms of both the increasing relevance of sustainability topics on the political agenda and increasing political concerns about, or even in opposition to, sustainability. At the same time, the sustainability thinking has undergone significant changes since its emergence more than 30 years ago.

Starting from various historical precursors, the idea of sustainable development has evolved into a significant political idea orienting political action in multiple areas and at multiple governance levels, especially in the last 30 years (Caradonna 2016; Meadowcroft et al. 2019). This process was initiated by the so-called Brundtland Commission and its Brundtland Report, as well as a series of world conferences, starting with the UNCED in Rio in 1992 and continuing with the Rio+10 Conference in Johannesburg and the Rio+20 Conference in Rio (Baker 2015). Notwithstanding the considerable differences between contexts, sustainability has entered governmental, economic, and civil society all over the world with remarkable speed. It has found expression in governance norms, organizational structures and practices, and thereby has become an irrevocable, permanent, and "normal" point of reference in various fields of social and political action (Burns 2012; Brand 2017). Yet this "sustainabilization" of governance has occurred rather quietly in the background in terms of a cultural transformation (Hammond 2020), without sustainability being high on the political agenda (Meadowcroft 2013). In recent years, however, we observed a politicization of sustainability in several respects. On the one hand, concrete sustainability problems such as climate change, energy transition, biodiversity loss, and sustainable food have increasingly become the focus of politics and appear on the agendas of numerous actors (Scoones 2016). Driven by the pressure of social movements and scientific experts who point out the urgency of action – with Fridays for Future and Scientists for Future being probably the most prominent examples – political parties and government actors across the political spectrum have discovered sustainability issues as topics for political campaigns and policy making. As a result, sustainability issues are increasingly moving to the center of political processes and are shaping top-level politics and policy making.

In addition to this issue-oriented politicization, the sustainability agenda as a whole has received a new boost in attention with the adoption of the UN 2030 Agenda for Sustainable Development. The SDGs have found their way into all areas of life and politics with a new transformative ambition. The turn to the 2030 Agenda has been accompanied by a number of shifts in the meaning of the idea that also have implications for the conceptualization and design of corresponding governance arrangements (Biermann, Kanie, and Kim 2017; Bornemann and Christen 2021). Exemplary here are the shifts in the scope of the sustainability agenda. With the 2030 Agenda, a comprehensive understanding of sustainability has finally prevailed, which makes the purely ecological interpretations that for a long time have dominated the discourse appear too narrow. With the 2030 Agenda and the broad system of goals formulated within them, sustainability has finally freed itself from its ecological embrace and become a broader transformational approach for society as a whole. Shifts can also be seen in terms of policy linkages. Although policy integration has always been a key conceptual element of sustainability-oriented thinking and action, the focus has shifted when it comes to the 2030 Agenda. It is no longer the question of how ecological goals can be incorporated into other sectoral policies that is central, but rather, it is the complex interactions between different goals and prioritization of goals that are considered to be particularly effective transformation levers from a systemic perspective (Le Blanc 2015; Bornemann and Weiland 2021). The newly emphasized breadth of the sustainability agenda forms a contrapoint to recent trends of a creeping "climatization" of sustainability policy making, that is, the tendency to identify sustainability policy with climate policy, hence allowing other issues and perspectives of sustainable development to lose importance and be pushed to the side.

In parallel with the recent politicization and partial reinterpretation of sustainable development, especially in the wake of the 2030 Agenda, there have been numerous deliberate attempts to devalue, if not entirely discard, the idea. In the political sphere, this includes open and direct opposition to sustainable development approaches and corresponding policies. In particular, the authoritarian-populist movements that have emerged in recent years are characterized by open opposition to the supposedly cosmopolitan-elitist idea of sustainable development and related themes, such as the energy transition (Kroll and Zipperer 2020); they display open hostility to scientific experts, who they state are the vanguard of a supposedly elite-driven sustainability policy against the "true interests of the true people." They even promote a fundamental ignorance of the scientific findings on which the diagnoses of numerous sustainability problems are based. The classic example of this is climate denialism or, at least, the pronounced climate skepticism of many populist movements (Lockwood 2018).

Criticism or open rejection of sustainable development is also forming within the left-wing political camp. In contrast to right-wing populist movements, however, this criticism is not based on fundamental doubts about the scientific basis of sustainability governance.

Rather, it questions whether sustainable development is (still) the right concept to guide the necessary profound societal transformations needed to address society's fundamental multiple socio-ecological crises. Sustainable development has not only failed to deliver, but is seen as complicit with existing political-economic interests: it is merely a new attempt to maintain and stabilize existing power relations (see Blühdorn 2016; Foster 2018). To overcome the persistent unsustainability of today's societies, fundamentally different guiding orientations such as "postgrowth" or "degrowth" are necessary, which also aim at changing existing power relations (Kallis and March 2015).

Apart from this critique of the neoliberal anchoring of sustainable development, which has become increasingly prominent in recent years, critical perspectives on sustainability are also being articulated, primarily in the context of the discussion about the Anthropocene (see Arias-Maldonado 2020). Given that with the transition from the Holocene to the Anthropocene humanity has become the most significant driver in the formation of fundamental geobiophysical processes, which in turn are approaching or have already exceeded planetary boundaries, sustainable development is, according to some critics, no longer a suitable guiding principle for shaping society. The Anthropocene requires far more radical forms of change and other principles for shaping transformations. Instead of sustainable development, the resilience and adaptability of societies in the Anthropocene need to become central goals for action (see the discussion by Grove and Chandler 2017). Some authors, however, call for rescuing the normative achievements and argue for a reconceptualization of sustainable development for the Anthropocene (Norström et al. 2014; Dryzek and Pickering 2019).

New encounters between democracy and sustainability

The fact that the changes in the democracy and sustainability discourse and practice can also affect the relationship between the two concepts and related phenomena has already been pointed out in the preceding sections. On the one hand, new dividing lines or tensions between democracy and sustainability emerge, or old ones are reactivated. These include, for example, new forms of eco-authoritarianism, that is, ideas according to which some sustainability issues that are overtaxing democratic processes or point to the limits of democratic problem-solving call for alternatives to democratic governance (Beeson 2010). Eco-authoritarian approaches articulate the idea that sustainable development – because of its redistributive and limiting implications – requires effective and expert-dominated governance arrangements that are decoupled from majority decision making. A new dividing line between democracy and sustainability is also emerging in that sustainability issues are increasingly becoming the subject of political polarization, putting democratic political institutions under radicalization stress.

On the other hand, the changes in the two discourses have also improved the conditions for the development of new convergences and lines of connection. Especially over the course of the simultaneous politicization of sustainable development and democracy issues, demands for sustainability and democracy meet in different policy arenas and enter into new practical interrelationships from which novel practices of sustainability-oriented and democratic governance can emerge (Eckersley 2020). From a theoretical point of view, new ways of thinking about the relationship between democracy and sustainability can emerge because of changed theoretical perspectives and evolving practices. For example, understanding democracy in the transnational sphere allows for considering the democratizing effects of transnational sustainability governance; considering sustainability in terms of enlarged inclusiveness sheds light on new opportunities for implementing sustainable development in a more participatory and cooperative manner.

Concept of the handbook

The *Handbook on Democracy and Sustainability* is built around the proposition that in contemporary societies, the relationship between democracy and sustainability has become ever more contingent, complex, and transitory than before. Both concepts are discussed and practiced in different regions of the world at different levels by different actors touting different goals and with various intentions. The question of whether and how democracy and sustainability go together cannot be answered on a general theoretical level alone. Instead, what is required is an inquiry into how the relationship is created and maintained in political discourses and practices. Rather than one particular relationship, spheres of different more or less contradictory and functional relationships between democracies and sustainability coexist in political theory, discourse, and practice, that is, (un)democratic (un)sustainability.

Thus, the overarching questions addressed by this handbook are as follows: How are democracy and sustainability related to each other in contemporary political theory, discourse, and practice? In what respects and to what extent are they mutually supportive – and where do tensions arise? How do they relate to broader theoretical debates and ideas? What is their role in current political discourses? And how do they manifest in practices of governance and policymaking – and with what effects?

In attempting to answer these questions, the handbook seeks to accomplish three goals. First, it provides both a comprehensive overview and partly fresh perspectives on the theoretical compatibilities and tensions between democracy and sustainability in contemporary societies. Second, it gathers recent empirical insights into the ways these concepts compete with and relate to each other in discourses and practices pertaining to various problem fields and spheres of action. Third, in so doing, the handbook provides the basis for critical and constructive reflections on the prospects and limitations, along with the design and implementation, of practical political strategies to foster the democratization of sustainability and the sustainabilization of democratic governance.

In addition to consolidating and summarizing the ongoing discussion, it extends the frontiers of knowledge in this field by including fresh perspectives and drawing on recent developments in theory and practice. The handbook is explicitly interdisciplinary and draws on the knowledge and experience of scholars from various disciplines, including political theory, policy research, philosophy, sociology, cultural studies, science and technology studies, and sustainability science. Rather than remaining on a merely theoretical level or being solely oriented toward empirical knowledge, the book combines various layers and fields of analysis: political theory, discourse, and practice in different empirical subject fields and in various practical action spheres. With this basic orientation, the handbook addresses an international and interdisciplinary readership that includes researchers, professionals, university teachers, and students.

Overview of the handbook

The individual chapters of the handbook are written by established or emerging experts in their respective fields. The authors wrote their contributions based on their own interpretations, knowledge, and expertise in the subject area, but they were encouraged to flesh out the complex relationships between the concepts and related phenomena when preparing their contributions. We organized the chapters into seven parts, each representing a distinct perspective on the relationship between democracy and sustainability. In the following, we provide an overview of the various parts and related chapters and highlight some emerging themes regarding the relationship between democracy and sustainability.

General introduction

In Part I of the handbook, *Origins and developments*, the three opening chapters map the terrain of democracy and sustainability from predominantly historical perspectives. Felix Heidenreich reconstructs the interlocking historical development of democratic thought and practice, which has led to a considerable differentiation of empirical and normative frameworks of democracy. Given that democracy is a constantly contested and evolving concept bringing forth ever new democratic practices, the relationship between sustainability and democracy must always be considered in its specific historical context. In view of the currently dominant liberal tradition, which has recently been subject to academic criticism and has come under fire from populist movements, Heidenreich suggests rediscovering the republican strand of democratic thinking and practice. Because of its emphasis on the primacy of collective goods over individual interests, republicanism might be more in line with the measures that need to be taken to cope with climate change.

In her historical-reconstructive analysis of the sustainability discourse (with a special focus on the UN discourse), Susan Baker emphasizes the differences in thinking about sustainability and how these continue to play out today in a multilayered and diversified landscape of ideas and practices. Thus, in contemporary political debates, controversies between reformist and growth-oriented ideas of weak sustainability and radically oriented, transformative ideas focusing on limitations come to the fore. Depending on the position, the implications for democracy also vary. While weak forms of sustainability are certainly compatible with liberal democracy, radical variants pose particular challenges to liberal democratic thought and practice and therefore support Heidenreich's argument for republican approaches.

Manuel Arias-Maldonado brings together the two debates on democracy and sustainability, both in a historical and systematic manner. Based on observations of a historically rather antagonistic relationship between democracy and environmentalism, he argues that sustainability has now arrived at the center of liberal democracies but that tensions remain between an outcome-related material principle of sustainability and process-related understanding of democracy. These tensions can be turned into productive relations if sustainability is included in democracies as an inalienable constitutional goal framing the democratic process. Conversely, sustainability must be democratized by understanding it as a principle open to interpretation that is constantly renegotiated and fixed. The reconciliation of sustainability and democracy is particularly necessary in light of the challenges of the Anthropocene, which is about fundamentally questioning the functional conditions of both democracy and sustainable development.

The chapters of Part II, *Theories and concepts*, revolve around two fundamental conceptual debates regarding the relationship between democracy and sustainability. The first targets the question of how well democratic systems actually fit with sustainability goals and what kinds of democratic practices and innovations can enable transformations toward sustainability. The second fundamental debate centers on values of freedom, well-being, and justice and how they are in conflict or in harmony with sustainable development.

Turning to the first strand of the debate on the suitability of democratic practices and sustainability goals, different arguments are put forward. At first, the normative core of sustainability – the representation of future generations – is brought together with the architecture of democratic institutions. Maija Setälä points out that inclusion has become ever more important with the increasing importance of territorial and temporal borders. However, while transnational externalities and affectedness can already be observed, the affectedness of future generations has not yet materialized. She discusses various options of "future-sensitive" politics, concluding that the institutional barriers to representing future generations need to be addressed to effectively implement long-term policies.

The present bias and reluctance to overcome the status quo is also an important starting point in a second thread of this scholarship focusing on the possible openings in democracies for social change. Henrike Knappe reconceptualizes political representation from a constructivist theoretical angle and points out how representation practices can actually empower those who are invisible and marginalized, including future generations. In a similar vein, Marit Hammond and Graham Smith explore the emancipatory potential of deliberation for change toward sustainability; the authors advocate for a systemic approach toward deliberation and the acknowledgment that deliberation can enable transformations toward sustainability on a more fundamental level than just being a tool in the policy toolbox. Deliberation has the emancipatory potential to structurally include marginalized voices and give way to alternative thinking. With a focus on plural temporalities, Rosine Kelz, Henrike Knappe and Alexander Neupert-Doppler make a similar point, outlining the traits in democracies that enable social change and transformation toward sustainability. The authors lay out the relationship between temporality, democracy, and sustainability. Outlining the different temporalities of openness of democracies, past orientation of sustainable futures, and opportunity seeking in transformations toward sustainability, they claim that only with a plurality of temporalities can we usefully think about democratic sustainabilities.

Regarding the second strand of the literature on freedom, justice, and sustainability, Marcel Wissenburg approaches the relationship between democracy and sustainability through the value of freedom. He argues that freedom is often used as an argument to prove that democracy is not compatible with sustainability. Instead, he argues that there is not one form of sustainability; instead, there are open-ended options for numerous sustainable futures within the realm of planetary boundaries. In that sense, liberal democracy is even conducive to achieving sustainability futures if reflective spaces for choosing between different sustainability options are created and sustainability futures are not closed off by technocratic decision making. Paul Burger and Marius Christen argue for well-being and justice as the normative bases of sustainable development. Going beyond merely descriptive approaches to sustainable development, they argue that we need normativity in the concepts of well-being and justice to think about desirable futures. Following the capabilities approach by Sen and Nussbaum, well-being is defined through the specific freedoms a person owns to choose in their life. This combination of subjective and objective layers of well-being makes this approach specifically attractive. Justice, then, is well-being achieved for all.

Part III, *Structures and dynamics*, explores how the basic structural conditions of contemporary societies and politics shape the ideas and practices of democracy and sustainability and the relationship between them. The chapters point to the enabling and limiting conditions for democracy and sustainability to emerge, prevail, and become related in productive ways. Ulrich Beck and Hartmut Rosa refer to the escalating dynamics of processes of cosmopolitanization, acceleration and increasing global risks as the key hallmarks of contemporary societies, and fundamental challenges to both democracy and sustainability. Unchecked economic growth and the rise of global capitalism threaten the democratic foundations from which they emerged while propelling ecological risks such as nuclear catastrophe, global warming, or the spread of new diseases. To deal with these challenges analytically and practically, they argue for an expansion of the existing repertoire of social theory, which allows for dealing with the accelerated and cosmopolitan transformation of society in a more reflexive way.

While Beck and Rosa focus on time and space, Beate Littig, Michael Jonas and Karl-Michael Brunner deal with the material economic structures. They argue that capitalist economies and their particular forms of production, distribution, and consumption profoundly shape the conditions of democracy and sustainable development. A core challenge lies in the increasing separation of the spheres of production (economy) and consumption (lifeworld), which are primarily brokered via anonymous markets, engendering an "imperial mode of living." Given that mainstream concepts of the "green economy" tend to merely reproduce existing structures, transformative change to move away from imperial lifestyles requires a profound democratization of economic structures, including the link between production and consumption.

Lena Partzsch discusses the central role of power in shaping the possibilities of transformative change toward sustainability. She argues for an expanded understanding of power in an analysis of sustainability transitions more generally and for understanding their democratic implications in particular. While scholars tend to focus (in a negative way) on how *power over* citizens prevents them from choosing a system that allows for greater sustainability, Partzsch argues to consider more comprehensively positive notions of power in the analysis and practice of sustainability-oriented transformations. By developing forms of power that promote individual freedom (*power to*) in sustainability transformations, the links to liberal democracy can be strengthened. By taking into account the forms of power directed at producing common goods (*power with*), republican traditions of democratic thinking and practice can be activated.

Jens Köhrsen explores how changing the supposed "resurgence of religion" changes power relations because it opens the doors for religious actors to participate in sustainable development. Given the vast number of followers, grassroots reach, and material resources of religious organizations, religions are increasingly regarded as a crucial factor for sustainable development. Although often avoiding open religious argumentation, religious actors actively participate in the governance of transformation processes toward more environmentally sustainable societies and, therefore, can be regarded as promoters of a democratization of these processes.

The chapters of Part IV discuss how *Actors and governance contexts* are crucial in shaping the way democracy and sustainability relate to each other and evolve over time. Actors build practices, self-understandings, and organization in sustainability governance and relate differently to democratic norms and practices. Governance contexts create enabling or disabling factors for democratic sustainability. The modern state is one of the most important and powerful actors to implement, govern, and administrate sustainability measures. Daniel Fiorino examines the critical role of effective governance that stretches over the governance systems of ecological, economic, and social sustainability. He sees effective governance as a fourth enabling system that has an integrative capacity; this underlines the argument to focus more on the *how* of sustainability instead of the *what* and *why* questions. Doris Fuchs and Sophie Dolinga investigate the influence of transnational corporations on global sustainability governance. They identify how business actors undermine comprehensive sustainability efforts and democratic principles alike. By analyzing their instrumental, structural, and discursive power, they come to the conclusion that social-ecological transformation can only be enabled by limiting the expansion of business power and promoting sufficiency. Jens Marquardt and Karin Bäckstrand approach private actors from a different angle; they investigate the democratizing effects of civil society organizations, cities, indigenous groups, and the business sector in climate governance. By examining the different roles attributed to nonstate actors, they explore how nonstate actors succeed or fail to secure these democratic norms. In the post-Paris era, nonstate actor involvement has the potential to enhance or undermine the democratic legitimacy of climate governance. Magdalena Bexell reviews the academic debate on democracy in global (sustainability) governance, finding that procedural accounts of global democracy have dominated the scholarship. However, reconciling procedural and substantive accounts of democratization is a fruitful way to better understand the different facets of democracy in global (sustainability) governance. Marit Rosol and Vincent Béal take us from the global context to the urban context of sustainability, one that was and still is praised for its potential of sustainability governance.

The authors investigate how the early hopes in environmental democracy were countered by technocratic governance and "postpoliticization" that put citizen participation on the margins. To deal with the tensions inherent in technocratic governance, they suggest a form of deliberative environmental policy analysis. Jennifer S. Bansard and Sandra van der Hel examine the relation between science and democracy and explore the ways in which knowledge production and value considerations are "locked-in." Finding that science and society are never fully separated, they examine the implications that a lack of diversity and stable inequalities have on knowledge production in the debates on the March for Science, negative emission technologies, and planetary boundaries.

Part V, *Issues and policy areas*, is dedicated to the question of how democracy and sustainability are referred to and linked in reference to selected issues and policy areas. The contributions in this part point to several problem-specific tensions in the relationship between sustainability and democracy that require more attention, but also point to pathways for change toward democratic sustainability. In her chapter, Amanda Machin asks how contemporary democracy should be rethought in the face of a changing climate. She explores five different "pathways" for a democracy that can better respond to climate change challenges: green representation, green deliberation, green cosmopolitanism, green localism, and green agonism. Each of these pathways has different priorities and distinct conceptions of human beings and their political interaction. Stefan Ewert and Susanne Stoll-Kleemann argue that although biosphere integrity is one of the four planetary boundaries that has already been exceeded, biodiversity loss with its many dimensions is a core problem when it comes to sustainability. The authors explore how certain forms of democracy and democratic legitimacy might have a positive effect on biodiversity and whether participation is key to solving this broader sustainability problem.

Philippe Doneys and Bernadette P. Resurrección investigate how democratic governance systems remain extremely gender unequal, hence undermining the potential pathways between democracy and sustainability. Furthermore, women's lack of political decision-making power also undermines the responses to environmental and climate change mitigation and adaptation. Katrin Sontag traces three dimensions of the relationship between migration, democracy, and sustainability. She explores the linkage between climate change and migration by focusing on climate change as a cause of human movement; and goes on by concentrating on the linkages between democracy and migration by pointing to the social inclusion in migration policies of the countries of arrival as well as the political rights of migrants in democracies in Europe. Basil Bornemann analyzes the politicization of the food sector through recent debates on "sustainable food" and "food democracy." He explores the links and controversies between both debates. Finally, he proposes an integrative framework to better understand how food systems can be democratic and sustainable at the same time. Markus Sperl, Anna Holzscheiter, and Thurid Bahr apply a rights perspective in their chapter on global health and human rights; they outline the virtues, challenges, and supporting and opposing actors of a human right to health and shed light on four debates in the contemporary global health literature: universal health coverage, democracy in global health institutions, controversies in sexual and reproductive health and rights, and the relationship between planetary and human health.

Both sustainability and democracy have been the drivers of innovative societal practices. Both have encouraged experiments to try out new forms of living and collective action with the aim of making communities and society more sustainable or more democratic.

Part VI, *Innovations and experiments*, reflects on the sustainability and democratic potential of these social innovations and experiments to fill in the gaps in the synergies and tensions between democracy and sustainability in experimentation practices. Tobias Gumbert traces the debate on behavioral economics and nudging and critically interrogates the alleged advantages of both for sustainability and democracy by pointing, for example, to the misrecognition of political and democratic values beyond environmental effectiveness. He explores the different contestations of nudging which is praised as a strategy to reach sustainability goals while at the same time preserving of freedom of choice. Anna Davies outlines the practices and models of collaborative consumption that emerge at the intersection of democracy and sustainability, for example, by the figure of the citizen consumer. She investigates how consumption has become political in the field of global environmental change and focusses on the diverse organizational structures of collaborative consumption practices and their implications for matters of democracy. Similarly, Viviana Asara shows us the diversity of environmental practice. In her case, she studies socio-environmental movements and their diverse movement strategies and democratic organizing. Those movements bear transformative potential, on the one hand, and show alternatives of relating to the human and nonhuman world, on the other hand.

The chapters of the concluding seventh part, *Challenges and perspectives*, deal with the current challenges of democracy and sustainability and their implications for the relationship between the two. Each chapter develops perspectives for the theory and/or practice of sustainability-oriented democratic governance. Stefan Wurster addresses the autocratic temptation that has increasingly emerged in recent years in connection with sustainability policies; it is based on the widespread belief that many autocratic regimes succeed surprisingly well in pursuing sustainability policies. In his empirically comparative analysis, Wurster shows that many democracies actually have serious sustainability deficits, while at least some autocracies have achieved considerable success in certain areas. He further explains why so many democracies have trouble taking the interests of future generations seriously and elaborates which political instruments could help achieve more sustainability in democratic ways. Frank Fischer deals with a classical challenge to the democratic process, which has gained new momentum in recent years, especially in the context of the emergence of "postpolitical" sustainability governance: the technocratic idea and practice, according to which particularly complex problems are detached from the democratic process and dealt with by experts. Based on a reconstruction of the relations between ecological politics, democracy, and technocracy, he points to the potential of a deliberative policy analysis for the study and processing of problems of ecological sustainability.

While Wurster and Fischer address challenges to democracy, Ayşem Mert and Jens Marquardt discuss challenges posed by the rise of the Anthropocene. Based on a reconstruction of different meanings and narratives of the Anthropocene, the authors discuss how these different narratives challenge thinking about the democratic foundations of sustainable development. While a science-driven, eco-modernist, and techno-determinist view limits the space for democratic intervention, a more open, inclusive, and reflexive use of the concept can strengthen democratic debates about the means and ends of sustainability. In this respect, the emergence of the Anthropocene discourse also has the potential to repoliticize sustainability action and rethink the democratic underpinnings of sustainability governance.

Ingolfur Blühdorn develops an integrated social theoretical perspective on the current challenges in the democracy-sustainability nexus. For the emancipatory social movements of the 1980s the democratization and ecologization of modern societies were still two inseparable dimensions of the same progressive project. More recent developments – marked by terms such as "postdemocratic turn" and "postecological turn" – point to a fundamental shift in the direction of late-modern societies. In his passage through the preconditions and consequences of this shift, Blühdorn reconstructs this ongoing reconfiguration in terms of a "second silent revolution" and as "second-order emancipation." A differentiated understanding of the current politics of nonsustainability and its (post)democratic conditions is necessary for any promising attempt to overcome it.

In the closing chapter, Barbara Adam develops a broad argumentative line that connects a diagnosis of the current temporal pattern of modern societies with considerations of how to shape political action under these conditions. She addresses the chasm between the technological production of increasingly expanding futures and a horizon of political concern, action, and predictive capacity growing ever shorter. In addition, she explores new potential openings for change that connect quests for control and certainty, here in contexts of uncertainty, with genuine care and concern for the future.

Future outlook

Taken together, the contributions to this handbook open up a broad spectrum of theorizations and analyses on the current relationship between democracy and sustainability. Disregarding all the differences in terms of content between the perspectives adopted, the contributions converge in the assessment that dealing with sustainability-oriented societal transformations is a serious challenge for democratic governance. In principle democratic societies, however, do have the capacity to meet the challenges of sustainable transformation. To activate these capacities, democratic institutions and practices themselves need to change.

Today's societies face major socio-ecological challenges, with climate change as the currently most dominant expression of these multiple challenges. There is common agreement that a major sustainability-oriented transformation is urgently needed throughout society. Sustainability policies, such as national climate policies or the European Green Deal, are supposed to initiate and steer changes in individual and social practices in various fields. Such transformation policies, on the one hand, meet great societal resistance. The yellow vest movement, but also the generational conflict addressed by Fridays for Future, shows that sustainability policies are controversial in their implementation and need the democratic public to problematize the winners and losers of different transformation paths, the question of social equity, and the priorities and speed of transformations. On the other hand, the transformation outlook also generates growing engagement and acceptance for sustainability. Fridays for Future and Climate Councils are examples of how the democratic public actively calls for and gets involved in the shaping of sustainability-oriented transformations, showing that the democratic public is an important factor in the understanding of sustainability-oriented transformations.

In an increasingly politicized environment, for the sake of their own legitimacy, governments must recognize that they cannot manage this great transformation alone. In practical terms, this implies that successful transformations cannot rely on top-down governance alone; instead, they need to be complemented with participatory bottom-up approaches and increased collaboration among actors. Governments can open up spaces for the democratic public to articulate their concerns and take part in sustainability transformations. The serious promotion of bottom-up approaches can also thwart populist movements because it counteracts the populist narrative of a struggle between "us," the people, and "them," the elites.

Based on the specific perspectives highlighted in the individual contributions, at least three overarching directions for further engagement can be identified. First, from a theoretical perspective, there is a need for further clarification of the relationships between the individual conceptual elements of democracy and sustainability, as well as comprehensive approaches to democratic and sustainability-oriented governance. On the one hand, this involves elaborating on existing conceptual linkages, such as "deliberation" as a principle anchored in thinking about both democracy and sustainability. On the other hand, there is a need to further address the tensions and develop bridging arguments. For example, the question of how to conceptualize democracy's promise of freedom in a way that is compatible with the notion of limitation, which is essential to sustainable development, remains open. Future theoretical work on clarifying the relationship between democracy and sustainability should also consider more deeply how the relationship is embedded in broader societal transformations, such as cultural value change or processes of digitalization, that are constantly changing the terms of the relationship itself.

Second, the handbook opens up numerous perspectives for empirical research. In addition to validating the theoretically postulated relationships between conceptual elements in real institutional settings, elucidating the specific references or nonreferences to sustainability and democracy in concrete policy discourses, actor strategies and policy programs are of particular interest to better understand the extent to which democratic sustainability is envisioned in real politics. Moreover, it is important to gain a more nuanced understanding of the democratic consequences and effects of concrete sustainability governance arrangements and practices and, conversely, a better understanding of the sustainability effects of concrete democratic arrangements and practices in individual policy fields.

Although there are fundamental and context-specific challenges in the relationship between democracy and sustainability that are not easy to overcome on a general level, some contributions finally point to basic approaches on how the relationship between democracy and sustainability can be productively developed and shaped in practice. For example, different contributions emphasize the need to broaden the perspective of governance design on the interactions between democratic and sustainability-oriented governance arrangements and practices. Other contributions stress the need to create spaces that enable sustainability and democracy to come together and generate innovative practices that simultaneously meet democratic and sustainability-related requirements. Both approaches call for new forms of meta-governance directed at shaping the very conditions under which sustainability-oriented and democratic governance come together on the ground.

References

Arias-Maldonado, M., 2020. Sustainability in the Anthropocene: Between Extinction and Populism. *Sustainability*, 12(6): 2538. https://doi.org/10.3390/su12062538.

Baker, S., 2015. *Sustainable Development*. 2nd ed. London and New York: Routledge.

Beeson, M., 2010. The Coming of Environmental Authoritarianism. *Environmental Politics*, 19(2), 276–294. https://doi.org/10.1080/09644010903576918.

Berkes, F., Colding, J., and Folke, C., eds., 2006. *Navigating Social-Ecological Systems. Building Resilience for Complexity and Change*. Cambridge: Cambridge University Press.

Biermann, F., Kanie, N., and Kim, R.E., 2017. Global Governance by Goal-Setting: The Novel Approach of the UN Sustainable Development Goals. *Current Opinion in Environmental Sustainability*, 26/27: 26–31. https://doi.org/10.1016/j.cosust.2017.01.010.

Biermann, F. and Möller, I., 2019. Rich Man's Solution? Climate Engineering Discourses and the Marginalization of the Global South. *Int Environ Agreements*, 19(2), 151–167.

Blühdorn, I., 2016. Sustainability – Post-Sustainability – Unsustainability. In T. Gabrielson, C. Hall, J.M. Meyer, D. Schlosberg, and G. Di Chiro, eds., *The Oxford Handbook of Environmental Political Theory*. Oxford: Oxford University Press, 259–273.

Bornemann, B. and Christen, M., 2021. A New Generation of Sustainability Governance: Potentials for 2030 Agenda Implementation in Swiss Cantons. *Politics and Governance*, 9(1): 187–199. https://doi.org/10.17645/pag.v9i1.3682.

Bornemann, B. and Weiland, S., 2021. The UN 2030 Agenda and the Quest for Policy Integration: A Literature Review. *Politics and Governance*, 9(1): 96–107. https://doi.org/DOI: 10.17645/pag.v9i1.3654.

Brand, K.-W., ed., 2017. *Die Sozial-Ökologische Transformation Der Welt: Ein Handbuch*. Frankfurt a.M.: Campus.

Burnell, P., 2012. Democracy, Democratization and Climate Change: Complex Relationships. *Democratization*, 19(5): 813–842. https://doi.org/10.1080/13510347.2012.709684.

Burns, T.R., 2012. The Sustainability Revolution: A Societal Paradigm Shift. *Sustainability*, 4(6): 1118–1134. https://doi.org/10.3390/su4061118.

Caradonna, J.L., 2016. *Sustainability: A History*. New York: Oxford University Press.

Christen, M. and Schmidt, S., 2012. A Formal Framework for Conceptions of Sustainability – A Theoretical Contribution to the Discourse in Sustainable Development. *Sustainable Development*, 20(6): 400–410. https://doi.org/10.1002/sd.518.

Christoff, P. and Eckersley, R., 2013. *Globalization and the Environment*. Lanham: Rowman & Littlefield.

Crenshaw, K., 1989. Demarginalizing the Intersection of Race and Sex: A Black Feminist Critique of Antidiscrimination Doctrine, Feminist Theory and Antiracist Politics. *University of Chicago Legal Forum*, 8.

Dahl, R.A., 2000. *On Democracy*. New Haven: Yale University Press.

Dobson, A., 1998. *Justice and the Environment. Conceptions of Environmental Sustainability and Theories of Distributive Justice*. Oxford: Oxford University Press.

Doherty, B. and de Geus, M., eds., 1996. *Democracy and Green Political Thought: Sustainability, Rights, and Citizenship*. European Political Science Series. London and New York: Routledge.

Dryzek, J., 2000. *Deliberative Democracy and beyond: Liberals, Critics, Contestations*. Oxford and New York: Oxford University Press.

Dryzek, J., 2013. *The Politics of the Earth: Environmental Discourses*. 3rd ed. Oxford: Oxford University Press.

Dryzek, J. and Pickering, J., 2019. *The Politics of the Anthropocene*. Oxford and New York: Oxford University Press.

Eckersley, R., 2000. Deliberative Democracy, Ecological Representation and Risk. Towards a Democracy of the Affected. In M. Saward, ed., *Democratic Innovation. Deliberation, Representation and Association*. London and New York: Routledge, 117–132.

Eckersley, R., 2004. *The Green State: Rethinking Democracy and Sovereignty*. Cambridge: MIT Press.

Eckersley, R., 2020. Ecological Democracy and the Rise and Decline of Liberal Democracy: Looking Back, Looking Forward. *Environmental Politics*, 29(2): 214–234. https://doi.org/10.1080/09644016.2019.1594536.

Foster, J., ed., 2018. *Post-Sustainability: Tragedy and Transformation*. London: Routledge.

Gadinger, F., 2016. On Justification and Critique: Luc Boltanski's Pragmatic Sociology and International Relations. *Int Polit Sociol*, 10(3): 187–205.

Gereke, M. and Brühl, T., 2019. Unpacking the Unequal Representation of Northern and Southern NGOs in International Climate Change Politics. *Third World Quarterly*, 40(5): 870–889.

Grove, K. and Chandler, D., 2017. Introduction: Resilience and the Anthropocene: The Stakes of 'Renaturalising' Politics. *Resilience*, 5(2): 79–91. https://doi.org/10.1080/21693293.2016.1241476.

Hammond, M., 2020. Sustainability as a Cultural Transformation: The Role of Deliberative Democracy. *Environmental Politics*, 29(1): 173–192. https://doi.org/10.1080/09644016.2019.1684731.

Holthaus, L., 2020. Who Practises Practice Theory (and How)? (Meta-)theorists, Scholar-practitioners, (Bourdieusian) Researchers, and Social Prestige in Academia. *Millennium*, 48(3): 323–333.

Hopwood, B., Mellor, M., and O'Brien, G., 2005. Sustainable Development: Mapping Different Approaches. *Sustainable Development*, 13(1): 38–52.

Irvine, J.A., Lang, S., and Montoya, C., eds., 2019. *Gendered Mobilizations and Intersectional Challenges. Contemporary Social Movements in Europe and North America*. London and New York: ECPR Press; Rowman & Littlefield.

Jackson, T., 2017. *Prosperity without Growth: Foundations for the Economy of Tomorrow*. Second edition. London and New York: Routledge.

Jacobs, M., 1999. Sustainable Development as a Contested Concept. In A. Dobson, ed., *Fairness and Futurity. Essays on Environmental Sustainability and Social Justice*. Oxford: Oxford University Press, 21–45.

Kallis, G. and March, H., 2015. Imaginaries of Hope: The Utopianism of Degrowth. *Annals of the Association of American Geographers*, 105(2): 360–368. https://doi.org/10.1080/00045608.2014.973803.

Keck, M.E. and Sikkink, K., 1998 *Activists Beyond Borders: Advocacy Networks in International Politics*. Ithaca: Cornell University Press.

Kenis, A., 2021. Clashing Tactics, Clashing Generations: The Politics of the School Strikes for Climate in Belgium. *Politics and Governance*, 9(2): 135–145.

Knappe, H., 2017. *Doing Democracy Differently. Political Practice in Transnational Civil Society Networks*. Berlin: Budrich UniPress Ltd.

Kroll, C. and Zipperer, V., 2020. Sustainable Development and Populism. *Ecological Economics*, 176. https://doi.org/10.1016/j.ecolecon.2020.106723.

Kuyper, J.W. and Bäckstrand, K., 2016 Accountability and Representation: Nonstate Actors in UN Climate Diplomacy. *Global Environmental Politics*, 16 (2): 61–81.

Lafferty, W.M., 2012. Governance for Sustainable Development: The Impasse of Dysfunctional Democracy. In J. Meadowcroft, O. Langelle, and A. Ruud, eds., *Governance, Democracy and Sustainable Development*. Cheltenham: Edward Elgar Publishing, 297–337.

Lafferty, W.M. and Meadowcroft, J., eds., 1997. *Democracy and the Environment. Problems and Prospects*. Reprinted. Cheltenham: Elgar.

Lawrence, P., 2019. Representation of Future Generations. In A. Kalfagianni, D. Fuchs, and A. Hayden, eds., Routledge Handbook of Global Sustainability Governance. New York: Routledge, 88–99.

Le Blanc, D., 2015. Towards Integration at Last? The Sustainable Development Goals as a Network of Targets. *Sustainable Development*, 23(3): 176–187. https://doi.org/10.1002/sd.1582.

Little, A. and Macdonald, K., 2013. Pathways to Global Democracy? Escaping the Statist Imaginary. *Rev. Int. Stud.*, 39(4): 789–813.

Lockwood, M., 2018. Right-Wing Populism and the Climate Change Agenda: Exploring the Linkages. *Environmental Politics*, 27(4): 712–732. https://doi.org/10.1080/09644016.2018.1458411.

Mason, M., 1999. *Environmental Democracy*. London: Routledge.

Meadowcroft, J., 2012. Pushing the Boundaries: Governance for Sustainable Development and a Politics of Limits. In J. Meadowcroft, O. Langelle, and A. Ruud, eds., *Governance, Democracy and Sustainable Development*. Cheltenham: Edward Elgar Publishing, 272–296.

Meadowcroft, J., 2013. Sustainable Development. In M. Bevir, ed., *The SAGE Handbook of Governance*. London: Sage, 535–551.

Meadowcroft, J., David Banister, D., Holden, E., Langhelle, O., Linnerud, K., and Gilpin, G., eds., 2019. *What Next for Sustainable Development? Our Common Future at Thirty*. Cheltenham: Edward Elgar.

Meadowcroft, J., Langhelle, O., and Ruud, A., eds., 2012. *Governance, Democracy and Sustainable Development: Moving beyond the Impasse?* Cheltenham: Edward Elgar.

Montanaro, L., 2018. *Who Elected Oxfam? A Democratic Defence of Self-Appointed Representatives*. Cambridge: Cambridge University Press.

Mulieri, A., 2013. Beyond Electoral Democracy? A Critical Assessment of Constructivist Representation in the Global Arena. *Representation*, 49(4): 515–527.

Näsström, S., 2015. Democratic Representation Beyond Election. *Constellations*, 22(1): 1–12.

Norström, A.V., Dannenberg, A., McCarney, G., Milkoreit, M., Diekert, F., Engström, G., Fishman, R., et al., 2014. Three Necessary Conditions for Establishing Effective Sustainable Development Goals in the Anthropocene. *Ecology and Society*, 19(3): art 8. https://doi.org/10.5751/ES-06602-190308.

Ophuls, W., 1977. *Ecology and the Politics of Scarcity: Prologue to a Political Theory of the Steady State*. San Francisco: Freeman.

Pichler, M., Brand, U., and Görg, C., 2020. The Double Materiality of Democracy in Capitalist Societies: Challenges for Social-Ecological Transformations. *Environmental Politics*, 29(2): 193–213. https://doi.org/10.1080/09644016.2018.1547260.

Rockström, J., Steffen, W., Noone, K., Persson, A., Stuart, F., Lambin, E., Lenton, T.M., et al., 2009. A Safe Operating Space for Humanity. *Nature*, 461(7263): 472–475. https://doi.org/10.1038/461472a.

Saretzki, T., 2007. Demokratie und Umweltpolitik: Konzeptionelle und methodologische Probleme der makroquantitativ ausgerichteten vergleichenden Umwelt- und Demokratieforschung. In K. Jacob, F. Biermann, P.-O. Busch, and P.-H. Feindt, eds., Politische Vierteljahresschrift, Sonderheft. Wiesbaden: VS Verlag für Sozialwissenschaften, 409–429.

Saward, M., 2007. General Introduction. In M. Saward, ed., *Democracy*. London and New York: Routledge, 1–20.

Saward, M., 2010. *The Representative Claim*. Oxford: Oxford University Press.

Schlosberg, D. and Collins, L.B., 2014. From Environmental to Climate Justice: Climate Change and the Discourse of Environmental Justice. *WIREs Clim Change*, 5(3): 359–374.

Scoones, I., 2016. The Politics of Sustainability and Development. *Annual Review of Environment and Resources*, 41(1): 293–319. https://doi.org/10.1146/annurev-environ-110615-090039.

Scruggs, L.A., 2003. *Sustaining Abundance: Environmental Performance in Industrial Democracies*. Cambridge: Cambridge University Press.

Sen, A., 1999. Democracy as a Universal Value. *Journal of Democracy*, 10(3): 3–17.

Severs, E., 2010. Representation as claims-making: Quid responsiveness? *Representation*, 46(4): 411–423.

Shearman, D.J.C. and Smith, J.W., 2007. *The Climate Change Challenge and the Failure of Democracy. Politics and the Environment*. Westport: Praeger.

Smith, G., 2003. *Deliberative Democracy and the Environment*. London and New York: Routledge.

Steffen, W., Richardson, K., Rockström, J., Cornell, S.E., Fetzer, I., Bennett, E.M., Biggs, R., et al., 2015. Planetary Boundaries: Guiding Human Development on a Changing Planet. *Science*, 347(6223): 1259855. https://doi.org/10.1126/science.1259855.

WCED, 1987. *Our Common Future*. Oxford: Oxford University Press.

Wodak, R. and Krzyżanowski, M., 2017. Right-Wing Populism in Europe and USA. *JLP*, 16(4): 471–484.

Wurster, S., 2013. Comparing Ecological Sustainability in Autocracies and Democracies. *Contemporary Politics*, 19(1): 76–93. https://doi.org/10.1080/13569775.2013.773204.

Zürn, M., Binder, M., and Ecker-Ehrhardt, M., 2012. International Authority and its Politicization. *International Theory*, 4(1): 69–106.

PART I

Origins and developments

2
ORIGINS AND DEVELOPMENTS OF DEMOCRATIC THINKING AND PRACTICE

Felix Heidenreich

Introduction

When we raise the question of the relationship between sustainability and democracy, we do so in a very specific context: on the one hand, "democracy" has become a ubiquitous rhetoric trope, an uncontested source of legitimation. Almost no political regime openly opposes democracy as a binding ideal. Even regimes such as North Korea, the People's Republic of China, or the Islamic Republic of Iran claim to be democratic. Authoritarian, nationalist, and populist leaders around the world pretend to install a "true" kind of democracy. Even the enemies of liberal democracy claim to be democrats who are responsive to the "true" preferences of the true people. On the other hand, we witness a global erosion of democracy. Not only authoritarian regimes such as China or Russia are gaining influence; more importantly, we have to state that even in countries where democracy appeared to be consolidated, liberal values such as tolerance, the Rule of Law, the protection of minorities, and the freedom of the press are under attack. The empirical findings are clear: more and more governments are questioning the freedom of the press and the independence of the courts (Freedom House 2018). The analysis of the "backsliding," "deconsolidation," "decline," or "erosion" of democracy has become a genre in Political Science (see e.g., Levitsky and Ziblatt 2018; Runciman 2018; Snyder 2018).

This complex picture – rhetorical ubiquity on the one hand and actual decline on the other – is not surprising when we take into account the complex history of the term. The fact that "democracy" has always been an essentially contested concept explains that it has, today, become hard to disentangle the polysemy of this core concept of our societies. First of all, it is important to remember that, going back to the origins of the debate on democracy, the term was originally used as vituperation. Up to the early nineteenth century, the democracy mainly named the vision of plebs in power. For our context, it is important to see that the unstable and therefore unsustainable character of this form of governance was, for many centuries, viewed as the central problem. I order to outline the basis for the debate on democracy and sustainability, this chapter will: 1) reconstruct the transformation of the concept of democracy; 2) then show that our contemporary use of the term can vary from modest and purely descriptive to more ambitious and normative theories; 3) I will then try to show that different patterns and models have very different implications and consequences concerning democratic practice; 4) a brief description of the contemporary challenges of democracy; 5) will be followed by some closing remarks on democracy and sustainability.

Democracy – from "plebs in power" to ubiquitous rhetorical topos

The most prominent and influential theorist who described democracy as a system in which the plebs, the uneducated under-classes forming unstable majorities, were in power is Plato. The idea of the philosopher-kings ruling the Republic based on true knowledge can be viewed as a counter-model to what he experienced as the violent rule of the *demos*. The death of his teacher Socrates, who was condemned for *asebia*, denying the Gods, is the most personal episode in this experience. The crime of killing an innocent philosopher (Socrates was forced to poison himself) could only be explained by the ignorance of the demos. The Platonic model of a hierarchy based on competence has provoked very different interpretations. The most prominent interpretation by Sir Raimund Popper draws a line from Plato to modern illiberalism and even totalitarianism (Popper 1945). Plato's idea of the Republic, however, remains an influential model since it links *stability* to the rule of experts. Plato thereby already raises the questions which become particularly relevant in modern, more complex societies: do politicians have to rely on experts – or even be experts themselves? Can political questions be answered in the same way scientific problems are solved?

It is unclear to what degree the Egyptian practice of concentrating competence in an elite of priests, an ideal Plato seems to have observed closely, served him as a model. Clearly, he believed that the most stable and successful political government would prefer truth and competence over majorities. Plato thought that expertise in "philosophy" (i.e., knowledge-seeking) and politics would operate in the same way. Mathematics constantly serves as the decisive paradigm for Plato in order to show that "correct" answers can be given, most prominently in his dialogue *Menon*. For Plato, all knowledge is of one kind, centered around the highest idea, the *Idea of the Good*, symbolized in his famous Cave Allegory as the sun which shines its light onto and into the enlightened philosophers. The question of how to apply abstract philosophical ideas to practical problems, however, remained unresolved. Plato seems to presuppose that the philosopher-kings do not only dispose of abstract knowledge but also of the competence to apply it.

His disciple Aristotle contradicted Plato and thereby founded what is since called "practical philosophy." He distinguished between a field of knowledge which he called "theoretical" (i.e., knowledge which aims to produce correct descriptions) on the one hand and "practical" knowledge needed in ethics and politics on the other. Practical questions – and in particular political questions – demand a different kind of competence. Aristotle called this second practical knowledge *phronesis*, prudence, the "knowing-how" of application. By introducing this decisive distinction, Aristotle overcame the Platonic idea that mathematics could serve as a paradigm for politics. In practical matters, there are no "correct" answers or solutions; there are only more or less appropriate ways of dealing with complex problems, he explained. The fact that there is something fuzzy, insecure, and unstable about politics, that political decisions are always made without fully understanding all consequences, turns out to be inevitable.

The most important consequence of this re-framing of politics by Aristotle consists in a different view on rhetoric. Whereas Plato condemned rhetoric as a despicable technique of fooling the listeners, of pretending competence where it actually doesn't exist, Aristotle tried to show that in practical matters, rhetoric is an inevitable craft that does not destroy true deliberation, but which helps to succeed in exchanging arguments. This is why Aristotle did not only analyze at great length the different techniques and skills which are applied in rhetoric.

He also, in contrast to Plato, believed that emotions could be a relevant and legitimate factor in politics, that politics is based not only on "pure" cognition but also on emotional states such as courage, anger, or passion.

In a way, Aristotle's critique of Plato already opens the path towards a more inclusive idea of politics. Nevertheless, Aristotle opposes "democracy" which in his terminology is a decadent form of what he calls "polity." The term "demos" had, in Ancient Greek, a negative connotation and continues to do so in Aristotle. Demos, even for Aristotle, is an amorpha and incompetent mass, a mob. The famous Aristotelean framework of different ways of organizing politics, the set of *monarchy-tyranny; aristocracy-oligarchy* and *polity-democracy,* however, gave political philosophy a new basis which remained influential up to the present: for the first time, different systems of governance were compared with regard to their performance.

It the context of the debate on democracy and sustainability it is important to see that in the case of Aristotle the decisive criterion was *stability*; his key question was the prevention of what is called "stasis" in Greek: uproar, insurgency, the collapse of social order. Therefore, the question of sustainability is at the origin of the debate on democracy but in a restricted sense: the main problem Aristotle was dealing with is *internal* stability, not the question of the relation of the social system to its natural environment. The question of collective survival was decided in war, not in the management of human and natural resources which still appeared to be almost inexhaustible.

The question of internal stability is still at the core of Polybius' famous analysis of the Roman Republic. In book six of his *Histories* he claims that the Roman Republic managed to remain stable because it had successfully integrated *monarchic, aristocratic,* and *democratic* elements by mixing the influence of the consuls, the Senate, and the assemblies of the many. The cycle of different forms of government had thereby been integrated into one complex construct, Polybius claimed. This text is usually seen as the first formulation of the idea of mixed government, a precursor of the modern separation of powers. The idea that the inevitable conflict between different social groups needed to be institutionalized in order not to escalate was highly influential when political philosophers such as Locke and Montesquieu developed the idea of the separation of powers many centuries later. The sophisticated application of this idea is the *first* element of modern democracy. Montesquieu is probably the most important and influential author who transforms Polybius' classical idea into a new constitutional framework. When he argues for the separation of legislature, executive power and jurisdiction, it is again *internal* stability that is at stake. Montesquieu's attempt to develop a stable system of powers checking, controlling, counter-balancing each other must also be understood as a response to Hobbes' *Leviathan*. Whereas Hobbes thought that only the unrestricted power (i.e., "sovereignty") of the State could prevent chaos, Locke and Montesquieu tried to conceptualize a dynamic idea of stability. *Stability*, however, should not be taken for *sustainability* in this context. Even in Montesquieu and Locke, the challenge is rather to prevent or hedge a latent civil war, not to prevent a self-destructive collective behavior.

Classical antiquity remained a constant source of inspiration. However, it is important to see that the modern debate could refer to other examples: authors such as Locke, Montesquieu, or Rousseau also could refer to experiences that had been gathered in Republics such as Florence, Geneva, or, more importantly, the *Republic of the Seven United Netherlands*, commonly referred to in historiography as the *Dutch Republic*. The experience of self-governance had also been important on the level of city councils, most prominently in the cities of the Hanseatic League. Urban elites organizing their own collective affairs is a setting we would not call democratic today since it excluded the vast majority of the population. However, the mechanisms of election and deliberation, the idea of equality amongst citizens in these early modern polities can be viewed as a prefiguration of modern democracy.

An outstanding example is, of course, the *Republic of Venice*, a polity that existed around a thousand years from 697 to 1797. The city built in a remote lagoon by people fleeing the barbarian invasion at the end of the Roman Empire was famous for saving the skills in marine technology of Ancient Rome. The *Republic of Venice* dominated the Mediterranean Sea for Centuries since it was the only political entity capable of producing and maintaining a fleet of galleys. The founding myth of Venice is centered around the claim that two merchants from Venice managed to save the mortal remains of Saint Marcus from Alexandria. The Republic of Venice used Saint Marcus, symbolized by a lion holding a book, as an integrating myth; for centuries, people all over Europe referred to Venice as *San Marco*. Venice as a symbol of Republican Self-Rule is important for one other, more practical reason: the famous *arsenale*, Europe's greatest shipyard and armory, was a collective effort of rich Venetians merchants, a *res publica* from which success and power resulted. It became a symbol of the importance of putting private interests second, of investing collectively in Common Goods, which could then – following a well-defined protocol – be used for private purposes.

The extraordinary fame the city gained also had an important impact since it spread the idea that collective self-rule could be successful. The doge was not a king and his famous *corno ducale* (a stiff horn-like bonnet called "ducal hat") was not a crown, but referred to the Phrygian cap, a symbol of Ancient democracy. The doge of Venice had wide-ranging executive powers, but he was also controlled by the council of the old families. Again, the model of mixed government seemed to work: the doge, the Senate, and the *gran consiglio* represented all three elements, monarchic, aristocratic, and democratic. The Venetian theorist Gasparo Contarini published a book on the *Commonwealth and Government of Venice* in 1543 in which the success of this arrangement was celebrated (Skinner 1997, 141).

Up to the eighteenth century the term "Republic" still operates as the opposite of "democracy." The practice of self-government, as it can be found in Venice, Geneva, or parts of Switzerland, implied an almost aristocratic element which can be compared to the Roman practice of attributing privileges to certain families. In Venice the "old families" (*famiglie vechie*) had a special status that allowed them to take part in all important decisions. Even the democratic revolutions of 1776 and 1789 excluded not only huge parts of the population, but above all people of color and women. Olympe de Gouges declared the *Rights of Women* as being an indispensable part of the revolutionary project, but the full inclusion of women came late and continues to be an unfulfilled promise.

Although the promise of democracy was unfulfilled, it became, in the great revolutions in America and France, fixated on paper for the first time: democracy as an ideal seems to be strongly linked to certain texts, declarations (of independence or of rights), and, more importantly, constitutions. The idea that rules, laws, and the constitution need to be written down and that everyone should have access to them is a *second* element of modern democracy. Antiquity knew some kind of "basic laws," but modernity is marked by the idea that the rules of the democratic game can and need to be fixed in a written constitution. Whereas in Antiquity, books served mainly as a tool for memorizing texts, the printing press had completely changed the cultural environment of politics: modern democracy is also based on modern media, above all the printing press. The idea that a set of transparent and coherent rules could serve as a common basis of a political community had an enormous impact. Constitutions can be viewed as collective techniques of self-binding, of limiting the collective range of options. This basic intuition dating from the constitutionalism of the eighteenth century today operates in the background of the debate concerning the option of defining sustainability as a constitutional obligation.

Besides the conceptualization of the Separation of Powers and the continuing efforts to base the political system on written constitutions, the Athenian model of self-government was overcome by a *third* decisive invention: political representation. In Athens, all citizens were expected to take part in the administration of public goods, and a system of lot was to assign public offices, such as those of judges. Of course, only a very small percentage of the population would count as citizens. However, those who were part of the *polis* had good reasons to think that they were *directly* governing themselves. In Switzerland, the so-called "Landsgemeinde," an assembly of all citizens of a Canton, is still practiced in places such as Glarus. The democratic revolutions of the eighteenth century, in contrast, established elections as the decisive mechanism for recruiting political elites (Manin 2010). Since this time, the idea of democracy and the role of elections are deeply linked: we cannot, today, imagine a democracy without elections, not even in a system marked by elements of direct democracy such as Switzerland. Free and fair elections are today the minimal criterion for democracy, even in countries with a strong tradition of referenda.

Rousseau is one of the first to critique this model of indirect self-rule. In his *Contrat social*, he argued that all political representation would cut the political body (*le corps social*) into two. From this point of view, elections consist not in expressing one's preferences but rather in giving away one's voice. Representation has often been viewed as an aristocratic element in modern democracies, excluding the poor, the uneducated, and those who belong to ethnic or religious minorities. The empirical findings are evident: a higher social status, more income, and higher levels of education make political participation, not only in the civil society but also in elections, more probable.

Even today, at least two competing conceptions of representation need to be distinguished: representation in a first understanding refers to *similarity* between the represented and the representing. From this point of view, delegates should do exactly what they are told by the voters and serve as their loyal appointees (*delegate-model*); in this sense, citizens also have a legitimate interest to see an adequate percentage of women, minorities, or other groups in their parliaments. To be represented then means to be mirrored, to be made present. A second interpretation is that the representatives do not have to be similar to whom they represent in order to act in their interest. This second model (*trustee-model*) would allow elderly specialists to represent the interests of a younger generation, and it would justify that legally trained experts are dominating the parliaments. Just as doctors do not need to suffer from the diseases they manage to heal, political representatives do not have the same identity as the people they are working for. Both concepts of representation seem partly legitimate: of course, voters want politicians to "be like them." They want elites to know the lives of ordinary people. On the other hand, the idea that elections should bring to power the "best," i.e., the most engaged, the brightest, the most competent, the most empathetic, expresses the aristocratic element of modern representations.

The nineteenth century could be reconstructed as a period that saw more and more inclusion; the census suffrage was more and more questioned, and the link between property and the right to vote was loosened in small steps. The right to vote for women came late, however. Some parts of Switzerland only introduced it in the 1970s after the federal government put huge pressure on the local administration. It is also important to remember that even in countries such as the USA, full democratic inclusion only began when the civil rights movement of the 1960s challenged the systematic exclusion of non-whites. In the USA, this practice continues today by other means such as gerrymandering. Another classical technique of exclusion from elections is the deliberate failure to organize elections. The quality of democratic rules is therefore strongly linked to the level of professionalism in practical matters. This is why the material dimension of democracy, the design of ballot boxes, the administration of voters or the aggregation of votes, has gained more attention in recent years. These "public things" (Honig

2017) that allow people to interact in a very concrete sense need to be fixed in many countries: modern democracy also presupposes a functioning infrastructure, a healthy public sphere, an undisputed electoral system. Democracy, we could conclude, is not only a contested and complex concept, but also a delicate practical endeavor.

Democracy – modest and ambitious definitions

The complex history of democratic practices might suggest that it is impossible to give an adequate definition of democracy. Mechanisms of self-government range, as we have seen, from the allocation of offices by lot in Athens to Republican elite rule in Venice to today's media-driven mass democracies that produce legitimacy through elections. It is therefore not surprising to see that the debate on the definition of democracy has not been closed. In order to shed some light on the complex debate, it seems helpful to distinguish, first of all, between formal, descriptive and modest definitions of democracy on the one hand and more material, normative and ambitious concepts on the other hand.

A minimal definition of democracy refers to the possibility to change the government by pre-defined, legitimate and legal mechanism: *If "the people," i.e., the citizens, cannot get rid of a government by elections or other peaceful means, the political system is not a democracy.* Historically this definition, often framed as "realist," can be found in the very influential writings of Alois Schumpeter (Schumpeter 1942). He claimed that the term democracy first and foremost refers to the idea of *competing for office*. If this competition ends, the free market of political propositions has collapsed, and democracy has ended, and power has been monopolized. Democracy in this sense also implies the existence of a legitimate opposition. The British system values this idea in a particular form: foreign guests are invited non only to talk to the Prime Minister but also to the leader of the opposition. The more general implication could be defined as the idea of a loyal opposition: opposing the government is not the same as rejecting the political system: democracy integrates the opposition into the system, gives it a legitimate place and a public role. Autocratic systems which claim to be democracies (such as the Russian Federation) show their true character via the absence of a legitimate opposition.

This first definition seems almost too modest, but it can serve as a litmus test that allows detecting anti-democratic ambitions of rulers: if their decisions, their behavior, or action aims at making the change of government impossible, they clearly try to destroy democracy. If, for example, a ruling president claims that only voter fraud could explain him losing the upcoming elections, this attack on the results of elections clearly is an attack on democracy itself. Other examples could be given to illustrate the usefulness of this minimalist definition: attacking the free press, intimidating voters, manipulating elections, or expelling the opposition from the country – all these measures clearly aim at making the change of the government by peaceful means impossible.

This minimal definition also makes more comprehensible a strong frustration among many voters: different circumstances can provoke the impression that the government never really changes, although elections have taken place. This can be the case in a consensus-based democracy like Switzerland, but it can also be the result of a fragmented party system in which coalitions may slightly change, but the government actually stays the same. The accusation of populists that a ruling "establishment" cannot be voted out of office uses (or even abuses) this intuition. This explains why it is so dangerous to claim that "there is no alternative" to policies that protect the global climate democracy always needs to make explicit the bad alternatives instead of claiming their non-existence.

Another advantage of this minimal or "realist" definition is the fact that all difficult normative questions are excluded. In this sense, the definition is primarily formal: it is sufficient to find out whether the opposition has a fair chance to compete with the government, all normative questions put aside. The more evidence can be found that the unlevelled playing field makes it impossible to change the government, no more details are needed.

This definition has, however, specific consequences once it is not used in order to describe reality but to prescribe how politicians should act. If democracy is reduced to competition around power and public offices, the idea of the common good may get lost. Democracy reduced to a market mechanism then probably ignores long-term challenges and only focuses on short-term advantages. It is, it could be argued, dangerous to convert this minimal definition into a normative model and to use exclusively economic categories in order to understand politics. If democracy is viewed as just a mechanism for negotiating conflicting interests, then the interests of coming generations can only be taken into account by constitutional courts or other expertocratic institutions.

A second, still modest but more substantial definition claims that democracy always implies two elements: the Sovereignty of the people to decide about their own destiny on the one hand and the Rule of Law on the other hand. Evidently, there is a tension between the right of the people to govern themselves by taking collectively binding decisions, and the restrictions defined by liberal individual rights protected by the Rule of Law. Whereas the first principle requires not only direct responsiveness but also a state capable of satisfying the preferences of its citizens, the second principle restricts the range of state intervention, even of politics in general. Popular initiatives and referenda are often considered to express the principle of Sovereignty in an ideal way: they seem to express what "the people" really want, as Rousseau claimed. Supreme Courts can be seen as the decisive players ready to defend the Rule of Law; they protect individual rights and limit the range of what can be decided. The idea of this fundamental tension has been theorized by different authors. Pierre Rosanvallon has proposed the terms of "democracy" (for the first element of sovereign collective decisions) and "counter-democracy" (for all the limitations, veto-players and mechanisms of hedging democratic power) (Rosanvallon 2006). Juergen Habermas has claimed that these two elements of democracy are interdependent: only if our individual rights are successfully protected by an independent judiciary we will feel sufficiently free and secure to express our opinion in the public sphere: only the Rule of Law will allow us to practice democratic self-rule. And only if the laws that define the parameters of the judiciary can be read as "our" laws will we accept their compulsory execution. Habermas' term to describe this mutual interdependence of the two basic elements of democracy is "equiprimordiality" (Habermas 1996).

This second definition seems particularly helpful in order to defend the idea of the Rule of Law against populist attacks. The populist narrative usually operates by claiming a contradiction (not a tension) between the Sovereignty of the people and the Rule of Law. Populist leaders often claim to "liberate" the "will of the people" from all the restrictions that "elites" and experts have installed by chaining democratic rule to complex laws or international treaties. This second definition helps to understand that democratic Sovereignty is never "unrestricted" or "without limits." Quite in contrast: from Polybius to Montesquieu, political philosophy has always tried to conceptualize the restriction of power and to prevent the tyranny of majorities. "Counter-democracy" in this sense is an essential part of democracy. Moreover, democratic freedom is never an unbound or limitless freedom; quite in contrast, restrictions, limitations, and checks are essential for a democratic concept of freedom. In the debate on democracy and sustainability, this idea is often transferred to the notion of natural resource limits: restricting democratic Sovereignty to "planetary boundaries" is, from this perspective, not in conflict with the ideal of democracy in general. The genealogy of democracy could be viewed, from this point of view, not as a process in which more and more freedoms have been gained. Quite in contrast, the history of democratization is also a history in which mankind has produced civilizational progress by introducing limitations to freedom, by introducing new prohibitions: the banning of torture, slavery, sexual abuse, racist speech, or sexist behavior. Democracy as a process of self-civilization from this point of view only continues if it intends to integrate the limits of the planet into its framework. This would also imply that democracy cannot and should not be separated from the idea of moral progress: raising moral standards then is something democracies always did and will continue to do.

A more ambitious definition of democracy is based on a different understanding of the ideal of equality. Whereas a modest definition would interpret the term of equality as referring to equality before the law (including general suffrage, of course), more ambitious democrats demanded not only a *formal* but *material* equality of citizens. Aristotle had already observed that extreme economic inequalities produced political instability and turmoil, a view that Martha Nussbaum referred to when she pleaded for an "Aristotelean social democratic" conception of democracy (Nussbaum 1990). The modern attempts to link legal and social justice do not only consider the question of stability, but also the idea of the dignity of man. From this point of view, the promise of democracy has been, from the beginning, to live in a society where all citizens are not only protected from slavery and legal dependence, but also from wage slavery and economic dependence. This debate has, in the last years, gained new importance as the inequality of wealth is rising to new all-time highs. Do we have to consider extremely unequal societies such as the US as oligarchies, even if the formal equality of citizens is protected by the judiciary? It is an open debate whether the ideal of democracy actually implies a certain level of economic equality amongst the citizens. Extremely unequal societies in which the promise of meritocracy is not kept and in which the recruitment of the elites depends very much on the inheritance of financial or cultural capital seem dysfunctional and unstable.

This third definition has another consequence of great importance: if democratic equality is not restricted to *legal* equality, *symbolic* inequalities gain importance. The promise of democracy can then be viewed as a promise of ever greater inclusion: inclusion of people of color, women, workers, immigrants, religious, or sexual minorities, of all those who are not part of the privileged class. The term "democracy" then does not refer to a mere system of government, but to a mindset, to a social utopia of a society without symbolic hierarchies and cultural exclusion. The mutual *recognition* of all citizens would then be a *conditio sine qua* non for democracy. This recognition however is always a matter of contestation, of struggle and conflict (Honneth 1996). Who deserves what kind of recognition for what? Can "identities" linked to race, class, and gender legitimize a specific status, even if it is a status of specific recognition?

The material and symbolic dimension of democracy continues to be contested. Just as in the case of the term "sustainability" there is no consensus on whether "democracy" implies only a formal mode of government (as Schumpeter would argue) or if it refers to a life-form, a way of interacting with the other citizens and maybe even with the natural world. In the first case, both democracy and sustainability become mere technical challenges, whereas the second understanding presupposes that both democracy and sustainability concern the whole of human existence.

In order to compare the performance of democracies with authoritarian regimes, a clear set of empirical indicators is needed. Besides abstract definitions, there are attempts to transfer the concept of democracy into a technical set of characteristics. These attempts allow empirical data to be obtained and the level of democratic quality in a given country to be quantified. The most prominent indicators in this field are the *Freedom House Index* and the *Bertelsmann Transformation Index*. They often find their basis in a list of five criteria established by Robert Dahl, namely effective participation, voting equality at the decision stage, enlightened understanding, control of the agenda, and inclusion (Dahl 1991; Dahl 2015). Although there is a never-ending debate on the theoretical presumption of these methods of operationalizing the term "democracy," there are important findings that show general global trends. In its report of 2019, Freedom House has described 13 years of democratic decline: between 2006 and 2018 the number of those countries with an improving democratic performance was lower than the number of countries which performed worse (Freedom House 2019).

Transferring such a complex term as "democracy" into a set of empirical data is not possible without accentuating specific aspects of democracy: every index has its blind spots. However, this does not at all devaluate the findings or lower the significance of the empirical research on democracy.

Empirical and normative models of democracy

The different definitions of democracy draw a line between democracies and non-democracies. However, we have already seen that democratic ideals can be realized in very different ways. Political science tries to understand how different democratic ideals, institutions, and practices form more or less coherent models.

One of the most influential comparative studies in political science is Arend Lijphart's book "Democracies: Patterns of Majoritarian and Consensus Government in Twenty-One Countries" which dates from 1984. His distinction between consensus and majoritarian models of democracy was highly influential. Starting from the empirical material of 36 countries, Lijphart argued that there are basically two ways of interpreting the ideal of democracy: collectively binding decisions can either try to integrate the opposition and refer to a broad consensus, or they can trump the minorities while promising that the opposition might win the next time. The consensus model has its most prominent example in Switzerland, where the government is formed by (almost) all parties of the parliament. Swiss democracy is also an instructive case since it shows that the consensus model usually goes hand-in-hand with a political culture that tries to find a solution everybody can accept. Political decisions then take longer, but their implementation is supported by all members of the polity. Lijphart argued that it is not a mere coincidence that the consensus model often goes hand in hand with a system of proportional elections: even smaller interest groups are integrated into parliament and heard in the public sphere.

The UK served Lijphart in order to illustrate the majoritarian counter model: here, a prime minister with a solid majority has almost no veto-players. The elections are majoritarian and are thus based on a "winner takes it all" mode, meaning that so-called "land-slide" victories are not uncommon. This system tries to establish strong majorities and produces a strict line between the supporters of the government and the opposition: cooperation between the cabinet and the shadow cabinet is not even intended. The practices of deliberation in the House of Commons are very competitive and allow the citizens to attribute responsibility clearly. The opposition is designed in order to formulate and articulate mistrust towards the government.

Both systems have clear advantages and disadvantages. So far, there is no clear evidence which of them is more conducive to successful transformations towards a sustainable society. A majoritarian model allows a high level of accountability, whereas the consensus-based rule tends to diffuse responsibility in long processes of consensus-finding. On the one hand, the case of Switzerland seems to show that a country can be very successful and operate even with four official languages if everyone is heard and all diverging interests are well balanced. Direct democracy can, however, seduce voters to put their short-term economic interests first. On the other hand, elections seem devaluated, since no matter how the results will be, at the end (almost) everybody will be back at the table anyhow. In general, it could be argued that the Swiss system moves slower but with more precision and accuracy.

Lijphart's distinction between the two models was groundbreaking when it was first published. Today it could be argued that many lines between the consensus- and the majority-level have been blurred. The rise of populist parties has established a very competitive and even agonistic mode of deliberation even in consensus-based democracies such as Switzerland. The distinction is, without any doubt, still valuable, but it seems that political polarization can change the political climate even in polities designed along the lines of the consensus model.

A less empirical and more normative distinction between three models was proposed by Juergen Habermas: the *republican model*, the *liberal model*, and the *model of deliberative democracy*. We have already seen in what way the idea of the *Res publica* was renewed in Italy, particularly in Venice and Florence. The republican model of democracy claims that sovereignty of collectively binding decisions should be allowed to trump individual preferences: the common good is more important and more legitimate than the private pursuit of happiness. Passion and love for the Republic are considered to be necessary virtues for a political community; political emotions in general, in particular the patriotic love for the own city or nation, are viewed as indispensable. In the republican tradition, political myth and the esthetic representation of the polity are therefore widespread. France often serves as an example of intense political emotions triggered by flags, hymns, or parades. Political input is considered to be more important than the protection from State-intervention. The public sphere, the *forum*, or the *piazza*, play an important role in order to generate collective decisions. The public sphere is not viewed as a mere marketplace, but as a common space where citizens live together. Often the republican tradition refers to Ancient models: Athens, the writings of Cicero, or the "free" cities of early modern Europe.

The liberal model, in contrast, views politics as a mechanism of deal-making: contrasting interests need to be balanced, and passion, even the love for the country, will only make this aggregation of interests more difficult. The liberal model often uses economic models in order to understand politics. Elections here are the most important mechanism: they lower the transactional costs and help to recruit the best personnel who is competent enough to do the job. Politics should not refer to common interests but protect the private interests of the citizens. The defense of private property and the restriction of State intervention are therefore essential to liberal thinking. The citizens are not primarily viewed as *citoyens*, but as stakeholders, paying taxes for the service of security and the implementation of laws. *Sovereignty* is primarily a quality of the individual, not of the collective. The liberal model often describes politics in economic terms: voting is framed as a kind of payment by the citizens; the political elites have to "deliver," "do their job," or "get things done." The competition between parties is conceptualized as a market mechanism in which offers need to meet the demands of the "clients," i.e., citizens.

The third model, according to Habermas, puts the idea first that democracy is about exchanging and enhancing arguments: democracy is mainly about deliberation, it claims. Habermas claims that this third model combines elements from the republican and the liberal tradition. It inherits the idea of individual rights from liberalism but integrates the idea that all citizens must have the possibility to take part in collective decision-making. The model of deliberative democracy has, since the 1980s, gained more and more importance. In many countries so-called "mini-publics" were implemented and politicians today have to lead a dialogue with the citizens. Integrating citizens into politics has, in part, become a business model, in many cases organized by private enterprises. As political decisions interfere in a more extensive way with the private life of citizens (e.g., the measures against the spreading of the corona crisis, or, more importantly, attempts to fight climate change), these mechanisms of producing the consent of citizens are more and more important.

While Habermas emphasizes the importance of a consensus, broad consensus in the case of the *republican model*, minimal or "overlapping" consensus as defined in the constitution of the *liberal model*, and procedural consensus in the *deliberative model*, another important approach, usually called "agonistic," claims that it is conflict, not consensus, which produces adherence to a polity. Democracy in this tradition is viewed as a *fundamental* competition, even as an ideological war and struggle (*agon*). Democracies are, from this point of view, always in a state of latent civil war (Mouffe 2013). Referring to the German right-wing theorist Carl Schmitt, Chantal Mouffe tries to develop a left-wing version of a radical democracy. Populism, the struggle of the underrepresented people against the elites, then suddenly becomes a progressive project (Mouffe 2018).

The decisive element of this approach consists in the distinction between a normal mode of *politics* on the one hand and a more fundamental mode called *the political* on the other. The usual everyday mode of democracy operates in a given framework, reproduces specific distinctions and excludes radical solutions through the way problems are framed. On this level, democracy is only about who wins the elections, who becomes the head of a political party and in what way certain policies need to be recalibrated. On the level of *the political*, however, the more fundamental question of *how we want to live* is asked: the frames and presuppositions themselves are questioned, new topics arise, and the mode of dealing with challenges is debated. It appears that the question of sustainability can be seen either as a matter of politics, or as a matter of the political, either in terms of an end-of-the-pipe solution or in terms of a fundamental transformation of our society. Does it question the way our democracy operates, the way we frame problems and try to cope with our challenges? Does sustainability transform democracy (Heidenreich 2018)?

In a comparable way many Marxist theorists continue to plea for a change of the "system," claiming that capitalism and sustainability are irreconcilable and that "everything" needs to change (e.g., Klein 2021). In the Marxist tradition, democracy is viewed as an unfulfilled promise as long as a fair and sustainable economic system is not established. Only the "end of capitalism" (Zizek 2017) will bring about a new, sustainable society, many Marxists claim. Although the theorists of radical democracy find a huge public resonance, their impact on the research in political science research is minimal. Terms like "capitalism" or "the system" seem unclear and contribute to generic and abstract speech in which differences between different countries (e.g., the US and Denmark, both "capitalist" countries) disappear. It is not unfair to state that Marxist theories of democracy are only to be found on the periphery of the academic field of political science.

The brief outline of different models of democracy does not give a full picture. Other approaches and theories could be added. There is, for example, a school of libertarian skepticism concerning State intervention in general, which dates back to the beginning of modernity and is still relevant, first and foremost in the US. Some of these libertarian approaches even question the idea of the modern state in general, hoping to re-privatize what has been turned into a public good in the seventeenth and eighteenth centuries. We can conclude that there will never be a consensus on how exactly democracy should look like.

The plurality of democratic ideals and practices

The tensions and ambivalences in the debate on the adequate concept of democracy are part of the concept of democracy itself, it seems. The expectations we have towards democracy are themselves to some extent contradictory. Citizens want to govern themselves freely, implement their decisions and define their common destiny. However, at the same time, they don't want to be subjugated to a tyranny of majorities and defend their private interests. Citizens want to exchange arguments but experience the frustrating fact that some issues are impossible to solve by rational discourse. Republican, liberal, and deliberative ideals are all equally relevant and are in a constant process of being balanced out. In the same way, we could argue that the two dimensions of *politics* and *the political* presuppose themselves: if there are no shared rules, mindsets, frames (*politics*), then there is nothing left to question (*the political*).

It therefore seems that the normative expectation implied in the term "democracy" is like an equation that can never be perfectly solved. Different democratic systems put their emphasis on different elements and thereby produce different frustrations. In this sense, the French historian Pierre Rosanvallon talks about an inevitable "malaise" in democracy: only totalitarian regimes promise complete satisfaction with politics, whereas grown-up democrats know that democratic politics will always remain partly frustrating. The challenge then is about finding intelligent ways of organizing this frustration.

Mark E. Warren has proposed leaving behind the debate about "models" of democracy and viewing our historical experience as a toolbox that contains different answers to different challenges. The variety of expectations embedded in the term "democracy" is so huge that we should rather use different approaches in different combinations: elections, referenda, processes of deliberation, contestation, even exiting – all these practices can be adequate for different situations (Warren 2017). Every democratic tool has its upsides and its disadvantages. The main challenge then is to find the right tool for the right problem. Complex international law may not be the adequate object for a referendum, whereas a local infrastructure might very well be decided directly. Complex moral questions (e.g., abortion rights) should only be discussed in well-defined deliberative settings to ensure that moral differences do not trigger mutual hate. Other political questions seem to be a good subject for mini-publics, whereas the religious rights of minorities are better discussed and protected in a constitutional court. The plurality of democratic decision-making presupposes a prudent attribution of topics and modes of decision-making.

However, democracies need an overlapping consensus to define what mode of decision-making should be applied in what case. It seems that in this regard, many of today's democratic societies are not only losing constitutional consensus, but even a collectively shared idea of reality: conspiracy theories and "fake news" are a new challenge to democratic problem-solving.

Whereas a plurality of democratic ideals seems legitimate and itself democratic, a plurality of "worlds" in which every group operates in its own echo chamber questions the idea of democracy fundamentally. As Hannah Arendt pointed out: in order to live and act together, we need to live in a common world. Bonnie Honig has shown that his common world is also a world of public things, of shared infrastructure, a public sphere in the general sense (Honig 2017).

Therefore, the pluralism of different normative visions of the world becomes problematic once these visions imply a different idea of the world altogether. The most obvious example of the problematic ramifications of this trend is climate change denial. Whereas Plato simply proposed to let "philosophers" (i.e., experts) rule and to exclude the foolish from politics, democracy has been reconstructed as a history of further and further inclusion. In particular the model of deliberative democracy is based on the assumption that everyone should be taken seriously, that the discourse should be "free of power" and that all arguments need to be taken into account. Today conspiracy theories have gained such an influence that some people doubt if democracy can implement the decisions necessary to organize the "great transformation" towards a sustainable future. Will only the rule of experts make this transformation possible, and should we therefore openly argue "against democracy" (Brennan 2017)? Plato's question of how to reconcile the inclusion of different views and the exclusion of non-sense seems to be back on the table.

Conclusion: the history and future of democracy and sustainability

Looking back at the origins and foundations of the debate about democracy, we can state that the term has changed its meaning fundamentally. This seems even to be true when we look at the last 40 or even 20 years. In the 1970s, many people viewed themselves as democrats, although they held racist or sexist views, opposed the public presence of homosexuality, gay marriage, or immigration. Today the term "democracy" has taken a more demanding meaning and implies the equality of ethnic or sexual minorities. Some of the contemporary rejection of democracy could be explained by this semantic shift: what was part of mainstream 50 years ago is now excluded – for good reasons.

As for now, it is unclear how the challenge of sustainability seriously will be integrated into our concept of democracy itself. Evidently, there is a correlation between populists and climate change deniers: Trump and Bolsonaro are the most evident examples. It seems plausible to suggest that republican conceptions of democracy are more in line with the measures that need to be taken in order to cope with climate change: in an age where collective action is needed and some individual freedoms need to be restricted, it seems promising to rediscover the republican tradition of democratic thinking.

However, some recent paradigm-shifting decisions by constitutional courts in the Netherlands and Germany seem to suggest that sustainability can be implemented based on liberal intuitions, namely the defense of individual freedom. An insufficient policy against climate change simply violates the rights of coming generations or those who already suffer from climate change ramifications. All attempts to reconcile democracy and sustainability from this point of view only intend to fulfill a promise already implicated in the early documents of modern democracy: equal rights for equal citizens, the freedom to live a life without being harmed directly or indirectly.

References

Brennan, J., 2017. *Against Democracy: New Preface by the Author*. Princeton: Princeton University Press.
Dahl, R., 1991. *Democracy and Its Critics*. New Haven: Yale University Press.
Dahl, R., 2015. *On Democracy*. New Haven: Yale University Press.
Freedom House, 2018. *Freedom in the World 2018. Democracy in Crisis*. Washington: Freedom House. www.freedomhouse.org
Freedom House, 2019. *Freedom in the World 2019. Democracy in Retreat*. Washington: Freedom House. www.freedomhouse.org
Habermas, J., 1996. *Between Facts and Norms. Contributions to a Discourse Theory of Law and Democracy*, translated by Regh, William. Cambridge: Polity Press.
Heidenreich, F., 2018. How Will Sustainability Transform Democracy? Reflections on an Important Dimension of Transformation Sciences. *GAIA – Ecological Perspectives for Science and Society*, 27(4): 357–362. https://doi.org/10.14512/gaia.27.4.7
Honig, B., 2017. *Public Things: Democracy in Disrepair*. New York: Fordham University Press.
Honneth, A., 1996. *Struggle for Recognition: The Moral Grammar of Social Conflicts*. Cambridge: MIT Press.

Klein, N., 2021. *How to Change Everything: The Young Human's Guide to Protecting the Planet and Each Other.* New York: Atheneum Books.
Levitsky, S. and Ziblatt, D., 2018. *How Democracies Die.* New York: Crown.
Manin, B., 2010. The Principles of Representative Government. Cambridge: Cambridge University Press.
Mouffe, C., 2013. *Agonistics: Thinking The World Politically.* London: Verso.
Mouffe, C., 2018. *For a Left Populism.* London: Verso.
Nussbaum, M., 1990. Aristotelian Social Democracy. In R.B. Douglass, G.M. Mara, and H.S. Richardson, eds. *Liberalism and the Good.* Routledge: London, 203–252.
Popper, K.R., 1945. *The Open Society and Its Enemies.* London: Routledge.
Rosanvallon, P., 2006. *Counter-Democracy.* Cambridge: Cambridge University Press.
Runciman, D., 2018. *How Democracy Ends.* London: Profile Books
Schumpter, A., 1942/2008. *Capitalism, Socialism, and Democracy.* Harper Perennial: New York.
Skinner, Q., 1978. *The Foundations of Modern Political Thought. Volume 1: The Renaissance.* Cambridge: Cambridge University Press.
Snyder, T., 2018. *The Road to Unfreedom: Russia, Europe, America.* London: Tim Duggan Books.
Warren, M.E., 2017. A Problem-Based Approach to Democratic Theory. *American Political Science Review*, 111(1): 39–53. https://doi.org/10.1017/S0003055416000605
Zizek, S., 2017. *Trouble in Paradise: From the End of History to the End of Capitalism.* London: Penguin.

3
SUSTAINABLE DEVELOPMENT
Between reformist change and radical transformation

Susan Baker

Introduction

The term 'sustainability' is commonly used synonymously with 'sustainable development'. In this chapter, 'sustainability' refers to the ability to continue to engage in an activity, process, or use of natural resources over the long-term. In contrast, 'sustainable development' refers to broader societal goals, addressing how equitable and just economic and social development should proceed, while taking account of ecological limits. This involves reconciling the complex interrelationship between the ecological, social, and economic dimensions of development, while adopting a global and, more recently, planetary perspective. Promoting sustainable development opens up debates about our relationship with the natural world, our ethical responsibilities to others, what constitutes social progress, and about the character of development, both in the North and the South, in the present and into the future (Baker 2015). While there are strong anthropocentric currents in the discourse, an extended, non-anthropocentric view would also include other life forms in sustainable development considerations. The focus is not upon individual advancement, but on protecting the common future of humankind as well as other life forms and planetary systems. An agenda for positive change, sustainable development also offers a critique of conventional thinking and practices.

Put this way, sustainable development is an aspiration that is difficult to disagree with. Yet, many would disagree even with the opening statement made in this chapter. For some, sustainable development is an oxymoron, or so hopelessly compromised in practice that it offers no conceptual or practical guide to reconciling the three core dimensions of development. Indeed, sustainable development 'is now like "democracy": it is universally desired, diversely understood, extremely difficult to achieve, and won't go away' (Lafferty 2004, 26).

This chapter traces the modern history of the concept of sustainable development, engaging with the debates on its usefulness and exploring the tensions between those for whom it offers a radical potential for societal transformation and those that point to its reformist foundations. A key tension is between those who argue that sustainable development promotes a growth-oriented model, and those who argue that sustainable development requires us to accept limits to growth. The chapter examines how commitment to sustainable development has played out through governance processes, with focus on institutionalisation through the United Nations.

It traces the history of UN engagement with the concept as a lens to examine how sustainable development is understood and the debates that it has generated.

Historical context

Sustainable development has long, historical roots going back to at least the eighteenth century, when the term was coined to address ways to meet a predicted shortage of timber, the key resource of the time, through policies that allowed the biological renewal of forests (for a study of the deep, historical roots of the term, see Mebratu 1998; Grober 2007). The classical economists Thomas Malthus (1766–1834) and William Stanley Jevons (1835–1882) were also troubled by resource scarcity, especially in the face of population rise (Malthus) and energy (coal) shortages (Jevons). In the 1950s, both Fairfield Osborn (Osborn, 1948; 1953) and Samuel Ordway (Ordway, 1953) raised concerns about limits to growth, especially given rising pollution, species loss, and decline in natural resources. Osborn's *Our Plundered Planet* (1948) is seen as playing a seminal role in the rise of neo-Malthusianism within the conservation movement, wherein population and economic growth are ultimately checked by absolute limits on resources, such as food, energy, and water. However, the approach was criticised for ignoring both the unequal impacts of resource scarcity, and thus matters of justice and equity, and the capacity of society to address limits, particular through technological innovations. The seminal work of population biologists and ecologists, including Rachel Carson (1962), Paul Ehrlich (1968), and Garett Hardin (1974), also focused attention on the damage humans were inflicting on the natural world. Growing environmental awareness also spurred the rise of the green movements of the 1970s, a period marked by growing conflict over industrial and economic development (Huber 2000; Tulloch and Neilson 2014). Furthermore, this period saw mounting critiques of the assumption that the North's development trajectory should form the basis of development planning for what is now termed the Global South. The dependency school of thought was instrumental in revealing the violence of dependent forms of development, where resource extraction enhanced the wealth of the few while structurally impoverishing the many (Baker 2015).

Already advocated by the classical economists, Adam Smith, John Stewart Mill, and David Ricardo, the term 'steady state economy' began to take hold. Such an economy features relatively stable size, with stability or mildly fluctuating levels in population and consumption of energy and materials. As advocated by Herman Daly, this leaves room for nature and provides for high levels of human well-being (Daly 1973). These ideas were also progressed in the *Limits to Growth* report published by the Club of Rome in 1972 (Meadows et al. 1972). Adopting a systems approach, the Report identified key global challenges, including depletion and pollution of the environment, population growth and uneven development, to warn about systems collapse once the limits to growth were reached. However, the Report was heavily criticised for seeking to impose restrictions on development, especially for the Global South, and for failing to take account of technical and social innovations. The term sustainable development was subsequently taken up in the *World Conservation Strategy – Living Resource Conservation for Sustainable Development* (IUCN et al. 1980). However, this failed to integrate social, economic, and environmental objectives, primarily focusing on achieving sustainable development through the conservation of living resources (Waas et al. 2011). Reconciling the economic, social, and environmental aspects of development was subsequently progressed by the UN, but here the faultiness of interpretation as to the meaning and usefulness of the concept of sustainable development begin to come sharply to the fore.

Discursive engagement

The UN has played a key role in advancing understanding of sustainable development and in its institutionalisation. The *United Nations Conference on the Human Environment* in 1972 succeeded in increasing environmental awareness and putting the environment on the international political agenda for the first time. It resulted in the Stockholm Declaration, which contained principles on the preservation and enhancement of the environment. It also led directly to the establishment of the UN Environment Programme (UNEP), the UN body responsible for environmental affairs, although competence for sustainable development is spread across an array of UN agencies and programmes, including the UN Development Programme (UNDP) and the Bretton Woods Institutions (World Bank and IMF). In 1983, the UN General Assembly established the World Commission on Environment and Development. Chaired by Gro Harlem Brundtland, the then former Norwegian Prime Minister, the Commission published its seminal report *Our Common Future* in 1987 (WCED 1987).

Our Common Future defines sustainable development as 'development that meets the needs of the present without compromising the ability of future generations to meet their own needs' (WCED 1987, 43). The Brundtland Report supported developing countries in their pursuit of economic and social improvements. It presented an optimistic view, driven by belief in the capacity of collective effort and of technological innovations to support our sustainable futures. However, Brundtland envisages building a common future on more fundamental processes of change, involving not just technological and institutional changes, but also social, economic, as well as cultural and lifestyle transformations (WCED 1987, 46). The Brundtland Report also addressed the issue of human population growth and growing per capita material expectations, reduction of which became central to the pursuit of sustainable development. This differs from the earlier IUCN approach, mentioned above, which linked the environment to conservation, not to development. In addition, the Report made it explicit that social and economic factors, especially processes operating at the international level, such as trade, influence whether the interactions between society and nature are sustainable.

The Brundtland Report is widely credited with advancing understanding of the concept of sustainable development by finding new ways to reconcile the economic, social, and environmental dimensions. In the years following its publication, sustainable development has become an institutionalised norm within the UN, and the dominant paradigm of major international environmental governance regimes, development agencies, financial institutions, business forum, and of key environmental organisations. However, the issue of limits to growth did not go away. Instead, debates began about whether the concept of sustainable development, as articulated by the Brundtland Report, presents a radical agenda for social change, or a reformist option. A useful way to investigate the debate is to distinguish between 'strong' and 'weak' forms of sustainable development.

In weak forms, reduction of a 'natural capital' asset is allowed, provided that another capital asset (or assets) is increased to compensate for such a reduction. The weak form allows for a high degree of substitutability between all forms of capital resources. While this imposes some degree of restriction on natural resource use, such restrictions are not based on concern for the ecosystems themselves, but rather, on concern about the ecosystems' ability to meet human needs. In contrast, those advocating strong forms of sustainable development argue that just protecting the overall amount of natural capital is insufficient because some critical natural capital cannot be replaced by other capital forms. This restricts the scale of human development relative to global carrying capacity. According to this view, when human development reaches global carrying capacity, no forms of natural capital are substitutable. Thus, there are absolute limits to human development. (Holden et al. 2014; Baker 2015). Some also reject the view that speaks of nature in terms of 'natural capital', as this term commodifies the natural world, subsuming nature under anthropocentric driven values. Thus, strong forms of sustainable development find resonance in philosophical discussions within deep ecology. The deep ecologist, Arne Naess, argued that, in the long run, environmental reforms of social and economic systems are not a viable solution to offset the accelerating destruction of the environment. Instead, the moral and ethical values that legitimise the domination of nature, which are deeply rooted in Western culture, need to be changed, along with recognition of the place of humans as a species within, as opposed to apart from or dominant over, nature (Naess 1973).

The publication of the Brundtland Report opened a major fault-line between two camps, those who interpreted the Brundtland approach as promoting weak forms of sustainable development and those who saw Brundtland as an opportunity to promote strong forms. The proponents of the first position argued that the interpretation of sustainable development adopted and promoted by the Brundtland Report addresses the linkage between poverty alleviation, environmental deterioration, and social equitability through promoting sustainable economic *growth* (see Tulloch and Neilson 2014). Because it promotes a growth-orientated model of development, the sustainable development discourse can be aligned with neoliberal thinking and its globalised, financialised, and demand-driven economic models (Carruthers 2005). This enabled economic actors to become critical catalysts in the promotion of sustainable development, engaging in various forms of corporate environmental responsibility (CER) and encouraging the growth of 'green consumerism', while continuing with 'business as usual'. Their role was legitimised through state-sanctioned use of market instruments, such as emissions trading schemes and payments for ecosystem services. Over time, the role of markets has become 'smuggled in as part of an apparently neutral and non-partisan perspective' (Tulloch and Neilson 2014). This, in turn, make efforts to promote sustainable development both a moral hazard and an ideological veil of ignorance, deflecting attention from the problem of growth, while purporting to address it. Moreover, its reformist approach served to block the radical discourses advocating systemic change, such as found in the limits to growth discourse (Dryzek 2005) and among those that saw ecological deterioration as a manifestation of the crisis inherent within the capitalist system (Pepper 1993; Lipietz 2013; Neilson 2013). From this perspective, the Report represents a key step in taming the sustainable development agenda, especially as presented by earlier environmental, feminist, and development organisations.

The representatives of the other position emphasised two key concepts contained within the Brundtland understanding of sustainable development: the concept of needs, in particular the essential needs of the world's poor, to which overriding priority should be given; and the idea of limitations imposed by the state of technology and social organisation on the environment's ability to meet present and future needs (WCED 1987, 43; see Baker 2015 for a fuller discussion). The concept of needs challenges the industrialised world to keep consumption patterns within the bounds of the ecologically possible and set at levels to which all can reasonably aspire. This reduction allows for necessary development in the South, where economic growth can have, in some contexts, net positive environmental, as well as social and economic, benefits (WCED 1987, 51). The idea of limits points to the Brundtland emphasis on limits to growth, and to the argument in *Our Common Future* that, while technology and social organisation can be both managed and improved to make way for a new era of economic growth, ultimate limits nonetheless do exist. These are imposed 'by the ability of the biosphere to absorb the effects of human activities' (WCED 1987: 8) and by the need to 'adopt lifestyles within the planet's ecological means' (WCED 1987: 9). In addition, attention is drawn to the normative principles set out in the Brundtland Report to guide development, including gender equality, intra-generational equity (within a generation), and inter-generational equity (between generations), and environmental justice.

More recent work from the Stockholm Resilience Centre on breaches of planetary boundaries and the need to find a safe operating space for humanity also lends support for calls to introduce a new economics and politics of limits (Rockström et al. 2009). The positions taken by the 'degrowth' literature also aligns limits to growth with the search for alternative forms of well-being. This draws its inspiration in part from the work of Herman Daly, who understood degrowth as a socially sustainable and equitable reduction of society's throughput (or metabolism) (Daly 1996). However, there are multiple streams of thought here, different interpretations as to what degrowth means, and varying views as to how this can be achieved (Martinez-Alier 2009). Nevertheless, they share in common a focus on the reduction of energy and material throughput to keep within existing biophysical constraints (in terms of natural resources and ecosystem's assimilative capacity); and they challenge the omnipresence of market-based relations in society (that is, commodification) and the growth-based roots of the social imaginary (see van den Bergh 2011; Kothari et al. 2015). De-growth also calls for the redistribution of resources between public and private consumption as well as within and between generations (see Kallis 2011, for a comprehensive treatment). While challenging the hegemony of growth, it also requires a redistributive downscaling of production and consumption in industrialised countries to achieve environmental sustainability, social justice, and well-being elsewhere (Kothari et al. 2015). The degrowth literature directly speaks to the limits to growth arguments advanced by strong sustainable development and a radical reading of Brundtland. This can be seen in particular in relation to calls to stay within ecological limits, to ensure that development is underpinned by normative principles, and in the commitment to enable pathways for development in the Global South to be realised through reductions in high consumption societies. However, while Brundtland focused on participation within existing liberal, democratic structures, and institutions, stressing the importance of including economic actors and civil society in policymaking processes, the emphasis in the degrowth literature is different. The degrowth agenda also includes identifying new forms of democratic institutions and practices that can make the degrowth transition possible. For some, re-appropriating technology, and self-instituting new spaces of choice and social interactions outside of market monetary exchange are key (Latouche 2009). Direct democracy, seen as involving spontaneous popular processes of autonomous 'self-institution' and a re-localised economy, are stressed (Cattaneo, et al. 2012). Others stress the fundamental links between liberal democracies, capitalism, and economic growth, calling for a replacement of the political-economic system (Fotopoulos 2007). The fault-line in interpretation, between those that see sustainable development as a growth-orientated model and those that argue that it embeds a 'limits to growth' perspective, is critical. From this stem major disputes as to the value of the concept of sustainable development itself, that is, whether it offers a new way of thinking about the interrelationship between economy, ecology, and society; or whether it is merely a tool for purporting to address environmental concerns, while simultaneously advocating growth. The issue at stake here is whether the ecological damage caused by growth – the increase in the production of goods and services – can be reduced or mitigated by technical, cultural, and institutional advances, the latter also including governance reform; or whether, irrespective of such changes, there are ultimate limits to growth in a planet characterised by finite resources and, what has now come to be termed 'planetary boundaries'. The issue of the distribution of the benefits of growth, both temporally within and between generations, and spatially, that is across regions, localities, and communities, is also a key concern. This speaks to the social pillar of sustainable development and concerns that a growth-orientated model of development is inherently uneven and unequal in its distributional consequences. In addition, the nature of the relationship between economic growth and the neoliberal democratic system is also in dispute.

In examining this core disjuncture between what sustainable development has come to mean it is critical to make a sharp distinction between the concept of sustainable development, especially that advanced in the radical reading of the Brundtland formulation, and the use to which the term has been put as institutionalisation and operationalisation took hold. Since Brundtland, an increasing number of organisations, agencies, and actors at various levels have subscribed to the notion of sustainable development. These include the European Union, the World Bank, IMF, WTO, national governments, sub-national regional and local authorities, as well as groups within civil society and economic actors, such as the World Business Council for Sustainable Development. It is difficult to argue against the claim that the adoption by key actors, including global business, has facilitated a process whereby the agenda of sustainable development has been tamed (Johnston et al. 2007). Institutionalisation has enabled the pursuit of sustainable development to become entwined with the economic growth agendas of neoliberalism, the dominant ideology shaping political and economic policy and governance in the contemporary period (Kambites 2014). The expansion of use has also brought attention to the cross-cutting nature of the tasks involved in promoting sustainable development, including in relation to international development, trade, urban and land use planning, environmental protection, energy policy, and agricultural and industrial policy, to name but a few. This has also facilitated the spread of a neoliberal interpretation of sustainable development within sectors, and across governance and regulatory regimes, such as those operating in trade and global environmental governance.

As mentioned above, examining historical developments in the institutionalisation of sustainable development provides a very helpful way to unfold how sustainable development has come to be understood in practice. It also provides a focused lens for investigating the debates that are generated when 'sustainable development' is used as a conceptual tool for integrating the environmental, economic, and social dimensions of development. Continuing with this investigation of the entanglement between institutional engagement, scientific conceptualisation, and critical debates, we turn to examine how the Brundtland Report was operationalised through the UN, examining its environmental Summits and its policy developments.

Institutionalisation

The Brundtland Report provided the momentum for the landmark UN Rio Earth Summit in 1992. Politically, the Summit was very successful, attracting world attention and eliciting an array of commitments from developed countries to support the promotion of sustainable development. It produced the *Rio Declaration on Environment and Development*, an action plan known as *Agenda 21*, the UN Framework Convention on Climate Change as well as the Convention on Biological Diversity and the Convention to Combat Desertification. The Rio Declaration contained 27 principles to serve as a basis for future policy and decision making (UNCED 1992). It acknowledged that people have the right to development but also the obligation to protect the environment, and since the environment is a public and common good, it also highlights the need for cooperation between the public and private sectors and civil society, and at a global level. It urged a new era of development marked by respect for the Earth's limited resources. The Declaration also detailed governance principles, stressing the importance of integrative and participatory practices in guiding development.

However, scathing criticism of both the Rio Summit and the entire international governance process that it subsequently spawned has come from within the radical green movement.

For example, *The Ecologist*, a then academic journal promoting strong forms of sustainable development and whose *Blueprint for Survival* (1972) was instrumental in shifting attention to the importance of small, decentralised and de-industrialised communities in promoting sustainable futures, questioned whose common future is being protected by the Rio process (Vol. 22 No. 4 – July/August 1992). It argued that powerful states use institutions such as the UN to transform their own interests into international environmental norms and governance systems, particularly in the negotiating stage of regime formation, where states have a powerful interest in ensuring that considerations of costs, benefits or problems of domestic implementation remain dominant factors in shaping outcomes (Breitmeier 1997). Radical greens argue that this is precisely what was happening at Rio and has continued since. As UN Summits continued over time, and actions plans began to be implemented, the Rio process, which builds upon negotiations between states, has redefined sustainability in ways consistent with the neoliberal agenda of dominant states, in turn, bolstering, legitimizing, and protecting this ideology from critique (Pitcher 2011). Institutions, especially Bretton Woods institutions, have also played a key role in this.

The dispute over interpretation is noticeable in relation to *Agenda 21*, the action plan for implementing sustainable development agreed at Rio. For some, *Agenda 21* signifies the privileging of economic growth as the basis for realising prosperity for all and where market principles are regarded as neutral mechanisms that will ensure both environmental protection and the allocation of social goods (Tulloch and Neilson 2014). Here social goals are subsumed within a project of globalised eco-efficient management (McAfee 2012). The environmental aspect also becomes infused with strong anthropocentric leanings (Jessop 2012), leanings already present in the weak reading of the Brundtland Report. In this, the pursuit of sustainable futures is presented as a problem of technological adjustment and innovation, rather than an issue of system or value changes. The dominant logic here is that poverty causes environmental degradation, and that environmental degradation can be reduced by reducing poverty, which implies that developing countries need economic growth, which in turn requires more liberal markets (Castro 2004; see also Purvis et al. 2018). This logic is at best simplistic (Lélé 1991), and at worst smuggling an inherently ideological agenda under the guise of benign necessity (Liverman 2004; Tulloch 2013). The more recent Transforming Our World: The 2030 Agenda for Sustainable Development (UN 2015) stands in the tradition of *Agenda 21* and bears strong resemblance to it, and is thus liable to similar critiques.

On the other hand, there is the view that through Agenda 21 a more democratic approach to environmental governance has emerged, with new and innovative procedures that have expanded the range and role of non-state actors involved in steering societal change (Gupta and Mason 2014). This includes the participation of business interests but also non-governmental organisation from with the environmental, development, and women's movements. Focusing in particular upon Chapter 28 of Agenda 21, known as Local Agenda 21 (LA21), attention is drawn to how implementation has strengthened sub-national, regional, and local engagement in sustainable development planning, increased capacity within the system of public administration, and enhanced social capital through civil society participation, all of which support the pursuit of sustainable development and help ensure that policy reflects local needs (Lafferty and Eckerberg 2009). This process is also seen as contributing to both the legitimacy and democratic nature of sustainable development policymaking (Young 1997).

The Rio Earth Summit was subsequently followed by the World Summit on Sustainable Development (WSSD), or Rio +10 conference in Johannesburg (2002). The WSSD pointed to the lack of implementation of commitments, including in relation to Agenda 21 and with respect to cooperation and aid to underdeveloped countries (Drexhage and Murphy 2010). It also pointed to the negative consequences of globalisation (UN 2002). The failure to address the ecological dimensions of sustainable development was evidenced by data on the further degradation of the environment and ecosystem losses. The Summit also introduced new implementation plans, including the Millennium Development Goals (MDGs) (UN 2010). In addition, the Summit highlighted the multi-stakeholder approach to implementation, including the role of governments and of business interests (UN 2002). However, it is widely regarded as having lacked political momentum (Klarin 2018).

The Johannesburg Summit unpacked sustainable development into twin components, sustainable consumption, and sustainable production. Looking at consumption, the distinction between weak and strong sustainable development is usefully applied here. The weak approach uses (energy) efficiency through technological innovation to promote sustainable consumption. Consumption levels are not addressed, but instead, faith is placed in finding technical solutions to ensure resource efficiency in delivering consumer goods. In contrast, stronger versions assume that changes in consumption levels and patterns are necessary to achieve sustainable development. Moreover, the strong approach reaches beyond consumption as an economic activity taking place in markets based on monetary values and stresses non-material contributions to a 'good life'; thus, it also addresses value issues. As this understanding advanced over the next decades, it increasingly took account of the social embeddedness of consumption decisions, promoting activities like neighbourhood exchange and community or subsistence work where increases in human well-being can be achieved through changing social structures (Seyfan 2009; Lorek and Fuch 2013). Such activities have the potential to change the logic of the dominant consumption-production systems (Lorek and Fuch 2013). To achieve this, Latouche calls for a 'decolonisation of the imaginary', an active process of liberating thought, desires, and institutions from the logic of growth, productivism, and accumulation for 'accumulation's sake' (Latouche 2015). This will allow material accumulation to no longer hold a prime position in the cultural imaginary (Demaria et al. 2019). This is in keeping with strong forms of sustainable development. However, it is fair to say that the UN approach, particularly that played out through the 10-Year Framework of Programmes on Sustainable Consumption and Production (10YFP) set up from the WSSD, promotes weaker forms (Baker 2015).

Marking the 20th anniversary of the Rio Earth Summit, the UN conference *From Rio to Rio +20* was held in Rio in 2012. Further decline in environmental quality was highlighted, with the loss of biodiversity, natural ecosystems, habitats, and species, and further pollution of air and water. Again, the ecological dimension of sustainable development proved to be continuously threatened. The Summit resolution, *The Future We Want* (UN 2012), in which a commitment to the promotion of the Green Economy was highlighted, attempted to address this threat. This emphasised how a low-emission economy, rational and efficient use of resources, and new efforts at social inclusion could be used to significantly reduce the risk of environmental damage and to improve social welfare and equity (UNEP 2015). The Green Economy model emphasises technological, managerial, and behavioural changes, and the importance of building in principles and parameters of sustainability into production, consumption and trade, while maintaining high rates of economic growth as the key driver of development (Kothari at al. 2015). Indeed, the Summit gave institutional legitimacy to those advocating a growth-oriented approach to sustainable development.

This 'greening of capitalism' also finds clear expression in the ecological modernisation agenda (Van der Heijden 2007). Ecological modernisation is both a theory of development and a strategy to advance the integration of environmental considerations into policy, in particular industrial and energy policy (Hajer 1995). Ecological modernisation seeks to decouple growth of GDP from energy and resource use (Hajer 1995). It represents a core way in which sustainable development has come to be interpreted in high consumption societies in the West. Like the Green Economy model of the UN, it formulates the promotion of sustainable development as a technical, managerial task of 'decoupling' through eco-efficiency. It is also explicit about not attempting to limit overall levels of production and consumption, but instead focuses on combining environmental awareness and market mechanisms to deliver sustainability, including through behavioural changes by green consumers (Spaargaren and Mol 2008). More recently, and in the context of climate change, it also advocates 'transition management' and reflexive forms of governance to steer society towards sustainable development, especially in the energy sector (Kemp and Loorbach 2006; Voss et al. 2009).

Because the social justice aspects of sustainable development are ignored by ecological modernisation, as is the distribution of wealth and society-nature relations (Langhelle 2000), it can only promote weak forms. The result is that ethical considerations are side-lined by attention to efficiency procedures. Furthermore, ecological modernisation, and its expression through green economy models, also sees growth as a solution to the planet's ecological crisis. This approach provides a distinctive advantage to advanced industrial society: it offers the hope that the environmental problem can be addressed without having to re-direct the course of societal development away from it unsustainable pathways (Blühdorn 2007). This politics of unsustainability sees both symbolic commitment to sustainable development and declaratory recognition of the seriousness of the problem of global environmental change, while at the same time is marked by a refusal to recognise their cause, let alone to address them (Blühdorn 2007).

Further efforts to refine the concept of sustainable development were made at the UN Conference on Sustainable Development in New York in 2015, which led to the resolution *Transforming Our World: The 2030 Agenda for Sustainable Development*. This presented 17 Sustainable Development Goals (SDGs) to be achieved by 2030 (UN 2015). They build on the earlier Millennium Development Goals (MDGs), which focus on poverty reduction and the satisfaction of basic needs but extend the focus on developing countries to a global agenda for sustainable development. While ending poverty remains a core objective, the SDGs set out a broader agenda that includes environmental, social, and economic sustainability, recognising the need to change policies and institutions if transformative change is to take place (Fukuda-Parr 2016). However, they also include a goal for growth that is sustainable and inclusive (Goal 8). Furthermore, there is no mechanism set out to address potential incompatibility and feedbacks, especially between economic development and ecological sustainability goals (Machingura and Lally 2017). Trade-offs also become apparent when examining the targets beneath each goal. Because they lack clarity on how to integrate the three dimensions, there is a danger that the SDGs will be implemented along the traditional economic pathway, further contributing to the dominance of the weak interpretation of sustainable development. This tension between using the concept of sustainable development to build new forms of development, or to use it as a tool to drive eco-efficiency management also plays out in the discourses and practices that address the links between sustainable development and women's agency. Here, it is argued, the global governance regime established under the UN process since Rio enabled a narrative of concern for gender equality without always confronting uncomfortable change (Arora-Jonsson 2014). The MDGs and the SDGs form part of what is referred to as 'governance through goals'. This approach, most evident within global environmental governance regimes, sees goal setting that function through weak institutional, intergovernmental arrangements, but which are not legally binding (Biermann 2017). These goals are largely detached from the international legal regimes for dealing with climate change and biodiversity loss established since Rio. While granting much leeway to national choices and preferences, their use also raises the need to develop mechanisms to track implementation progress (Young 2017). The shift to governance through goals has led to considerable effort to develop an array of indicators for measurement. Similar initiatives, such as Life Cycle Assessment, ISO 26000, the Global Reporting Initiative, and triple bottom line analysis, had previously found their way into the business world (Elkington 1997). Goal setting can be criticised for lack of effectiveness and for encouraging cherry-picking in setting prioritises and implementation plans. When viewed through the lens of strong sustainability the critique would be more radical (for a fuller treatment see Geels 2010; Baumgartner 2011; Hoffmann 2011). Here, the preoccupation with targets and timetables is criticised for shifting attention to means, not ends. This deflects attention away from value changes and the call to rethink the dominant economic model (Milne and Gray 2013). They also feed into the dominant tendency to see the promotion of sustainable development as a technical and managerial task, based around measures and indicators of material efficiency, sustainable yield levels, and performance.

Ongoing frustration with the entrapment of the sustainable development agenda has led to claims that we have reached the end of 'sustainability' as a discourse of development and as a policy paradigm. For some, we now enter a new and much bleaker age, characterised by irreversible climate change and biodiversity loss, by brutal inequalities and by suffering, both physical and emotional – and which cannot be rectified. Reaching the 'Anthropocene' calls for acceptance that human beings have decisively altered the atmosphere and set in motion a now-inevitable mass extinction as drastic as any produced by Earth system changes over geological time (Foster 2008). For others, there is the possibility that the recognition of the Anthropocene may finally take modern societies into a new era 'ripe with human-directed opportunity' (Crutzen and Schwägerl 2011). This can give a new legitimacy to techno-environmentalism, where sustainability no longer means identification of, and subordination to, ecological limits and imperatives, but 'an inherently open principle' that frames the debate on the kind of nature and society 'we wish to have' (Arias-Maldonado 2013, 17). However, this anthropocentrism – unmoderated and unmediated by humility – can represent a new and dangerous expression of hubris. This is not the kind of Anthropocene that is envisaged by the ethical principles of strong sustainable development. For yet others, abandonment of the concept of sustainable development offers space to trigger a deep crisis within environmentalism itself that will force an end of pretending (Foster 2008) and move capitalist consumer societies beyond their current state of denial (Benson and Craig 2014; Blühdorn 2017).

Understanding the fault lines

The fault lines of interpretation, examined in this chapter by exploring the UN's engagement in promoting sustainable development, once again underline the 'fluidity' of the concept of sustainable development. After all, the search for a unitary and precise meaning of sustainable development may well rest on a mistaken view of the nature and function of political concepts (Lafferty 1995). As many commentators have argued, sustainable development is best seen as similar to other contested concepts such as 'democracy', 'liberty', and 'social justice' (O'Riordan 1985; Jacobs 1995; Lafferty 1995). For concepts such as these, there is both a readily understood 'first level meaning' and general political acceptance, but there also lies a deeper contestation. In liberal democracies, the debates around such contested concepts form an essential component of the political struggle over the direction – and steering – of social and economic development, that is, of change (Lafferty 1995). The existence of substantive political arguments is part of the dynamics of liberal, democratic politics, and the process of conscious steering of societal change. Such arguments are important as they can stimulate creative thinking and practice – in this case about 'development' and our relationship to nature and the natural world. This also helps us realise that sustainable development is not a blueprint for change, but an open-ended, future-orientated response, with both policy and ethical dimensions. Open dialogue about the vision of sustainable futures and how to realise this in practice has, as mentioned above, stimulated debates about the type of democratic processes and practices that best serve the promotion of sustainable development. At one level, sustainable development, particularly in its strong forms, can be seen as foundational to any democratic political system. This is not least because the survival of democracy would be very difficult in an unequal, resource-constrained and overheated world (FDSD 2020). However, the type of democracy, and thus the role of the state, the power of the economic system and the responsibility of economic interests, and the value of environmental citizenship and civil society participation, all remain open to debate.

But herein also lies a danger, because such debates and their outcomes are the product of asymmetrical power distribution that sees some given voice, while others not; some voices heard while others struggle to be recognised. In this context, the term sustainable development becomes what Alamo calls 'sanitised' (Alaimo 2012, 559). It presents a 'win–win' approach that effectively neutralises radical critique, depoliticising sustainability by presenting the three dimensions of development, the economic, social, and environmental, as if they were already reconciled. This risks that the critical, indeed even emancipatory potential of sustainable development will be lost. What is at stake here is the exercise of power by vested interests that enables the continuation of the present social, economic, and political system in the face of the disruptive potential that the pursuit of sustainable development holds.

This debate over the meaning and use of sustainable development also finds resonance in long-standing political and ideological cleavages between those who hold that social change can be brought about through reforming the existing status quo, and those that argue that structural changes to the existing order are needed to address social and economic inequalities. There are thus conflicting interpretations as to how to realise social change. This is giving rise to a growing literature that suggests that the root cause of the divide is that quest for growth is a structural feature of capitalism in all its varieties (Harvey 2007; Spangenberg 2010; Blühdorn 2017). So, addressing limits to growth, and deemphasising the economic so as to give attention to the ecological and social dimensions of development, calls for systemic political, institutional, and cultural change. This change is needed in order to create a different system, where expansion will no longer be a necessity and where economic rationality and the goals of efficiency and maximisation will not dominate all other social rationalities and goals (Latouche 2009; van den Bergh 2011).

Conclusion

This chapter used a historical reconstruction to examine how the concept of sustainable development has been interpreted and institutionalised, focusing on UN engagement at the global level. This reconstruction helped unpack the debates that evolved about the meaning of the concept and about the political, social, economic, and value changes that are required to promote sustainable futures. A heuristic device that constructed sustainable development into weak and strong forms was used to frame the different views and to lend order to the analysis.

Through UN engagement, the concept of sustainable development has come to permeate the official discourse not just of international bodies and institutions, but also nation-states, civil society organisations, and economic actors, where it remains replete with declaratory aspirations. This has given rise to a major fault line in interpretation as to what the commitment to promote sustainable development entails, one that maps on to longer-established political and ideological cleavages. However, it is one that may also be based on a failure to distinguish between forms of sustainable development, and between the sustainable development imaginary and its use in institutional contexts.

Strong forms of sustainable development call forth a complex, and interrelated social and political project that seeks to change the direction of development, both at the macro-level of economic and political institutions and at the micro-level of personal values and aspirations. It also calls upon us to exercise our moral responsibilities to both present and future generations, and to nature and other life forms. As articulated though the Brundtland formulation, it requires that we hold the Earth in trust for future generations. Because it has strong normative value, it demands that our policies and actions adhere to the moral imperatives of addressing the needs of others, in ways that favour the principles of justice and equity, and that respects limits to growth. The concept acknowledges environmental limits – as recently articulated in the planetary boundary approach and in the degrowth movement. Such limits also serve a justice agenda: they enable the creation of the conditions necessary for ecologically legitimate development, particularly in the Global South. Strong sustainable development thus challenges conceptions of development that prioritise individual self-advancement and replaces it with a focus on our common fate. This means that the promotion of the common good takes precedent over the wants of the favoured few. It may indeed help us address what Blühdorn calls 'the increasing fixation on self-realisation, self-determination and self-experience' (Blühdorn 2017, 53). From a governance perspective, it also requires that participation of the marginal be given attention (Meadowcroft 2007). Such voices include poor people, nature, and future generations. Strong forms of sustainable development mandate the empowerment of the marginal and those most directly affected by environmental degradation to hold public and private power and authority accountable to present and future generations and other life forms. In doing this, it also calls into questions the nature and practices of liberal democracy itself, debating whether participation within existing structures is sufficient for transformation, or whether new forms of direct, and delocalised practices are required.

As an agenda of transformation, the strong sustainable development imaginary runs contrary to those focusing on relative changes. Undoubtedly, weak forms of sustainable development have come to dominate, entrapped in market-orientated approaches and subordinated to neoliberal hegemony. Declaratory commitment to sustainable development is well embedded and institutionalised, and policy outputs have become more sophisticated, wider in scope, and more detailed in treatment. However, while institutionalisation has made a push towards technical solutions and monitoring, the inherently political and ethical nature of sustainable development is often ignored, replaced by technical and managerial tasks, more recently associated with transition management. As such, progress in addressing the interlinkages between the environmental, social, and economic dimensions of development remains weak, even if acknowledgement of these interlinkages is now well established. Thus, the strong forms of sustainable development made possible by one reading of the Brundtland conceptualisation of sustainable development have become marginalised as the deepening of institutional engagement has unfolded.

However, while there is a large gap between, on the one hand, the sustainable development imaginary, and its aspirations and, on the other, the actions and practice that have been put in place, such as through the UN process, this does not in itself justify the abandonment of the concept. In progressing our understanding, attention needs to be turned to the importance of making a distinction between aspiration and value and how these come to be realised in practice and in institutional context. Because international political and economic processes have restricted the agenda of sustainable development, this does not mean that the promotion of sustainable development is itself a limited agenda for change. Whether it is currently politically co-opted should not have a bearing on whether it is a worthwhile ethical and social objective. Despite its widespread appropriation by technocrats and market enthusiasts, sustainability is not an apolitical idea, but a rich and powerfully normative concept that lays the foundation for a new vision of development. Speaking more generally, we can see that there are several key norms, such as gender equality, that have been co-opted – so that the emancipatory demands of the women's movement have been subsumed under a call for labour market participation, yet often without the structural changes that make women equally valued. This does not mean that we would wish to abandon the emancipatory demands of feminism. In a similar way, we abandon at our peril the transformative potential embedded in the commitment to promote a common future based on the principles and practices of strong forms of sustainable development.

References

Alaimo, S., 2012. Sustainable This, Sustainable That: New Materialisms, Posthumanism, and Unknown Futures. *PMLA: Publications of the Modern Language Association of America*, 127 (3), 558–564.

Arias-Maldonado, M., 2013. Rethinking Sustainability in the Anthropocene. *Environmental Politics*, 22 (3), 428–446.

Arora-Jonsson, S., 2014. Forty Years of Gender Research and Environmental Policy: Where Do We Stand? *Women's Studies International Forum*, 47, 295–308.

Baker, S., 2015. *Sustainable Development*. London: Routledge.

Baumgartner, R.J., 2011. Critical Perspectives of Sustainable Development Research and Practice. *Journal of Cleaner Production*, 19, 783–786.

Benson, M.H. and Craig, R.K., 2014. The End of Sustainability. *Society & Natural Resources*, 27 (7), 777–782.

Biermann, F., Kanie, N., and Kim, R.E., 2017. Global Governance by Goal-setting: The Novel Approach of the UN Sustainable Development Goals. *Current Opinion in Environmental Sustainability*, 26–27, 26–31.

Blühdorn, I., 2007. Sustaining the Unsustainable: Symbolic Politics and the Politics of Simulation. *Environmental Politics*, 16 (2), 251–275.

Blühdorn, I., 2017. Post-Capitalism, Post-Growth, Post-Consumerism? *Global Discourse* 7(1): 41–60.

Breitmeier, H., 1997. International Organisations and the Creation of Environmental Regimes. In O.R. Young, eds. *Global Governance: Drawing Insights from the Environmental Experience*. Cambridge: MIT Press, 87–114.

Carruthers, D., 2005. From Opposition to Orthodoxy: the remaking of sustainable development. In J. Dryzek and D. Schlosberg, eds. *Debating the Earth: The Environmental Politics Reader*. New York: Oxford University Press, 285–300.

Carson, R., 1962. *Silent Spring*. Boston: Houghton Mifflin Company.

Castro, C.J., 2004. Sustainable Development: Mainstream and Critical Perspectives. *Organisation and the Environment*, 17, 195–225.

Cattaneo, C., D'Alisa, G., Kallis, G. and Zografos, C., 2012. Degrowth Futures and Democracy. *Futures*, 44 (6): 515–523.

Crutzen, P. and Schwägerl, C., 2011. Living in the Anthropocene: Toward a New Global Ethos [online]. Available from: http://e360.yale.edu/feature/living_in_the_anthropocene_toward_a_new_global_ethos/2363/.

Daly, H.E., 1973. *Toward a Steady-State Economy*. San Francisco: W.H. Freeman.

Daly, H.E., 1996. *Beyond Growth: The Economics of Sustainable Development*. Beacon Press.

Demaria, F., Kallis, G. and Bakker, K., 2019. Geographies of Degrowth: Nowtopias, Resurgences and the Decolonization of Imaginaries and Places. *Environment and Planning E: Nature and Space*, 2 (3).

Drexhage, J. and Murphy, D., 2010. Sustainable Development: From Brundtland to Rio 2012. New York: UN and International Institute for Sustainable Development.

Dryzek, J.S., 2005. *The Politics of the Earth: Environmental Discourses*, 2nd edn. Oxford: Oxford University Press.

Ehrlich, P., 1968. *The Population Bomb*. New York: Ballantine.

Elkington, J., 1997. *Cannibals with Forks: The Triple Bottom line of 21st Century Business*. Oxford: Capstone.

Foster, D., 2008. *The Sustainability Mirage: Illusion and Reality in the Coming War on Climate Change*. London: Routledge.

Fotopoulos, T., 2007. Is Degrowth Compatible with a Market Economy? *The International Journal of Inclusive Democracy*, 3 (1).

Foundation for Democracy and Sustainable Development (FDSD), 2020. *The Challenge* [online]. Available from: www.fdsd.org.

Fukuda-Parr, S., 2016. From the Millennium Development Goals to the Sustainable Development Goals: Shifts in Purpose, Concept, and Politics of Global Goal Setting for Development. *Gender & Development*, 24 (1), 43–52.

Geels, F.W., 2010. Ontologies, Socio-technical Transitions (to Sustainability), and the Multi-level Perspective. *Research Policy*, 39: 495–510.

Grober, U., 2007. Deep roots – A conceptual history of 'sustainable development'(Nachhaltigkeit) Berlin Wissenschaftszentrum für Sozialforschung (WZB) paper Nr. P 2007–002.

Gupta, A. and Mason, M., 2014. A Transparency Turn in Global Environmental Governance. In A. Gupta, and M. Mason, eds. *Transparency in Global Environmental Governance: Critical Perspectives*. Cambridge: MIT Press, 3–38.

Hajer, M., 1995. *The Politics of Environmental Discourse: Ecological Modernisation and the Policy Process*. New York: Clarendon Press.

Hardin, G., 1974. Living on a Lifeboat. *BioScience*, 24 (10), 561–568.

Harvey, D., 2007. Neoliberalism as Creative Destruction. *Annals of the American Academy of Political and Social Science*, 610, (1).

Hoffmann, U., 2011. Some reflections on climate change, green growth illusions and development space. United Nations Conference on Trade and Development.

Holden, E., Linnerud, K., and Banister, D., 2014. Sustainable Development: Our Common Future Revisited. *Global Environmental Change*, 26, 130–139.

Huber, J., 2000. Towards Industrial Ecology: Sustainable Development as a Concept of Ecological Modernization. *Journal of Environmental Planning and Policy*, 2(4), 269–285.

IUCN, 1980. International Union for Conservation of Nature and Natural Resources, *UNEP, and WWF, 1980. World Conservation Strategy: Living Resource Conservation for Sustainable Development. International Union for Conservation of Nature and Natural Resources: Gland, Switzerland, 1980* [online]. Available from: https://portals.iucn.org/library/efiles/documents/WCS-004.pdf.

Jacobs, M., 1995. Justice and Sustainability. In J. Lovenduski and J. Stanyer, eds. *Contemporary Political Studies*. Belfast: Proceedings of the Political Studies Association of the UK, Vol. 3, 1470–1485.

Jessop, B., 2012. Economic and Ecological Crises: Green New Deals and No-growth Economies. *Society for International Development*, 55 (1), 17–24.

Johnston, P., Everard, M., Santillo, D., and Robèrt, K-H., 2007. Reclaiming the Definition of Sustainability. *Environmental Science and Pollution Research*, 14 (1), 60–66.

Kallis, G., 2011. In Defence of Degrowth. *Ecological Economics*, 70 (5), 873–880.

Kambites, C.J., 2014. Sustainable Development: The 'Unsustainable' Development of a Concept in Political Discourse. *Sustainable Development*, 22 (5), 336–348.

Kemp, R. and Loorbach, D., 2006. Transition Management: A Reflexive Governance Approach. In J.P. Voss, D. Bauknecht, and R. Kemp, eds. *Reflexive Governance for Sustainable Development*. Cheltenham: Edward Elgar, 103–130.

Klarin, T., 2018. The Concept of Sustainable Development: From its Beginning to the Contemporary Issues. *Zagreb International Review of Economics & Business*, 21 (1), 67–94.

Kothari, A., Demaria, F., and Acosta, A., 2015. Buen Vivir, Degrowth, and Ecological Swaraj: Alternatives to Sustainable Development and Green Economy. *Development*, 57 (3–4), 362–375.

Lafferty, W.M., 1995. The Implementation of Sustainable Development in the European Union. In J. Lovenduski and J. Stanyer, eds. *Contemporary Political Studies*. Belfast: Proceedings of the Political Studies Association of the UK, 1, 223–232.

Lafferty, W.M. eds., 2004. *Governance for Sustainable Development. The Challenge of Adapting Form to Function*. Cheltenham: Elgar.

Lafferty, W.M. and Eckerberg, K., 2009. *From the Earth Summit to Local Agenda 21 Working Towards Sustainable Development*. London: Earthscan.

Langhelle, O., 2000. Why Ecological Modernisation and Sustainable Development Should Not be Conflated. *Journal of Environmental Policy and Planning*, 2 (4), 303–322.

Latouche, S., 2009. *Farewell to Growth*. Cambridge: Polity Press.
Latouche S., 2015. Imaginary, Decolonization of. In G. D'Alisa, F. Demaria, and G. Kallis, eds. *Degrowth: A Vocabulary for a New Era*. Abingdon: Routledge, 117–120.
Lélé, S.M., 1991. Sustainable Development: A Critical Review. *World Development*, 19 (6), 607–621.
Lipietz, A., 2013. Fears and Hopes: The Crisis of the Liberal Productivist Model and its Green Alternative. *Capital & Class*, 37(1), 127–141.
Liverman, D., 2004. Who Governs, at What Scale and at What Price? Geography, Environmental Governance, and the Commodification of Nature. *Annals of the Association of American Geographers*, 94(4), 734–738.
Lorek, S. and Fuchs, D., 2013. Strong Sustainable Consumption Governance – Precondition for a Degrowth Path? *Journal of Cleaner Production*, 38, 36–43.
Machingura, F. and Lally, S., 2017. *The Sustainable Development Goals and their trade-offs*. London: Overseas Development Institute.
Martinez-Alier J., 2009. Social Metabolism, Ecological Distribution Conflicts, and Languages of Valuation. *Capitalism Nature Socialism*, 20 (91), 58–87.
McAfee, K., 2012. Nature in the Market-World: Ecosystem services and Inequality. *Development*, 55 (1), 5–33.
Meadowcroft, J., 2007. Who is in Charge Here? Governance for Sustainable Development in a Complex World. *Environmental Policy and Planning*, 9 (3–4), 193–212.
Meadows, D.H., Meadows, D.L., Randers, J. and Behrens III, W.W., 1972. *The Limits of Growth* [online]. Available from: http://collections.dartmouth.edu/published-derivatives/meadows/pdf/meadows_ltg-001.pdf.
Mebratu, D., 1998. Sustainability and Sustainable Development: Historical and Conceptual Review. *Environmental Impact Assessment Review*, 98 (18), 493–520.
Milne, M.J. and Gray, R., 2013. W(h)ither Ecology? The Triple Bottom Line, the Global Reporting Initiative, and Corporate Sustainability Reporting. *Journal of Business Ethics*, 118 (13–29).
Naess, A., 1973. The Shallow and the Deep, Long-range Ecology Movement. A Summary. *Inquiry*, 16 (1–4), 95–100.
Neilson, D., 2013. Reworking the Scientific Socialist Prognosis in the 21st Century: Mid-range Contingency and a Counter-hegemonic Model of Development. *Knowledge Cultures*, 1(2), 73–93.
Ordway, S., 1953. *Resources and the American Dream, Including a Theory of the Limit of Growth*. New York: Ronald Press Company.
O'Riordan, T., 1985. What does sustainability really mean? Theory and development of concepts of sustainability, Sustainable Development in an Industrial Economy, proceedings of a conference held at Queens' College, Cambridge, 23–25 June, Cambridge: UK Centre for Economic and Environmental Development.
Osborn, F., 1948. *Our Plundered Planet*. London: Faber and Faber.
Osborn, F., 1953. *The Limits of the Earth*. Boston: Little and Brown.
Pepper, D., 1993. *Eco-socialism*. London: Routledge.
Pitcher, B., 2011. Radical Subjects after Hegemony. *Subjectivity*, 4, 87–102.
Purvis, B., Mao, Y., and Robinson, D., 2018. Three Pillars of Sustainability: In Search of Conceptual Origins. *Sustainability Science*, 14, 681–695.
Rockström, J. et al., 2009. Planetary Boundaries: Exploring the Safe Operating Space for Humanity. *Ecology and Society*, 14 (2), 32.
Seyfang, G., 2009. *The New Economics of Sustainable Consumption: Seeds of Change*. London: Palgrave.
Spaargaren, G. and Mol, A., 2008. Greening Global Consumption: Redefining Politics and Authority. *Global Environmental Change*, 18 (3), 350–359.
Spangenberg, J.H., 2010. The Growth Discourse, Growth Policy and Sustainable Development: Two Thought Experiments. *Journal of Cleaner Production*, 18 (6), 561–566.
Tulloch, L., 2013. On Science, Ecology and Environmentalism. *Policy Futures in Education*, 11 (1), 100–114.
Tulloch, L. and Neilson, D., 2014. The Neoliberalisation of Sustainability. *Citizenship, Social and Economics Education*, 13 (1), 26–38.
UN, 2002. *Report of the world summit on sustainable development (A/CONF.199/20)* [online]. Available from: www.unmillenniumproject.org/documents/131302_wssd_report_reissued.pdf.
UN, 2012. *The Future we Want. Resolution adopted by the general assembly on 27 July 2012 (A/RES/66/288)* [online]. Available from: http://daccess-dds-ny.un.org/doc/UNDOC/GEN/N11/476/10/PDF/N1147610.pdf?OpenElement.

UN, 2015. *Transforming our world: the 2030 Agenda for Sustainable Development* [online]. Available from: www.un.org/ga/search/view_doc.asp?symbol=A/RES/70/1&Lang=E.

UNCED (United Nations Conference on Environment and Development), 1992. *Rio Declaration on Environment and Development* [online]. Available from: www.un.org/documents/ga/conf151/aconf15126-1annex1.htm.

UNEP, United Nations Environmental Programme, 2015. *Green Economy* [online]. Available from: www.unep.org/greeneconomy/AboutGEI/WhatisGEI/tabid/29784/Default.aspx.

United Nations Millennium Declaration. A/55/L.2. www.un.org/millennium/declaration/ares552e.htm. September 8, 2000

Van den Bergh, J.C.J.M., 2011. Environment Versus Growth – A Criticism of "Degrowth" and a Plea for "A-growth". *Ecological Economics*, 70 (5), 881–890.

Van der Heijden, H.-A., 2007. Environmental Movements, Ecological Modernisation and Political Opportunity Structure. *Environmental Politics*, 8 (1), 199–221.

Voss, J-P., Smith, A. and Grin, J., 2009. Designing Long-term Policy: Rethinking Transition Management. *Policy Sciences*, 42, 275–230.

Waas, T., Hugé, J., Verbruggen, A. and Wright, T., 2011. Sustainable Development: A Bird's Eye View. *Sustainability*, 3, 1637–1661.

WCED, United Nations World Commission on Environment and Development, 1987. *Our Common Future*. Oxford: Oxford University Press.

Young, O.R., 1997. Rights, Rules and resources in World Affairs. In O.R. Young, eds. *Global Governance: Drawing Insights from the Environmental Experience*. Cambridge: MIT Press, 87–114.

Young O.R., 2017. Conceptualization: Goal-setting as a Strategy for Earth System Governance. In N. Kanie and F. Biermann, eds. *Governing Through Goals: Sustainable Development Goals as Governance Innovation*. Cambridge: MIT Press, 31–52.

4
DEMOCRACY AND SUSTAINABILITY
An evolving relationship

Manuel Arias-Maldonado

Introduction

How does sustainability relate to democracy? This is not a question that can be answered lightly. For once, it requires the previous clarification of the concepts at play: what is meant by sustainability in relation to which understanding of democracy. Depending on how these concepts are defined, different answers will be given by different people. On the other hand, the relationship between sustainability and democracy has a diachronic quality: it has evolved in time both normatively and empirically. This means that their mutual compatibility has been perceived differently in different moments, but also in relation to changes in socionatural relations – fear related to population growth is not the same as climate change, nor is the latter synonymous with the wider challenge represented by the Anthropocene. Finally, changes in existing democracies must be considered too, as the rise of national-populism or the digitization of the public sphere impact on how democracies work and hence on the way in which they foster or hinder sustainability.

Democracy and sustainability maintains an uneasy relationship. The problem was impeccably formulated by Robert Goodin almost three decades ago: "To advocate democracy is to advocate procedures, to advocate environmentalism is to advocate substantive outcomes: what guarantee can we have that the former procedures will yield the latter sort of outcomes?" (Goodin 1992, 168). For many observers, in fact, democratic procedures have *not* produced sustainable outcomes: climate change and many other environmental problems remain unaddressed and actually threaten the long-term survival of human societies. Thus the belief that we live in "an age of unsustainability" (Dauvergene 2016) which results from the "politics of simulation" that prevent social radical change (Blühdorn 2007). In the Anthropocene, the maladjustment between democracy and sustainability is compounded by a pervading sense of urgency that speaks of extremes, emergencies, exceptions (Lynch and Veland 2018). More cautiously, others recognise that the popularity of the idea of sustainability is matched by a persistent shortfall in practice (Dryzek and Pickering 2019, 82). Democratic societies may be more sustainable than in the past, but they are not sustainable yet and it is not clear that they are advancing towards this goal with the required speed. To complicate matters further, democracies share the planet and thus global environmental problems with autocracies and flawed democracies: international cooperation may falter as a result. Still, the withdraw of the US from the Paris Agreement on

Climate Change under the presidency of Donald Trump demonstrates that consolidated democracies can also contribute to multilateral failure.

When confronted with this stubborn reality, critics have deployed a number of strategies. On the one hand, a focus on the shortcomings of liberal democracy leads to the belief that a different kind of democratic organization can deliver better results – hence the emphasis on deliberation or participation (Smith 2001). The greening of liberal democracy is another possibility, by way of supplementing traditional representation with institutional devices that are able to integrate other interests in the political process, such as those of future generations or the nonhuman world (Goodin 1996). A more radical strategy is that of dispensing with democracy altogether: if the latter is perceived as the obstacle to sustainability, a shift to authoritarianism in the name of survivalism may be warranted (Beeson 2010). Finally, sustainability itself may be resignified in order to solve the equation: either depriving it from its more transformative undertones or questioning its usefulness in the current socio-ecological predicament (Blühdorn 2019).

Outside the academia, a political debate on sustainability has also taken place. The latter has been increasingly relevant for the self-understanding of liberal democracies, while it has helped to articulate demands for social justice in the Global South. Sustainability began as a fringe issue that gained ground in the public debate during the 90s, once the concept of sustainable development was launched by the UN and years of sustained growth in a globalized world made room for so-called post-materialist worries (see Inglehart 2018). As of late, the increasing salience of the climate crisis has obscured sustainability in favor of the narrower goal of decarbonization. However, the climate movement has put environmental concerns in the center of the public agenda, highlighting the relevance of scientific knowledge as a basis for political debate as well as the materiality of global warming and its potential effects. At the same time, the emphasis on urgency *and* science may undermine the established relationship between sustainability and democracy – and yet the discourse is in flux and it is too soon to know how the current discussion will evolve.

The chapter is divided into four sections. The first outlines the troubles that afflict the relationship between sustainability and democracy. The second spells out the eco-authoritarian argument. The third section elaborates the argument that democracy and sustainability can and must be reconciled. Fourth, and by way of conclusion, the impact of the Anthropocene hypothesis on the paradigm of sustainability is discussed.

Sustainability and democracy: means against ends?

The compatibility of democracy and sustainability cannot be taken for granted: a persistent state of unsustainability in the face of the climate crisis should be enough testimony of the tension that plagues their relationship. The question is whether democracy can provide for sustainability, which is a particular societal state – or, even, whether democracy *allows for* sustainability. If there is a handicapped relationship between them, where exactly lies the problem? Is democracy hindering sustainability?

At first sight, the key lies in the frayed relationship between democratic means and substantial ends. In principle, democratic *procedures* cannot possibly guarantee green *outcomes*. And that is the reason why some strands of environmental thought have mistrusted democracy: a decision-making procedure that is open to all kind of arguments may easily frustrate those who seek a non-negotiable result (see Ophuls 1977). The more sustainability is defined as a set of given policies that lead to pre-fixed outcomes, then, the less compatible it will be with an open democratic procedure that does not guarantee any pre-ordained outcome. Moral consequentialists demanding the realization of substantive goals may thus feel that democracy is an obstacle, despite the fact that democracy's openness makes it easier for new voices and values to emerge. Another way of putting this is that by presenting certain values as non-negotiable, democratic procedures are actually emptied out.

This is the case, at least, if a procedural view of democracy as a collective decision-making device based on the majority rule is adopted. From this standpoint, a democratic procedure is a method for determining the content of legally binding decisions, so that the preferences of the citizens have some formal connection with the outcome in which each citizen counts equally (Barry 1979, 156). A number of criteria must be met for a full procedural democracy to exist: political equality, effective participation, a sufficient understanding on the part of citizens, enough participative inclusion (Dahl 1979). In a proceduralist conception of democracy, means seem to prevail over ends. And yet a number of underlying principles – from equity to rationality, tolerance and liberty – make it possible for the procedure to exist. None of them, however, assure that particular demands will be accepted. If democratic rules are respected and sustainability is treated as just another substantive goal, there is no way to assure that greens will achieve the results they aim for. In sum: sustainability and democracy clash because the latter cannot guarantee the realization of the former.

Nevertheless, attempts have been made to establish a more firm relationship between democratic procedures and sustainable outcomes. Three arguments stand out:

1. *The preconditional argument.* It suggests that democracy is committed to the conditions that make its procedures possible: they include rationality or tolerance, but also environmental conditions without which no dialogue is feasible. Sustainability might thus be seen as a generalizable interest not subjected to deliberation (see Saward 1996).
2. *The value-emergence argument.* Green values such as the need to pursue sustainability will naturally emerge in the course of the democratic process given its objective reasonableness (Hayward 1998, 161). If democracy works well, it will be green. Thus, the preference for deliberative models of democracy that are supposed to give priority to the best arguments at play (see Jacobs 1997).
3. *The deontological argument.* Democracy, runs this argument, is committed to the integration of all relevant interests in the political process. This includes the interests of future generations and the nonhuman world, which must thus be represented in the political realm (Mills 1996) or recognised in the form of rights associated to the liberal principle of autonomy (Eckersley 1996, 214).

Yet none of them is truly convincing as far as a *necessary* connection between sustainability and democracy is concerned: ecological sustainability is the pre-condition for any political regime, and not just for a democratic one, to exist; nothing can guarantee that the best arguments are chosen in the course of a democratic deliberation, no matter how evident its logical or normative superiority may seem; an enlargement of the moral community via rights or special forms of representation are already substantive outcomes rather than procedural guarantees and thus cannot be excluded from democratic consideration. Despite the value of these attempts, they can also be appraised as a case of theoretical wishful thinking (Humphrey 2004, 116).

On the face of it, then, there is an unavoidable tension between some green values and some democratic values, which makes itself manifest in the relationship between sustainability and democracy. If sustainability is understood as providing strong protection to nonhumans or bringing about a truly radical transformation of society, democracy will be found wanting. Thus the suggestion that the "sacred cow" of democracy, incapable as it is to solve the ecological crisis, should be replaced with a platonic philosopher-king (Westra 1993). Whenever sustainability is defended as a conception of the good that is not open to negotiation or compromise, democracy will struggle to achieve it. The latter has not to do with the *best* outcome as defined by a set of participants, but with the *right* outcome as defined by a sufficient majority of them. Respecting the formal procedure for taking that decision, in turn, makes it also legitimate. Hence the conclusion that "there is no logically or conceptually *necessary* connection between a commitment to the natural environment and a commitment to democracy" (Ball 2006, 132). The resulting conundrum led Bryan Norton to suggest that greens must decide whether they want to be "first and foremost, environmentalists or, first and foremost, democrats (while admitting its many and varied weaknesses)" (Norton 2002, 23).

However, a different account of the relationship between sustainability and democracy emerges if attention focuses on the conceptual indeterminacy of the former. It should be remembered that it was not until the second half of the 1980s that the concepts *sustainability* and *sustainable development* rose to prominence with the Bruntland Report evacuated by the United Nations World Commission on Environment and Development. It defined sustainable development as "development that meets the needs of the present without compromising the ability of future generations to meet their own needs" (WCED 1987, 43). These concepts were thus indeterminate from the beginning: to defend sustainability entails deciding *what* ought to be sustained, for *whom*, for *how long*, and for *what reason* (Redclift 1993). Normative judgements are therefore indispensable for giving sustainability social and political meaning, despite the development of conceptual and empirical tools that have made it easier to measure unsustainability and to differentiate between different versions of the general principle of sustainability: natural capital, carrying capacity, ecological footprint, ecosystem services, material flows, socio-ecological metabolism. This scientific sophistication notwithstanding, there is no such thing as a unified theory of sustainability (Atkinson et al. 2007, 1). Rather, there exists a broad discourse of sustainability that contains a number of interpretations of what sustainability means and what it requires (Dryzek and Pickering 2019, 83). As the proper meaning of sustainability remains the subject of continued disagreement, it should be seen as a "contested concept" similar to those such as democracy, liberty, or social justice (Jacobs 1999; Bosselman 2008). Sustainability is thus a normative principle rather than a particular theory.

Such openness is highly relevant for understanding sustainability's relationship with democracy. If we define sustainability as any kind of socionatural relationship that is balanced enough to be maintained in the indefinite future, it is far from settled *how* this equilibrium will be reached. Scientific knowledge, notwithstanding its key role in providing environmental insights, does not have the last word. The reason is apparent:

> Sustainability cannot be determined objectively because defining sustainability involves value judgements with respect to which qualities of which resources should be sustained by which means, as well as for and by whom. Differences in human values make people's answers to these questions, and hence their definitions of sustainability, differ.
>
> *Sikor and Norgaard 1999, 49*

As a result, a general orientation towards sustainability does not determine the critical features of each specific adjustment, i.e. the degree in which natural forms are going to be protected, the priority to be assigned to social justice, the political means through which sustainability is pursued. That remains to be decided. The well-known distinction between *strong* and *weak* sustainability illustrates this in connection to one of the key dimensions of *any* version of sustainability, i.e. the degree in which natural capital can or should be substituted by man-made or cultivated capital. In strong or very strong versions of sustainability, such substitution is highly restricted – and vice versa (Neumayer 2010). Translated into simpler terms, strong versions of sustainability should lead to societies more respectful of the nonhuman world.

In the absence of a single version of sustainability, then, democracy may be necessary as a vehicle for achieving the latter – sorting out which values are to be given priority in the pursuit of it. However, such openness runs the risk that no particular sustainability is secured while the democratic conversation about the topic takes place. And it certainly means that sustainability remains a fuzzy term that does not imply any commitment to the kind of structural change that radical ecologists and many scientists regard as essential if serious harm and societal collapse are to be prevented (Meadowcroft 2013, 991). As John Dryzek (2013) observed, sustainable development can be seen as an imaginative (as opposed to prosaic) and reformist (as opposed to radical) discourse. In this respect, it could be said that climate change has simplified matters – either the planet remains habitable or it does not. But it still remains open how decarbonization is to be implemented: politics cannot be taken out of the picture. Furthermore, the emerging consensus about the need to fix the climate may not serve traditional green outcomes, such as the protection and welfare of nonhumans. But is there any alternative to democracy?

The eco-authoritarian temptation

A belief in the inability of democracy to deliver sustainability can lead to a disbelief in democracy. This is how the eco-authoritarian temptation emerges: an exceptional situation is invoked as the reason for the temporary suspension of democratic rule on behalf of human survival. Authoritarianism thus represents a supposed guarantee against unsustainability and a shortcut for delivering sustainability without the complications associated to democratic political processes. This anti-democratic temptation was once strong enough to generate a strain of thought, namely the so-called eco-authoritarianism that flourished in the 1970s. An ideological reflection of a decade in which ecological fears were incorporated into mainstream culture, eco-authoritarianism is also a latent possibility of environmentalism – one that is bound to resurface in times of ecological distress.

Eco-authoritarianism adopted theoretical shape in the variegated contributions from William Ophuls (1977), Paul Ehrlich (1969), Robert Heilbroner (1975), and Garret Hardin (1977). In Hobbesian fashion, Ophuls argued that the natural condition of society is that of the dearth of the resources upon which the human existence depends. As a result, an orderly distribution of scarce resources is the very foundation of politics. The approach's Malthusian undertones have much to do with the idea of a "population bomb" (Ehrlich 1969) about to explode. When ecological scarcity manifests itself, the community's survival becomes the basic political problem and political goods such as democracy or individual liberty cannot be enjoyed. Democracy turns out to be unfeasible under the pressure exerted by worsening ecological conditions and resources must be protected by political institutions that are able to coerce citizens into obedience (Heilbroner 1975, 86–90; Ophuls, 1977, 152). The suggestion is that of a green Leviathan: "Only a government possessing great powers to regulate individual behavior in the ecological common interest can deal effectively with the tragedy of the commons" (Ophuls 1977, 154). This strong, centralised state is to be ruled by "if not a class of ecological guardians, then at least a class of ecological mandarins who possess the esoteric knowledge needed to run it well" (Ophuls 1977, 163). Plato's philosopher king is replaced by the ecological expert: technocratic rule becomes the only path to sustainability. Thus Gilley's definition of authoritarian environmentalism's ideal as "a public policy model that concentrates authority in a few executive agencies manned by capable and uncorrupt elites seeking to improve environmental outcomes" (Gilley 2012, 288).

The ideal rests upon a number of questionable assumptions. The first is a rigid view of ecological limits, from which the very notion of ecological scarcity is derived. Such view is contestable: although there are absolute ecological limits to human activity, societies can and have often overcome natural limits by applying technological or institutional solutions (see Meadowcroft 2012). Second, it is assumed that a coercive centralized state is more capable of delivering sustainable results than democratic governments. But cooperation seems to be necessary for complex societies to go sustainable at a planetary level – and that makes it impossible to separate legitimacy from effectiveness, since only policies that are perceived as legitimate will be massively adopted (Saward 1998, 175). Third, the green Leviathan is supposed to possess the knowledge that is needed to achieve sustainability, although how that knowledge is produced remains unexplained. The reason may be that eco-authoritarian rule seems to endorse a single formula for sustainability, namely that of a steady-state economy that provides for small communities which in turn reduce their ecological impacts by radically diminishing their degree of activity. On the other hand, the eco-authoritarian argument takes for granted that implementing a closed version of sustainability would be easy on account of the mandarinate's technical knowledge, and yet a number of normative decisions would still have to be made – about birth control, the treatment of animals, the scope of personal liberties, and so on.

It follows that politicizing nature brings about a paradoxical de-politicization. Insofar as sustainability is deemed a technical problem to be solved by experts, no necessary connection between sustainability and democracy can be established. Such rationale can also be linked to the kind of moral consequentialism practiced by those environmentalists who present the moral end of protecting nature's intrinsic value as prior to moral deliberation and the collective social inquiry (see Minteer 2002, 45). Therefore, a decision will not be legitimate unless it respects such moral priority. Survivalism is not the only potential foundation for eco-authoritarianism – moral consequentialism can engender it too.

Is eco-authoritarianism a thing of the past? Not quite. Global warming is slowly creating new fears that resemble those of the 1970s, while liberal democracies themselves are threatened by the rise of populism and the return of nationalism. Weaker forms of eco-authoritarianism that looks at China as a powerful autocracy that exhibits ecological awareness are emerging (Beeson 2010). Whereas democratic regimes struggle to enact the structural changes required by global warming, the suspicion grows that "humanity will have to trade its liberty to live as it wishes in favour of a system where survival is paramount" (Shearman and Smith 2007, 4). As Dan Shahar explains, new eco-authoritarians now claim that:

> governments should not act as central planners but should nevertheless be granted full discretion to carry out public programs and to intervene in the personal and economic activities of citizens, without having to abide by limitations emerging from citizens' private and democratic right.
>
> *Shahar 2015, 346–347*

As market liberalism is uncapable of achieving sustainability, the authoritarian alternative becomes a risk worth taking if the climate crisis is to be effectively dealt with. Interestingly, though, technocratic rule has also been subjected to criticism by environmental thinkers who believe that expert rule may deprive citizens of the opportunity to decide how the Anthropocene should be confronted and/or designed. The latter could thus "usher a dangerous new world of undisputed scientific authority and anti-democratic politics" (Leach 2013). To be sure, this would be a different kind of authoritarianism – one that is better understood through categories such as governmentality or biopower. Yet it also chimes with the argument that liberal democracies are shifting towards "post-democracy" (Crouch 2004) and "post-politics" (Swyngedow 2013). In Blühdorn's phrasing:

> A strategy to avoid socio-political conflict is the continued depoliticization of eco-political issues – framed as matters of scientific knowledge, technological innovation and managerial perfection.
>
> *Blühdorn 2019, 269*

In this view, the technocratization of socionatural relations promote societal adaptation to a permanent condition of unsustainability. Mostly, the charge of managerialism is directed against ecomodernists who emphasize the need to rely on technology in order to achieve sustainability (see Asafu-Adjaye et al. 2015). That there exists a negative relationship between ecomodernism and democracy is however not proven, as it depends on how the latter is defined. It has even been suggested that ecomodernism is actually a "social democratic response to global ecological challenges", as it advocates state regulation and intervention in a capitalist economy in order to promote shared interests (Symons 2019). And yet if democracy must be intensely participatory to count as democracy, and sustainability must be strong to count as sustainability, the connection between them remains contingent and not necessary.

Reconciling sustainability and democracy

There are different ways in which the connection between sustainability and democracy can be strengthened. Whether a necessary link between them can be established at a theoretical level, is a different matter: nothing prevents autocracies from being sustainable, nor guarantees that democracies will prevent unsustainability. For their relationship to be firm, a pluralistic conception of sustainability must be embraced that requires a political system that takes pluralism into account while at the same time puts limitations to popular government for the sake of socio-ecological efficiency. This means that a narrow understanding of sustainability is discarded in favor of the recognition that a society can become sustainable in different, albeit not countless, ways. As an open-ended process, sustainability cannot be closed to ideas, findings, or technologies. This does not prevent radical approaches to social change from being defended – they are just not accepted as an inevitable pathway to sustainability. On the other hand, there is the question of how likely it is that democracies, as opposed to autocracies, commit themselves to the pursuit of sustainability. It seems that democracies are better equipped for that task – not only do they perform better on average terms, they also feature vibrant public spheres where the need to go sustainable can be articulated in a persuasive manner (see Torgerson 1999). Moreover, green activists and theorists are committed to democratic procedures: the association between sustainability and democracy may not work in theory, but it certainly works in practice.

Now, the claim that democracies are unsustainable begs a logical reply: unsustainable as compared to what? An overlooked aspect of this topic concerns the opposition between the *ideals* of sustainability and democracy, on the one hand, and the *reality* of them, on the other. On this regard, the sustainable society advocated by radical environmentalists possesses a utopian imprint: a final state of humanity where socionatural harmony is restored while a great deal of current social activities are curtailed – travel, trade, technological innovation, and so forth (see De Geus 1999). As a result, sustainable society turns into some kind of myth dissociated from real political processes. Needless to say, utopian accounts of sustainability play an important role in the realm of cultural production as they open up new political possibilities that can in turn influence social practices (see Garforth 2018). Yet if their descriptions are taken as the standard according to which the environmental performance of liberal democracies are to be judged, they may distort the way in which the latter is perceived and appraised.

On the other hand, empirical research shows that democracies present a better environmental performance than non-democratic regimes. This is unsurprising, as democratic institutions provide public goods more successfully than autocratic ones (Bättig and Bernauer 2009). A number of reasons have been suggested as an explanation: the high value that democracies places on the quality of life, their greater long-term future orientation, the responsiveness of its institutions, the opportunities for civil society to demand environmental action, the electorate's ability to change governments, or the process of political learning (see Esty and Porter 2005). Yet as Hanusch (2018) points out, there seems to be no conclusive explanations for the differences in environmental performance *among* democracies. Factors such as cyclical issue attention, the periodicity of elections, or the degree of parliamentarian fragmentation are considered – but the question remains open.

A more general interrogation follows pertaining to the manner in which liberal democracy can facilitate or hinder the achievement of sustainability. On this topic, there is a rich tradition of green criticism that points to a number of shortcomings that negatively affect the ability of democracies to tackle unsustainability: from the lack of political representation of those who are potentially affected by decisions that bear ecological costs (Eckersley 2004), to the undue influence that the contest for power has on the evaluation of the different interests at stake (Burnheim 1995), the orientation towards short-term solutions on account of the electoral cycle (Gleditsch and Sverdrup 2003), or the environmental costs of orthodox GDP-driven economic policies unable to measure genuine human well-being (Barry 2012). None of this suggests that democracy is to be dispensed with, but it certainly leads to the conclusion that liberal democracy must be deeply reformed if not replaced by some kind of "post-liberal democracy" (Eckersley 1992; Barry 2001). It could even be the case that the empirical transformation of democracy, as decision-making is increasingly assumed by governance networks, suggests a new compatibility between sustainability and democracy (see Sørensen and Torfing 2005).

A different version of the critique of liberal democracy emphasizes how the problems of the Anthropocene exacerbate existing vulnerabilities in democratic theory and practice in a moment when representative democracies are exposed to anti-establishment protest that questions their legitimacy (Di Paola and Jamieson 2018). Populism poses a challenge for liberal democracies as it locates the democratic will of the people as the main source of political legitimacy, thus contesting the mechanisms through which the latter filter popular sovereignty – constitutions and rights, bodies of experts that include judges, administrative procedures, non-majoritarian institutions, and so forth. An old problem thus adopts a new form: while sustainability requires popular consent, a polity that reinforces the will of the people may weaken the voice of expert knowledge while also questioning the need to implement transformative policies oriented towards sustainability. Hence the dilemma:

> if democracies fail to successfully address climate change and other problems of the Anthropocene, their legitimacy will be challenged on public utility grounds. If they aggressively attempt to address them, their legitimacy will likely be challenged on expressed preference grounds.
>
> *Di Paola and Jamieson 2018, 403*

In addition to this, there is the tendency of liberal democracies to be paralyzed by the action of so-called veto players, i.e. agents who can prevent reforms to be enacted and thus make it difficult for democracies to depart from the status quo (see Tsebelis 2002). Whether they result from constitutional design, as in the US, or from fragmented parliaments, as in Europe, enacting structural reforms is becoming increasingly difficult. The political effects of digitization must also be contemplated, as the latter seems to facilitate the rejection of expertise while reinforcing the plebiscitary elements of party politics, giving priority to emotional expressivism over reasoned debate (see Pörksen 2018). Perhaps the democracies of the Anthropocene will have to be more democratic in some respects (integrating more voices in the political process) and less in others (securing the role of experts) (Di Paola and Jamieson 2018, 423). For this to happen, though, sustainability must be constitutionalized: transformed into a shared principle that, while demanding specification, cannot be just ignored or neglected. The growing salience of the climate movement might push this forward.

It follows that the connection between sustainability and democracy is reinforced when both are seen as essentially open-ended, dynamic, and reflexive. These features also suggest that autocratic solutions cannot work, as eco-authoritarian advocates engage in the debate at the level of problem-solving effectiveness, thus assuming in advance that "we know what the problems are and what needs to be done" (Dryzek and Pickering 2019, 149). Yet problem-solving does not stand in logical priority to the continuous task of finding out what the problems are. The fact that environmental problems relate to each other in complex ways only increases the need for a reflexive approach that is capable of dealing with dynamism and uncertainty. This also entails that sustainability is a process rather than an end-state, as it requires constant adaptation and sensitivity to change (see Baker 2006, 7–8).

Sustainability can thus be seen as an inherently open principle for guiding social action, as it signals a general orientation for society that can in turn be pursued in several ways. Any of them will typically require a combination of state regulation, expert knowledge, public policies, and civil engagement. Ultimately, there are two sides to sustainability: it is a *principle* that demands a social orientation towards a balanced socionatural relation, as well as a *framework* that encompasses the conflict between different versions of such general principle. To put it differently, sustainability is a *concept* that can be decontested in different ways, thus resulting in a number of *conceptions* (Jacobs 1999).

A distinction can thus be made between two general views of sustainability, depending on how they deal with the openness and indeterminacy that are inherent to the task of making socionatural relations sustainable in the future (see Arias-Maldonado 2012). In more detail:

1. *Closed sustainability*. In this case, the particular shape of sustainability is technically or ideologically predetermined and removed from public debate. Technical feasibility or ideological fulfillment is given priority over democratic deliberation. As a consequence, no necessary link is established between sustainability and democracy. It could even be argued that closed conceptions of sustainability can only be realised in the absence of democratic checks and balances.
2. *Open sustainability*. Sustainability is conceived as a necessary societal goal whose content and conditions are not pre-given. It is thus inherently open and democratic, since only a democratic society guarantees the necessary conditions for its achievement. Given that society's future knowledge, preferences, technological capabilities, and environmental conditions are by definition uncertain and dynamic, sustainability cannot possibly be closed in advance.

A similar distinction is that between a *political* and a *metaphysical* conception of sustainability (Elliott 2007). Inspired by the Rawlsian "overlapping consensus" and drawing in Norton

(2005), Elliott separates a political conception that does not rely on controversial religious or philosophical views but rather on fundamental ideas that all reasonable members of a democratic polity can accept from a metaphysical conception that precisely relies on them. Following this, value pluralism is to be accepted as the paradoxical basis for sustainability (Norton 2005). It is paradoxical because sustainability itself is a value that cannot be negotiated, since different traditions of thought or ideologies will define it differently – just like freedom, equality, or justice. Hence sustainability must be assumed as a meta-consensus (Dryzek and Niemeyer 2006), a general goal that binds all members of the polity but do not compel them to embrace any particular version of it. In other words, an open approach to sustainability is justifiable insofar as the latter is conceived as a societal goal rather than as a scientific concept to be defined through observation or experiment (Robinson 2004, 382).

An open view of sustainability thus requires a democratic polity, but it is important not to conflate its *relative* openness with an *absolute* one that fails to appreciate the ecological dimension at play. Unlike justice or liberty, the practical outcomes of sustainability possess an existential quality: sustainability must *work* in a way that justice or liberty do not. That is why sustainability needs to be "ecologically attuned", so that "any view of sustainability that clashes with the ecological conditions for human and non-human flourishing must be ruled out" (Dryzek and Pickering 2019, 89). Despite it being open, then, sustainability is not endlessly open because the reality it refers to is not that open either. Moreover, society cannot stay in an unsustainable path while the conflict between different views of sustainability is democratically sorted out. This suggests that democracies must ensure that certain ecological standards are met at all times. Such ecological minimum would thus work like the "safe space for humanity" invoked by Rockström et al. (2009) in connection to the "planetary boundaries" that should not be trespassed. They are not an undisputable standard either and can themselves be subjected to criticism, but at least provide a departure point for avoiding the risk of runaway scenarios from which no safe retreat is possible.

Reflexivity and adaptability feature as the two main characteristics of an open, democratic approach to sustainability. Whereas reflexivity can be defined as the capacity to reconsider core values (Dryzek and Pickering 2019, 18), adaptability has been understood as a way of dealing with socionatural relations through experimentation, multiscalar analysis, and place-sensitivity (Norton 2005, 92). Given that human needs and expectations may change alongside environmental conditions, sustainability cannot be pursued in the absence of these two guiding principles. Whether liberal democracy is apt to the task, is a different question. As Norton puts it: "The practical problem is whether it is possible to design and implement a deliberative decision process that can operate effectively in complex and pluralistic situations" (Norton 2005, 403). The aim of inclusion is to enhance reflexivity by way of including insights from communities affected by environmental change and signals from the non-human world (see Eckersley 2000; Dryzek 1995). Yet a selective reflexivity that attends to particular groups or entities is better served by supplementing liberal democracies with participatory-cum-deliberative devices that operate in parallel to the wider public debate. At the same time, though, the epistemic dimension of liberal democracies might need to be reinforced in order to prevent the populist erosion of scientific knowledge, perhaps by providing experts with greater visibility or by engaging them in formal discussions with the public. An enlarged participation does not automatically mean more sustainability. Likewise, the emotive dimension of sustainability might be worth exploring in order to increase public support.

It should be noted, though, that liberal-democratic *regimes* are also liberal-democratic *societies*, i.e. communities whose members act and interact under the protection of the law in ways that foster scientific, moral, political, economic, and technological innovation. Likewise, collective actors are free to engage in collective mobilization oriented to persuade others about the value or merit of a given goal or value. It is thus not true that citizens can only express themselves politically in the ballot box – for some time now we are living in a "movement society" (Meyer and Tarrow 1998). Digitization and social networks have made it even easier for individuals and groups to express their political demands in the public sphere (see Margetts et al. 2016). Although none of these developments *benefit* environmentalism in a particular way, they do not *damage* it either – on the contrary, it provides sustainability advocates with new instruments. Democratic institutions do not exhaust democratic possibilities.

For that reason, environmental thinkers have paid attention to liberal civil society as a site for advancing sustainability in a variety of ways. There is the question of educating citizens, be it through public campaigns or via the affective impact of environmental shocks such as heatwaves or hurricanes (see Shapiro 2018). Ecological citizenship has been defended as a way to emphasize duties over rights in the practice of democratic citizenship – thus encouraging sustainable behaviors that include ethical shopping or traveling (see Dobson 2003; Jackson 2007). On the other hand, it is within liberal societies that initiatives like the Transition Movement can exist: a number of people trying to build local sustainable communities meant both as a way of living and as a blueprint for the inspiration of others (see Hopkins 2008). Likewise, democracy becomes indispensable whenever environmental justice is deemed an essential part of the green agenda and thus of sustainability itself (see Ellis 2019). Once again, nothing guarantees that sustainability will be effectively promoted, but there does not seem to be a better vehicle for advancing sustainability than the one offered by imperfect, albeit improvable and ever-changing, liberal democracies.

Towards a conclusion: sustainability and democracy in the Anthropocene

As the planet continues to warm and other challenges associated to the Anthropocene make themselves present, from ocean acidification to loss of biodiversity, doubts arise as to the usefulness of the sustainability paradigm. Climate change, after all, is not just another environmental problem: if it is not tackled, the planet will most likely become unhabitable. This means that there will be no opportunity to rebuild human civilization along more sustainable lines – unsustainability spells apocalypse. Thus Blühdorn's interrogation: "Why is a paradigm that has provided so extensive evidence of its failure to deliver radical structural change nevertheless not abandoned in favor of a more effective approach?" (Blühdorn 2019, 260). In other words: how good is sustainability if it cannot guarantee survival?

Such doubts are compounded by suspicions about sustainability's neutralization by established interests. According to this view, sustainability would have been co-opted by dominant discourses and thus deprived of its transformative potential. This has led to the announcement of "the end of sustainability" (Benson and Craig 2014, 777), even though just a few years earlier it was said that "environmentalism is morphing into sustainability" (O'Riordan 2009, 313). As for the alternative, "resilience" has been suggested as providing "a superior framework for analysing sustainability in the context of irreversibility, surprise and non-marginal change" (Adger 2007, 79). Yet resilience, a term that designs the ability of a system to endure external shocks without losing its qualities, sounds ecologically static and politically conservative – it lacks sustainability's range. Resilience can be a feature among others in sustainable societies, but it is doubtful that it can ever replace sustainability. On the other hand, sustainability does not *necessarily* call for radical structural change – only some conceptions of it do that, while others go for imaginative reform instead.

Yet it cannot be denied that climate change and the Anthropocene have an impact on how sustainability is conceived, perceived, and enacted. On the one hand, planetary pressures simplify the normative justification of sustainability: as climate change threatens the habitability of the Earth, there seems to be no need for sophisticated arguments on behalf of sustainability. The feeling that there is time yet to re-arrange socionatural relations in a desirable way, though, has led to the controversial interrogation about the "good Anthropocene" (see Arias-Maldonado 2019). And while the existential risk posed by climate change and other Anthropocene manifestations will revitalize the eco-authoritarian argument, the link between democracy and sustainability is still strong enough. As Dauvergne (2016, 387) suggests, the narrative of sustainability is too valuable to be surrendered, especially if the distinction between the general principle and its particular versions is kept in mind.

It should not be forgotten that, as this chapter has tried to show, the relationship between democracy and sustainability is itself historical and subject to change. As environmentalism progressed from the fringes to the mainstream, its internal pluralism increased and a dialogue with the liberal tradition was initiated that widened the formerly narrow understanding of sustainability (see Humphrey 2003). At the same time, liberal societies adopted the goal of achieving a balanced relationship with their environments, thus opening up a conversation about how sustainability can be achieved by democratic means and without necessarily abandoning democracy itself or the search for social well-being. Strong versions of sustainability were soon contested by alternatives such as the justice-centered sustainable development or the innovation-oriented paradigm of ecological modernization (see Baker 2006; Mol, Sonnenfeld and Spaargaren 2009). It was argued that this normalization of the sustainability discourse meant that the ecological crisis had turned "from apocalypse to way of life" (Buell 2003).

Ironically, climate change and the other challenges of the Anthropocene are now calling for an urgent societal response that is testing the validity of the sustainability paradigm – the apocalyptic frame has been reintroduced in the public sphere. Arguably, the Anthropocene needs to be more reflexive and more integrated with other social values (Dryzek and Pickering 2019, 19). Yet it must also deliver structural change in a complex, interconnected global society – an ambitious goal that asks for a reinforcement of scientific expertise and multi-level governance. The Anthropocene might even be a valuable resource for democratic renewal if horizons of space, time, community, and agency are expanded as a response to the challenges posed by the new epoch (Eckersley 2017). For democracy to deliver sustainability in the Anthropocene, then, a delicate balance must be reached: between representation and participation, between public engagement and private consent, between technocratic efficiency and political legitimacy. If that fails, perhaps sustainability and democracy end up parting their ways. Let us hope they don't.

References

Adger, N., 2007. Ecological and Social Resilience. In G. Atkinson et al. eds, *Handbook of Sustainable Development*. Cheltenham and Northampton: Edward Elgar, 78–90.
Arias-Maldonado, M., 2012. *Real Green. Sustainability After the End of Nature*. Aldershot: Ashgate.
Arias-Maldonado, M., 2019. Towards a Good Anthropocene? In M. Arias-Maldonado and Z. Trachtenberg, eds. *Rethinking the Environment for the Anthropocene: Political Theory and Socionatural Relations in the New Geological Epoch*. London: Routledge, 137–150. https://doi.org/10.4324/9780203731895.
Asafu-Adjaye, J., et al., 2015. *An Ecomodernist Manifesto*. Available from: www.ecomodernism.org/.
Atkinson, G., Dietz, S., and Neumayer, E., 2007. *Handbook of Sustainable Development*. Cheltenham and Northampton: Edward Elgar.
Baker, S., 2006. *Sustainable Development*. London and New York: Routledge.

Ball, T., 2006. Democracy. In A. Dobson and R. Eckersley, eds. *Political Theory and the Ecological Challenge*. Cambridge: Cambridge University Press, 131–147.

Barry, B., 1979. Is Democracy Special? In P. Laslett and W.G. Runciman, eds. *Philosophy, Politics and Society. Fifth Series*. Oxford: Basil Blackwell, 155–196.

Barry, J., 2001. Greening Liberal Democracy: Practice, Theory and Political Economy. In J. Barry and M. Wissenburg, eds. *Sustaining Liberal Democracy. Ecological Challenges and Opportunities*. Houndmills: Palgrave, 59–80.

Barry, J., 2012. *The Politics of Actually Existing Unsustainability*. Oxford: Oxford University Press.

Bättig, M., and Bernauer, T., 2009. National Institutions and Global Public Goods: Are Democracies More Cooperative in Climate Change Policy? *International Organization*, 63 (2), 281–308.

Beeson, M., 2010. The Coming of Environmental Authoritarianism. *Environmental Politics*, 19 (2), 276–294.

Benson, M., and Craig, R., 2014. The End of Sustainability. *Society and Natural Resources*, 27 (7), 777–782.

Blühdorn, I., 2007. Sustaining the Unsustainable: Symbolic Politics and the Politics of Simulation. *Environmental Politics*, 16 (2), 251–275.

Blühdorn, I., 2019. Sustainability – Post-Sustainability – Unsustainability. In T. Gabrielson, C. Hall, J.M. Meyer, and D. Schlosberg, eds. *The Oxford Handbook of Environmental Political Theory*. Oxford: Oxford University Press, 259–273.

Bosselmann, K., 2008. *The Principle of Sustainability*. Aldershot: Ashgate.

Buell, F., 2003. *From Apocalypse to Way of Life: Environmental Crisis in the American Century*. New York: Routledge.

Burnheim, J., 1995. Power-Trading and the Environment. *Environmental Politics*, 4 (4), 49–65.

Crouch, C., 2004. *Post-democracy*. Cambridge: Polity.

Dauvergne, P., 2016. The Sustainability Story: Exposing Truths, Half-Truths, and Illusions. In S. Nicholson and S. Jinnah, eds. *New Earth Politics: Essays from the Anthropocene*. Cambridge: MIT Press, 387–404.

Dahl, R., 1979. Procedural Democracy. In P. Laslett and W.G. Runciman, eds. *Philosophy, Politics and Society. Fifth Series*. Oxford: Basil Blackwell, 97–133.

De Geus, M., 1999. *Ecological Utopias. Envisioning the Sustainable Society*. Utrecht: International Books.

Di Paola, M., and Jamieson, D., 2018. Climate Change and the Challenges to Democracy. *University of Miami Law Review*, 369. Available from: h9ps://repository.law.miami.edu/umlr/vol72/iss2/5.

Dobson, A., 2003. *Citizenship and the Environment*. Oxford: Oxford University Press.

Dryzek, J., 1995. Political and Ecological Communication. *Environmental Politics*, 4 (4), 13–30. https://doi.org/10.1080/09644019508414226.

Dryzek, J., 2013. *The Politics of the Earth: Environmental Discourses*. 3rd ed. Oxford: Oxford University Press.

Dryzek, J., and Niemeyer, S., 2006. Reconciling Pluralism and Consensus as Political Ideals. *American Journal of Political Science*, 50 (3), 634–649.

Dryzek, J., and Pickering, J., 2019. *The Politics of the Anthropocene*. Oxford: Oxford University Press.

Eckersley, R., 1992. *Environmentalism and Political Theory*. New York: State University of New York Press.

Eckersley, R., 1996. Greening Liberal Democracy. The Rights Discourse Revisited. In B. Doherty and M. de Geus, eds. *Democracy and Green Political Thought*. London: Routledge, 212–236.

Eckersley, R., 2000. Deliberative Democracy, Ecological Representation and Risk. Towards a Democracy of the Affected. In M. Saward, ed., *Democratic Innovation. Deliberation, Representation and Association*. London and New York: Routledge, 117–132.

Eckersley, R., 2004. *The Green State*. Cambridge: The MIT Press.

Eckersley, R., 2017. Geopolitan Democracy in the Anthropocene. *Political Studies*, 65 (4), 983–999.

Ehrlich, P., 1969. *The Population Bomb*. New York: Sierra Club.

Elliott, K., 2007. Norton's Conception of Sustainability. *Environmental Ethics*, 29 (1), 3–22.

Ellis, E., 2019. Democracy as Constraint and Possibility for Environmental Action. In T. Gabrielson, C. Hall, J.M. Meyer, and D. Schlosberg, eds. *The Oxford Handbook of Environmental Political Theory*. Oxford: Oxford University Press, 505–519.

Esty, D., and Porter, M., 2005. National Environmental Performance: An Empirical Analysis of Policy Results and Determinants. *Environment and Development Economics*, 10, 391–434.

Garforth, L., 2018. *Green Utopias. Environmental Hope Before and After Nature*. Cambridge: Polity.

Gilley, B., 2012. Authoritarian Environmentalism and China's Response to Climate Change. *Environmental Politics*, 21 (2), 287–307.

Gleditsch, N., and Sverdrup, B., 2003. Democracy and the Environment. In M. Redlicft and E. Page, eds. *Human Security and the Environment: International Comparisons*. Cheltenham: Edward Elgar, 45–70.

Goodin, R., 1992. *Green Political Theory*. London: Polity.
Goodin, R., 1996. Enfranchising the Earth, and its Alternatives. *Political Studies*, XLIV, 835–849.
Hanusch, F., 2018. *Democracy and Climate Change*. Abingdon: Routledge.
Hardin, G., 1977. The Tragedy of the Commons. In G. Hardin and J. Baden, eds., *Managing the Common*. San Francisco: W.H. Freeman and Company, 16–30.
Hayward, T., 1998. *Political Theory and Ecological Values*. Cambridge: Polity.
Heilbroner, R., 1975. *An Inquiry into The Human Prospect*. London: Calder & Boyars.
Hopkins, R., 2008. *The Transition Handbook*. Totnes: Green Books.
Humphrey, M., ed., 2003. *Political Theory and and the Environment: A Reassessment*. Londres: Frank Cass.
Humphrey, M., 2004. Ecology, Democracy and Autonomy: A Problem of Wishful Thinking. In Y. Levy and M. Wissenburg, eds. *Liberal Democracy and Environmentalism. The end of environmentalism?* London: Routledge, 115–126.
Inglehart, R., 2018. *Cultural Evolution*. Cambridge: Cambridge University Press.
Jackson, T., 2007. Sustainable Consumption. In G. Atkinson, S. Dietz, and E. Neumayer, eds. *Handbook of Sustainable Development*. Cheltenham and Northampton: Edward Elgar, 254–268.
Jacobs, M., 1997. Environmental Valuation, Deliberative Democracy and Public Decision-making Institutions. In J. Foster, ed. *Valuing Nature? Economics, Ethics and Environment*. London: Routledge, 223–243.
Jacobs, M., 1999. Sustainable Development as a Contested Concept. In A. Dobson, eds. *Fairness and Futurity. Essays on Environmental Sustainability and Social Justice*. Oxford: Oxford University Press, 21–45.
Leach, M., 2013. Democracy in the Anthropocene? Science and Sustainable Development Goals at the UN. *Huffington Post*, 28 March.
Lynch, A., and Veland, S., 2018. *Urgency in the Anthropocene*. Cambridge: The MIT Press.
Margetts, H., John, P., Hale, S., and Yasseri, T., 2016. *Political Turbulence. How Social Media Shape Collective Action*. Princeton and Oxford: Princeton University Press.
Meadowcroft, J., 2012. Pushing the Boundaries: Governance for Sustainable Development and a Politics of Limits. In J. Meadowcroft, O. Langhelle, and A. Rudd, eds. *Governance, democracy and sustainable development: Moving beyond the impasse?* Cheltenham: Edward Elgar, 272–296.
Meadowcroft, J., 2013. Reaching the Limits? Developed Country Engagement with Sustainable Development in a Challenging Conjuncture. *Environment & Planning C: Government & Policy*, 31, 988–1002.
Meyer, D., and Tarrow, S., 1998. *The Social Movement Society: Contentious Politics and the New Century*. Boulder: Rowman and Littlefield.
Mills, M., 1996. Green Democracy: The Search for an Ethical Solution. In B. Doherty and M. de Geus, eds. *Democracy and Green Political Thought*. London: Routledge, 97–114.
Minteer, B., 2002. Deweyan Democracy and Environmental Ethics. In B. Minteer and B. Pepperman Taylor, eds. *Democracy and the Claims of Nature. Critical Perspectives for a New Century*. Lanham: Rowan & Littlefield, 33–48.
Mol, A., Sonnenfeld, D., and Spaargaren, G., eds., 2009. *The Ecological Modernisation Reader*. London: Routledge.
Neumayer, E., 2010. *Weak versus Strong Sustainability. Exploring the Limits of Two Opposing Paradigms*. 3rd edition. Cheltenham: Edward Elgar.
Norton, B., 2002. Democracy and Environmentalism: Foundations and Justifications in Environmental Policy. In B. Minteer and B. Pepperman Taylor, eds., *Democracy and the Claims of Nature. Critical Perspectives for a New Century*. Lanham: Rowan & Littlefield, 11–32.
Norton, B., 2005. *Sustainability. A Philosophy of Adaptative Ecosystem Management*. Chicago: The University of Chicago Press.
Ophuls, W., 1977. *Ecology and the Politics of Scarcity*. San Francisco: W.H. Freeman and Company.
O'Riordan, T., 2009. Reflection on the Pathways to Sustainability. In W.N. Adler and A. Jordan, eds. *Governing Sustainability*. Cambridge: Cambridge University Press, 307–328.
Pörksen, B., 2018. *Die grosse Gereiztheit. Wege aus der kollektiven Erregung*. Munich: Carl Hansen Verlag.
Redclift, M., 1993. Sustainable Development: Needs, Values, and Rights. *Environmental Values*, 2 (1), 3–20.
Robinson, J., 2004. Squaring the Circle? Some Thoughts on the Idea of Sustainable Development. *Ecological Economics*, 48 (4), 369–384.
Rockström, J., et al., 2009. A Safe Operating Space for Humanity. *Nature*, 461, 472–475.
Saward, M., 1996. Must Democrats be Environmentalists? In B. Doherty and M. de Geus, eds. *Democracy and Green Political Thought. Sustainability, Rights and Citizenship*. London: Routledge, 79–96.

Saward, M., 1998. *The Terms of Democracy*. Cambridge: Polity.

Shahar, D., 2015. Rejecting Eco-Authoritarianism, Again. *Environmental Values*, 24 (3), 345–366.

Shapiro, M., 2018. *The Political Sublime*. Durham and London: Duke University Press.

Shearman, D., and Smith, J., 2007. *The Climate Change Challenge and the Failure of Democracy*. Westsport: Praeger.

Sikor, T., and Norggard, R., 1999. Principles for Sustainability: Protection, Investment, Co-operation and Innovation. In J. Köhn, J. Gowdy, F. Hinterberger, and J. van der Straaten, eds. *Sustainability in Question. The Search for a Conceptual Framework*. Cheltenham: Edward Elgar, 49–65.

Smith, G., 2001. Taking Deliberation Seriously: Institutional Design and Green Politics. *Environmental Politics*, 10 (3), 72–93.

Sørensen, E., and Torfing, J., 2005. Network Governance and Post-Liberal Democracy. *Administrative Theory & Praxis*, 27 (2), 197–237.

Swyngedouw E., 2013. The Non-political Politics of climate Change. *ACME: An International Journal for Critical Geographies*, 12 (1), 1–8.

Symons, J., 2019. *Ecomodernism. Technology, Politics and the Climate Crisis*. Cambridge: Polity.

Torgerson, D., 1999. *The Promise of Green Politics*. Durham: Duke University Press.

Tsebelis, G., 2002. *Veto Players. How Political Institutions Work*. Princeton: Princeton University Press.

World Commission on Environment and Development., 1987. *Our Common Future*. Oxford: Oxford University Press.

Westra, L., 1993. The Ethics of Environmental Holism and the Democratic State: Are they in Conflict? *Environmental Values*, 2 (2), 125–136.

PART II

Theories and concepts

5
INCLUSION, PARTICIPATION AND FUTURE GENERATIONS

Maija Setälä

Introduction

Democratic political systems are under strain. Among many other problems, they should make urgent decisions on how to make their economic and social systems more sustainable. According to Brundtland Commissions' report, sustainable development "[…] meets the needs of the present without compromising the ability of future generations to meet their own needs" (World Commission on Environment and Development 1987, 43). The exacerbation of environmental problems such as climate change and loss of biodiversity seems to make the goal of sustainable development increasingly hard to reach.

While there has been public awareness of the severity of the human-caused environmental problems for several decades already, political response to them seems inadequate so far. Representative democratic governments seem to recognize the problems, but they have difficulties in devising and pursuing policies that would efficiently address them. This raises the question whether current forms of democratic participation are conducive to sustainable policymaking and what could be done in order to improve their capacity in this respect. The problem of democratic short-termism or myopia has often been discussed as a problem of intergenerational justice (e.g. Caney 2018). Indeed, the problems of short-termism are likely to be most severe in cases of intergenerational conflicts, i.e. in situations where current generations should make sacrifices in order to ensure the well-being of future generations (e.g. Hara et al. 2019).

The aim of this chapter is analyzing the reasons for why current patterns of democratic inclusion and participation often seem defective in terms of future generations and their interests. The obvious problem is that future generations do not exist and therefore they are, by definition, excluded from the democratic process. Moreover, certain institutional characteristics, most notably electoral competition, in current representative systems may further aggravate the tendencies towards short-termism. The chapter argues democratic deliberation is essential for enhancing consideration of long-term effects of policies without compromising democratic legitimacy.

I will first discuss how the key concept of this chapter, namely inclusion, is understood in different theories of democracy. I will especially focus on the role of so-called all-affected principle in democratic theory. Thereafter, I will point out some theoretical and empirical problems that arise when trying to enhance the inclusion of future generations and their interests in representative democracies. Finally, I will show how inclusive deliberative forums, especially so-called deliberative mini-publics, can facilitate consideration of future interests and discuss their potential roles in the context of representative democracies and supranational government.

The issue of inclusion in democratic theory

Currently, the concept of democracy is typically used to refer to a political system where decisions are made by representatives who are elected in free and fair elections with universal suffrage (e.g. Dahl 1989). In addition to the procedure of free and fair election of decision-makers, democracy requires that all adult citizens living in a particular geographical unit should have equal rights to participate in elections and to act politically. Moreover, citizens should have equal democratic rights and freedoms, most notably freedom of expression and right of political association.

In this view of liberal, representative democracy, inclusion means that all those adult individuals who are bound by collective decisions should have the right to participate in processes of making them – or at least in electing representatives making those decisions. This idea is often referred to as *the all-bound* principle. Because collective decisions legally and coercively bind people living in a specific, territorially defined political unit, people living within the borders of that unit should have a say in making those decisions. This seems to imply that all adult individuals living permanently within a jurisdiction of, for example, a nation state. Dahl (1989, 207) argues that "[t]he criteria of the democratic process presuppose the rightfulness of the unit itself." According to Dahl, the legitimacy of the *demos* follows from history and politics, and democratic theory or procedures cannot provide a definite answer to the conflicts related to defining boundaries of democratic units. However, there are some controversial aspects even in this traditional understanding of the *demos*, for example, when it comes to the rights of migrants to participate (Dahl 1989). In addition, there are concerns about the detrimental effects of societal and economic inequalities on the functioning of democratic systems. Formal democratic rights do not ensure that everyone actually has an equal say in decision-making.

Young (2000, 50–52) makes a distinction between two different forms of political exclusion, namely external and internal exclusion, both of which can be observed in current representative systems. External exclusion means exclusion of individuals or groups who should be entitled to participate in decision-making. Examples of external exclusion include exclusive patterns of policymaking such as back-door brokering and the dominance of powerful interest groups in public discussion. Internal exclusion refers to variety of practices through which affected individuals' or groups' interests and viewpoints are not properly taken into account in the political discourse or political process. For Young, democracies are just only as long as they strive to overcome patterns of external and internal exclusion. Representation of marginalized groups could be ensured e.g. through quotas in representative bodies. More inclusive institutions would not only ensure articulation of various affected interests in decision-making, but it would also have emancipatory and developmental effects when affected groups can articulate their own viewpoints and interests.

During the past decades, the idea of liberal, representative democracy has been challenged on different grounds. Theories of participatory and deliberative democracy point out that the liberal conception of democracy fails to account properly for the key aspect of democracy, namely the idea of popular self-government. In more practical terms, participatory and deliberative democrats argue that citizens ought to have more opportunities to participate in making decisions affecting their everyday lives (e.g. Pateman 2012) and more opportunities for political participation in the context of large-scale representative democracies (Barber 1984).

Although there are some overlapping themes in the theories of participatory and deliberative democracy, they also differ in certain important respects (cf. Mutz 2006; Floridia 2017). The differences between these theories can also be understood in terms of different understandings of the notion of inclusion. While participatory theory requires inclusive participation and empowerment in different contexts of life, deliberative democracy emphasizes the role of inclusive public deliberation in collective decision-making. In such deliberative process, claims of those affected by decisions are weighed equitably by their merits. Compared to deliberative democracy, participatory democracy is more "proceduralist" in the sense that it emphasizes intrinsic values such as political equality involved in democratic participation (Saffon and Urbinati 2013). Participatory theorists often highlight the positive by-products or side-effects of participation, i.e. its capacity to enhance the quality of life and individual development (cf. Elster 1986). Theories of deliberative democracy emphasize, not just the procedural values of democracy such as political equality, but also the capacity of democratic processes to yield "better" collective decisions measured by their epistemic quality and justice. However, the instrumental value of democratic deliberation depends on the inclusiveness of deliberative processes. In this respect, concern for processes and outcomes are by no means mutually exclusive in the theory of deliberative democracy.

The question of inclusion – or the definition of the *demos* – has become more acute in democratic theory and practice during the recent decades. This is because the definition of the *demos* by geographical boundaries seems increasingly problematic in the globalized world with a nexus of spatial and temporal interdependencies Michal Zürn (2000, 187–189) has discussed the problem of inclusion in terms of two types of incongruence problems, namely so-called input and output incongruence. Input incongruence refers to the lacking capacity of some individuals or groups to influence decisions affecting their lives, which basically reduces their capacity to rule themselves. Output incongruence means that democratic polities fail to achieve collectively defined goals due to political – or other types of – decisions made outside its jurisdiction. Some kind of multi-level governance seems to be a remedy to the problems of input and output incongruence. It would allow participation and representation of a wider range of affected groups in making collective decisions and democratic will-formation in political units of a different scale. As a consequence, the idea of multi-level governance seems to rest on some kind of an assessment of the geographical scope of causal effects of political decisions This is obviously against Dahl's (1989) purely proceduralist view that precludes the use of such substantive criteria when defining the *demos*.

While the all-bound principle is based on the legal effects of decisions, *the all-affected principle* is based on an assessment of the causal effects of decisions (Näsström 2011; Beckman 2013). In other words, democratic decision-making should allow inclusion or representation of all those who are legally bound but also those who are (in significant ways) causally affected by a particular decision. The all-affected principle is based on the view that democracy is not just a formal procedure, but it needs to be linked with a more substantial conception of justice in order to be legitimate. The all-affected principle seems to be especially relevant whenever political decisions harm or threaten the vital interests of people who are excluded from decision-making processes leading to them.

There are various criticisms of the all-affected principle (e.g. Beckman 2013). One of the critical questions pertains to the idea of "being affected" – what does it mean and who is entitled to define the group of affected people? The all-affected principle is often used to justify more inclusive institutions that provide participatory opportunities for groups that are currently excluded. However, the all-affected principle could be actually interpreted to require more exclusive definitions of the *demos* (Lagerspetz 2015). The most fundamental problem is that the all-affected principle defines democratic citizenship in terms of having stakes in the issue rather in terms of equal rights. Giving voice primarily to affected groups could actually lead to situations where those with high stakes have a bigger say in the issue. This seems to lead to conclusions that contradict the central idea of democracy, namely political equality.

At the same time, for example, Näsström (2011) defends the all-affected principle. She cautions against falling into the "people trap," in other words, defining democracy in terms of pre-established political units such as nation states. The all-affected principle remains normatively relevant because collective decisions – or non-decisions – made in democratic systems may harm people living outside territorial boundaries. Sometimes the question is about serious harms with respect to the vital interests of the affected groups. Näsström (2011) argues further that the exclusion of affected groups may lead to situations that are not only unjust, but non-acceptable from the democratic perspective. Most notably, political exclusion of affected groups may undermine their capacity to govern themselves. In the most obvious cases of domination such as colonial rule, the incapacity to self-rule is a result of intentional efforts to control other subjects. Sometimes the incapacity of self-government is an unintended consequence of collective decisions. Consider, for example, a situation where extreme weather conditions caused by human-induced climate change destroy communities' livelihood and the capacity to self-rule.

However, the *demos* is not just constrained by geographical borders, but necessarily also by time. In this respect, the non-representation of future people can be regarded as a specific instance incongruence problem recognized in democratic theory. Similarly to attempts to use all-affected principle to justify multi-level governance in geographical terms, one could try to delineate the temporal limits of political units. This would be in line with the view that the time span of our responsibilities for future generations depends on the type of (the negative) effects of our decisions (Caney 2018). In particular, if the causal effects of policies appear to be short-lived and reversible, it may be perfectly justified for the current people to consider the issue only from their own perspectives (Beckman 2013).

If the (negative) effects or, in more economic terms, externalities reach far to the future and are irreversible, it seems to be a requirement of justice that interests of those affected in the future are considered in the decision-making process. For example, a decision to build a nuclear power plant will have irreversible material consequences that could affect people living hundreds or even thousands of years from now. The extensive use of fossil fuels may cause drastic changes in the climate that affect communities and societies indefinitely. In addition to such well-established cases of "long-term" problems, there is a possibility that decisions made to address urgent or "short-term" problems can have anticipated or non-anticipated impacts that reach far in the future. Therefore, it seems relevant to ask whether the interests of those living in the future should be considered in decision-making. And if so, how could it happen in practice?

Indeed, future generations seem to be in a worse position than those affected across borders. While negative externalities reaching across geographical borders can already be observed and experienced, the problems of future generations have not been materialized yet. In this respect, future problems largely remain "out of sight." In case of transnational externalities, there is at least a chance that those affected can articulate their own interests in a public debate, even though they may lack formal democratic rights. In other words, these affected groups have some, although often limited, political leverage such as discursive power, or sometimes even bargaining power in transnational politics.

This is obviously not the case when it comes to future generations. While there may be democratic ways of addressing incongruence problems by adopting new forms of democratic governance at transnationally or globally, there does not seem to be room for intergenerational democracy. As Beckman (2013) points out, the specific measures taken to ensure it set limits on democratic self-government among the present people. In this respect, the kinds of democratic remedies for the exclusion of affected groups adopted by the defenders of transnational, multi-level democracy seem to be out of question in the case of future generations. However, Caney (2018) argues that the fact that future generations cannot have democratic opportunities to influence policies does not remove our moral responsibilities to them.

How to square a circle? Sensitivity to future interests in democratic participation and deliberation

Institutional drivers and responses to short-termism

To summarize the discussion above, political decision-making has a variety of consequences that reach beyond the spatial and temporal limits of the *demos*. Although one may identify certain issue areas where these kinds of effects are rather obvious, it is not always possible to do so *a priori*. While harms caused by political decisions made across the borders can often be made visible and affected groups are often capable of defend their own interests, this is not possible for future generations. In this respect, future generations remain a much more profound challenge to democratic inclusion than marginalized groups within the *demos* or affected group across borders.

In addition to this reality, there are some aspects in current representative democracies that aggravate the problem of short-termism. However, this is not to say that representative democracies would be more myopic than, for example, authoritarian regimes. Jacobs (2016) has analyzed the so-called drivers of short-termism in representative democracies, such as poor information, uncertainty of future consequences of policy choices and opposition of potential cost-bearers of more long-term policies. Yet the most important driver is probably electoral competition that seems to incentivize politicians and parties to act according to short-term interests of their constituents. Elected representatives are likely to be tempted to "pander" their potential voters in order to secure electoral support (Chambers 2009). In order to succeed in elections, candidates and parties often need to mobilize support by appealing to concrete benefits to their potential voters rather than uncertain rewards for future generations.

However, representative systems also involve various institutional designs that may help elected representatives to consider the future consequences of polices. There institutional mechanisms that encourage consideration of long-term policy consequences. First, the delegation of authority to independent agencies can be regarded as a way to enhance long-term policymaking. Admittedly, this seems like a rather undemocratic way of improving the quality of decision-making. Second, parliamentary committees should allow a space for careful consideration of policy choices from different perspectives. In order to secure a space for the exchange of arguments, committee work is often secret or only partly open to public (e.g. Elster 1998). Third, certain principles applied in law-making, such as those requiring generality, durability and prospectivity of laws, should encourage law-makers to consider the impact of public decisions from the perspective of all those who are affected by them (Vermeule 2007, 33).

There are also ways in which future interests can be represented in political processes. Elected representatives may adopt a role in defending their interests. Using Mansbridge's (2003) terms, elected representatives can act as surrogate representatives for future generations. According to Mansbridge, surrogate representation simply means that legislators discursively represent some constituents outside their own districts. Obviously, one might ask whether surrogate representation is a sufficient method of representing future generations. Even if representatives were motivated to do so, there is a risk that representatives' interpretations of future generations' interests are colored by the interests of their constituents to whom they are actually accountable in elections.

As a remedy for these types of problems, Dobson (1996) has suggested that there should be specific quota for representatives for future generations within parliaments. In order to ensure the democratic legitimacy, Ekeli (2005) proposed that the parliamentary representatives for future generations should be democratically elected. However, this suggestion entails a risk that the tendencies towards short-termism created by electoral mechanism would occur also in case of representatives for future generations. There are also suggestions and actual practices involving "independent offices for future generations" (Smith 2015) that articulate and defend the interests of future generations, especially in situations where some policy choices might work against them. In this respect, the tasks of offices for future generations would be similar to "ombudsmen" for particular marginalized groups who may not be able to defend their own interests, such as the disabled, the young or the elderly.

Obviously, independent officials for future generations lack the most essential procedural features of democratic representation, namely delegation and accountability. Furthermore, in contrast to proxy representatives of marginalized groups, officials for future generations are even less anchored in the civil society since their "constituents" do not exist yet. In this respect, they are likely to fail to represent the diversity of societal viewpoints among future generations, which should not be regarded as unitary entities but individuals and groups with different interests and perspectives. The lack of representation of these perspectives is obviously a problem from the normative perspective requiring inclusiveness of democratic decision-making (Smith 2019).

But, as Smith (2019) point out, because of the lacking connection to the civil society, these kinds of institutions are also likely to suffer from a lack of sociological legitimacy as well. As a consequence, there may be very few defenders for offices for future generations in situations when they are challenged in the public. And these institutions are likely to be challenged whenever their recommendations are against strong presentist interests. Indeed, the actual experiences seem to confirm the view of their vulnerability of independent officials for future generations. Israel and Hungary established offices for future generations in the 2000s, but these institutions have either been weakened or abolished. Smith (2015; 2019) has suggested that the democratic legitimacy of offices for future generations could be strengthened by enhancing citizen participation in conjunction with these institutions.

Political participation on behalf of future generations

Obviously, also other actors than elected representatives or non-elected authorities can defend and represent the interests of future generations. There are several instances where civil society actors have taken an active role in defending future people's interests in the public discourse. Using Saward's (2010) terminology, they have made "claims of representation" of the interests of future generations. Consider, for example, Greta Thunberg's role in representing the future generations' voice in the public discourse on climate change. Obviously, this kind of representation falls beyond what is understood as democratic representation because it lacks electoral authorization and accountability. Therefore, the legitimacy of the claims made by such representatives are likely to be challenged, especially by those groups whose current interests would be harmed by more long-term policies.

One might also question the likelihood that current people would actively act on behalf of future generations, especially if the harms pertain to people in the distant future. Based on a review of behavioral decision research, Weber (2006, 116) points out consequences that will materialize in the future are not very likely to give rise to emotional reactions that are necessary for triggering collective action. As Weber (2006, 110) argues: "Abstract representations of consequences in the distant future lack the concrete associations that are connected to emotional reactions, essentially by definition."

This seems to indicate that problems materializing in the distant future are not very likely to mobilize people to act politically. Obviously, emotional reactions towards future generations can be activated – there are, for example, various artistic ways of doing this. A potentially powerful way of evoking empathetic concern and perspective-taking with regard to future generations is to frame issues in terms of problems caused for our children or grandchildren. This is likely to cause emotional reactions because of people's evolutionary tendency to care for their offspring (Preston 2013). Moreover, the recent political protests regarding climate change in different parts of the world demonstrate how those who are likely to be affected by the consequences, namely the young, are ready to engage in political action on this issue.

In addition to protests, the increasing concern for climate change has been channeled in more conventional ways in Western democracies. For example, in the European Parliamentary election of Spring 2019, the issue of climate change was obviously the issue motivating especially the young people to turn out to polls (Zalc et al. 2019). In representative democratic systems providing opportunities of Citizens' Initiatives, there have been recent initiatives to address climate issues. For example, the Swiss "glacier initiative" demanding carbon neutrality in 2050 collected sufficient support to be submitted to a popular vote in Autumn 2019 (Swissinfo 2019). In Finland, a few climate-related agenda initiatives that have been submitted to the parliament, for example, initiatives for the ban of clear-cutting of state-owned forests and for flight taxes (see www.kansalaisaloite.fi).

The increasing political action around climate issues demonstrates that the risks of climate change are not necessarily so abstract and distant any more. Extreme weather conditions experienced in different parts of the world in recent years and the increasingly alarming reports by scientists seem to have raised wide-spread concern for the living conditions of the next generations. Indeed, one might argue that the awareness and the concern of climate change has now reached the point where a large share of the public in advanced democracies, especially the young, is increasingly willing to engage in collective action to bring about the societal and political changes that are necessary.

However, civil society activism and political protests demanding measures to tackle climate change are not sufficient to bring about political change in established representative democracies. The presentist biases of current representative institutions may contribute this. Namely, it may still be a better strategy for candidates and parties to focus on other, more tangible issues that are more likely to mobilize voters in elections, for example immigration, housing or health care. The issue of climate change is only one issue among many that democratic systems need to resolve and many of them seem to affect people's lives even more directly. Moreover, when it comes to policies aimed to tackle climate change, conflicts may arise with other important claims such as the need for employment or affordable housing or transport. Some established democracies have experienced a backlash as a reaction to some of the suggested measures to reduce CO_2 emissions. For example, the Yellow Vests movement in France was a reaction to the governmental decision of raising diesel taxes. The movement represented especially lower middle classes whose claims were largely fueled by the societal inequalities and austerity policies (Chamorel 2019). This example already highlights the fact that claims made in support of intergenerational injustices may backlash because of intragenerational injustices.

Similar conflicts regarding economic welfare and the sustainable use of natural resources are visible in different parts of world, taking different forms depending on the political system and the characteristics of social cleavages in the society. Those willing to mobilize around issues such as the climate change take advantage of the available political opportunity structures (cf. Tilly 1978) in the political system. While there are differences between representative democratic systems in this respect, overall they still provide many more opportunities for civil society activism than authoritarian regimes. Moreover, it may very well be that those who are most vulnerable to environmental crises caused by human-induced climate change need to address more mundane issues related to day-to-day survival (cf. Curato 2019), which limits their capacity to organize themselves to address the root causes of these problems.

From participation to deliberation: the prospects of more future-sensitive democracy

While representative systems provide spaces for competing claims appealing to intra- and intergenerational justice, the legitimacy of democratic decision-making depends on whether these claims are considered critically and even-handedly against other, competing claims. In other words, some kind of a deliberative process seems to be necessary in order to make judgements about the weight and urgency of different political demands. For example, Habermas (1996, 170–172) has emphasized the importance of parliamentary deliberation for making political judgements of this kind. As pointed out earlier, parliamentary procedures may not be optimal in terms of fostering deliberation since parties and representative are often too much wedded to their own constituents' interests. Factors such as party discipline further limit the prospects of deliberation in the parliamentary arena.

Obviously there are also a variety of societal (e.g. economic equality and access to universal education) as well as institutional factors (e.g. proportional representation and institutions allowing for inclusive agenda-setting) that facilitate the quality of deliberation in the parliamentary arena and within the political system more generally. However, empirical evidence suggests that parliamentary procedures are, even at their best, a combination of deliberation based on merits of arguments, and bargaining (Holzinger 2004).

This leads to the argument put forward by several authors (e.g. MacKenzie 2016b) that democratic deliberation, especially when it takes place among randomly selected ordinary citizens, is a better way to ensure the future-sensitivity in democratic decision-making. Organized citizen deliberation, especially in so-called deliberative mini-publics (Grönlund et al. 2014), seems to have a lot potential in this respect. Deliberative mini-publics are democratic innovations that are designed to facilitate inclusive deliberation. There are various formats of mini-publics, such as Citizens' Juries and Citizens' Assemblies, that differ especially in terms of their size. However, there are certain design features that are common to all mini-publics, most notably the use of random selection in the recruitment of the participants, interaction with experts and moderated small group deliberations (Setälä and Smith 2018; Farrell et al. 2019).

There are a variety of mechanisms contributing to the capacity of mini-publics to consider issues of intergenerational and intragenerational justice. Mini-publics entail a diversity of societal viewpoints, discussion rules and moderated discussions, which should ensure external and internal inclusion. Inclusive deliberation can even be expected to foster consideration of a variety of viewpoints and interests. Arguably, deliberative mini-publics could even help consideration of future generations' viewpoints. There are different mechanisms contributing to this. From the epistemic perspective, the most obvious mechanism is that deliberation increases sensitivity to factual arguments on the consequences of policies. Because deliberative mini-publics involve different forms of interaction with experts, participants in mini-publics should be more able to account for also the long-term impacts of policy choices, including those that pertain to future generations.

But a mere exposure to facts and scientific evidence is not enough, since individuals tend to be very selective and biased in information processing. Yet, deliberation in mini-publics could be a remedy to these biases as well. Studies in social psychology suggest that the diversity of viewpoints in a deliberative group may help correct biases of reasoning. In a group consisting of diverse individuals, individuals' biases are checked by other individuals with different biases, which increases factual accuracy of judgements (Mercier and Landemore 2012). In addition, people tend to start checking their own biases already in anticipation of a situation where they need to justify their viewpoints to others representing different viewpoints. In this respect, deliberation in diverse groups has an instrumental value of improving the epistemic quality of judgements. For example, much of the debate on climate change pertains to factual claims on the effects of CO_2 emissions. In this debate, political actors have the tendency to interpret facts based on their pre-established views and own interests. In other words, the interpretations of climate facts are vulnerable to a variety of biases, such as in-group bias, self-serving bias and attribution bias (Morrell 2010; 2014). Inclusive deliberation based on exchanging and weighing different viewpoints in a diverse group is thus likely to be an efficient method of correcting biases in interpretations of facts related to climate change.

The capacity of deliberative processes is not limited to increasing factual knowledge and correcting biases of reasoning, but it can also enhance the capacity of moral judgement. There are variety of ways in which inclusive deliberation, e.g. in mini-publics, may enhance balanced consideration of future generations' interests. First, deliberation is likely to reduce the scope of short-sighted and self-serving behavior. Deliberators cannot appeal to their own interests only, but they need to justify their claims in terms of more general principles of justice or common good. Second, inclusion of different viewpoints in the deliberative process enhances deliberators' sensitivity to variety of societal viewpoints, as well as the effects of policies on different types of individuals and groups. Jürgen Habermas (1996, 162) regards "ideal role-taking" as a part of moral discourse. "Ideal role-taking" (originally introduced by G.H. Mead (1934) means a process of placing oneself in others' positions and trying to understand their perspectives (Grönlund et al. 2017). In a deliberative process leading to political decision-making, ideal role-taking should extend to all those who are potentially affected by the decision.

Third, and perhaps most importantly, deliberation entails assessment of political claims and arguments by their merits only. Social hierarchies or power resources should not influence the judgements made in a deliberative process. Deliberators should judge political claims equally based on the generalizability of the underlying moral principles. Therefore, the exclusion of future generations and their lack of power resources should not influence the judgements concerning the claims made on their behalf. Deliberative process should thus bring about better judgements on whether different claims are justified and how they should be prioritized, including those claims made on behalf of future generations.

However, because future generations do not exist, current policy choices can only have potential consequences on their lives. And because of their non-identities, future generations' interests cannot be articulated or represented in a deliberative process in substantial or agent-specific ways. As Heyward (2008) points out, future generations' interests can only be construed in "Rawlsian" or identity-independent terms, associated with "token" future people. In more practical terms, future interests are likely to remain under-represented in deliberative processes because future generations are not there to articulate and defend their own interests. Moreover, there are no guarantees that any of the actual deliberators takes an active role in representing the interests of "token" future people.

Therefore, specific measures may be needed in order to evoke future generations' interests in the context of a deliberative process. Measures to evoke future generations' interests could involve alternative scenarios or other concretizations of the future combined with the requirement of justifying decisions for future generations or imagining oneself in their position (MacKenzie 2016a, 34). The most systematic way of enhancing the representation of future people's interests is probably the so-called future design model, developed in Japan by Hara et al. (2019). In this model for citizen deliberation, the purpose is to create imaginary future generations and incorporating the viewpoints of future generations into the present. In the pilot project testing this model, half of the deliberators were asked to address the issue from the perspective of the people living in the future, namely in the year 2060, while the other half engaged in a normal deliberation from their present perspective. In addition, participants were given information on certain long-term issues, such as climate change, and their effects.

In other words, the representation of future generations was ensured by asking some of participants to "time-travel" – without ageing – to a future point of time. Hara et al. (2019) observe a number of differences when it comes to the topics, values and priorities among future generations groups and present generations groups. Interestingly, deliberation on policy priorities *between* groups representing present and future generations helped detect some intergenerational conflicts. Although procedures such as the future design may appear rather experimental, there seem to be legitimate reasons to elicit representations of future generations' viewpoints and interests in long-term planning or in situations when policy choices can be expected to have irreversible and negative long-term consequences.

Even without such specific designs, there are many reasons to believe that deliberative mini-publics are more sensitive to future generations' interests than current institutions of representative democracy. This may be one of the reasons of the sudden interest in deliberative mini-publics as a response to the climate crisis among both civil society movements and some democratic governments. The demands for reforming the political system and the adoption of democratic innovations such as deliberative mini-publics seem to be based on the view that existing institutions of representative democracy are inadequate to deal with the long-term problems that we face. There are actual experiences of Citizens' Assemblies on climate change in several established democracies, for example, in Ireland, Canada, France, Germany and in the UK. In the UK, there have been several local-level Citizens' Assemblies on climate change. The nation-wide Citizens' Assembly on climate change, organized in the UK in early 2020, was commissioned by six different parliamentary committees. It is also a response to the large-scale Extinction Rebellion demonstrations and protests. In France, on the other hand, the nation-wide Citizens' Assembly is part of series of national discussions that were organized largely as a response to the Yellow Vest protests.

Indeed, it seems that many representative governments have realized the difficulties of balancing claims of intra- and intergenerational justice and feel that they may need new forms of democracy in order to resolve these conflicts in a legitimate way. A one-off deliberative Citizens' Assembly may be important for helping focus attention to a particular political issue and provide policy-makers and citizens with some advice on the issue. In this way, deliberative mini-publics like Citizens' Assemblies may be instrumental for societal changes required by climate crisis without sacrificing democratic legitimacy.

However, one may ask whether these types of instruments are likely to have the desired long-term impacts on the political system and people's attitudes. Rather than changing long-term patterns of policymaking, deliberative mini-publics could actually serve as a method of "defusing" difficult issues and removing them from a political agenda. This leads to another issue with deliberative mini-publics, which pertains to their role in the democratic systems. Can deliberative mini-publics be a remedy some of the obstacles for deliberation in representative systems? How should deliberative mini-publics be coupled with other democratic procedures in order to secure they help improve the quality of political decision-making?

When it comes to the use of deliberative mini-publics in conjunction with parliamentary decision-making, there are various ways in which deliberative mini-publics can be coupled, for example, to parliamentary committees (e.g. Hendriks 2016). However, unfortunately there are also plenty of examples of mini-publics that have been poorly connected to actual policymaking processes and, for this reason, their impact has remained negligible. Therefore, the prospects of deliberative mini-publics to enhance inclusive processes of deliberation and critical reflection are contingent on how they are connected to different policymaking processes (Setälä 2017).

Mini-publics should not be used to help policy-makers to promote their pre-established political agenda, but rather encourage policy-makers to consider different political arguments by their merits. When it comes to the use of deliberative mini-publics in conjunction with representative decision-making, there are various promising models around. When mini-publics are advisory and make recommendations to elected representatives, policy-makers should at least give a public justification on how they will react to the recommendations of a mini-public. Recommendations of mini-publics could also influence policies more directly, or they could be used to scrutinize the decisions made by elected representatives. In addition to elected representatives, mini-publics could advise voters as well. For example, Warren and Gastil (2015) have suggested that deliberative mini-publics could be used as trusted sources of voter information. There is already empirical evidence on the capacity of mini-publics to facilitate learning and reflection on specific issues, most notably from the Citizens' Initiative Review (CIR) processes in Oregon and elsewhere.

More systemic effects are possible only when deliberative mini-publics are used regularly and are institutionalized. For example, MacKenzie (2016b) has suggested that the interests of future generations could be protected by a randomly selected second parliamentary chamber. There would be rather quick rotation of the members of the chamber, the main task of which would be to scrutinize law-making by elected representatives. The chamber would have powers to delay legislation, which would encourage the elected representatives to anticipate the potential objections raised in the deliberative process.

Obviously, intergenerational justice requires collective decision-making, not just within nation states, but also between them. However, as pointed out by Dahl (1999), there are also democratic risks when delegating powers to supranational bodies, especially when they are lacking democratic procedures. To address these types of concerns, there are suggestions for radical democratization of supra-national governance, e.g. through randomly selected deliberative forums (e.g. Dryzek, Bächtiger and Milewicz 2011). In addition, enhancing inclusiveness of deliberative processes is likely to have epistemic benefits because inclusive deliberation helps grasp the consequences of policies from a variety of social perspectives. In fact, inclusive and deliberative institutions at supra-national level have a potential to enhance more future-regarding policymaking since issues of expansive geographical impacts often have extended temporal impacts as well (Caney 2018).

Concluding remarks

This chapter has shown the variety of interpretations and the problems of the concept of inclusion in democratic theory. The consideration of affected interests seems to be necessary for ensuring that democratic decision-making does not lead to injustices or domination. This may require including people outside the current geographical borders of nation states as well as more systematic consideration of the interests of future generations.

The consideration of the interests of future generations sets a profound challenge to democratic theory and practice. Notably, the current forms of electoral democracy seem to aggravate the tendencies towards short-termism. Rather than vote-maximizing behavior and power-based bargaining, consideration of future generations requires evidence-based, inclusive deliberative processes in which arguments are assessed by their merits. Moreover, the legitimacy of many long-term policies requires sensitivity to both intergenerational and intragenerational injustices. This is possible only if inclusiveness of different viewpoints in ensured in the process – and this may only be possible if current political inequalities are somehow leveled.

Randomly selected bodies for citizen deliberation – or deliberative mini-publics – seem to provide a democratically legitimate way to account for causal complexities of issues and variety of affected interests. The capacity of deliberative mini-publics to deal with intergenerational conflicts could be enhanced by specific measures that help evoke future generations' interests. When properly coupled with existing policymaking institutions, deliberative mini-publics have potential to address problems of short-termism arising in the context of representative democracies. In addition to representative democracies, there is a need for such deliberative bodies in context of supra-national decision-making where forums for inclusive deliberation are often entirely lacking.

References

Barber, B., 1984. *Strong Democracy. Participatory Politics for a New Age*. Berkeley: University of California Press.

Beckman, L., 2013. Democracy and Future Generations. Should the Unborn Have a Voice? In J.-C. Merle, ed. *Spheres of Global Justice: Volume 2*. Dordrecht: Springer, 775–788.

Caney, S., 2018. Justice and Future Generations. *Annual Review of Political Science*, 21, 475–493.

Chambers, S., 2009. Rhetoric and the Public Sphere: Has Deliberative Democracy Abandoned Mass Democracy? *Political Theory*, 37 (3), 323–350.

Chamorel, P., 2019. Macron Versus the Yellow Vests. *Journal of Democracy*, 30 (4), 48–62.

Curato, N., 2019. *Democracy in a Time of Misery. From Spectacular Tragedy to Deliberative Action*. Oxford: Oxford University Press.

Dahl, R.A., 1989. *Democracy and its Critics*. New Haven and London: Yale University Press.

Dahl, R.A., 1999. Can International Organizations be Democratic? In I. Shapiro and C. Hacker-Cordón, eds. *Democracy's Edges*. Cambridge: Cambridge University Press, 19–36.

Dobson, A., 1996. Representative Democracy and the Environment. In W.M. Lafferty and J. Meadowcroft, eds. *Democracy and the Environment*. Cheltenham: Edward Elgar Publishing, 124–139.

Dryzek, J.S., Bächtiger, A. and Milewicz, K., 2011. Toward a Deliberative Global Citizens' Assembly. *Global Policy*, 2 (1), 33–43.

Ekeli, K.S., 2005. Giving a Voice to Posterity – Deliberative Democracy and Representation of Future People. *Journal of Agricultural and Environmental Ethics*, 16, 429–450.

Elster, J., 1986. The Market and the Forum: Three Varieties of Political Theory. In J. Elster and A. Hylland, eds. *Foundations of Social Choice Theory*. Cambridge: Cambridge University Press, 103–133.

Elster, J., 1998. Deliberation and Constitution Making. In J. Elster, ed. *Deliberative Democracy*. Cambridge: Cambridge University Press, 97–122.

Farrell, D.M., et al., 2019. *Deliberative Mini-Publics: Core Design Features*. Centre for Deliberative Democracy & Global Governance, University Canberra. Working Paper Series No. 2019/5 www.governanceinstitute.edu.au/magma/media/upload/ckeditor/files/Deliberative%20Mini-Publics%20Core%20Design%20Features.pdf

Floridia, A., 2017. *From Participation to Deliberation. A Critical Genealogy of Deliberative Democracy*. Colchester: ECPR Press.

Grönlund, K., Bächtiger, A. and Setälä, M., eds., 2014. *Deliberative Mini-Publics*. Colchester: ECPR Press.

Grönlund, K., Herne, K. and Setälä, M., 2017. Empathy in a Citizen Deliberation Experiment. *Scandinavian Political Studies*, 40 (4), 457–480. http://onlinelibrary.wiley.com/doi/10.1111/1467-9477.12103/full

Habermas, J., 1996. *Between Facts and Norms*. Cambridge: The MIT Press.

Hara, K., et al., 2019. Reconciling Intergenerational Conflicts with Imaginary Future Generations: Evidence from a Participatory Deliberation Practice in a Municipality in Japan. *Sustainability Science*, 14, 1605–1619.

Hendriks, C., 2016. Coupling Citizens and Elites in Deliberative Systems: The Role of Institutional Design. *European Journal of Political Research*, 55 (1), 43–60.

Heyward, C., 2008. Can the All-affected Principle Include Future Persons? Green Deliberative Democracy and the Non-identity Problem. *Environmental Politics*, 17 (4), 625–643. doi: 10.1080/09644010802193591

Holzinger, K., 2004. Bargaining by Arguing. An Empirical Analysis Based on Speech Act Theory. *Political Communication*, 21, 195–222.

Jacobs, A.M., 2016. Policy Making for the Long Term in Advanced Democracies. *Annual Review of Political Science*, 19, 433–454. doi:10.1146/annurev-polisci-110813-034103

Lagerspetz, E., 2015. Democracy and the All-Affected Principle. *Res Cogitans*, 10 (1), 6–23.

MacKenzie, M., 2016a. Institutional Design and Sources of Short-termism. In A. Gosseries and I. González-Ricoy, eds. *Political Institutions for Future Generations*. Oxford: Oxford University Press, 24–49.

MacKenzie, M., 2016b. A General-purpose, Randomly Selected Chamber. In A. Gosseries and I. González-Ricoy, eds. *Political Institutions for Future Generations*. Oxford: Oxford University Press, 282–299.

Mansbridge, J., 2003. Rethinking Representation. *The American Political Science Review*, 97 (4), 515–528.

Mead, G.H., 1934. *Mind, Self and Society*. Ed. Charles M. Morris. Chicago: University of Chicago Press.

Mercier, H. and Landemore, H., 2012. Reasoning is for Arguing: Understanding the Successes and Failures of Deliberation. *Political Psychology*, 33 (2), 243–258.

Morrell, M.E., 2010. *Empathy and Democracy*. University Park: Penn State University Press.

Morrell, M.E., 2014. Participant Bias and Success in Deliberative Mini-Publics. In K. Grönlund, A. Bächtiger and M. Setälä, eds. *Deliberative Mini-Publics*. Colchester: ECPR Press, 157–176.

Mutz, D.C., 2006. *Hearing the Other Side. Deliberative Versus Participatory Democracy*. Cambridge: Cambridge University Press.

Näsström, S., 2011. The Challenge of the All-Affected Principle. *Political Studies*, 59 (1), 116–134.

Pateman, C., 2012. Participatory Democracy Revisited. *Perspectives on Politics*, 10 (1), 7–19.

Preston, S.D., 2013. The Origins of Altruism in Offspring Care. *Psychological Bulletin*, 139 (6), 1305–1341.

Saffon, M.P. and Urbinati, N., 2013. Procedural Democracy, the Bulwark of Equal Liberty. *Political Theory*, 41 (3), 441–481.

Saward, M., 2010. *The Representative Claim*. Oxford: Oxford University Press.

Setälä, M., 2017. Connecting Deliberative Mini-Publics to Representative Decision-Making. *European Journal of Political Research*, 56, 846–863.

Setälä, M. and Smith, G., 2018. Deliberative Mini-Publics. In A. Bächtiger, J. Dryzek, J. Mansbridge and M. Warren, eds. *The Oxford Handbook of Deliberative Democracy*. Oxford: Oxford University Press, 300–314.

Smith, G., 2015. *The Democratic Case for an Office for Future Generations*. London: Foundation for Democracy and Sustainable Development.

Smith, G., 2019. The Legitimacy of Independent Offices for Future Generations. *Political Studies*, online first.

Swissinfo, 2019. Swiss set to vote on 'Glacier Initiative', Swissinfo, 28 November 2019, www.swissinfo.ch/eng/environment_swiss-set-to-vote-on--glacier-initiative-/45399020, accessed 29 November 2019.

Tilly, C., 1978. *From Mobilization to Revolution*. Reading: Addison-Wesley.

Vermeule, A., 2007. *Mechanisms of Democracy. Institutional Design Small Writ*. Oxford: Oxford University Press.

Warren, M.E. and Gastil, J., 2015. Can Deliberative Minipublics Address the Cognitive Challenges of Democratic Citizenship? *The Journal of Politics*, 77, 562–574.

Weber, E., 2006. Experience-based and Description-based Perceptions of Long-term Risk: Why Global Warming Does Not Scare Us (Yet). *Climatic Change*, 77, 103–120.

World Commission on Environment and Development, 1987. *Our Common Future*. Oxford: Oxford University Press.
Young, I., 2000. *Inclusion and Democracy*. Oxford: Oxford University Press.
Zalc, J., Becuwe, N. and Buruian, A., 2019. The 2019 Post-Electoral Survey. Have European Elections Entered a New Dimension. Eurobarometer Survey 91.5 of the European Parliament: Brussels: European Union. www.europarl.europa.eu/at-your-service/en/be-heard/eurobarometer/2019-european-elections-entered-a-new-dimension.
Zürn, M., 2000. Democratic Governance Beyond the Nation-State: The EU and Other International Institutions. *European Journal of International Relations*, 6, 183–221.

6
POLITICAL REPRESENTATION AND SUSTAINABLE FUTURES

Henrike Knappe

Introduction

Matters of political representation in sustainability politics are often closely associated with the representation of future generations as a normative baseline of sustainability. Although the future of planet Earth and coming generations is at the center of global sustainability politics since the late 1980s, the political representation of future generations remains either a rather abstract metaphor or struggles with given democratic systems' presentism. This problem of an abstract notion of the future can also be traced in the history of global environmental politics. Despite the significant number of environmental treaties negotiated since the 1960s, "irreversible environmental change" – especially climate change and biodiversity loss – is considered to be "one of the greatest examples of *regulatory* failure by states" (Christoff and Eckersley 2013). For many decades, global environmental and climate change was something happening in the distant future and therefore not of immediate urgency. In recent years, this diffuse responsibility towards the future has developed into a more serious and urgent issue. Leading scientists have suggested that we have entered the time of the Anthropocene (Crutzen and Stoermer 2000), a new geological era in which, for the first time, humans are the most powerful force on Earth, affecting its fate for countless generations to come. The techno-scientific debate that has taken shape around the Anthropocene in recent decades puts forward science-based arguments of responsibility for future generations, which rest upon assumptions of human efficacy and obligation in the Anthropocene, and limits on the extent to which planetary resources can continue to be exploited (Lövbrand et al. 2015). However, also in the Anthropocene, the representation of future generations remains difficult. What has been criticized by some social scientists and post-colonial scholars is that the Anthropocene debate depoliticizes planetary futures by naturalizing the geological past and future that it describes as universal and free from any political power or injustice (Yusoff 2018). Contrasting the Anthropocene debate with the one on sustainable development, Lövbrand et al. (2020) find that the debate has lost its optimistic undertone:

> In contrast to the hopeful and reassuring concept of sustainable development that has guided international environmental cooperation since the early 1990s, the

> Anthropocene is wedded into a language of fear and sorrow in view of irreparable loss of Artic ice sheets, mass species extinction, acidified oceans and degraded lands.
>
> Lövbrand et al. 2020, 5

With the Anthropocene, the catastrophic futures of the climate crisis and biodiversity loss have already arrived in the present. Still, global environmental politics is driven by the narrative of sustainable development, while in parallel catastrophic effects of climate change break into the present. This parallelism must make us think differently about the notion of future generations, long-term futures and how to politically represent them in the present.

This chapter argues that democratic representation is necessary for realizing sustainable futures. True democratic inclusive representation changes the very imagination of sustainable futures and makes them more equal and diverse. Furthermore, the chapter develops further the question of how representation could look in the twenty-first century troubled by the climate crisis.

The chapter is divided into three parts. At first, I lay out the general tensed relationship between political representation and sustainable futures. Here, I will focus on the problems of long-term futures for democratic politics and how standard representation theory's proposals to solve these problems look like. Then I introduce the most recent debates on constructivist approaches in representation theory and explore how they can help to think about repertoires of political representation in global environmental politics. Finally, the last section of this chapter will zoom into the more concrete questions of representation practices. Here, the analysis centers on doing representation in the age of the Anthropocene. I finish with some conclusions on the relationship between representation and sustainability politics.

Future generations in democratic representation

Greta Thunberg is one of the most prominent representatives of younger and future generations in contemporary politics. In one of her most prominent speeches in front of the United Nations audience in September 2019 she told member states of the UN "I shouldn't be up here. I should be back in school …".[1] She requested state representatives to do their proper job and criticized that they failed to represent younger people and future generations, like her. Thunberg refused to act as a representative of future generations and at the same time she performatively *did* represent future generations by going up on this stage and talking about the grief younger and future generations have to expect due to state leaders' unwillingness to act against climate change. Thunberg speaks about future generations as affected groups that suffer from political decisions taken in the here and now. With this claim, she points to the necessity to democratically represent future generations in global environmental politics. However, Thunberg's case shows how difficult it is do integrate sustainability concerns into established political processes and institutions. Although temporalities and future horizons are always part of sustainability governance mechanisms (Bornemann and Strassheim 2019), futures are not necessarily governed in view of sustainability efforts. Although climate future horizons are getting shorter and shorter, the regulatory inertia that was attested to global environmental politics for many decades now is still prevalent. Although the Paris agreement was a big breakthrough in global climate politics, national and international politics do not show much ambition in reaching the goals set in the Paris agreement. Democratic theorists argue that this has to do with the long-term nature of the future. While young climate activists have mobilized mass demonstrations since the beginning of 2019 under the heading of "Fridays for Future", they see themselves confronted with national and international governing bodies that are stuck in myopia or democratic short-termism (Setälä 2021, Chapter 5 in this volume; Caney 2018) and elected politicians who rather govern for the present times than for long-term futures because of the pressure of getting re-elected by present voters. Many scholars argue that this short-termism is built into democratic institutions that are bound to short election cycles (Caney 2016). Many people who are affected by the long-term consequences of climate change do not yet exist. Although they build affected groups and thus can be seen as a legitimate constituency following the democratic ideal of the all-affected principle (Näsström 2011; Lawrence 2019), they cannot actively elect representatives. Therefore, representation of future generations is always indirect and/or by (self-) appointment.

Theorists of democracy and justice for future generations have dealt with the problems of myopia, and long-term futures for decades now (Dobson 1997; Lafferty and Meadowcroft 1997). In her classic text, Hannah Pitkin notes that representation is thought of as making someone or something present that is not literally present (Pitkin 1967: 8). Representation is then thought of as a dyadic relationship between the representative and the constituency. Dobson (1997) argues that because direct representation of future generations is not possible, proxy representatives can be a viable option. Proxy representatives as representatives of future generations in parliaments could be either selected by random sampling or by deliberate choice. While random sampling would mirror the "full range of interests of future generations" he has doubts that the presentist orientation of current voters would really enable a representation of future generations by a random sample of proxy voters. The second alternative of selecting a "sustainability lobby" is for Dobson more convincing as they have their "eyes firmly fixed on the future" (Dobson 1997, 133) and thus a representation of future generations by proxy representatives can better be fulfilled. This is a choice to put representational power in the hands of experts. Its argumentation underlies the assumption that it matters who the representative is. In Dobson's argumentation, this representative would be somebody who has the interests of future generations fully at heart and would convincingly act for them.

Some years after Dobson published his text, Thompson (2010) suggests to cope with the presentist problems in democracies by introducing the concept of "democratic trusteeship". He argues in contrast to Dobson, that citizens and their representatives *can* act as trustees of future generations. Trusteeship is a sub-category of substantive representation. Pitkin distinguishes substantive representation further into mandated representation and trusteeship representation. Whereas in mandated representation the wishes of the represented should be the yardstick for any action of representatives, the trustee's judgment is the only relevant criterion for taking decisions (Pitkin 1967, 165). Once trustees are elected, they are independent in their actions (Pitkin 1967, 146–147). Trusteeship, as conceptualized by Burke as "virtual" representation, depends on representatives who ideally act with wisdom, but without the consent of their constituency (Burke 1774). Acting with this wisdom, current generations should then secure that future generations have "as much capacity for collective decision-making as present citizens have" (Thompson 2010, 26). Thompson limits the scope of responsibility for future generations here. While Dobson argued that with all uncertainty of futures it is still safe to say that future generations would want a "viable environment in which to live and the possibility of satisfying their basic needs" (Dobson 1997, 132), Thompson limits the knowable interest of future generations to the functioning of a democratic system. One could of course argue that a democratic system can only exist within a viable environment and with people having their basic needs satisfied. Still, the emphasis is shifted, focusing on the functioning of the political system. Similar differences in the representation of future generations can be found in current climate litigation cases. While many former cases, for example in 2018 in Colombia or 2015 the case Juliana vs. the United States[2] referred to the right of future generations of life and a healthy environment, a current case of April 2021 by Germany's Federal Constitutional Court lays an emphasis on the violation of freedom that comes with enforced and drastic measures to reduce CO_2 emissions in the future if the legislature is not installing measurements to more effectively reduce CO_2 emission already until 2030. This is similar to Thompson's argumentation that future generations must have the capacity to still make their own political decisions. A broader assumption we find in both classic argumentation of Dobson's proxy representation and also Thompson trusteeship model is that current generations, either with expertise or with wisdom can effectively represent future generations. However, one could wonder why in both texts there is no consideration of younger people as possible descriptive representatives. Pitkin distinguishes descriptive "standing for" from substantive "acting for" (Pitkin 1967, 116). Descriptive representation then means that the representative shares the group identity with her or his constituency, in this case the group of young and future generations. They do not only have their eyes on the future, but it is also their very own and existential self-interest to represent future generations. They will be the future generations that outlive all other age groups of society.[3] This becomes even more evident, when we observe how the capacity of current representatives to transcend their own presentist interests clearly failed, exemplified in the regulatory failure of states in environmental politics in the recent decades (Christoff and Eckersley 2013). This disappointment was one mobilizing effect of the mass demonstrations of Fridays for Future in 2019 and with this huge climate movement, the question again came to fore of who really represents future generations and if the younger generations should have a role in this, as directly affected citizens. It is interesting, that standard representation theory of future generations barely notices the role of younger people as representatives of future generations. In further elaborating on the trusteeship model Thompson also suggests installing "age-differentiated political rights" in order to balance out the presentism. However, he does not argue for a lowering of voting age, but for a limiting of voting age at the top and for giving parents extra votes for their children (Thomspon 2010, 33). This might be a sensible thought to consider, but it also shows a general skepticism towards the younger generation to represent future generations and towards descriptive representation as an effective way to install justice in democracies. Other scholars directly argue against descriptive representation of young people as not more effective than any other representative in representing "their constituents substantial interests" (Karnein and Roser 2015, 80). In the face of the climate crisis and the lack of political will to reach the climate goals of the Paris agreement, one begs to differ. The notion of representation that underlies such conceptions is rooted in a realist understanding of fixed interests that the representative merely needs to mirror and amplify.

However, standard notions of representation in electoral systems seem unfit to cope with instability (Knappe 2020b) and the crises of Anthropocene futures. Newer approaches of representing future generations (Smith 2020; Tamoudi et al. 2020) try to complement this very static understanding and refer to the contextual nature and political struggles of and over futures (Knappe 2020a; Tamoudi 2020). Here, representation is seen as something that emerge within dynamic participation processes (Smith 2020) and which particularly because of this dynamic character can have transformative effects (Hammond and Smith, Chapter 7 in this volume). This resonates with a reality which is more and more unstable, uncertain and dynamic. While environmental scholars in recent decades were bothered with the long-term nature of the future, now, with entering the Anthropocene, futures are not long-term anymore. They are rapturous and uncertain. This also bears democratic problems, as Hajer (2009) points out. When we are faced with open and uncertain futures, when we don't know how things will turn out, politicians rather opt for the "managerial reflex" as Hajer puts it:

> All too often "fragmentation", "volatility", and "crisis" are invoked to suggest that in such periods "management" has to prevail over democratic deliberation. Situations that are open, where it is unclear if they are going to result in turmoil or will slowly wither away, do not seem to go well with a commitment to democratic governance. But is that necessarily so? Are there political repertoires that do not revert to the managerial reflex?
>
> *Hajer 2009, 10*

In analyzing the democratic problems in the era of the Anthropocene, Eckersley criticizes that many scholars and politicians now follow the "governance fantasy of rational steering" (Eckersley 2017, 986). Lövbrand et al. (2015) argue that in view of urgent and catastrophic futures of the Anthropocene, a post-political agenda is proposed. While Anthropocene scholars mainly refer to established expert institutions in governing the Anthropocene "the space for political contestation, debate and reorientation is ... restricted" (ibid.). Uncertain futures create a form of managing governance that limit disagreement and democratic debate to decisions over "the choice of technologies, the detail of the managerial adjustments, and the urgency of their timing and implementation" (ibid., 214). This de-politicization of futures is a democratic problem, as it limits the democratic input into political processes from public deliberation and inclusive representation. In the next section, I argue for a constructivist and performative perspective on representation and show how they can advance and stimulate the discussion on political representation of sustainable futures.

Imaginaries of a demos: political representation as a performative act

Constructivists' fundamental critique of such standard notions of representation lies in the refusal of the inherent realist "fantasy of a reality that is self-evident, unmediated by social processes, and sovereign so that it can be imagined to provide an origin and point of reference for assessing the accuracy and faithfulness of any attempt to represent it" (Disch 2011, 104). Following this major claim, that representation not only transmits pre-existing interests (Urbinati 2008), recent constructivist representation theory works with three major hypotheses. First, representation is seen as a creative act that necessitates a certain agency and creativity on the part of the representative. Representation is not just a mirroring of already existing interests. Second, representation must always be partial and selective. Representation reflects a specific perspective of the representative who chooses to frame her or his claims in a certain way. Third, representation has constitutive power. Because representation is creative and selective, it can be a powerful act of defining constituencies, drawing lines between the members and non-members of constituencies and thereby creating realities and visibilities of the represented.

Representation as a creative act

In research on transnational democracy, the conceptualization and normative justification of non-electoral representation focusses on the performative character of representation, i.e. representation as a creative act. In his prominent work on representative claims, Michael Saward (2006) argues that political representation is not an act of passively mirroring an external reality, but an act of creating subjects, worlds or identities: "A representative – or someone making a representative claim – has necessarily to be creative. He or she has to mould, shape, and in one sense create that which is to be represented." (Saward 2006, 310). This idea of representation as a creative act is also prominent in feminist theories of representation. Spivak for example notes, that forms of aesthetic representation and political representation are "complicit" (Spivak 1999). Feminist scholars of representation are thus much interested in the "relationship between aesthetic or semiotic representation (things that 'stand for' other things) and political representation (persons who 'act for' other persons)" (Mitchell 1995, 11, cited in Disch 2016, 781).

There are three German words for representation: *vorstellen* (conceptual representation), *darstellen* (aesthetic representation) and *vertreten* (political representation). Vorstellen is the philosophical term to describe "conceptual representation of the world by the mind" (Disch 2016, 800). Darstellen is described as "things that 'stand for' other things" (ibid., 781) like portraits stand for real persons or maps stand for geographic regions. Finally, vertreten means that persons "act for" other persons (ibid.). Criticizing the existence of an autonomous subject, post-structuralists denied conceptual representation and thus concluded that it also does not make sense to engage in political representation. Spivak (and many after her) made clear, that because of the complicity between aesthetic and political representation, political representation can take place without conceptual representation because it is "not transparent to the world but constitutive of it" (ibid., 800). To put it differently, even if we assume that people cannot imagine (vorstellen) the world in an *accurate* and realistic sense and always *construct* their own images, they still can engage in political representation. Representation is then not a simple mirroring of the world, but a creation of a world through aesthetic features.

Disch paraphrasing Spivak argues that "acts of political representation follow on the more or less explicit constitution-by-picturing of the subject to be represented" (Disch 2016, 793). This picturing can be made through rhetoric, cartographically through mapping a terrain or symbolically (ibid.). The presenting of images of the future, charts, scenarios and maps always also feeds into political representation and is used to pursue specific political goals. Thus, the intersection between aesthetic and political representation is where struggles over political authority materialize. Would-be representatives claim political authority by picturing or creating an image of the subjects which they purport to represent. Thus, investigations into the use of images, a certain language or specific symbols are not mere illustrations or mirrors of actual politics; the exploration itself and the objects of investigation are complicit in constituting present and future power relations. This phenomenon can be observed in the universal economic narratives of development and progress, or in the Anthropocene narrative of universal humankind and human agency. The aesthetic representation of climate futures for example show charts, diagrams and curves of the rather long-term impacts done by scientists in the Global North (Chaturvedi and Doyle 2015). Only recently is climate change also associated with the contemporary images of disasters in the Global South. This scientific bias in climate change representation is also a regional bias of the Global North. Political representative claims being articulated with the picturing of scientific data mainly generated in the Global North (see Bansard and van der Hel 2021, Chapter 20 in this volume) serve the notion of long-term climate change futures that are catastrophic but still seem to remain too abstract for political decision-makers in the Global North.

Viewing representation as a creative act helps us to better understand how representational roles are assigned – that is, which actors have the agency and knowledge to claim representation, how representative norms are re-interpreted and re-signified in, and by whom. Couching representation in constructivist terms enables us to critically reconstruct the dynamics of representation practice. For example, how roles such as "the passive constituency" are constructed, how norms of representational inclusion are stabilized, re-interpreted or avoided, and how "the represented" and the "representatives" are constituted and thus mobilized in the very act of representing.

Representation is partial

The creative act of representing constituencies involves the decision to represent in a certain manner and with a specific meaning: "The representation is selective: it proposes that we see the world from a certain perspective and that we arrange what can be seen in a certain way" (Ankersmit 1996, 39–40). In the context of the Anthropocene and the climate crisis, Chakrabarty reminds us to become suspicious if representative claims are made that demand to be universal: "narratives that presume to speak for all of humanity without any attention to the problems that divide and differentiate people along certain axes of power, leav[e] some groups with much less capacity for self-representation than some powerful minorities" (Chakrabarty 2015, XIV).

Pointing to those differences and inequities, and criticizing the supposedly universal narratives of humankind, was and is the contribution of post-colonial scholars. The "unevenness of development" (DeLoughrey et al. 2015) that comes with great injustice and inequities stemming from economic growth in global capitalism makes universalist narratives an instrument of power on an unequal playing field. In keeping with this claim about the instrumentalization of the universal-humankind narrative, and pointing to humankind's diversity, differences and inequities, Chakrabarty also hints at the entangled nature of representations. How people, politicians or stakeholders make representative claims is closely related to their power, position and background. There is no "outside" position from which universal claims for humanity can be made. Representation is *always* partial. Thus, matters of political representation do not rest upon the question of the best possible or most accurate representation, but rather on the question of who has access to representational practices and how representative claims can be made *differently*.

In referring to the similarities between aesthetic and political representation Saward argues that the representation is always distinct from the "original". It is not the function of the representation to copy the original; rather, representations are different perspectives and images of the world that are contested in political struggle:

> The signified or the object is not the same as the thing or district itself (the referent). It is rather a picture, a portrait, an image of that electorate. It is no closer to being that thing itself than a Rembrandt self-portrait was to Rembrandt himself. Competing significations are, arguably, what political debate and dispute is all about. [...] Political figures, parties, lobby groups, social movements – as makers of representative claims, their business is aesthetic because it is political.
>
> *Saward 2006, 310*

Consequently, representation is an act of power over the interpretation of a certain case: "[s]peaking for others involves choosing between alternatives, not only between good and bad alternatives but rather between various interpretations that could be represented otherwise" (Berger and Esguerra 2018, 219). When we follow the argument, that representation is a choice of one interpretation over the other, this can open up new practices of representing futures and future generations. The argument that futures are unknown and uncertain is thus not as relevant, because representation is not about accuracy, but about a deliberate choice for a certain future and the transformation there to it.

Representation constitutes realities

What follows from this is that the constituency is endogenous to the process of political representation: "It is only through representation that a people comes to be as a political agent, one capable of putting forward a demand. Thus, representation cannot be regarded as either supplementary or compensatory; it is 'the essence of democracy' (p. 330)" (Disch 2011, 104). Post-colonial feminist scholars start from a similar assumption but depart into a more power-critical direction in arguing that this kind of representation is also always a hegemonial act. They emphasize the "boundary drawing" of representation (Castro Varela and Dhawan 2012, 276). While representation can be seen as the "essence of democracy" in mobilizing the political agency of "the people" (Disch 2011, 104), representation at the same time also means excluding persons from belonging to "the people". Before the implementation of women's suffrage, women were marked as "Other" who were systematically invisible in representation. The argument that women *can* and should be represented by men made women invisible as political subjects in their own right. Currently migrants are systematically excluded from representational practices (Sauer 2011, 131). This constitutes realities as such excluded groups are made invisible and irrelevant for political goals. In turn, representation can be seen as "imperfect yet meaningful democratic practices" (Little and Macdonald 2013, 789) where actors constantly struggle over voice while making representations: "Who is speaking, who is spoken of, and who listens, is a result, as well as an act of political struggle" (Alcoff 1991, 15).

In sum, constructivist representation theory thus argues that representation should be seen as a creative act. The representative does not merely mirror existing interests but *creates* her or his own claims and thereby shapes constituencies. Representatives from different parties or political organizations will differently portray societal groups such as young people, women or workers and thereby will create their own image of such groups or even "invent" and make visible new groups, such as, for example, during the Corona pandemic "the lost generation of young people" or "the underpaid care workers". What comes with this notion of representation as a creative act is that representation can never be an accurate picture of reality. Political representation will always reflect the perspective of the representative and will always exclude certain people and groups. However, and that is the third argument put forward, such acts of representation constitute realities. Through speaking for specific groups in a certain way, representation gets performative. It makes some groups more visible, louder. It silences other groups. And more generally speaking, political representation is not only a reactive practice, but a proactive construction of political realities which can strengthen the own authority.

After having laid out the central points in the theory scholarship on constructivist representation, I will now turn to the above-mentioned political repertoires of representation under conditions of crisis and uncertainty that mark the era of climate crisis and the Anthropocene. So, speaking with Hajer (2009), what are the political repertoires of representation that can cope with uncertain futures of climate crises? What are the transformative potentials and challenges in political representation while facing uncertain futures?

Voices of the invisible: transformative repertoires of representation

Zooming into concrete performative representation practices, we can find studies in IR, but also theory development on the different categories of representation unfolding in dynamic settings. In the theory work on representation, Mansbridge for example suggests the new form of "anticipatory representation" as "in most instances interactive and more continually reflexive" (Mansbridge 2003, 518). Consequently, the normative criteria for judging its democratic quality must be systemic and not dyadic (concerning the relationship between representative and constituency). Rather, the "functioning of the entire representative process – including political parties, political challengers, the media, interest groups, hearings, opinion surveys, and all other processes of communication" (Mansbridge 2003, 519, quoted by Disch 2011, 105) must be taken into account. A similar argument is made with regard to transnational non-electoral representation. Representation is seen as an active process of "render[ing] others politically present" (Montanaro 2018, 7). Such rather flexible and interactive transnational representation practices can be mainly found in civil society organizations and their politics vis-à-vis international organizations or widespread constituent groups (Knappe 2020b). This dynamic process of making representation also involves the acceptance or rejection of specific representative claims by audiences and constituencies. Political power struggles occur in the creative process of making representation, and these are reflected in the subsequent reactions to the representation that has ensued from that process: "Indeed, we can pinpoint three characteristics and potential effects that are crucial to the power dynamics of the representative claim: audience-creation, reading-back and silencing" (Saward 2006, 303). Saward points here to the power asymmetries in political representation. While makers of representative claims can actively avoid contestation and dialogue by creating audiences that are in favor of the representative claims made and silence affected communities by highlighting that their absences for example is necessary or unavoidable. At the same time, such powerful acts by representatives cannot make them immune against "reading back", meaning any kind of contestation and even the articulation of counter-claims (ibid.).

Empirical studies in IR also emphasize the power dimension inherent in representation practice. Holzscheiter (2016), for example, studies the case of global civil society advocacy vis-à-vis child labor activists, and suggests that analyses of political representation must account for the "power-dimension inherent to the interrelation between formal and performative aspects of representation, that is [,] between civil society actors' power to represent and their power over representation". Hajer (2006) investigates the multi-signification in performing representation practices in EU governance and also points to the complicated and ambiguous nature of transnational representation, which needs to be backed by a lot of informal practices in order to clarify the fundamental meanings of policy negotiations for all actors involved (Hajer 2006, 43–44).

Adding to these difficult power asymmetries, transnational environmental politics face the double democratic challenge of transnationality and trans-temporality: political representatives can be held accountable neither by a clear-cut geographical community such as a nation-state, nor by a clearly defined temporal community, because the impacts of political decisions stretch into the lives of future generations. Trans-temporal and transnational distances between decision makers and "affected environments" (Christoff and Eckersley 2013, 168) render many forms of political representation almost impossible.

> Local place and time are increasingly overlaid with abstract space and time, producing more abstract social relations along with a biophysical world that is increasingly exploited, disassembled, transported, reassembled, and consumed in different parts of the planet.
>
> *Christoff and Eckersley 2013, 162*

Furthermore, abstract space and time conceals the diversity of possible future worlds that could be articulated, were the future representations more open to including different actors in sustainability politics. Thus, beyond questions of feasibility, sustainability scholars point increasingly to issues of power, accessibility and plurality (Lövbrand et al. 2015; Vervoort and Gupta 2018; Knappe et al. 2019b). Similar to IR research on performativity (Holzscheiter 2016), a scholarship on environmental futures (Lövbrand et al. 2015; Beck and Mahony 2017; Granjou et al. 2017; Mert 2019; Oomen et al. 2021) has developed against the background of the unfolding climate crisis and the introduction and quite rapid career of the Anthropocene concept. Futures in this context are not necessarily regarded as long term. Rather, the non-linear and rapturous, even catastrophic character of futures plays an important part in studying the representation of environmental futures. scholars go one step back and ask how environmental futures are constructed in the first place (Beck and Mahony 2017; Oomen et al. 2021) and who gets to represent them (Biermann and Möller 2019; Knappe et al. 2019a; Lövbrand et al. 2020). Performativity in this context is understood as "images of and expectations for 'the future' [that] structure decision-making and social organization" (Oomen et al. 2021, 2).

Inviting a "reflection on what democratic governance could look like in an era marked by fragmentation, instability, and volatility" (Hajer 2009, 10), representation theorists have suggested investigating, for example, who has access to representational systems, who has the resources to make representative claims (Saward 2010), and/or how reflexive are processes of representation (Disch 2011)? Similarly, with regard to future generations, Karnein argues for the process quality of representation, for sincere deliberations and imaginations about what future generations would want. In this regard, the actual outcome is not as relevant as "the reasons for choosing one course of action over another" (Karnein 2016, 93). "The important point is that we would have to justify our decisions to future generations *as if they were present today*" (ibid. italics in the original).

The very transformative nature of representation then comes from the ability to make counter-proposals for representations that would "challenge hegemonic subject formations" (Disch 2016, 794, referencing Spivak 1999). Furthermore, representation should be regarded as a transformative practice rather than a practice of accuracy (ibid.). Projecting such representations into the future, Crawford (2003) states that:

> [t]hrough the imagining of possible worlds, we may come to understand our own world better, to recognize its historical construction, and to imagine new configurations, possibilities that are not constrained by pre-existing ideas and precedent logics of what is past and considered politically feasible in the here and now.
>
> *Crawford 2003, 198*

Mateo (2019) argues that representation always builds and forms identities, and in this regard social realities can be transformed by fictionally staging future possible realities such as for example gender equality via equal representation of women in parliaments. Although gender equality is not a reality in the wider society the parliament represents, the parliament can transform this unequal reality by giving way to an equal representation of women in parliament. Similarly, Sauer (2011, 129) identifies the feminist transformative perspectives in representation in the combination of *Darstellen* (aesthetic representation) and *Handeln* (political action) in the form of institutional change and mobilization. She argues for processes that critically question representation practices and that broaden the political space, make the excluded visible in demonstrating non-representation.

Conclusions

This chapter has given an overview of how democratic representation is linked to sustainable futures. The difficulties of implementing institutions that safeguard the rights of future generations point to the tensions between democracy and sustainability that arise from the assumptions that futures are generally uncertain and far away. Stepping back and re-examining the very concept of representation by introducing constructivist representation theory, we might reconsider these tensions. The constructivist notion of representation as a creative and partial political act that constitutes realities introduces a more critical account of representation shedding light on the power asymmetries built into representation practices. However, it can also bring us further into thinking of how representation of sustainable futures might look. Constructivist representation theory views representation as a proactive practice that in itself creates notions of the future. In rendering this notion productive, representation can be an empowering and mobilizing practice that allows citizens to create their own plural visions of the future. When we approach the argument that representation is performative from a democratic theory lens, we can argue that this can also have empowering effects. As Lisa Disch argued, representation can mobilize political agency (2011). Representatives can mobilize groups that can define and crystallize their interests within the process of representation. Articulating claims can bring up political discourses. Even if representation is controversial, it can give the represented the opportunity to put forward counter-claims and become representatives themselves.

Furthermore, if we take the performativity seriously, then specifically descriptive representation can also mobilize constituencies and transform realities. Or as one producer behind the Netflix series *Bridgerton* commented on featuring more and more black characters as protagonists in their series: this brings about "something you have never seen before". And she doesn't mean the sheer visibility of persons of color in on the screen, but the emergence of new stories. As in the example of *Bridgerton*, the regency era (1810–1820, early nineteenth century) in England is re-imagined as a place where black people existed as equals with whites. Thus, reimagining a past that never existed and questioning "what would have been if" is a critical representation practice. This "as-if" can also be applied to the future. The future is a place of imagining a not-yet that needs to be filled with just and plural representations.

Notes

1 www.npr.org/2019/09/23/763452863/transcript-greta-thunbergs-speech-at-the-u-n-climate-action-summit?t=1618300459892 (last accessed 4/13/2021)
2 http://climatecasechart.com/climate-change-litigation/
3 While feminist political theorists argue that descriptive representation has a democratizing potential for political systems Cress (2018), most scholars of standard representation theory rather argue that descriptive representation has no benefits to substantive representation (Karnein and Roser 2015).

References

Alcoff, L., 1991. The problem of speaking for others. *Cultural Critique* 20 (5).
Ankersmit, F.R., 1996. *Aesthetic Politics: Political Philosophy Beyond Fact and Value*. Stanford: Stanford University Press.
Beck, S. and Mahony, M., 2017. The IPCC and the politics of anticipation. *Nature Climate Change* 7 (5), 311–313.
Berger, T. and Esguerra, A., 2018. Conclusion: power, relationality and difference. In T. Berger and A. Esguerra, eds. *World Politics in Translation: Power, Relationality and Difference in Global Cooperation*. London and New York: Routledge, 216–231.

Biermann, F. and Möller, I., 2019. Rich man's solution? Climate engineering discourses and the marginalization of the Global South. *International Environmental Agreements: Politics, Law and Economics* 19 (2), 151–167.

Bornemann, B. and Strassheim, H., 2019. Governing time for sustainability: analyzing the temporal implications of sustainability governance. *Sustainability Science* 14 (4), 1001–1013.

Burke, E., 1774. Speech to the Electors of Bristol.

Caney, S., 2016. Political institutions for the future: a fivefold package. In I. González-Ricoy and A. Gosseries, eds. *Institutions for future generations*, First edition. Oxford: Oxford University Press, 135–155.

Caney, S., 2018. Justice and future generations. *Annual Review of Political Science* 21 (1), 475–493.

Castro Varela, M.D.M. and Dhawan, N., 2012. Postkolonialer Feminismus und die Kunst der Selbstkritik. In E. Gutiérrez Rodríguez, and H. Steyerl, eds. *Spricht die Subalterne deutsch?: Migration und postkoloniale Kritik*, 2. Aufl. Münster: Unrast-Verl, 270–290.

Chakrabarty, D., 2015. Foreword. In E.M. DeLoughrey, J. Didur and A. Carrigan, eds. *Global Ecologies and the Environmental Humanities: Postcolonial Approaches*. New York and London: Routledge, xiii–xv.

Chaturvedi, S. and Doyle, T., 2015. *Climate Terror: A Critical Geopolitics of Climate Change*. Basingstoke: Palgrave Macmillan.

Christoff, P. and Eckersley, R., 2013. *Globalization and the Environment*. Lanham: Rowman and Littlefield.

Crawford, N.C., 2003. Feminist futures. In Weldes, J. (ed.) *To Seek Out New Worlds*. New York: Palgrave Macmillan, pp. 195–220.

Cress, A., 2018. Feministische Repräsentationskritik: (Dis-)Kontinuitäten von den ersten deutschen Frauenbewegungen bis in die Gegenwart. *FEMINA POLITICA – Zeitschrift für feministische Politikwissenschaft*, 27 (2–2018), 25–39.

Crutzen, P.J. and Stoermer, E.F., 2000. The "Anthropocene". *Global Change Newsletter* 41, 17–18.

DeLoughrey, E.M., Didur, J. and Carrigan, A., eds., 2015. *Global Ecologies and the Environmental Humanities: Postcolonial Approaches*. New York and London: Routledge.

Disch, L., 2011. Toward a mobilization conception of democratic representation. *American Political Science Review* 105 (1), 100–114.

Disch, L., 2016. Representation. In L. Disch and M.E. Hawkesworth, eds. *The Oxford Handbook of Feminist Theory*. Oxford: Oxford University Press, 781–802.

Dobson, A., 1997. Representative democracy and the environment. In W.M. Lafferty and J. Meadowcroft, eds. *Democracy and the Environment: Problems and Prospects*, Reprinted. Cheltenham: Elgar, 124–139.

Eckersley, R., 2017. Geopolitan democracy in the Anthropocene. *Political Studies* 65 (4), 983–999.

Granjou, C., Walker, J. and Salazar, J.F., 2017. Guest Editorial to the special issue 'Politics of Anticipation: On knowing and governing environmental futures'. *Futures* 92, 1–4.

Hajer, M.A., 2006. The living institutions of the EU: Analysing governance as performance. *Perspectives on European Politics and Society* 7 (1), 41–55.

Hajer, M.A., 2009. *Authoritative Governance: Policy-making in the Age of Mediatization*. Oxford: Oxford University Press.

Holzscheiter, A., 2016. Representation as power and performative practice: global civil society advocacy for working children. *Review of International Studies* 42 (2), 205–226.

Karnein, A. and Roser, D., 2015. Saving the planet by empowering the young? In A. Mason, I. Dimitrijoski, J. Tremmel and P.H. Godli, eds. *Youth Quotas and Other Efficient Forms of Youth Participation in Ageing Societies*. Basel: Springer, 77–92.

Knappe, H., 2020a. Globale Zukunftsvisionen und die Repräsentation alternativer Zukünfte. In N. Tamoudi, S. Faets and M. Reder, eds. *Politik der Zukunft*. Bielefeld: transcript-Verlag, 87–106.

Knappe, H., 2020b. Representation as practice: agency and relationality in transnational civil society. *Journal of International Relations and Development* 12 (4), 467.

Knappe, H., Holfelder, A.K., Beer, D.L. and Nanz, P., eds., 2019a. The politics of making and un-making (sustainable) futures. *Sustainability Science* 13 (2), 273–274.

Knappe, H., Holfelder, A.K., Löw Beer, D. and Nanz, P., 2019b. The politics of making and unmaking (sustainable) futures: Introduction to the special feature. *Sustainability Science* 14 (4), 891–898.

Lafferty, W.M. and Meadowcroft, J., eds., 1997. *Democracy and the Environment: Problems and Prospects*, Reprinted. Cheltenham: Elgar.

Lawrence, P., 2019. Representation of future generations. In A. Kalfagianni, D. Fuchs, D. and A. Hayden, eds. *Routledge Handbook of Global Sustainability Governance*. New York: Routledge, 88–99.

Little, A. and Macdonald, K., 2013. Pathways to global democracy? Escaping the statist imaginary. *Review of International Studies* 39 (4), 789–813.

Lövbrand, E., Beck, S. and Chilvers, J., et al., 2015. Who speaks for the future of Earth?: How critical social science can extend the conversation on the Anthropocene. *Global Environmental Change* 32, 211–218.

Lövbrand, E., Mobjörk, M. and Söder, R., 2020. The Anthropocene and the geo-political imagination: re-writing Earth as political space. *Earth System Governance* 4.

Mansbridge, J., 2003. Rethinking representation. *American Political Science Review* 97 (4), 515–528.

Mateo, M.M., 2019. Füreinander Sprechen. Zu einer feministischen Theorie der Repräsentation. *Leviathan* 47 (3), 331–353.

Mert, A., 2019. Democracy in the Anthropocene: a new scale. In F. Biermann and E. Lövbrand, eds. *Anthropocene Encounters: New Directions in Green Political Thinking.* Cambridge: Cambridge University Press, 128–149.

Mitchell, W.J.T., 1995. Representation. In F. Lentricchia and T. McLaughlin, eds. *Critical Terms for Literary Study.* Chicago: University of Chicago Press, 1–12.

Montanaro, L., 2018. *Who Elected Oxfam?: A Democratic Defence of Self-Appointed Representatives.* Cambridge: Cambridge University Press.

Näsström, S., 2011. The challenge of the all-affected principle. *Political Studies* 59 (1), 116–134.

Oomen, J., Hoffman, J. and Hajer, M.A., 2021. Techniques of futuring: on how imagined futures become socially performative. *European Journal of Social Theory* 82, 136843102098882.

Pitkin, H.F., 1967. *The Concept of Representation.* Berkeley: University of California Press.

Sauer, B., 2011. "Only paradoxes to offer?" Feministische Demokratie- und Repräsentationstheorie in der "Postdemokratie". *Österreichische Zeitschrift für Politikwissenschaft,* (2), 125–138.

Saward, M., 2006. The representative claim. *Contemporary Political Theory* 5 (3), 297–318.

Smith, G., 2020. Enhancing the legitimacy of offices for future generations: the case for public participation. *Political Studies* 68 (4), 996–1013.

Spivak, G.C., 1999. *A Critique of Postcolonial Reason.* Harvard: Harvard University Press.

Tamoudi, N., 2020. Das Problem mit der Zeit: Zukünftige Generationen und die Heuristik der Zukunft. In N. Tamoudi, S. Faets and M. Reder, eds. *Politik der Zukunft: Zukünftige Generationen als Leerstelle der Demokratie,* 1. Auflage. Bielefeld: transcript Verlag, 109–128.

Tamoudi, N., Faets, S. and Reder, M., eds., 2020. *Politik der Zukunft: Zukünftige Generationen als Leerstelle der Demokratie,* 1. Auflage. Bielefeld: transcript Verlag.

Thompson, D.F., 2010. Representing future generations: political presentism and democratic trusteeship. *Critical Review of International Social and Political Philosophy* 13 (1), 17–37.

Urbinati, N., 2008. *Representative Democracy: Principles and Genealogy.* Chicago: University of Chicago Press.

Vervoort, J. and Gupta, A., 2018. Anticipating climate futures in a 1.5°C era: the link between foresight and governance. *Current Opinion in Environmental Sustainability* 31, 104–111.

Yusoff, K., 2018. *A Billion Black Anthropocenes or None.* Minneapolis: University of Minnesota Press.

7
DELIBERATION AND SUSTAINABILITY
From policy instrument to emancipation

Marit Hammond and Graham Smith

Introduction

The relationship between deliberation and sustainability is contested. One prominent articulation of the relationship sees deliberation as an established policy instrument in the sustainability governance toolbox (Bäckstrand et al. 2010). Policy makers, practitioners, activists and academics commonly articulate the virtues of deliberation in improving policy making for sustainability. Deliberative technologies such as citizens' panels, juries and assemblies, consensus conferences, and forms of stakeholder engagement and the like are celebrated as ways of realising deliberation within the policy process (Voß 2016). Deliberation is taken to improve decision making and build political legitimacy by enhancing reflection on the diversity of environmental values and knowledge. Sustainability is a major social problem; deliberation a method of improved problem-solving.

While this is an important development, it reflects a partial story of the relationship between deliberation and sustainability. The focus on deliberation as policy instrument neglects the origin of deliberative democracy as a critical social theory that challenges broader systemic injustices. While deliberation may have significant problem-solving capacities, the emancipatory ambition of deliberative democracy is more extensive, aiming to recast established expressions of social and economic power. Democratic communication is a broader social phenomenon, not just a means to an end. Combine this with a recognition of sustainability as on ongoing process, then deliberation can be understood as a key property of social systems that enable forms of democratic reflexivity; a foundation for more reflexive, adaptable, and ecologically attuned societies.

The first section of this chapter explains the nature of deliberation and its attraction for those concerned about sustainability. It brings into focus the difference between deliberation as sustainability governance instrument and its more radical interpretation as critical social theory that offers a more systemic approach to the sustainability challenges we face. The second section explains the emergence of deliberative democracy, how it lost its emancipatory impulse and the dangers that the focus on a more instrumental reading of deliberation may undermine more radical democratic change and thus the capacity to embrace more inclusive and emancipatory conceptions of sustainability. The final section of the chapter explores how recovering the original emancipatory understanding of deliberation points us towards broader considerations of the role of institutions, culture and democratic systems in our endless search for sustainability.

Deliberation as a policy instrument or emancipatory theory?

Deliberation is a particular way of ordering and doing things. It is a form of communication that is fair, reasoned, inclusive, public, and free from the distortions that emerge from the exercise of social and economic power. Deliberation is 'authentic' to the extent that it induces reflection in a non-coercive manner (Dryzek 2000). This sets the bar for legitimacy much higher than typical political discourse, whether in governments, parliaments, civil society or the media. For genuine deliberation to occur, participants must have equal standing, justify their positions to others through reason, commit to being open to changing their own views in light of others' arguments, and be sincere and orientated to the common-good. Manipulation and the maximisation of self-interest over common concerns have no place (Benhabib 1996; Dryzek 2000). Deliberation has an equalising function – redressing forms of political domination such as the undue influence of resources, status, background and structural biases. With this ambitious normative core, deliberation rests on the inclusion of otherwise marginalised voices, restricting opportunities to bypass democratic processes or capitalise on powerful social positions (Curato et al. 2018).

Why the interest in deliberation amongst those committed to sustainability? Concern for sustainability often places advocates in opposition to entrenched social norms, practices and interests that perpetuate unsustainability (Jordan et al. 2010, 4; Hanson 2018). Deliberation offers a way of challenging established norms, practices and interests by embedding 'ecological rationality' (Dryzek 1990) – ensuring that the full range of ecological values and different types of ecological knowledge are expressed, justified and considered (Baber and Bartlett 2018). Advocates of deliberation draw on both theoretical and empirical evidence to suggest that self-interested motives that often drive unsustainability are difficult to justify under the scrutiny of free and fair deliberation (Smith 2003; Mackenzie 2018). As Offe and Preuss (1991) argue, deliberation is fact-regarding, other-regarding and future-regarding. Sustainability brings alternative perspectives and interests into conflict, including within the environmental movement itself (think, for example of the worldviews of conservationists and preservationists; radicals and reformers). Deliberation does not wish away this conflict, but rather creates the conditions for political judgements that take into consideration different perspectives on the non-human world (Smith 2003, 53). Deliberation provides the space to challenge embedded assumptions about endless economic growth and technological solutionism.

It is these characteristics of deliberation that have captured attention within sustainability governance. When faced with entrenched social and economic power, deliberation promises a way of opening up decision making in a more inclusive and democratic manner. Over recent years, deliberation has emerged as an increasingly important instrument in the sustainability governance toolbox. The promise is better and more legitimate decision making (Newig et al. 2018). Better in the sense that policy will be made that reflects the plurality of environmental values and situated knowledges. More legitimate because participants and the broader public will recognise the process of deliberation as being inclusive, free and fair. In some ways this resonates with the long-standing political commitment to stakeholder participation that is common amongst advocates of sustainable development, not least official UN agreements such as Agenda 21 (Meadowcroft 2004). The difference for deliberative democrats, however, is that it is not just a question of who is at the table (all affected stakeholders), but the mode of interaction and the forms of social power that this expresses (democratic deliberation).

In practice, this means a great deal of interest and experimentation in creating conditions under which participants in the policy process can engage in more deliberative exchanges. A range of deliberative designs have emerged that bring together and facilitate varying combinations and types of stakeholders, citizens, scientists and policy makers. Whole industries have developed to deliver this new approach to participatory technologies. Just one example is the range of processes that fall under the umbrella of 'deliberative mini-publics', such as citizens' juries, citizen assemblies, planning cells and consensus conferences (Setälä and Smith 2018). These highly facilitated bodies bring together a random selection of citizens to work on a particular policy challenge. Participants hear from and question a range of experts and interest groups, deliberate amongst themselves and come to recommendations. Random selection ensures a broad diversity of perspectives on the issue under consideration; facilitation ensures fairness in the deliberative process.

Such mini-publics have been used across a range of sustainability issues at varying levels of governance. Organisations such as MASS LBP (Canada),[1] newDemocracy (Australia)[2] and the Jefferson Center (US)[3] have run citizens' juries and panels on, for example, urban planning, rural climate challenges and nuclear waste disposal. The Danish Board of Technology (DBT) has a long record of organising consensus conferences as a means of incorporating the perspectives of the lay public within the assessment of new scientific and technological developments that raise significant social and ethical concerns.[4] DBT was the coordinator of the World Wide Views project which in 2009 engaged over 4,000 citizens in 38 countries to deliberate on the future of climate policy (Rask et al. 2012). Deliberative polls have been used to bring large numbers of people together to deliberate on a range of issues, including regional planning for Texas utility companies (Fishkin 2009).[5] In Poland, citizens' assemblies have been organised at municipal level on climate change and flood prevention.[6] The Irish Citizens' Assembly, famous for its recommendation to liberalise the constitutional status of abortion, which was then supported by a national referendum, also spent a couple of weekends considering and making recommendations on how to strengthen Irish climate policy.[7] The recent French Citizens' Convention on Climate commissioned by President Macron,[8] the Climate Assembly UK commissioned by six parliamentary select committees[9] and Scotland's Climate Assembly promised in Scotland's Climate Change Act (2019)[10] indicate the extent to which this model of deliberative engagement has entered the mainstream.[11] Evidence from these experiments with mini-publics suggests that citizens are willing and able to deliberate on highly complex and controversial issues; and that they reach judgements that are sensitive to ecological and social concerns. The case for deliberation as a way of promoting reflection and consideration on sustainability is strong.

Deliberation in this context is very much a problem-solving method (Wironen et al. 2019). Deliberation offers a solution to the problem of how to create the conditions under which values and knowledge claims that are typically given short shrift are considered in the policy making process. Deliberation promises to provide a space in which often marginalised ecological values and knowledge are heard and given fair consideration.

But this 'problem-solving' perspective on deliberation has shortcomings. The rhetorical influence of deliberation within the policy process far outpaces its actual impact. Deliberative workshops and forums have proliferated, but the extent of policy effect is rather limited. These initiatives are only one part of the policy process and only one input into decision making; inserted often as a one-off shot. The deliberations from these processes have recommendatory force: the assumption is that the quality of the process and recommendations will influence decision makers (Fishkin 2009). The quality of deliberative engagement may be high, but it has to fare against the rest of the policy process that has non-deliberative characteristics: electoral-party motivations and the power of interest groups win out too often at the expense of deliberation. Critics worry that the timing, framing and impacts of deliberative mini-publics are too influenced by power struggles in the conventional policy process (Lafont 2015; Böker 2017). The very forces that undermine sustainability, such as powerful vested interests, undermine deliberation. One answer to the question of impact is to empower deliberative processes. This is what we have seen in Poland, for example, where municipal mayors have agreed to implement recommendations from citizens' assemblies where they realise at least 80 percent support amongst participants (Gerwin 2018).[12] In Gdansk, a more effective flood defence system has been implemented on this basis. But political elites are typically suspicious of empowering deliberation to this extent, not least because of the loss of power on their part. Facilitated citizen deliberation is recognised as a useful ingredient to add; but it is not seen as the whole cake.

A more fundamental critique questions the celebration of deliberation as policy instrument – as a sophisticated approach to problem solving. The tendency to consider deliberation as the property of mini-publics (or some other deliberative method) inserted into the policy process loses sight of the emancipatory potential of deliberative democracy as a critical social theory (Böker 2017). Deliberation definitely has problem-solving and coordination capacities, but it is also the basis of an emancipatory theory that aims to structurally recast established expressions of social and economic power. Deliberation is a broader mode of social and political communication on which a fairer democratic society should be ordered. Deliberative democracy thus emerges as a critique of existing democratic practices; as a response to the contemporary crises of democracy, whether this be conceptualised as the impact of speculative capitalism, authoritarian populism or institutional racism (White 2017; Curato et al. 2018). The idea of deliberation as a policy instrument to be exploited in an otherwise technocratic policy process undersells its potential as a force for social change, not least for sustainability.

But just as deliberation is 'radicalised', so too sustainability. The policy instrument approach assumes a set of fairly-well defined outcomes to be achieved. The Sustainable Development Goals are the most obvious global expression of this technocratic perspective. Instead, a more political interpretation recognises that sustainability is not an end state that can be defined clearly, but is rather a site of confrontation, contestation and negotiation about different ways of living in relation to the nonhuman world. Coordination of social action in such a context requires high levels of reflexivity and capacities to adapt, characteristics of political systems that are poorly served by current democratic practices. For deliberative democrats, deliberation is a key property of social systems that will enable forms of democratic reflexivity and adaptation: an ongoing inclusive social process of coordination and conflict over potential futures. The dual crises of unsustainability and democratic practice require more than deliberation as policy instrument.

How did we get here?

These different approaches to understanding the potential of deliberation reflect the evolution of the theory of deliberative democracy and its relationship with environmental politics. The move from critical social theory with ambitions of systemic change to policy instrument occurred as deliberative democracy established itself in the mainstream. Tracing the evolution of the theory helps put current practice into its wider theoretical context and direct renewed attention to broader systemic change.

Democratic theorists do not always advocate for social change. In the 1950s and 60s, theorists such as Joseph Schumpeter, Anthony Downs and William Riker used economic methods to justify minimal forms of liberal democracy, in which the role of citizens is little more than voting for competing governing elites – hence the term democratic or competitive elitism. This limited conception of democracy appeals to those, including some prominent scientists, who believe that a more technocratic and centralised approach is necessary to deliver sustainability (Lovelock 2010; Maxton and Randers 2016). Yet such an articulation of democracy is problematic on a number of fronts. First, reducing participation to regular elections limits democratic principles of inclusiveness and empowerment to their bare minimum. Second, such a technocratic approach assumes that sustainability can be shorn of its normative core; that the diversity of perspectives and significant social conflicts over what sustainability entails can simply be ignored. And third, competitive elitism severely overestimates the capacity of central control to realise the reflexivity and social coordination necessary for responding to sustainability challenges in a complex society.

The social movements of the 1960s, such as the civil rights, environmental, feminist and peace movements, paved the way for new theorising on democracy that challenged the stranglehold of competitive elitism's conservative account. Theorists were inspired by the participatory politics of that era and its demands for empowerment of marginalised social groups. Participatory democrats challenged authority in all realms of life – not just the traditional political realm, but also the economic, social and even personal – arguing that citizens should be empowered to govern their own lives. The negative perception of the apathetic and politically incompetent citizens cast by democratic elitists was replaced by that of citizens learning to govern their lives through participating collectively in political, economic and social organisations (Pateman 1970; Barber 2004). For many, the politics of sustainability took on a participatory hue. For example, Ostrom's (1990) influential account of governing the commons explicitly articulated the centrality of community control over non-renewable resources. Communities have the local knowledge and motivation to ensure sustainability that distant bureaucrats and officials lack.

Emerging in the 1980s and 90s, deliberative democracy draws on the insights of participatory democrats, but with a more explicit account of the structural barriers to emancipation and more stringent normative criteria of the conditions for emancipation. Jürgen Habermas (1984) provides an extensive analysis of how a pernicious 'instrumental rationality' has taken hold of liberal societies to the detriment of 'communicative rationality' through which citizens can freely and fairly negotiate social conflicts. Deliberative democracy thus cast itself in opposition to entrenched economic and social power structures that reduce the scope for communication. Many green political theorists found themselves inspired by deliberative democracy. John Dryzek was an early pioneer, arguing that instrumental rationality is the source of much ecological destruction. In contrast, communicative rationality is necessarily 'ecologically rational' in the sense that it presupposes the basic ecological conditions for human life (Dryzek 1987). This focus on forms of rationality has led to differences of emphasis within deliberative democracy between a central focus on the emancipation of citizens through their active participation in deliberative processes and a broader concern about the articulation of competing discourses across the public sphere and their transmission into political decision making (Dryzek and Niemeyer 2008; Owen and Smith 2015). Our own tendency is towards the former. As Amy Gutmann argues: 'the legitimate exercise of political authority requires justification to those people who are bound by it, and decision-making by deliberation among free and equal citizens is the most defensible justification anyone has to offer for provisionally settling controversial issues' (Gutmann 1996, 344).

Often highly philosophical and abstract in its analysis, an 'institutional turn' has looked to make deliberative democracy more practically relevant through a search for the institutions through which deliberative democratic ideals might be realised – or at least approximated. This turn to institutions focused on how the design of institutions enables or disables deliberation. For example, studies of parliaments show how different party systems, architectures and parliamentary practices affect the deliberative quality of proceedings (Steiner et al. 2009). Mini-publics became a particular fascination. Practical work with mini-publics had emerged in the 1970s. Deliberative democracy scholars saw in the application of random selection and facilitation a means of ameliorating the impact of broader social and economic power imbalances and a space within which ordinary citizens are willing and capable of deliberating on highly complex policy problems (Setälä and Smith 2018). A sophisticated research agenda has emerged, one that suggests that mini-publics are helpful in resolving political stalemate and enhancing inclusion (Beauvais and Warren 2019) in ways that are both 'extremely useful to policy-makers' (Delap 2001, 39) and welcomed by citizens (Jacquet 2019).

The attraction of getting things done in the here-and-now meant that many academics and practitioners came to view mini-publics as the standard bearers of deliberative democracy. This emerging research and practice agenda can be interpreted in two ways: mini-publics and other participatory processes are instrumentally valuable for making better policy; or such participatory institutions are an expression of an altogether different way of doing politics, recalling the earlier principles of participatory democracy. The more deliberation became a professionalised and commercialised practice of interest to public authorities (Hendriks and Carson 2008), the more the problem-solving approach and thus the instrumental use of deliberation have tended to dominate, particularly in relation to sustainability governance. In a couple of decades, the weight of research moved from deliberative democracy as emancipatory social theory to how to design deliberative processes that are more informed and reflective to help solve concrete political problems – not least sustainability concerns.

The problem-solving function of deliberation is important to responding to the crisis of unsustainability, but given that the crisis is systemic, dangers exist that attention is focused on particular policy gains with less attention to broader and more critical engagement across society at large. The danger is that mini-publics and the like help stabilise or even reinforce outdated structures and practices of policymaking rather than transforming these processes in ways that are necessary for sustainability. In the name of deliberative democracy and sustainability, deliberative policy instruments are integrated into existing institutions in ways that legitimate the very structures that have driven us to into the crises of democracy and unsustainability in the first place. We patch up failing institutions rather than recognise the need for transformation.

A more recent 'systems' turn in deliberative democracy has restored attention to questions of deliberation at scale rather than the characteristics of individual institutions, but still not necessarily recovered the theory's original critical ethos (Mansbridge et al. 2012). To enable sustainability, systems considerations must bring into focus questions of whether and how deliberation can inform, induce reflection, and mediate across divides, but importantly also channel critical contestation, not only within mini-publics and other carefully designed institutions, but scaled up to societies as a whole (Niemeyer 2014; Owen and Smith 2015; Curato and Böker 2016). Our attention needs to turn to the question of what deliberation looks like not just inside highly orchestrated, designed spaces, but in the messy and imperfect, but often less constrained, public sphere (Chambers 2009).

Where next for deliberation and sustainability?

The theoretical and empirical connection between deliberation and sustainability is well established. The research agenda on how particular institutions, such as deliberative mini-publics, are able to deal with sustainability issues is equally advanced – as is the practice on the ground. But if we are to take the emancipatory and sustainability potential of deliberative democracy seriously, the next step in the research agenda will need to be more critical and systemic in its ambitions. It will need to return to the earlier theoretical endeavours, but ask what does this mean in practice? It is one thing to argue for a more systemic approach to deliberation; another entirely to work out the cultural and institutional implications. One danger is that it becomes too speculative – unlike the analysis of single mini-publics, thinking systemically is harder to ground empirically. But the reality of unsustainability demands that we take what Erik Olin Wright (2010) terms a 'real utopias' approach: laying the foundations for a set of concrete, emancipatory alternatives to business as usual. This will necessarily take us beyond mini-publics to questions of how to restructure entrenched political, economic, social – and even familial – institutions and practices such that they embed the inclusiveness and reflexivity necessary for the collective search for, and action towards, sustainability.

We can only begin to offer a sketch of what this challenging intellectual and practical agenda might look like.

Taking a more systemic approach to deliberative democracy certainly does not mean abandoning interest in mini-publics and other participatory institutions that create protected spaces for citizen deliberation. But it means thinking more radically about how they might be integrated into the broader political system. Extinction Rebellion (XR) in the UK offers one such proposition. Not only is it demanding that the British government declare a climate emergency and act immediately to halt biodiversity loss and reduce greenhouse gas emissions to net zero by 2025, but that government must establish and be led by the decisions of a Citizens' Assembly on Climate and Ecological Justice.[13] XR makes the case that system change is necessary. An empowered citizens' assembly needs to be at the centre of political governance, given the inability of political elites to respond to the climate and ecological emergency. Whatever we think of this demand, it takes us beyond deliberation as policy instrument. Debates have also turned to the question of whether legislative chambers should be sortition-based: Michael MacKenzie, for example, makes a sustained argument for why a randomly-selected second chamber would promote and defend the interests of future generations through the institutionalisation of deliberation (MacKenzie 2017). Others contend that simply changing the composition of the legislature is not enough and more radical restructuring of the body and surrounding institutions is necessary if the practice of sortition and rotation is to become an established part of our governing institutions (Owen and Smith 2019). The idea of empowering sortition-based institutions in this way is not comfortable for some deliberative democrats, who are concerned about the loss of well-established forms of electoral accountability. The sustainability crisis requires us to confront and carefully consider our well-entrenched perspectives on what makes for legitimate democratic design.

Relatively novel institutions such as independent offices for future generations are also deserving of attention and consideration (Smith 2020; 2021). In principle, such offices have the capacity to facilitate critical reflexivity within polities given that they are not subject to electoral cycles or the nefarious influence of powerful sectional interests that motivate short-termism within established political institutions. It is telling that the first two such offices in Israel and Hungary were abolished and had their power curtailed respectively. This suggests they made the life of elected officials uncomfortable. The recent creation of international interest in the Future Generations Commissioner for Wales indicates that this institutional form may still have an important role to play within democratic systems.[14] The requirement under the Wellbeing of Future Generations (Wales) Act for the Commissioner to promote public involvement in its own activities and the work of other public bodies suggests a recognition of the importance of public dialogue in developing and implementing long-term policy and ensuring its broader public legitimacy. Such bodies may become important focal points for critical reflection on sustainability within and across political systems.[15]

Our analytical gaze must also confront actions and activities within the economic realm, too often ignored by democratic theorists. Long established (cooperatives, mutuals) and newer (social enterprises, B-corps) forms of economic enterprise are structured to promote deliberation within and beyond the confines of the legal entity and have become important actors within sustainability niches that deliver economic returns without compromising social and environmental concerns. But the regulatory and legal context within which they operate systemically privileges economic enterprises that are accountable primarily to shareholders (Smith and Teasdale 2012). Attention to such regulatory and legal frameworks may not be the usual focus of deliberative democrats, but their impact is critical to embedding a set of economic practices that support a broader deliberative culture within which sustainability is a primary driver.

Deliberative culture – understood as the norms of fairness, inclusiveness and open communication – is not simply a product of orchestration and facilitation by the state (Böker 2017). More organic and informal, citizen-led and dispersed public deliberation on visions for the future is critical (Hammond 2019; 2020). Such developments connect with the adoption of 'prefigurative politics' by many environmentalists who aim to build alternative forms of production and consumption: concrete projects such as alternative food systems or community energy initiatives (Yates 2015). The ambition is to realise solutions in the here-and-now: seeking 'to create the new society "in the shell of the old" by developing counterhegemonic institutions and modes of interaction that embody the desired transformation' (Leach 2013, 1). Rooted in communities, the question is how such activities can be scaled up in ways that foster deliberation and critical reflection on the necessary social and economic changes for sustainability.

What these reflections on different institutional forms and social practices points to is the need to think both about the ways in which institutions across political, social and economic realms enable a 'deliberative stance' amongst citizens (Owen and Smith 2015), such that they are in a position to critically reflect on alternative futures, and to consider what it means to embed a 'deliberative culture' (Böker 2017) more systemically within and across political systems.

Conclusion

Deliberation has many virtues for those wishing to promote sustainability. Its significance can be traced through the growing number of deliberative initiatives that are integrated into policy processes to deal with particular sustainability challenges. While examples exist of where such deliberative interventions have made a difference to policy outcomes, most of the time the impact of such initiatives is unclear. The concern is that deliberation is used as a window dressing for the politics as usual. This is an uncomfortable situation when we consider that the origins of deliberative democracy are as an emancipatory social theory, one which promises to challenge entrenched interests and the patterns of unsustainability caused by the instrumentalization of the environment. A return to the more emancipatory roots of deliberative democracy entails an expansion of our vision of deliberation beyond policy instrument to the foundation of a more reflexive, socially just and ecologically sustainable society. This is a ridiculously challenging research agenda – and an even more challenging political one. But simply crafting occasional opportunities for citizens to deliberate within established policy processes is a long way from the emancipatory agenda that is necessary if we are to come to terms with the evermore pressing sustainability challenges we face now and in the future.

Notes

1 www.masslbp.com/
2 www.newdemocracy.com.au
3 https://jefferson-center.org/
4 https://tekno.dk/
5 https://cdd.stanford.edu/
6 https://climateassemblies.org/
7 https://2016-2018.citizensassembly.ie/en/
8 www.conventioncitoyennepourleclimat.fr/
9 www.climateassembly.uk/
10 www.climateassembly.scot/
11 https://theconversation.com/citizens-assemblies-how-to-bring-the-wisdom-of-the-public-to-bear-on-the-climate-emergency-119117
12 https://climateassemblies.org/
13 https://rebellion.earth/the-truth/demands/
14 https://futuregenerations.wales/
15 A broader literature on how to design democratic institutions for the long-term has emerged in recent years. See, for example, Iñigo González-Ricoy and Axel Gosseries (2017); Boston (2016); Smith (2021).

References

Baber, W.F. and Bartlett, R.V., 2018. Deliberative Democracy and the Environment. In A. Bächtiger, J. Dryzek, J. Mansbridge and M.E. Warren, eds. *The Oxford Handbook of Deliberative Democracy*. Oxford: Oxford University Press, 755–767.

Bäckstrand, K., Khan, J., Kronsell, A. and Lövbrand, E., 2010. The Promise of New Modes of Environmental Governance. In K. Bäckstrand, J. Khan, A. Kronsell and E. Lövbrand, eds. *Environmental Politics and Deliberative Democracy: Examining the Promise of New Modes of Governance*. Cheltenham: Edward Elgar, 3–27.

Barber, B.R., 2004. *Strong Democracy: Participatory Politics for a New Age*. Berkeley: University of California Press.

Beauvais, E. and Warren, M.E., 2019. What can deliberative mini-publics contribute to democratic systems? *European Journal of Political Research*, 58 (3), 893–914.

Benhabib, S., 1996. Toward a Deliberative Model of Democratic Legitimacy. In S. Benhabib, eds. *Democracy and Difference. Contesting the Boundaries of the Political*. Princeton: Princeton University Press, 67–94.

Böker, M., 2017. Justification, critique, and deliberative legitimacy: the limits of mini-publics. *Contemporary Political Theory*, 16 (1), 19–40.

Boston, J., 2016. *Governing the Future: Designing Democratic Institutions for a Better Tomorrow*. Bingley: Emerald.

Chambers, S., 2009. Rhetoric and the public sphere: has deliberative democracy abandoned mass democracy? *Political Theory*, 37 (3), 323–350.

Curato, N. and Böker, M., 2016. Linking mini-publics to the deliberative system: A research agenda. *Policy Sciences*, 49 (2), 173–190. https://doi.org/10.1007/s11077-015-9238-5.

Curato, N., Hammond, M. and Min, J.B., 2018. *Power in Delibrative Democracy: Norms, Forums, Systems*. Basingstoke: Palgrave Macmillan.

Delap, C., 2001. Citizens juries: reflections on the UK experience. *PLA Notes*, 40, 39–42.

Dryzek, J.S., 1987. *Rational Ecology: Environment and Political Economy*. Oxford: Blackwell.

Dryzek, J.S., 1990. *Discursive Democracy: Politics, Policy, and Political Science*. Cambridge: Cambridge University Press.

Dryzek, J.S., 1995. Political and ecological communication. *Environmental Politics*, 4 (4), 13–30.

Dryzek, J.S., 2000. *Deliberative Democracy and Beyond: Liberals, Critics, Contestations*. Oxford: Oxford University Press.

Dryzek, J.S., 2010. *Foundations and Frontiers of Deliberative Governance*. Oxford: Oxford University Press.

Dryzek, J.S., 2016. Institutions for the Anthropocene: governance in a changing earth system. *British Journal of Political Science*, 46 (4), 937–956.

Dryzek, J.S. and Niemeyer, S., 2008. Discursive representation. *American Political Science Review*, 102 (4), 481–493.

Eckersley, R., 1996. Greening Liberal Democracy: The Rights Discourse Revisited. In Brian Doherty and Marius de Geus, eds. *Democracy and Green Political Thought: Sustainability, Rights and Citizenship*. London: Routledge, 212–236.

Eckersley, R., 2000. *Deliberative Democracy, Ecological Representation and Risk: Towards a Democracy of the Affected*. Abingdon: Routledge.

Fishkin, J.S., 2009. *When the People Speak: Deliberative Democracy and Public Co*. Oxford: Oxford University Press.

Gerwin, M., 2018. *Citizens Assemblies: Guide to Democracy that Works*. Krakow: Open Plan Foundation [online]. Available from: https://citizensassemblies.org/

González-Ricoy, I. and Gosseries, A., eds., 2017. *Institutions for Future Generations*. Oxford University Press.

Gutmann, A., 1996. Democracy, Philosophy, and Justification. In Seyla Benhabib (Ed.) *Democracy and Difference*. Princeton: Princeton University Press, 340–347.

Habermas, J., 1984. *The Theory of Communicative Action. Vol. I: Reason and the Rationalization of Society*, T. McCarthy (trans.). Boston: Beacon.

Hammond, M., 2019. A cultural account of ecological democracy. *Environmental Values*, 28 (1), 55–74.

Hammond, M., 2020. Sustainability as a cultural transformation: the role of deliberative democracy. *Environmental Politics*, 29, 173–192.

Hanson, L., eds., 2018. *Public Deliberation on Climate Change: Lessons from Alberta Climate Dialogue*. Edmonton: AU Press.

Hendriks, C.M. and Carson, L. (2008). Can the market help the forum? Negotiating the commercialization of deliberative democracy. *Policy Sciences*, 41 (4), 293–313. https://doi.org/10.1007/s11077-008-9069-8.

Jacquet, V., 2019. The role and future of deliberative mini-publics: a citizen perspective. *Political Studies*, 67 (3), 639–657.

Jordan, A., Huitema D. and van Asselt, H., 2010. Climate Change Policy in the European Union: An Introduction. In A. Jordan, D. Huitema, H. van Asselt, T. Rayner and F. Berkhout, eds. *Climate Change Policy in the European Union: Confronting the Dilemmas of Mitigation and Adaptation?* Cambridge: Cambridge University Press, 3–26.

Lafont, C., 2015. Deliberation, participation, and democratic legitimacy: should deliberative mini-publics shape public policy? *Journal of Political Philosophy*, 23 (1), 40–63.

Leach, D.K., 2013. Prefigurative politics. In D.A. Snow, D. della Porta, B. Klandermans and D. McAdam, eds. *The Wiley-Blackwell Encyclopedia of Social and Political Movements*. Malden: Blackwell.

Lovelock, J., 2010. Humans are too stupid to prevent climate change. *The Guardian*, 29 March.

MacKenzie, M.K., 2017. A General Purpose, Randomly Selected Chamber. In I. González-Ricoy and A. Gosseries, eds. *Institutions for Future Generations*. Oxford University Press, 282–298.

MacKenzie, M.K., 2018. Deliberation and Long-Term Decisions: Representing Future Generations. In A. Bächtiger, J.S. Dryzek, J. Mansbridge and M.E. Warren, eds. *The Oxford Handbook of Deliberative Democracy*. Oxford: Oxford University Press, 251–272.

Mansbridge, J., Bohman, J., Chambers, S., Christiano, Y., Fung, A., Parkinson, J., Thompson, D.F. and M.E. Warren, 2012. A Systemic Approach to Deliberative Democracy. In J. Parkinson and J. Mansbridge, eds. *Deliberative Systems*. Cambridge: Cambridge University Press, 1–26.

Maxton, G. and Randers, J., 2016. *Reinventing Prosperity: Managing Economic Growth to Reduce Unemployment, Inequality and Climate Change*. Vancouver: Greystone.

Meadowcroft, J., 2004. Participation and Sustainable Development: Modes of Citizen, Community and Organisational Involvement. In W.M. Lafferty, ed. *Governance for Sustainable Development: The Challenge of Adapting Form to Function*. Cheltenham, UK/Northampton, MA: Edward Elgar, 162–190.

Newig, J., Challies, E., Jager, N.W., Kochskämper E. and Adzersen, A., 2018. The environmental performance of participatory and collaborative governance: a framework of causal mechanisms. *Policy Studies Journal*, 46 (2), 269–297.

Niemeyer, S., 2014. Scaling up Deliberation to Mass Publics: Harnessing Mini-Publics in a Deliberative System. In K. Grönlund, A. Bächtiger and M. Setälä, eds. *Deliberative Mini-Publics: Involving Citizens in the Democratic Process*. Colchester: ECPR Press, 177–202.

Offe, C., and Preuss, U.K., 1991. Democratic Institutions and Moral Resources. In D. Held, ed. *Political Theory Today*. Cambridge: Polity, 143–171.

Ostrom, E., 1990. *Governing the Commons: The Evolution of Institutions for Collective Action*. Cambridge: Cambridge University Press.

Owen, D. and Smith, G., 2015. Survey article: deliberation, democracy, and the systemic turn. *Journal of Political Philosophy*, 23 (2), 213–234.

Owen, D. and Smith, G., 2019. Sortition, Rotation and Mandate: Conditions for Political Equality and Deliberative Reasoning. In J. Gastil and E.O. Wright, eds. *Legislature by Lot: An Alternative Design for Deliberative Governance*. London: Verso.

Pateman, C., 1970. *Participation and Democratic Theory*. Cambridge: Cambridge University Press.

Rask, M., Worthington, R. and Lammi, M., eds., 2012. *Citizen Participation in Global Environmental Governance*. London: Earthscan.

Setälä, M. and Smith, G., 2018. Minipublics and Deliberative Democracy. In A. Bächtiger, J.S. Dryzek, J. Mansbridge, and M.E. Warren, eds. *The Oxford Handbook of Deliberative Democracy*. Oxford: Oxford University Press, 300–314.

Smith, G., 2003. *Deliberative Democracy and the Environment*. London: Routledge.

Smith, G., 2020. Enhancing the legitimacy of offices for future generations: the case for public participation. *Political Studies*, 68 (4), 996–1013.

Smith, G., 2021. *Can Democracy Safeguard the Future?* Cambridge: Polity.

Smith, G. and Teasdale, S., 2012. Associative democracy and the social economy: exploring the regulatory challenge. *Economy and Society*, 41 (2), 151–176

Steiner, J., Bächtiger, A., Spörndli, M. and Steenbergen, M.R., 2009. *Deliberative Politics in Action: Analysing Parliamentary Discourse*. Cambridge: Cambridge University Press.

Voß, J.P., 2016. Reflexively Engaging with Technologies of Participation: Constructive assessment for public participation methods. In J. Chilvers and M. Kearnes, eds. *Remaking Participation: Science, Environment and Emergent Publics*. London and New York: Routledge, 238–260.

White, S.K., 2017. *A Democratic Bearing: Admirable Citizens, Uneven Justice, and Critical Theory*. Cambridge: Cambrdige University Press.

Wironen, M.B., Bartlett, R.V. and Erickson, J.D., 2019. Deliberation and the promise of a deeply democratic sustainability transition. *Sustainability*, 11 (4), 1023–1041.

Wright, E.O., 2010. *Envisioning Real Utopias*. London. Verso.

Yates, L., 2015. Everyday politics, social practices and movement networks: daily life in Barcelonas social centres. *The British Journal of Sociology*, 66 (2), 236–258.

8
TEMPORALITY AND DEMOCRATIC SUSTAINABILITY

Rosine Kelz, Henrike Knappe and Alexander Neupert-Doppler

Introduction

Despite their importance for the idea of sustainability, notions of temporality often remain implicit rather than explicitly spelled out in debates about sustainable politics. Bringing different understandings of temporality to the fore can contribute to clarifying how social and intergenerational justice are central to the concept of sustainability. Moreover, a focus on temporality can also foster an understanding of the normative links between sustainability and democratic politics. As normative ideas, sustainability and democracy advocate for the possibility of an open future – a future that is formable and more just and ecologically feasible (Kelz 2019). Neither democracy nor sustainability are fixed or timeless ideas. Instead, they are better understood as evolving processes. However, present formulations of democratic and sustainable politics are constrained by the effects of previous political decisions and societal practices that have formed our material and institutional environments. With the current environmental and climate crises, contemporary perceptions of the future have been altered: we have become more aware of how the aggregate of present and past actions of (some) humans can affect the planetary future. The effects of human development over the past centuries, including intensive agricultural production, the overuse of natural resources and the use of nuclear and fossil fuels, make the future less certain and diminish possibilities for the survival and thriving of diverse human and nonhuman lives. While it seems like the human capacity to alter the planet is increasing, there is also a growing awareness of the human incapacity to fully foresee and control the forms and effects of these accumulating alterations (Crutzen and Stoermer 2000). A changing planetary environment will also limit future policy discretion, as policy makers will be forced to address existential threats brought on, by example, by more frequent extreme weather events, like flooding and draught (Steffen et al. 2015). In light of such seemingly uncontrollable planetary futures of global ecological crises, we explore in this chapter the role of ideas of the future for notions of sustainability and democracy.

As normative ideas, rather than concrete practices, both sustainability and democracy are inherently oriented towards an alterable open future. The modern conception of democracy entails the idea that it always has to remain possible to renegotiate the current institutional arrangements and challenge political decisions, if these are deemed unjust or not fully inclusive (Buchstein and Jörke 2003). In other words, to be characterized as democratic, regimes must always remain open to critique and future renegotiation. Democracy, understood in this way, entails the promise of a better, that is, more just and inclusive, political future (Kelz 2019). Similarly, sustainability can be understood as an open concept. Even though many contemporary notions of sustainability highlight the connections between more ecological, socially just, and inclusive futures, the concept leaves under-defined *what* needs to be sustained, *for whom*, and *how*. Part of a democratic politics of sustainability is therefore the continuous renegotiation of the goals of sustainability and its appropriate tools (see Arias-Maldonado, Chapter 4 in this volume; Gottschlich 2017).

At first sight, it seems like temporality is an already well-explored topic within sustainability politics discourses, given their explicit future orientation (Bornemann and Strassheim 2019). Every foundational document from the Club of Rome to the Brundtland Definition to the Sustainable Development Goals uses the future as a point of reference. Moreover, questions of intergenerational justice are widely discussed in sustainability scholarship (see e.g. Caney 2018; Lawrence 2018). Nonetheless, global sustainability politics is often characterized by a limited notion of abstract space and time, and universal narratives of the future of humankind which are based on the modern notion of universal human progress. There is a "lack of critical reflection on time and temporality" (Faets et al. 2018: 283) not only in many scholarly debates around sustainability, but also in public discourse on the subject. As Faets et al. write, time in this context is often referred to as universal, linear, and transcendent, a "theoretical construction" disconnected from real people and contexts (Ibid.). A more nuanced engagement with theories of time and temporality is thus a necessary step to better understand the ways societies understand the future. Practices of articulating diverse ideas of possible futures, in turn, are constitutive for political organization and collective socio-political action. In our understanding, transformation towards more sustainable, just, and democratic societies would involve a temporal orientation in which the future is valued differently than it is today (Adam and Groves 2007). In the face of the closing down of futural horizons by unfolding ecological crises, this temporal reorientation would seek to establish an understanding of the future as a realm that remains politically malleable. Moreover, we contend that the practice of de-politicizing the future (Knappe et al. 2019) has led us to the current climate and ecological crises and now paralyzes political responses that could avert the worst to come. A political reframing of the future, therefore, also involves the multiplication of temporal and historical perspectives. This, as Lövbrand et al. suggest with reference to the academic debate on the Anthropocene, involves "resist[ing] unified accounts of 'the human' and instead work[ing] to situate people and social groups in the rich patterns of cultural and historical diversity" (Lövbrand et al. 2015, 216). To make historical accounts and notions of better futures more diverse, it is necessary to foster "a vibrant public space where manifold and divergent socio-ecological relations and nature concepts can be exposed and debated" (Ibid.).

To flesh out this argument, this chapter begins with a rough sketch of dominant notions of historical time. We contrast temporal narratives that construe history as linear and the future as pre-determined with philosophical critiques that have sought to re-describe history in non-linear terms and understand the future as a realm of the unexpected and new. We then argue that political future-making – with regard to sustainability and democracy – involves a specific understanding of temporality and history, which aims to decenter linear thinking in order to be more inclusive of different temporal experiences. This makes it necessary to consider the past not just as preceding the present but as an integral part of any present and future politics. Past catastrophes and injustices continue to be felt in the present and must play a more important role in the consideration of sustainability measures and efforts for more participative politics. As we can observe from climate change negotiations, the ignorance and/or denial of colonial pasts can stabilize, reinforce, and broaden inequalities in the future. Based on these observations, we go on to ask how, if futures are open and pasts are still present, we should deal with these kinds of contingencies. With reference to the notion of Kairós, we argue that the present can be understood not just as a bridge between past and future but as a space of opportunities that needs to be politically negotiated.

Historical time and notions of the future as "closed" and "open"

In modern Western thought the future has been generally understood as pre-determined. This understanding of the future, it is often argued, "satisfies a Judeo-Christian desire that time and history – both past and future – represent a continuous unity of progress and fulfilment" (Martinon, 2007, 15). Time, in this tradition, is thought of as "one-dimensional." The modern Western notion of history seeks to encompass the whole of humanity's existence in one cohesive narrative of universal progress – from the ancient past to an end point in the future (Koselleck 2002). Building on the eschatological tradition in Western thought, early modern philosophers understood history as "the fulfillment of a telos that one can rationally anticipate in advance in the form of an idea" (Cheah and Guerlac 2009, 15). As Hannah Arendt writes, this "modern historical consciousness" bestows "upon mere time-sequence an importance and dignity it never had before" (Arendt 2006, 65).

During the twentieth century, however, this understanding of history, and the pre-determined future it entails, has become the target of criticism. For Arendt, for example, the insistence on "mere time-sequence" discourages genuine political agency because it downplays the role of unforeseen events, which spring from the interactions of political actors, in bringing about the "new." The teleological understanding of history, however, has not only been criticized as a philosophical notion that discounts the future as a realm of the genuinely new. The perpetual violence of European (neo-)colonial rule, two World Wars and the Holocaust have disproven the idea of a unified history of perpetual human progress (see e.g., Arendt 1978, 212; Chakrabarty 2012; Allen 2016). History, instead, has been increasingly perceived as internally riven and marked by radical breaks. Not only did universalistic theories not fully account for the massive oppression, violence, and destruction that accompanied European "progress," Eurocentric ideas of progress themselves have become recognized as at least partly responsible for the rise of imperialism, totalitarianism, and environmental depletion. Moreover, universal historical narratives, like current abstract narratives about "our" future in sustainability and planetary health discourses, tend to overlook the diversity of human experiences and therefore contribute to stabilizing existing power asymmetries:

> narratives that presume to speak for all of humanity without any attention to the problems that divide and differentiate people along certain axes of power, leaving some groups with much less capacity for self-representation than some powerful minorities. [...] Universal narratives often act as ruses of power of agentive forces and institutions [...] (such as the World Bank or certain bodies of the United Nations or even the IPCC) that – precisely because of uneven development – have a relatively greater capacity to project themselves as acting on behalf of all while many of their actions end up privileging nations, groups, and classes that are already powerful.
>
> *Chakrabarty 2015, XIV*

At stake in these critiques is not only the notion of linear, teleological temporality, but also that of *unified* time. Advances in technology and science, economic growth, and socio-political developments are no longer understood as closely intertwined and proceeding at a similar pace. Instead, these spheres have become regarded as increasingly independent and governed by different temporal logics, which are not synchronized with each other (Rosa 2003). The notion of temporal discord and the need for re-synchronization have also been guiding themes of the early development of sustainability theories. Originally "sustainability" had an explicitly economic connotation and was used to describe practices that would synchronize the temporal patters of (natural) resource use (e.g., in forestry) with the natural temporal patterns of regeneration (Muraca 2010, 25). Going beyond this call for "resynchronization" of economic and ecological temporalities, we want to suggest that if sustainability is understood as a discourse that involves issues of social justice and democratic representation, it needs to pay closer attention to divergent temporal logics. As Eckersley (2017) points out, issues of justice and democracy are closely intertwined when it comes to the uneven impacts of the Anthropocene, such as ecological degradation and climate change:

> the worst impacts are typically felt by marginal communities who lack political recognition and representation. This is not only a problem of environmental injustice. It is also a quintessentially democratic problem of political representation and accountability, and it represents one of the core democratic challenges produced by "the globalisation of modernization."
>
> *Eckersley 2017, 991*

To open up political space for political representation of historically excluded groups, sustainability politics need to involve a rethinking of predominant temporal narratives (see also Knappe and Schmidt 2021).

Giving up on teleological history, however, does not necessarily lead to a normative understanding of the future as open. If teleological history no longer carries us towards a better, foreseeable future, for some, another foundation that delimits the insecurities of political contingency has to be found. In the past decades the connection between liberal government and capitalist market economy has provided such a new foundation. The sense of necessity or inevitability that restricts what kinds of future are thinkable here is moved from a historical narrative to an economic one (see e.g., Fukuyama 1992; Séville 2017). From Margaret Thatcher's famous "There is no alternative" proclamation to current austerity reforms, the political future is presented as delimited by economic necessities. Even though history as such does not play its former role as a major driving force, the teleological spirit remains alive here in the belief that economic growth is necessary and infinite. Institutional politics, then, is no longer driven by historical, but rather economic, necessity: the future – in terms of economic and political systems – remains closed.

This narrative of a perpetual present, however, has also been destabilized in light of more recent crises and a general perception of growing insecurity.[1] The uncertainty of the future is perceived in many states of the Global North (primarily) as a potential threat which needs to be managed. If the political and economic status quo is presented as being without any realistic or desirable alternative, the role of institutional politics becomes restricted to a defense against potential future shocks or the managing of unpreventable external change (ranging from the sudden appearance of a virus to the very foreseeable, as well as unforeseen, effects of environmental catastrophes in the course of a changing climate). From such a perspective, the present of some privileged populations has to be maintained and made "resilient" against the impositions of a potentially catastrophic future (see e.g., Walker and Cooper 2011). However, if radical political and economic change is precluded, solutions for ecological crises such as climate change can only be articulated in narrow terms of managerial, technological (e.g., innovation that would reduce emissions or sequester CO_2; climate engineering), or "personal" solutions (e.g., green consumption). Here, the notion of political agency of individuals is delimited to their role as consumers and voters in a narrow, managerial form of institutional democracy. In such a framework, sustainability is framed as a technical problem that is largely divorced from ideas of justice and democratic representation. In difference to such thin formulations of sustainability, broader, more "open" notions of sustainability are connected to a deepending and broadening of democracy and are linked to the need to cultivate an attitude of care towards the unknowable, but formable future. This cultivation needs to involve both the formulation of desirable future(s) and a critical engagement with dominant narratives of the past and the present (Knappe 2020). For this, the question of which societal groups have been historically excluded from future-making practices has to be addressed: whose views of a better future have been and are currently being heard, and who is excluded from political practices that shape the future?

The role of the past in present and future

As argued above, a socially just and democratic understanding of sustainability needs to include different temporal notions. In what follows, we argue for a specific perspective on the past, which we see as necessary for a just and democratic sustainability politics. As Mary Kathryn Nagle points out, when actors in the environmental movement in the US in the 1970s were pushing for laws that would protect the environment for future generations, they "neglected to address the then-existing legal framework that justified the colonial conquest of what now constitutes 'American' lands on the basis that Tribal Nations had failed to commercially exploit them" (Nagle 2018, 674). Not revising the narrative that "land constitutes an object to be colonially conquered and commercially exploited […] [and] that anyone who fails to engage in such exploitation should lose their property rights in the land" (Ibid., 682) results in the continuation of injustice and discrimination against indigenous populations and the increasingly catastrophic consequences of climate change. Environmental protection efforts based on these outdated narratives remain short-term and selective. Environmental activists have to fight repeatedly against practices such as the extraction of fossil fuel energy sources that cause climate change, as the Dakota Access Pipeline Protests of 2016/2017 demonstrate. Putting environmental claims into a broader historical perspective, for example by questioning the very definition of (colonial) land use, can politicize environmental cases and create opportunities for departing from common policymaking practices and establishing alternative futures.

Postcolonial scholars argue that ignoring the colonial past means ignoring current serious inequalities that inevitably prestructure climate change:

> The fact is that we live in a world that has been profoundly shaped by empire and its disparities. Differentials of power between and within nations are probably greater today than they have ever been. These differentials are, in turn, closely related to carbon emissions. The distribution of power in the world therefore lies at the core of the climate crisis.
>
> *Ghosh 2016, 146*

The violence of European (neo-)colonial rule in the Global South still manifests today as economic dependencies, civil wars, and environmental catastrophes. The continuance of this oppressive and violent past is often forgotten in the narratives of universal progress, where "population groups are [framed as] lagging behind" (SDG UN progress report 2016) and merely in need of catching up.

Specifically, in cases of environmental depletion such as industrial pollution, the slow pace at which it progresses conceals the violence of the phenomenon and therefore masks its causes and those who are responsible for the damage. Such slow catastrophes "are marked above all by displacements" (Nixon 2013, 7). For example, people are forced to leave their home because health issues occur in regions of massive industrial pollution, and people face droughts and lack of access to food and water as a result of other forms of environmental depletion. Such spatial and temporal displacements let these catastrophes sink into oblivion, at least for the actors who once caused the harm and control the narrative of those events. For those affected by such slow violence, the past still governs the present in the sense that depletive processes wreak havoc on their lives long after they are set in motion. When the causes of the phenomena that lead to such suffering are so difficult to detect, they are often long ignored (by those responsible for them).

This continuation of colonial power and hegemonic global politics results in a much higher vulnerability to climate change in countries of the Global South. Colonialism has left many formerly colonized countries in a situation of gross indebtedness and dependence in an inequitable global market that has forced them to restructure their economic systems around sectors such as tourism, agriculture, or fishing, which are now particularly threatened by climate change. Global warming is an existential matter: "A world warmed by no more than 1.5°C, to be clear, is one in which existing Caribbean societies have a future" (Sealey-Huggins 2017, 2445). However, the marginalization, if not denial of the colonial legacy as a topic at global climate negotiations has allowed Western countries in particular to further water down the 1.5°C goal (Ibid.), which will inevitably contribute to even more catastrophic futures for several countries of the Global South. The COP15 talks in Copenhagen in 2009 are considered unsuccessful not only because they failed to follow up on the Kyoto Protocol, they were also a major catastrophe for the Global South:

> Di-Aping pointed out that the 2°C target was the limit of the ambitions of wealthy countries in Copenhagen. Troublingly, this extent of average warming globally would result in deadly temperatures in excess of 3.5°C for many parts of Africa.[2]
> *Sealey-Huggins 2018, 104*

Sealey-Huggins concludes that if the COPs in Copenhagen and later in Paris in 2015 had been held in a more equitable manner, a more robust climate governance regime could have resulted (Ibid.). However, this would have made a thorough analysis of historical catastrophes and injustices necessary. Only by tracing the continuum of past injustices such as colonialism could all parties at the negotiating table understand how the current situation is shaped by historical events. This would broaden the circle of responsibility for current and future climate change-induced catastrophes. However, there are many reasons why this looking back is blocked by Western states in global climate change negotiations. It would implicate many states in the Western world in the environmental catastrophes of the Global South, revealing horrors and injustices that could no longer be ignored. With these revelations, responsibilities for a successful climate change politics would be very differently attributed. Tracking the developments of climate change catastrophes such as hurricanes, floods, and droughts that are mainly occurring in the Global South, to the past of industrial pollution and colonial exploitation would clearly point to Western states as the sole causes or descendants of perpetrating states.

What does this mean for a political and democratic future-making? It can mean that remembrance of the past and recognition of the injustices that continue to govern the present are practiced as political acts of resistance. Remembering entails a disruptance of the linear narrative and making visible the "unimaginable." Jenny Edkins (2003) argues that survivors of major catastrophes have often witnessed unimaginable and collectively traumatizing events. They've experienced the contingency of social order and the disruption of seemingly linear time. However, they are seldomly listened to after the event:

> Events of the sort we call traumatic are overwhelming, but they are also a revelation. [...] They question our settled assumptions about who we might be as humans and what we might be capable of. Those who survive often feel compelled to bear witness to these discoveries. On the whole, the rest of us would rather not listen. A frequent excuse is that the horrors survivors testify are too terrible. They are "unimaginable": we need not listen because we cannot hear.
>
> *Edkins 2003, 5*

If linear time is that of the formal political process and also a tool to stabilize power by reaffirming that there has never been an alternative to our present or future, then remembering disrupts this dominant linear temporality by giving way to plural temporalities and counter-histories.[3] Sustainability politics must acknowledge that climate change itself is a temporally uneven phenomenon that not only looms ahead for all of us but has already landed for a less fortunate segment of the population. By looking into more than just the (Western) future (of climate change), we can see where climate change is already an event of the past and present:

> in the global south the day of reckoning already exists. The metaphoric flood is in the past, not in a climate-changing future. [...] Just because one looks to the future, and the rights of future citizens, does not mean that the people of the present are uniformly better off.
>
> *Chaturvedi and Doyle 2015, 47*

The argument that intra- and intergenerational justice needs to be linked is made in broader scholarship on sustainability (Lafferty and Langhelle 1999; Ott 2018). However, we want to further enrich this argument by demonstrating that "the many different existential needs and environmental problems facing poor people currently living on the planet" (Ott 2018, 20) can be traced back to a past of colonialism, exploitation, and dependence. This past has a lasting effect on regions in the Global South. Rather than only speaking about a looming ecological catastrophe that threatens future generations, the exaggerated reality of environmental destruction and changing climates in poorer regions also has to be acknowledged and used to fuel political action.

It is in this spirit that we can take account of Walter Benjamin's notion that we are driven into the future less effectively by envisioning a better future for our grandchildren than by looking back at the catastrophic injustices of the past. He argues that looking back at history as a disjointed account of past catastrophes rather than a story of progress can prompt the recognition that the future needs to differ from the past. A crisis brings both disaster and opportunities for transformation. Such a consideration of opportunities concerns past, present, and future. Moreover, the past does not only motivate us to work towards a different future, it can also be approached as a realm of missed opportunities that might still be realized (in the future). From this perspective, the past itself might be reconsidered as a source of novelty for the political sphere. As Elizabeth Grosz writes:

> This is indeed the primary political relevance of the past: it is that which can be more or less endlessly revived, dynamized, revivified precisely because the present is unable to actualize all that is virtual in it. The past is not only the past of this present, but the past of every present, including that which the future will deliver. It is the inexhaustible condition not just of an affirmation of the present but also of its criticism and transformation. Politics is nothing but the attempt to reactive that potential, or virtual, of the past so that a divergence or differentiation from the present is possible.
>
> Grosz 2004, 178

If we think of history as a linear progression, all of the horrors of the past are qualified as sacrifices for the future. Complicating that perspective by recognizing missed opportunities in historical review, the past opens up to the future.

Contingency and Kairós – future practices between past and future

If we acknowledge the ongoing importance of the past for our present ability to create different and multiple political futures, the question is not only how we can include the past in our understanding of the present, but also how we can learn from history to shape current political action. Here the question of opportunities and the concept of Kairós comes into play. Named after the Greek god of opportunity, Kairós is "the cognitive form of the propitious moment (Kairós) […] [as] a passing opportunity to do something that one intended to do anyway" (Luhmann 1991/1993, 150). In reference to political activities, this concept suggests that political actors and structures have to be prepared for an opportunity in which change becomes possible. Such opportunities might have been missed before, and it is therefore part of a productive engagement with the past to learn to understand why that was the case, so that opportunities can be seized when they arise in the future.

The notion of Kairós can provide insight into the question of how the contingency of history can be handled. Accepting contingency does not rule out a future-directed politics. An alternative to linear notions of history is to see the suddenness of windows of opportunity. Four aspects of the idea of Kairos are important: first, Kairós-time is closely linked to the concept of crisis; second, crises can be the occasions on which it is worth concentrating political activities; third, activities can then unfold a constituent power to create something new; and fourth, opportunities are (always) chances for certain actors to realize their goals (Neupert-Doppler 2019).

So what does it mean to think about the potential functions of opportunities in the context of crises, constellations of forces, and constituent power? Crises are not just brief interruptions within a continuous linear development. Instead, they can be breaks with continuity which allow for historical path changes. When existing policies or institutions are in crisis, opportunities for renewal open up. Which periods are perceived as crises, however, also depends on the duration of the affected system. Colonialism, capitalism, and industrialism, for example, have been interwoven parts of a socio-economic system which has spanned centuries. The current global ecological crises therefore do not denote that a satisfactory situation deteriorates; instead, a crisis is a challenge to an existing socio-political system. A crisis is thus defined as the political articulation of an existing pressing problem; it is a demand for political action. It follows that not every catastrophe constitutes a crisis in this political sense. After centuries of industrialism, the limits of growth were reached in the twentieth century. However, environmental degradation only becomes defined as an environmental crisis – and thus a potential Kairós for change – because of public discourses brought on by environmental movements, natural and social sciences, and politicians from the 1970s to the present. The vision of a sustainable use of natural resources of course predates this recent period and is present in many religions and cultures, including European stories of utopias (Neupert-Doppler 2020). But it was only when these possibilities became acute in the environmental crisis that a window of opportunity for sustainability emerged. This is important for the politicization of the future. It is through politicization that crises become opportunities. For example, the right time for a new climate policy can only arise, when the climate crisis has been politicized by a movement for climate justice. A change in awareness prepares opportunities for political change. As Immanuel Wallerstein notes, "it is when their demise is in sight that a system is in crisis, and must therefore be in transition to something else. This is the right time to which the concept of Kairós refers" (Wallerstein 1991, 146).

Kairós is a time in which a number of circumstances align. First, there is a crisis situation. Second, there is a moment of decision in which new paths are crafted that depart from the past, although the repercussions of previously established paths cannot be completely avoided. This shows the particular closeness between Kairology, sustainability and democracy. If the recognition of crises necessitates that the future be perceived as open, the question, then, is how these open futures are dealt with in democracies. As we have seen, political theorists like Arendt and Benjamin agree that disruptions of linear history can be used to create the possibility of a "real", that is genuinely new, future. Of course, this does not happen by itself, but requires political action, spurred by a concentration of forces. Arendt conceptualized revolution as a constitution, pointing to the fact that it is a constellation of forces that turns a crisis into Kairós. A seized Kairós is characterized by a concentration of political forces in a crisis which is sufficient to create something new, to go a new way. Michael Hardt and Antonio Negri also address this third aspect of the Kairós. They also differentiate between the ordinary Chronos time and the Kairós time of decisive events (Hardt and Negri 2004, 392). The latter makes it possible to develop constitutive power in order to establish new relationships and institutions (Ibid., 383).

What can political practice learn from the theory of Kairós about why some political opportunities are taken while others are missed? Niklas Luhmann emphasizes the difference between seized and missed opportunities: "The propitious moment for a political decision on the abolition of nuclear power stations lay in the days following Chernobyl – neither before not after. The propitious moment for advancing German reunification lay immediately after the opening of the borders" (Luhmann 1991/1993, 151). From these examples we can extract the importance of having a coordinated constellation of forces ready to respond in a moment of crisis. While the groups that wanted to end the use of nuclear power were not strong enough to enforce such a termination when Chernobyl occurred and missed their Kairós in 1986, the West German government that wanted a unified nation was strong enough to take advantage of the crisis in East Germany and seized their Kairós in 1989. Nevertheless, the Chernobyl crisis is a good example of a partial use of opportunity. Although an exit from nuclear power did not succeed, the constituent power of ecologically-oriented forces was strong enough to push for the creation of the Ministry of the Environment, Nature Conservation and Nuclear Safety in Western Germany, which was established five weeks after Chernobyl. Although there had been representatives of ecological thinking both inside and outside parliament and other governmental bodies since the 1970s, it was the crisis that gave them the opportunity to force the establishment of a new ministry.

Such power to act must be prepared in advance, but the question of when the time is right to activate potential power is one of contingent circumstances. The politically new is usually not completely detached from what has been and what exists. The past plays a role here, insofar as the new must differ qualitatively from the old and solve problems from previous developments. The motives and resources for political action also extend from previous circumstances. Political future-making practices assert the open nature of the future by considering the problematic past and responding to a kairological present. The Kairós as the moment of the political, then, is akin to an Arendtian understanding of constitutive power. From this perspective, establishing new institutions, such as ministries, would only provide the necessary pre-conditions that can help enable novel political action. In the example of Chernobyl, the call for sustainability governance gained an addressee in the state apparatus with the formation of the Federal Environment Ministry in 1986.

The Kairós-Theory should not be misunderstood as a recommendation to wait and see. Only when there is a political debate about different visions of sustainable futures can agents of change make democratic decisions and recognize their opportunities. Politics struggles with historical burdens, sudden opportunities and non-linear processes: "The logic of the political process tends to discount (if not exploit) the future, to underestimate the remaining time for preventive design and to miss the right time (Kairós) for setting the course" (Offe 2001, 478 – translated). One way to prepare for the possible appearance of an opportunity could be future-making practices that experiment with implementing alternatives on a small scale be transferred to larger scales. This is what the concepts of prefigurative politics and preparation politics stand for. The theory of prefiguration focusses on local pasts, local realities, and local futures. Carl Boggs introduced the term in 1977: "By 'prefigurative,' I mean the embodiment, within the ongoing political practice of a movement, of those forms of social relations, decision-making, culture, and human experience that are the ultimate goal" (1977).

If sustainability is thought of as a process, transformative politics must start in the present. Transformation theories today include examples of prefigurative politics: "thus, for example, today in decentralized, ecological energy villages and regions, forms of solidarity economy, different cooperatives, [and] new social and democratic forms of participation and ways of life" (Reissig 2014, 86, translated). Local experiments with renewable energy, solidarity-based economy, and democratic participation are not the transformation of society as a whole, but they help to gather the knowledge and experience that are needed in Kairós.

We believe that local prefiguration politics and global sustainability politics can complement each other. In the local framework, solutions can be tried out which have the potential for implementation on a broader scale, if the right Kairós moment arises. Different levels of action, topics, and divergent time horizons complement each other in transformation processes. "Today in particular, transformation requires or includes a large number of progressive changes at the local, regional and global level" (Reissig 2014, 86, translated). Local experiments, the conditions of which depend on local pasts, can open up new development paths for sustainable futures. Future practices are characterized by preparation for the transfer of experimental experiences to larger contexts that take place in Kairós.

> Whether it is ultimately germs of the new that are being dealt with can only be measured by whether they are effectively overcoming the structure of the old growth

and development model (albeit partially) and embodying and promoting the seeds of
a new socio-ecological and solidarity-democratic direction of development.

Reissig 2014, 86, translated

Different levels of change complement each other: national laws for decentralizing the energy supply can, for example, create opportunities for regional experiments. Upscaling the experiences of prefigurative politics to national and global politics could be more of a challenge. Future-making practices, in our conceptualization, take past disasters and missed opportunities into account, respond to current opportunities, and open up alternative futures. In open situations, pasts are valued differently and future expectations are uncertain. Sustainability policies can be implemented if policy makers are prepared with actionable concepts on the one hand and are able to identify favorable opportunities on the other. Thus, how change is conceived of by agents of that potential change is significant. We suggest thinking about the future not by leaving the past and present behind, but by remembering pasts, kairological presence of the mind and openness to possible futures as necessary conditions for the future governance of sustainability in democratic societies. Despite the given contingency, an open and shapeable future does not leave actors without direction. They can, for example, use prefigurative politics to prepare for moments of Kairós that allow them to diverge from the paths of the past.

Conclusion and outlook

In this chapter, we have critically engaged with different notions of temporality that are crucial to the relationship between sustainability and democracy. Because we consider it necessary to take "time" and "future" seriously in sustainability scholarship and politics, we've made three main points. First, we've showed how an alternative, non-linear understanding of time developed in twentieth-century European philosophy, makes it possible to conceive of the future as open and different from the present and the past. Here, an understanding of historical processes as not being pre-determined is central. Second, we've argued that past events, and more specifically catastrophes and injustices, must play a more important role in future-making politics such as the forming of sustainability measures. As we can observe from climate change negotiations, the ignorance or denial of colonial pasts can stabilize, reinforce, and broaden inequalities in the future. So can, for example, economic inequalities translate into inequalities in climate change affectedness if historical injustices are not taken into consideration. Third, we've addressed the question of how to deal with contingencies of temporalities if futures are open and pasts are still present. We've argued that this temporal understanding of contingency and non-linearity highlights the role of the present in sustainable future making which serves not just as a bridge between past and future, but as a space of opportunities that need to be politically negotiated.

Living with the reality of the climate crisis makes the re-thinking of, and debate about, temporalities even more relevant. Therefore, (further) critical studies of time could make a relevant contribution to the extensive debate about the Anthropocene (see Mert and Marquardt, Chapter 32 in this volume) and how we can approach sustainability in our given political democratic systems. The reality of anthropogenic climate change brings the interlacing of "human" and "non-human" times further into the foreground of social awareness. Political responses to climate change, or the lack thereof, show us how complicated it still seems to be to think of the timescales of human actions as interrelated with the time scales of planetary processes (Markley 2012, 43–45). With a shift to thinking in geological timescales, a temporal narrative emerges where human history no longer provides the predominant temporal scale.

Instead, modernity appears as a disruptive event within a much larger temporal horizon of geological eras. Integrating geological timescales, different human histories, and the emergence of rapid techno-scientific development – an event which has brought forth destructive techniques and practices like the use of fossil fuel and nuclear power – is a challenge for contemporary social and political practices. We still have to explore what it could mean to understand politics as a temporal practice that is impacting a much larger timescale that cannot be experienced.

Notes

1 One of the most recent examples of this is the Corona pandemic for which, in light of a sudden external pressure, drastic political measures that severely affect the economy have been taken in several countries. It remains to be explored, however, whether these measures and debates during the crisis (e.g., about health care systems) will translate into more long-term political change, where underlying systemic issues of social inequality could be addressed. If we were to ask why similarly drastic measures have not been taken to address the climate crisis, one obvious answer lies in the different time scales of both the perceived threat and the necessary response.
2 Lumumba Di-Aping represented the Group of 77 and China bloc of 130 nations at the Copenhagen summit (Sealey-Huggins 2018, 104).
3 With counter-histories, we are referring to different philosophical and historical debates that criticize hegemonic historicism and discuss alternative forms of writing history. One of the most prominent examples of this is the Subaltern Studies Group, a group of South Asian historians who studied the subaltern consciousness in order to bring it in opposition to hegemonic historical writing. The approach of the group was famously criticized by Spivak (1999) who argued that their approach would essentialize the subaltern subject and smoothly fit it into the logics of Western hegemonic politics. Dipesh Chakrabarty, who links postcolonial thought to issues of climate change, was a member of the Subaltern Studies Group and has also written extensively on postcoloniality and history (2009).

References

Adam, B. and Groves, C., 2007. *Future Matters: Action, Knowledge, Ethics*. Brill, Leiden.
Allen, A., 2016. *The End of Progress. Decolonizing the Normative Foundations of Critical Theory*. New York: Columbia University Press.
Arendt, H., 1978. *The Life of the Mind*. New York: Harcourt Brace Jovanovich.
Arendt, H., 2006. *The Concept of History. Between Past and Future*. New York: Penguin.
Bennett, J., 2010. *Vibrant Matter. A Political Ecology of Things*. Durham and London: Duke University Press.
Boggs, C., 1977. *Marxism, prefigurative communism and the problem of workers' control* [online]. Available from: https://libcom.org/library/marxism-prefigurative-communism-problem-workers-control-carl-boggs.
Bornemann, B. and Strassheim, H., 2019. Governing time for sustainability: analyzing the temporal implications of sustainability governance. *Sustainability Science*, 14(4), 1001–1013.
Buchstein, H. and Jörke, D., 2003. Das Unbehagen an der Demokratietheorie', Leviathan, 31.
Caney, S., 2018. Justice and future generations. *Annual Review of Political Science*, 21 (1), 475–493.
Chakrabarty, D., 2009. *Provincializing Europe. Postcolonial Thought and Historical Difference* (New Edition) (Princeton Studies in Culture / Power/History), Princeton: Princeton University Press.
Chakrabarty, D., 2012. Postcolonial studies and the challenge of climate change. *New Literary History*, 43, 1–18.
Chaturvedi, S. and Doyle, T., 2015. *Climate Terror: A Critical Geopolitics of Climate Change (New Security Challenges Series)*. Basingstoke, Hampshire: Palgrave Macmillan.
Cheah, P. and Guerlac, S., 2009. Introduction: Derrida and the time of the political. In P. Cheah and S. Guerlac, eds. *Derrida and the Time of the Political*. Durham and London: Duke University Press, 1–40.
Crutzen, P.J. and Stoermer, E.F., 2000. The "Anthropocene". *Global Change Newsletter*, 41, 17–18.
DeRoo, N., 2013. *Futurity in Phenomenology. Promise and Method in Husserl, Levinas, and Derrida*. New York: Fordham University Press.
Edkins, J., 2003. *Trauma and the Memory of Politics*. Cambridge: Cambridge University Press.

Eckersley, R., 2017. Geopolitan democracy in the Anthropocene. *Political Studies*, 65 (4), 983–999.
Faets, S., Tamoudi, N. and Reder, M., 2018. Fresh perspectives on intergenerational justice. Comments on social criticism, temporality, and future narratives. In *Jahrbuch Praktische Philosophie in globaler Perspektive 2*, 279–304.
Fukuyama, F., 1992. *The End of History and the Last Man*. New York: Free Press.
Ghosh, A., 2016. *The Great Derangement: Climate Change and the Unthinkable*. Chicago: University of Chicago Press.
Gottschlich, D., 2017. *Kommende Nachhaltigkeit. Nachhaltige Entwicklung aus kritisch-emanzipatorischer Perspektive*. Baden-Baden: Nomos.
Grosz, E., 2004. *The Nick of Time: Politics, Evolution, and the Untimely*. Durham: Duke University Press.
Kelz, R., 2019. Thinking about future/democracy: towards a political theory of futurity. *Sustainability Science*, 14 (4), 905–913.
Knappe, H., 2020. Globale Zukunftsvisionen und die Repräsentation alternativer Zukünfte. In N. Tamoudi, S. Faets and M. Reder, eds. *Politik der Zukunft. Zukünftige Generationen als Leerstelle der Demokratie*. Transcript Verlag, Bielefeld, 87–108.
Knappe, H., Holfelder, A.-K., Löw Beer, D. and Nanz, P., 2019. The politics of making and unmaking (sustainable) futures: Introduction to the special feature. *Sustainability Science*, 14(4), 891–898.
Knappe, H. and Schmidt, O., 2021. Making representations: the SDG process and major groups' images of the future. *Global Environmental Politics*, 21(2).
Koselleck, R., 2002. *The Practice of Conceptual History: Timing History, Spacing Concepts*. Stanford: Stanford University Press.
Lafferty, W.M. and Langhelle, O., 1999. Future challenges of sustainable development. In W.M. Lafferty and O. Langhelle, eds. *Towards Sustainable Development*. London: Palgrave Macmillan, 213–239.
Lawrence, P., 2019. Representation of future generations. In A. Kalfagianni, D. Fuchs and A. Hayden, eds. *Routledge Handbook of Global Sustainability Governance*. New York: Routledge, 88–99.
Lövbrand, E., Beck, S. and Chilvers, J. et al., 2015. Who speaks for the future of Earth?: How critical social science can extend the conversation on the Anthropocene. *Global Environmental Change*, 32, 211–218.
Luhmann, N., 1991/1993. *Risk: A Sociological Theory*. New York: De Gruyter.
Marchart, O., 2010. *Die politische Differenz*. Berlin: Suhrkamp.
Martinon, J.P., 2007. *On Futurity: Malabou, Nancy and Derrida*. London and New York: Palgrave Macmillan.
Mert, A. and Marquardt, J., 2021. Reframing the Anthropocene: democratic challenges and openings for sustainability. In B. Bornemann, H. Knappe and P. Nanz, eds. *Handbook of Democracy and Sustainability*. London: Routledge.
Muraca, B., 2010. *Denken im Grenzgebiet: Prozessphilosophische Grundlagen einer Theorie starker Nachhaltigkeit*. Freiburg/München: Verlag Karl Alber.
Nagle, M.K., 2018. Environmental justice and tribal sovereignty. Lessons from Standing Rock. *The Yale Law Journal Forum*, 667.
Negri, A. and Hardt, M., 2004. *Multitude. Krieg & Demokratie im Empire*. Frankfurt a. M. and New York: Campus.
Neupert-Doppler, A., 2019. *Die Gelegenheit ergreifen – Eine politische Philosophie des Kairós*. Wien: Mandelbaum.
Neupert-Doppler, A., 2020. Utopische Naturverhältnisse, historische Transformationen und die Kairós-Zeit. In B. Görgen and B. Wendt, eds. *Sozial-ökologische Utopien – Diesseits oder jenseits von Wachstum und Kapitalismus*, München: Oekom, 29–46.
Nixon, Rob., 2013: *Slow Violence and the Environmentalism of the Poor*. Cambridge: Harvard University Press.
Offe, C., 2001. Wessen Wohl ist das Gemeinwohl?. In K. Gunther and L. Wingert, eds. *Die Öffentlichkeit der Vernunft und die Vernunft der Öffentlichkeit*, Frankfurt a. M.: Suhrkamp, 459–489.
Ott, K., 2014. *Umweltethik*, Hamburg: Junius.
Ott, K., 2018. Sustainability: theory and policy. In B. Klauer, R. Manstetten, T. Petersen and J. Schiller, eds. *Sustainability and the art of long term thinking*. London and New York: Routledge, 16–31.
Reissig, R., 2014. Transformation – ein spezifischer Typ sozialen Wandels. Ein analytischer und sozialtheoretischer Entwurf. In M. Brie, eds. *Futuring – Perspektiven der Transformation im Kapitalismus und über ihn hinaus*. Münster: Westf. Dampfboot, 50–100.
Rosa, H., 2003. Social acceleration: ethical and political consequences of a desynchronized high-speed society. *Constellations*, 10, 3–33.

Sealey-Huggins, L., 2017. '1.5°C to stay alive': climate change, imperialism and justice for the Caribbean. *Third World Quarterly*, 38(11), 2444–2463.

Sealey-Huggins, L., 2018. The climate crisis is a racist crisis. structural racism, inequality and climate change. In G. Yancy, A. Johnson, R. Joseph-Salisbury, B. Kamunge and C. Sharpe, eds. *The Fire Now. Anti-Racist Scholarship in Times of Explicit Racial Violence*. London: ZED Books, 99–113.

Séville, A., 2017. *"There is no Alternative" Politik zwischen Demokratie und Sachzwang*. Frankfurt and New York: Campus Verlag.

Spivak, G.C., 1999. *A Critique of Postcolonial Reason*. Cambridge: Harvard University Press.

Steffen, W., Richardson, K., Rockström, J., Cornell, S.E., Fetzer, I., Bennett, E.M., Biggs, R., Carpenter, S.R., de Vries, W., de Wit, C.A. Folke, C., Gerten, D., Heinke, J., Mace, G.M., Persson, L.M., Ramanathan, V., Reyers, B. and Sörlin, S., 2015. Planetary boundaries: guiding human development on a changing planet. *Science*, 347(6223), 1259855.

Walker, J. and Cooper, M., 2011. Genealogies of resilience: from systems ecology to the political economy of crisis adaptation. *Security Dialogue*, 42(2), 143–160.

Wallerstein, I., 1991/2001. *Unthinking Social Science – The Limits of Nineteenth-Century Paradigms*. Philadelphia: Temple University Press.

9
SUSTAINABILITY, DEMOCRACY AND THE VALUE OF FREEDOM

Marcel Wissenburg

Democracy and sustainability

It has often been argued that the free choice that defines democracy is counterproductive for sustainability: liberal democracy (as it is, North and South) tolerates and even fosters selfishness, it limits the citizens' and politicians' view to short-term goals and superficial success, and it results in at best indecisiveness, at worst incremental unsustainability (see e.g. Blühdorn 2008). Without denying any of this, I will argue here that freedom as offered by liberal democracy is in fact conducive, perhaps even necessary, for the realization of sustainability – because sustainability is not just about ecological facts but also, primarily, about a normative choice for the society and environment that we deem worth living in. This first section aims to elucidate these claims step-by-step.

There is no guarantee that democracy, an open-ended process, will give birth to sustainability, a goal. There is also no guarantee that it will not. Democracy is not a necessary or sufficient condition for sustainability, nor is sustainability required for democracy, as illustrated by authoritarian environmentalist regimes, by authoritarian environmental thinkers, and by the ominous absence of words like right, liberty, freedom and democracy from all IPCC reports.

To say that the source of the tension between sustainability and democracy lies in the inability of an open-ended process to generate 'the right choice', and to propose forms of direct, participatory or deliberative democracy as improvements that would make 'the right choice' more likely to be made, misses the point. If 'the right choice' were a choice on *facts* (the correct fact, the correct calculation, the best algorithm), then the problem of squaring sustainability and democracy would have a mathematically sound solution. But it doesn't. The issue isn't about facts only, it is first and foremost about humanity's ability to *(re)create*, *make*, our body politic and our living environment – together forming our 'body ecologic'. In other words: the source of the tension between democracy and sustainability is *freedom*, the very open choice we have for the kind of society and environment that we want to live in. There is not *one* sustainable society – there is an endless range of options open to us, from a global Manhattan for countless billions of humans fed on processed algae to a global Yellowstone Park with room for several million humans only (Wissenburg 1998).

While there are many conceptions of sustainability, many 'sustainabilities', they all contain a hard core of shared variables.[1] Each conception of sustainability is the property of a combination of at least four sets of variables: (1) the desirable numbers and types of subjects (humans, possibly other animals or natural entities); (2) the desirable levels and development of technology, including but not exclusively means and modes of production; (3) the desirable levels and types of resources and resource use; and (4) the desirable levels and types of wellbeing, or whichever other measure is used for the quality of life. Sustainability is about balancing these variables for present and future generations. Positing that there are many 'sustainabilities' in no way constitutes a denial of the reality of limits to growth, carrying capacity or, a popular term in the Anthropocene discourse, 'planetary boundaries' (Lambacher 2016; Lenton 2016; Jennings, Kish and Orr 2020) – but to see those boundaries as predetermining only one possible future would be a modern-day version of the naturalistic fallacy.

There is, then, no one single perfectly sustainable society out there waiting to be discovered. While there are indisputably countless *unsustainable* societies, there are, given the huge number of variables involved, arguably countless *sustainable* societies as well. The choices we make among these variables obviously close off paths, delete possible futures, but they open up possibilities as well.

Democracy allows us to channel this freedom of choice and forces us to rank and compare alternative futures, sustainable or other, on the basis of their moral import and not just feasibility or efficacy. Here then are some important commonalities between democracy and sustainability that become visible once we accept the openness of the future: both suggest a need to avoid 'bad' choices and to make 'good' ones; both thereby stress the importance of deliberation and uncertainty in political decision making (cf. Strunz and Bartowski 2018); and both acknowledge diversity, respectively in theories of the good life and biologically feasible future bodies ecologic.

The claims just made are broad, sweeping. The remainder of this chapter is devoted to adding precision, reservations and constraints. After I introduce the décor for my argument for freedom, mainstream liberal political philosophy, I will further argue for sustainabilities rather than sustainability, and describe how the contradiction and synergy between republican and liberal freedom define liberal democracy. I then argue that choosing between sustainabilities requires that we distinguish carefully between assessments based on quantity, on more or less freedom, and quality, on the values attached to different freedoms. This distinction I then use to catalogue the main critiques of and alternatives to mainstream liberal thought in three crucial respects: (1) where it concerns the value of nature other than as capital, on the basis of which limits to the freedom of exploitation and consumption are suggested; (2) where the value of freedom is at stake, both 'in itself' (freedom of choice *per se*) and as a property of distinct freedoms; and (3) where alternative forms of collective decision-making, hence of self-binding, are suggested.

Concepts and conceptions

Freedom and autonomy: these are among the first things humans desire, after and sometimes before food and shelter – 'give me liberty or give me death' has been the rallying call of virtually every revolution since the eighteenth century. They are defining, constitutive features of modern democracy and they are the greatest moral challenge for the legitimacy of any conception and politics of sustainability.[2] Modern democracy is limited democracy: the majority rule of all over all in all affairs is limited on the one hand by the creation of pockets of self-rule protected against interference (known as liberal freedom), on the other by rules and institutions protecting collective self-rule against degenerating into universal egoism (known a republican freedom). Modern democracy is procedural, open-ended, essentially unpredictable. Sustainability may be an essentially contested concept, but in any of its incarnations it is definite, a goal. The tension is obvious (indeed, the *raison d'être* of this volume) and its cause is at least in part freedom. Freedom (and therefore democracy) and sustainability are neither perfectly compatible nor communicating vessels; their relation is neither win-win nor zero-sum. Like democracy and sustainability, freedom comes in many forms, shapes and guises. Understanding the complex relation between democracy and sustainability, their incompatibilities and synergies, requires careful analysis rather than an 'other things being equal' reliance on a shared intuition of what freedom would be, requires and gives. The result, and as I will argue the nature, of such an analysis may well be advocacy: either explicit defence of one conception of freedom over another, or a bias built into the structure of the discourse.

This chapter aims to offer a telescopic analysis of freedom, broadly matching and comparing several major conceptions of freedom with different conceptions of sustainability and democracy – a microscopic analysis would require more than one book. I want to avoid defending just one kind of freedom, democracy or sustainability as 'the' right choice, and advocate openness and flexibility – but I do take position. My point of departure for this dialectic is philosophical liberalism, specifically the liberalism of John Bordley Rawls (1921–2002) – 'not because it is easy, but because it is difficult', to paraphrase John F. Kennedy. Philosophical liberalism, particularly Rawls's, has been the dominant vocabulary of moral discourse for the past 50 years. It is relative to Rawls that both liberals and non-liberals (ecologists, republicans, virtue ethicists, etc.) still position themselves; the ubiquity of Rawls's ideas is what makes it difficult, and therefore so enlightening, to (try to) distance oneself from them.

It is, especially in the context of questions of sustainability, crucially important to remember that freedom is more than political freedom or liberty. There is also the freedom of the bird in the sky: physical freedom, power, the ability to do things, which in the case of humans goes beyond what the body can do, thanks to science and technology (Jennings, Kish and Orr 2020). It is not the freedom to consume or to exploit resources in itself that has made sustainability the problem it is today, but primarily humanity's ability to move beyond the use of rocks, sticks and bone. While this chapter focuses on liberal perspectives on ways to square democracy and sustainability, it does so in the knowledge that our ability to shape our *political* environment is just one aspect of our ability to shape our *entire* environment: the body politic is part of the body ecologic.

So much for what we could (metaphorically) call the independent variable in this chapter, freedom. The elements of the dependent variable, 'the complex relation between democracy and sustainability', require clarification too.

Sustainabilities

There are literally scores of conceptions, definitions and interpretations of sustainability. In environmental political thought, these distinctions often refer back not just to environmental economics but also to environmental ethics. The by now classic dichotomy ecocentrism/anthropocentrism or deep/shallow green describes the extremes of the ethical reasons ('for whom' and 'why') to value the natural environment, thereby also the 'what' that is to be sustained. For example, the three conceptions of environmental sustainability that Andrew Dobson (1998, 33) distinguished,[3] now adopted by countless others, is economical on the surface: (1) sustainability of 'critical natural capital' assumes strong substitutability of natural capital both by other bits of nature and by non-natural capital; (2) sustainability of 'natural value' assumes minimal substitutability;[4] and (3) sustainability of 'irreversible nature' represents a mean, still limiting substitution. Yet the grounds for the distinction between these three are not based on what is economically, physically or biologically possible, but on ethical categories. 'Critical natural capital' represents an anthropocentric or environmentalist perspective on nature, 'natural value' represents ecocentrism or (political) ecologism, and 'irreversible nature' represents an anthropocentrism reined in by ecocentric concerns.

In this chapter, no (intentional) choice between any of these or other conceptions of sustainability will be made. It is, however, good to keep in mind that different sustainabilities imply different sets and distribution patterns of freedoms, or vice versa, different political constellations are more or less compatible with different conceptions of sustainability. For example, a society that wants to square high-tech and a high GDP with fifteenth-century emission levels will probably demand fairly strict control on the kinds of technology admitted, thus limits to freedom of trade, and a fairly egalitarian tax regime, whereas a low-tech, modest welfare sustainable society will either need strict population control or a very strict all-pervasive ideology demanding restraint and (self-)control. This chapter opened with another example: it is not too common to see ecological sustainability as easily compatible with modern-day liberal democracy.

In spite of their diversity, though, what virtually all conceptions of sustainability have in common is that they, by definition, limit the freedom of present generation humans for the benefit of future generations. In fact, without obligations to future generations, the Brundtland definition of sustainable development and the UN Sustainability Goals, both unapologetically anthropocentric and environmentalist programmes, would hardly make sense (cf. also Thiele 2016, 14) other than as programmes for global justice.

Democracy

The oldest sources in political philosophy (Cicero 1866; Plato 1974; Aristotle 1981) equate democracy with mob rule: the unreflective, purely self-interested, rule of all over all in all affairs. Modern democracy, as said above, is limited democracy. On the one hand, modern democracies offer mixtures of rules and institutions to ensure the sustainability of a public's (Dagger 1997; 2001) collective self-rule, in particular by embracing fallibility and uncertainty about science, facts and values, and by creating room for deliberation (Strunz and Bartowski 2018, 1159). Benjamin Constant (1819) referred to the result as republican freedom, the freedom of the Ancients.

But modern democracy is limited in another way as well – creating what Constant called the freedom of the Moderns, liberal freedom: a private sphere where individuals rule themselves and cooperate on their own terms without interference from the collective.[5] That individual need not be an isolated ego, an island entire of itself – rather, he or she is a relational atom, defined by (the absence of) specific relations with others as e.g. a family creature. In other words, while modern democracies may be defined in part by liberal freedom, they are not by definition liberal democracies; it all depends on which freedoms are attributed to which understanding of the individual (cf. Brennan 2018).

Finally, modern democracy is characterized by the *mix of*, as much as the constant *tension between*, republican and liberal freedom. The result is constant mitigation, adaptation and evolution of institutions, and a constant redrafting of the borders between the private sphere where freedom of production and consumption exist, and the public sphere where its limit are defined. One of the moving forces behind this evolutionary process is the changing relation with our natural environment (Wissenburg 2016): again, societies aren't just bodies politic but bodies ecologic.

Freedom and the value of freedom

Democracy channels our freedom to choose between (un)sustainable futures; it thereby also selects, shapes and eliminates freedoms. Which freedoms are compatible with which sustainabilities (if at all), which combinations are preferable, and why? No sensible answer to these questions is possible without a transparent vocabulary – because like sustainability and democracy, there are countless conception of the concept of freedom.

Above, I already introduced two such conceptions: republican and liberal freedom. Another very popular but also highly controversial distinction, that between negative and positive liberty,[6] was introduced by Isaiah Berlin (1969). Negative liberty denotes the absence of human-made obstructions to doing X, while positive liberty is the ability to act upon one's will. The distinction is controversial because Berlin gave different and contradictory interpretations to positive freedom. He argued that embracing the superficially attractive idea of positive freedom put one on a slippery slope towards a paternalistic and totalitarian understanding of it as a duty to realize (read: dictate) the individual's 'real' or 'true' will or 'objective interest' (cf. MacCallum 1967). Although the negative/positive dichotomy seems ineradicable in politics and civil society, a more technical and neutral distinction is slowly finding its way into the handbooks: that between formal and effective freedom, where formal freedom is the absence of (human-made) obstacles to doing X and effective freedom is having the means to do X.

A further useful distinction is that between freedom and autonomy (and, by implication, between formal and effective autonomy): freedom is external to the acting subject, and concerns the choices or courses of action available, while autonomy is internal, and refers to the capacity or ability to choose. One can be free without being autonomous: while in a coma, we retain all the freedom of the citizen. And one can be autonomous without being free, for instance as a prisoner.

Of course, further, more subtle and quite often politically important distinctions between conceptions of autonomy can be made – for example the one Bob Goodin (1992, 125) made between autonomy as the choice *of* oneself (the choice for personality and character), *for* oneself (self-legislating) or *by* oneself (authenticity, even autogenesis, of any choice including the choices of and for oneself). For lack of space, these will not be pursued here.

One final distinction is, however, absolutely vital: that between freedom and the *value* of freedom (Van Hees and Wissenburg 1999). The two are quite often used as two faces of freedom, the one being 'better' or 'more' than the other: having the freedom to vote, on this view, makes one 'more free' than having the freedom to wear one's coat inside out, or the freedom to kill with impunity, because the freedom to vote would be more meaningful. Likewise, in environmental political thought, it is often argued that limits to consumption, production or procreation make one in the end *more* free, in meaningful ways, or *differently* free, if one renames the two as quantitative 'option freedom' and qualitative 'action freedom' (Pettit 1999; 2001; for similar interpretations of freedom as a qualitative property, see e.g. Dagger 1997; Hannis 2016; Lambacher 2016; Bader 2018; Beresford 2020). In this vein, Lambacher (2016, 392) argues that 'green freedom is about contributing to a *quality* of life that people help to create, for themselves and others' (his italics).

For politicians and pamphleteers, it has proven notoriously difficult to part with the distinction between positive and negative freedom; for academics (myself included), it still proves to be notoriously difficult to clearly distinguish between freedom and the value of freedom. The problem with conflating the two, and with the option/action freedom dichotomy, is that they equate and compare apples and oranges. Quantity is not the same as quality, value not the same as number, amount not the same as weight. For the sake of clarity, it is better to keep the two strictly separate. An individual, then, really *is* more free the more courses of action are open to her, *regardless* of the (dis)value of those choices. And it's not just clarity that's served by strictly separating the two. There is no better way to highlight that the choice between two equally large but different sets of freedoms is *not* immaterial; no better way also to show that this choice is a moral and political choice, not a technical one.

Liberalism and its critics

Perhaps unsurprisingly, analyses of the relation between freedom and other concepts (like democracy and sustainability) tend to start either from a liberal perspective or (e.g. Eckersley 2004; Hannis 2016) from a critique of liberalism; a common point of reference for all is John Rawls's liberalism (1993; 1999). Very briefly, for the uninitiated: Rawlsian liberalism assumes that individuals want to realize as much as possible the very different, often incompatible plans that they have with their lives, and the very different, incompatible 'theories of the good' behind those plans. (Rawls refers to this as 'irreducible moral pluralism'.) A society made up of such individuals can only be viable and sustainable if its basic institutions are procedurally just. This means that laws, organizations, institutions should guarantee a fair distribution of the burdens and benefits of social cooperation. Fairness, finally, stands for impartial principles that reflect an overlapping consensus between 'reasonable' doctrines, that is, theories of the good that respect the limits to what can reasonably be argued and proven.

Rawlsian liberalism is a natural ally for both the advocates of weaker forms of environmental sustainability, such as Brundtland and the UN, and for liberal democracy. Sustainability is brought on board by the idea that society is a cooperative venture of overlapping generations. This cooperation requires commitment to a just savings principle, a demand that whenever feasible, each generation sets aside a reasonable portion of its accumulated resources for future generations, on the condition that the latter do so as well (Rawls 1999). Liberal democracy is part and parcel of the Rawlsian constitution: the principles of justice Rawls defends are by and large covered by the liberal (rather than republican) freedoms that limit democracy.

Roughly since Goodin (1992), environmental political theorists have been testing Rawlsian liberalism for its green potential, resulting either in proposals for its adaptation or for its replacement by a greener, more sustainable alternative. In at least three respects do such proposals relate to notions of freedom: (1) where it concerns the value of nature other than as capital, and limits to the freedom of exploitation and consumption are suggested; (2) where the value of freedom is at stake, both 'in itself' (intrinsic value) and as a property of distinct freedoms; and (3) where alternative forms of collective decision-making, hence of self-binding, are suggested.

The value of nature

Mainstream conceptions of sustainability are weak (or 'environmentalist') in conceiving of nature almost exclusively as resources, as instruments or capital for humans. The same applies to mainstream liberalism (e.g. Dobson 1998; 2007; Bell 2002; Eckersley 2004; Garner 2019). The notion of 'the intrinsic value of nature' may itself be philosophically controversial (Wissenburg 1998), but the conviction that there must be more to trees than firewood, that nature can legitimately be seen as having more, different or other value, is a central tenet of environmental ethics and environmental political theory. Consequently, a large share of the critique of liberalism has been aimed at its weak conception of sustainability.

A first type of response has been the development of other understandings of nature's value – one could say, changing the *input* of sustainability and liberalism. Some of these responses are normative. The most radical normative response ascribes intrinsic value to nature (for more on this, see Garner 2019), while the most limited response attempts to fit nature into the Rawlsian framework via his 'primary social goods', the stuff (in this case nature and natural resources) needed for the realization of individuals' life plans. In between these extremes one will find authors like Daly (1992), Dobson (1998) and O'Neill (1993) involved in the earlier mentioned debate on sustainability and substitutability.

Substantively different responses are ontological rather than normative. The best known and evolved among these is probably Simon Hailwood's (2004; 2015) alternative reading of nature as other, with humanity having the option of being *positively* alienated from nature (Hailwood 2015), that is, sufficiently distant to learn to control both it and humanity itself.

Obviously, different valuations of nature would imply different (stricter) limits to the freedom to use nature, thus to the set of morally admissible sustainable worlds – at least, if such considerations get *access* to the public debate in the first place (cf. Bell 2002). Rawlsians argue that the proper place for 'substantive' conceptions of nature is the private sphere, together with aesthetic, religious and sexual preferences, not the public sphere, because that would violate the 'burdens of judgment', as Rawls (1993) calls it, the limits of what beliefs one can reasonably demand others to accommodate in the public domain. In far less diplomatic (and far clearer) terms, the libertarian, Jan Narveson expresses this point as follows: 'your particular faith, sensitivities or convictions cannot limit my (…) rights – I may tear down my house even if it is some famous guy's birth place, or even if it would harm "ecological integrity" or *some such thing that we ordinary folk do not understand*' (my italics, MW), and: 'Environmental concern that extends beyond concern for humans is not a matter of right or wrong, but a mere matter of taste'. The ecologist could respond here with the observation that excluding 'substantive' conceptions of nature privileges an equally substantive but shallow, materialist and instrumentalist conception of nature as the exclusive, mandatory basis of society's nature management policies – but that would only confirm the orthodox liberal judgment that (e)valuations of the value of nature cannot reasonably be part of the public values of a free society (Wissenburg 2019b).

An alternative way around the objection of bias might be to expand the community of justice, the polity, by including entities with an interest in other uses and non-uses of nature than as capital for humans. Thus, authors like David Schlosberg (2007) argue that an ecosystem can be a moral subject whose interests should be taken into account alongside humans' in the public debate on the design and adaptation of our body ecologic. By the same token, animal advocates (Donaldson and Kymlicka 2011; Garner 2005; 2013) have argued for the inclusion of sentient species in the polity. Both strategies are already reflected in current legal practices where nature, natural entities or individual animals are given constitutional and civil rights (cf. Tanasescu 2015).

The Narvesonian and the Rawlsian would counter that in pleas for the extension of membership, their advocates once more need to appeal to substantive and 'unreasonable' doctrines. Does 'interest', for instance, really mean the same for a human, for a donkey or for a wilderness area? An increasing body of empirical research on animals supports the thesis that animals may well be sufficiently similar to humans to qualify as much as humans as morally relevant subjects. Although Narveson (2001) would qualify this as a necessary but still insufficient condition for political inclusion, it does suggest that a new reflective equilibrium among liberal scholars may eventually support animal interests, further limiting the range of admissible sustainabilities. For other entities though, like rivers, ecosystems, or 'the climate', the objection against 'substantive doctrines' still stands. This is what brought green libertarian Tal Scriven (1997) to the paradoxical conclusion that there is no room whatsoever in the public sphere for even moderately green conceptions of a sustainable world – and that it is at the same time almost irrational for an individual not to adopt and practice strong ecological convictions.

The value of freedom

The value of freedom plays a central role in at least two strands of environmentalist critique on Rawlsian liberalism. First, there is the question of the *intrinsic* value of freedom per se. For classical liberals and libertarians in particular, freedom has an absolute value: a world in which one can choose to ride a bicycle to work is better than one where one is obliged to bike to work, even and particularly if that would have been one's choice anyway – because being given freedom enables one to live as a human, not a slave, because it is an expression of respect for the individual as a moral subject, capable of choice and responsibility.

The intrinsic value of freedom is obviously a huge obstacle for the realization of any conception of sustainability that requires coordinated collective action, in other words, restrictions on individual freedom of action. In fact, it is an insurmountable obstruction for libertarians, who reject virtually all claims to authority not supported by voluntary and informed consent. The fact that, less obviously, sustainability policies may also *create* choices (therefore freedoms) that did not exist previously, like the freedom to guarantee future generations a decent life, does not alter anything: sidestepping consent remains a violation of the most basic of human rights, even if consent would have been the only sensible choice.

In more mainstream versions of liberalism, there is room for a collective overruling individual freedom, for example on the basis of a social contract, the protection of basic liberties, the reasonableness of the rule imposed, etc. (for more see Raz 1990). Yet if one accepts that freedom has intrinsic value, consent remains a prima facie requirement for collective action, and lack of consent can only be overruled (e.g. by democratic majorities) with very good substantive reasons – but what counts as a good reason to limit freedom?

This then brings us to the second role that the value of freedom plays in liberalism: that of the value of *distinct* freedoms. Here the critique of liberalism is often self-critique, arguing for restrictions on more formal freedoms like consumer freedom, the freedom to fly, travel, trade, or property rights, in favour of what would be more meaningful, therefore more valuable effective freedoms. Liberal perfectionism, as inspired by Raz (1986), offers this option – as does Piers Stephens's (2001a; 2001b; 2015) Millian liberalism. In more recent years, Martha Nussbaum's capabilities have been used in a similar way,[7] as have human rights and 'development rights' (Dryzek, Norgaard and Schlosberg 2013: 80).

It is important to note that at the heart of such attempts to rank or prioritize freedoms is neither the distinction between formal and effective (or negative and positive) freedom, nor the degree to which one freedom would be more or less conducive to sustainability than another. At issue is rather, on the one hand, the question what constitutes a good life (and which freedoms that requires), and on the other, how desirable is the sustainable body ecologic that is required to realize that particular conception of the good life. Less abstractly put: a world where, given present biotechnology, each adult consumes 700 grams of meat every week can be both pleasant and sustainable – but at least for the latter goal, other resources and prospects will have to be sacrificed, up to and including the freedom to procreate.

The question of the value of freedom, respectively distinct freedoms, cannot be settled with reference to facts, forecasts or scenarios. It is a collective choice problem, a choice between not just the feasible and the unfeasible but also the desirable and the undesirable. Which brings us to the third respect in which critics of liberal freedom hope to support (their particular conceptions of) sustainability: can democracy be improved upon?

Reflective rationality

As said above, to locate the tension between sustainability and democracy in the inability of an open-ended process to generate 'the right choice' is to miss the point. The choice for a body ecologic is not one for technocrats, since it is not a purely technical issue. Nor is it a choice for epistocrats because there is no one unique moral truth or (by implication) one unique ideal society. Strict majoritarianism (or 'unlimited' democracy) is no alternative either, at least not from a liberal point of view. The acceptance of moral pluralism as both empirically given and epistemologically unavoidable does not imply that anything goes, or that an ethical norm or ideal is better simply because it has more supporters. Not every normative point of view is equally sensible.

The choice between sustainable futures, between desirable bodies ecologic, is a moral one and, given irreducible moral pluralism, a political one. What I mean by that is two things. First of all, in Weberian terms, it is not a goal-rational choice for the most efficient or effective way to realize a given ideal but a choice between ideals, requiring reflection on the goals to be chosen themselves. Second, given moral pluralism, that reflection cannot in advance assume the possibility or even desirability of a compromise but must admit for the possibility that decisions may need to be made on inconclusive, unsatisfactory, non-consensual reasons (cf. Mouffe 2005).

Liberals and their critics may disagree on how well real-existing liberal democracies do in facilitating reflective rationality, especially where sustainability versus freedom is concerned, but they agree that improvement is possible. I will discuss two broad avenues for alternatives: more democracy, and less.

Environmentalist critics of liberal democracy often point to its protection of individual freedoms, making sustainability a matter of individual choice and virtue, where the real public interest is that we *ensure* sustainability. Republican freedom would offer better chances for a sustainable future than liberal freedom. The most comprehensive alternative offered from this perspective is green republicanism (Barry 2012; 2016; Cannavò 2016; 2020), which advocates the promotion of commitment to the *res publica*, the public interest (including an interest in sustainability), via on the one hand public virtues, on the other the creation of decision-making structures that require active participation. At the heart of green republicanism we thus find a commitment, shared with many non-republicans (from Dryzek and Fishkin to Rawls and Habermas), to the promotion of *deliberative* over simple aggregative democracy, and to the creation of forums for reflection, debate and qualitative testing of arguments rather than merely increased quantitative participation.

Deliberative democracy is not a panacea for all imperfections of liberal democracy, certainly not where sustainability is concerned. For one, like any other form of democracy, it is an open-ended procedure, therefore still no guarantee for sustainability as a goal (Humphrey 2007). More importantly, it is fairly difficult to guarantee the quality and impartiality of reflection in real-world settings: participants are often unrepresentative of a community, in age, gender, available time, education, experience, eloquence, commitment, trust, etc. Finally, even representative composition is no guarantee for the quality of reflection.

In addressing this last problem, two approaches have become most popular: Jürgen Habermas's and John Rawls's. Jürgen Habermas introduced the notion of a *herrschaftsfreier Diskurs*, a domination-free discourse (1981), where no physical, emotional, intellectual or other obstacles impede the reflection to identify the presumably shared standards for the right, the good and the beautiful that we refer to when we disagree, in concrete cases, on what is right, good or beautiful. The jury is still out on whether or not Habermas must presume that there are actual objective standards to be discovered – but if that is what he believes, then he also basically denies that moral pluralism is irreducible.

John Rawls's notion of an overlapping consensus between reasonable doctrines (Rawls 1993), while sharing the same roots in Kantian philosophy, is less reductive. According to Rawls, no ultimate standards for the right, the good and the beautiful are likely to be developed – but agreement on ways to accommodate the resulting diversity of theories of the good life is possible, if and in so far as the 'burdens of judgment' are embraced. The burdens of judgment define the limits to how conceptions of the good can reasonably be defended (and imposed on others). They include for example the possibility of contradictory and inconclusive evidence, conceptual indeterminacy and different priorities for shared values. This alone guarantees that new ideas, experiences and discoveries make any overlapping consensus temporary and inconclusive.

Rawls's and Habermas's views remain controversial. They help to exclude extreme (and extremists') views but, as agonistic thinkers argue, by pre-empting any discussion on what counts as reasonable, they may also exclude too much and too many. How unreasonable, really, are thinkers like Zerzan (2012) who argue that life would be more fulfilling if humanity returned to a Holocene way of life, or the ecomodernists (Asafu-Adjaye 2015; cf. Symons 2019) who rely heavily on as yet non-existent technology to create a sustainable high-tech high-welfare world for ten billion people or more? And another objection to Rawls and Habermas: both offer laboratory solutions. Actual, real-life deliberation processes that meet their standards seem impossible, and might well in fact be undesirable, given the imperfections of real existing humans.

Where forms of deliberative democracy confront the choice for future bodies ecologic via republican freedom, a different tradition would instead address it via liberal freedom. The latter is the path of, among others, free market environmentalists Anderson and Leal (1991), libertarians (Nozick 1974; Sagoff 1974, 1992; Rothbard 1982; Rasmussen and Den Uyl 1991; Narveson 2001), left-libertarians (Otsuka 2003), and, most recently, libertarian paternalism (Thaler and Sunstein 2003). As we have already seen above, this tradition rejects the idea that any conception of the sustainable society or any majority decision (cf. Brennan 2018) can overrule or limit individual freedom. Instead, the execution of each individual's freedoms defines and delineates the room for feasible sustainable societies.

That is not to say that, on these views, all environmental interests are by definition always overruled by each and any individual preference. Individual freedom has 'only' prima facie priority. Exceptions are imaginable – at least for some thinkers in this tradition – on at least four intellectually related grounds. First, where a collective good cannot be realized without the risk of free-riders (Gauthier 1986), individual freedom may be trumped if that good is arguably more important to the overall system of liberty. There are circumstances imaginable where some measures aimed at sustainability might qualify on this count. Second, an exception will be made where the execution of individual liberties does straightforward harm to others – pollution, up to and including emission of greenhouse gases, probably qualifies. Third, the same applies where legitimate use of natural resources inevitably also affects 'ecosystem services', goods produced by an ecosystem like clean air or running water that cannot be privatized. Fourth, limits on 'original acquisition' (extracting resources from nature) can be defended, for instance when nature is understood as 'originally' collective property or, as in the case of the famous Lockean proviso, where original nature is unowned. The argument in both cases is that other interested parties are, by privatizing, undeservedly denied access to that specific resource (Wissenburg 1998; 2018; Bell 2002).

Conclusion

Our discussion of freedom has, I think, shown that (liberal) democracy is not so much *at odds* with sustainability, but is instead conducive and perhaps necessary for its realization – so that the debate on sustainability becomes one on sustainabilities (plural), so that the choice for desirable bodies ecologic is not prematurely voided by technocrats and epistocrats, and so that room is created for reflective rationality, for ethics and the political (Wissenburg 2016; 2019a). Two further observations seem relevant here.

First, realistically speaking, no policy aimed at sustainability stands a chance of being considered legitimate, both in the political and the moral sense, unless it reflects genuine 'green' preferences of citizens. No public support for a policy means no moral high ground, no democratic basis for interference.

Second, equally realistically, that the tension between freedom and sustainability (or carrying capacity, or ecological footprint) is so often misconstrued does not mean that it is not there. There are countless physically possible sustainable bodies ecologic; there are infinitely many that are impossible, therefore infeasible. But the set of possible sustainable worlds is not at any time a fixed given. Planetary boundaries define how much Earth there is, not what we must do within those boundaries – nor do they mean that those boundaries cannot be stretched. As Rasmus Karlsson (2020; cf. Karlsson and Symons 2014) argued, designing a sustainable society does not have to remain limited to the management of natural resources, but can and should extend to the *liberation* of nature.

Notes

1 Sustainability is not so much a family concept where similarities between remote family members peter out at the edges of the tribe – but more a horde concept, where members stick together and mingle (cf. Wissenburg 2006).
2 My point of reference in this chapter is liberal democracy broadly understood, characterized in particular by majoritarian decision-making, general elections, the *trias politica*, checks and balances and constitutions. Most political systems in Western and Middle Europe, the Americas, Oceania, sub-Saharan Africa and the Indian sub-continent are incarnations of this model. My argument is first and foremost an argument against epistocracy and technocracy, in other words, it suggests that theocracies, post-communist oligarchies and other authoritarian regimes do not do justice to the normative nature of the politics of sustainability. It can also be read as a warning for 'developing' liberal democracies challenged by relative poverty and powerful oligarchs, to the effect that the more open (in Popper's sense of the word) a society and particularly its political agora is to different values, lifestyles and theories of the good, the better it can identify feasible sustainable futures compatible with long-term development.
3 Note that before Dobson (1998), ecologists ('deep greens') tended to disqualify sustainability as by definition incompatible with the protection of nature as intrinsically valuable, and saw it as an expression of anthropocentric egoism. The discourse has changed; all sides now embrace sustainability, though in quite different form. These days, there is no clear competition for sustainability as the central concern of environmental politics and thought, though the concept of resilience may eventually challenge the hegemony.
4 Ecologists might argue that the two extremes are perfectly illustrated by the two sides in the 2009 movie *Avatar*, with the colonizing anthropocentric humans religiously pursuing strong, and the exploited local ecocentric Na'vi weak, substitutability.
5 See Brennan (2018, 336) for a list of freedoms characteristic of liberal democracy.
6 The terms freedom and liberty will be used as interchangeable in this chapter.
7 Remarkably, although Nussbaum repeatedly rephrases her list of ten basic capabilities, the term sustainability has never become part of it.

References

Anderson, T.L. and Leal, D., 1991 *Free Market Environmentalism*. Boulder: Westview Press.
Aristotle, 1981. *The Politics*. Revised edition, Harmondsworth: Penguin.
Asafu-Adjaye, J. et al., 2015. *An Ecomodernist Manifesto*. Available from: www.ecomodernism.org/ [Accessed 7 June, 2019].
Bader, R.M., 2018. Moralized Conceptions of Liberty. In D. Schmidtz and C.E. Pavel, eds. *The Oxford Handbook of Freedom*. Oxford: Oxford University Press.
Barry, J., 2012. *The Politics of Actually Existing Unsustainability: Human Flourishing in a Climate-Changed, Carbon-Constrained World*. Oxford: Oxford University Press.
Barry, J., 2016. Citizenship and (Un)Sustainability: A Green Republican Perspective. In S.M. Gardiner and A. Thompson, eds. *The Oxford Handbook of Environmental Ethics*. Oxford: Oxford University Press.
Bell, D., 2002. How can Political Liberals be Environmentalists? *Political Studies* 50, 703–724.
Beresford, A., 2020. The Virtue Ethics Alternative to Freedom for a Mutually Beneficial Human-Earth Relationship. In C.J. Orr, K. Kish and B. Jennings, eds. *Liberty and the Ecological Crisis*. London: Routledge, 96–109.
Berlin, I., 1969. *Four Essays on Liberty*. Oxford: Oxford University Press.
Blühdorn, I., 2008. *The Politics of Unustainability*. London: Routledge.
Brennan, J., 2018. Democracy and Freedom. In D. Schmidtz and C.E. Pavel, eds. *The Oxford Handbook of Freedom*. Oxford: Oxford University Press, 335–349.
Cannavò, P., 2016. Environmental Political Theory and Republicanism. In G. Teena, C. Hall, J.M. Meyer and D. Schlosberg, eds. *The Oxford Handbook of Environmental Political Theory*. Oxford: Oxford University Press.
Cannavò, P., 2020. Limits and Liberty in the Anthropocene. In C.J. Orr, K. Kish and B. Jennings, eds. *Liberty and the Ecological Crisis*. London: Routledge, 82–95.
Cicero, M.T., 1866. *De Re Publica / De La République*. First bilingual edition, translation by J.V. Le Clerc. Paris: Hachette (original 51 BC).
Constant, B., 1819. *The Liberty of Ancients Compared with that of Moderns*. Available from: https://oll.libertyfund.org/titles/constant-the-liberty-of-ancients-compared-with-that-of-moderns-1819 [Accessed 7 June, 2019].
Dagger, R., 1997. *Civic Virtues*. Oxford: Oxford University Press.
Dagger, R., 2001. Republicanism and the Politics of Place. *Philosophical Explorations* 4 (3), 157–173.
Daly, H., 1992. *Steady-State Economics*. 2nd ed. London: Earthscan.
Dobson, A., 1998. *Justice and the Environment: Conceptions of Environmental Sustainability and Dimensions of Social Justice*. Oxford: Oxford University Press.
Dobson, A., 2007. *Green Political Thought*. 4th ed. London: Routledge.
Donaldson, S., and Kymlicka, W., 2011. *Zoopolis: A Political Theory of Animal Rights*. Oxford: Oxford University Press.
Dryzek, J.S., Norgaard, R.B and Schlosberg, D., 2013. *Climate-Challenged Society*. Oxford: Oxford University Press.
Eckersley, R., 2004. *The Green State: Rethinking Democracy and Sovereignty*. Cambridge: MIT Press.
Garner, R., 2005. *The Political Theory of Animal Rights*. Manchester: Manchester University Press.
Garner, R., 2013. *A Theory of Justice for Animals*. Oxford: Oxford University Press.
Garner, R., 2019. *Environmental Political Thought*. London: Red Globe Press.
Gauthier, D., 1986. *Morals by Agreement*. Oxford: Oxford University Press.
Goodin, R.E., 1992. *Green Political Theory*. Cambridge: Polity Press.
Habermas, J., 1981. *The Theory of Communicative Action. Volume 1: Reason and the Rationalisation of Society*. Boston: Beacon Press.
Hailwood, S., 2004. *How to Be a Green Liberal*. Chesham: Acumen.
Hailwood, S., 2015. *Alienation and Nature in Environmental Philosophy*. Cambridge: Cambridge University Press.
Hannis, M., 2016. *Freedom and Environment: Autonomy, Human Flourishing and the Political Philosophy of Sustainability*. London: Routledge.
Humphrey, M., 2007. *Ecological Politics and Democratic Theory: The Challenge to the Deliberative Ideal*. London: Routledge.

Jennings, B., Kish, K., and Orr, C.J., 2020. Introduction. In C.J. Orr, K. Kish and B. Jennings, eds. *Liberty and the Ecological Crisis*. London: Routledge, 1–14.

Karlsson, R., 2020. Conflicting Temporalities and the Ecomodernist Vision of Rewilding. In J.C. Pereira and A. Saramago, eds. *Non-Human Nature in World Politics: Theory and Practice*. New York: Springer Nature.

Karlsson, R., and Symons, J., 2014. Scalability and Realist Climate Insights. *Weather, Climate and Society* 6, 289–292.

Lambacher, J., 2016. The Limits of Freedom and the Freedom of Limits. In T. Gabrielson, C. Hall, J.M. Meyer and D. Schlosberg, eds. *Oxford Handbook of Environmental Political Theory*. Oxford: Oxford University Press, 385–397.

Lenton, T., 2016. *Earth System Science: A Very Short Introduction*. Oxford: Oxford University Press.

MacCallum, G.C., 1967. Negative and Positive Freedom. *The Philosophical Review* 76 (3), 312–334.

Mouffe, C., 2005. *The Return of the Political*. Revised ed. London: Verso.

Narveson, J., 2001. *The Libertarian Idea*. Peterborough: Broadview Press.

Nozick, R., 1974. *Anarchy, State, and Utopia*. New York: Basic Books.

O'Neill, J., 1993. *Ecology, Policy and Politics: Human Well-Being and the Natural World*. London: Routledge.

Otsuka, M., 2003. *Libertarianism Without Inequality*. Oxford: Oxford University Press.

Pettit, P., 1999. *Republicanism: A Theory of Freedom and Government*. Oxford: Oxford University Press.

Pettit, P., 2001. *A Theory of Freedom: From the Psychology to the Politics of Agency*. Cambridge: Polity Press.

Plato, 1974. *The Republic*. 2nd ed. Harmondsworth: Penguin.

Rasmussen, D.B., and Den Uyl, D.J., 1991. *Liberty and Nature: An Aristotelian Defense of Liberal Order*. La Salle: Open Court.

Rawls, J.B., 1993. *Political Liberalism*. New York: Columbia University Press.

Rawls, J.B., 1999. *A Theory of Justice*. Revised ed. Cambridge: Harvard University Press.

Raz, J., 1986. *The Morality of Freedom*. Oxford: Clarendon Press.

Raz, J., ed., 1990. *Authority*. Oxford: Basil Blackwell.

Rothbard, M.N., 1982. Law, Property Rights, and Air Pollution. *Cato Journal* 2 (1), 55–99.

Sagoff, M., 1974. On Preserving the Natural Environment. *Yale Law Journal* 84 (2), 205–267.

Sagoff, M., 1992. Free-Market versus Libertarian Environmentalism. *Critical Review* 6 (2–3), 211–30.

Schlosberg, D., 2007. *Defining Environmental Justice: Theories, Movements, and Nature*. Oxford: Oxford University Press.

Scriven, T., 1997. *Wrongness, Wisdom and Wilderness: Towards a Libertarian Theory of Ethics and the Environment*. Albany: State University of New York Press.

Stephens, P.H.G., 2001a. The Green Only Blooms amid the Millian Flowers: A Reply to Marcel Wissenburg. *Environmental Politics* 10 (3), 43–47.

Stephens, P.H.G., 2001b. Green Liberalisms: Nature, Agency and the Good. *Environmental Politics* 10 (3), 122.

Stephens, P.H.G., 2015. On the Nature of "Nature": The Real Meanings and Significance of John Stuart Mill's Misunderstood Essay. *Environmental Ethics* 37 (3), 359–376.

Strunz, S. and Bartowski, B., 2018. Degrowth, the Project of Modernity, and Liberal Democracy. *Journal of Cleaner Production* 196, 1158–1168.

Symons, J., 2019. *Ecomodernism: Technology, Politics and the Climate Crises*. Cambridge: Polity Press.

Tanasescu, M., 2015. *Environment, Political Representation, and the Challenge of Rights: Speaking for Nature*. London: Palgrave Macmillan.

Thaler, R.H. and Sunstein, C.R., 2003. Libertarian Paternalism. *The American Economic Review* 93 (2), 175–179.

Thiele, L.P., 2016. *Sustainability*. 2nd ed. Cambridge: Polity Press.

Van Hees, M. and Wissenburg, M., 1999. Freedom and Opportunity. *Political Studies*, 47 (1), 67–82.

Wissenburg, M., 1998. *Green Liberalism: The Free and the Green Society*. London: UCL Press/Routledge.

Wissenburg, M., 2006. Ecological Neutrality and Liberal Survivalism: How (not) to Discuss the Compatibility of Liberalism and Ecologism. *Analyse & Kritik* 26 (2), 125–145.

Wissenburg, M., 2016. The Anthropocene and the Body Ecologic. In P.H. Pattberg and F. Zeli, eds. *Environmental Governance in the Anthropocene: Institutions and Legitimacy in a Complex World*. London: Routledge, 15–30.

Wissenburg, M., 2018. The Foundation of Rights to Nature. In M. Oksanen, A. Dodsworth and S. O'Doherty, eds. *Environmental Human Rights: A Political Theory Perspective*. London: Routledge, 66–84.

Wissenburg, M., 2019a. Geo-engineering: A Curse or a Blessing for Liberal Democracy? In M.A. Maldonado and Z. Trachtenberg, eds. *Rethinking the Environment for the Anthropocene: Political Theory and Sociocultural Relations in the Geological Age*. London: Routledge, 153–165.

Wissenburg, M., 2019b. The Concept of Nature in Libertarianism. *Ethics, Policy & Environment* 22 (3), 287–302.

Zerzan, J., 2012. *Future Primitive Revisited*. Port Townsend: Feral House.

10
SUSTAINABILITY, WELL-BEING AND JUSTICE

Paul Burger and Marius Christen

Introduction

Looking at most influential scientific literature on sustainable development (SD),[1] one might easily get the impression that SD is only about overfishing, resource depletion, climate change, biodiversity loss, water scarcity and the like. Concepts like resilience, carrying capacity, planetary boundaries, (e.g. Berkes et al. 2006; Rockström et al. 2009a; Rockström et al. 2009b; Folke and Gunderson 2010; Steffen et al. 2015) or the Anthropocene (Lewis and Maslin 2015 for an overview, Hamilton et al. 2015; Dryzek and Pickering 2018) take a dominating role in the academic discourse on sustainability. According to that line of reasoning, a development is sustainable if it stays within the thresholds given by the earth's carrying capacities or the according system's resilience levels. The ecology is treated as the primary and foundational goal-dimension of SD. Concepts such as resilience or planetary boundaries function as frame conditions for realizing societal goals.

Another strand of scientific SD literature, however, holds normative concepts, such as justice and well-being, to be key to the idea of sustainability. The Brundtland Report was crystal clear on the ultimate purpose of SD: ensuring all contemporary and future human beings the possibility to lead a decent, humane life (WCED 1987, 41). Accordingly, staying within planetary boundaries is not the primary, final or intrinsic goal of SD but is instrumentally necessary to realize goals regarding well-being and justice (among many Pearce 1989; Norton 2005; Grunwald 2011; Burger and Christen 2011; Christen and Schmidt 2012; Christen 2013; Stumpf et al. 2015; Schmieg et al. 2017; Burger 2018).

Besides conceptual reflection, in practice, it matters which line of SD reasoning one follows. While well-being and justice are classic informants for public decisions, sustainability is a rather new sort of informant, bringing especially the relations between human good life and its (economic, social and ecological) conditions as well as intergenerational justice into the picture. Whether sustainability is conceptualized on the basis of resilience or on the basis of well-being and justice is of utmost practical relevance: in the first case, it figures as an alternative to the classic informants, and in the second case, it links to them and transforms them.

This chapter positions itself within the normatively informed line of SD reasoning, arguing for the second option. First, we will provide arguments for why well-being and justice should be treated as the normative bases of SD and how the relation to more descriptive concepts, such as planetary boundaries, should be conceived thereby. Second, we lay out the many facets of well-being and justice that are relevant for conceptions of and analytic work on SD. As there is no generally accepted well-being or justice approach, we provide an overview of the different well-being and justice considerations. We will thereby argue for the Capability Approach (CA) as a promising foundational basis for SD. Finally, we use these outlines to provide an argument for why democracy is an indispensable foundational element of SD.

Well-being and justice as the foundational layer of SD: an argument from and for normativity

Doubtless, human societies all over the globe face substantial risks stemming from overusing planetary resources and from overloading the sink capacities of planetary and local eco-systems. Given these risks, it seems rational to conclude that the focal concern for changing today's non-sustainable societies should be ecological capacities. Notwithstanding the severity of these risks, however, we see three main reasons against taking concepts such as resilience or the Anthropocene as the foundational basis for SD.

A first argument is based on the history of the idea of SD. Dealing with global ecological risks has been a motivating factor for developing the idea of 'sustainable development' since the Brundtland Report. Although this includes 'living within the ecological boundaries', the 'living' is decisively framed such that it includes poverty alleviation as well as more global justice. Coupling the normative idea of a good life for all with the necessity to realize it within the given ecological conditions is the major innovation of the Brundtland Report (Christen and Schmidt 2012). In this tradition, SD goes substantially beyond the paradigm of von Carlowitz, which considers sustainability primarily as environmental management (Christen et al. 2019).

We call the second reason the argument from desirability. Being independent from concrete political ideas, it is based on the idea that SD is future-oriented and is thought to be the general role model for shaping the realm of desirable futures. Accordingly, any conception of sustainability has to be able to positively shape that realm of desirable futures in some way. We doubt that resilience or carrying capacities satisfy this requirement. Proponents of carrying capacities argue that carrying capacities should be taken as a foundational layer of SD because exceeding them will threaten the provision of ecological functions that are necessary for any desirable future. The most famous example is the life-supporting system functions of the earth's ecosystem. We ought to stay within the earth's carrying capacities, the argument goes, because we have to safeguard life-supporting system functions if we want to have a future at all. So far, we fully agree. However, the argument is incomplete. The reason for safeguarding them is not because they are valuable per se but because they are a precondition for *human* survival. The argument for the desirability of staying within the carrying capacities is an argument to safeguard specific system functions for human living.

Resilience or carrying capacities only provide negative thresholds for desirable futures. They define minimal conditions for any future with human beings, whether desirable or not. Desirability, however, consists of more than mere survival. In addition, not just any system function is worthwhile to safeguard, and there could even be structures that we need to overcome for sustainable transformation (Derissen et al. 2011). In order to be able to assess which system functions should be safeguarded, we need normative arguments that allow the distinguishing of desirable from non-desirable futures.

The third and most relevant argument to hold normative concepts, such as justice and well-being, as fundamental to the idea of sustainability comes from axiology (Christen 2013). The question is on what type of reasons academic approaches to SD should be based. There are only two such types available, namely, descriptive/explanatory and normative reasons. Since the time of the British philosopher David Hume, though, we know that it is invalid to derive or defend a normative claim based on purely descriptive notions (Hume 1978). Under penalty of a naturalistic fallacy, what constitutes a desirable future cannot be deduced from non-normative properties and functions alone, even if they are crucial for the earth system. This is why resilience and the like cannot provide the *foundational* basis for sustainability. They have no normative power. Descriptive notions or considerations help to *further* frame reasonably desired futures, but they cannot provide the basic reasons why we should value a specific system property or any other aspect of a desirable future.

The structure of this argument is as follows:

1. Why should we value resilience (carrying capacity etc.)?
   Because not trespassing resilience ensures life-supporting functions.
2. Why should we value life-supporting functions?
   Because life-supporting functions are a necessary prerequisite to live a decent human life.
3. Why should we value the possibility to live a decent human life?
   The possibility to live a decent human life has intrinsic value. It does not stand for anything else. Rational questioning comes to an end here.

The argument demonstrates that one must first establish the primary constitutive element, the intrinsic value for desirable futures. Based on such a foundational, necessarily normative basis, one can go further and identify secondary constitutive elements (i.e. instrumental goods) necessary to realize the first. At this point, resilience or carrying capacities enter the argumentative construction of SD, as they shape frame-conditions for realizing intrinsic values.

Whereas the first argument refers to the political discourse, the second and third provide the reasons for normativity as the primary foundational basis for sustainability. These arguments *for* normativity are, in turn, arguments *from* normativity. The semantic locution 'for ... from' is thought to display the inherent relation between sustainability and normativity. The arguments offer reasons to base SD on normative grounds and they do so by standing on a normative ground already.[2]

Going back to the Brundtland Report, two clarifications need to be added. First, although the report frames the general goal as having the opportunity to live a decent life (ibid. 41), it conceptualizes 'decent life' by 'satisfaction of needs' (WCED 1987, 43). We will not follow that line in the next sections. Instead, we propose reading the term 'decent life' within the Brundtland Report in a pre-analytic, intuitive manner, as a kind of 'placeholder' analogue to 'well-being'. The specific content for 'decent life' has yet to be given. Second, the same holds true for the term 'justice', which is not further qualified in the Brundtland Report. In addition, the distinction between intra- and intergenerational justice must be introduced. Accordingly, one can take the pre-analytic normative orientation from the report and caution against a hasty conceptualization by means of needs or a specific understanding of justice.

Although both well-being and justice are important aspects of a decent life, it is important to distinguish between them. While the intrinsic value of a good life is related to the individual level, justice concerns the aggregated or interpersonal level. Well-being is an individualistic concept: individuals are the bearers of well-being. Justice, in contrast, concerns *all* individuals, that is, 'those here and those who are to come' (WCED 1987, 41). Neither well-being nor justice are well-defined concepts per se. There are not only a number of competing scientific theories for both, there are also different facets to look at. This manifold is an invitation to explore it more deeply. We first turn our attention to approaches to well-being before discussing the relevance of approaches to justice for SD.

Well-being and sustainability

We start this section by providing arguments for why we do not consent to needs as a conceptualization of well-being and why we dismiss the term 'socially acceptable' (or compatible) (1). We then introduce and discuss the distinction between normative and descriptive approaches to well-being and point to two generally accepted conceptual traits in today's understanding of well-being (2). Third, we present two major scientific approaches to well-being, Hedonism and Eudaemonism, by considering important links to sustainability as well as advocating for a specific version of Eudaemonism, the Capability Approach (3). We finish with an argument for how to understand the sketched diversity (4).

(1) Due to the Brundtland tradition 'needs' or 'satisfaction of needs' is widely used within the SD literature. The problem with satisfaction of needs as a criterion for desirable futures is the arbitrariness of needs (or preferences) people claim to have (for example 'needing a private airplane'). We should be able to distinguish between legitimate and non-legitimate needs, a requirement that obviously demands some normative ground beyond needs. To circumvent this problem of normativity, the term 'need' can be conceptualized as expressing a psychological property people have as human beings (cf. the famous hierarchy of needs by Maslow 1943). However, this would again amount to building criteria for desirable futures on descriptive properties. Instead, a feasible option for needs as currency of well-being would be to go along the so-called basic needs approach (Stewart 1985; Brock and Miller 2019 for an overview of normative considerations regarding needs). It captures a list of factors expressing minimal material and non-material goods to which a human being is *morally entitled*. As a moral approach, this is totally different from the Maslowian needs pyramid. However, such an approach is hardly able to capture well-being as human flourishing, as will be further discussed below.

Instead of needs, the term 'socially acceptable' (cf. Fournis and Fortin 2017 related to renewable energies) is often used as a target factor in SD literature. According to that criterion, actions fostering SD need to take the interests of affected people into account to rule out veto-acting (e.g. Moula et al. 2013). Although the interests of affected people are obviously important, we find it misleading to take 'socially acceptable' as a placeholder for well-being within SD. First, this does not provide a positive criterion for well-being. Second, what is socially accepted is by no means always in line with all people having the opportunity to live a decent life. Third, it is not a normative term capturing what ought to be the case at all. Rather, it describes a societal state of affairs. In contrast, well-being captures what is ultimately good for a person (Crisp 2017). Hence, we dismiss both conceptualizing well-being in terms of needs and of the socially acceptable.

(2) Above, we mentioned an important distinction for dealing with well-being when we referred to needs as a psychological property and to basic needs as a moral category. This disparity between property and moral basis is one of the difficult parts of dealing with well-being. For the sake of argument, imagine that you are a member of a survey panel. One question of the survey is 'How satisfied are you with the overall course of your life?'; that is, how do respondents perceive their state of well-being. Alternatively, you might be asked a battery of questions on how important different aspects are for your daily life (see Figure 10.1). There is no normative power in these questions. They aim to get information on the current mental states of people. There is, properly speaking, no evaluative thread there (cf. Haybron 2019 for an extended argument). Happiness or life satisfaction expresses a psychological state of affairs. This changes when someone is claiming that happiness is a *good* measure for well-being or when it is argued that public policy *should* have the goal to safeguard or enhance people's happiness. Life-satisfaction or well-being are then no longer expressing mental states but conceptualizations of

> *How important are the following to you?*
>
> (1) Good health
> (2) Having and maintaining good relations
> (3) Freedom and control over my life
> (4) Safety
> (5) Living according to my own identity
> (6) Having privacy
> (7) Having access to a clean natural environment
> (8) Having or being able to find a job
> (9) Spending time outside of work/housework to my satisfaction
> (10) Being comfortable
> (11) Being able to enjoy natural and cultural beauty
> (12) Having a varied life and pleasant experiences
> (13) Being appreciated and respected by others
> (14) Having nice possessions
>
> Answers are to be given on a five-point response scale:
> *not at all important; not important; indifferent; important; very important*

Figure 10.1 Eudemonic item battery for well-being/quality of life as used in SHEDS (Weber et al., 2017), adapted from Steg and Gifford (2005); own illustration

the intrinsic good 'well-being'. Accordingly, it is of utmost importance to distinguish whether one talks about well-being as a mental state without any normative power or about well-being as the intrinsic good of human life.

Developing that argument further, we come to distinguishing two widely accepted traits of well-being. First, there is the just-introduced difference between a descriptive and a normative understanding. When we ask why we should follow policy A rather than B, we are on the normative side and have to base the argument on its contribution to well-being. However, we can also simply ask people how well-off they are. Answers to that question will be descriptive because they display mental states of affairs. Second, when talking about well-being, we refer to individuals. Individuals are the bearers of well-being (i.e. they are well-off or not-so-well-off). The term 'well-being' might be said to capture what is (intrinsically) good for an individual. Well-being has, accordingly, an irreducible normative and subjective component howsoever it is further conceptualized. This also gives us a strong argument against objectivist theories of well-being claiming that well-being criteria hold true independent of subjective assertion (for a critical view cf. Varelius 2004; for a defence of objectivist theories of well-being cf. Fletcher 2016). Rather, well-being seems to call for considering the interplay of mental and axiological aspects.

(3) Variations among conceptual approaches to well-being depart at that point: given that there is an irreducible subjective component, the questions that arise are to what degree it is subjective, in what exactly its subjectivity consists and how the relation between subjectivity and normativity is to be understood.

One popular option is to say that well-being is purely subjective and its kernel is the individual's striving for pleasure, which in turn is then seen as the basis for normativity. Alternative options may challenge both assumptions. Drinking a glass of well-aged malt whiskey, an aficionado can experience a lot of pleasure. However, drinking a bottle of it will most certainly cause severe health issues that cannot be captured by subjective standards of experiencing pleasure – and that stands in opposite to the normative claim inherent in 'health'. Hence, there might be good reasons for *not* relying a conception of well-being *purely* on subjective grounds even though well-being is concerned with how well-off individuals are.

There are two major scientific approaches to well-being along these axes: Hedonism and Eudaemonism. The hedonic school and the eudaemonic school both look upon well-being as a relation between what is good for a person and the harm the individual could suffer. An individual can then be said to be well-off if there are more good than bad things for her. The differences between the two schools emerge along the categories they take to be the basis for the goods. Hedonism is based on subjective grounds only. It either takes pleasure in the tradition of Jeremy Bentham or utility (what is useful and contributes to one's satisfaction or happiness) in the tradition of Georg Edward Moore as the metric for well-being. Well-being on the individual level then equates to the satisfaction of the individuals' preferences. Another option would be to take happiness as currency for well-being, expressing emotional individual well-being. Hedonism is not only purely subjectivist but also unidimensional. There is only one measure of well-being (e.g. life-satisfaction or happiness).

The school of Eudaemonism questions this unidimensional understanding of well-being. A good may contribute to self-realization, flourishing or realization of purposeful activities. The basic idea goes back to the Greek philosopher Aristotle, who argued that there is more to well-being than only pleasure or happiness. The 'more' consists of the qualities typical for the constitution of human beings. This approach has been renewed in recent decades along at least three different lines. First, there is psychological Eudaemonism, including a number of different sub-versions. One such version is expressed, for example, by the item battery displayed in Figure 10.1 (taken from Swiss Household Energy Demand Survey, cf. Weber et al. 2017, adapted from Steg and Gifford 2005). The idea is to have a multidimensional set of qualified items that shape expectations about well-being for individuals. The approach is fully subjectivist – it is about what people expect to constitute a good life. Another sub-version looks at people's emotional state by including several dimensions (e.g. the recently developed PERMA-model, Seligman 2011; Butler and Kern 2016).

Their strengths lie in capturing the multidimensional aspects of people's well-being. However, there is a general objection against purely subjective approaches to well-being. One can be fully satisfied with one's life without having access to health facilities, education, information or clean water (the phenomenon is known as adaptation behaviour, cf. Haybron 2019). If well-being encompasses what is intrinsically good for a person, then it has to include objective qualities, not only subjective beliefs. Following that line, quality of life also includes objective features, such as having access to the type of facilities mentioned.

The second eudaemonic line of reasoning, which brings in such objective features, stems from the field of social indicator research (cf. Michalos 2011; Noll 2011 discussing Stiglitz et al. 2009), although most scholars in that field would refrain from qualifying themselves as eudaemonists. However, the qualities in question encompass access to education, health facilities, mobility and energy issues, income distribution, social security and more. The general argument here claims that qualities like material and immaterial goods determine whether people are well-off.

The third line is philosophical Eudaemonism as advocated by the Capability Approach (CA) with its two sub-versions. The first, presented by Amartya Sen, puts the freedom to choose what is valuable for a person's life at centre stage. Expressed in eudaemonic terms, Sen claims that having reasonable opportunity spaces for choices is the cornerstone of self-realization, that is, for being able to lead a purposeful and reasonable life (Sen 1993; 1999a; 2009). Similar to social indicator research, opportunity spaces ask for inputs (goods and services). The second version, presented by Martha Nussbaum, claims that human flourishing or self-realization requires freedoms within a number of specific and identifiable fields (Nussbaum 2000; 2006; 2011). This results in a list of capabilities (Figure 10.2) that resemble psychological

---
- Capability for physical survival
- Capability for bodily health
- Capability for bodily integrity
- Capability for the exercise of imagination
- Capability for emotional response and exploration
- Capability for practical reason
- Capability for love and friendship
- Capability for connection with nature and other species
- Capability for play
- Capability for the exercise of control over environment, including political control
---

Figure 10.2 Nussbaum's capability list (1999)

expectation-Eudaemonism. However, the CA – in both versions – departs from the other presented types of Eudaemonism in two important respects. First, it is an explicitly normative approach. Second, it adds an objective layer, like social indicator research, and includes a subjective layer according to which individuals make choices for what they reasonably deem to be a valuable life. The objective part is related to having choices at all, provided by some opportunity spaces. This objective part can be directly related to policy instruments. The famous Human Development Index (HDI) displays this idea, as it measures relevant objective factors deemed to be relevant for individuals having choices. The subjective part, however, is not considered.

Happiness, life satisfaction or the CA provide us with theoretically informed approaches for operationalizing the fundamental target factor of SD. They give criteria for informing the goal dimension of public decisions. However, they normally do not consider what is needed to *realize* well-being, namely resources. Following, for example, the Sustainable Livelihood Approach, there are at least four additional types of resources beside natural resources (capitals) to be taken into account, namely social capital (e.g. social relations), human capital (e.g. education), economic capital (e.g. property, income) and physical capital (e.g. infrastructure) (cf. Lienert and Burger 2015). Whether they should be considered when discussing the notion of well-being could be debated. However, they have to be considered when discussing *the realization of* well-being. At this point, an inherent relation between two essential elements within SD becomes visible, namely between well-being as a target factor and resources as enabling factors to achieve the goal in question. This speaks in favour of extending the CA towards SD (cf. below).

Additionally, and picking up the non-normative line in well-being research, recent studies, especially within the field of (sustainable) consumption, have established evidence of the relation between expectations towards well-being, experiencing one's state of well-being and sustainability driven changes. Put in technical terms for empirical research, there are, on the one hand, attempts to understand the impact of policy measures or new technologies on the dependent variable understood as welfare, overall life satisfaction, happiness, capability spaces or having access to resources and facilities (cf. Haybron and Tiberius 2015 on well-being policy). On the other hand, consumption or sufficiency research studies in what respect quality of life preferences (i.e. what individuals expect or want to achieve) play an explanatory role in understanding decisions as well as routines (Perlavicuite and Steg 2012; Nordbakke and Schwanen 2014; Burger et al. 2019). Example candidates include comfort, time and the usefulness of one's activity. This highlights the importance of being clear within SD research: do we talk about the normative goal dimension and hence the policy-relevant content of what makes up desirable futures, or do we talk about societal and psychological states of affairs relevant to understanding drivers and barriers for societal transition? Both are relevant for SD, but for different purposes.

(4) There is common ground as well as competition among the different aspects of and approaches to well-being. You cannot be hedonist and eudaemonist at the same time. Neither can you opt for the CA and conceive happiness as the relevant feature of well-being. However, empirical studies informed by different approaches can, notwithstanding their conceptual exclusiveness, provide important complementary information. Looking empirically at development curves in overall life-satisfaction offers information on how people experience their life, whereas HDI-development statistics are not able to do so. None of the normative currencies reveal possible determinants of consumption choices, because they all treat well-being as the target factor. The difference between normative well-being criteria and what people expect to constitute a good life matters. The former is relevant with regard to target factors of public decisions (defining and fostering SD). The latter is relevant, for example, when it comes to the change of consumption patterns. Well-being is a multi-dimensional topic and should be treated in a multi-dimensional way in general and in the field of SD in particular. Looking upon the CA as the most promising approach for conceptualizing well-being, we seek to emphasize its many existing open edges, e.g. to psychological Eudaemonism.

Justice and sustainability

As discussed, SD implies the claim that *all* individuals should be able to enjoy a certain level of well-being – those here and those who are to come. This requires transgressing the individual perspective on people's well-being and brings forth the need to balance (the realization of) well-being between individuals. The tension between claims that all human beings should be able to enjoy well-being and that well-being might be differently distributed among a group of individuals brings forth issues of justice.

As with well-being, there are a number of justice approaches and different facets to be considered. Notwithstanding the existing diversity and based on the most influential work of John Rawls (1971), there is much agreement that justice is about distributing advantages (and disadvantages) and constructing respective institutional arrangements.[3] Moreover, a complete theory of justice is expected to address three main fields (Page 2007; Christen 2013): it specifies how justified distribution ('principles') of what relevant goods ('metric') between which claim holders ('scope') looks like. Justice, hence, is not only about justly distributing goods. Rather, it also reflects who is entitled to receive benefits and what kind of goods or benefits should be considered. The latter closely links justice to well-being. Both deal with the question what really matters, but from different standpoints. The variety of justice approaches results from differently conceptualizing the three fields. Below, we present major contributions to these fields, indicate their relevance for sustainability (similarly Stumpf et al. 2015) and advocate for the CA as most promising option when relating the three fields to SD.

(1) By what principle or criterion should a distributional situation be judged just? There are three main options for answering this question: distribution might be justified by the principle of equality, the principle of priority or by some kind of threshold.

Egalitarianists argue for the first option. They hold that justice is about equality, be it equality of resources and goods (Rawls 1971; Dworkin 1981) or of opportunity spaces (Sen 1992). Consequently, any instance of inequality must be assessed as unjust. Rawls calls this the first principle of justice, claiming that each person has an equal right for the same share (1971, 266).

The second option has its origin in Rawls' work. It states that inevitable inequalities should be dealt with under the criteria of 'the greatest benefit of the least advantaged' (ibid.). This can be described as the principle of priority, according to which goods should not be equally distributed but primarily given to those who need them most.

Both the principles of equality and of priority have been criticized in the philosophical debate (Arneson 2013). The main objection is that they both neglect how well-off people *really* are. If we assume equality to be the relevant criterion for the justness of distribution, then a situation in which all have the same amount of goods but not enough to survive or to lead a decent life would have to be assessed as just.

This brings us to the third option, claiming that distribution is just if all get enough; that is, if all reach a threshold of decent life. Nussbaum's version of the CA is a prominent example of such a threshold-account. She claims that only if all people reach a certain level of capabilities are they able to lead a decent or truly human life (2000; 2006; 2011). A threshold as the criterion for distribution states how goods should be distributed.

Which option one favours has significant implications for one's understanding of SD. The principle of equality, for example, can lead to the claim that well-being should be equally distributed within and among generations. However, given the existing differences between more or less industrialized countries and respective diverging requirements to realize well-being today, equality between generations could be in opposition to equality within generations. The principle of priority, in turn, is most relevant, for example, within the Agenda 2030 in issues such as poverty alleviation. Applying it to future generations, however, could lead to strongly discounting future generations, as proposed by Anand and Sen (2000). A threshold account of justice – as proposed by the CA, for example – allows for more contextualized distribution, taking into account different starting points. Moreover, a decline of well-being (at least in terms of material well-being) over generations is justifiable as long as all generations are able to enjoy a decent life.

(2) The question of the metric of justice – what should be distributed? – was prominently raised by Amartya Sen (1980). There are important overlaps between this question and theories of well-being. Like theories of well-being, the debate about different metrics of justice circles around the question of what well-being is all about. Both ask what ultimately matters for individuals to be well-off. In the justice debate, we find four main routes to the problem of metrics: utility, resources and goods, need satisfaction and opportunities (Sen 1980).

Utilitarianism is an example of the first option. Broadly speaking, it assumes that what we finally owe to each other is determined by subjective mental states, identified in terms of utilities (satisfaction of preferences) or happiness (cf. section above). If most people receive the most utility or happiness or life-satisfaction, this is the optimal – or most just – distribution. Accordingly, justice is about the distribution of satisfaction of preferences or happiness.

Rawlsianism is a prominent example of the second option, primary goods. Rawls assumes that all citizens have an interest in having more rather than less primary goods, such as rights and opportunities, power, income and wealth, and the social bases of self-respect (2001, 58f.). In a similar way, Ronald Dworkin speaks of 'equality of privately-owned resource' (1981). Both only look at these inputs, not at what people are able to do with these goods. Sen criticized the focus on goods and resources and proposed to ask 'what these goods *do* to human beings' (1980, 218).

The third option picks up that criticism and considers basic needs as a relevant metric of justice (cf. section above), understood as the moral attributes of human beings to reach a minimal threshold of a humane life. What should be distributed is the opportunity to satisfy the basic needs one is entitled to (Doyal and Gough 1991). Such an account defines for all human beings what their most relevant needs ought to be without considering subjective differences. It defines a minimal standard for legitimate claims but is not based on an active and positive understanding of human life. For this reason, the basic needs approach has been criticized both for being too objectivistic and too narrow.

Such a critique is presented by the CA, the fourth option for a metric trying to merge objective and subjective components. Capabilities (as introduced in the section above) are reasonable opportunity spaces – beings and doings people can choose and have reason to value (Sen 1993; 2009). The CA draws on the distinction between means and ends and states that what ultimately matters are ends, conceptualized as freedoms or opportunity spaces (Sen 1999a). In addition to this objective part, it adds the subjective part of what people have reasons to value for living a valuable life. On that basis, Nussbaum (2000) develops a universal threshold approach, allowing for contextualized applications.

The debate about metrics of justice is of decisive importance for SD. It lays the conceptual background upon which to decide what should be sustained for future generations – one of the core questions of sustainability (Dobson 1996; Christen and Schmidt 2012). Rawls' primary goods approach, for example, can be nicely linked with the capital approach in SD. Capitals-based conceptions of SD (Pearce et al. 1989) assume that what should be guaranteed to living people and sustained for future generations are opportunity spaces defined by capital stocks, such as human, societal, natural and economic capitals. Following the argument presented in the section above, we opt for the fourth option, taking capabilities as an auspicious basis for SD (Burger and Christen 2011; Rauschmeyer et al. 2013). Resources or capitals are of secondary or deduced importance and to be defined in relation to intrinsic values, such as capabilities. As a consequence, questions of substitution of resources, often seen as most important to sustainability (Neumayer 1999), are only of secondary significance. Resources and capitals should be sustained, because they figure as enabling conditions for opportunity spaces. The CA provides a promising basis for such an argument.

(3) The third question for theories of justice concerns the 'who': whose claims should be considered? There are two important interpretations of that question. The first asks whether justice is only about distribution between human beings or whether non-human entities should also be considered. In environmental ethics we find arguments that justice claims should not be limited to human beings (Brennan and Lo 2016). However, for the sake of our argument, we refrain from going into that topic and stick to an (enlightened, cf. Kopfmüller 2001) anthropocentric understanding of SD.

The second interpretation of the 'who' question relates to distribution between generations (i.e. intergenerational justice). While intragenerational justice considers claims between individuals living at the same time – for example, inequalities between the rich and the poor – intergenerational justice relates different generations. Due to its future orientation, inter-temporal issues are crucial for SD.[4] However, whether temporal extension of justice is even possible (i.e. whether present generations can be dutybound by not-yet-living people) is contested (Meyer 2020). If not, it also questions the very idea of sustainability. If there is a lack of reciprocity between future living people and contemporaries, how can we today be bound by future generations' claims – and why, then, should we sustain anything for future generations?

A prominent form of this concern is the so-called non-identity problem (Parfit 1984). Assume that today's policies will have direct or indirect effects not only on the level of future well-being but also on the composition of future generations – that is, on how many people will live and what their lives will look like. The problem is, in brief: 'How can any person have a claim to compensation for a wrong that was a condition of her existence?' (Cohen 2009, 81).

Today, we can neither know who will exist nor what concrete claims future individuals will have in quantity and in quality. One strategy to circumvent this problem is to avoid interpersonal comparisons and to base intergenerational justice not on a reciprocal basis but on a universal principle (Barry 1999; Christen 2013). This is to assume that justice claims are bound to people wherever and whenever they live. Every human being, no matter when and where it exists, has a right to a decent life. Accordingly, justice obligations do not rely on concrete claims made by someone with an identity vis-à-vis another person. Rather, to oblige present people, it suffices to accept that right-holders will live in the future. Advocates of a positive threshold of a good life, such as the CA, argue that threshold approaches have the advantage of coping with the problem of future obligations by building on a universal but nevertheless contextualizable account of human beings.

One's understanding of SD will depend on the choices made along the sketched variations. We advocated for the CA as a promising approach to dealing with the questions in the three fields of justice. However, there is (yet) no ready-made solution to all theoretical challenges when looking at the link between justice and SD, especially with regard to environmental, economic and societal factors providing conditions and circumstances for the long-term provision of human good life (Christen and Schmidt 2012). In justice theory, such relations between normative and descriptive aspects are conceived of in terms of non-ideal justice. While ideal theories of justice assume that the rules of justice are followed by all obliged actors (strict or full compliance) and that the circumstances allow reaching the conditions of justice, non-ideal theories question these two assumptions (Rawls 1971, 8f., 144ff.). They postulate that not all actors follow rules of justice and that there are trade-offs and conflicts in implementing justice. For example, there are conflicts between providing democratic rights to all citizens and the scarcity of financial resources needed for guaranteeing other state obligations (Farrelly 2007). While ideal theories rationalize general rules of justice only in normative terms, non-ideal theories also consider practical questions of implementation. Non-ideal theories aim for and result in recommendations that are not only desirable but (ideally) also achievable (Stemplowska 2008; similarly, Swift 2008). The existing conditions for human good life on earth – that is, limited resources and fragile ecosystems – build constraints regarding the achievability of SD and lead to trade-offs between potentially conflicting sustainability goals. Hence, taking justice and existing conditions simultaneously into account, doubt is cast on ideal or optimal solutions – rather, we must seek well-balanced pathways towards more sustainable futures. Accordingly, SD is not a field of ideal justice theory only. Rather, a sustainability conception should complement its underlying justice approach with non-ideal aspects that consider practical constraints for realizing a global human society as just as possible. With regard to the CA as a normative fundament for SD, this amounts in the challenges, for example, of linking capabilities to resources and considering the effects of capability realization for the provision of future capabilities – challenges that yet remain unsolved.

Putting the bricks together: sustainability, well-being, justice and democracy

We argued that SD is about desirable futures and that arguments for what desirability consists of are inherently normative and based on some understanding of well-being and justice. On this basis, we conclude our chapter by asking if and in what respect democracy is an element of any desirable future and should be seen as an aspect of a normatively well-justified conception of SD. Given the currently often-contested role of democracy around the world, it matters a great deal whether we include democracy in the normative basis of SD, or not.

There are, however, at least two meanings of the term 'democracy' (e.g. Sen 1999b; Christiano 2018) we should differentiate when arguing for including democracy in SD. A first meaning is related to 'being able to participate in public decisions' as part of being able to live a good life. The human rights declaration is the most salient expression of such a normative understanding. The second meaning is functional: 'democracy' refers to an institutional form of public decision-making based on societal deliberation as well as on some form of citizen participation. In what follows, we do not consider these functional aspects and the related institutional settings. There are many highly diverse institutional forms of democracy, and there is no point in including them in a general normative understanding of SD (but cf. Wallimann et al. 2017). Focusing on the normative meaning of democracy, we see two arguments to include democracy in whatever institutional form in the realm of SD.

The first is an 'argument from well-being to democracy'. Properties like having a say in affairs concerning one's own life, autonomy regarding one's preferences, the ability to express one's opinion and the ability to live according to one's own values are seen as goods having intrinsic value. Importantly, these goods play a role in any conception of well-being, be it hedonic (belonging e.g. to being emotionally well-off) or eudaemonic (belonging e.g. to human individual flourishing). The CA strongly and explicitly relies on such an idea of freedom and tries to substantiate it by the concept of capabilities – a further good argument for this approach. As 'political freedom is part of human freedom' (Sen 1999b, 10), the according individual goods (as, for example, stated by the Human Rights Declaration) are to be protected under all circumstances by appropriate institutional settings. Democracy as a participatory decision-making setting is the institutional reflection of this aspect of well-being, howsoever the institutional setting for public decisions is designed. The institutional setting 'democracy' sets the societal frame-conditions for realizing political freedom as part of human freedom and decent life.

The second argument to include democracy in SD is an 'argument from justice'. There is scholarly agreement that only democratic arrangements can be just and legitimized (Valentini 2012). As mentioned in the section above, justice is not only about how to distribute what for whom, but also, in the tradition of Rawls (1971), about the institutional setting enabling fair distributions. Whereas the argument from well-being points to political freedom as an intrinsic good, the argument from justice highlights enabling and collective conditions to realize a decent life. Obviously, according public goods, such as having access to health and education facilities or energy provision, are not per se provided for all. Democracy sets the societal frame-conditions for public deliberation on distribution in such a way that varieties of problem perceptions and different interests (expressing e.g. different values) are publicly displayed, debated and balanced in order to ideally identify the most informed, balanced and fairest outcome.

Against this backdrop, the relation between democracy and sustainability can be framed as follows. First, democracy is a fundamental brick of sustainability because it guarantees political freedoms-for all as an intrinsic value of what makes a humane life today and in the future. Second, democracy is a fundamental brick of sustainability because it is indispensable for deliberation on the just and legitimized distribution of goods and services within and across generations by providing societal opportunity spaces to find fair balances between conflicting goods. Although democracy as an institutional setting does not display an intrinsic value (but cf. Taylor 1995, chapter 7 on irreducibly social goods, Deneulin 2008 for a defense of intrinsic social values), it nevertheless possesses necessary instrumental value just like life-supporting functions of ecosystems (cf. on necessary instrumental values Schultz et al. 2013).

The concepts outlined here – sustainability, well-being, justice and democracy – are conceptually tied. We understand 'sustainability' as a criterion for public choices to transform today's societies based on well-being as an intrinsic goal of human development and on justice as a criterion to look at distribution of well-being within and across generations. Despite, this irreducibly normative fundament, the implementation of SD has to take environmental and societal frame-conditions into account. Within that scope, democracy is on the one hand related to the intrinsic value of 'political freedom' belonging to well-being, and on the other hand figures as necessary instrumental good for enabling all individuals to live a decent life. How democratic institutional settings should look like to facilitate SD goes beyond the scope of this chapter. However, future research considering democratic settings for global solutions beyond the currently state-wise settings should take into account and build on the normative basis of SD as outlined in this chapter.

Notes

1. Although one could argue that 'sustainability' refers to the conceptual content of 'sustainable development', we do not distinguish between these terms in this chapter.
2. 'Normative' and the related 'ought' can have two different meanings: 'what ought to be the case from a moral perspective' or 'what ought to be the case from the perspective of prevailing social or individual norms'. We use 'normative' in our argument only in the first, not in the second, sense, linking the moral 'ought' to intrinsic values.
3. Besides distributive justice, there are also other forms of justice, especially political justice dealing with the justness of political institutions and retributive justice concerned with compensation for wrongdoing. However, dealing with all aspects of justice would go beyond the scope of this chapter.
4. The scope of intergenerational justice also comprises claims of past generations (Meyer 2020). This is relevant in specific sustainability issues, for example, with regard to compensation for extensive CO_2-emissions in the past.

References

Anand, S. and Sen, A., 2000. Human Development and Economic Sustainability. *World Development*, 28 (12), 2029–2049.

Arneson, R., 2013. Egalitarianism. In E. N. Zalta, ed. *The Stanford Encyclopedia of Philosophy*. https://plato.stanford.edu/archives/sum2013/entries/egalitarianism/

Barry, B., 1999. Sustainability and Intergenerational Justice. In A. Dobson, eds. *Fairness and Futurity. Essays on Environmental Sustainability and Social Justice*. Oxford: Oxford University Press, 93–117.

Berkes, F., Colding, J., and Folke, C. eds., 2006. *Navigating Social-Ecological Systems. Building Resilience for Complexity and Change* (Reprinted). Cambridge: Cambridge University Press.

Brennan, A. and Lo, Y.-S., 2016. Environmental Ethics. In E. N. Zalta, ed. *The Stanford Encyclopedia of Philosophy*. https://plato.stanford.edu/archives/win2016/entries/ethics-environmental/

Brock, G. and Miller, D., 2019. Needs in Moral and Political Philosophy. In E. N. Zalta, eds. *The Stanford Encyclopedia of Philosophy*. https://plato.stanford.edu/archives/sum2019/entries/needs/

Burger, P., 2018. Sustainability, Sustainability Assessment, and the Place of Fiscal Sustainability. In D. Malito, G. Umbach, and N. Bhuta, eds. *The Palgrave Handbook of Indicators in Global Governance*. London: Palgrave Macmillan, 139–159.

Burger, P. and Christen, M., 2011. Towards a Capability Approach of Sustainability. *Journal of Cleaner Production*, 19, 787–795.

Burger, P., Sohre, A., and Schubert, I., 2019. Governance for Sufficiency: A New Approach to a Contested Field. In P. Hamman, eds. *Sustainability Governance and Hierarchy*. London and NewYork: Routledge, 157–177.

Butler, J. and Kern, M. L., 2016. The PERMA-Profiler: A brief multidimensional measure of flourishing. *International Journal of Wellbeing*, 6 (3), 1–48.

Cohen, A. I., 2009. Compensation for Historic Injustices: Completing the Boxill and Sher Argument. *Philosophy and Public Affairs*, 37 (1), 81–102.

Christen, M., 2013. *Die Idee der Nachhaltigkeit. Eine werttheoretische Fundierung*. Marburg: Metropolis-Verlag.

Christen, M. and Schmidt, S., 2012. A Formal Framework for Conceptions of Sustainability – a Theoretical Contribution to the Discourse in Sustainable Development. *Sustainable Development*, 20, 400–410.

Christen, M., Seele, P., and Zapf. L., 2019. Sustainability's Promise of Salvation? A Kuhnian Reconstruction of Sustainability from Resource Management to Contingency Management. In T. Meireis, G. Rippl, eds. *Cultural Sustainability. Perspectives from the Humanities and Social Sciences*. London: Routledge, 109–123.

Christiano, T., 2018. Democracy. In E. N. Zalta, ed., The Stanford Encyclopedia of Philosophy. https://plato.stanford.edu/archives/fall2018/entries/democracy/

Crisp, R., 2017. Well-Being. In E. N. Zalta, eds., The Stanford Encyclopedia of Philosophy (Fall 2017 Edition), https://plato.stanford.edu/archives/fall2017/entries/well-being/.

Deneulin, S., 2008. Beyond Individual Freedom and Agency: Structures of Living Together in the Capability Approach. In F. Comim, M. Qizilbash, and S. Alkire, eds. *The Capability Approach. Concepts, Measures and Applications*. New York: Cambridge University Press, 105–124.

Derissen, S., Quaas, M. F., and Baumgärtner, S., 2011. The relationship between resilience and sustainability of ecological-economic systems. *Ecological Economics*, 70 (6), 1121–1128.

Dobson, A., 1996. Environmental sustainabilities: an analysis and a typology. *Environmental Politics* 5 (3), 401–428.

Doyal, L. and Gough, I., 1991. *A Theory of Human Need*. London: Palgrave.

Dryzek, J. and Pickering, J., 2018. *The Politics of the Anthropocene*. Oxford: Oxford University Press.

Dworkin, R., 1981. What is equality? Part 2: Equality of resources. *Philosophy and Public Affairs* 10 (4), 283–345.

Farrelly, C., 2007. Justice in ideal theory: a refutation. *Political Studies* 55, 844–864.

Fletcher, G., 2016. Objective List Theories. In G. Fletcher, eds. *Routledge Handbook of Philosophy of Well-Being*. New York: Routledge, 590–632.

Folke, C. and Gunderson, L., 2010. Resilience and global sustainability. *Ecology and Society* 15 (4), 43.

Fournis, Y. and Fortin, M-J., 2017. From social 'acceptance' to social 'acceptability' of wind energy projects: towards a territorial perspective. *Journal of Environmental Planning and Management* 60 (1), 1–21.

Grunwald, A., 2011. Conflict-resolution in the context of sustainable development. In O. Parodi, I. Ayestaran, G. Banse, eds. *Sustainable Development – Relationships to Culture, Knowledge and Ethics*. Karlsruhe: KIT Publishing, 19–32.

Hamilton, C., Bonneuil, C., and Gemenne, F., eds., 2015. *The Anthropocene and the Global Environmental Crisis: Rethinking Modernity in a New Epoch*. London and New York: Routledge.

Haybron, D., 2019. Happiness. In E. N. Zalta, eds. *The Stanford Encyclopedia of Philosophy*. https://plato.stanford.edu/archives/win2019/entries/happiness/

Haybron, D. and Tiberius, V., 2015. Well-being policy: what standard of well-being? *Journal of the American Philosophical Association* 1 (4), 712–733.

Hume, D., 1978. *A Treatise of Human Nature*. Oxford: Clarendon Press.

Kopfmüller, J. et al., 2001. *Nachhaltige Entwicklung integrativ betrachtet. Konstitutive Elemente, Regeln, Indikatoren*. Berlin: edition sigma.

Lewis, S. and Maslin, M., 2015. Defining the anthropocene. *Nature* 519, 171–180.

Lienert J. and Burger, P., 2015. Merging capabilities and livelihoods: analyzing the use of biological resources to improve well-being. *Ecology and Society* 20 (2).

Maslow, A., 1943. A theory of human motivation. *Psychological Review* 50 (4), 370–396.

Meyer, L., 2020. Intergenerational Justice. In E. N. Zalta, eds. *The Stanford Encyclopedia of Philosophy*. https://plato.stanford.edu/archives/sum2020/entries/justice-intergenerational/.

Michalos, A. C., 2011. What did Stiglitz, Sen and Fitoussi get right and what did they get wrong? *Social Indicators Research* 102, 117–129.

Moula, M.M. et al., 2013. Researching social acceptability of renewable energy technologies in Finland. *Journal of Sustainable Built Environment* 2 (1), 89–98.

Neumayer, E., 1999. *Weak versus Strong Sustainability. Exploring the Limits of Two Opposing Paradigms*. Cheltenham: Edward Elgar.

Noll, H-P., 2011. The Stiglitz-Sen-Fitoussi-Report: old wine in new skins? Views from a social indicators perspective. *Soc Indic Res* 102, 111–116.

Nordbakke, S. and Schwanen, T., 2014. Well-being and mobility: a theoretical framework and literature review focusing on older people. *Mobilities* 9, 104–129.

Norton, B. G., 2005. *Sustainability. A Philosophy of Adaptive Ecosystem Management*. Chicago: UCP.

Nussbaum, M., 2000. *Women and Human Development. The Capabilities Approach*. Cambridge: CUP.

Nussbaum, M., 2006. *Frontiers of Justice. Disability, Nationality, Species Membership*. Cambridge: Belknap Press.

Nussbaum, M., 2011. *Creating Capabilities. The Human Development Approach*. Cambridge: Belknap Press.

Page, E. A., 2007. Intergenerational justice of what: welfare, resources or capabilities? *Environmental Politics* 16 (3), 453–469.

Parfit, D., 1984. *Reasons and Persons*. Oxford: Clarendon Press.

Pearce, D., Barbier, E.B., and Markandya, A., 1989. *Blueprint for a Green Economy*. London: Earthscan.

Perllavicuite, G. and Steg, L., 2012. Quality of life in residential environments. *Psychology* 3 (3), 325–340.

Rauschmeyer, F. and Lessmann O., 2013. The capability approach and sustainability. *Journal of Human Development and Capabilities: A Multi-Disciplinary Journal for People-Centered Development* 14 (1), 1–5.

Rawls, J., 1971. *A Theory of Justice*. Cambridge: Harvard University Press.

Rawls, J., 2001. *Justice as Fairness. A Restatement*. Cambridge: Belknap Press.

Rockström, J., Steffen, W., and Noone, K., 2009a. A safe operating space for humanity. *Nature* 461, 472–475.

Rockström, J. et al., 2009b. Planetary boundaries: exploring the safe operating space for humanity. *Ecology and Society* 14 (2), 32.

Schmieg, G. et al., 2017. Modeling normativity in sustainability: a comparison of the sustainable development goals, the Paris agreement, and the papal encyclical, *Sustainability Science* 13, 785–796.

Schultz, E. et al., 2013. A sustainability-fitting interpretation of the capability approach: integrating the natural dimension by employing feedback loops. *Journal of Human Development and Capabilities* 14 (1), 115–133.

Seligman, M. E. P., 2011. *Flourish: A Visionary New Understanding of Happiness and Well-Being*. New York: Free Press.

Sen, A., 1980. Equality of What? In S. McMurrin, eds., *Tanner Lectures on Human Values*. Vol. I, Cambridge: Cambridge University Press, 197–220.

Sen, A., 1992. *Inequality Reexamined*. Oxford: Oxford University Press.

Sen, A., 1993. Capability and Well-Being. In M. Nussbaum, A. Sen, eds., *The Quality of Life*. Oxford: Clarendon Press, 30–53.

Sen, A., 1999a. *Development as Freedom*. Oxford: Oxford University Press.

Sen, A., 1999b. Democracy as a universal value. *Journal of Democracy* 10 (3), 3–17.

Sen, A., 2009. *The Idea of Justice*. London: Penguin Group.

Steffen, W. et al., 2015. Planetary boundaries: guiding human development on a changing planet. *Science* 347 (6223), 736.

Steg, L. and Gifford, R., 2005. Sustainable transportation and quality of life. *Journal of Transport Geography* 13, 59–69.

Stemplowska, Z., 2008. What's ideal about ideal theory. *Social Theory and Practice* 34 (3), 319–340.

Stewart, F., 1985. *Planning to Meet Basic Needs*. London: Palgrave Macmillan.

Stiglitz, J. Sen, A., and Fitoussi, J-P., 2009. Report by the Commission on the Measurement of Economic Performance and Social Progress. http://citeseerx.ist.psu.edu/viewdoc/download?doi=10.1.1.215.58andrep=rep1andtype=pdf

Stumpf, K. H. et al., 2015. The justice dimension of sustainability: a systematic and general conceptual framework. *Sustainability* 7, 7438–7472.

Swift, A., 2008. The value of philosophy in nonideal circumstances. *Social Theory and Practice* 34 (3), 363–387.

Taylor, Ch., 1995. *Philosophical Arguments*. Oxford: OUP.

Valentini, L., 2012. Justice, disagreement and democracy. *British Journal of Political Science* 43 (1), 177–199.

Varelius, J., 2004. Objective explanations of individual well-being. *Journal of Happiness Studies* 5, 73–91.

Wallimann-Helmer, I., Meyer, L., and Burger, P., 2017. Democracy for the future: A conceptual framework to assess institutional reform. *Jahrbuch für Ethik und Wissenschaft* 197–220.

Weber, S. et al., 2017. *Swiss Household Energy Demand Survey (SHEDS): Objectives, design, and implementation*, SCCER CREST Working paper.

World Commission on Environment and Development (WCED), 1987. *Our Common Future*. Oxford: Oxford University Press.

PART III

Structures and dynamics

11

ESCALATING SIDE EFFECTS

The transformation of modern society through processes of cosmopolitanization, acceleration and increasing global risks

Ulrich Beck and Hartmut Rosa

Introduction[1]

One of the key hallmarks of the political, social, economic, and cultural development of the twenty-first century is the spatial, temporal, economic, ecological, and socio-cultural transformation of society through processes of escalation. What was once rightfully called a "revolution" has globally permeated into the dynamics of the conditions, as it were – we are witnessing an escalating "revolution of the side effect." First of all, this involves a decoupling of the social and political from geography, that is, a universal expansion of ranges, linkages, and opportunities. *Spatially*, these transformation processes are frequently discussed under the banner of *globalization*. This intends to express that the distant causes and distant effects of social processes and interactions are increasing, first, in terms of their range, second, in terms of their intensity, third, in terms of their speed, and, fourth, in terms of their depth of penetration (Held et al. 1999, 14–31). What this means is that entrepreneurial decisions, for instance, but also university reforms or cultural events and the like, are ever-more frequently linked (increasing intensity) with events and decisions in ever-more distant parts of the globe (increasing extensity) that affect, to an ever-increasing and profound degree, the nature of these business, university, or cultural entities (increasing depth of penetration). For this reason, we can speak of a paradigm shift inasmuch as processes of globalization no longer impinge on national or cultural institutions and practices from the outside but rather that these institutions and practices are already globalized from within, as it were, in terms of their logic of operation. This creates new kinds and dynamics of social relations and types of social action that are characterized by various modes of simultaneous inclusion and exclusion. The distant other is also here, and we are also elsewhere. This is what Ulrich Beck has referred to as the social-scientific fact of *"cosmopolitanization"* as opposed to the philosophical norm of cosmopolitanism. Cosmopolitanization is thus the sociological face of globalization, which is to be subjected to investigation (Beck 2006).

The fact that processes of exchange and interaction are continuously picking up speed is an essential element of the encompassing transformation through processes of acceleration, which characterize the *temporal dimension* of the (late-)modern tendency toward escalation.

These processes of acceleration can be subdivided into processes of technical acceleration (especially of transportation, communication, and production), the acceleration of social change (i.e., an increase in the rate of socio-cultural change), and the acceleration of the pace of life (characterized by an increase in episodes of action and experiences per unit of time) (Rosa 2013a).

Both of these transformation processes – cosmopolitanization and acceleration – are an expression of a global risk capitalism, the triumph of which is threatening its own nationally rooted democratic foundations. Both the increase in the rate of innovation and the increase in the range of side effects are a signum of modernity's tendency toward economic escalation, which is inherent in capitalism's logic of valorization: by necessity, capitalist economies must grow, accelerate, and innovate to reproduce their structure. In so doing, they generate the global side effects that today threaten and alter the world order, respectively.

To explain the concept of *escalation of side effects*, it is useful to distinguish three types of side effects: (1) simple side effects, which sociology has traditionally investigated and addressed as a public issue as [an outcome of] social change through technical-economic innovation; (2) reflexive side effects, which pose a challenge to institutional foundations and resources (e.g., climate change, 9/11, the financial crisis, the euro crisis); and (3) side effects of side effects or, in other words, the side effects of global risks, which create transnational publics as well as pressure to act and open up alternative lines of action previously deemed unthinkable.

Against this backdrop, the common notion of revolution seems oddly idyllic and antiquated. The revolution of side effects is not only local, regional, or national but also global. It affects not only a historical regime of political rule but also our understanding of the concept of the political and of society itself. It is not just a temporally, spatially, and socially limited exception but escalates as risk capitalism escalates. Inaction does not bring this revolution of side effects to a halt but rather keeps it going. This revolution does not originate in the centers of democratically legitimated politics but in the profit calculus of economies and in the laboratories of technology and science. It happens unintentionally, in the absence of a revolutionary consciousness. The fact that this revolution is overthrowing the world order is an insight that must first be disclosed, step-by-step, against the prevailing consciousness of immanent social change in science, politics, and everyday life – in line with the motto, "We are not revolutionary, reality is".

Economic growth and an escalating volume of financial markets are thus key features of global risk capitalism. And they themselves are intrinsically tied to the escalation of ecological problems: both ecological risks and threats (from nuclear catastrophe to the greenhouse effect, to the spread of new diseases and genetic mutations) as well as the scarcity of resources (from oil to wood and fish to water) are increasing in terms of range, relevance, and speed of intensification.

Taken together, all these escalatory processes are resulting in transforming the material and institutional structures of the world and the world becoming virtually *inconceivable* in the process, that is to say, proving elusive to theoretical conceptualization. That the magnitude of this change exceeds the grasp of our categories is most clearly manifested in linguistic decay, in key terms that no longer open the doors to understanding. Take your pick: the right–left dichotomy aligning political parties, the distinction between natives and foreigners, nature as set apart from society, the family, First and Third World, centre and periphery, the European Union – wherever we turn, empty phrases, broken coordinates, gutted institutions.

It is no coincidence that the prefix "post" is the catchword of our time: postmodernity, postfeminism, postdemocracy, postnational constellation, posthistoire. "Post" is the white cane of intellectuals – the small word employed to express the illegibility of the world.

When we consider the momentous events and trends in recent decades – the nuclear disasters of Chernobyl and Fukushima, the attacks of 9/11, climate change, the financial and euro crises – we notice that they all have three features in common: First, they were *inconceivable* before they happened; second, they were *global* in nature and in their consequences; and third (with the exception of 9/11), they were *not intentional* but rather epitomize a kind of "revolution of the side effect" – a revolution that they, by their own occurrence, further escalate and proliferate. These were global events that let us experience the ever-denser interconnectedness of spheres of action and of the places where we live; events that we can no longer comprehend with the tools and categories that have underpinned thought and action within a national framework.[2]

Regaining a grasp on the socio-historical dimension of these developments by adopting an appropriate historical perspective of this transformation, as the theories of world risk society and social acceleration attempt to do, is antithetical to mainstream social theory and politics on the one hand, which have been doing the exact opposite by focusing (and even doing so with intellectual pride!) on the *reproduction* of social and political order – with a view to the class system (Pierre Bourdieu), the system of power (Michel Foucault), bureaucracy (Max Weber), or the (autopoietic) [social] system (Niklas Luhmann). On the other hand, this theory perspective is also antithetical to the Marxian paradigm and Jürgen Habermas' critical theory inasmuch as they posit that social and political transformations are triggered and propelled only by crises, revolutions, or at least political controversies but not by the silent side-effects of successful modernization.

The transformation (and precisely *not* reproduction!) of social and political order through this order's inherent tendency toward escalation thus confronts not only political actors but also the social sciences in general and sociology in particular with problems. Conventional models for explaining social developments, which are usually geared toward national contexts – the long-dominant theories of modernization being a case in point – no longer seem to be convincing; we can no longer identify simple chains of cause and effect or laws of development. An alarm signaling the need to revise sociological theories, categories, and research routines is perhaps the fact that sociology was not only taken by surprise by crucial developments at the turn of the twenty-first century (e.g., the fall of the Iron Curtain and the collapse of the Eastern Bloc, the development of the internet and the digitization of financial markets, the revival of religion in the public sphere, [or] the economic center of capitalism shifting from the Euro-Atlantic region to Asia) but that it has to date also been unable to integrate them convincingly into social theory. All this notwithstanding, a large number of contemporary approaches have been making an effort to realign sociology's analytical toolbox and overcome accordingly models geared toward societies constituted on the basis of the nation state ("container sociology," Beck 2000, especially 23–26). We would now like to briefly examine these approaches in more detail before we offer a proposal of our own to reconceptualize the accelerated and cosmopolitan transformation of society and reconfigure sociology's analytical repertoire.

Theories of functional differentiation/systems theory

Niklas Luhmann was one of the first to realize, and to apply this insight very systematically, that talk of *the* German and *the* American society could not be justified sociologically, as processes of communication know no national boundaries. He and his followers therefore always speak of world society, the decisive feature of which they identify as *functional* differentiation. In this reading, the key lines of division are not borders between nation states but the boundaries between functional systems such as economy, politics, law, science, art, and so forth (Stichweh 2000; for a comparative overview, see Wobbe 2000). Increasing complexity then appears as an inevitable side effect of the ever-progressing differentiation into ever-more specialized subsystems. This approach reaches its explanatory limits in areas where we observe new, pronounced tendencies toward *dedifferentiation*, that is, in areas where, for instance, economy and politics, entertainment and culture, science and religion, or war and law begin to fuse in new ways on the one hand and when it comes to understanding the rapid transformations of social and political order on the other. For systems theory, nothing fundamental has happened since the transition from an estate-based to a functionally differentiated society, hence since the onset of modernity. Conceptually, systems theory proves unable to grasp the fundamental rupture that has been taking place within modernity in recent decades.

World systems theory/theory of capitalism

When it comes to systematically conceptualizing and analyzing the global transformation processes of global risk capitalism, *theories of capitalism* are promising candidates by their very nature. They derive these tendencies and their inherent logic of escalation systematically from the process of the (self-)valorization of capital. As early as in the *Communist Manifesto*, Marx and Engels impressively described capital's tendencies toward acceleration and globalization (Marx and Engels 1848/2010, 16):

> The need of a constantly expanding market for its products chases the bourgeoisie over the entire surface of the globe. It must nestle everywhere, settle everywhere, establish connexions everywhere. The bourgeoisie has through its exploitation of the world market given a cosmopolitan character to production and consumption in every country. To the great chagrin of Reactionists, it has drawn from under the feet of industry the national ground on which it stood. All old-established national industries have been destroyed or are daily being destroyed. They are dislodged by new industries, whose introduction becomes a life and death question for all civilised nations, by industries that no longer work up indigenous raw material, but raw material drawn from the remotest zones; industries whose products are consumed, not only at home, but in every quarter of the globe. In place of the old wants, satisfied by the production of the country, we find new wants, requiring for their satisfaction the products of distant lands and climes. In place of the old local and national seclusion and self-sufficiency, we have intercourse in every direction, universal inter-dependence of nations. And as in material, so also in intellectual production. The intellectual creations of individual nations become common property. National one-sidedness and narrowmindedness become more and more impossible, and from the numerous national and local literatures, there arises a world literature. The bourgeoisie, by the rapid improvement of all instruments of production, by the immensely facilitated means of communication, draws all, even the most barbarian, nations into civilisation.

Drawing on the Marxist tradition, authors such as David Harvey, Giovanni Arrighi, and particularly Immanuel Wallerstein have made an effort to interpret processes of globalization and the resulting dynamics of inequality and socio-economic dislocations as a consequence of unleashed flows of capital, which time and again are able to exploit local, regional, and global inequalities in distribution and development for [the sake of] increasing profits (Harvey 2006; Arrighi 2010; Wallerstein 2011). However, this endeavour has reached [its] limits and run into contradictions. For one, Wallerstein presupposes, and treats as a constant, the duality of national and international. What he fails to recognize in so doing is the transformations driven by cosmopolitanization, that is, that the [common] dualisms of national and international, us and them, inside and outside are unravelling, and their new hybrid forms must be newly deciphered both conceptually and empirically. [His] world-systems analysis is a model of the *national writ large* and as such is only to [very] limited extent capable of overcoming methodological nationalism.

For another, this vein of theory and research misunderstands the political nature of global risk and world risk capitalism. Global risk must not be mistaken for catastrophe but rather understood as the current anticipation of future catastrophes, to prevent them from happening. Risk holds a message: "It is high time for action!" To avoid the unthinkable worst-case scenario, that which had just recently been inconceivable now becomes politically conceivable and possible, for example, opting out of nuclear energy. The end of the end of politics inherent in this is what neo-Marxist approaches have so far failed to recognize (Beck 2005).

As powerful as such approaches have proven to be in analyzing economic relationships, they become problematic when they find seek to explain *all* social and cultural changes and developments by reference to the logic of capital valorization or to downplay them as being merely contingent and thus as insignificant by these theorists' measure.

New network theories

An attempt of a different nature to come to terms conceptually with the complexity and dynamics of the late-modern world is *network theories*, which have rapidly gained currency, veritably mushrooming, over the last two decades. Network theories have a plausible commonsensical root in the observation of the prevalence of network structures in nearly every area of life – from the internet and Facebook via the terror network to the neuronal network of our brain. Network theorists, from Manuel Castells to Bruno Latour, therefore suggest that we no longer embark on social analyses from the vantage point of actors, states, enterprises, or generally of institutions as fixed entities that maintain relationships but rather to move relationship patterns and structures to the center of attention. In this way, they seek to take account of flexibility, dynamism, and "fluidity," that is, the high rate of change and the instability of the late-modern social world. Networks are characterized by the fact that they are formed by relationships, actually consist of relationships, which can be intensified or weakened at will, that they have no top and no center, and that the *network nodes* (involved actors or institutions) can flexibly be activated and deactivated or included and excluded. For actors, institutions, and places, it is important to be part of the proper networks in order to steer the respective streams (of capital, commodities, information, tourists, and so on) in one's own direction. In this respect, inclusion and exclusion in networks depends to an increasingly lesser extent on physical space itself: those excluded find themselves being endlessly removed from what goes on in the network irrespective of spatial distance. In this sense, Manuel Castells, for instance, diagnosed that we are witnessing the transition to a new era dominated by a new space–time regime ruled by network logic (Castells 1996). It comes with change in the modes and the significance of politics, production, as well as cultural experience.

Whereas Castells speaks of the emergence of a "new network society" in this sense, other network theorists take a much more radical approach. The French sociologist Bruno Latour, one of the founders of *actor–network theory* (ANT), for instance, suggests abandoning the concept of society altogether and the distinction between nature and culture along with it. In his view, we can get an appropriate grasp on the (late-)modern world only if we replace traditional basic sociological concepts of action, structure, society, social classes or strata, and so forth with an unconditional analysis of "the things themselves," which prove to be dynamic networks of varying, interconnected "actants." Actants are all entities, whether human or non-human, that influence an occurrence (Latour 2005; see also the contribution by Laux 2014).

As fascinating as such approaches may be, so far evidence is still lacking that they do actually equip us to understand and explain the transformations of the social and political order of the twenty-first century. There is reason for doubt, as the "transformation" of key categories of the social and political – class, nation, power and domination, state, democracy, family, love, and so on – are not within the view of this [line of] thinking and researching. Moreover, network-theoretical approaches so far lack the conceptual means to systematically grasp processes of cosmopolitanization and acceleration. Whatever the case may be, the majority of the available work done so far consists of theoretical debates and statements of intent, to the extent that it reaches beyond the narrow confines of science and technology studies (STS) [at all].

Complexity theory

Finally, attempts that show a similar radicality are those that seek to account for the complexity of the global world in accordance with complexity theory as developed in mathematics and computer sciences. In this vein, social systems can be modeled and analyzed like other complex systems such as the weather. Authors such as John Urry (2002) advocate for accepting, in line with chaos theory, that the social world is not only not determined but can as a matter of principle also not be fully described in terms of causality. Rather, in many respects, the social world is unpredictable and imponderable. Yet this is not to say that we can observe no stability or regularity of any kind: just as weather systems, for instance, prove unpredictable in the long term while they do form stable high- or low-pressure systems and stable flow conditions in the short and sometimes medium term that result in a degree of local stability and predictability for a given period of time, the social world can also be understood as an entropic, non-linear system (or an entire series of such systems) that indeed makes it possible to identify recurring patterns and temporary islands of stability. In this vein, the Western nation and welfare state would, for example, resemble a very stable high-pressure system that is gradually coming under the influence of low fronts while the globally circulating flows of capital can be compared to the largely steady westerlies.

And as in other chaotic systems, we can identify more or less persistent path dependencies in regard to social flows (e.g., of tourists or migrants, ideas and information, of capital, commodities, and labour, drugs and weapons) and the effect of attractors of various strengths that seem to exert a pull on those flows for a while. Just as in other complex systems, there are likewise also positive and negative feedback processes, that is, self-reinforcing effects of attraction or repulsion. Thus, a booming location attracts, say, capital, jobs, luxury goods, information, young people, intellectuals, tourists, which makes it even more attractive for all these flows, whereas a declining region conversely loses all this and becomes even less attractive. The crucial issue in this context is that the chains of cause and effect do not follow a simple linear pattern so that small causes sometimes have enormous impact, whereas in other cases huge efforts achieve no notable effect.

Just as a single flapping of a butterfly's wings in the skies over the Russian taiga under very specific conditions can trigger a thunderstorm over Cologne, the emergence of seemingly harmless (and, besides, also years old) Mohammad cartoons in Denmark can spark a war in Pakistan or a riot in Algeria, whereas massive international aid programs and even extensive military operations (such as in Afghanistan) can ultimately turn out to largely be to no avail.

Whatever the case, one is just as unpredictable as the other. As the aforementioned examples illustrate, this approach can indeed produce fascinating ex post descriptions of social processes. What falls by the wayside, however, is the sociological aspiration to render the world *comprehensible* and the redefinition of key *social-scientific* categories and methodologies that this would require. This amounts not only to abandoning hope that social processes, phenomena, and developments could actually be *explained* by means of precise analysis (instead of merely being described) but also to undermining the idea that the world could be shaped politically (and [thus], at least to a limited extent, in some planned fashion). In the following, this verdict leads us to develop our own proposal for conceptualizing late-modern relations in a way that makes it possible to handle these theoretically and politically.

Reflexive dynamization: a new conceptual approach

In contrast to the latter proposals discussed above, the theories of world risk society, reflexive modernization, and social acceleration developed by the authors of this chapter hold onto sociology's traditional explanatory aspirations as well as to a concept of society in the sense of a historically evolving, transforming social (process-)formation that calls for hermeneutic interpretation. However, they do share the belief that living up to this aspiration and comprehending societies of the twenty-first century is only possible by applying a conceptual and analytical sociological toolbox that takes account of global change. In so doing, it is of fundamental importance to overcome methodological nationalism and the container sociology associated therewith – according to which the nation state is perceived as the container within which society happens – and to integrate the escalation and transformation processes of modernity described above into sociology's basic conceptual apparatus. Understanding these processes requires that we think of modern society, first, as a societal formation that can stabilize itself only dynamically and, second, as one whose modes of dynamic stabilization are challenged by the acceleration, cosmopolitanization, and risks of a transformation driven by its tendencies toward escalation. This manifests itself in the contradiction that modernity must continuously grow, accelerate, and innovate to reproduce its structure, yet that this process simultaneously induces transformation and risky developments with unknown outcomes. This mode of dynamic stabilization through destabilization (or destabilization through stabilization) is most conspicuous in the (capitalist) economy. In all known varieties of this economic system, a lack of growth entails a loss of jobs, business closures, and decreasing public revenue along with increasing public expenditure, ultimately resulting in crises of social security systems and a delegitimization of the political system. At the same time, this primacy of economic growth is unintentionally linked with growing endangerment, which as a "revolution of side effects" endogenously calls into question the premises and coordinates of the social order – *without* there being a discernible new mode of stabilizing such destabilization.

Yet we can in fact observe such a mode of dynamic (de-)/stabilization in areas other than the economy as well: in the field of knowledge (which in modernity is organized as the dynamically expanding activity of science, which simultaneously increases the realm of the unknown), the arts (which no longer have as their core activity the mimetic replication of nature or the old masters but rather the outdoing of what has been done before as well as the engagement in cosmopolitanization, innovation, and risk-seeking), and in legislation (the limitations of which, however, are reflected in the overlap between national and transnational legislation), to mention but a few (in detail, see Beck and Lau 2004; Beck and Wehling 2012; Rosa 2013b).

In this light, the transition from modernity to late modernity or from first to second modernity, in which the transformational tendencies induced by escalation begin to erode the stable reproduction of institutions, can be grasped in two ways. First, *reflexivity* proves to be the crucial engine of modernity's dynamization. This leads to the modern principles of dynamization applying themselves to their own institutional foundations: not only the mode of production but also the (welfare-state, political, familial, educational, etc.) institutions that organize it are exposed to compulsions to escalate and thus under pressure to rationalize, differentiate, and/or accelerate. Hence, we can identify the transition to second modernity in areas where the basic institutions of modern society that were once assumed to be stable – the nation state, the separation of state and religion, the monopoly over the means of violence, the workings of parliamentary democracy, territorially and nationally defined family and intimate relationships, and so forth – are themselves being refashioned under the pressure of the imperatives of transformation (see Beck and Beck-Gernsheim 2014).

Such transitions can be observed, for instance, where democratic political opinion formation and decision making no longer appear to be pacemakers of social development but merely action that lags behind, seeks to put out the blaze, and is reactive toward technical, cultural, and particularly economic developments and risks (see Rosa and Scheuerman 2009; Beck 2013b, 22–38). What we see here is that not all spheres of society are equally capable of being dynamized, which results in severe problems of desynchronization. And we can indeed describe all the major crises of our global present in terms of such desynchronization crises: in addition to the crisis of democracy outlined above, these are the following: (1) *the financial and economic crisis*, rooted in the speed of transactions in financial markets, which has become independent of the pace of production and consumption, a pace that can be accelerated only to a limited degree; (2) *the ecological crisis*, caused by the escalating consumption of resources and filling sinks with pollutants that overwhelm the intrinsic temporality [*Eigenzeit*] and reproduction periods of nature; and lastly (3) the mental crisis, manifested in diseases involving anxiety, stress, burnout, and depression, which can be understood as overwhelming the intrinsic temporality of the human psyche.

Second, in the modern formation defined in this way, the principles of movement and standstill overlap in a highly peculiar way: beginning in the eighteenth century and in the Euro–Atlantic West, growth, acceleration, and intensification of innovation became the defining modus of stabilization. The aspect of movement came to dominate cultural perception: The transition to modernity was perceived as embarking on a path forward and was associated with *ideas of progress* pertaining to technical, economic, cultural, and political development. Growth, acceleration, and innovation promised substantial improvements in living conditions and social conditions, but above all an increase in the scope of individual and collective autonomy. In twenty-first-century risk capitalism, by contrast, progress also means progressing *self-endangerment* and acceleration, including the acceleration of *(un)desired risks*, an experience that resembles a frenetic standstill in thought and action. Growth, acceleration, and the intensification of innovation now seem less a promise and more *compulsions* and *threats* that have to be accommodated simply to maintain the status quo. This can be described as a transition from the production of wealth to the production of risk: economic growth must continue, but no one (in the so-called Western countries) still ties their hopes to this growth enabling us to (permanently) overcome poverty and scarcity and it mitigating existential competition. Quite to the contrary, it is perceived as a certainty that global competition and the struggle over increasingly scarce resources will intensify. Similarly, technical acceleration can be expected to advance further – yet the belief that once prevailed around [the] 1970[s] that this could turn a shortage of time into a surplus thereof has completely vanished. The process of scientific and technical innovation will continue as well, as it is indispensable for maintaining the dynamic of reproduction and transformation. It will likely bring us a fusion of bio and computer technology; yet this, too, is a prospect that would carry the revolution of side effects to extremes. Paradoxically, poverty, lack of time, and new threats to civilization and our lives seem to result from the very principles of (capitalist) growth, acceleration, and scientific-technical innovation.

The result of these side effects becoming rampant in the "world risk society" (see Beck 2013a) is a cultural self-perception in which the events of global transformation are no longer experienced as progression toward a promising future on the horizon but as a panicked attempt, as it were, to run away from a catastrophic abyss that is hard on our heels. This perception is certainly not equally dominant in all parts of the world – yet in Europe, Japan, and North America, this upending of perspective becomes manifest in the fact that, for the first time in the history of modernity, a majority of parents are no longer driven by the expectation that their children will one day be better off than they are but by fear that their children will do worse. It is a perception that is rooted in the logic of dynamic (de-)stabilization itself and can be sensed even in those parts of the world that can still view themselves as progressing along a forward trajectory.

For sociology, this presents a dual challenge: on the one hand, it faces the task of ridding its conceptual toolbox from the inbuilt priority of reproducing the national–international order and to open it up toward [addressing] the highly ambivalent transformation [of society] through escalation and self-endangerment. On the other hand, sociology encounters the truly political question of how and by means of which institutions we might rein in or even overcome the risks and the repercussions of desynchronization as well as the compulsions toward escalation unfolding a life of their own before all this comes to dominate – beyond our control – modernity's promise of autonomy, as outlined above. Our approach offers conceivable answers to the first challenge by developing a *methodological cosmopolitanism* and to the second by outlining the concept of a *democratic cosmopolitanism*.

Notes

1 This chapter is a slightly modified English translation of Ulrich Beck and Hartmut Rosa (2016): Eskalation der Nebenfolgen: Kosmopolitisierung, Beschleunigung und globale Risikosteigerung. In Jörn Lamla, Henning Laux, Hartmut Rosa and David Strecker (eds.), *Handbuch der Soziologie*, Konstanz: UVK, pp. 465–474. © regarding text contributions by Ulrich Beck: All rights reserved by Suhrkamp Verlag Berlin.
2 By contrast, the theory of world risk society (Beck 1992; 2013a) consciously focuses on these unintended ways in which modernity endangers itself and raises the question of how the social order based on the nation state unravels in the face of the catastrophes that threaten it and how this categorically transforms our understanding of power, social inequality, and the political.

References

Arrighi, G., 2010. *The Long Twentieth Century. Money, Power and the Origins of Our Time*. London: Verso.
Beck, U., 1992. *Risk Society. Toward a New Modernity*. London: Sage
Beck, U., 2000. *What is Globalization?* Cambridge: Polity Press.
Beck, U., 2005. *Power in the Global Age: A New Political Economy*. London: Polity Press.
Beck, U., 2006. *Cosmopolitan Vision*. Cambridge: Polity.
Beck, U., 2013a. *World at Risk*. Cambridge: Polity Press.
Beck, U., 2013b. *German Europe*. Cambridge: Polity Press.
Beck, U. and Beck-Gernsheim, E., 2014. *Distant Love: Personal Life in the Global Age*. Cambridge: Polity Press.
Beck, U. and Lau, C., eds., 2004. *Entgrenzung und Entscheidung: Was ist neu an der Theorie reflexiver Modernisierung?* Frankfurt/M: Suhrkamp.
Beck, Ulrich and Wehling, P., 2012. The Politics of Non-Knowing: An Emerging Area of Social and Political Conflict in Reflexive Modernity. In F.D. Rubio and P. Baert, eds. *The Politics of Knowledge*. London and New York: Routledge, 33–57.
Castells, M., 1996. *The Rise of the Network Society*. Malden, MA: Blackwell Publishing.

Harvey, D., 2006. *Spaces of Global Capitalism. Towards a Theory of Uneven Geographical Development*. London; Verso.

Held, D., McGrew, A.G., Goldblatt, D. and Perraton, J., 1999. *Global Transformations. Politics, Economics and Culture*. Cambridge: Polity.

Latour, B., 2005. *Reassembling the Social: An Introduction to Actor-Network-Theory*. Oxford and New York: Oxford University Press.

Laux, H., 2014. Soziologie der Existenzweisen: Bruno Latour. In J. Lamla, H. Laux, H. Rosa and D. Strecker, eds. *Handbuch der Soziologie*. Konstanz: UVK: 261–279.

Marx, K,, and Engels, F., 1848. The Communist Manifesto [online]. Available from: www.marxists.org/archive/marx/works/download/pdf/Manifesto.pdf.

Rosa, H., 2013a. *Social Acceleration. A New Theory of Modernity*. New York and Chichester: Columbia University Press

Rosa, H., 2013b. Historischer Fortschritt oder leere Progression? Das Fortschreiten der Moderne als kulturelles Versprechen und als struktureller Zwang. In U. Willems, D. Pollack, H. Basu, T. Gutmann and U. Spohn. *Moderne und Religion. Kontroversen um Modernität und Säkularisierung*. Bielefeld: Transcript, 117–142.

Rosa, H. and Scheuerman, B., 2009. *High-Speed Society: Social Acceleration, Power and Modernity*. University Park, PA: University Press.

Stichweh, R., 2000 *Die Weltgesellschaft*, Frankfurt/M: Suhrkamp.

Urry, J., 2002. *Global Complexity*, Oxford: Polity.

Wallerstein, I., 2011. *The Modern World-System, 4 volumes*. Berkeley: University of California Press.

Wobbe, T., 2000. *Weltgesellschaft*, Bielefeld: transcript.

12
CAPITALISM, CONSUMERISM AND DEMOCRACY IN CONTEMPORARY SOCIETIES

Karl-Michael Brunner, Michael Jonas and Beate Littig

Introduction

Capitalist economies and their particular forms of production, distribution and consumption have profound effects on the development of democracy. In this chapter, we examine the impact of current forms of consumerism on the development of democratic practices in contemporary societies, especially Europe and the United States. In these societies, consumption and production form the two sides of a coin (Warde 2005) and, along with the distribution that goes with them, involve complex interrelationships and processes of power. A whole range of production work steps are woven into everyday consumer practices, while energy, raw materials, tools and machines are used and consumed in the process. In contrast, the spheres of production (economy) and consumption (lifeworld) have increasingly gone their separate ways over the course of time and are now primarily brokered via anonymous markets. Looking to the future, any discussion of this topic thus needs to consider both these spheres, the power and governance structures in the markets as well as their ties to democracy and sustainable development. Our analysis of the corresponding interrelationships that come into play focuses on the transformation of contemporary liberal democracies. While we view the green economy as the mainstream concept that offers the greatest compromise when it comes to socio-economic change, we also recognize its incapacity to meet the demands of a comprehensive socio-ecological transformation and a departure from the dominant "imperial mode of living" (Brand and Wissen 2018).

Consumerism as socio-ecological problem and the response of the green economy

Development of consumerism

Consumerism is seen as a main cause and driver of the current socio-ecological crisis. In the social and economic sciences, consumerism usually refers to a material, market-mediated consumer culture in which personal needs and well-being are satisfied through the acquisition and consumption of goods and services. However, the underlying conception of consumerism is by no means unequivocal; opinions differ in particular between neoclassical economics and sociology of consumption scholars.

From a neoclassical economics perspective, consumption is a quasi byproduct of production. This view places the actual purchase act or decision to purchase specific goods or services at the center of the economic model of consumption; what happens to the procured goods or services in subsequent everyday life is of less interest in economic terms. The purchasers are viewed as individuals who make such decisions of their own free will. Accordingly, the purchase decision is driven by the pursuit of individual preferences, whose origins and forms are not examined further. In the meantime, this view has become the subject of heterodox criticism even among economists, particularly from environmental and ecological economists (Raworth 2017).

From a social sciences perspective, consumerism is more than just the mere purchase or use and consumption of commodified products. The modern-day consumerism phenomenon is better conveyed in the broader concept of the consumer culture, which describes the socio-cultural handling of material goods, attaches meanings to consumption and indicates and reproduces the socio-economic status of consumers (Sassatelli 2007). Although the social and socio-economic functions and origins of the consumption phenomenon were already discussed at the end of the nineteenth century by Thorstein Veblen ([1899] 1967), a corresponding, broad social sciences discourse started to develop in the 1960s with the critique of the overconsumption of goods in the "affluent society" (Galbraith 1958). Since then, consumption has been viewed as a central element in everyday practices in capitalist societies. According to Pierre Bourdieu's (1984) habitus theory, the prevailing consumer culture facilitates social distinction through the realization of lifestyle-specific taste preferences and thus reproduces the capitalist production and consumption rationale. In this respect, the spheres of production and private consumption are intrinsically linked. The American sociologist Juliet Schor uses the "work-and-spend cycle" argument to emphasize that modern consumerism can only be analyzed in connection with economic progress. In her influential book *The Overworked American* (Schor 1991), she argues that (not only in the United States) productivity growth no longer translates into more free time for the workforce, it results at best in more pay – and thus more consumer spending. She also shows in her later book *The Overspent American* (Schor 1998) that increased consumption is habit-forming and changes consumer preferences. At the same time, her empirical findings point to a positive correlation between watching a lot of TV and consumer spending; a finding that illustrates the malleability and targeted manipulation of consumer preferences and habits. A corresponding shift in the competitive aspirations of consumers is also evident – away from a horizontal ("keeping up with the Joneses") to a vertical orientation on the affluent, highly consumerist lifestyles of the top 20 percent of the (American) population. Schor explains this new form of consumerism primarily with the rise in social inequality that has been brought about by the neo-liberal policies since the 1980s and 1990s and has encouraged the consumptive competition for status. Yet, growing social inequality also means poverty, makes it more difficult for the poorer groups in society to maintain their status and increasingly excludes them from the purchase of consumer goods. Loans, debts and cheap products can at least temporarily reduce the threat of loss of status and thus maintain the rationale of consumerism. Yet increasing levels of debt can even trigger a global economic crisis – as the bursting of the US real-estate bubble in 2008 showed.

The ongoing rapid digital transformation of the economy, the generating and analysis of big data leads to new forms of (not only) consumer manipulation, mainly driven by private transnational companies. Digital information technologies allow for direct, personalized marketing practices and increased online shopping, even more facilitated by "moneyless" credit card paying. Yet the discussion of the consequences of digitalization for sustainable development of economy, society and humankind has just started (WBGU 2019). Whether digital sharing platforms will contribute to the reduction of material and energetic throughput or whether the convenience of shopping online will even increase it, is widely unclear (Santarius 2017). The effects of social media on consumerism is ambivalent, too: it can help to promote the attitudes of "must haves" as well as of sufficiency. So far, digitalization is often celebrated as the tool of environmental sustainability (Kuntsman and Rattle 2019), but negative effects are also evident (e.g. the growth of e-waste). Nevertheless, there are rising voices that ask for democratic control of digitalization and the use of digitalization to push on sustainable development; the initiative of the German Advisory Council for Global Change (WBGU) to focus in the Rio+30 conference in 2022 on the issues of digitalization and sustainability could help to make them heard internationally.

The green economy as hegemonic guiding principle of sustainable development

The criticisms of the twentieth-century consumer societies that developed with the establishment of Fordist manufacturing systems into mass consumer societies (cf. section 2.2) were initially led by the environmental movements that sprung up around the globe in the 1970s. Growing mountains of trash, high levels of air and water pollution, and the first oil crisis directed scientific and political attention to the limited absorption and re-creation capacities of our ecological systems and finiteness of our natural resources (Meadows 1972). The unintended environmental side-effects of mass production in the early industrialized nations thus became the target of the consumerism critics and led, at least to some extent, to a modernization of production, primarily through end-of-pipe environmental protection measures (filters, catalysts, etc.), and a politicization of Western consumer behavior. This ultimately manifested itself in 1992 at the UN's legendary Rio de Janeiro Earth Summit, where the establishment of sustainable production and consumption was launched as a global policy guideline. Chapter IV of the *Agenda 21* action plan refers to the need "[t]o promote patterns of consumption and production that reduce environmental stress and will meet the basic needs of humanity" (UNCED 1992). Women are a particular target group for the promoters of environmentally-friendly consumption since the gendered division of work in the home means they are (still) considered chiefly responsible for everyday household purchasing decisions; a notion criticized by feminists as a feminization of environmental protection that contributes to the reification of traditional gender roles (Littig 2018).

The broad guiding principle of sustainable development was reinforced in 2012 at the Rio+20 anniversary summit by the term "green economy". A "green new deal" should serve henceforth to reconcile economy and ecology and, not least, to address the consequences of the post-2008 economic and financial crisis. According to the *Future We Want* outcome document, the green economy should focus on technical innovations and energy/resource efficiency as drivers for growth, new jobs and the eradication of poverty and be supported, where needed, by moderate state control (UNCED 2012).

The notion of the green economy has long since gained broad consensus and has established itself as a hegemonic guiding principle, advocated by many international organizations. The EU's framework strategy, *Europe 2020*, also makes reference to the green economy and sees itself as a "new strategy for jobs and smart, sustainable and inclusive growth" (European Commission 2010). The new European Commission and the current president's "green deal" reinforce these goals. However, mainstream politics are currently challenged by growing international social movements, just to name the Degrowth-movement and Fridays for Future. Especially the latter has been successful at least on the discursive level, claiming for more radical climate policies and for global climate justice.

The green economy concept, which comprises various ideas relating to growth, efficiency and prosperity, was further affirmed by the UN's sustainable development goals (SDGs) (UN 2015). Adopted in 2015, a central goal of these SDGs is to promote "sustainable economic growth, employment and decent work for all" (Goal 8), which ties in closely with the goal to ensure "responsible consumption and production patterns" (Goal 12).

While the green economy builds worldwide on green economic growth, green full-employment societies and access by broad groups of society to green consumer products and services, its advocates also recognize that a sustainable management of resources and decoupling of economic growth and environmental consumption cannot be achieved through technological innovation and resource efficiency in production alone. When it comes to e-mobility, a (often euphoric) poster child for the green economy, they point to the need for a multimodal approach and innovative digitally-assisted sharing options for electric cars, bikes and scooters (European Commission 2011). While they do not call the actual use of private motor vehicles into question, limiting their criticism instead to the damage to the environment caused by carbon emissions from petrol vehicles, they omit to mention the production and (battery) disposal problems, high electricity consumption and infrastructure required for e-vehicles. In comparison to technical and incremental innovations, approaches like sufficiency – a new, low-resource notion of prosperity – or far-reaching social innovations supported by broad sections of the population still play a marginal role in the political mainstream of the green economy. Moreover, ecological modernization is often linked with the neoclassical concepts of freedom of consumer choice, where restrictions should be kept to an absolute minimum and influence only exerted – if at all – by incentives and gentle "nudging" (Keller, Halkier, and Wilska 2016; see section 3.2). Accordingly, the state assumes the role of a gently intervening, facilitating regulator, who sets incentives, offers appropriate (financial) compensation, but largely avoids the use of regulatory policy.

Some achievements (irrespective of social demands) towards environmental sustainability have clearly been made since the 1992 Rio summit. These include the (albeit modest in global terms) growth in renewable energies, increase in energy efficiency and growing reuse of resources and materials. While technological improvements have led to reductions in material and energy intensity, some of the gains are eaten up by growth effects, including the "rebound effect" (Santarius 2017). In many cases, manufacturing pollution is shifted to nations with lower social and environmental standards, thus significantly improving the environmental records of the externalizing nations (Lessenich 2019).

Although the green economy can so far be seen more as a political declaration of intent towards environmental modernization, it has at least spurred the critics. Brand and Wissen (2018) label it an exclusive "modernization project" that mainly benefits the early industrialized nations in the capitalist centers and the aspiring middle classes in the emerging nations. This will, in the end, uphold and perpetuate the global proliferation of the imperial mode of living. The core thinking behind this concept is that everyday life in the capitalist centers essentially shapes societal relationships and relationships with nature elsewhere. The Global North depends in essence on unlimited extractivism and the labor capacity, natural resources and wells in the Global South. This relationship of dependency and exploitation reproduces itself through inequality, power and hegemony and even in some cases by direct force (Barth, Jochum and Littig 2019).

Resource-intensive consumerism and modes of production: past and present

Historical roots

The consumer practices that currently dominate in the northern hemisphere's liberal democracies are rooted in development processes that date back to the expansion of the European empires including the conquering of South and Central America from the fifteenth century onwards, the expansion of the slavery-based economy, the introduction of the workshop system in Europe, the industrial revolution as well as the introduction of Fordist mass production. Further relevant elements are a progressive increase and internationalization of raw materials and goods flows as well as the separation of production and reproduction (Komlosy 2013). The existing resource extraction and exploitation practices (Adebanwi 2017) in the northern nations and their southern colonies were hereby intensified and remain in place to this day.

The special position enjoyed by the European habitats is clearly illustrated in the relevance of meat consumption. While people in the rest of the world followed a primarily vegetarian diet from the fifteenth to the eighteenth centuries, Europe experienced periods of prosperity, which benefited its entire population, the majority of whom had a diet based on regionally produced meat. In the eighteenth century, growing population numbers necessitated a radical switch to a plant-based diet. It was not until the mid-nineteenth century that scientifically managed animal husbandry and the large-scale import of meat permitted a return to the excessive consumption of meat (Braudel 1979a). In its present hegemonic form, meat consumption is no longer practiced solely by (primarily male) consumers in Europe and North America but is also considered worth emulating by (primarily male) members of the aspiring middle classes, for instance in Asian nations.

In the eighteenth century, eating habits began to change radically, and different crops like rice, maize, wheat and even potatoes (with exceptions) spread worldwide. Like the potato, maize was initially used to feed the poor – along with staples like salt, pepper, eggs, fish and sugar, the latter imported from slave-based production in the sugar colonies. Drinking water supplies were inadequate both in dry and urban regions. Even cities that stood on the banks of major rivers did not have sufficient drinking water because these rivers were used extensively for waste and wastewater disposal. There were also huge differences when it came to housing, clothing or furnishings.

During this period, the forerunners to a public sphere emerged in some Western European countries in the form of social inner spaces. Access to these spaces, which developed into protected communication zones for the bourgeois male in the gap between the patriarchal private sphere and government power, was largely determined by wealth. However, the French Revolution (ca. 1790) led to the strengthening of arenas in the emerging public sphere across Europe (Honneth 2014), quasi concluding the era of bourgeois enlightenment.

Industrialization was yet another fundamental development process that began in Great Britain and went on to shape not only the United States but also other European regions. In quantitative terms, the textile industry was the most influential of the early industrial sectors and satisfied the increase in demand for yarn and cloth that arose during the industrial revolution through population growth, urbanization and the rise in paid work (König 2000). While the cotton was supplied by its colonies, it was processed in Great Britain, which thus entered into competition with the respective manufacturing industry in India, ultimately outstripping the latter in the late eighteenth century with the aid of its mechanical prowess (Braudel 1979b). Since it was largely no longer able to compete effectively in the protectionist European markets, Great Britain intensified its trade relations with the American colonies (and soon-to-be-formed

United States) and India. This expansion in world trade served – alongside rationalization, mechanization and the assertion of capitalist economic modes – as the main driving force for the industrial revolution. Aside from the industrial strongholds in Great Britain, industry development in Europe was initially niche-based. Mines and factories lay isolated in traditional peasant farming environments where living conditions were shaped by a subsistence economy. The substitution of charcoal with cheaper hard coal led to a huge surge in industrial regions like the Ruhr area in Germany with its large-scale iron and steel production and processing plants. This was accompanied by a massive exploitation of natural resources, rapid urbanization, population growth and proletarianization processes which forced new (capitalist industry) working hours and modes on the working classes over many decades (Thompson 1967). It was also the period that saw the emergence of a so-called leisure class (Veblen [1899] 1967), a time in which conspicuous consumption served as a means of expression of the bourgeoisie and which had its own urban centers of trade with luxury goods like the covered arcades in Paris.

The nineteenth century was also the period in which the middle classes won the right to political participation in a patriarchal society, as evidenced in the extension of suffrage to all men (but not women) and the granting of the right of assembly or right to form political associations. The emergence of political public spheres is *de facto* linked to the formation of the nation states in the nineteenth century, whose outwardly limited and inwardly borderless communication spaces now allowed the identification and open negotiation of topics of mutual interest (Honneth 2014).

In the decades around the turn of the twentieth century, economic growth in the European industrial nations was accompanied by a strong expansion in world trade. The growth of key industrial nations like Great Britain, the United States and Germany stemmed chiefly from export industries like metal processing or mechanical engineering, not from consumer goods industries. These nations imported raw materials and foodstuffs from non-industrialized (colonial) regions. The industrial goods they exported to them were used to build the emerging supplier industries in these regions. These processes were interrupted by World War I.

From Fordism to post-Fordism

But it is these industrialization processes that led after World War I and from the 1920s onwards to initial surges of mass production and consumption, first in the United States and then in the European industrial nations – where they were not, however, initially able to replace the then widespread manual-industrial bulk manufacturing system and its subsistence economy consumer practices. Referred to using the term Fordism, these industrialization processes would not have managed to develop and assert themselves without the extraction of natural resources, in particular crude oil (Zündorf 2008). Oil production began in the mid-nineteenth century in the United States, which remained the primary oil-producing nation until World War II when it ceded this position to the Arab states. In relation to the production processes, the relevant term Fordism means mass production and rationalization. Its practices of production-friendly construction, standardization, increase in material, energy and information flows, automation, mechanization and, last but by no means least, shift-based, 24/7 production – penetrated – albeit in different ways – all industrial processes and procedures. The new Fordist production paradigm brought both mass production and mass consumption. A form of social contract between employers and employees bound these together and transformed – first in the United States in the 1920s – some of the profits of mass production into mass consumption (automobiles, household goods, etc.). It was the "roaring twenties", a period in which the public were slowly gaining more democratic rights – as reflected in the extension of the right to vote to women but also the emergence of consumer (protection) rights and cooperative organizations – which thus illustrated the weak democratic structures in the economic sphere. At the same time, however, the emergence and journalistic orientation of mass media (like the daily press or radio) and the global economic crisis triggered development processes in the public sphere that fended off democracy (Dewey 1927). Economic prosperity in the United States in the 1920s was sustained chiefly by strong domestic demand, this situation was not repeated in the European economic spheres. In addition to the emerging industrial sector, Europe also had a strong traditional economic sector, the like of which could never have evolved in the United States. At the same time – and in contrast to the United States – real earnings in Europe were rising at a far slower rate than productivity growth in the industrial sector, thus preventing a comparable spread of mass consumption. In the period between the two world wars, around half of the workforce in France and Germany (but not Great Britain) was still employed in the traditional economic sector. Most of the money earned in wages or salaries in the industrial market economy sectors was used to cover direct living costs and was spent in the traditional sector. In 1907, on average around half of all consumer expenditure in Germany went on foods, around one-fifth on housing and household needs and just over one-tenth on clothing. Most of the foods consumed by private households reached consumers via short trade routes with limited transport overheads. Most of the expenditure on clothing also flowed into the traditional sector. Consumers did not usually purchase ready-made garments. They bought fabric instead, which was made into clothes either at home or in sewing workshops (Lutz 1989).

The fragility of the emerging industrial capitalist democracies can be seen not least in the seizure of power by the National Socialists in Germany and the strengthening of radical right-wing political currents in a number of European nations, a situation that reached its absolute low point in the actions of the German Reich in World War II and the Shoah.

The post-war reconstruction phase in the early 1950s saw massive economic growth in all European industrial nations, a trend that would later be repeated in Asia. It was only from this time onwards that we can really talk of the existence of Fordist or modern states in Europe that were founded on the division of labor and mechanization and bound to the principles of mass prosperity and loyalty (Lutz 1989). In many European nations, the traditional sector was swiftly absorbed by the industrial market economy. Paid work became the primary form of labor in the Western democracies. It cemented the previous distinction between productive/unproductive labor as well as the assertion of male employment as the standard and the near total banishment of the female workforce into unpaid reproductive work. These processes triggered a period of economic prosperity in many Western industrial nations, the ecological and social impacts of which ultimately became apparent from the 1970s onwards. By 1971, there were clear signs of an end to post-war Fordism (Streeck 2012): markets were saturated with mass-produced, standardized consumer goods, economic crises were common, and growth had reached its limits. This led to a fundamental restructuring of manufacturing processes and ranges, an influx of women into the labor market, de-standardization and sustained, intensified globalization, but no slow-down whatsoever in the continued and increasing extraction of natural resources and living beings. The diversification of product ranges and associated conversion of the markets from satisfying needs to realizing wishes prevailed on a large scale. These processes are characterized by increased product differentiation, accelerated stock turnover and precise marketing, which establish a new type of sociation in contemporary post-Fordist societies. This new type of sociation by excessive consumption (Joy 2010) can be seen, for instance, in the unlimited consumption of meat (in combination with husbandry practices that show disregard for animal life), the rising air traffic levels in the mass tourism and independent travel sectors (in combination with a disproportionate emission of harmful pollutants) or the increasing demand for low-cost clothing or electronics (in combination with unjust working conditions and massive pollution of the environment above all in Asian and African countries).

This type of sociation also replaces political participation with individualized consumerism: post-modern patterns of consumption are individualistic and no longer collectivist, "alienated rather than synergistic, and private rather than public" (Banerjee and Linstead 2001, 698). Elements thereof progressively penetrate public patterns of interaction and communication. The result is a gradual re-privatization of the public sphere, which increasingly risks becoming just a meeting place for consumers who act solely on their own (Honneth 2014).

These trends do not point towards fundamental socio-ecological change (Jonas 2017). On the contrary, the modern-day capitalist economy is not sustainable either in intra-generational or inter-generational terms. Measured by international treaties like the Paris Climate Agreement, it is becoming increasingly clear that "politically palatable options of focusing on marginal lifestyle changes and technical efficiencies" (Welch and Southerton 2019, 32) will not suffice. Efforts to broaden sustainable patterns of consumption are being thwarted by the global rise in resource-intensive consumption: the global consumer class is growing at a rate of 140 million people per year (Kharas 2017). The persistence of social sustainability problems indicates that the global escalation in unsustainable patterns of production and consumption must be molded by a radical transformation of the imperial forms of life if we are to meet the equality imperatives of sustainable development.

Socio-ecological transformation paths in consumer democracies

How should socio-ecological transformation in consumer democracies be achieved if it is to meet the goals of sustainable development on the one hand and be democratic on the other? In this section, we identify key positions in the debate on the relationship between consumerism, democracy and sustainability and examine their transformation potential. Since a full discussion of the many and diverse elements in this debate would exceed the scope of this article, we have restricted ourselves thereby to providing a brief outline of these positions and potentials.

Consumption lock-in between post-politics and bottom-up democratization

This position assumes a societal lock-in in which the current economic or political structures stabilize unsustainable production and consumption patterns. There are two variants to this position. The first, a post-political "democracy of unsustainability" (Blühdorn 2018), expresses fundamental doubts in the link between sustainability and democracy. These relate: a) to the potential limitations of a liberal democracy (e.g. sluggishness or fixation on the present) in addressing urgent sustainability problems as well as to the close ties between the development of modern European democracy; and b) to environmentally destructive industrialization in general. Seen from this perspective, democracy and democratization would have themselves become the greenhouse of the growth paradigm and the accelerant for the destruction of nature (Blühdorn 2018, 160) in order to serve the rights of participation of the majority and hinder political distribution conflicts. Mitchell (2011) talks in this regard of a "carbon democracy", thus pointing to the biophysical materiality of democratic institutions and participation (Pichler, Brand and Görg 2018). In the neo-liberal, post-political constellation, democracy has metamorphosed into a means of politically organizing and legitimating global social inequality and exclusion, i.e. into a "democracy of unsustainability". While the social movements of the 1960s and 1970s still viewed ecologization and democratization as an indivisible unit and called for an ecologically sustainable democracy, opinions of this indivisibility are now ambivalent. For one thing, there are increasing doubts as to whether a technocratic, management-like solution to the environmental question can actually be achieved by democratic means. Moreover, the cultural basis to formulate political regulations in the name of higher values or collective goals would diminish in a "liquid modernity" (Bauman 2000), since identity would be increasingly linked to consumerism, and the middle-class ideal of the stable identity would crumble. According to Blühdorn (2018, 167), the individualistic liberal principle has clearly gained the upper hand over its integrative, egalitarian, social and communal counterpart. The "sociation by consumption" (2012, 35) postulated by Streeck also pertains to the champions of democratic environmental transformation encountered primarily in the educated middle classes. Consumerism in the post-Fordist era appears to be an important means of self-enactment and articulation for flexible, multilayered and conflicting identities and also fulfils a key subjectivation function for pro-sustainability milieus. According to Blühdorn, critical and creative people tend to cultivate more resource- and energy-intensive lifestyles than the average person and are thus also more likely to defend consumerism in this form. In a growth economy, the lower-income classes could also participate in this world. However, this focus on the material dimension – which transcends class and is problematic in sustainability policy terms – and its associated identity building ultimately fall under pressure in a *de facto* post-growth society, become more socially selective, lead to the exclusion of financially weak groups within a society and strengthen right-wing populist currents. Under these conditions, democracy would shift from a mechanism of inclusion to one of exclusion to maintain unsustainable lifestyles and modes of business and stabilize the imperial mode of living. The state is thus seen not as an architect of socio-ecological change but rather an actor trying to maintain the satisfaction rationale of growth and consumption under increasingly aggravated conditions.

The democracy of unsustainability position paints a very self-contained picture of politics and society in an unsustainable economy when politics increasingly loses its legitimacy. Social milieus that support sustainability are themselves seen as inseparable from unsustainable styles of life, while activists who criticize the system are branded as naïve illusionists.

The theory behind the imperial mode of living (Brand and Wissen 2018) shares – albeit with a different slant – the diagnosis of unsustainable sociation by consumption but considers this system to be challenged by critical social movements fighting for a democratization of society's relations to nature. This approach assumes that the current unsustainable production and consumption patterns are a result of the capitalist economy and its focus on profits at the expense of people and nature. While a fundamental crisis in the relationships between society and nature is postulated, this does not mean that the former questions this system to any great extent. Institutional and specific societal normalization processes regulate these relationships and thus appear quasi "natural". The destructive nature of society's handling of nature remains latent and is viewed as manageable (and hence acceptable), since the costs are spatially and temporally externalized. A politicization of society's relationship to nature can be prevented for a certain period of time. In the tradition of historical materialism, the state is viewed as a fundamental component of social power and governance structures, which it seeks to stabilize and legitimize in corresponding institutions. The international institutions of neo-liberal imperial globalization used by strong economic and political elites to secure the status quo also work to this effect. The imperial mode of living means "living well at other's expense" (Lessenich 2019). Hence, everyday life in the capitalist centers is largely facilitated by the structure of societal relationships and society's relationship to nature elsewhere through the unlimited access to labor capacity and natural resources/wells. In line with the work of Antonio Gramsci, it is assumed that the capitalist mode of social formation can only be reproduced if it is anchored in everyday practices and thought, thus becoming quasi "normal". Consumerism as social participation assumes a central role in this normalization process. But the imperial mode of living is challenged by social initiatives which politicize ecology as a social issue and develop counter-hegemonic concepts. Such groups demonstrate the outlines of a supportive, fair way of life that focuses on democratizing society's relationships with nature (Brand and Wissen 2018). Their guiding principle is an emphatic understanding of democracy with elements like freedom of realization, equality in decision making, solidarity, cooperation, etc. The liberal democracy is thereby more of a hindrance than a means of socio-ecological transformation: what is actually needed is a "democratization of democracy" and a reconstruction of the state as an institution towards a full democratization of society.

> Democratization furthermore requires the politicization of the power relations and inequalities that are reproduced *through* contemporary liberal democracies – particularly through the separation of the political from the economic. A democratization of democracy implies acknowledging the biophysical limits of economic growth and democratic procedures to negotiate these limits.
>
> Pichler, Brand and Görg 2018, 15

Societal relations to nature are seen from this perspective as contingent and contested. In other words, counterhegemonic movements that promote a radical, democratic transformation towards sustainability can develop even under the hegemony of the imperial mode of living and the attractiveness of its unsustainable patterns of consumption. One problem with this approach is its elevation of what can be extremely heterogeneous movements and initiatives (whose influence on the imperial mode of living has not yet been studied empirically) to the new "transformation subject" at the edges of society. When it comes to the democratization of democracy, the proponents of this approach still need to spell out how this democratization would be organized and institutionalized in a highly complex society and how the existing relations of power should be changed (cf. section 3.3).

The green economy: consumerist democracy as choice?

In green economy concepts and the ecological modernization approach, consumers are frequently addressed – in the neoclassical economics sense – as the drivers of market activity and at the same time – alongside business – as the people who are responsible for a sustainable economy. In doing so, these concepts draw on the notion of competent, responsible or even "reflexive" consumers, who act rationally and make informed choices based on the information available to them. This ideal is embraced by many players in business, politics and civil society, even though it does not usually reflect everyday consumer practices. In its underlying concepts, consumerism (as already indicated in section 1.1) is frequently reduced to individual decisions, without giving adequate consideration to societal relationships, social and cultural contexts or even routines and (infra)structural restrictions. The green economy banks on responsible purchase and consumption decisions, i.e. on a moralization of this behavior and the sustainable use and consumption of the goods in question. Yet the marketing of moralized goods and the much-lauded consumer power contribute more to individualizing sustainable development and making sustainability a matter of lifestyle and distinction practices (Brunner 2014). "Soft" political instruments should encourage changes in consumer attitudes and enable "reflexive" consumers to assume responsibility. Labeling schemes are seen thereby as key control instruments. Intermediaries (consumer organizations, professional experts and the like) help mediating between production and consumption by influencing motivations, values, knowledge and the coordination of actors in the market for sustainable products. Such transition intermediaries can positively influence sustainability processes by linking actors and activities (Kivimaa et al. 2019). But state interventions in the markets should be kept to a minimum. The success of this market-oriented strategy in bringing about change has as yet been modest, even with regard to the "greening" of manufacturing to achieve eco-efficient production, green supply chains and green jobs. While incremental changes can be identified in some fields (e.g. food), they are very demanding, advance at a slow pace and have not made the (food) system fundamentally sustainable (Brunner and Littig 2017). Moreover, the concept fails to answer the question of sufficiency, an issue that is paramount for an inter- and intra-generational, fair transformation of the economy. It also restricts democracy to the political system and "freedom" of consumer choice; a potential democratization of the capitalist economy is not foreseen.

Transformation from the bottom up: from sustainable consumer experiments to radical democratic post-growth movements

While advocates of the "democracy of unsustainability" see civil activists as defenders of the unsustainable status quo in times of increased struggle, and proponents of the green economy regard them as potentially sustainable market participants, others (e.g. approaches critical of capitalism) view civil society as the driver of more or less radical socio-ecological change. Top-down approaches to socio-ecological change need to be augmented or replaced by bottom-up citizens' and consumer initiatives to drive this change forward (Wilhite 2016). Yet the bandwidth of civil movements, initiatives and experiments surrounding sustainability is large. Jaeger-Erben, Rückert-John and Schäfer (2015) investigated the spectrum of "social innovations for sustainable consumption practices" in Germany and found a "great variety of bottom-up initiatives, organizational settings as well as innovative services which are also described with terms like collaborative consumption, sharing economy, communing and presuming" (Jaeger-Erben, Rückert-John and Schäfer 2015, 785). These can range from swap networks or DIY workshops to community farms or energy cooperatives, each of which differs (at times significantly) in their innovativeness or communality. Some sustainable consumption alternatives are less demanding than others when it comes to their differences in diffusion strength and transformation potential. Boström and Klintman (2018) subdivide political consumerism into alternative consumption (consuming differently) and anticonsumerism (consuming less). Many of the innovations studied by Jaeger-Erben, Rückert-John and Schäfer fall more into the alternative consumption category and only differ from individual sustainable consumption in the green economy in their collective nature. Empirical findings are rather sobering when it comes to the transformation potential of such initiatives: Frenken and Schor (2017) identify fairly ambivalent economic, social and environmental effects for the sharing economy, which so far do not live up to the partly emphatic expectations. Digital platforms could change the relationship between ownership and the provision of goods and services, but up to now, there are tendencies of decommodification as well as intensified commodification (Welch and Southerton 2019). Very often, consumers as "digital prosumers" become unpaid quasi-employees of a company (Staab 2017). There does not, however, appear to be a "one size fits all" approach that can accommodate the variety of civil society transformation approaches. Harold Wilhite talks in this regard of "intentional communities" that are rarely explicitly critical of capitalism, noting however that "many of them nonetheless either explicitly or implicitly challenge one or more of the pillars of capitalism: economic growth, individual ownership, consumerism and traditional market exchange" (Wilhite 2016, 103). A common characteristic of these communities is that they are based on civil society self-organization (Adloff 2018, 301) and are often organized as grassroots democracies. Energy cooperatives, for example, are not aimed specifically against the capitalist economy but they do work according to democratic principles and thus represent a non-capitalist element that increasingly enhances capitalist goods with public and cooperative alternatives (Boddenberg and Klemisch 2018, 280). At the radical-democratic end of the civil society initiative scale lie those social initiatives and approaches that question the imperial mode of living and focus on democratizing society's relationships with nature (Brand and Wissen 2018). These should afford an escape from the pressure for growth in capitalist societies and lead to new welfare models and a dematerialization of production and consumption. They also question the "half democracy" in which the principle of democratic self-determination only applies to the public sphere of the political system. The economy itself should be based on and controlled by democratic principles. This should also apply to the ostensibly "private, apolitical" area of reproduction, which is questioned in particular in gender relations terms (Biesecker and Hofmeister 2010). It remains to be seen, however, whether these social movements and initiatives can mobilize the necessary support for radical socio-ecological change (Adloff 2018). In the case of socio-ecological innovations, it is also questionable whether the social experimental spaces for sustainable practices can move out of their niches to bring about change at regime level and thus facilitate a sustainable economy. At present, this only appears to be happening to a limited extent.

Conclusions

The most widespread concept of socio-ecological change in modern-day liberal-democratic consumer societies is that of the green economy/ecological modernization, a concept which builds on incremental improvements but is not linked to a trend towards a "sustainability transition" as a "fundamental change in structure, culture and practices" (Rotmans and Loorbach 2010, 109). While its potential to bring about transformation has hitherto been limited, a future rise therein that is triggered by crisis developments – including increased requirements for political control – cannot be entirely ruled out. It is doubtful whether the post-political democracy of unsustainability, which ultimately postulates a doomsday scenario for unsustainable trends in the economy, politics and society (and whose central sociation mode lies in unsustainable patterns of consumption), adequately represents the ambivalence to these trends or the learning processes triggered by sustainability challenges in various sectors of society and on diverse (even political) levels. If the state as a "partner in crime" to the economy and society for growth and the status quo fails at least in the post-political and anti-capitalist approaches as a top-down agent of change and also constitutes a relatively weak "sustainability pioneer" in the green economy approaches, this change could potentially be expedited by radical-democratic bottom-up approaches. The central role played by environmental and other movements in socio-ecological transformation is undisputed. However – and as we have shown – their transformative effect is limited. Fundamental socio-ecological change in highly complex societies is an extremely demanding undertaking. There is neither a master plan nor *one single* actor that can deliver this change. All manner of different actors with different powers of action and their own respective levels of institutionalization and rationales come up against each other to negotiate profound conflicts of values, interests and power in the societal debate on sustainability, the outcome of which is unpredictable. Such processes are emergent, heterogeneous, contradictory, contentious and embattled (Brand 2017).

Currently, the Green Economy is the hegemonic framing of international sustainability discourses and politics and there are only weak signs for more radical transformations in contemporary societies. More and more emerging economies are buying into this development model (McNeill and Wilhite 2015). Recent climate change policy programs in countries like Germany and Austria (or GB) show that sustainable production and consumption policies are for the most part market-oriented, based on incremental improvements, and avoid tackling the problem of over-consumption. Sufficiency policies are nowhere to be seen in the countries of the North. Comparative empirical studies on sustainable welfare show a relative decoupling of CO_2 emissions from social and individual welfare in many countries, but no evidence of an absolute decoupling. The main problem of rich countries lies in "unsustainable consumption", as "all other prosperity indicators correlate negatively with 'clean consumption'" (Fritz and Koch 2016, 47). Although the Green Economy has delivered limited sustainability outcomes so far, it will remain the politically most palatable sustainability strategy of liberal democracies in the near future.

References

Adebanwi, W., 2017. Africa's 'Two Publics': Colonialism and Governmentality. *Theory, Culture & Society*, 34 (4), 65–87.
Adloff, F., 2018. Zivilgesellschaft in der sozialökologischen Krise. *Forschungsjournal Soziale Bewegungen*, 31 (1–2), 298–309.
Banerjee, S.B. and Linstead, S., 2001. Globalism, Multiculturalism and Other Fictions: Colonialism for the New Millennium. *Organization*, 8 (4), 683–722.
Barth, T., Jochum, G. and Littig, B., 2019. Machtanalytische Perspektiven auf (nicht-)nachhaltige Arbeit. *WSI-Mitteilungen*, 72 (1), 3–12.
Bauman, Z., 2000. *Liquid Modernity*. Cambridge: Polity Press.
Biesecker, A. and Hofmeister, S., 2010. Focus: (Re)productivity. Sustainable Relations Both Between Society and Nature and Between the Genders. *Ecological Economics*, 69 (8), 1703–1711.
Blühdorn, I., 2018. Nicht-Nachhaltigkeit auf der Suche nach einer politischen Form. Konturen einer demokratischen Postwachstumsgesellschaft. *Berliner Journal für Soziologie*, 28, 151–180.
Boddenberg, M. and Klemisch, H., 2018. Bürgerbeteiligung in Zeiten der Postdemokratie – Das Beispiel der Energiegenossenschaften. In J. Radtke and N. Kersting, eds. *Energiewende: Politikwissenschaftliche Perspektiven*. Wiesbaden: Springer, 269–288.
Boström, M. and Klintman, M., 2018. Mass consumption and Political Consumerism. In M. Böstrom, M. Micheletti and P. Oosterveer, eds. *The Oxford Handbook of Political Consumerism*. Oxford: Oxford University Press, 855–975.
Bourdieu, P., 1984. *Distinction. A social Critique of the Judgement of Taste*. Cambridge: Harvard University Press.
Brand, K.W., 2017. Theoretischer und historischer Interpretationsrahmen. In K.W. Brand, ed. *Die sozialökologische Transformation der Welt. Ein Handbuch*. Frankfurt: Campus, 35–152.
Brand, U. and Wissen, M., 2018. *The Limits to Capitalist Nature: Theorizing and Overcoming the Imperial Mode of Living*. London: Rowman & Littlefield.
Braudel, F., 1979a. *Civilization and Capitalism, 15th–18th Century. The Structure of Everyday Life*. Berkeley: University of California Press.
Braudel, F., 1979b. *Civilization and Capitalism, 15th–18th Century. The Perspective of the World*. Berkeley: University of California Press.
Brunner, K.-M., 2014. *Nachhaltiger Konsum und soziale Ungleichheit*. Wien: AK.
Brunner, K.-M. and Littig, B., 2017. Nachhaltige Produktion, nachhaltiger Konsum, nachhaltige Arbeit. The Greening of Capitalism? In K.W. Brand, ed. *Die sozial-ökologische Transformation der Welt. Ein Handbuch*. Frankfurt: Campus, 215–242.
Dewey, J., 1927. *The Public and its Problems*. New York: H. Holt and Company.
European Commission, 2011. *Roadmap to a Single European Transport Area – towards a competitive and resource efficient transport system, EC Transport White Paper* [online]. https://ec.europa.eu/transport/themes/strategies/2011_white_paper_en.
European Commission, 2010. *Europe 2020. A European Strategy for Smart, Sustainable, and Inclusive Growth*. Brussels: EU.
Frenken, K. and Schor, J., 2017. Putting the Sharing Economy into Perspective. *Environmental Innovation and Societal Transitions*, 23, 3–10.

Fritz, M. and Koch, M., 2016. Economic Development and Prosperity Patterns Around the World: Structural Challenges for a Global Steady-State-Economy. *Global Environmental Change*, 38, 41–48.

Galbraith, J.K., 1958. *The Affluent Society*. Boston: Houghton Mifflin.

Honneth, A., 2014. *Freedom's Right. The Social Foundation of Democratic Life*. New York: Columbia University Press.

Jaeger-Erben, M., Rückert-John, J. and Schäfer, M., 2015. Sustainable Consumption Through Social Innovation: A Typology of Innovations for Sustainable Consumption Practices. *Journal of Cleaner Production*, 108, 784–798.

Jonas, M., 2017. Transition or Transformation of Societal Practices and Orders? A Plea for a Critical Praxeological Approach of Radical Societal Change. In M. Jonas and B. Littig, eds. *Praxeological Political Analysis*. London: Routledge, 116–133.

Joy, M., 2010. *Why we Love Dogs, Eat Pigs and Wear Cows. An Introduction into Carnism*. San Francisco: Conari.

Keller, M., Halkier, B. and Wilska, T.A., 2016. Policy and Governance for Sustainable Consumption at the Crossroads of Theories and Concepts. *Environmental Policy and Governance*, 26, 75–88.

Kharas, H., 2017. *The Unprecedented Expansion of the Global Middle Class: An Update*. Washington: Brookings Institute.

Kivimaa, P., Boon, W., Hyysalo, S. and Klerkx, L., 2019. Towards a Typology of Intermediaries in Sustainability Transitions: A Systematic Review and Research Agenda. *Research Policy*, 48, 1062–1075.

Komlosy, A., 2013. Transitions in Global Labor History, 1250–2010: Entanglements, Synchronicities, and Combinations on a Local and a Global Scale. *Review Fernand Braudel Center*, 36 (2), 155–190.

König, W., 2000. *Geschichte der Konsumgesellschaft*. Stuttgart: Franz Steiner.

Kuntsman, A. and Rattle, I., 2019. Towards a Paradigmatic Shift in Sustainability Studies: A Systematic Review of Peer Reviewed Literature and Future Agenda Setting to Consider Environmental (Un) Sustainability of Digital Communication. *Environmental Communication*, 13 (5), 567–581.

Lessenich, S., 2019. *Living well at Other's Expense: The Hidden Costs of Western Prosperity*. Cambridge: Polity Press.

Littig, B., 2018. Good Work? Sustainable Work and Sustainable Development: A Critical Gender Perspective from the Global North. *Special Issue of Globalizations: Labour in the Web of Life*, 15 (4), 565–579.

Lutz, B., 1989. *Der kurze Traum immerwährender Prosperität*. Frankfurt: Campus.

McNeill, D. and Wilhite, H., 2015. Making Sense of Sustainable Development in a Changing World. In A. Hansen and U. Wethal, eds. *Emerging Economies and Challenges to Sustainability*. London: Routledge, 34–49.

Meadows, D., 1972. *The Limits to Growth. A Global Challenge. A Report for the Club of Rome Project on the Predicament of Mankind*. New York: Universe Books.

Mitchell, T., 2011. *Carbon Democracy: Political Power in the age of oil*. New York: Verso.

Pichler, M., Brand, U. and Görg, C., 2018. The Double Materiality of Democracy in Capitalist Societies: Challenges for Social-Ecological Transformations. *Environmental Politics*, 29 (2), 193–213.

Raworth, K., 2017. *Doughnut Economics: Seven Ways to Think Like a 21st-Century Economist*. London: Random House.

Rotmans, J. and Loorbach, D., 2010. Towards a Better Understanding of Transition and Their Governance. A Systemic and Reflexive Approach. In J. Grin, J. Rotmans and J. Schot, eds. *Transitions to Sustainable Development: New Directions in the Study of Long Term Transformative Change*. New York: Routledge, 105–220.

Santarius, T., 2017. *Digitalization, Efficiency and the Rebound Effect* [online]. www.degrowth.info/de/2017/02/digitalization-efficiency-and-the-rebound-effect/.

Sassatelli, R., 2007. *Consumer Culture: History, Theory and Politics*. London: SAGE.

Schor, J., 1991. *The Overworked American. The Unexpected Decline of Leisure*. New York: HarperCollins.

Schor, J., 1998. *The Overspent American. Why We Want What We Don't Need*. New York: HarperCollins.

Staab, P., 2017. The Consumption Dilemma of Digital Capitalism. *Transfer*, 23(3), 281–294.

Streeck, W., 2012. Citizens as Customers: Considerations on the New Politics of Consumption. *New Left Review*, 78, 27–47.

Thompson, E.P., 1967. Time, Work-Discipline, and Industrial Capitalism. *Past & Present*, 38, 56–97.

UNCED (United Nations Conference on Environment and Development), 1992. *Agenda 21*. https://sustainabledevelopment.un.org/outcomedocuments/agenda21.

UNCED (United Nations Conference on Environment and Development), 2012. *Future We Want*. https://sustainabledevelopment.un.org/index.php?menu=1298.

UN (United Nations), 2015. *Sustainable Development Goals.* www.un.org/sustainabledevelopment/.
Veblen, T., (1899) 1967. *The Theory of the Leisure Class.* New York: Penguin Press.
Warde, A., 2005. Consumption and Theories of Practice. *Journal of Consumer Culture,* 5 (2), 131–153.
WBGU (German Advisory Council for Global Change), 2019. *Towards our Common Digital Future. A Flagship Report. BerlIn WBGU.* www.wbgu.de/en/publications/publication/towards-our-common-digital-future.
Welch, D. and Southerton, D., 2019. After Paris: Transitions for Sustainable Consumption. *Sustainability: Science, Practice and Policy,* 15 (1), 31–44.
Wilhite, H., 2016. *The Political Economy of Low Carbon Transformation.* London: Routledge.
Zündorf, L., 2008. *Das Weltsystem des Erdöls: Entstehungszusammenhang, Funktionsweise, Wandlungstendenzen.* Wiesbaden: VS.

13
POWER AND DEMOCRACY IN THE TRANSITION TO SUSTAINABILITY

Lena Partzsch

Introduction

A growing number of scholars studying power and sustainability are questioning the potential of representative democracy to address the ecological crisis. They argue, for example, that sustainability efforts reinforce asymmetries based on class, race, gender, and other social constructs. These scholars direct attention to economic structures and ideational discourses, which have produced a world in which the distribution of benefits and burdens is deeply and unfairly skewed (Lövbrand et al. 2009; Stripple and Bulkeley 2013). Change is only considered possible if it fits with the interests and rationalities of a few dominant actors and the neoliberal hegemony, which agents intentionally, or unintentionally, reproduce (Fuchs et al. 2016; Okereke et al. 2009). Complementing these studies, I have made and continue to make a strong claim for acknowledging the capacity of agency, or agents, in debates about power and sustainability (Partzsch and Weiland 2015; Partzsch 2017).

While admitting that structure and agency are mutually constitutive in an ongoing process (Cerny 2000; Hayward and Lukes 2008), I am interested in the types of relations through which agents can bring about a 'turnaround' and how this can happen in a democratic way. In this respect, I present key components of the debate on power and agency by identifying different perceptions of power that are common to sustainability research along three ideal-type conceptions: *power over* (coercion and manipulation), *power to* (resistance and empowerment) and *power with* (cooperation and learning) (Allen 1998; Haugaard 2011). In addition to my earlier works, I outline links of power and agency to democracy and sustainability in this chapter.

I begin by introducing the three conceptions of power. I then illustrate in three sections how studies on the transition to sustainability have applied them. At the end of each section, I outline how each conception relates to democracy. Actors are not equal, and asymmetries among participants and forms of exclusion persist in initiatives to greater sustainability. There are tensions between power, democracy and sustainability. However, this does not mean that transitions to sustainability cannot be democratic. Whether we are able to conceptualize a transition to be democratic, or whether we exclude this option, depends on how we define power and how we perceive agency.

Conceptions of power

Power over, *power to* and *power with* stand for three ideal-type concepts. They reflect how scholars perceive power and agency, and how agents may, or may not, come to influence decision-making processes in sustainability politics (see Table 13.1). *Power over* describes the direct and indirect ability to influence the actions and even the thoughts of others. It is based on the well-known grouping of four 'faces of power' (Digeser 1992). Following this conception of power, decisions are democratic, if power wielders represent the interests of and can be held accountable by their constituencies. Scholars who apply this concept are mainly busy explaining gridlock and limits of modern democracies when it comes to a transition to sustainability (Blühdorn 2020).

Power to corresponds to the ability of agents 'to get things done' (Parsons 1963, 232). This is a perception generally shared by liberal democracy. If every (wo)man is the architect of her, or his, own fortune, there is no ruler to be held accountable. Democracy hence unfolds especially in direct forms of democracy (Blühdorn 2020; Heidenreich 2018). By contrast, *power with* means collective empowerment through convincing and learning with and from each other. It refers to processes of developing shared values, finding common ground and generating collective strength (Partzsch and Fuchs 2012). This conception of power admits for individuals deliberately sacrificing their personal freedom along republican traditions of democracy that underscore the common good (Heidenreich 2018). Recent suggestions for a 'geopolitan democracy' (Eckersley 2017) and 'green republicanism' (Heidenreich 2018) assume that such an exercise of power is possible. However, most scholars studying power in transitions to sustainability tend to focus on *power over*. They find deficits of addressing the ecological crisis, on the one hand, and of realizing democratic demands, on the other hand. Against this backdrop,

Table 13.1 Power and responsibility for change

	Definition	Who is responsible for change?
Power with	Power is understood as the ability to act in concert, based on learning and cooperating with one other.	The collective, i.e. nation-state and international community
Power to	Power is the ability to act in an indirect relational way.	Individual actors and groups, i.e. NGOs, businesses, consumers
Power over (four dimensions)		
First dimension	Power is the potential of powerful actors to directly determine the actions of others.	Dominant actors
Second dimension	Power manifests itself through some issues not making it on to the political agenda or being discarded before (observable) negotiations start.	Dominant actors and structures
Third dimension	Power is exercised by means of influencing, forming and constituting ideas and intentions.	Dominant actors, structures and discourses
Fourth dimension	Power is inherent (inscribed) in social constructions of subjectivity and individuality that are described in historical terms.	'New thinking' that does not reproduce system and positions

Source: Author

I start elaborating the conception of *power over* and related requirements for democracy in the next section.

Power over: 'top down' transition to sustainability

Power over describes power over other actors, structures and discourses. Weber (1978/1922) established the famous understanding of power as carrying out his (or her) own will in an asymmetric relation,[1] and in the original debates, starting with Dahl (1957), power was self-evidently understood as power over others – A gets B to do something that B would not otherwise do.[2] A distinction is usually made between four dimensions or 'faces' of power.

In the first dimension, which is based on Dahl's understanding, power is exercised directly and *visibly*. Power can be measured in terms of votes in parliament (e.g. for and against environmental regulation). Any kind of state force implementing sustainability by 'top down' regulation (e.g. binding carbon emission reduction targets) means exercising direct, potentially visible *power over* others (e.g. over emitting industries). When scholars measure the power (over) of business actors and non-governmental organizations (NGOs) in terms of how successful their demands in specific negotiation processes are, they apply this concept of *visible power over* and understand the exercise of power to be zero-sum within a specific agenda (Betsill 2006; Lund 2013). If there is no external intervention, the structural gap between more and less powerful actors increases, as such, a zero-sum logic prevails between blockers and advocates of a transition to sustainability. As environmental NGOs generally have fewer resources than business representatives, their advocacy is inferior to the polluters' lobby, except for situations in which external events, such as environmental accidents, weaken business actors (e.g. the Fukushima nuclear disaster, see Ho 2014). Admitting that actors are unequal, means admitting that current systems of liberal democracy, which are not hedged against business advocacy, have democratic deficits. These deficits become even more serious, if we consider the other three dimensions of *power over*.

The second dimension of *hidden power (over)* is less actor-centred. It refers to structural power not directly opposed by anyone. Bachrach and Baratz (1962) point to the fact that some issues never come onto the political agenda and are rejected before observable negotiations begin. This is the case for many sustainability issues. For example, forest and water problems receive far less attention than climate change (Simonis 2006). Narain (2010) explains how, in climate politics, negotiations about a temperature ceiling also affect developing countries in a 'hidden' way, even if their emissions were not on the official agenda: a global temperature ceiling leaves little leeway to developing countries for a carbon-rich course of development.

The traditional conception of structural hidden *power over* in the international arena addresses coercion resulting from the capital mobility of transnational corporations. Threats to shift investments abroad do not even need to be voiced in order to influence institutional politics in their favour (Altvater and Mahnkopf 1999; Strange 1988). More recent studies point to the fact that business also exercises structural hidden *power over* through self-regulation and public–private partnerships that allow business actors to actively set rules (Auld 2015; Ponte and Daugbjerg 2015). Non-state agents, including business actors and NGOs, set their own standards, while public authorities have faced challenges in facilitating the implementation of environmental and human rights-based norms outside their jurisdictions. For instance, the EU has started to use 'voluntary' certification schemes to verify compliance with sustainability criteria, such as biofuel production outside its own territory (Kemper and Partzsch 2018; Ponte and Daugbjerg 2015). As a consequence, power in the global political economy has been diffused, leaving non-state actors with considerable power in sustainability politics.

Scholars analyse inherent power asymmetries and identify winners and losers resulting from these processes, i.e. democratic states losing capacity for environmental regulation (e.g. Altvater and Mahnkopf 1999; Strange 1988).

In the *third dimension*, *power over* results from ideal systemic factors. Here scholars take a look at power relations that are linked to latent conflicts of interests (Lukes 1974). Such conflicts are neither open nor simply hidden. *Invisible* power has an effect through norms and ideas. It is reflected in discourse, communication practices, cultural values and institutions that manipulate actions and thoughts (Lukes 1974). Görg and Brand (2002) identify 'Myths of Global Environmental Management' (author's translation of German book title) in this sense. Based on this perspective, scholars criticise sustainability for its win-win story line and for neglecting, or deferring, questions of social justice (Jessop 2012). Global power asymmetries manifest themselves through the win-win rhetoric, rather than contributing to a sustainability transition (see already Hajer 1995).

Neo-Gramscian International Political Economy rejects the simple differentiation between 'advocates' and 'blockers' of a transition to sustainability. Bedall (2011) shows, for example, how dominant NGOs within the heterogeneous civil society secure the neoliberal hegemony in the field of climate politics, especially the *Climate Action Network* (*CAN*) – instead of pushing a counter-hegemonic project. Scholars, such as Levidow (2013, 211), blame the EU for using the concept of sustainability as a means to depoliticise its 'global plunder of resources'.

With reference to Foucault (1982) and Bourdieu (1987), we can capture links between knowledge, power and politics in a *fourth dimension* of power (Digeser 1992). Such critical and (post-)structuralist approaches are increasingly prevailing in sustainability research (Lövbrand et al. 2009; Stripple and Bulkeley 2013). Power is understood in a way that, in the final analysis, everything is socially constructed, including subjectivity or individuality. Individual actors are seen as products of practices and of the kind of problematization that is inherent to a specific period. In his later works, Foucault points to the fact that power is not only repressive, i.e. has a suppressive effect. Power also has a productive effect related to knowledge (*power to*); by persistently reproducing their own subjectivities, actors mainly reproduce existing systems and positions (Guzzini 2007).

Discourse analytical studies address the interrelation between knowledge and power under the catchword of eco-governmentality (for example Bäckstrand and Lövbrand 2006; Methmann 2013). These scholars demonstrate how certain rationalities of governing generate environmental problems, which Foucault (1982) describes as governmentality. Oels (2010), for example, shows how the Intergovernmental Panel on Climate Change (IPCC) constituted climate change as a global management problem and enabled an expansion of state power. Following Foucault, Oels (2010) understands this global management as governmentality ('bio-power'). Since the 1990s, she argues, there has been a change in governmentality to an advanced liberal thinking, which constitutes climate change as a problem of state failure that we are supposed to address with the creation of new markets. This change in governmentality has reduced the leeway of public actors for climate mitigation (*power over*). Instead, climate issues are left to the market. Nonetheless, despite the dismissal of (state) agency, the climate regime is productive (*power to*, see below), because – although it does not protect the climate – it (re-)produces a specific system and positions. For example, contracting states are constituted as '*responsible* and *calculating* members of the climate community' (Oels 2010, p. 186, author's translation), without actually being able to prevent global warming. States reproduce their positions in an ecologically destructive system. Like other perspectives of *power over*, such Foucauldian studies on 'productive' power hence demonstrate how dominant structures are reproduced and how dominant discourses have prevented a transition to sustainability.

Asking for *power over* in the research on environmental politics and sustainability reveals the failure of representative democracy to overcome asymmetries among actors, structures and discourses that mainly reproduce themselves and hence continue to drive the ecological crisis. We assume a bi-directional power relation between governments that exercise *power over* citizens on the one hand and citizens, who elect governments and can hold them accountable through election, legal action through the courts etc., on the other hand. While 'top down' environmental regulation is basically possible, there is visible, hidden, invisible and unconscious power that prevents constituencies from choosing systems that allow for greater environmental sustainability and social justice. Different imperatives (internal security, international competitiveness, economic prosperity, etc.) are more important for the state's legitimation and stability (Blühdorn 2020). In consequence, humanity is doomed to exercising 'geological agency' (Eckersley 2017, 984) in the sense of producing irreversible and systemic changes on a planetary scale. By contrast, if we want to understand, how agents can enable change towards greater sustainability, we need power perspectives that allow for self-determined agency. As we will see below, this can be a perspective that highlights individual freedom (*power to*) and is hence linked to liberal democracy, or it can be a perspective that admits for individuals deliberately sacrificing their personal freedom (*power with*) along republican traditions that underscore the common good (Heidenreich 2018).

Power to: empowerment and resistance

Power to refers to the agency of individuals and separate groups, such as environmental NGOs and 'green' businesses. Pitkin (1972, 177) emphasises that

> (o)ne man ... may have *power to* do or accomplish something by himself, and that power is not relational at all; it may involve other people if what he has power to do is a social or political action, but it need not.

Pitkin's understanding of *power to* assumes that actors are self-determined, i.e. they have the self-confidence and capabilities to pursue their decisions (see also Eyben et al. 2006). For instance, an actor can simply start a more sustainable life by going by bike or by growing organic food, without any permission or interference from others. *Power to* is therefore often linked to Parsons' (1963) understanding of power that highlights a productive agency, especially in cases where actors' goals are opposed or resisted. The number of these *alternative* agents (environmental NGOs, 'green' businesses and ethically minded consumers) is ultimately limited as long as unsustainable systems, which they oppose, remain dominant. Agents who exercise *power to* criticise the practices, and the authority, of the dominant unsustainable system and refuse to reproduce their own positions in this system. Students who demand climate action with 'Fridays for Future'-school strikes are a recent example. They resist compulsory school attendance (on Fridays) to oppose the dominant political and economic system. Agents empower from and resist to structures. Their non-conformism is perceived to be for the 'good' of society, such as in the case of climate mitigation and sustainability.

From this perspective, studies have explored the potential of NGOs as 'climate savers' (Walk 2008, author's translation), and often their political action is considered legitimate and urgently required, for instance, in resisting nuclear power (Ho 2014) or genetically modified organisms (GMOs) (Andrée 2011). Studies on the role of 'green' businesses and the potential of corporate social responsibility sometimes also share an understanding of *power to* (Assadourian 2006). In such studies, business enterprises can take the very same role like NGOs; they may have *power to* accomplish something all by themselves and protect the environment in their daily practices, for example, by saving water (Kemper and Partzsch 2019). This type of power is not directly relational.

However, Pitkin's definition of non-relational power is highly controversial. In particular, Barnett and Duvall (2005) understand *power to* in the same way as outlined above for the fourth dimension of *power over*. They argue that this concept of power is tied to social relations of constitution, and consider 'how social relations define who are the actors and what are the capacities and practices they are socially empowered to undertake' (Barnett and Duvall 2005, 5). This means that structures define who the agents are and what they are able to do. For example, in many societies, cars are a status symbol, or organic food is mainly consumed by more affluent people. Scholars emphasise buying organic certified (non-GMO) products helps them demonstrating ethical consciousness 'to get a (better) job, a partner or social standing' (Hoskins 2014, 198). Similarly, journalists have argued that 'Fridays for Futures'-activists are puppets of environmental NGOs, i.e. that they are themselves effects of socialisation to structures. Following Lukes (1974), certain issues, such as environmental degradation and social injustices, are not simply hidden from political agendas, but there also exists manipulation of the 'very wants' (Lukes 1974, 3) of disadvantaged actors. Heidenreich (2018) outlines tensions between liberalism and sustainability in this regard: '[M]odern liberal assumption of a privatized idea of the *Good Life* [...] that allows maximized individual freedom is incompatible with the need to lower consumption' (Heidenreich 2018, 358).

In order to contribute to a real turnaround, actors would need to newly define the system and positions. In the structure-agency debate, Mikhail Gorbachev, last leader of the Soviet Union, serves as an example of an agent whose 'new thinking' about the nature of international relations provoked a radical change process and led to a structural transformation which was the end of the Cold War (Nye 2008, 8; Wendt 1992, 419–422). Climate activists can only contribute to turning around the conventional system of transport and mobility by going by bike, if they do not simultaneously continue to have a car as a status symbol (that reproduces their position and the conventional system). Likewise, actors would need to support those certification initiatives that do not reproduce the conventional system of industrial agriculture, and that create alternatives such as organic farming systems (Partzsch and Kemper 2019).

While constructivists have mainly been busy explaining how subjectivity is socially constituted, many of them acknowledge both *subject* ('me') and *self* ('I') (Wight 1999, 130). A 'reflexive turn' (Beck et al. 2014) in environmental and sustainability politics would imply a continuous reflection of the selves about their subjectivities. In this vein, Eckersley (2017) develops an account of hyper-reflexive 'geopolitan democracy' as the appropriate approach to navigating the Anthropocene. If the self can initiate transformational change, and if actors are not simply subject to dominant structures (of either the conventional or an alternative system), such hyper-reflexive situations of transformational change can be considered essentially democratic.

Power with: cooperation and learning

While *power to* allows transformational actors to potentially turn around systems by altering their own positions and creating alternatives, *power with* means bringing about a change through cooperation and learning with and from each other. It refers to processes of developing shared values, finding common ground and generating collective strength *within* systems (Allen 1998; Eyben et al. 2006; Partzsch and Fuchs 2012). Against the backdrop of the structure–agency debate, and from the perspective of *power with*, actors with a transformational orientation have substantial agency, if they act in concert (Partzsch 2017). In this vein, a turnaround of the conventional system may only follow a collective change in societal thinking and behaviour, instead of only a few agents changing their own positions. For instance, we would need an agricultural reform, rather than a few actors growing organic food. Car traffic would need to lose its societal acceptance, instead of only a few transformational actors going by bike.

Power with is often linked to Arendt's (1970, 44) definition of power. She defines power as joint action in the public sphere:

> Power corresponds to the human ability not just to act but to act in concert. Power is never the property of an individual. ... When we say of somebody that he is 'in power' we actually refer to his being empowered by a certain number of people to act in their name.

From this perspective, those who advocate sustainability do serve everybody's interest and act in their name; transformational agents sacrifice themselves on behalf of the collectivity (for instance, by taking the effort of using the bike instead of the car; by accepting more labour-intense forms of agriculture). In this vein, non-environmentalists are described as 'free riders' or 'laggards' (instead of describing them as actors with competing interests and values) (e.g. Jänicke 2008).

However, different from such research, Arendt does not take a stand on the result of the exercise of power in either a positive or negative way. What interests her is joint action. Finding agreement becomes an end in itself and does not (only) serve the assertion of particular interests (Arendt 1970). Thus, it is not *power over* that transformational leaders exercise, because it is not about accomplishing a particular idea or position over others. In other words, *power with* does not refer to the diffusion of already existing (predefined) norms. Rather, it implies mutual learning processes that allow actors to reflect and question self-perceptions and to actively build up a new awareness of individuals or groups (Eyben et al. 2006, 8–9; Gaard 2010, 71). In this vein, actors would need to collectively agree on the content of sustainable agriculture etc. in processes of *power with*, instead of following predefined standards, for instance, already existing standards of organic agriculture. This would require a process of re-evaluating common norms and values in society. Competing state imperatives (domestic security, international competitiveness, etc.) could then eventually be deferred for the sake of greater sustainability.

Habermas' (1998) deliberative democracy builds on Arendt's concept of power. Deliberation can be defined very broadly as 'communication that induces reflection on preferences, values and interests in a non-coercive fashion' (Dryzek 2000, 76). Deliberative democracy is often conceived as the most viable model of democracy (Bäckstrand 2012, p. 514). Besides scientific experts, NGO and social movements play a central role in deliberative accounts of global democracy. Eckersley's (2017, 996) model of 'geopolitan democracy [...] seeks to build enhanced reflexivity from the bottom up in ways which will temper parochialism and build greater public trust in science and more scientific trust in the common-sense experience and imagination of lay publics'. Heidenreich (2018, 359) agrees that 'democracy will have to change'. Different from liberal democracy, to which the freedom of individuals (and their self-interests) are most central, he argues in favour of a 'green republicanism' (Heidenreich 2018, 361). The republic is entitled, so he argues, to ask for 'sacrifices' of its citizens. In this vein, individuals are not irrelevant in processes of *power with*; however, individuals only unfold their power when acting together with other fellow citizens.

Like in the case of *power to*, *power over* also affects agency and agents in processes of *power with*. Arendt's definition of power is characterized by her understanding of the polity, and should not be considered independently (Canovan 1978; Göhler 2009). She refers to Aristotle and the ancient polis when she describes politics as a relation among equals who govern themselves. However, only the citizens, those who presided over the household, had access to the public sphere of the polis. This means that Arendt's power conception is based on ancient times' exclusion and displacement of then 'non-citizens' such as women, slaves, etc. into the private sphere of the household, including supposedly non-political issues such as economics and bodily health. Therefore, Arendt's conception of power is often said to be based on a utopian or elite version of polity (Canovan 1978); she simply assumes that people have basic capabilities at their disposal to act upon in the public sphere. Eckersley's 'geopolitan democracy' and Heidenreich's 'green republicanism' run the risk of falling into the same trap. *Power with* is undemocratic in situations in which actors have unequal capabilities to represent their own individual and specific interests in the public sphere, and in situations in which some stakeholders are excluded from processes of *power with*. Moreover, there is no guarantee that mutual learning leads to greater sustainability. Instead, it is possible that competing imperatives (for example, domestic security) may prevail (Blühdorn 2020).

Conclusion: tensions between power, democracy and sustainability

If we apply concepts of *power over* and understand sustainability as a 'top down' approach, the democratic state is the only legitimate actor to enforce a political and societal transition. However, the majority of studies that I associate with *power over* assume that the state cannot enforce a transition against the interests or rationalities of those actors, structures or discourses that are currently dominant and that basically account for the ecological crisis. Therefore, studies essentially explain gridlock in this regard, while it remains unclear who or what can provoke change (for example, Fuchs et al. 2016; Lövbrand et al. 2009; Oels 2010; Stripple and Bulkeley 2013).

If we want to allow for, and better understand, a transition to sustainability, scholars need to acknowledge agent-based concepts of *power to* and *power with*. Most political scientists, among them those who share understandings of *power over*, acknowledge that there are (rare) situations in which agency is possible (e.g. Wendt 1992; Wight 1999). Understanding which conditions allow agents to exercise *power to* would be essential for realising a 'reflexive turn' (Beck et al. 2014) and democratic transition to sustainability. In parallel, we need to further develop concepts such as 'geopolitan democracy' (Eckersley 2017) and 'green republicanism' (Heidenreich 2018), which demonstrate *power with*, by identifying such processes empirically. Only if these processes accomplish sustainability based on greater agency, rather than exclusion of actors, can these processes enhance agency and a transition to sustainability can be considered democratic.

Greater agency and new forms of democracy might still be unimaginable, but business as usual is unthinkable. Dominant actors, structures and discourses have led to, and *de facto* continue to aggravate, the ecological crisis. We need to conceptualise the 'agency of everybody', as well as its preconditions and limits, in order to explore possibilities of individual and collective empowerment for the sake of 'saving the planet'. Environmental protection might not make everybody a winner but is inevitable for the survival of humanity.

Notes

1 Weber (1978/1922) defines power as the 'probability that one actor within a social relationship will be in a position to carry out his own will despite resistance, regardless of the basis on which this probability

exists'. Power is essentially seen as an 'asymmetric relation between at least two objects of actions (A and B) (…). Without the relation to actor A, actor B would not act in the way he does' (Maluschke 1995, 400; author's translation).

2 'A has power over B to the extent that he can get B to do something that B would not otherwise do' (Dahl 1957, 201).

References

Allen, A., 1998. Rethinking power. *Hypatia*, 13 (1), 21–40.
Altvater, E., and Mahnkopf, B., 1999. *Grenzen der Globalisierung. Ökonomie, Ökologie und Politik in der Weltgesellschaft*. Münster: Westfälisches Dampfboot.
Andrée, P., 2011. Civil society and the political economy of GMO failures in Canada: a neo-Gramscian analysis. *Environmental Politics*, 20 (2), 173–191.
Arendt, H., 1970. *On Violence*. New York: Harcourt, Brace & World.
Assadourian, E., 2006. International agierende Unternehmen im Wandel. In Worldwatch Institute, eds. *Zur Lage der Welt 2006. China, Indien und unsere gemeinsame Zukunft*. Münster: Westfälisches Dampfboot, 286–319.
Auld, G., 2015. *Constructing Private Governance. The Rise and Evolution of Forest, Coffee, and Fisheries Certification*. New Haven: Yale University Press.
Bachrach, P., and Baratz, M.S., 1962. Two faces of power. *The American Political Science Review*, 4 (56), 947–952.
Bäckstrand, K., 2012. Democracy and global environmental politics. In P. Dauvergne, eds. *Handbook of Global Environmental Politics, second edition*. Cheltenham: Edward Elgar Publishing Limited, 507–518.
Bäckstrand, K., and Lövbrand, E., 2006. Planting trees to mitigate climate change. Contested discourses of ecological modernization, green governmentality and civic environmentalism. *Global Environmental Politics*, 6 (1), 50–75.
Barnett, M., and Duvall, R., 2005. Power in global governance. In M.N. Barnett and R. Duvall, eds. *Power in Global Governance*. Cambridge: Cambridge University Press, 1–32.
Beck, S., et al., 2014. Towards a reflexive turn in the governance of global environmental expertise. The cases of the IPCC and the IPBES. *GAIA*, 23 (2), 80–87.
Bedall, P., 2011. NGOs, soziale Bewegungen und Auseinandersetzungen um Hegemonie. Eine gesellschaftstheoretische Verortung in der Internationalen Politischen Ökonomie. In A. Brunnengräber, ed. *Zivilisierung des Klimaregimes. NGOs und soziale Bewegungen in der nationalen, europäischen und internationalen Klimapolitik*. Wiesbaden: VS Verlag für Sozialwissenschaften, 59–84.
Betsill, M.M., 2006. Transnational actors in international environmental politics. In M.M. Betsill, K. Hochstetler, and D. Stevis, eds. *International Environmental Politics*. New York: Palgrave MacMillan, 172–202.
Blühdorn, I., 2020. The legitimation crisis of democracy. Emancipatory politics, the environmental state and the glass ceiling to socio-ecological transformation. *Environmental Politics*, 29 (1), 38–57.
Bourdieu, P., 1987. *Sozialer Sinn. Kritik der theoretischen Vernunft*. Frankfurt a.M.: Suhrkamp.
Canovan, M., 1978. The contradictions of Hannas Arendt's political thought. *Political Theory*, 6 (1), 5–26.
Cerny, P.G., 2000. Political agency in a globalizing world. Towards a structurational approach. *European Journal of International Relations*, 6 (4), 435–463.
Dahl, R.A., 1957. The concept of power. *Behavioral Science*, 2 (3), 201–215.
Digeser, P., 1992. The fourth face of power. *The Journal of Politics*, 54 (4), 977–1007.
Dryzek, J.S., 2000. *Deliberative Democracy and Beyond. Liberals, Critics, Contestations*. New York: Oxford University Press.
Eckersley, R., 2017. Geopolitan democracy in the Anthropocene. *Political Studies*, 65 (4), 983–999.
Eyben, R., Harris, C., and Pettit, J., 2006. Introduction: exploring power for change. *IDS Bulletin*, 37 (6), 1–10.
Foucault, M., 1982. The subject and power. *Critical Inquiry*, 8 (4), 777–795.
Fuchs, D., et al., 2016. Power: the missing element in sustainable consumption and absolute reductions research and action. *Journal of Cleaner Production*, (132), 298–307.
Gaard, G., 2010. Women, water, energy: an ecofeminist approach. In P.G. Brown and J.J. Schmidt, eds. *Water Ethics. Foundational Readings for Students and Professionals*. Washington: Island Press, 59–75.

Göhler, G., 2009. 'Power to' and 'power over'. In Stewart R. Clegg and Mark Haugaard, eds. *The Sage Handbook of Power*. Los Angeles: Sage, 27–39.

Görg, C., and Brand, U., eds., 2002. *Mythen globalen Umweltmanagements. Rio + 10? Und die Sackgassen nachhaltiger Entwicklung*. Münster: Westfälisches Dampfboot.

Guzzini, S., 2007. The concept of power. A constructivist analysis. In F. Berenskoetter and M.J. Williams, eds. *Power in World Politics*. New York: Routledge, 23–42.

Habermas, J., 1998. *Between Facts and Norms. Contributions to a Discourse Theory of Law and Democracy*. Cambridge: MIT Press.

Hajer, M.A., 1995. *The Politics of Environmental Discourse. Ecological Modernization and the Policy Process*. London: Oxford University Press.

Haugaard, M., 2011. Editorial. *Journal of Political Power*, 4 (1), 1–8.

Hayward, C., and Lukes, S., 2008. Nobody to shoot? *Power, Structure, and Agency: A Dialogue*, 1 (1), 5–20.

Heidenreich, F., 2018. How will sustainability transform democracy? Reflections on an important dimension of transformation sciences. *GAIA – Ecological Perspectives for Science and Society*, 27 (4), 357–362.

Ho, M.-S., 2014. The Fukushima effect: explaining the resurgence of the anti-nuclear movement in Taiwan. *Environmental Politics*, 23 (6), 965–983.

Hoskins, T.E., 2014. *Stitched Up. The Anti-Capitalist Book of Fashion*. London: Pluto Press.

Jänicke, M., 2008. *Megatrend Environmental Innovation. On the Ecological Modernization of the Economy and the State*. Munich: Oekom-Verlag.

Jessop, B., 2012. Economic and ecological crises: green new deals and no-growth economies. *Development Policy Review*, 55 (1), 17–24.

Kemper, L., and Partzsch, L., 2018. A water sustainability framework for assessing biofuel certification schemes. Does European hybrid governance ensure sustainability of palm oil from Indonesia? *Journal of Cleaner Production*, 26 (192), 835–843.

Kemper, L., and Partzsch, L., 2019. Saving water while doing business. corporate agenda-setting and water sustainability. *Water*, 11 (2), 297.

Levidow, L., 2013. EU criteria for sustainable biofuels: accounting for carbon, depoliticizing plunder. *Geoforum*, 44 (1), 211–223.

Lövbrand, E., Stripple, J., and Wiman, B., 2009. Earth system governmentality. *Global Environmental Change*, 19 (1), 7–13.

Lukes, S., 1974. *Power: A Radical View*. London: Macmillan.

Lund, E., 2013. Environmental diplomacy: comparing the influence of business and environmental NGOs in negotiations on reform of the clean development mechanism. *Environmental Politics*, 22 (5), 739–759.

Maluschke, G., 1995. Macht/Machttheorien. In D. Nohlen, ed. *Wörterbuch Staat und Politik*. Bonn: Bundeszentrale für Politische Bildung, 399–403.

Methmann, C., 2013. The sky is the limit: global warming as global governmentality. *European Journal of International Relations*, 19 (1), 69–91.

Narain, S., 2010. Keine gemeinsame Teilhabe an der Welt. *Aus Politik und Zeitgeschichte* (32–33), 3–7.

Nye, J.S., 2008. *The Powers to Lead*. New York: Oxford University Press.

Oels, A., 2010. Die Gouvernementalität der internationalen Klimapolitik. Biomacht oder fortgeschritten liberales Regieren. In M. Voss, ed. *Der Klimawandel – Sozialwissenschaftliche Perspektiven*. Wiesbaden: VS Verlag für Sozialwissenschaften, 171–186.

Okereke, C., Bulkeley, H., and Schroeder, H., 2009. Conceptualizing climate governance beyond the international regime. *Global Environmental Politics*, 9 (1), 58–78.

Parsons, T., 1963. On the concept of political power. *Proceedings of the American Philosophical Society*, 107 (3), 232–262.

Partzsch, L., 2017. 'Power with' and 'power to' in environmental politics and the transition to sustainability. *Environmental Politics*, 26 (2), 193–211.

Partzsch, L., and Fuchs, D., 2012. Philanthropy: power with in international relations. *Journal of Political Power*, 5 (3), 359–376.

Partzsch, L., and Kemper, L., 2019. Cotton certification in Ethiopia. Can an increasing demand for certified textiles create a 'fashion revolution'? *Geoforum*, 99 (Feb.), 111–119. Available from: www.sciencedirect.com/science/article/pii/S0016718518303543.

Partzsch, L., and Weiland, S., eds., 2015. *Macht und Wandel in der Umweltpolitik. Sonderband der Zeitschrift für Politikwissenschaft*. Baden-Baden: Nomos.

Pitkin, H.F., 1972. *Wittgenstein and Justice. On the Significance of Ludwig Wittgenstein for Social and Political Thought*. Berkeley: University of California Press.

Ponte, S., and Daugbjerg, C., 2015. Biofuel sustainability and the formation of transnational hybrid governance. *Environmental Politics*, 24 (1), 96–114.

Simonis, U.E., 2006. Die Reform der Umweltpolitik der Vereinten Nationen. In J. Varwick and A. Zimmermann, eds. *Die Reform der Vereinten Nationen. Bilanz und Perspektiven*. Duncker & Humblot: Berlin, 229–241.

Strange, S., 1988. *States and Markets*. London: Blackwell.

Stripple, J., and Bulkeley, H., eds., 2013. *Governing the Climate. Rationality, Practice and Power*. Cambridge: Cambridge University Press.

Walk, H., 2008. *Partizipative Governance. Beteiligungsformen und Beteiligungsrechte im Mehrebenensystem der Klimapolitik*. Wiesbaden: VS Verlag für Sozialwissenschaften.

Weber, M., 1978/1922. *Economy and Society: An Outline of Interpretive Sociology*. eds. R. Guenther and C. Wittich. Berkeley and Los Angeles: University of California Press.

Wendt, A., 1992. Anarchy is what states make of it: the social construction of power politics. *International Organization*, 46 (2), 391–425.

Wight, C., 1999. They shoot dead horses don't they? Locating agency in the agent-structure problematique. *European Journal of International Relations*, 5 (1), 109–142.

14
POSTSECULARITY AND SUSTAINABLE DEVELOPMENT

Jens Köhrsen

Introduction

To date, there is only a small – though rising – consideration of religion in academic debates about sustainability. This is astonishing given the potentials often attributed to religion. More than 80 percent of the world's population adheres to a religious tradition (Pew Research Center 2017). Religious traditions can reach people in the remotest of places (Sheikh 2006; Mangunjaya and McKay 2012) and have an impact on their worldviews and moral attitudes. Moreover, in many places, religious leaders and organizations enjoy a high credibility. They have an important voice in public debates and can sometimes influence political decision-making through their diplomatic networks (Casanova 1994). Finally, the biggest religious communities have massive financial and organizational resources that they can draw upon to promote sustainability transitions (Gardner 2002). In sum, it appears that religions have much to offer for sustainability transitions (Ives and Kidwell 2019).

One cause for the disregard of religion may be related to the historical importance of secularization theories, which assumed that the social relevance of religion would diminish over time. The ongoing modernization processes – involving, *inter alia*, industrialization, urbanization, rationalization, as well as rising levels of material well-being, health, and education – implied that religion would lose importance for modern individuals and societies (Bruce 2011; Pollack 2018). It would disappear from public and political life and diminish into a private affair for its remaining followers. Apart from secularization theories, normative secularist views perceived religion as part of the problem rather than the solution for the development of societies. In this perspective, religious traditions had contributed to poverty, social inequality, violent conflicts, resource exploitation, and polluting behavior. Consequently, religions formed rather a barrier than a means for sustainable development.

However, in the last decades, views have changed. While the secularization thesis dominated academic debates about religion until the 1990s, today, notions assuming a "resurgence of religion" prevail. Although, scholars disagree about the extent of this "resurgence" and what actually qualifies as religion (Tenbruck 1993; Asad 2009; Woodhead 2011; Pollack and Rosta 2017), many researchers agree that religion continues to inform the lives of vast population segments and remains present in public life (Casanova 1994; Casanova 2003; Davie 2010). In most parts of the world, there is no evidence of a fading of religion. However, as there has also not been an overwhelming rise in religion, the idea of a "resurgence" mostly refers to the recovered attention for religion by researchers and the public. In the context of this new awareness for religion, Jürgen Habermas introduced the notion of post-secularity (Habermas 2001; Habermas 2006; Habermas 2008). He argued that post-secular societies would not ban religions from the public sphere but accept them as equal discussion partners. Recognizing them in this vein means that religions have the potential to make important contributions to ongoing debates about social and political issues.

This changing perception has also opened doors for religious actors in the field of development. Today, religious actors are active in different fields of sustainable development and are sometimes even perceived as the "great hope" in the context of the sustainable development goals. Against the backdrop of these changes, this chapter examines the relationship between religion, democracy, and sustainability and critically scrutinizes the notion of post-secularity. I argue that religious actors increasingly participate in public debates on environmental sustainability while facing at the same time the need to self-secularize their communication. Public debates on environmental sustainability mostly constitute secular arenas, forcing their participants to leave out their religion. Consequently, religious actors tend to act as secular rather than religious actors in these arenas, thereby contradicting the assumption of a "post-secular" society.

The first section of this chapter addresses the "resurgence" of religion by focusing on the increasing integration of religious actors into global development politics. It discusses the religious engagement in sustainable development and shows that the notion of "post-secularity" is misleading to describe the increasing presence of religious actors in this domain. Though global development circles increasingly consider the development abilities of religious actors (e.g., grassroots reach), their specifically religious features remain problematic to these mostly secular circles. The second section discusses the relationship between religion, democracy, and sustainability. As we lack empirical research that directly explores the relationship between these three variables, the section focuses on studies that have separately scrutinized the relationships between: (a) democracy and religion; and (b) sustainability and religion. For both relationships, I show that religion assumes an ambivalent role: it can facilitate or block democratization and sustainable development processes. The third section seeks to bring the three variables – religion, democracy, and sustainability – together by placing emphasis on religious actors' public campaigning activities for environmental sustainability. The final section summarizes the insights gained from the aforementioned sections, critically reflects on the notion of post-secularity and sketches a research outlook.

Towards post-secular development politics?

Developments such as the global spread of new religious movements, the Iranian revolution, and the 9/11 terror attacks have generated a new public visibility of religion and challenged secularization theories. While secularization theories, proclaiming that processes of modernization would diminish the societal relevance of religion, dominated public and academic discourses about religion until the 1980s, most academics nowadays agree on the ongoing relevance of religion.

This "rediscovery" of religion is also relevant for the global sustainable development agenda, as it has generated a novel focus on religion in international development politics.[1] While religion was originally perceived as a hindrance for development, international development agencies have started to consider the potentials of religion for development and have increasingly regarded religious organizations as relevant partners for development activities

(Marshall 2001; Clarke 2006; Haynes 2007; Ter Haar and Wolfensohn 2011; Koehrsen and Heuser 2020):

> [...] various secular development agencies – including the World Bank, IMF, ILO and several UN agencies – sought to engage with faith-based organisations in initiatives designed to improve developmental outcomes for the world's poorest people.
>
> *Haynes 2007, 13*

Religious organizations – often described in this context as faith-based organizations or religious NGOs – have become important collaboration and dialogue partners for international development agencies. In 2012, Beinlich and Braungart (2019) found that 9 percent of the NGOs accredited at the *United Nations Economic and Social Council* are religious organizations. Depending on the survey, between well over half and up to three quarters of these organizations have a Christian background (cf. Berger 2003; Haynes 2013; Lehmann 2016 Beinlich and Braungart 2019). Beinlich and Braungart (2019) identified 60 percent of these organizations as Christian, followed by organizations with a Muslim (13 percent), Jewish (9 percent), Buddhist (4 percent), and Hindu (3 percent) faith background.

Religious organizations are active in different fields of sustainable development, involving, for instance, projects on gender equality (Sustainable Development Goal [SDG] 5), sustainable cities and communities (SDG 11), as well as peace and justice, strong institutions (SDG 16) (Koehrsen and Heuser 2020; Marshall 2001; Berger 2003; Lunn 2009; Green et al. 2012; Heist and Cnaan 2016; Ware et al. 2016). To organize, and conduct projects, they frequently collaborate with secular NGOs and organizations from other faith-backgrounds (see also Boehle 2010b).

Religions are regarded as bringing in specific resources for promoting development (Heuser and Koehrsen 2020). First, religious leaders and organizations frequently enjoy a high credibility in the Global South, whereas local populations and governments often distrust secular organizations and perceive their activities as Western foreign interventions (Cordier 2009; Palmer 2011; Petersen 2012b, 775). Second, unlike state organizations, they have direct access to the grassroots-level through local religious communities and can often reach the most remote places and populations (Berger 2003; Rice 2006; Cordier 2009; Petersen 2012a; Amri 2014). Third, given their grass-roots connections, they are more likely to be responsive to the needs of local people (Occhipinti 2015, 332). Finally, they bring in more holistic conceptions of development: while development was for a long time conceptually limited to economic growth and material prosperity, for religious organizations, development involves more than material welfare and includes, for instance, spiritual, psychological, and social well-being (Lunn 2009; Boehle 2010a; Deneulin and Rakodi 2011; Hoffmann 2020; Kloß 2020). Thus, these organizations have promoted alternative concepts of development.

However, there are also challenges for religious organizations engaging in sustainable development. Perceptions of religion as inciting conflict and primarily searching for souls (proselytism) can hamper its involvement (Kaag 2007; Lunn 2009; Thaut 2009; Petersen 2012a, 135–136; Petersen 2012b, 771–774; Heist and Cnaan 2016; Lynch and Schwarz 2016). Most importantly, the secularity of the international field of development challenges religion. Despite the rising integration of religious organizations, this field has remained a secular sphere in which incorporating religion is problematic (Clarke 2008, 4–5; James 2009b; Glaab 2017). The United Nations, which is the main hub for development activities, is a secular organization that has no formal place for religion (Haynes 2013; Glaab 2019). Haynes states with regard to the role of religion at the United Nations:

> most FBOs [Faith-Based Organizations] struggle at the UN [United Nations] to be taken seriously, with no automatic right to be heard in global policy debates (…) they must necessarily adopt and adapt to the terms and rationale of liberal – that is, non-religious – discourse, even when they do not agree with it.
>
> Haynes 2013, 23

In these contexts, religious organizations will not be heard if they stick to religious arguments. They must adapt to the secular framing and communicate in a non-religious fashion (James 2009b, 10; Haynes 2020). However, at the same time, religious organizations have to take into account the expectations of their religious constituencies that ask for underpinning the faith dimension of development (James 2009a; James and Crooks 2009). Consequently, religious organizations are forced to tackle different expectations and act as boundary agents that mediate between the expectations of their religious constituencies and the secular field of international development (Koehrsen and Heuser 2020).

In this context, it would be misleading to refer to the field of international development as a "post-secular" political arena (for a criticism on the concept, see also Beckford 2012). The field has remained secular while integrating religious organizations only in their capacity to adapt to this secular framing. This might change if the secularity of this field becomes subject to negotiations and conflict (Glaab 2022). As such, there are demands for developing religious literacy among secular development actors (Narayanan 2016). Establishing religious literacy and openness for religious arguments within the field of international development could be interpreted as paving the way for a "post-secular" development agenda.

Democracy – religion – sustainability: ambivalent relationships

This section discusses the relationships between: (a) democracy and religion; and (b) sustainability and religion. I will show that in both cases there is no straight answer to the question whether religion influences democracy and sustainability in a positive or negative way. Depending on the given context, it may support or hinder transition processes towards democracy and sustainability.

Democracy and religion

Studies have produced divergent results regarding the impact of religion on democracy. While some scholars state that religious belief and practice facilitate positive attitudes towards democracy (Meyer et al. 2008), other authors argue that there are democratic and undemocratic aspects of religion. For instance, Ben-Nun Bloom and Arikan (2013) suggest that the private aspects of religion (e.g., prayer, belief) diminish support for democracy, whereas the communal aspects (e.g., community practice) increase democratic attitudes. By contrast, Minkenberg (2007) states that those religions that have a holistic approach to society – such as Catholicism, Islam, and Orthodox Christianity – tend to hamper the emergence of democracy. However, he acknowledges that these religious traditions can change over time to be more in tune with democratic values. Religious traditions are not only subject to transformation processes; they are also multi-vocal. Heterogeneous interpretations of the given traditional foundations will in some cases exhibit features that are beneficial for democracies and in other cases not (Stepan and Robertson 2003). Overall, the picture is highly complex: it involves differences between religious traditions, and within religious traditions, transformations of religious traditions over time, and different aspects of religion (private vs. communal). Nevertheless, a general mismatch between religion and democracy does not become evident.

Today's democracies exhibit differing relationships to religion. Although democracies require a basic separation of church and state, this does not imply that democracies must be necessarily secular. As such, Driessen (2010) points to the existence of different church-state arrangements, many of which offer substantial entry points for religion to participate in political discourses without hampering democratic processes. For instance, there are Christian Democracies in Western Europe that are marked by the presence of strong Christian Parties. These parties sometimes maintain close relationships to churches, but may nevertheless show a pragmatic stance towards their Christian heritage (Kalyvas and van Kersbergen 2010).

Some authors even argue that democracies have religious foundations. Democratic ideas originated from religious teachings (Maddox 2012) and secular democratic states still draw upon religious foundations in the form of civil religion (e.g., implicit religious values, rituals, and symbols) (Bellah 1967). At the same time, the internal structure of religious communities is not necessarily democratic, as it involves religious leaders who can exert significant power in their communities and sometimes evolve authoritative self-images (Ingram 1981).

Traditionally, there has been a tendency to increasingly detach religion from democratic politics in Western countries. Consequently, the "resurgence" of religion challenged the "secularization" of Western politics. In particular, the rise of "political Islam" sparked critical views, perceiving it as an antagonist of the Western world and to liberal democracy (Huntington 1996). Thus, the electoral success of Islamist parties in countries like Algeria, Morocco, and Tunisia after the Arab Spring created anxieties. However, research has shown that these Islamist parties often act in a pragmatic rather than ideological-religious fashion and show openness for democratic processes and structures (Driessen 2012; Dalmasso and Cavatorta 2013). Interestingly, in Europe, a study finds that Muslims show stronger pro-democratic attitudes than Christians (Vlas and Gherghina 2012). These studies counter the frequent assumption that Islam inhibits processes of democratization.

Sustainability and religion

Sustainable development means different things to different actors and includes different pillars (Lele 1991; Garud and Gehman 2012; Luederitz et al. 2016). I will focus on environmental sustainability in this as well as the following section. Similar to the aforementioned relationship between religion and democracy, religion can facilitate or block environmental sustainability.

Different contributions have outlined the negative impact of religious traditions on the environment (White 1967; Artur and Hilhorst 2012; Barker and Bearce 2013; Wexler 2016). Lynn White (1967) spearheaded this perspective. In 1967, he published a groundbreaking article in the journal *Science* in which he argued that Western Christianity is responsible for the ecological crisis: Christian anthropocentrism with its idea of human supremacy over nature has led to the massive exploitation of the earth. Some researchers have argued that although religion may not necessarily encourage environmental exploitation, it may still be far from having a positive effect. Religious worldviews may block environmental protection efforts by interpreting environmental degradation as the will of God. In doing so, they are unlikely to encourage their followers to act against environmental degradation (Artur and Hilhorst 2012; Haluza-DeLay 2014; Roscoe 2016). For instance, evangelicals interpreting environmental degradation as a step towards the second coming – the return of Jesus – will be unwilling to stop this process (Barker and Bearce 2013). Moreover, quantitative research has scrutinized the relationship between conservative evangelicals and climate change skepticism in the US (Evans and Feng 2013; Ecklund et al. 2017). Though conservative evangelicals tend to show a stronger tendency towards climate change skepticism than non-religious populations, climate change skepticism is more strongly associated with political ideology and skeptical views of science. Finally, research has also started to study the impact of religions on climate change through population growth (Skirbekk and Pędziwiatr 2018). Many religions tend to spur population growth by encouraging family creation and opposing contraception measures.

Nevertheless, religions do not only have negative environmental impacts. Most researchers in the academic field of religion and ecology oppose this grim picture by presenting optimistic narratives about the pro-environmental potentials of religion. Though presenting a tough criticism of Western Christianity, Lynn White already indicated these potentials in his famous article. He suggested that only a new religion or significant modification of existing Christianity can solve the environmental crisis: "More science and more technology are not going to get us out of the present ecologic crisis until we find a new religion, or rethink our old one" (White 1967, 1206). White highlights Francis of Assisi, who "tried to depose man from his monarchy over creation and set up a democracy of all God's creatures" (White 1967, 1206). Hence, a reinterpretation of Christian tradition could help to change humanity's attitudes towards nature and stop environmental exploitation. White's argument marked an important starting point for a trend denominated as "greening of religion" (Kanagy and Willits 1993; Shibley and Wiggins 1997). The "greening of religion" means that religious traditions and communities over time become more environmentally aware and engaged. Since the 1980s, scholars have observed the development and expansion of new theologies that propose an environmentally-friendly reading of the given scriptures in the major religious traditions – such as Buddhism, Christianity, Hinduism, Islam, and Judaism (Gottlieb 2006b; Tucker 2006; Tucker 2008; Sivaraska 2009; Abdul-Matin 2010; Boff 2011; Gerten and Bergmann 2012; Blanc 2017). Chaplin (2016) observes similarities in these greening tendencies. Religious traditions increasingly perceive nature as a mirror or a manifestation of the divine. Given this transcendent dimension of nature, humans should act as stewards of nature instead of exploiting it. Based on these observations, Chaplin speaks of a "global greening of religion."

Scholarship about religion and ecology tends to subscribe to the idea of a "greening of religions" and to stress the pro-environmental potentials of religions. In this vein, scholars point to a rise in ecological activities of religious communities, such as public statements, consultations with national governments, recycling or tree planting projects, and environmental education (Shibley and Wiggins 1997; DeHanas 2009; Mohamad et al. 2012; Amri 2014). Religious communities can contribute with these and other activities to broaden sustainability transition processes. In general terms, one can distinguish between three types of religious environmental activity (Koehrsen and Huber 2021): (a) public campaigning; (b) materialization of transitions; and (c) dissemination of environmental values and worldviews. The first type, public campaigning, refers to the public presence and political influence of religious actors (Casanova 1994; Habermas 2008). Depending on their public visibility and political influence, religious actors can have an impact on public debates and political decision-making. They can use this power to promote (or hinder) environmental protection via public statements, media presence, and lobbying towards decision-makers (Gardner 2006; Johnston 2010). The second type, materialization, implies the implementation of transition projects (Gottlieb 2006a; Harper 2011; Mohamad et al. 2012). Examples include the installation of solar panels; the improvement of energy efficiency in religious buildings; a focus on regional consumption; or the implementation of recycling programs. Finally, the third type of engagement refers to the dissemination of pro-environmental values and worldviews. Scholars often stress this as the specific contribution of religion to sustainability transitions, since politics, science, and economy cannot undertake the dissemination of values and worldviews (Gardner 2003; Gardner 2006; Holmes 2006; Tucker 2006; Gottlieb 2008; Bergmann 2009). By propagating pro-environmental values and worldviews through sermons and religious education, religious communities can influence the lifestyles of broad population segments (Shibley and Wiggins 1997; Djupe and Hunt 2009).

Despite the notion of "a global greening of religion," scholarship supposes differences between religious traditions (Kearns 1996; Shibley and Wiggins 1997; Lorentzen and Leavitt-Alcantara 2006; Douglass Warner 2008; Wardekker et al. 2009; McCright and Dunlap 2011; Peifer et al. 2014; Taylor et al. 2016; Ecklund et al. 2017; Skirbekk et al. 2017). In particular, some scholars suggest a strong "greening" process among mainline Christians (e.g., Catholics, Lutherans, Calvinists). Though the macro-level of these communities – the umbrella organizations and leaderships – do indeed show a strong engagement, studies about the environmental attitudes among adherents do not support this assumption (Clements et al. 2014; Taylor et al. 2016; Carlisle and Clark 2018). As such, there appears to be a gap between the strong engagement on the macro-level and the absence of a "greening" on the micro-level: the followers. This gap could be explained by observing local congregations as potential meso-level brokers of the macro-level "greening" towards the micro-level. Exploratory studies suggest that a transmission of the greening on the meso-level scarcely takes place, as local congregations only modestly engage in environmental protection (Koehrsen and Huber 2021). Potential reasons for this lack of engagement among local congregations could be a lack of resources, institutional inertia, and the perception of other issues as more pressing.

Public campaigning as a case for the interlinkage between religion, sustainability and democracy

The previous section has described three potential types of religious environmental engagement: (a) public campaigning; (b) materialization of transitions; and (c) dissemination of environmental values and worldviews. Regarding the relationship with democracy, the most important type is public campaigning. This section describes firstly the potentials of religious actors to shape public debates and political decision-making processes about environmental sustainability. In a second step, it addresses the challenges of religious actors. These become manifest in the stigmatization of religion in environmental circles and the competitive struggles among religious actors.

Religious actors can draw upon their public visibility and credibility to influence public debates about environmental sustainability. By publishing pro-environmental statements, they can create normative pressure on local populations as well as political decision-makers. With regard to the behavior of local populations, these can become particularly relevant in societies where broad populations actively practice a faith tradition. For instance, in Indonesia – the country with the world's largest Muslim population – powerful national Muslim organizations (i.e. Majelis Ulama Indonesia, Nahdlatul Ulama, and Muhammadiyah) circulated public statements, requesting the government to act against environmental degradation and to stick to international climate goals (Mangunjaya and McKay 2012; Amri 2014; Koehrsen 2021). To increase the populations' environmental awareness, Muslim leaders published eco-*dakhwas*: public messages connecting environmental protection with Islam and traditional Indonesian culture (Gade 2012). Additionally, regional councils of Islamic scholars issued *Fatwas* (non-binding legal opinions), declaring environmentally harmful activities (e.g., illegal logging and mining) as *haram* (forbidden) (Mangunjaya and McKay 2012, 302–303). Beyond these leading Muslim organizations, grassroots student initiatives have started to campaign on university campuses in Indonesia, using badges and t-shirts with ecological statements to raise awareness among fellow students (Nilan 2020). In this way, Muslim organizations have contributed to raise public concern about environmental protection in Indonesia.

Public statements of religious actors can also create pressure on political decision-makers. For instance, the encyclical "Laudato Si" by Pope Francis generated a new normative horizon for the climate policy of Catholic politicians. After the publication of the encyclical, politicians and journalists questioned Australian prime minister Tony Abbott about disregarding the Pope's position in his climate policy (e.g., repeal of carbon tax) despite claiming a strong Catholic identity (Grattan 2015; Priestley 2015; *The Guardian* 2015). This example illustrates how public statements of religious actors produce, even in "secular" democracies, an unprecedented need for justification and allows for the interrogation of prevalent climate policies.

Moreover, religious actors can use their relationship with political decision makers and engage in trust building to influence political processes. One example for this is the engagement of religious actors at the United Nations Framework Convention for Climate Change (UNFCCC) (Glaab 2017). The UNFCCC constitutes the legal platform of national governments to negotiate political measures addressing climate change. In recent years, religious actors have become more and more visible in the meetings. Though sharing a similar normative stance like many radical civil society actors (e.g., Greenpeace), religious actors avoid open protest and work within the institutions of the UNFCCC. They prefer developing relationships and trust with governmental actors and using diplomacy to shape decision-making. By taking this trust-building pathway within existing institutions rather than engaging in political protest, they feel that they will have higher chances of influencing political decision-making processes.

Apart from the aforementioned potentials, religious actors also face challenges when engaging in public debates on environmental sustainability. An important challenge are internal religious struggles. Religious actors may assume opposing opinions in public debates about environmental sustainability. These may also include positions that portray rising environmental concern as problematic. An example is the evangelical Cornwall Alliance in the US with its petition "Forget 'Climate Change', Energy Empowers the Poor!" and its initiative "Resisting the Green Dragon" (Chaplin 2016). This alliance critically questions the focus on environmental protection, fearing that the needs of humans are increasingly ignored (e.g., job-loss in extraction industries; disengagement from poverty reduction programs in the Global South). Thereby, it opposes evangelicals that seek to promote environmental protection. Consequently, evangelical opinion leaders pursue to influence public views on climate change and US climate policy in different ways.

Another major challenge consists in the secular framing of environmental debates. Research indicates that receiving attention from secular actors can be challenging. Religious actors frequently face stigma and feel the need to self-secularize in order to contribute to these debates. An example for this is a study conducted by Nita on the *London Islamic Network for the Environment*. The study describes how Muslim activists from this network face marginalization among environmental groups for being religious (Nita 2014, 233–235). Secular environmental groups tend to discourage their members from expressing their religion and, sometimes, even deny religious groups access to their activities. Interestingly, even environmental activists driven by religion may exclude it from their communication. As such, a study on pioneering actors in the energy transition of the German city of Emden illustrates how a spiritual apprehension of nature motivates their environmental engagement (Koehrsen 2018). However, fearing social stigma, these actors do not discuss this religious dimension of nature with other actors. Religion appears to be a factor that environmental actors often – actively or passively – exclude.

Similarly, the above-mentioned study on religious actors at the UNFCCC indicates that these actors usually adapt their language to the secular and often scientifically framed contexts of the UNFCCC and tend to downplay their religious identity (Glaab 2021; see also Haynes 2020). In total, the secular framing of public environmental debates, sometimes even accompanied by open hostility against religion, leads religious actors to self-secularize their communication.

In sum, the aforementioned examples of public environmental activities illustrate that religious actors seek to participate in public opinion processes and shape environmental politics. They assume different positions in these democratic processes and engage via diverse channels, involving public statements, trust building with political decision-makers, and the stimulation of emotional sensibilities. Yet, in the secularized contexts of environmental debates in Global North societies and international settings such as the United Nations, religious actors tend to adapt to the "non-religious" communication standards, avoiding religious terminology and argumentation. This contradicts the narrative of post-secularity, as religious actors often feel restrained to engage their own religious language in democratic public spheres.

Conclusion

This chapter discussed the relationship between religion, democracy, and sustainability. To understand the "new" role of religion in democratic processes and sustainability, it first addressed the "resurgence of religion." While secularization theories have long dominated academic and public debates, religion has received novel attention. Paralleling the increased visibility of religion, religious actors play a rising role in the field of sustainable development. Here, they engage in achieving different SDGs and bring in specific abilities such as their grassroots reach and credibility.

In a second step, this chapter explored the relationships between: (a) democracy and religion; and (b) sustainability and religion. Research in these domains shows that these relationships are ambivalent. Scholarship on the relationship between democracy and religion paints a complex picture. Under specific conditions, religions may help to ferment democracies.

In terms of its impact on environmental sustainability, research has shown that religion can have a negative impact on the environment and counter-act environmental awareness. As such, religious actors may ferment climate change scepticism, thereby influencing public opinion and blocking political decision-making processes directed against climate change. However, at the same time, many scholars suppose that religion can play an important role in promoting environmental sustainability and suggest a "greening of religions," meaning that faith traditions become more environmentally friendly over time. Religions can become relevant in three ways for environmental sustainability: (a) public campaigning; (b) materialization of transitions; and (c) dissemination of environmental values and worldviews.

Considering the relationship between religion and democracy, public campaigning is the most relevant type of religious activity and was, therefore, explored in the third step of this contribution. Various examples illustrate that religious actors can act as democratic actors that seek to have a voice in the public debates about environmental sustainability. Religious actors have developed different strategies, such as trust building and the dissemination of public messages, in order to reach decision-makers and the wider public. Frequently, they take a normative stance, publicly propagating the protection of the environment. In other cases, they shed critical light on the rising environmental focus and lobby for a stronger dedication to questions of poverty eradication.

Although public and political arenas seem to show an increasing openness towards "religion," the ongoing marginalization of religion renders its inclusion in the democratic debates challenging. Religious actors frequently feel that their participation in democratic public arenas requires self-secularization, meaning that they have to leave out religious language and arguments. While religious actors are welcomed to bring in those features of their religion that are regarded as helpful for reaching the objectives of sustainable development (e.g., grassroots reach, organizational facilities), crucial religious elements such as their worldviews, values, and concepts of transcendence tend to be perceived more critical – mismatching the secular and democratic standards of international development – and are therefore left out. This limits the democratic participation of religion, as the inclusion of religious actors often involves the exclusion of their religion, thereby leading religious actors to engage as secular actors in these arenas. Thus, the notion of post-secularity appears to be misleading.

Further research may study what the increasing integration of religious actors means for the democratic negotiation of sustainability politics. To what extent are religious actors able to influence democratic decision-making processes regarding sustainability transitions? More generally, in what way does their participation alter the working principles of "secular" democracies? Does their participation perhaps make it possible to renegotiate the boundaries between religion and "the secular," potentially opening up post-secular spaces?

Note

1 Apart from the "rediscovery" of religion, two other factors have facilitated the integration of religion in "secular" development contexts: (a) structural adjustment programs, rolling back governmental welfare services and allowing civil society organizations (including religious organizations) to step in; and (b) the belief that religion can effectively make a difference in development activities in the Global South.

References

Abdul-Matin, I., 2010. *Green Deen. What Islam Teaches about Protecting the Planet / Ibrahim Abdul-Matin*. 1st ed. San Francisco: Berrett-Koehler.
Amri, U., 2014. From theology to a praxis of "eco-jihad". The role of religious civil society organizations in combating climate change in Indonesia. In R.G. Veldman, A. Szasz, and R. Haluza-DeLay, eds. *How the world's religions are responding to climate change. Social scientific investigations*. London: Routledge, 75–93.
Artur, L., and Hilhorst, D., 2012. Everyday realities of climate change adaptation in Mozambique. *Global Environmental Change*, 22 (2), 529–536.
Asad, T., 2009. *Genealogies of Religion: Discipline and Reasons of Power in Christianity and Islam*. Baltimore: The Johns Hopkins University Press.
Barker, D.C., and Bearce, D.H., 2013. End-times theology, the shadow of the future, and public resistance to addressing global climate change. *Political Research Quarterly*, 66 (2), 267–279.
Beckford, J.A., 2012. SSSR presidential address public religions and the postsecular: critical reflections. *Journal for the Scientific Study of Religion*, 51 (1), 1–19.
Beinlich, A.-K., and Braungart, C., 2019. Religions NGOs at the UN. A quantitative overview. In C. Baumgart-Ochse and K.D. Wolf, eds. *Religious NGOs at the United Nations. Polarizers or mediators?* Abingdon: Routledge, 26–46.
Bellah, R.N., 1967. Civil religion in America. *Daedalus*, 1–21.
Ben-Nun Bloom, P., and Arikan, G., 2013. Religion and support for democracy: a cross-national test of the mediating mechanisms. *British Journal of Political Science*, 43 (2), 375–397.
Berger, J., 2003. Religious non-governmental organisations: an exploratory analysis. *Voluntas: International Journal of Voluntary and Nonprofit Organisations*, 14 (1), 15–39.
Berger, P.L., 1999. *The Desecularization of the World. Resurgent Religion and World Politics*. Washington: Wm. B. Eerdmans Publishing Company.
Bergmann, S., 2009. Climate change changes religion. *Studia Theologica – Nordic Journal of Theology*, 63 (2), 98–118.
Blanc, J., 2017. *Ökokatholizismus. Sozialethische Untersuchungen zu ausgewählten Ländern und Institutionen in Europa*. Marburg: Metropolis-Verl.

Boehle, J., 2010. The UN system and religious actors in the context of global change. *CrossCurrents*, 60 (3), 383–401.
Boff, L., 2011. *Ecología. Grito de la tierra, grito de los pobres*. 5th ed. Madrid: Trotta.
Bruce, S., 2011. *Secularization. In Defence of an Unfashionable Theory*. Oxford: Oxford University Press.
Carlisle, J.E., and Clark, A.K., 2018. Green for God: religion and environmentalism by cohort and time. *Environment and Behavior*, 50 (2), 213–241.
Casanova, J., 1994. *Public Religions in the Modern World*. Chicago: University of Chicago Press.
Casanova, J., 2003. Beyond European and American exceptionalisms: towards a global perspective. In G. Davie, L. Woodhead, and P. Heelas, eds. *Predicting Religion. Christian, secular, and alternative futures*. Aldershot: Ashgate Publishing, 17–29.
Chaplin, J., 2016. The global greening of religion. *Palgrave Communications*, 2. Available from: https://doi.org/10.1057/palcomms.2016.47.
Clarke, G., 2006. Faith matters: faith-based organisations, civil society and international development. *Journal of International Development*, 18 (6), 835–848.
Clarke, G., 2008. Faith-based organisations and international development. An overview. In G. Clarke and M. Jennings, eds. *Development, civil society and faith-based organisations. Bridging the sacred and the secular*. Basingstoke: Palgrave Macmillan, 17–45.
Clements, J.M., Xiao, C., and McCright, A.M., 2014. An examination of the "Greening of Christianity" thesis among americans, 1993–2010. *Journal for the Scientific Study of Religion*, 53 (2), 373–391.
Cordier, B. de, 2009. Faith-based aid, globalisation and the humanitarian frontline. An analysis of Western-based Muslim aid organisations. *Disasters*, 33 (4), 608–628.
Dalmasso, E., and Cavatorta, F., 2013. Democracy, civil liberties and the role of religion after the Arab awakening: constitutional reforms in Tunisia and Morocco. *Mediterranean Politics*, 18 (2), 225–241.
Davie, G., 2010. Resacralization. In B.S. Turner, ed. *The new Blackwell companion to the sociology of religion*. Malden: Wiley-Blackwell, 160–177.
DeHanas, D.N., 2009. Broadcasting green. Grassroots environmentalism on Muslim women's radio. *The Sociological Review*, 57 (2 suppl), 141–155.
Deneulin, S., and Rakodi, C., 2011. Revisiting religion: development studies thirty years on. *World Development*, 39 (1), 45–54. Available from: www.sciencedirect.com/science/article/pii/S0305750X10001269.
Djupe, P.A., and Hunt, P.K., 2009. Beyond the Lynn White thesis: congregational effects on environmental concern. *Journal for the Scientific Study of Religion*, 48 (4), 670–686.
Douglass Warner, K., 2008. The greening of American Catholicism: identity, conversion, and continuity. *Religion and American Culture-a Journal of Interpretation*, 18 (1), 113–142.
Driessen, M.D., 2010. Religion, state, and democracy. Analyzing two dimensions of church-state arrangements. *Politics and Religion*, 3 (01), 55.
Driessen, M.D., 2012. Public Religion, Democracy, and Islam: Examining the Moderation Thesis in Algeria. *Comparative Politics*, 44 (2), 171–189.
Ecklund, E.H., et al., 2017. Examining links between religion, evolution views, and climate change skepticism. *Environment and Behavior*, 0 (0), 0013916516674246.
Evans, J.H., and Feng, J., 2013. Conservative Protestantism and skepticism of scientists studying climate change. *Climatic Change*, 121 (4), 595–608.
Gade, A.M., 2012. Tradition and sentiment in Indonesian environmental Islam. *Worldviews*, 16 (3), 263–285. https://doi.org/10.1163/15685357-01603005.
Gardner, G.T., 2002. *Invoking the spirit. Religion and spirituality in the quest for a sustainable world* [online]. Available from: www.worldwatch.org/system/files/EWP164.pdf [Accessed 10 October 2016].
Gardner, G.T., 2003. Engaging religion in the quest for a sustainable world. In Worldwatch Institute, ed. *State of the world, 2003. A Worldwatch Institute report on progress toward a sustainable society*. New York: W.W. Norton, 152–175.
Gardner, G.T., 2006. *Inspiring Progress: Religions' Contributions to Sustainable Development*. New York: W.W. Norton.
Garud, R., and Gehman, J., 2012. Metatheoretical perspectives on sustainability journeys. Evolutionary, relational and durational. *Research Policy*, 41 (6), 980–995.
Gerten, D., and Bergmann, S., eds., 2012. *Religion in Environmental and Climate Change. Suffering, Values, Lifestyles*. London and New York: Continuum.
Glaab, K., 2017. A climate for justice? Faith-based advocacy on climate change at the United Nations. *Globalizations*, 14 (7), 1110–1124.

Glaab, K., 2019. Faithful translation? Shifting the boundaries of the religious and the secular in the global climate change debate. In T. Berger and A. Esguerra, eds. *World politics in translation. Power, relationality, and difference in global cooperation*. London: Routledge, 175–190.

Glaab, K., 2022. The green, the secular, and the religious. The legitimacy of religious environmentalism in global climate politics. In J. Köhrsen, J. Blanc, and F. Huber, eds. *Global religious environmental activism: case studies of emerging conflicts and tensions in earth stewardship*. London: Routledge.

Gottlieb, R.S., 2008. You gonna be here long? Religion and Sustainability. *Worldviews: Global Religions, Culture, and Ecology*, 12 (2), 163–178.

Gottlieb, R.S., 2006a. Religious environmentalism in action. In R.S. Gottlieb, ed. *The Oxford handbook of religion and ecology*. Oxford: Oxford University Press, 467–509.

Gottlieb, R.S., ed., 2006b. *The Oxford Handbook of Religion and Ecology*. Oxford: Oxford University Press.

Grattan, M., 2015. *Can the Pope get Tony Abbott serious about climate change* [online]. Available from: http://theconversation.com/abbott-has-papal-disconnect-on-fossil-fuels-renewables-43555 [Accessed 5 December 2015].

Green, M., Mercer, C., and Mesaki, S., 2012. Faith in forms. Civil society evangelism and development in Tanzania. *Development in Practice*, 22 (5–6), 721–734.

Habermas, J., 2001. *Glauben und Wissen. Friedenspreis des Deutschen Buchhandels 2001*. 1st ed. Frankfurt: Suhrkamp.

Habermas, J., 2006. Religion in the public sphere. *European Journal of Philosophy*, 14 (1), 1–25.

Habermas, J., 2008. Notes on post-secular society. *New perspectives quarterly* (25).

Haluza-DeLay, R., 2014. Religion and climate change. Varieties in viewpoints and practices. *Wiley Interdisciplinary Reviews: Climate Change*, 5 (2), 261–279.

Harper, F., 2011. Greening faith: turning belief into action for the earth. *Zygon*, 46 (4), 957–971. Available from: http://dx.doi.org/10.1111/j.1467-9744.2011.01231.x.

Haynes, J., 2007. *Religion and Development. Conflict or Cooperation?* Basingstoke: Palgrave Macmillan.

Haynes, J., 2013. *Faith-Based Organisations at the United Nations. 2013/70*. Florence: European University Institute.

Haynes, J., 2020. World vision and 'Christian values' at the United Nations. In J. Koehrsen and A. Heuser, eds. *Faith Based Organizations in Development Discourses and Practices*. London: Routledge, 86–112.

Heist, D., and Cnaan, R., 2016. Faith-based international development work. A review. *Religions*, 7 (3), 19.

Heuser, A., and Koehrsen, J., eds., 2020. *Does Religion make a Difference? Religious NGOs in International Development Work*. Baden-Baden/Zürich: Nomos.

Hoffmann, C., 2020. From missionaries to Ecumenical co-workers: a case study from Mission 21 in Kalimantan, Indonesia. In J. Koehrsen and A. Heuser, eds. *Faith Based Organizations in Development Discourses and Practices*. London: Routledge.

Holmes, R., 2006. Caring for nature: what science and economics can't teach us but religion can. *Environmental Values*, 15 (3), 307–313.

Huber, F., and Koehrsen, J., 2020. Das Ergrünen von Religionen. Ökologische Nachhaltigkeit in religiösen Gemeinschaften. In A. Henkel and T. Barth, eds. *10 Minuten Soziologie: Nachhaltigkeit*. Bielefeld: transcript.

Huntington, S.P., 1996. *The Clash of Civilizations and the Remaking of World Order*. New York: Simon & Schuster.

Ingram, L.C., 1981. Leadership, Democracy, and religion: role ambiguity among pastors in southern Baptist churches. *Journal for the Scientific Study of Religion*, 20 (2), 119.

Ives, C.D., and Kidwell, J., 2019. Religion and social values for sustainability. *Sustainability Science*. Available from: https://doi.org/10.1007/s11625-019-00657-0.

James, R., 2009a. *What is Distinctive about FBOs?* [online]. International NGO Training and Research Centre. Available from: http://dspace.africaportal.org/jspui/bitstream/123456789/24075/1/What%20is%20distinctive%20about%20FBOs.pdf?1 [Accessed 10 June, 2017].

James, R., 2009b. What is distinctive about FBOs? How European FBOs define and operationalise their faith. *Praxis Paper*, 22 (3).

James, R., and Crooks, B., 2009. *Faith-Based Organisational Development (OD) with Churches in Malawi* [online]. International NGO Training and Research Centre. Available from: http://dspace.africaportal.org/jspui/bitstream/123456789/26272/1/Praxis%20Note%2047%20-%20Faith%20and%20organisational%20development.pdf?1 [Accessed 10 June, 2017].

Johnston, L.F., 2010. The religious dimensions of sustainability: institutional religions, civil society, and international politics since the turn of the twentieth century. *Religion Compass*, 4 (3), 176–189.

Kaag, M., 2007. Aid, Umma, and Politics. Transnational Islamic NGOs in Chad. In B. Soares and R. Otayek, eds. *Islam and Muslim politics in Africa*: Springer, 85–102.

Kalyvas, S.N., and van Kersbergen, K., 2010. Christian democracy. *Annual Review of Political Science*, 13 (1), 183–209.

Kanagy, C.L., and Willits, F.K., 1993. A "greening" of religion? Some evidence from a Pennsylvania sample. *Social Science Quarterly*, 74 (3), 674–683.

Kearns, L., 1996. Saving the creation: Christian environmentalism in the United States. *Sociology of Religion*, 57 (1), 55–70.

Kloß, S., 2020. Giving and development: ethno-religious identities and 'holis-tic development' in Guyana. In J. Koehrsen and A. Heuser, eds. *Faith based organizations in development discourses and practices*. London: Routledge, 113–138.

Koehrsen, J., 2018. Eco-spirituality in environmental action: studying dark green religion in the German energy transition. *Journal for the Study of Religion, Nature and Culture*, 12 (1), 34–54.

Koehrsen, J., and Heuser, A., 2020. Beyond established boundaries: faith based organizations in development discourses and practice. In J. Koehrsen and A. Heuser, eds. *Faith based organizations in development discourses and practices*. London: Routledge.

Koehrsen, J., 2021. Muslims and climate change. *WIREs Climate Change*, 12 (3), 1–19.

Koehrsen, J. and Huber, F., 2021. A field perspective on sustainability transitions: the case of religious organizations. *Environmental Innovations and Sustainability Transitions*, 40, 408–420.

Lehmann, K., 2016. *Religious NGOs in International Relations. The Construction of 'The Religious' and 'The Secular'*. London and New York: Routledge.

Lele, S.M., 1991. Sustainable development: a critical review. *World Development*, 19 (6), 607–621.

Lorentzen, L.A., and Leavitt-Alcantara, S., 2006. Religion and environmental struggles in Latin America. In R.S. Gottlieb, ed. *The Oxford handbook of religion and ecology*. Oxford: Oxford University Press, 510–534.

Luederitz, C., Abson, D.J., Audet, R. and Lang, D.J., 2017. Many pathways toward sustainability: Not conflict but co-learning between transition narratives. *Sustainability Science*, 12 (3), 393–407. https://doi.org/10.1007/s11625-016-0414-0.

Lunn, J., 2009. The role of religion, spirituality and faith in development: a critical theory approach. *Third World Quarterly*, 30 (5), 937–951.

Lynch, C., and Schwarz, T.B., 2016. Humanitarianism's proselytism problem. *International Studies Quarterly*, 60 (4), 636–646.

Maddox, G., 2012. *Religion and the Rise of Democracy*. London and New York: Routledge.

Mangunjaya, F.M., and McKay, J.E., 2012. Reviving an Islamic approach for environmental conservation in Indonesia. *Worldviews: Global Religions, Culture, and Ecology*, 16 (3), 286–305.

Marshall, K., 2001. Development and religion. A different lens on development debates. *Peabody Journal of Education*, 76 (3–4), 339–375.

McCright, A.M., and Dunlap, R.E., 2011. Cool dudes: the denial of climate change among conservative white males in the United States. *Global Environmental Change*, 21 (4), 1163–1172.

Meyer, K., Tope, D., and Price, A.M., 2008. Religion and support for democracy. A crossnational examination. *Sociological Spectrum*, 28 (5), 625–653.

Minkenberg, M., 2007. Democracy and religion: theoretical and empirical observations on the relationship between Christianity, Islam and Liberal democracy. *Journal of Ethnic and Migration Studies*, 33 (6), 887–909.

Mohamad, Z.F., Idris, N., and Mamat, Z., 2012. Role of religious communities in enhancing transition experiments. A localised strategy for sustainable solid waste management in Malaysia. *Sustainability Science*, 7 (2), 237–251.

Narayanan, Y., 2016. Religion, sustainable development and policy: principles to practice. *Sustainable Development*, 24 (3), 149–153.

Nilan, P., 2020. Muslim youth environmentalists in Indonesia. *Journal of Youth Studies*, 1–16.

Nita, M., 2014. Christian and Muslim climate activists fasting and praying for the planet. Emotional translation of "dark green" activism and green-faith identities. In R.G. Veldman, A. Szasz, and R. Haluza-DeLay, eds. *How the world's religions are responding to climate change. Social scientific investigations*. London: Routledge, 229–243.

Occhipinti, L.A., 2015. Faith-based organisations and development. In E. Tomalin, ed. *The Routledge handbook of religions and global development*. London and New York: Routledge, 331–345.

Palmer, V., 2011. Analysing cultural proximity. Islamic Relief Worldwide and Rohingya refugees in Bangladesh. *Development in Practice*, 21 (1), 96–108.

Peifer, J.L., Ecklund, E.H., and Fullerton, C., 2014. How evangelicals from two churches in the American Southwest frame their relationship with the environment. *Review of Religious Research*, 56 (3), 373–397.

Petersen, M.J., 2012a. Islamizing aid. Transnational Muslim NGOs after 9.11. *Voluntas: International Journal of Voluntary and Nonprofit Organizations*, 23 (1), 126–155.

Petersen, M.J., 2012b. Trajectories of transnational Muslim NGOs. *Development in Practice*, 22 (5–6), 763–778.

Pew Research Center, 2017. *The Changing Global Religious Landscape* [online]. Available from: www.pewforum.org/2017/04/05/the-changing-global-religious-landscape/ [Accessed 7 March, 2019].

Pollack, D., 2018. Säkularisierung. In D. Pollack, *et al.*, eds. *Handbuch Religionssoziologie*. Wiesbaden: Springer VS, 303–327.

Pollack, D., and Rosta, G., 2017. *Religion and Modernity: An International Comparison*. Oxford: Oxford University Press.

Priestley, A., 2015. *Can the Pope get Tony Abbott serious about climate change* [online]. Available from: www.womensagenda.com.au/talking-about/top-stories/item/5913-can-the-pope-get-tony-abbott-serious-about-climate-change [Accessed 5 December, 2015].

Rice, G., 2006. Pro-environmental behavior in Egypt: is there a role for Islamic environmental ethics? *Journal of Business Ethics*, 65 (4), 373–390.

Roscoe, P., 2016. Method, measurement, and management in IPCC climate modeling. *Human Ecology*, 44 (6), 655–664.

Sheikh, K.M., 2006. Involving religious leaders in conservation education in the Western Karakorum, Pakistan. *Mountain Research and Development*, 26 (4), 319–322.

Shibley, M.A., and Wiggins, J.L., 1997. The Greening of Mainline American Religion: A Sociological Analysis of the Environmental Ethics of the National Religious Partnership for the Environment. *Social Compass*, 44 (3), 333–348.

Sivaraska, S., 2009. *Wisdom of Sustainability. Buddhist economics for the 21st century*. Chiang Mai: KOA Books.

Skirbekk, V., *et al.*, 2017. *Religious belief and environmental challenges in the 21st century* [online]. Available from: www.populationenvironmentresearch.org/pern_files/papers/Religious%20belief%20and%20environmental%20challenges%20in%20the%2021st%20century.pdf [Accessed 28 September 2019].

Skirbekk, V., and Pędziwiatr, K., 2018. *Sustainability and climate change in major religions with a focus on Islam* [online]. Available from: www.researchgate.net/publication/329656310 [Accessed 1 September 2019].

Stepan, A.C., and Robertson, G.B., 2003. An "Arab" More Than a "Muslim" Democracy Gap. *Journal of Democracy*, 14 (3), 30–44.

Taylor, B., van Wieren, G., and Zaleha, B.D., 2016. Lynn White Jr. and the greening-of-religion hypothesis. *Conservation Biology*, 30 (5), 1000–1009.

Tenbruck, F.H., 1993. Die Religion im Maelstrom der Reflexion. *Kölner Zeitschrift für Soziologie und Sozialpsychologie. Sonderheft* (33), 31–67.

Ter Haar, G., and Wolfensohn, J.D., 2011. *Religion and Development. Ways of Transforming the World*. London: Hurst & Co.

Thaut, L.C., 2009. The Role of Faith in Christian Faith-Based Humanitarian Agencies. Constructing the Taxonomy. *Voluntas: International Journal of Voluntary and Nonprofit Organizations*, 20 (4), 319–350.

The Guardian, 2015. *Liberals 'disgusted' after Larissa Waters asks if Tony Abbott will listen to Pope on climate change* [online]. Available from: www.theguardian.com/australia-news/video/2015/jun/22/liberals-disgusted-after-greens-larissa-waters-asks-if-catholic-tony-abbott-will-listen-to-pope-on-climate-change-video [Accessed 5 December 2015].

Tucker, M.E., 2006. Religion and Ecology. Survey of the field. In R.S. Gottlieb, ed. *The Oxford handbook of religion and ecology*: Oxford University Press, 398–418.

Tucker, M.E., 2008. World Religions, the Earth Charter, and Sustainability. *Worldviews: Global Religions, Culture, and Ecology*, 12 (2), 115–128.

Vlas, N., and Gherghina, S., 2012. Where does religion meet democracy? A comparative analysis of attitudes in Europe. *International Political Science Review*, 33 (3), 336–351.

Wardekker, A., Petersen, A.C., and van der Sluijs, Jeroen P., 2009. Ethics and public perception of climate change. Exploring the Christian voices in the US public debate. *Global Environmental Change*, 19 (4), 512–521.

Ware, V.-A., Ware, A., and Clarke, M., 2016. Domains of Faith Impact: How "Faith" is Perceived to Shape Faith-Based International Development Organisations. *Development in Practice,* 26 (3), 321–333.

Wexler, J., 2016. *When God isn't green. A world-wide journey to places where religious practice and environmentalism collide.* Boston: Beacon Press.

White, L., 1967. The historical roots of our ecologic crisis. *Science,* 155 (3767), 1203–1207.

Woodhead, L., 2011. Five concepts of religion. *International Review of Sociology – Revue Internationale de Sociologie,* 21 (1), 121–143.

PART IV

Actors and governance contexts

15
THE MODERN STATE AND SUSTAINABILITY
Challenges to governance

Daniel Fiorino

Introduction

The concept of sustainability has become a staple of contemporary political and economic discourse. Definitions abound. The best-known is that of the World Commission on Environment and Development (Brundtland Commission), as "development that meets the needs of the current generation without compromising the ability of future generations to meet their needs" (WCED 1987, 43). This constitutes a vision more than anything else. Among other illustrative definitions of sustainability are: "the capacity to continuously produce the necessities of quality human existence within the bounds of the natural world of undiminished quality" (Paehlke 2006, 58); "an interdependent concern with: promoting human welfare; satisfying human needs; protecting the environment; considering the fate of future generations; achieving equity between rich and poor; and participating on a broad basis …" (Lafferty and Meadowcroft 2000, 19); and "the integration of environmental objectives into non-environmental policy sectors" (Lafferty and Hoven 2003, 1).

What all of these share is concern with the future, especially with not foreclosing options for future generations; the need to incorporate ecological issues into economic, political, and social decision making; a process engaging all of society; equity and empowerment; and preventing long-term and irreversible degradation to ecosystems. All of this poses profound challenges to modern states and effective governance, the role of which is often neglected in the sustainability literature.

This chapter considers the relationships among sustainability, the state, and governance. It begins with the concept of sustainability and its neglect of the role of effective, quality governance. Next is the topic of ecological governance, a precondition for sustainability. Following that are discussions of patterns of governance and regime types that determine capacities for sustainability: do different forms of the state have more or less of a capacity to lead a transition to sustainability? The final section considers some of the tensions surrounding the role of the state in sustainability.

Linking governance with sustainability

Linking sustainability with governance means bringing the concept down to earth: making it relevant to practical issues of governing and the state normatively and empirically. A start is in systems thinking and its advantages for sustainability. Systems thinking recognizes the dynamism existing in ecological, political, economic, and social systems. It distinguishes a given system from its environment. It allows us to think about levels, with some systems nested within others. It incorporates the concepts of self-regulation, adaptation, emergence, evolution, and resilience; all apply to natural and human systems (see Hjorth and Bagheri 2006 on a systems-based approach).

The typical view of sustainability consists of three interdependent, overlapping systems: the ecological, economic, and social. Each one defines a system-level imperative. The *ecological imperative* is "to remain within planetary biophysical capacity" (Robinson and Tinker 1997, 77). The *economic imperative* is "to ensure and maintain adequate standards of living for all people" (77). The *social/political imperative* is "to provide social structures, including systems of governance, which effectively propagate the values people wish to live by" (77). Each system is crucial in itself; failure in one undermines others. Political instability impedes economic success; ecological devastation leads to economic insecurity and political instability; economic crisis can cause poor resource use and degrades ecosystems. The governance challenge is "to sustain each system internally as well as to maintain an appropriate balance among them" (Fiorino 2010, 80).

The problem with the standard three-system formulation of sustainability is that it lumps too much into the social system and thus neglects governance. The social system typically includes procedural (transparency, participation, civil rights) and substantive dimensions (access to health care, education, housing). More problematically, it mixes governance with these other issues. To appreciate the roles of governance and the state, we should view governance as a fourth, enabling system.

Governance is defined here as "a process of – more or less institutionalized – interaction between public and/or private entities ultimately aimed at the realization of collective goals" (Lange et al. 2013, 406). In these terms, governance exists only when it has a purpose: the "realization of collective goals." Consistent with recent thinking in public administration, governance includes more than just government. Government institutions and processes are central, but interactions with others matter. Governance "is more or less institutionalized." Despite the critical role governance systems play in sustainability transitions, they are neglected in much of the literature.

Differentiating governance from the social system allows us to focus better on particular characteristics of governance and its role in sustainability. Indeed, the research suggests that the quality and stability of governance systems are a critical part of a transition to sustainability – of sustaining each of the other systems while also maintaining the appropriate balance among them. The process of maintaining the ecological system while sustaining an appropriate balance with the other systems – a function of the political process at multiple scales – is ecological governance.

This chapter presents the challenge as one of making a transition to sustainability, in the sense that sustainability is a journey more than a destination. This will consist in coming decades of, as examples, shifts from fossil fuel to clean energy, expanding sustainable farming, protecting ecosystems, promoting water efficiency and reuse, and other more specific transitions. None of this occur without a capacity for local, regional, and national ecological governance.

Ecological governance and the state

Ecological governance is a relatively recent addition to the responsibilities of the modern state. James Meadowcroft (2012a) writes that, until late in the last century, the core activities of the modern state were to maintain internal order and protect against external threats; promote economic prosperity; and deliver welfare services. The security, prosperity, and welfare states now have expanded to encompass the ecological state. Yet expectations for the ecological state are hardly firmly established; Meadowcroft writes that "the environment remains the most vulnerable of these core domains of state activity because it is the newest and least institutionally embedded" (2012a, 76). This is most obvious in the United States, which for decades has been the scene of challenges to sustainability by a neo-liberalism that is hostile to the ecological state (Layzer 2012).

Ecological governance emerged as a core function of industrial countries nationally in the 1970s. Pioneer countries were those of northern Europe, the British Commonwealth, the United States, and Japan. They established ministries and regulatory agencies, adopted laws and policies, set goals, and generally incorporated environmental issues into the core roles of the state (Janicke and Weidner 1997; Duit, Feindt, and Meadowcroft 2016). More recently, this institutionalization of policies and goals extended to developing and emerging economies in Eastern Europe, China, Brazil, Latin America, and India in a learning process from pioneer countries (Sommerer and Lim 2016). In these countries, the environment is even less firmly embedded on national agendas. Still, it is a widely accepted role for the state and occupies a prominent place in national policy agendas.

For most of the second half of the last century, ecological governance focused on the goal of environmental protection. As governments made progress on air or water pollution and waste management, another even more challenging set of problems emerged. The policy literature views this as a shift from a first to a second and third generation of environmental issues. Governments worried not just about point sources of air and water pollution (power plants, sewage treatment works, steel and auto makers) but diffuse, harder-to-control non-point sources. Farm and urban stormwater run-off accounted for more water degradation. Growing evidence of the effects of climate change forced a reassessment of energy, transport, food, and other systems. In the United States this is seen as a transition through three environmental epochs (Mazmanian and Kraft 2009): from regulation, to efficiency and innovation, and then to an as yet-unfulfilled sustainability epoch.

Moving from environmental protection to sustainability imposes different demands on the modern state (Dovers 1996). To start, sustainability calls for longer time frames. Political systems tend to operate in the short term, where public attention is focused and policy decisions are made. It also forces a high degree of policy integration, most famously by linking economy and ecology as well as social issues like education and health care. Given the dominance of economic goals in modern states, ecological issues often end up on the losing end of calculations. Another qualitative difference is irreversibility. Environmental sustainability involves choices about ecosystems, species, the climate system, and resources that, once a line is crossed, often cannot be reversed. Sustainability also challenges policy makers with lots of scientific complexity and uncertainty. As Dovers points out, these features are present in more traditional challenges to governance, but rarely have they all been present to the same degree or as consistently as in sustainability policies.

What matters now is moving from a concern about environmental protection to one for environmental sustainability. Environmental protection is about managing or limiting the effects of human activities on ecology and public health: controlling air or water pollution, managing waste, protecting ecosystems and species, and reducing chemical risks. It avoids major changes in economic systems in favor of minimal intervention through technology requirements or product standards and limits. An illustration is the practice of environmental impact assessment. Although it was a major innovation in environmental policy at the time, it is incremental, a way to assess proposed actions and conduct analysis that considers how to minimize harm (Andrews 2017). Despite its value, it does not offer a path to a fundamental economic and ecological transformation.

A focus on environmental sustainability raises more basic questions. It is not necessarily a radical process aiming to sweep away existing social, economic, and political systems and replace them with something fundamentally different (Dryzek 2013; Fiorino 2018b; Bornemann and Christen 2019). It does call for changes in economic systems: from fossil fuels to clean energy, to new ways of cultivating crops and using water, to designs for green chemistry, and to new modes of transport. Rather than seek ways to make coal-fired electricity cleaner, for example, a sustainability perspective would aim to eliminate coal from the energy system. Rather than fine-tune the internal combustion engine to improve fuel efficiency and reduce emissions, the goal in a sustainability context is to electrify everything, generate electricity with clean energy, and aggressively promote energy efficiency.

What has driven this transition in ecological governance from concerns with environmental protection to sustainability? Certainly, the prominence of economic goals is a factor. Ecological goals are constantly pitted against economic ones: growth, competitiveness, and jobs, and the sustainability concept itself reflects this framing. Indeed, the core idea is that economics and ecology may be reconciled in positive ways, and a belief that this idea has empirical foundations.

Even more important in driving the change in goals from environmental protection to environmental sustainability is awareness of local, regional, and global ecosystem limits. Although the evidence on climate change makes these limits especially obvious, other factors highlight them as well: water stress, ecosystem degradation, deforestation, species loss, and others. Grasping the role of the state and governance calls for an understanding of limits. Indeed, if there were no ecological limits, there would be no need to worry about at least some elements of sustainability (Meadowcroft 2012b; Fiorino 2018b).

Recognizing planetary limits

Driving this concern with environmental sustainability over environmental protection is a growing awareness of planetary limits. This is not new. The idea of limits joined the ecological lexicon in *The Limits to Growth* (Meadows et al. 1972). Indeed, the first decade of modern environmentalism (the 1970s) stressed the need for political and economic change. Critics doubted that democracies could do the job (Heilbroner 1974; Ophuls 1977). As it turned out, democracies mostly have protected the environment better than authoritarian regimes (Dasgupta and De Cian 2018), although criticizing specific democracies was more the point for many of these writers, with liberal-pluralist-capitalist states like the US as their target (an example is Shearman and Smith 2007).

The limits case has gained renewed traction in recent decades, largely due to evidence on climate change, but with more understanding of other environmental limits and health effects as well. Governments are contending with a scientific consensus that human activity, mostly related to energy and agriculture, is responsible for growing concentrations of greenhouse gases in the atmosphere and adverse effects on the systems on which human well-being depends. Added to this is a better appreciation of threats to local, regional, and global ecosystems, species, and resources.

The challenge for the state is illustrated in the concept of planetary boundaries. This builds on previous assessments of limits but reorients it in terms of a *safe operating space* for humanity. It identifies nine planetary boundaries that underpin the quality of life: atmospheric concentrations of carbon dioxide, rates of biodiversity loss, the nitrogen and phosphorous cycles, changes in land use, global freshwater use, aerosol loadings, stratospheric ozone depletion, chemical pollution, and ocean acidification. Three of the nine boundaries already have been exceeded: carbon dioxide, the nitrogen cycle, and biodiversity loss. For ocean acidification, land use, phosphorous, and freshwater, boundaries are being stretched, and long-term trends are worrisome (Rockstrom et al. 2009).

These trends pushing the edge on planetary limits are more than an ecological and health issue, although these matter (MEA 2005). The larger issue is that they threaten the foundations of human well-being. Over time, climate change damages health, disrupts agriculture, increases droughts in some places and flooding in others, produces more extreme weather, adds to economic insecurity and political stability, and causes other adverse effects. Deforestation, species loss, desertification, lost wetlands, and other ecological harm makes life more difficult, expensive, and insecure. It is not fearmongering to assert that stretching and exceeding local, regional, and global limits will have devastating consequences. A driver of ecological harm is economic growth, at least in the forms it has occurred so far; any failure to change the patterns of growth is a dangerous path. Whether or not this will requires some form of negative growth is up for debate (Fiorino 2018b).

Indeed, a 2019 report from the Intergovernmental Science-Policy Platform on Biodiversity and Ecosystem Services (IPBES) documents the severe impacts land and sea use, climate change, and pollution are having on global ecosystems. These are more than just ecological or health issues. As statement issued with the report states "We are eroding the very foundations of our economies, livelihoods, food security, health and quality of life worldwide" (IPBES 2019). In combination, all these factors place demands on the capacities at local, regional, and global scales of governance.

The role of the state in sustainability

In the emergence of ecological governance discussed earlier, a core set of environmental responsibilities were added to the existing state roles in security, prosperity, and social welfare. Since the late 1960s, governments around the world – first in the early industrial nations and more recently in the emerging economies – enacted laws, created ministries and regulatory agencies, trained professionals, and added environmental standards to the activities of agencies and firms. Nearly all the early innovation was in democratic countries, with authoritarian ones lagging. Even now, it appears that democracies perform better on the environment than do authoritarian regimes. (This evidence is summarized in Fiorino 2018a and discussed in more detail later in the chapter.)

As the urgency of climate change and other issues increased, and as most governments have been ineffective in managing them, we have seen two kinds of challenges to these views. One holds that government is largely irrelevant, that is, unreliable, inconsistent, and unnecessary in making the needed change – that the private sector can lead the charge on its own. The other is that only highly centralized, authoritarian regimes can force the necessary changes in behavior, economies, politics, and societies. Both pose criticisms of democratic governance: one asserts that government should get out of the way and let the private sector, technology, and markets do the job; the other claims that profound change will only occur if governments suspend democratic consent, concentrate authority, and limit private property rights. It is worth reflecting on these two views in thinking about governance, the state, and sustainability.

Can the private sector alone lead a sustainability transition?

Can the private sector lead a sustainability transition on its own, with government tagging along as a helper? Proponents of this view cite the greening of industry that occurred in recent decades, especially to opportunities for new markets and operating efficiency, growing awareness among consumers and investors, and market-driven technology change (WBCSD 2010). In this view, government should get out of the way and let private firms lead a sustainability transition.

There is much to be said for this argument. Leading firms are greening supply chains, reporting on goals, engaging customers and communities, wooing socially responsible investors, and cleaning up operations in impressive ways. Yet government still matters, for many reasons:

- Much of this progress is founded on government setting and enforcing core standards that are applied universally and that competitors must meet, the so-called level playing field.
- Many past "voluntary" practices began with government forcing firms to account for the social costs of their actions; examples are restrictions on disposal of hazardous waste and community-right-to-know laws, both of which pushed firms toward pollution prevention.
- Unguided markets alone do not establish the requisite price on pollution (such as carbon) or on resources (such as water) that are allocated inefficiently or unfairly.
- Many problems call for large-scale, collective action where government authority is essential: cleaning up the Chesapeake Bay or Mediterranean Sea or mitigating climate change.
- Only government can marshal the resources and has the motivation to invest in public goods, such as basic research and development, where private incentives are lacking.
- Sustainability demands global cooperation. Although the private sector contributes, only the state can make international commitments and take the domestic actions to fulfill them.

There is no doubt private firms must play a part in a sustainability transition, especially in market economies. Still, it is hard to imagine such a transition without government in a major role. Most environmental problems are the result of market failures. Government may use market tools to advance sustainability, with carbon cap-and-trade, transferable fishing quotas, and water quality trading. In such cases, however, government action is necessary to assign a price to resources that are not valued in markets or to establish the conditions in which private firms will act sustainably.

Is a transition to authoritarian regimes necessary?

A contrary view is that only authoritarian regimes can solve our ecological crises. This is nothing new. In the 1970s, the early days of modern environmentalism, many writers wanted to suspend democratic institutions and processes to change lifestyles, force economic sacrifice, limit property rights, and overcome the power of vested interests. Political scientist William Ophuls called for centralized, expert regimes that are "more authoritarian and less democratic" and "much more oligarchic" (162). He added: "democracy as we know it cannot possibly survive" (152). In *An Inquiry Into the Human Prospect*, Robert Heilbroner argued human greed had to be controlled by monastic government combining "religious orientation with a military discipline" (1974, 176–177). Similar doubts emerge in climate change. James Lovelock, the inventor of the Gaia Hypothesis, stated in a 2010:

> Even the best democracies agree that when a major war approaches, democracy must be put on hold for the time being. I have a feeling that climate change may be an issue as severe as a war. It may be necessary to put democracy on hold for a while.
>
> *Hickman 2010*

To be sure, this will be a very long war; the challenge of climate change is not one that is easily solved.

There is appeal in imaging a society ruled by enlightened ecological autocrats making climate change, ecosystem preservation, and sustainable resource use an overriding priority. The catch in this vision is that no such regime ever existed; it is hard to imagine how one might emerge and establish legitimacy. Indeed, the experiences of the former Soviet Union and the Eastern Bloc should give us pause. Research strongly suggests democracies are equally or more capable on environmental and climate issues than are authoritarian regimes (Buitenzorgy and Mol 2011; Kneuer 2012; Fredriksson and Neumayer 2013; Stehr 2015). Likely advantages are free flows of information, electoral accountability, low corruption, a higher quality of administration, the rule of law, political pluralism, and typically more dynamic and innovative economies. Democracies are better at engaging in international problem-solving and less likely to go to war (Fiorino 2018a). Still, these are complicated relationships; many factors affect this relationship, depending on the issue and policy (for nuanced views, see Wurster 2013 and Battig and Bernauer 2009).

A great deal of evidence highlights the superior capabilities of democracies for ecological governance. Many democracies do a better job of environmental protection on multiple dimensions than do their non-democratic alternatives. The *Environmental Performance Index* (EPI) is a comprehensive, data-driven assessment of national performance. Updated every other year, it evaluates national performance with both health and ecological indicators. Consistently, the top-ranked countries in the EPI are rated as "full" democracies in the Economist Intelligence Unit's *Democracy Index*. In the 2018 EPI, for example, Switzerland, France, Denmark, Malta, and Sweden make up the top five. All are rated full democracies in the *Democracy Index*. The *Climate Change Performance Index* evaluates climate, energy, and policy performance (CCPI 2019). Of the top ten, the *Democracy Index* rates six as full and three as flawed democracies (EIU 2019). Only one country rated as non-democratic – Morocco – was among the top ten climate performers.

Policy research generally concludes that democracies do better on the environment, despite the reservations of critics. For example, a study of five indicators of degradation (including air and water pollution and deforestation) found "a rise in democracy reduces environmental degradation and improves environmental performance" (Li and Reuveny 2006). Studying Europe and Latin America, Kathryn Hochstetler found "liberal democracies are more likely to make commitments to policies and institutions intended to protect the environment than are non-democracies" (2012, 206). A study of climate policies attributed democracies' better performance to having governance systems that are "participatory, consensus-oriented, accountable, transparent, responsive, effective and efficient, equitable and inclusive, and on accordance with the rule of law" (Kneuer 2012, 879). Democracies engage in global problem-solving; "All other things being equal … a more democratic world also will be a world with stronger environmental commitment" (Neumayer 2002, 158). There are exceptions to these findings, but most research supports the case for democracy (Fiorino 2011).

In thinking about sustainability, there is little support for the idea of tossing democracy for unproven, risky alternatives. This is why seeing governance as a fourth, enabling system matters. Not only is the current generation passing down a well-regulated climate or healthy ecosystems to future ones, they are handing down governance systems. Losing democracy is a long-term, perhaps irrevocable, choice that binds future generations. As Ludwig Beckman writes: "the powers taken away from parliaments today are taken away from future parliaments as well" (2008, 620). Obligations to future generations include governance as well as the other sustainability systems.

In summary, the state is a necessary participant in a sustainability transition, and there is limited evidence to support the case against democracy. By definition, sustainability is an enterprise in which all sectors of society will need to be engaged, so private sector participation is essential. At the same time, only government can define incentives, make the global commitments, protect common pool resources, and establish the moral authority to lead a sustainability transition. As for the form of governance, the normative and practical benefits of democracy are compelling.

Are some democracies more suited to a sustainability transition?

Although the research suggests overall that democracies perform better on environmental issues, these conclusions should be qualified. Some studies suggest the effects of democracy vary (Mayer 2017). Much research finds the democracy advantage applies more to consolidated than to emerging democracies. Researchers view this in terms of "accumulated stocks" of democracy with advantages that accrue over time (Gallagher and Thacker 2008). More consolidated democracies have been found to perform best in managing air and water pollution, ecosystem loss, climate change, and deforestation (Hochstetler 2012; Kneuer 2012; Fredriksson and Neumayer 2013).

The relevance of the institutional characteristics of democracies also is debated. Although many studies conclude that parliamentary systems perform better, this is not a consistent finding (Fiorino 2011). Some research suggests that political systems with more veto players (actors who can block policy change) have fewer, weaker climate policies (Madden 2014). The United States is the poster child for this evidence; it is full of veto players and ranks among the weakest in terms of climate action policies of any rich country. Still, its federal system, while a source of veto players, has been a saving grace for United States climate policy. While the Trump administration unraveled national policies, states like California, New York, Massachusetts, and Hawaii were making major strides, on a par with global climate and energy leaders (Vogel 2017; Stokes and Breetz 2018).

Patterns of governance also appear to matter. Environmental sustainability is an integrating concept; it demands capabilities for linking multiple policy sectors in positive ways. The most compelling need for policy integration is in finding and carrying out positive relationships among the economic and ecological systems. The more a political system can identify and reach consensus on these positive relationships, the more likely it will be to govern sustainably. Research suggests that integrating systems do better on many environmental indicators and have a stronger capacity for sustainability than do the more adversarial, pluralist democracies (Fiorino 2011, 378–380).

In an early illustrative study, Lyle Scruggs assessed industrial countries on a range of environmental indicators. He found no evidence that parliamentary systems perform better than presidential ones; being federalist or unitary or having a bicameral or unicameral legislature does not seem to matter. What does appear to make a difference are the patterns of governance in a system. An illustration is comparing pluralist political systems, like the United States and Canada, and more neo-corporatist ones, such as Germany and Sweden. The study:

strongly suggests that countries characterized by strong, centralized interest groups and a more "consensual" approach to policy making ... have enjoyed better environmental performance than countries where economic groups are less comprehensively organized and policymaking is less consensual.

Scruggs 2003, 123

In this comparison of more adversarial/pluralistic systems in which choices are fragmented and compartmentalized to more consensual/collaborative systems that are able to integrate choices, the latter appear to have a capacity for ecological governance and a transition to sustainability.

A theme in environmental sustainability research and the state is that quality of governance matters (Fiorino 2018b, 74–97). Early World Bank work on growth, governance, and air quality found "governance has strong, independent effects on environmental quality" (Dasgupta et al. 2006, 1598). A related study concluded that responding to environmental problems will "require serious attention to the long-run development of public sector administrative and decision-making capacity" (Dasgupta et al. 2005, 416). Research at the Free University of Berlin on environmental policy capacity added to this line of findings (Janicke and Weidner 1997).

Indeed, the positive effects of democracy may be due to their delivering stable, uncorrupt, quality governance (Povitkina 2018). The oft-studied Environmental Kuznets Curve (EKC), where growth initially harms then later improves environmental quality, may reflect the effect of growth on governance, which in turn is linked to a consolidation of democratic institutions and processes (Welzel 2013).

A recent review of sixty quantitative studies found that "Greater democracy, more civil liberties, and experience with democratic systems of government generally lead to greater environmental protection policies, including greater participation in international environmental agreements and better performance outcomes" (Dasgupta and De Cian 2018). On environmental innovation, the same study concluded "weak institutions increase uncertainty and are likely to have adverse effect on innovation while efficient institutions may expedite the process of registering new patents, diffusion of knowledge, enforcement of property rights, and reduce the uncertainty of new projects" (83). Competent, consistent, reliable governance is essential for sustainability.

Tensions relating to the state and sustainability

There are good reasons to doubt the capacity of any political system to be sustainable. As Dovers argues, the challenge is profoundly different from what governments faced in the past. In particular, economic growth has become such a priority that it is hard to avoid the conclusion that the form of growth must either change at its core or be greatly moderated if planetary limits are not to be exceeded.

Modern states confront many tensions in managing a sustainability transition. One is that of maintaining legitimacy in adopting and carrying out a sustainability agenda. The second is the collective action problem: how do countries (or states and provinces, for that matter) justify making hard choices and departing from the status quo when others are not acting to solve global problems? Third, how do political leaders balance pressures for short-term economic prosperity against the need to transform economies and societies in the many ways that will be necessary?

Maintaining legitimacy

Whether democratic, authoritarian, or something in-between, governments need to be seen as legitimate in exercising their authority. A reason consolidated democracies tend to do better on the environment is that they appear to have managed the legitimacy issue better than others. In the western democracies during the 1970s, for example, governments were able to respond to concerns about pollution and overcome industry opposition. Transitional democracies are less successful.

Evidence of the challenges in maintaining legitimacy comes in the rise of authoritarian populism in both established and transitional democracies. A combination of factors – lingering effects of the Great Recession, economic inequality, globalization, technology-induced job losses, and large-scale immigration – led voters in many democracies to support authoritarian populists. In some cases, such as Hungary and Italy, parties founded on right-wing populism are in power. In others – France, Greece, Germany, even the United Kingdom – these parties garner enough votes to influence mainstream parties, even if they do not run governments. They often oppose acting on issues like climate change for many reasons: hostility to multilateralism, *us* versus *them* attitudes that undermine the capacity for collective action (often focused on immigration), stress on short-term economic issues, and skepticism toward or actual rejection of scientific evidence (Lockwood 2018, 1).

One study of right-wing populist parties in Europe found them to be "hostile towards policies supporting multilateralism and international cooperation" (Schaller and Carius 2019, 1). These parties portray climate change as an elite issue and policy action as harmful to ordinary voters, who could face higher energy costs and lower job prospects. Many parties reject mainstream climate science and the role of the Intergovernmental Panel on Climate Change as a neutral expert. The notable exception is Hungary's Fidesz, which accepts the need to act on climate. In most others, climate action policies are seen as being harmful, expensive, and as contrary to national interests.

Despite the many criticism of liberal democracies and their environmental capacities, there is ample support for their advantages: better governance; free expression and flows of information; dynamic and innovative economies; many points of access and influence (pluralism); responsive and accountable governance; less corruption; and higher engagement in global problem-solving (Fiorino 2018a). The evidence on the advantages of consolidated democracies demonstrates that quality matters. For many reasons, the rise of authoritarian populism and other challenges to the legitimacy of modern liberal democracies should be cause for concern.

A reason many critics see advantages in authoritarian systems is a belief that they can solve the legitimacy problem more easily than democracies. They imagine governance by ecologically enlightened autocrats who can force hard choices on a selfish society with short time horizons. But authoritarian systems need to maintain legitimacy, and there is no evidence they are able to find it by pushing strong environmental agendas or subordinating economic goals to ecological ones.

Organizing for collective global action

Oluf Langhelle writes that "Sustainable Development is notoriously complex in the sense that it demands the cooperation of all countries in a globalized, competitive, capitalist system" (2017, 201). It poses what is easily the largest, most complex collective action problem in history.

A common argument from opponents of policies for mitigating greenhouse gas emissions is that acting when other countries do not is economically harmful. On the other hand, not acting when others do may confer short-term advantages. Why adopt policies leading to higher energy prices or requiring more investment in alternative energy or agriculture when competitors are not doing the same? Why give up the short-term benefits from timber sales when others refuse to act?

This underscores a need for multilateral action for transboundary issues and climate change in particular. Consider this from the perspective of politics in the United States. Global action is far more difficult if the US does not participate; it is the largest economy, prominent in global diplomacy, a source of scientific expertise and technology, and the cause of some fifteen percent of emissions. At the same time, the domestic case is tougher in the United States if other major states like China, India, and Brazil are not part of the solution. Domestic fears of economic loss make it tough for any one country to get too far ahead of others. David Victor (2016) states it well: "What the United States does at home will also eventually have an effect on the world, as few nations will go far in making the costly reductions if other economic powerhouses are not doing the same."

The political demands of sustainability are formidable. Global action is required. National governments must be able negotiate and act in classic two-level game, involving "the simultaneous imperatives of both a domestic political game and an international game" (Putnam 1988, 427). Combined with the three sustainability imperatives set out above, the challenges to governance are formidable.

Acting for the long term

Another dilemma all political systems face is acting beyond the short-term horizons of voters, interest groups, and elections (Boston 2017). As Al Gore wrote decades ago, "The future whispers while the present shouts" (1993, 170). Asking people to focus on ecosystem degradation, species loss, and climate is hard when immediate issues of job security and health care are on their minds.

A defining feature of sustainability is long time scales. This is most obvious with respect to climate change. The causes have been brewing for nearly two centuries, since the industrial revolution of the mid-nineteenth century. Due to an accumulation of atmospheric greenhouse gases, the extent of the problem only began to become apparent well into the twentieth century. Early scientific assessments of climate change relied on a 2050 planning horizon for scenarios and planning; more recent ones use 2100 as a time horizon. Although effects are being felt now, larger concerns look to late in the century and beyond for avoiding the worst impacts of climate change.

The challenge with issues like climate change is that action needs to be taken now to avoid potentially catastrophic consequences in the future. Public opinion research suggests the evidence on climate change – extreme weather, flooding and drought, new patterns of disease, wildfires, heat stress, and so on – is raising awareness of the problem (Leiserowitz et al. 2018). Still, public opinion is changing slowly, and many of impacts already have been baked into the climate system.

Improving governance for sustainability

Sustainability poses new, difficult challenges to governance in the modern state. Ecological governance is a recent addition to the core responsibilities of the state, one that still is vulnerable. In competition among ecological and economic goals, short-term economic interests reflecting the status quo too often prevail over the long-term requirements for environmental sustainability. Yet the pressing issues of climate change, water stress, ecosystem degradation, pollution, land use, and others, pose sustainability imperatives on which the quality of human well-being depends. Modern states cannot avoid the challenge of ecological governance and environmental sustainability. What lessons may be drawn from research and experience on sustainability, governance, and the state?

One lesson is that governance constitutes a fourth sustainability system. Its role is to sustain the ecological, economic, and social systems while maintaining an appropriate balance among them. In most countries, economic goals receive preference over ecological and social ones – thus the record of ecological harm and rising social inequality in recent decades. Based on assessments like the *Environmental Performance Index* and *Climate Change Performance Index*, some countries do better on the environment than others. Understanding why is essential for improved governance.

Second, although there are no hard rules on reasons for variations in performance, it does appear that democracies perform better on many ecological indicators than authoritarian systems. They are more open, interact with other democracies, allow for accountability and responsiveness, and are capable of producing more dynamic, innovative economies. Their core advantage is that they govern better, with a civil service, rule of law, strong institutions, stability, continuity, and less corruption.

This is not to say that authoritarian systems cannot deliver on environmental quality. They need to deliver, to be sure. According to the *Democracy Index*, one-third of the world population lives under authoritarian regimes; they account for some 40 percent of global greenhouse gas emissions. To many, recent environmental policies in China may hold out some promise. Consistent with the lessons of the EKC, China appears to have at least leavened goals for rapid growth and is giving attention to the state of the environment, especially dangerous levels of air and water pollution (Schreurs 2011). Still, arguing for a transition to authoritarianism to save the planet is off the mark. Considering all the practical and normative benefits of democracy, it offers the most likely path to sustainability.

Third, political systems vary in their success at ecological governance and meeting the goal of sustainability. The research suggests explanations for these variations in both performance and policies, but there is much more to learn. Why would a consolidated democracy like the United States be a middling performer on the *Environmental Performance Index* and rank among the worst in the *Climate Change Performance Index*? Why does California rank among the top energy and climate performers in the world? Why do small social democracies like Sweden do so well?

The concept of sustainability has been criticized as being vague, contradictory, elusive, naïve, too anti-growth, too pro-growth, and on many other accounts. Yet it has survived for over three decades as the term for managing prosperity, equity, and human well-being within nature's limits. The challenges it presents and problems it raises "will remain at the heart of international politics for the foreseeable future" (Meadowcroft and Fiorino 2017, 338). Writing on sustainability has focused to a large degree on the *what* and *why* of the concept. By focusing on the governance capacities of modern states, we can give needed attention to the crucial *how* of sustainability.

References

Andrews, R.N.L., 2017. Environmental Impact Assessment: Can Procedural Innovation Improve Environmental Outcomes? In J. Meadowcroft and D.J. Fiorino, eds. *Conceptual Innovation in Environmental Policy*. Cambridge, MA: MIT Press, 77–101.

Battig, M.B., and Bernauer, T., 2009. National Institutions and Global Public Goods: Are Democracies More Cooperative in Climate Change Policy? *International Organization*, 63, 281–308.

Beckman, L., 2008. Do Global Climate Change and the Interest of Future Generations Have Implications for Democracy? *Environmental Politics*, 17, 610–624.

Borneman, B., and Christen, M., 2019. Sustainabilizing the Government Machinery? Explaining Sustainability-Oriented Transformations of Internal Governance in Swiss Cantons. In P. Hamman, eds. *Sustainability Governance and Hierarchy*. London: Routledge, 115–135.

Boston, J., 2017. *Governing for the Future: Designing Democratic Institutions for a Better Tomorrow*. Bingley: Emerald.

Buitenzorgy, M., and Mol, A.P.J., 2011. Does Democracy Lead to a Better Environment? Deforestation and the Democratic Transition Peak. *Environmental and Resource Economics*, 48, 59–70.

Climate Change Performance Index (CCPI), 2019. Available from: www.climate-change-performance-index.org/

Dasgupta, S., and De Cian, E., 2018. The Influence of Institutions, Governance, and Public Opinion on the Environment: Synthesized Findings from Applied Econometrics Studies. *Energy Research and Social Science*, 43, 77–95.

Dasgupta, S., Hamilton, K., Pandey, K.D., and Wheeler, D., 2006. Environment During Growth: Accounting for Governance and Vulnerability. *World Development*, 34, 1597–1611.

Dasgupta, S., Laplante, B., Wang, H., and Wheeler, D., 2005. Confronting the Environmental Kuznets Curve. In R.N. Stavins, eds. *Economics of the Environment: Selected Readings*. 5th ed. New York: W.W. Norton, 399–422.

Dovers, S.R., 1996. Sustainability: Demands on Policy. *Journal of Public Policy*, 16, 303–318.

Dryzek, J.S., 2013. *The Politics of the Earth: Environmental Discourses*. 3rd ed. Oxford: Oxford University Press.

Duit, A., Reindt, P.H., and Meadowcroft, J., 2016. Greening Leviathan: The Rise of the Environmental State. *Environmental Politics*, 25, 1–23.

Economist Intelligence Unit (EIU), 2019. *Democracy Index 2018*. Available from: www.eiu.com/Handlers/WhitepaperHandler.ashx?fi=Democracy_Index_2018.pdf&mode=wp&campaignid=Democracy2018

Fiorino, D.J., 2010. Sustainability as a Conceptual Focus for Public Administration. *Public Administration Review*, 70 (Supplement), 78–S88.

Fiorino, D.J., 2011. Explaining National Environmental Performance: Approaches, Evidence, and Implications. *Policy Sciences*, 44, 367–389.

Fiorino, D.J., 2018a. *Can Democracy Handle Climate Change?* Cambridge: Polity Books.

Fiorino, D.J., 2018b. *A Good Life on a Finite Earth: The Political Economy of Green Growth*. Oxford: Oxford University Press.

Fredriksson, P.G., and Neumayer, E., 2013. Democracy and Climate Change Policies: Is History Important? *Ecological Economics*, 95, 11–19.

Gallagher, K.P., and Thacker, S.C., 2008. Democracy, Income, and Environmental Quality. University of Massachusetts, Political Economy Research Institute (PERI), Working Paper 164.

Gore, A., 1993. *Earth in the Balance: Ecology and the Human Spirit*. New York: Penguin.

Heilbroner, R., 1974. *An Inquiry Into the Human Prospect*. New York: W.W. Norton.

Hickman, L., 2010. James Lovelock: Humans Are Too Stupid to Prevent Climate Change. Interview. *The Guardian*.

Hjorth, P., and Bagheri, A., 2006. Navigating Trends Towards Sustainable Development: A Systems Dynamic Approach. *Futures*, 38, 74–92.

Hochstetler, K., 2012. Democracy and the Environment in Eastern Europe and Latin America. In P. Steinberg and S. VanDeveer, eds. *Comparative Environmental Politics*. Cambridge, MA: MIT Press, 199–230.

Intergovernmental Science-Policy Platform on Biodiversity and Ecosystem Services (IPBES), 2019. *IPBES Global Assessment Report on Biodiversity and Ecosystem Services*. Available from: outlook.office.com/owa/?realm=american.edu#exsvurl=1&ll-cc=1033&modurl=0&wa=wsignin1.0

Janicke, M., and Weidner, H., eds., 1997. *National Environmental Policies: A Comparative Study of Capacity-Building*. New York: Springer.

Kneuer, M., 2012. Who Is Greener? Climate Action and Political Regimes: Trade-Offs for National and International Actors. *Democratization*, 19, 865–888.

Lafferty, W.M., and Hoven, Eivind., 2003. Environmental Policy Integration: Towards an Analytical Framework. *Environmental Politics*, 12, 1–22.

Lafferty, W.M., and Meadowcroft, James., 2000. *Implementing Sustainable Development: Strategies and Initiatives for High-Consumption Societies*. Oxford: Oxford University Press.

Lange, P., Driessen, P.P.J., Sauer, A., Bornemann, B., and Burger, P., 2013. Governing Towards Sustainability – Conceptualizing Modes of Governance. *Journal of Environmental Policy and Planning*, 15 (3), 403–425.

Langhelle, O., 2017. Sustainable Development: Linking Environment and Development. In J. Meadowcroft and D.J. Fiorino, eds. *Conceptual Innovation in Environmental Policy*. Cambridge, MA: MIT Press, 181–206.

Layzer, J.A., 2012. *Open for Business: Conservatives' Opposition to Environmental Regulation*. Cambridge, MA: MIT Press.

Leiserowitz, A., Maibach, E., Rosenthal, S., Kotcher, J., Ballew, M., Goldberg, M., and Gustafson, A., 2018. *Climate Change in the American Mind: 2018*. Yale University and George Mason University, December. Yale Program on Climate Change Communication. Available from: https://climatecommunication.yale.edu/wp-content/uploads/2019/01/Climate-Change-American-Mind-December-2018.pdf

Li, Q., and Reuveny, R., 2006. Democracy and Environmental Degradation. *International Studies Quarterly*, 50, 935–936.

Lockwood, M., 2018. Right-Wing Populism and the Climate Change Agenda: Exploring the Linkages. *Environmental Politics*, 27 (4), 712–732.

Madden, N.J., 2014. Green Means Stop: Veto Players and Their Impact on Climate-Change Policy Outputs. *Environmental Politics*, 23, 570–589.

Mayer, A., 2017. Will Democratization Save the Planet? An Entropy-Based, Random Slope Study. *International Journal of Sociology*, 47, 81–98.

Mazmanian, D.A., and Kraft, M.E., 2009. The Three Epochs of the Environmental Movement. In D.A. Mazmanian and M.E. Kraft, eds. *Toward Sustainable Communities: Transition and Transformations in Environmental Policy*. 2nd ed. Cambridge, MA: MIT Press, 1–32.

Meadowcroft, J., 2012a. "Greening the State?" In P. Steinberg and S. VanDeveer, eds. *Comparative Environmental Politics*. Cambridge, MA: MIT Press, 63–88.

Meadowcroft, J., 2012b. Pushing the Boundaries: Governance for Sustainable Development and a Politics of Limits. In J. Meadowcroft, O. Langhelle and A. Rudd, eds. *Governance, Democracy, and Sustainable Development: Moving Beyond the Impasse*. Cheltenham: Edward Elgar, 272–296.

Meadowcroft, J., and Fiorino, D.J., eds., 2017. *Conceptual Innovation in Environmental Policy*. Cambridge, MA: MIT Press.

Meadows, D.H., Meadows, D.L., Randers, J., and Behrens III., W.W., 1972. *The Limits to Growth: A Report for the Club of Rome's Project on the Predicament of Mankind*. New York: Universe Books.

Millennium Ecosystem Assessment (MEA), 2005. *Living Beyond Our Means: Natural Assets and Human Well-Being*.

Neumayer, E., 2002. Do Democracies Exhibit Stronger International Environmental Commitment? A Cross-country Analysis. *Journal of Peace Research*, 39, 139–164.

Ophuls, W., 1977. *Ecology and the Politics of Scarcity: Prologue to a Political Theory of the Steady State*. San Francisco, CA: W.H. Freeman.

Paehlke, R.C., 2006. Environmental Values and Urban Life in America. In N.J. Vig and M.E. Kraft, eds. *Environmental Policy: New Directions for the Twenty-First Century*. 6th ed. Washington: CQ Press, 57–77.

Povitkina, M., 2018. The Limits of Democracy in Tackling Climate Change. *Environmental Politics*, 27, 411–432.

Putnam, R.D., 1988. Diplomacy and Domestic Politics: The Logic of Two-Level Games. *International Organization*, 42, 427–460.

Robinson, J., and Tinker, J., 1997. Reconciling Ecological, Economic and Social Imperatives: A New Conceptual Framework. In T. Schrecker, eds. *Surviving Capitalism: The Social and Economic Challenges*. New York: St. Martin's Press, 71–94.

Rockstrom, J., et al., 2009. Planetary Boundaries: Exploring the Safe Operating Space for Humanity. *Ecology and Society*, 14, 32.

Schaller, S., and Carius, A., 2019. *Convenient Truths: Mapping Climate Agendas of Right-Wing Populist Parties in Europe*. Berlin: Adelphi.

Schreurs, M.A., 2011. Climate Change Politics in an Authoritarian State: The Ambivalent Case of China. In J.S. Dryzek and R.B. Norgaard, eds. *The Oxford Handbook of Climate Change and Society*. Oxford: Oxford University Press, 449–463.

Scruggs, L., 2003. *Sustaining Abundance: Environmental Performance in Industrial Democracies*. Cambridge: Cambridge University Press.

Shearman, D.J.C., and Smith, J.W., 2007. *The Climate Change Challenge and the Failure of Democracy*. Westport, CT: Prager.

Sommerer, T., and Lim, S., 2016. The Environmental State as a Model for the World? An Analysis of Policy Repertoires in 37 Countries. *Environmental Politics*, 25, 92–115.

Stehr, N., 2015. Climate Change: Democracy is Not an Inconvenience. *Nature*, 525 (7570), 449–450.

Stokes, L.C., and Breetz, H.L., 2018. Politics in the U.S. Energy Transition: Case Studies of Solar, Wind, Biofuels, and Electric Vehicles. *Energy Policy*, 113, 76–86.

Victor, D., 2016. *What to Expect from Trump in Energy Policy*. Brookings Institution. Available from: www.nationalreview.com/2016/11/trump-energy-policy-what-expect/.

Vogel, D., 2017. *California Greenin': How the Golden State Became an Environmental Leader*. Princeton, NJ: Princeton University Press.

Welzel, C., 2013. *Freedom Rising: Human Empowerment and the Quest for Emancipation*. New York: Cambridge University Press.

World Business Council for Sustainable Development (WBCSD), 2010. *Vision 2050: The New Agenda for Business*. Available from: file:///C:/Users/danie/Downloads/Vision2050-FullReport.pdf.

World Commission on Environment and Development (WCED), 1987. *Our Common Future*. Oxford: Oxford University Press.

Wurster, S., 2013. Comparing Ecological Sustainability in Autocracies and Democracies. *Contemporary Politics*, 19 (1), 76–93.

16
CORPORATE POWER AND THE SHAPING OF SUSTAINABILITY GOVERNANCE

Doris Fuchs and Sophie Dolinga

Introduction

The sustainability transformation as a cross cutting subject necessarily touches and involves various actors and sectors. Among these, however, *business actors*,[1] especially transnational corporations (TNCs), currently play a particularly prominent role and influence significantly the way sustainability governance evolves over time. This is due to two intertwined phenomena. First, the public debate about unsustainability often focusses on production and consumption patterns, which makes economic actors particularly central players in efforts to improve sustainability. Much hope is being placed on innovation, market mechanisms, so called green growth and (well-informed) consumers to make societies more sustainable. This dominant approach to apprehend sustainability is shaped by the enormous political power corporations wield in today's multilevel governance structures, which indicates the second noteworthy phenomena. As we will argue, this exercise of power can take various forms. Business actors not only sit at the table of central negotiations regarding sustainability measures and thus can impact directly political decision-making, but they have prior influence as well. More indirectly, business power shapes public discourse by affecting how political and private spheres, political actors and interests, policy problems and objectives are conceived. This in turn influences which choices of policy measures, targets, and instruments seem appropriate.

Integrating these two aspects in its inquiry, this contribution aims to examine critically the role of business actors in global sustainability governance. Specifically, we argue that corporations influence the current pathway to (un)sustainability in multiple ways that often undermine comprehensive sustainability efforts as well as democratic principles. In support of our argument, we delineate major developments in business power and their impact on sustainability governance using a three-dimensional power framework. With the help of this framework, we juxtapose the political influence and interests of TNCs with societal sustainability objectives and identify specific and fundamental barriers to transformation.

We proceed as follows. The next section sets up the context of our inquiry pondering requirements for a successful sustainability transformation. Section 3 presents our three-dimensional perspective on corporate political power and delineates relevant trends with a particular focus on sustainability governance. Section 4, then, links the insights gained back to questions of democracy and sustainability highlighting threats to both. We conclude with a discussion of opportunities and challenges for a more promising pathway towards more sustainability and an associated change in the political role of corporations and their influence.

Choosing a democratic pathway towards comprehensive sustainability

Any transformation towards more sustainable societies is a highly complex task. Sustainability in the sense of guaranteeing an adequate satisfaction of needs of present and future generations (WCED 1987) challenges all spheres of today's societies.[2] In the following, we will briefly discuss two major requirements for such a sustainability transformation.

A comprehensive approach to sustainability

The notions of *sustainable development* or in more recent times of *sustainability transformation* are much cited in public and scholarly debates. A prominent example is the United Nations' resolution presenting the 2030 Agenda and the 17 Sustainable Development Goals under the title "Transforming our world" (United Nations 2015). As with many widely used terms, different interpretations and meanings can be attributed to the notion of sustainability. Often the debate about a sustainability transformation focusses on delimitable spheres, like energy or mobility, or on specific symptoms and crises, like pollution or droughts, rather than broader social, political and economic dynamics and causes. In other words, sector-specific short-term strategies have become a dominant approach to sustainability transformation, ignoring root causes of unsustainability and power relations that hinder change (Görg et al. 2017).

In view of such limited approaches to societal change and a focus on political-strategic shifts that seek only partial improvements, Brand (2016) has developed the concept of a *critical-emancipatory transformation*, which focuses on a broad, structural analysis of the causes of current crises and obstacles to socio-ecological transformation. Such a perspective helps identify, for example, shallow or paradoxical instruments employed to promote sustainability. In a similar manner, Blühdorn et al. (2020) highlight the systematic "unsustainability of sustainability governance". What such critical perspectives most fundamentally show, then, is the complexity of current sustainability challenges, the need to go beyond symptom control and to address questions of power, inequality, and democracy if the objective is an effective, substantial and just sustainability transformation (Brie et al. 2016; Dörre et al. 2019).

Participation to guide the sustainability transformation

A comprehensive sustainability transformation demands fundamental changes in the organisation of societies, their (infra-)structures, practices, underlying logics, and power relations. The sheer scope and complexity of the task makes clear that there is no fixed, universal path towards more sustainable societies. What is needed is a continuous, reflexive societal search process that is interwoven with questions concerning social values, such as justice, well-being, and responsibility.

Both challenges of sustainability transformation, its complexity and moral dimension, can be addressed through democratic political processes with participation at their centre. Participation, in a broad sense, can be understood as all voluntary and non-professional action in the political sphere (Van Deth 2014). An entire research strand in the field of sustainability research is devoted to its crucial role for sustainability transformation and identifies various benefits of strong participation. For instance, a participatory approach enables a better assessment of needs of the affected population, draws on knowledge concerning local conditions, leads to an increased acceptance and legitimacy of policies and their associated costs and allows a more effective implementation (Heinrichs et al. 2011).

Building on participatory and deliberative theories of democracy (e.g. Habermas 1981), a legitimate pathway towards sustainability needs to be based on equal participation opportunities granted to all people concerned. In this context, deliberation can be a valuable participatory instrument helping to reach decisions that go beyond the aggregation of individual interests and reflect the common will (Habermas 1981; Lövbrand and Khan 2010). This orientation towards the general good is of great importance to the sustainability debate that addresses questions that transcend individual interests such as global responsibility, the life of future generations or the inherent value of nature.

A lack of opportunities for participation and, in particular, power asymmetries favouring particular rather than public interests in relevant processes weaken fundamental democratic principles. In regard to business actors in sustainability governance, analyses of opportunities for and barriers to sustainability transformation must shed light on the distribution of power in sustainability governance.

The multi-faceted influence of business power in sustainability governance

In order to examine the complex role and diverse influence of corporate actors in the shaping of sustainability governance, the analysis draws on a differentiated power perspective. Specifically, we use a three-dimensional power framework that adopts both an instrumental perspective, analysing more direct impacts, as well as structural and discursive perspectives, taking into account broader contextual factors. In the following, we briefly delineate this framework before applying it to current and past developments in business actors' role in sustainability governance and their underlying sources.

A three-dimensional power framework

Our perspective on power differentiates between instrumental, structural, and discursive forms of political power and considers their material as well as ideational sources (see also Arts 2003; Fuchs 2005; Levy and Newell 2005). Of course, such a differentiation is sensible primarily for analytical purposes. In practice, the lines between the different dimensions of power tend to be blurred.

The *instrumental power* dimension focuses on the influence on political output via political decision makers. It is best represented by activities like lobbying and campaign finance, via which corporate lobbyists try to affect legislation and votes (Hall and Wayman 1990; Bouwen 2002).[3] It is also reflected in the *revolving door*, i.e., the frequent transition of political decision makers and top bureaucrats into the private sector and vice versa. This form of power highly depends on actor-specific resources including financial, organizational, and human resources, but, importantly, also access to decision makers. In general, scholars have noted increasingly open doors of policy makers (even those on the left side of the political spectrum) for business representatives. Two reasons for this development exist: the access of global companies to political decision makers has been facilitated by an increasing complexity of technical and economic questions and simultaneously emptier public coffers and associated reductions in bureaucratic capacities (Clapp 1998). At the same time, the overall neoliberal *Zeitgeist* has meant that business actors generally were perceived as capable and efficient actors important for technological, innovation-based solutions (Fuchs and Kalfagianni 2010).

Structural power, in turn, focuses on the input side of the political process. It asks why certain issues reach the political agenda, and most importantly can highlight why some never do (Bachrach and Baratz 1962). The dependence of policy makers on corporate investment and jobs exemplifies such an agenda-setting power of business actors. Political decisions for higher corporate taxes, for example, are unlikely in a world of nations (and sub-national units) competing for corporate investment.[4] This form of businesses' structural (material) power has a connotation of passiveness. It exists because of corporate control over transnational financial and organizational resources in an economically liberal world, and often does not even become visible, as politicians tend to have an understanding of corporate positions on specific policy issues relating to their business activities (e.g. taxation, labour regulations, environmental guidelines). In today's global economy, however, businesses' structural (material) power can also be seen in the ability of corporations to exercise rule-setting power themselves (Fuchs 2005). Via private (or in some instances public-private) standards and regulations, corporate actors affect a broad range of stakeholders all along their supply chains, today, sometimes replacing or pre-empting public governance (Cutler et al. 1999; Ronit 2012; Grabs and Ponte 2019).

The dimension of *discursive power*, finally, allows us to recognize and assess the ideational power corporate actors exercise via communication and reference to norms and ideas (Lukes 1974). In an ideational and (post)structuralist understanding, the way a problem is framed and which solutions seem necessary or appropriate is never neutral but the result of exercises of power. Specific assumptions and interpretations become dominant and shape discourses and practices, which in turn impact perceptions, values and identities (Hajer 1995; Koller 1991). In other words, discursive power is a very subtle and yet broad form of power. It influences the political process in a fundamental and at the same time subliminal way and intervenes at a very early stage, i.e. before negotiations even start, shaping identities and interests, which makes it difficult to contest (Fuchs 2005). A crucial ideational source of discursive power is the perceived legitimacy and authority of actors (although in a world of largely private media, material resources help enormously in exercising this kind of power as well, of course). If corporations are perceived as legitimate actors in sustainability governance, they can wield influence on what is discussed and in which way (Levy and Newell 2005; Fuchs and Kalfagianni 2010).

The depicted framework provides a basis for a comprehensive and differentiated analysis of corporate political power, in general, and corporate influence on sustainability governance, in particular. Besides considering different sources of power and channels for the exercise of power, the framework importantly also considers the entire range of the political process, which goes far beyond the legislative processes frequently analysed.

Current trends of business power in sustainability governance

In the last half century, TNCs have developed into significant players in numerous fields of governance. The area of sustainability governance is no exception, but rather a particularly relevant example that illustrates the versatile and strong influence of these actors, as we show below.

Instrumental power

Influencing political outcomes through extended lobbying and financing clearly is part of corporate everyday activities in sustainability governance, be it national or international (including EU) regulations on car emissions, genetically modified organisms, or climate change policy, for example (Fuchs et al. 2017; Brulle and Aronczyk 2020). Statistics on lobbying spending illustrate the dominance in political processes business actors have compared to civil society actors, leading to a strong power asymmetry in this context.[5] The Corporate Europe Observatory has found that businesses spend four times more on lobbying on the agriculture policies in the European Union alone, than civil society actors spend across policy issues, for instance (Corporate Europe Observatory 2011). Similarly, Brulle (2018) shows in his study that business actors related to fossil fuels outspent environmental organisations and the renewable energy sectors by a ratio of about 10:1 in the context of lobbying on climate policy in the US, with corporations spending more than US$ 2 billion.[6]

That companies can invest large amounts of money in lobbying is a function of their enormous material resources (and tax laws allowing them to deduct expenses for public/political relations). Trends towards increased capital concentration in various market sectors enable such a strong accumulation of financial resources and thus increase the imbalance in resources between corporate and civil society actors. For instance, high capital concentration can be observed in many food segments where a small number of corporations controls major parts of the market: In the US only four corporations hold 85 percent of the market in beef processing, for example (Clapp 2016).

However, as pointed out above, access to political decision makers, reinforced by the neoliberal *Zeitgeist*, is crucial for businesses' lobbying power. In sustainability governance, this influence goes along with a political preference for technical solutions, hoping that relevant innovations will allow the parallel pursuit of growth and sustainability. Consequently, business actors have been able to establish themselves as players in a broad range of areas of sustainability governance, highlighting their ability to promote marketable solutions. Again, moreover, the asymmetry in power between corporations and civil society (and small and medium sized businesses) not merely due to financial resources but also due to access to decision-makers is noteworthy. In preparation of the TTIP negotiations, which included many sustainability related issues and controversies, representatives of the EU Commission had 560 official lobbying contacts, 520 of which were exclusively with individual TNCs or with business associations, for instance (CEO 2014). In sum, not only the extent of corporate instrumental power in sustainability governance requires attention, but also the existing imbalance between different non-state actors.

Structural power

The structural power of TNCs in sustainability governance has increased as well, over the course of the last decades, in both, its passive and active forms (Fuchs 2005). However, developments in the active form, i.e. rule-setting power, deserve particular attention (Cutler et al. 1999; Brühl et al. 2004). Especially in sustainability governance, *self-regulation* has become an increasingly relevant activity of business actors. Without input or control from public authorities, companies adopt rules as part of private governance initiatives in order to regulate sustainability standards of production and consumption processes (Gullbrandsen 2010). Through self-regulation, corporations claim control over rule-setting and pre-empt public regulation. While such self-regulation also implies (self-defined, and more or less stringent) constraints for the regulating actors themselves, its corresponding imposition of regulations on and impacts for other actors along supply-chains represents an exercise of power, and specifically one that assures the implementation of rules fitting businesses' interests. Relevant examples range from fashion to the agri-food sector and include standards and labels directed at the consumer as well as certification systems limited to business-to-business relations. In some cases, relevant labels and certificates were created to decrease the influence of more stringent ones, such as the many competing labels in the wood sector that the timber industry and retails sector created as a response to the Forest Stewardship Council (Cashore et al. 2005). In other cases, they are used to document corporate social and environmental sustainability after public efforts to develop relevant regulations failed, often due to opposition by corporate actors. The Global Gap, a certification scheme for agri-food supply chains, for instance, was developed by food retailers, after the international Codex Alimentarius negotiations, against which business actors had lobbied, were abandoned (Smythe 2009).

One may think that such corporate self-regulation nevertheless can help to tackle environmental and social sustainability challenges. However, many studies have documented the lack of relevant performance criteria and sustainability impacts of such initiatives. In one of the first empirical studies, in this context, King and Lenox (2000) found no evidence of a positive influence of membership in the chemical industry's Responsible Care program on the rate of environmental improvement of a company, but a higher likelihood by dirtier firms to participate in the program. Similarly, Fuchs and Kalfagianni (2010) have shown the Global Gap's emphasis on documentation of pesticide use rather than its reduction and the absence of standards relating to fair pay, for example. At the same time, they highlighted its ability to determine access to global markets on the production side and consumer choice sets on the consumption side. To the extent that such private rule-setting pre-empts public rule-setting or weakens initiatives developed with civil society participation, scholars and practitioners need to critically reflect on the consequences of the expansion of this active form of corporate structural power in sustainability governance.

Discursive power

The discursive power of business actors plays a crucial role in public and political perceptions of sustainability issues and possible solutions. Fundamentally, there is not a unique perspective on sustainability but a variety of frames competing for hegemony in the public discourse (Dryzek 1999). In accordance with the neoliberal *Zeitgeist* identified above, tackling sustainability issues through the market sphere (e.g. emission trading schemes or the marketing of so called "green" products) has been the dominant approach in most countries of the Global North (and the EU) in the last decades. In order to guarantee its reproduction and undermine alternative approaches, business actors draw on specific resources and strategies to promote corresponding ideas and norms in public discourse. They exercise discursive power through advertising campaigns, media communication, and in the context of sponsorships of events and institutions, including educational institutions through all age ranges (Fuchs and Kalfagianni 2010). Indeed, scholars have documented comprehensive communication strategies, such as those by the Global Climate Coalition, a business lobby group opposed to climate action in the US. The Global Climate Coalition engaged in the production and broad distribution of the video "The Greening of Planet Earth", claiming exclusively positive effects of rising CO_2-emissions, for instance (Levy and Newell 2005). Nowadays, communication strategies not only include the publication of own media content, but also work much more subtly. The economic pressure from advertiser in the news media, for example, increasingly blurs the line between advertising and editorial content and leads to growing interference by companies in media coverage (Nyilasy and Reid 2011).

Furthermore, the image of actors is another central source and target of discursive power. As pointed out above, the potential impact of business actors is closely linked to their perceived legitimacy. The public and state regulators seem to place increasing trust in business actors' capability to provide desired outcome (Scharpf 1998; Cashore 2002). Based on the assumption that the complex challenges of sustainability transformation require decentralised and flexible governance instruments, business actors put forward their role as the better and more competent regulator compared to public authorities (Reinicke 1998). In addition, as mentioned above, business actors succeeded to gain a role as experts, especially for technical issues, which led them to become seemingly neutral advisors. However, the perception of business actors' capabilities to provide desired results does not automatically include trust in their willingness to do so. To gain trust, businesses depend on a good public image to enhance their perceived legitimacy as not only competent but committed and reliable regulator in favour of sustainability. The massive increase in Corporate Social Responsibility strategies illustrates this trend well, while also revealing a close link between self-regulation and discursive power.

Next to self-regulation, corporate actors pursue branding and philanthropic activities in efforts to increase their legitimacy. Thus, businesses reshape their image from car companies to mobility providers or support environmental and social civil society projects. Or they finance think tanks and business initiated non-governmental organizations (BINGOs) to piggyback on the legitimacy of science and civil society and gather further discursive power for their positions. Finally, corporate actors also exercise discursive power in the reshape of the image of other actors, portraying governments as incompetent or intergovernmental organisations (IGOs) as undemocratic and inefficient, for example (Ong and Glantz 2000; Smith 2000).

In sum, discursive power is an extremely important part of the political toolbox of corporations in sustainability governance. Again, the asymmetry in its potential exercise between corporations and civil society as well as small and medium sized enterprises needs to be noted. While civil society actors may benefit from a higher degree of trust placed in them by the public, the ability to buy media space and time, to fund scientific studies and BINGOs supporting their views and interests puts corporations in a highly advantaged position here. This situation creates enormous challenges for sustainability governance, as section 5 will argue. First, however, we would like to sketch the pathways that led to the present situation.

The rise of corporate power

As stated above, business actors have acquired a central position in governance processes. They can draw on different power resources and have an important potential impact in order to promote their interests. When it comes to instrumental, structural or discursive power, businesses outpower other actors like civil society organisations by far. This situation of imbalance in power reproduces further imbalance. Today, we are at a stage where businesses sit at the table of international organisations and national governments, take over regulatory tasks without public control and have influential communication channels at their disposal. It is unlikely that they will use this position to restrain their own power.[7] In the context of transformation efforts, moreover, it must be borne in mind that we are dealing with politically powerful actors that benefit from the status quo. In order to better comprehend businesses' power position in the current governance setting, we have to understand the developments which led to it.

Scott Bowman (2010) documents how, in the beginning of the twentieth century, great public tasks had to be carried out requiring companies with resources of a previously unknown size, for instance to build the US–American railroad system. This situation led politicians to overcome their concern about the size of economic actors and to allow "incorporation". Interestingly, those large companies were meant to exist only until the accomplishment of the task. But instead of disintegrating after the work was finished, companies kept expanding. Eventually, business actors reached a previously unknown size, influence and wealth in the wake of globalisation. Today's large companies have annual sales revenues greater than the GDP of a substantial number of countries (Ferguson and Mansbach 1999). For example, Volkswagen has reached an annual turnover of around US$ 270 billion in 2018,[8] close to Finland's GDP of about US$ 276 billion.[9]

The political and societal acceptance of economic actors of such a size was made possible by the stabilisation of a (neo-)liberal world order and its emphasis on private ownership and market competition (Brand et al. 2000). Further integration of markets on a global scale and increased privatization of public domains are only two further developments, which also illustrate this normative context (Harvey 2007). (Neo)liberal thinking, in turn, meant that politicians and society tended to place a lot of trust in markets and market actors, when it comes to the solving of political problems and the pursuit of public objectives, increasing business' instrumental, structural, and discursive power as delineated above and further stabilised by corresponding exercises of this power.

For sustainability governance, two prominent narratives illustrate these dynamics well: the compatibility of economic growth and sustainability, often referred to as *green growth*, and the potential promotion of structural change by consumer choices. The deep anchoring of economic growth in the sustainability debate, which manifests itself not least in the listing of growth as one of the UN Sustainability Development Goals (SDG 8), is of particular benefit to market-based actors. Economic growth as high political goal is widely established and rarely questioned (Schmelzer 2015). Correspondingly, politicians and media coverage place a lot of focus on growth indicators such as (change in) GDP. Although this indicator provides (incomplete) information on a country's overall economic performance, it does not provide information on its population's quality of life (Fuchs et al. 2020). For instance, environmental disasters, which can cause destruction and death, often increase GDP, as reconstruction measures boost production. Moreover, many aspects that are central to human well-being, such as health or an intact environment, or the distribution of income in a society do not fall within the scope of the classic added-value indicator (Costanza et al. 2009). Furthermore, studies show that a growing economy correlates with an enhanced experience of wellbeing only up to a certain level of per capita incomes (Kubiszewski et al. 2013).

Diverging perspectives, which emphasise, for instance, limits to growth have existed for a long time but did not foster fundamental political change (Meadows et al. 1972). However, they prepared the ground for many further studies illustrating the paradox of a notion of *green growth* and the transnational civil society and scholarly movement around the notion of *degrowth* (D'Alisa et al. 2014). Even though the debate received a certain amount of political and media attention, there was no notable political or entrepreneurial change of strategy. Politicians, investors, and a large share of society remain constrained to ideas of the neoliberal *Zeitgeist* such as growth, efficiency, and profit-maximisation. Accordingly, governments choose sustainability strategies that are based on dominant neoliberal premises and demand no fundamental changes, promoting the sale of electric cars rather than far-reaching changes in mobility practices. Importantly, such strategies trying to combine growth and sustainability also buy into an unfounded idea: the idea of decoupling economic growth from resource consumption, which has not yet been achieved (EEB 2019). GDP is still the number one predictor of a society's ecological footprint. The growth-imperative (Jackson 2009) and the acceptance of an externalisation of environmental and social costs (Lessenich 2016) continue to provide a basis of exploitation of man and nature for profit in a (neo)liberal world and are reproduced in the current market-focused approach to sustainability.

Another dominant narrative in sustainability governance focusses on consumption behaviour and individual responsibility, reflected in the notion of *consumer sovereignty* (Fellner and

Spash 2015). This narrative claims that consumers bear the most influence in the market, exercising control over production patterns through their consumption choices. This argument is based on the idea that the market will provide more sustainable products and finally transform production patterns, if the demand for sustainable products increases sufficiently. In this manner, a huge solution potential to the unsustainable state of societies today is seen in individual behaviour change and the market. In turn, sustainability becomes marketable and thus profitable for businesses. Reproduced and strengthened is this narrative inter alia through media and advertisements promoting "green" products and lifestyles. Similar to the weaknesses of GDP, discussed above, the narrative of consumer sovereignty can be easily challenged. Scholars have shown that information asymmetries and other structural contexts constraining consumer choice impose serious limits on the actual influence that consumers can exercise on production practices (Princen 2002). Individual behavioural choices are always embedded in structures and thus are not as free as the idea of consumer *sovereignty* suggests (Grunwald 2018). Oligopolistic market structures add to this situation. Still, the individualistic and consumer choice-oriented approach has long dominated sustainability governance, due to its clear responsibility attribution and its fit with the (neo)liberal ideational climate.

The undermining of a comprehensive sustainability approach and democracy

The current dynamics in sustainability governance described above have a significant impact on how potential alternative approaches to today's sustainability challenges are perceived. In the following, we will show how the dominant developments hinder a comprehensive and cause-oriented perspective on sustainability, broad participation in the transformation process, and, thereby, prevent opportunities for successful sustainability governance.

Counteracting a comprehensive approach to sustainability transformation

Under the narratives of *green growth* and *consumer sovereignty*, governments have pursued a variety of attempts at sustainability governance. Adopted policies range from emission and efficiency standards for cars, buildings, and household appliances to regulations on pesticide use and organic food – to name only a few. However, the result is disastrous. Overall, resource consumption and emissions (especially in industrialized countries) still exceed sustainable ecological footprints by far, which is illustrated by the continuously advancing Earth Overshoot Day,[10] symbolising the point at which a country lives beyond its (regenerative) means. Why is this the case, if our cars and fridges are so much more energy efficient than they were ten or 20 years ago?

At least part of the answer lies in rebound-effects as well as in the attitude-behaviour and behaviour-impact gaps. The rebound-effect means that eco-efficiency efforts, like the use of modern power-saving technologies, are generally outweighed by increased consumption volumes (Steinberger et al. 2010). While our cars may have become more energy efficient, we also tend to drive or fly more, for example. The concept of the attitude-behaviour gap points to the frequent divergence between individuals' professed environmental values and their consumption decisions (Kollmuss and Agyeman 2002). It highlights that high environmental awareness does not necessarily lead to environmental friendly everyday behaviour, as consumption choices are also determined by habit, context, and competing objectives, for example. Moreover, the occasional purchases of a "greener" products tend to be outweighed by a few (or many) more impactful consumption decisions, in which environmental concerns do not matter at all (Barr et al. 2010). Finally, the concept of the behaviour-impact gap addresses the minor or missing ecological effects of pro-environmental behaviour, highlighting the limits to the impact of individual consumption decisions due to (infra)structural constraints. Thus, a significant share of the ecological footprint in developed countries is determined by societal resource use that is beyond the individual's control (Csutora 2012).

These dynamics depict some of the core obstacles to consumer sovereignty and green consumerism as a solution strategy for the sustainability crises. A focus on consumption choices responsibilises the individual consumer, who is constantly confronted with a functional and normative overload (Maniates 2001). Gathering all of the relevant product information already requires more time than any consumer has, not to mention the difficulties of transparency of and access to relevant information. More fundamentally, while consumers are told to purchase environmentally or socially fairer products, on the one side, they are constantly bombarded with messages to purchase more and more, on the other. The extensive and ever-present use of advertising forms action-guiding structures, creating desires for new products and, in the end, resource-intensive lifestyles (Grunwald 2018). An example is how commercials link desires for relaxation and recreation with products like yoga outfits or long-distance travel. Commercial advertising, even advertising for "green" products, turns the focus of consumers to needs satisfaction through (resource) consumption.

As consequence of these observable dynamics and trends, critical sustainability scholars have argued that sustainability governance will need to focus on sufficiency next to efficiency (Princen 2005). Besides buying "greener" or fairer products, we simply also need to buy less. The most resource-saving activity and therefore effective contribution to recovery is to fundamentally rethink lifestyles and considerably reduce consumption (Paech 2012). *Sufficiency* raises the question of the necessary and reasonable level of consumption. In doing so, it fundamentally questions the equation of consumption and well-being and thereby opposes to the pursuit of economic growth at all costs. Talking about sufficiency and socially as well as ecologically bearable levels of consumption is a complex issue connected to questions of justice and responsibility. Therefore, scholars encourage broad public discussions about limits to consumption, about establishing minimum as well as maximum consumption standards for all. These limits are reflected, for example, in the concept of *consumption corridors*, which define a societally negotiated space for sustainable consumption (Blättel-Mink et al. 2013; Di Giulio and Fuchs 2014). Such a comprehensive approach based on sufficiency and consumption limits, however, does not fit with currently dominant economic structures and interests. There simply is no profit-oriented business plan for a world of consistent sufficiency.

Undermining principles of participatory democracy

The increase in corporate power and the dominant role of economic actors have an important impact on participatory democratic principles in sustainability governance. People's political participation as well as the pursuit of public welfare are threatened by the expansion of corporate power in various ways.

Most fundamentally, the enormous asymmetry in political influence between corporate actors and civil society noted above reveals a dysfunction in our democratic decision-making processes. This imbalance of power underlines how far we have moved away from the democratic ideal of equal representation of interests. Furthermore, the dominance of market actors and market logic in public discourse means that individuals are primarily addressed as "consumers" rather than citizens. The narrative of consumer sovereignty, permanently reproduced and spread through advertising, advocates the idea that every product purchase can have an important societal impact. The power individuals have as citizens fades into the background. Maniates (2001) warns that the focus on individual behaviour distracts from political claims and actions and thus neglects political transformation potentials. Thereby, he reveals the fundamental weakness of the political consumption argument, and the extent to which it buys into the neoliberal paradigm. Various forms of political participation can enable people to intervene more much more directly in the relevant processes than the indirect route via the market. As citizens, individuals can exercise political power through elections, active involvement in parties and politics, protests and civil disobedience, or public/societal participation processes, as they occur more and more often, especially at the municipal level (Celikates 2016; Della Porta 2018; Bohn and Fuchs 2019). Fortunately, recent developments signal a reinvigoration of political activism.

In sum, the ideal of a democratically decided, comprehensive pathway towards a sustainability transformation faces a fundamental challenge. It is hindered by enormous power asymmetries in the system with the most powerful actors (and discourses) opposing necessary (qualities of) deliberation and decision-making processes. This is not to say that more powerful civil society actors or enhanced political participation would automatically lead to the implementation of comprehensive sustainability measures, of course. However, empirical studies have shown that citizens are willing to support stringent measures of sustainability governance relating to consumption if they are convinced of the need for and benefit of such measures, and if it is clear that such consumption restrictions apply to all, thus limiting collective action problems (Di Giulio and Defila 2020).

Where can we go from here?

The key question now is, how can we change course towards a comprehensive and democratic sustainability governance. The established procedures in sustainability governance and their underlying power structures seem extremely stable as they are. Even crises or regular warnings about the inadequacy of current sustainability measures by science or civil society appear to barely be able to challenge the status quo. In 2007 and 2008, large parts of the industrialized world experienced a severe financial crisis. In its wake, however, banks (as well as other TNCs) have only grown larger, and trust in market mechanisms still prevails. In 2018 and 2019, the Intergovernmental Panel on Climate Change (2018) warned that current commitments by states to tackle climate action are nowhere near sufficient and Fridays for Future organised demonstrations with thousands of participants in many cities across the world. And yet, across the political spectrum, criticism of the growth paradigm still appears to be unspeakable. Due to its dominance, the focus on business actors and marketable solutions undermines other perspectives that highlight the structural causes of the unsustainable character of large parts of western societies. Alternatives that do not fit with market logics and corporate interests remain in niches and struggle to gain importance. In this section, however, we will ponder some instruments and ideas that may allow us to challenge, more or less fundamentally, the dominant market regime.

First, limits and regulations can help to counteract the expansion of business power in sustainability governance. On the one hand, policies and initiatives can limit how corporations can wield their power or tackle different sources of businesses' power. Regarding the instrumental power dimension, this could mean to push for transparency in lobbying, more regulated and transparent party financing and greater diversification of actors in negotiation processes. Setting stringent public production standards, which incorporate social and environmental costs instead of non-transparent self-regulation of corporations, could limit their structural power.

Additionally, corporate discursive power could be limited by supporting public media, making public relations and advertising expenditures non tax-deductible, and establishing advertising-free public spaces (especially in educational institutions). Simultaneously, political participation by civil society needs to be enhanced and the depoliticization of sustainability governance countered. Awareness raising, funding of civil-society initiatives and facilitation of easily accessible and inclusive public participation processes are only a few examples to encourage a vivid public debate on sustainability.

Second, we need to start talking about sufficiency and limits to consumption. As shown above, technological innovation and improvements in eco-efficiency, as much as they are important to increase resource efficiency, will not allow us to overcome the sustainability crisis by themselves. The concepts of sufficiency and consumption corridors introduced above provide a promising way forward as they focus on the conditions that would allow current and future generations to flourish on this planet. Talking about sufficiency and limits to consumption means talking about justice and about what humans need to be able to lead a good life. In practical terms, this can mean to start public debates on what we need, how we want to live and what we understand by well-being. Since there are no absolute answers to such complex and highly normative questions, initiating extensive public deliberations, tackling major power imbalances in decision-making processes, and thereby deepening democracy are key conditions for truly participatory and comprehensive sustainability governance. In close connection which such deliberations, we will need policies, which facilitate sufficient lifestyles, such as the provision of adequate infrastructures or service provisioning systems. More fundamentally, we will need to develop economic structures and business models that actually allow the pursuit of a good life for all humans living now, and in the future, and not just the privileged ones.

Of course, one may consider such suggestions utopian. Given what we said about the political power of corporations, why would we expect such strategies to be politically feasible? Indeed, there are huge challenges involved here. Nevertheless, there is already a variety of civil-society initiatives that show what change in sustainability governance can look like. They implement eco-friendly and solidary food systems such as community-supported agriculture, try alternative economic approaches like local exchange trading systems, or bring more transparency to businesses' political activities by tracking down corporate spending. And perhaps increasing citizens' awareness of the extent of corporate political power as well as of their rights, political weight, and responsibility as citizens (not only as consumers) in the light of the worsening sustainability can provide a basis for courageous policy initiatives, after all. And perhaps we can try to get money out of politics, one step at a time.

Notes

1 In the following analysis, we understand *business* or *corporate actors* as independent organisations based on private ownership and the pursuit of profit and engaging in economic activities. They can be distinguished from civil society which we define as the totality of non-state and non-market actors.
2 At this point, it must be emphasised that sustainability transformation does not affect all societies and parts of societies in the same way. The strong historical and current inequalities in resource access and consumption as well as the persistent global power asymmetries make a uniform approach – in practice as well as in science – inappropriate (Hanaček et al. 2020; Vanhulst and Beling 2020). In the following, we refer mainly to transformation in the early industrialized societies of the Global North.
3 Clearly, lobbying today affects not only how policy makers will vote on a given legislative proposal, but also which issues policy makers put on the negotiating table. This is an example, therefore, of how the line between instrumental and structural (agenda-setting) power is blurred.
4 Ganghof (2005) has nicely shown how corporate tax rates have uniformly moved in one direction, i.e. downward, across OECD countries.

5 As mentioned above, we distinguish businesses from civil society actors, which are typically cast as the competitor to corporate interests in the political game. However, it should be borne in mind that these two categories do not form homogeneous entities but include a variety of actors with sometimes conflicting interests and different resources. Regarding businesses, we have witnessed an increasing willingness of corporate actors to act independently or as a group of like-minded (and sized) corporations over the last decades (Fuchs 2005). This has meant that business associations, and especially small- and medium-sized businesses have lost influence relative to corporations as well.
6 This calculation is a conservative estimation based on reported lobbying spending and thus do not include lobbying in its broad sense. The vast majority of lobbying expenditure came from the transport, utility, and fossil fuel sectors (Brulle 2018).
7 Such an assumption does not imply that a given CEO may not care deeply about sustainability issues but reflects broader mechanisms like the pressure of reporting gains at short-term intervals that he or she experiences.
8 Volkswagen Group annual report 2018: www.volkswagenag.com/presence/investorrelation/publications/annual-reports/2019/volkswagen/de/Y_2018_d.pdf.
9 World Bank national accounts data 2018: https://data.worldbank.org/indicator/NY.GDP.MKTP.CD?end=2018&locations=FI&most_recent_value_desc=true&start=1966.
10 www.overshootday.org/

References

Arts, B., 2003. *Non-State Actors in Global Governance*. Max-Planck-Projektgruppe, Recht der Gemeinschaftsgüter 003/4, Bonn: Max-Planck-Gesellschaft.
Bachrach, P. and Baratz, M., 1962. Two faces of power. *APSR*, 56, 947–952.
Barr, S., Shaw, G., Coles, T. and Prillwitz, J., 2010. A holiday is a holiday. *Journal of Transport Geography*, 18, 474–481.
Blättel-Mink, B., Brohmann, B., Defila, R., Di Giulio, A., Fischer, D., Fuchs, D., Gölz, S., Götz, K., …, 2013. *Konsum-Botschaften*. Stuttgart: Hirzel.
Blühdorn, I., Butzlaff, F., Deflorian, M., Hausknost, D. and Mock, M., 2020. *Nachhaltige Nicht-Nachhaltigkeit*. Berlin: transcript.
Bohn, C. and Fuchs, D., 2019. Partizipative Transformation? In Bohn, C., Fuchs, D., Kerkhoff, A., Müller, C., eds. *Gegenwart und Zukunft sozialökologischer Transformation*. Baden-Baden: NOMOS, 7–24.
Bouwen, P., 2002. Corporate lobbying in the European Union. *Journal of European Public Policy*, 9(3), 365–390.
Bowman, S., 2010. *Modern Corporation and American Political Thought*. University Park: Pennsylvania State University Press.
Brand, U., 2016. How to get out of the multiple crisis? *Environmental Values*, 25(5), 503–525.
Brand, U., Brunnengräber, A., Schrader, L., Stock, C. and Wahl, P., 2000. *Global Governance. Alternative zur neoliberalen Globalisierung?* Münster: Westfälisches Dampfboot.
Brie, M., Reißig, R. and Thomas, M., eds., 2016. *Transformation*. Berlin: LIT.
Brühl, T., Feldt, H., Hamm, B., Hummel, H. and Martens, J., eds., 2004. *Unternehmen in der Weltpolitik*. Bonn: Dietz.
Brulle, R., 2018. The climate lobby. *Climate Change*, 149, 289–303.
Brulle, R. and Aronczyk, M., 2020. Environmental Counter Movements. In Kalfagianni, A., Fuchs, D. Hayden, A., eds. *Routledge Handbook of Global Sustainability Governance*. London: Routledge, 218–230.
Cashore, B., 2002. Legitimacy and privatization of environmental governance. *Governance*, 8(4), 503–529.
Cashore, B., Van Kooten, G., Vertinsky, I., Auld, G. and Affolderbach, J., 2005. Private or self-regulation? *Forest Policy and Economics*, 7(1), 53–69.
Celikates, R., 2016. Democratizing civil disobedience. *Philosophy & Social Criticism*, 42(10), 982–994.
Clapp, J., 1998. The privatization of global environmental governance. *Global Governance*, 4, 295–316.
Clapp, J., 2016. *Food*. Cambridge: Polity.
Costanza, R., Hart, M., Talberth, J., Posner, S., 2009. Beyond GDP. *The Pardee Papers*, 4, 1–37.
Csutora, M., 2012. One more awareness gap? *Journal of Consumer Policy*, 35, 145–163.
Cutler, C., Haufler, V. and Porter, T., eds., 1999. *Private Authority and International Affairs*. Albany: SUNY Press.
D'Alisa, G., Demaria, F. and Kallis, G., eds., 2014. *Degrowth*. London: Routledge.
Della Porta, D., 2018. Protests as critical junctures. *Social Movement Studies*, 1–20.

Di Giulio, A. and Defila, R., 2020. The 'Good Life' and Protected Needs. In A. Kalfagianni, D. Fuchs and A. Hayden, eds., *The Routledge Handbook of Global Sustainability Governance*. London: Routledge.

Di Giulio, A. and Fuchs, D., 2014. Sustainable consumption corridors. *GAIA*, 23(1), 184–192.

Dörre, K., Rosa, H., Becker, K., Bose, S. and Seyd, B., eds., 2019. *Große Transformation?* Wiesbaden: Springer.

Dryzek, J., 1999. Transnational democracy. *Journal of Political Philosophy*, 7(1), 30–51.

EEB, 2019. *Decoupling Debunked*. Brussels: EEB.

Fellner, W. and Spash, C., 2015. The role of consumer sovereignty in sustaining the market economy. In L. Reisch and J. Thøgersen, eds. *Handbook of research on sustainable consumption*. Cheltenham: Edward Elgar, 394–409.

Ferguson, Y. and Mansbach, R., 1999. Global politics at the turn of the millennium. *International Studies Review*, 1(2), 77–107.

Fuchs, D., 2005. *Understanding Business Power in Global Governance*. Baden-Baden: NOMOS.

Fuchs, D., Gumbert, T. and Schlipphak, B., 2017. Euroscepticism and big business. In B. Leruth, N. Startin and S. Usherwood, eds. *The Routledge handbook of Euroscepticism*. London: Routledge, 317–330.

Fuchs, D. and Kalfagianni, A., 2010. The causes and consequences of private food governance. *Business and Politics*, 12(3), doi:10.2202/1469-3569.1319.

Fuchs, D., Schlipphak, B., Treib, O., Long, L.A. and Lederer, M., 2020. Which way forward in measuring the quality of life. *Global Environmental Politics*, 20(2), 12–36.

Ganghof, S., 2005. The Politics of (Income) Tax Structure. Paper presented at the Yale Conference on Distributive Politics, April 29–30.

Görg, C., Brand, U., Haberl, H., Hummel, D., Jahn, T. and Liehr, S., 2017. Challenges for social-ecological transformations. *Sustainability*, 9(7), 1045.

Grabs, J. and Ponte, S., 2019. The evolution of power in the global coffee value chain and production network. *Journal of Economic Geography*, 19(4), 803–828.

Grunwald, A., 2018. Warum Konsumentenverantwortung allein die Umwelt nicht rettet. In A. Henkel, N. Lüdtke, N. Buschmann and L. Hochmann, eds. *Reflexive Responsibilisierung*. Bielefeld: transcript, 421–436.

Gulbrandsen, L.H., 2010. *Transnational Environmental Governance: The Origins and Effects of the Certification of Forests and Fisheries*. Cheltenham: Edward Elgar Publishing.

Habermas, J., 1981. *Theorie des kommunikativen Handelns*. Frankfurt a.M: Suhrkamp.

Hajer, M., 1995. *The Politics of Environmental Discourse*. Oxford: Oxford University Press.

Hall, R. and Wayman, F., 1990. Buying time. *APSR*, 84(3), 797–820.

Hanaček, K., Roy, B., Avila, S. and Kallis, K., 2020. Ecological economics and degrowth. *Ecological Economics*, 169.

Harvey, D., 2007. Neoliberalism as creative destruction. *Annals of the American academy of political and social science*, 610(1), 21–44.

Heinrichs, H., Kuhn, K., and Newig, J., 2011. *Nachhaltige Gesellschaft*. Wiesbaden: VS, 27–45.

IPCC, 2018. *Global Warming of 1.5°C*. Geneva: World Meteorological Organization.

Jackson, T., 2009. *Prosperity Without Growth?* London: Earthscan.

King, A. and Lenox, M., 2000. Industry self-regulation without sanctions. *Academy of Management Journal*, 43(4), 698–716.

Koller, P., 1991. Facetten der Macht. *Analyse und Kritik*, 13, 107–133.

Kollmuss, A., Agyeman, J., 2002. Mind the gap. *Environmental Education Research*, 8(3), 39–260.

Kubiszewski, I., Costanza, R., Franco, C., Lawn, P., Talberth, J., Jackson, T. and Aylmer, C., 2013. Beyond GDP. *Ecological Economics*, 93, 57–68.

Lessenich, S., 2016. *Neben uns die Sintflut*. München: Hanser Berlin.

Levy, D. and Newell, P., eds., 2005. *The Business of Environmental Governance*. Cambridge: MIT.

Lövbrand, E. and Khan, J., 2010. The deliberative turn in green political theory. In K. Bäckstrand, J. Khan, A. Kronsell and E. Lövbrand, eds. *Environmental politics and deliberative democracy*. Cheltenham: Edward Elgar, 47–65.

Lukes, S., 1974. *Power, a Radical View*. London: Macmillan.

Maniates, M., 2001. Individualization: plant a tree, buy a bike, save the world? *Global Environmental Politics*, 1(3), 31–52.

Meadows, D.H., Meadows, D.L., Randers, J. and Behrens, W., 1972. *The Limits to Growth*. New York: Universe Books.

Nyilasy, G., Reid, L., 2011. Advertiser pressure and the personal ethical norms of newspaper editors and ad directors. *Journal of Advertising Research*, 51(3), 538–551.

Ong, E. and Glantz, S., 2000. Tobacco industry efforts subverting international agency for research on cancer's second-hand smoke study. *The Lancet*, 355, 1253–1259.

Paech, N., 2012. *Befreiung vom Überfluss*. München: oekom.

Princen, T., 2005. *The Logic of Sufficiency*. Cambridge: MIT Press.

Princen, T., 2002. Distancing: Consumption and the Severing of Feedback. In Princen, T., Maniates, M. and Conca, K. eds. *Confronting Consumption*. Cambridge: MIT Press, 103–131.

Reinicke, W., 1998. *Global Public Policy*. Washington: Brookings.

Ronit, K., 2012. *Private Voluntary Programs in Global Climate Policy*. New York: United Nations University Press.

Scharpf, F., 1998. Demokratie in der transnationalen Politik. In U. Beck, eds. *Politik der Globalisierung*. Frankfurt a.M.: Suhrkamp, 151–174.

Schmelzer, M., 2015. The growth paradigm. *Ecological Economics*, 118, 262–271.

Smith, M., 2000. *American Business and Political Power*. Chicago: University of Chicago Press.

Smythe, E., 2009. In Whose Interests? Transparency and Accountability in the Global Governance of Food: Agribusiness, the Codex Alimentarius, and the World Trade Organization. In Clapp, J. and Fuchs, D., eds. *Corporate Power in Global Agrifood Governance*. Cambridge: MIT Press, 93–123.

Steinberger, J.K., Krausmann, F. and Eisenmenger, N., 2010. Global patterns of materials use: A socio-economic and geophysical analysis. *Ecological Economics*, 69(5), 1148–1158. https://doi.org/10.1016/j.ecolecon.2009.12.009.

United Nations., 2015. *Resolution adopted by the General Assembly on 25 September 2015. Transforming our world*. www.un.org/ga/search/view_doc.asp?symbol=A/RES/70/1&Lang=E.

Van Deth, J., 2014. A conceptual map of political participation. *Acta Politica*, 49(3), 349–367.

Vanhulst, J. and Beling, A., 2020. Post-Eurocentric sustainability governance. In A. Kalfagianni, D. Fuchs and A. Hayden, eds. *Routledge handbook of global sustainability governance*. London: Routledge, 115–128.

WCED, 1987. *Our common future*. Oxford: Oxford University Press.

17
DEMOCRACY BEYOND THE STATE

Non-state actors and the legitimacy of climate governance

Jens Marquardt and Karin Bäckstrand

Introduction

Translating intergovernmental commitments like the Paris Agreement or the Sustainable Development Goals (SDGs) into national policies and action faces numerous challenges relating to democratic legitimacy. A major question is if and how non-state actors – such as civil society organizations, businesses, or indigenous peoples – can secure global democratic legitimacy and thus contribute to the democratization of global environmental governance. Do they represent a transmission belt between citizens and multilateral institutions? Are national governments representative and accountable to their constituencies concerning actions on global threats like climate change? How can democratic debates and decision-making be organized around transboundary collective action problems? And what role does the diverse group of "non- and sub-state actors"[1] play in multi-level climate governance in the midst of a pandemic that disrupts global governance routines?

In response to the broader theme of democracy and sustainability, this chapter sheds light on how and under what conditions non-state actor participation can increase the democratic legitimacy of global climate governance. Based on a number of empirical illustrations, we explore the various possibilities for non-state actors to democratically engage with states' submissions of national climate plans (or their Nationally Determined Contributions, NDCs) to the United Nations Framework Convention on Climate Change (UNFCCC). These NDCs should outline the states' commitments to tackling climate change. Still, an NDC synthesis report (UNFCCC 2021) described them as insufficient to prevent global temperature increase of well below 2 degrees until the end of the century. While national governments are primarily responsible for formulating, and implementing their NDCs, regional meetings, as well as the global climate governance arena, provide additional forums for cooperation and contestation beyond the domestic context. Increasingly complex interdependencies between national, transnational, and multilateral actors shape the evolution of the NDCs (Hermwille 2018) and reflect a form of "hybrid multilateralism" (Bäckstrand and Kuyper 2017). While the spheres of "bottom-up" flexible transnational climate governance and "top-down" intergovernmental climate diplomacy are increasingly aligned, the submission of climate plans by states is combined with mechanism of transparency and review of commitments by the UNFCCC (Bäckstrand et al. 2017; Hale 2020).

Non-state climate action is characterized by a diversity of public and private actors, issues of inequality as well as power struggles, competing interests, and ideological contestation (Nasiritousi 2019; Marquardt and Nasiritousi 2021). Non-state action can be public, private, or take hybrid forms such as in public-private partnerships (Bäckstrand, 2008; Van Asselt and Bößner 2016, 55). Private actors include companies, non-governmental organizations (NGOs), indigenous peoples, and trade unions ranging from grassroot movements such as Fridays for Future to sub-state networks such as the C40 Cities Climate Leadership Group. Public authorities such as regional governments, cities, or municipalities are increasingly active in climate politics through transnational networks but also share non-state actor characteristics in the UNFCCC context (Betsill and Bulkeley 2006, 141). According to Angel Hsu et al. (2015), action by subnational authorities involves more than 7,000 cities with a combined population of 794 million people. Not surprisingly, scholars in International Relations have shown a long interest in non-state climate action (Andonova et al. 2009; Hoffmann 2011; Abbott 2012; Betsill and Corell 2014), particularly since the adoption of the Paris Agreement in 2015 (Hsu et al. 2020; Kuramochi et al. 2020; MacLean 2020)

Beyond these academic debates, the establishment of the Global Climate Action portal (GCP, originally known as Non-state Actor Zone for Climate Action, NAZCA) and the Lima–Paris Action Agenda (LPAA) in the lead up to the adoption of the Paris Agreement further consolidated non-state action into international climate commitments and agreements (Bäckstrand et al. 2017). While such a strong push for non-state actor engagement in decarbonization efforts underlines the Paris Agreement's hybrid character (Hsu et al. 2020), others have criticized the agreement as a form of "dangerous incrementalism" (Allan 2019) which overburdens non-state actors with responsibilities, and shifts commitments to non-binding climate plans submitted by states. Blurring the lines between global commitments and national contexts, these national climate plans have already become a primary target for democratic debate and contestation. The formulation and implementation of the NDCs opens up different forums for stakeholder engagement and fosters non-state actor involvement across different governance levels (Tørstad et al. 2020).

This chapter assesses if and how non-state actors can secure democratic values in the NDC process. We analyze how they affect the democratic legitimacy of climate governance through their engagement with the formulation of states' climate plans at the international, regional, and national level.[2] Synthesizing previous research, we present illustrative cases and take Sweden as a primary example due to the country's renowned performance in climate politics (Burck et al. 2019). Historically heralded as an environmental pioneer, Sweden aims to become one of the world's first fossil-free welfare states by 2045.

In the following, we first revisit the burgeoning literature on democracy beyond the state to examine the linkages between legitimacy and democratic theory. We build on the scholarship on how to enhance democratic values beyond the state and in non-electoral settings to draw lessons from examples in UN diplomacy, regional forums, and national contexts. We argue that a focus on democratic values like participation, representation, accountability, transparency, and deliberation represents a promising approach to evaluate the democratic legitimacy in complex governance settings. This approach allows us to explore how the process of formulating, and reviewing states' domestic climate plans can enhance democratic debates in a multi-level governance context, evaluate if non-state actor involvement in the NDC process can increase the democratic legitimacy of climate politics, and critically reflect on the democratic limitations and constraints of the NDC process.

Democratic legitimacy and non-state actors in climate governance

International Relations scholars have long discussed to what extent civil society and non-state actors can increase the democratic legitimacy of global governance, through participation, voice, and representation in international negotiations (Scholte 2002; Machin 2013). Civil society can enhance global democratization by representing public interests, acting as a transmitter of citizens' concerns, giving voice to marginalized groups, future generations, and non-human species, serving as watchdogs to improve accountability, and enhance transparency by monitoring governments' compliance with international agreements (Bäckstrand 2011). Three decades of UN climate and sustainable development summits have consolidated models of "stakeholder democracy," where engagement by non-state actors such as women, youth, trade unions, and NGOs was institutionalized through civil society deliberation and representation (Bäckstrand 2006). The expansion of civil society participation at global governance settings in general and at climate summits in particular fosters a transnational public sphere and principles of deliberative democracy (Stevenson and Dryzek 2014).

In contrast, skeptics to global democracy claim that global civil society actors struggle to reduce democratic deficits, because many NGOs are not an independent sphere from the state and the market (Scholte 2002; Bernauer and Betzold 2012). It is, therefore, problematic to view civil society as a democratizing force against unaccountable global governance since civil society itself can be undemocratic, unelected, and unaccountable (Brühl 2010). NGOs do not have democratic credentials, as they are not legitimated through electoral mechanisms. They are largely self-selected and are frequently not accountable to their constituencies, isolated from broader public interests, and, at worst, promote their own political agendas (Green 2013). For example, many professionalized NGOs in the Global North are represented by Western, male, and middle-class elites, which act as lobbyists closely aligned with governments, losing their critical activist role as credible representatives of marginalized stakeholder groups (Scholte 2011; Agné et al. 2015). If the democratic credentials of civil society are in doubt, the prospect for other non-state actors like businesses, industries, and trade-unions, looks even bleaker.

Scholars of global cosmopolitanism argue that an international climate regime lacks democratic legitimacy due to the absence of a global demos and an elected world government (Held and Hervey 2011). Others warn that the dominance of expert knowledge and technocratic approaches erodes legitimacy (Jasanoff 2010). Yet, there are numerous models to advance the democratization of global climate governance through new modes of democratic participation for marginalized groups, civic engagement, and the inclusion of a variety of non-state actors (Bäckstrand and Kuyper 2017; Feindt and Weiland 2018). However, democratic legitimacy hinges on more than participation. As a consequence, scholars have developed approaches like liberal intergovernmentalism (Keohane et al. 2009; Friedman et al. 2013), multi-stakeholder democracy (Bäckstrand 2006; Macdonald 2008; Gleckman 2018), deliberative democratization (Stevenson and Dryzek 2014), and radical participatory democracy (Machin 2013).

While all these models have their relative merits, we choose to evaluate democratic legitimacy here based on a set of five key democratic values often discussed in global governance literature. Given the explorative character of this analysis and the evolving post-Paris climate governance regime, such an open conceptualization allows us to investigate how democratic values unfold in the NDC process. At its core, the democratic values approach traces how those affected by decisions are involved in the decision-making process (Tallberg and Uhlin 2011; Bäckstrand and Kuyper 2017; Kuyper et al. 2018). In contrast to more institutional, actor-oriented, or deliberative approaches towards democracy, the democratic values approach assesses democratic legitimacy at various governance levels in an open-ended manner. Non-state actors are treated far less state-centric than in other models of democracy. The approach addresses the global democratic deficit by evaluating if a set of values is met in formal and informal institutions (Bäckstrand and Kuyper 2017, 7). By providing a specific understanding of what core values constitute democracy, the democratic values approach pays tribute to the contested nature of democracy (Dingwerth 2007; Tallberg and Uhlin 2011; Bexell 2014). Klaus Dingwerth (2014) also highlights that conceptualizing democracy as a set of values allows us to shed light on the interrelations between those values.

We focus on participation, representation, accountability, transparency, and deliberation. We argue that these values provide a profound foundation from which we can evaluate the democratic legitimacy of climate governance. Studies in (global) environmental politics have focused on these five values which are particularly relevant for non-state actors in global environmental regimes (Bäckstrand and Kuyper 2017; Kuyper et al. 2018). Participation is secured when citizens affected by political decisions have the opportunity to be involved in the decision-making process. This includes the ability to set the agenda, shape rule-making, and evaluate decisions. In order to connect participants with sites of authority, participation largely depends upon forms of representation which can be conducted through national government officials or a variety of non- and sub-state actors. Representation concerns whether a wide range of stakeholders affected by climate politics, including businesses, civil society actors, and cities, are well-represented in the decision-making process. Accountability means that those affected by decision-making should have the right to hold those in power accountable "to a set of standards, to judge whether they have fulfilled their responsibilities in light of these standards, and to impose sanctions if they determine that these responsibilities have not been met" (Grant and Keohane 2005, 29). Yet, any attempt for meaningful accountability requires transparency to those affected by decisions. We define transparency here "as the means of disclosure of actions taken by public actors and institutions" (Bäckstrand and Kuyper 2017, 9). Finally, deliberation provides those affected by decisions with a rationale for how authority is exercised and how it is connected to modes of public reasoning. This means that "representatives of those affected have an opportunity to put their reasons forward and have a response" (Bäckstrand and Kuyper 2017, 8).

Table 17.1 summarizes the five democratic values discussed here. They form a normative foundation for assessing the democratic legitimacy of climate governance, which we apply to the NDC process.

These democratic values offer an idealized form of democracy against which the NDC process can be evaluated. Doing so, we can substantiate claims related to the democratic quality of the global climate regime – or the lack thereof – by discussing if democratic values can be

Table 17.1 Five dimensions of the democratic values approach

Participation	People affected by political decisions should have the opportunity to get involved in the decision-making process.
Representation	The views, preferences, and ideas of affected stakeholders should be represented in the debates leading to political decisions.
Accountability	Participating stakeholders need to hold those who pledge commitments and make decisions accountable for their promises and action.
Transparency	Transparency through access to information allows those affected by decisions to track progress and monitor commitments.
Deliberation	Decisions are publicly justified and discussed to allow debates around their rationale and give affected people the opportunity to participate in a responsive discourse.

secured in the implementation process. Following a highly explorative approach we discuss the fulfillment of these values as well as their absence in the multi-level NDC process. We do not attempt to measure or quantify democratic legitimacy. Instead, we discuss these values for the context of non-state actor involvement in the NDC process based on a qualitative and selective approach. We do so by analyzing policy documents, reports, and workshop documentations from different non-state actors at the global, regional, and national level. For the global level, we investigated input from observer organizations on the Marrakech Partnership for Global Climate Action brought forward in 2016 and 2019. For the regional context, we focused on UNFCCC documents related to regional climate workshop particularly in Africa and Latin America. For the domestic level, we concentrated on Sweden's climate policy framework and the Fossil Free Sweden initiative.

Non-state actor involvement in multi-level climate governance

Involving non-state actors, such as NGOs (Betsill and Corell 2008), businesses (Newell 2000), cities (Bulkeley and Betsill 2003), or the climate justice movement (Hadden 2015) has been "a distinct feature of global climate governance" (Bäckstrand et al. 2017) for more than 30 years. Non-state actors have challenged "the limitations of the traditional state-centric system" (Princen and Finger 1994, 217) already in the early 1990s, and they have "transformed the process of international environmental cooperation" (Raustiala 1997, 724) by conducting research, presenting marginalized positions, monitoring state commitment, communicating to different publics, and acting as watchdogs during international negotiations. The literature on non-state and sub-state action in climate governance has proliferated and expanded across research fields and disciplines, particularly in the aftermath of the Paris Agreement (Hsu et al. 2020; Kuramochi et al. 2020; MacLean 2020; Streck 2020). A general search on Web of Science results in more than 1,650 relevant publications,[3] published between 1999 and 2020. Figure 17.1 summarizes the development of the field over time.

Civil society organizations as one type of non-state actors have long been described as watchdogs or outsiders to the international negotiations (Fisher and Galli 2015). Yet, their multiple roles in agenda setting, lobbying, advocacy, monitoring, and implementation have become more institutionalized in the UNFCCC regime. The Paris Agreement formally recognizes non-state actors as crucial to limiting global warming well below 2°C. Going

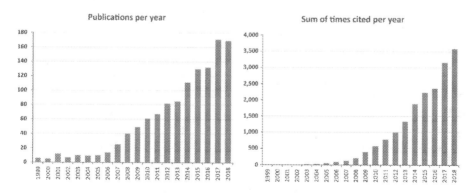

Figure 17.1 Research on non-state actor involvement in climate governance
Source: Data from Web of Science, retrieved January 9, 2019

beyond traditional categories of top-down vs. bottom-up governance, the agreement enacts a governance arrangement of "hybrid multilateralism" where the states' national climate plans and non-state action become increasingly intertwined under the umbrella of the international agreement, orchestrated and steered by the UNFCCC (Bäckstrand and Kuyper 2017; Streck 2020). Within the hybrid arrangement, non-state actors fulfill two key functions: First, they monitor and evaluate the implementation of the NDCs under an international transparency and review framework (Gupta and van Asselt 2019). Second, the UNFCCC facilitates an "increasingly dynamic interplay between multilateral and transnational climate action" (Bäckstrand et al. 2017, 562) to mobilize their mitigation potential and help closing the global emissions gap.

While some scholars praise the Paris Agreement for offering no less than "a model for effective global governance in the twenty-first century" (Slaughter 2015), others argues that the agreement's design to shift responsibilities to non-state actors could undermine ambitious climate action by states (Allan 2019). Sander Chan et al. (2019) contrast the optimistic arguments related to greater non-state action in sustainability governance with potential governance risks that are rarely recognized. For example, current tendencies towards aggregation of non-state commitments might easily disregard non-quantifiable action. Yet, with the NDCs at its heart (Held and Roger 2018, 532), the Paris Agreement calls for non-state actor participation at various levels. Although not legally binding as targets under the Kyoto Protocol, all countries have to prepare, communicate, and maintain an NDC that reflects their "highest level of ambition" (UNFCCC 2015, Article 4). The Paris Agreement also establishes a "bottom-up pledge and review approach" (Zaman 2018) as well as an iterative process designed to review, adjust, and catalyze action over time. As such, the Paris Agreement and the state-driven UNFCCC process gives non-state actors numerous opportunities for engagement (Pattberg et al. 2018). The key question remains if such a design leads to true and meaningful participation beyond the status quo of a state-driven international climate change regime (Dryzek and Pickering 2017).

Non-state actors and the global climate regime

In the run-up to the Paris Agreement, considerable efforts have been taken to strengthen the inclusion of non-state action into a global climate regime. In 2014, the UN General Secretary urged business leaders, civil society organizations, and mayors to join the global fight against climate change. Aiming to foster action by non-state actors and considered as a back-up option in case of negotiation deadlock, the LPAA established the NAZCA platform, later known as the Global Climate Action portal (GCP). As of December 2020, more than 27,500 voluntary commitments by over 18,500 non-state and sub-state actors, as well as cooperative action by networks, were registered in the online repository, covering a broad range of topics. The GCP lists initiatives like the Global Covenant of Mayors for Climate and Energy which aims to facilitate transitions to a low emission resilient society, but also long-known programs such as a Greenpeace campaign to promote a shift in cooling technology towards natural refrigerants. Besides, 700 major cities, regions, companies, and investors pledged their commitment to implement the Paris Agreement (Obergassel et al. 2016). In 2020, the UNFCCC convened the "Race to Zero November Dialogues," a series of virtual dialogues between Parties and non-state actors to foster exchange about decarbonization in the absence of the postponed COP26.

Non-state actors played an important role already in the run-up to the Paris negotiations, and countries adopted measures to "bridge the ambition gap" between NDCs and the Paris commitments even well ahead of the Paris Agreement (Hale 2016). The Marrakech Partnership for Global Climate Action was initiated as a parallel track to intergovernmental negotiations and led by two "high-level champions" to foster collaboration between governments and other stakeholders during the pre-2020 period, enhance ambition, and support immediate emissions reduction until 2020 "to support the success and overachievement of the […] NDCs" (Held and Roger 2018, 533). At COP25, the Global Climate Action was extended to 2025 to bolster non-state action after 2020, and after the Coronavirus outbreak new ways to engage digitally with non-state actors have been advanced (UNFCCC 2019c). Interactions between states and non-state actors have developed into a regular segment of events during the COPs, where an annual Yearbook of Global Climate Action has been launched since 2017 (UNFCCC 2019d). The shift to a systematic and institutionalized inclusion reflects a "growing recognition that nation states are no longer the only actors tackling global warming" (Christoff 2016, 780). Instead, ambitious climate action is required by all governments and non-state actors, "including civil society, the private sector, financial institutions, cities and other sub-national authorities, local communities and indigenous peoples" (UNFCCC 2015).

The Paris Agreement largely builds on state-driven action, yet recognizes "the importance of the engagements of all levels of government and various actors" (UNFCCC 2015, para.15) to combat climate change. Non-state actors have different options at their disposal to shape the NDCs: they can influence policy outcomes either by carrying out tasks delegated to them by states, lobbying and advocacy or by forming transnational governance initiatives (Nasiritousi 2019; Streck 2020). For example, non-state actors joined the state-led NDC Partnership (hosted by the World Resource Institute and the UNFCCC), which brings together countries and international organizations to mobilize more ambitious climate action. As non- and sub-state actors have moved into the spotlight of climate politics around the world, how does it affect the democratic legitimacy of global climate action? The above-mentioned innovations to integrate non-state action into the state-led NDC process and the intergovernmental negotiations holds promises and pitfalls for effective and democratically legitimatized climate governance.

In terms of participation, non-state actors have multiple options to shape the development of the NDCs within and beyond the UNFCCC regime. Numerous forums and high-level meetings invite not only submissions of positions papers, and interventions at high-level segments, but also concrete mitigation pledges and good practices. For example, the Yearbook of Global Climate Action (UNFCCC 2019d) and the Global Climate Action Summit (United Nations 2019) connect non-state actors to the UNFCCC process to showcase action beyond the nation-state. Yet, these forums and pledges are rarely representative, largely dominated by non-state actors from OECD countries and with limited input from civil society organizations (UNFCCC 2019d). In 2016 and 2019, country delegations and observer organizations were asked to submit inputs on the Marrakech Partnership for Global Climate Action that was adopted at the UN climate summit in Marrakech in 2016. Among others, stakeholders suggested that Parties to the UNFCCC should develop "multi-stakeholder platforms" through which non-state actors can continuously engage in the NDCs (UNFCCC High-Level Champions 2019). While organizations such as the World Business Council for Sustainable Development used this opportunity to underline their commitment to help design and implement the NDCs, others formulated more specific ideas to improve the NDC process. For example, Local Governments for Sustainability (ICLEI) demanded meetings with government representatives responsible for the NDCs during the Regional Climate Weeks (ICLEI 2019). The UNFCCC constituency for youth organizations (YOUNGO) proposed to break down the NDCs to local contexts to make it easier, particularly for youth and children, to shape implementation (YOUNGO 2019). In late 2019, Global Climate Action was extended by Climate Action Pathways which outline the "transformational actions and milestones across the thematic and cross-cutting areas"

(UNFCCC 2019a) of the Marrakech Partnership for Global Climate Action. In 2020, the High-level Champions of Global Climate Action invited submissions by states and non-state actors "to gather feedback on how to improve the Marrakech Partnership for enhancing ambition" (Muñoz and Topping 2020).

With a particular focus on women, indigenous people, and youth, the UNFCCC aims to empower these vulnerable and often marginalized groups. However, representatives from these groups often criticize the Global Climate Action process itself where they are less represented than businesses or cities (Allan 2018). Such a setting has direct implications for the democratic value of representation. Non-state actors from the Global South as well as civil society organizations, are less represented than cities and businesses as well as organizations from the Global North (UNFCCC 2019d). While actors with significant financial resources and often larger carbon footprints – such as megacities or carbon-intensive industries – make pledges and set the agenda, civil society organizations, or indigenous groups are far less represented in initiatives like the Global Climate Action platform (UNFCCC 2020a). This requires a critical reflection on why certain groups are not part of the formalized UNFCCC process. David Held and Charles Roger (2018, 534) warn that despite the faith in a participatory regular pledge-and-review process and peer pressure, "we might also see a vicious circle, as pledges, pressure, and actions repeatedly fall short of what is needed."

Hierarchical patterns of accountability seem less appropriate for the complex multilateral climate regime that has become more intertwined with transnational action (Widerberg and Pattberg 2017). Broadening climate mitigation pledges to non-state initiatives can increase overall accountability of global climate action, but this approach also runs the risk to decrease pressure on state legislators. Platforms such as the GCP or the Global Climate Action Summit encourage non-state actors to take on voluntary commitments and thereby close the emission gap left by the insufficient state targets, but the accompanying COP decision to the Paris Agreement makes it clear that these additional mechanisms are not a substitute for state action but a complement. Despite the voluntary character of non-state commitments, a shift can be seen towards their institutionalization. For example, NGOs are increasingly seen as implementing entities to the Paris Agreement in addition to their role as critical watchdogs (United Nations 2019; Streck 2020). While such a development holds all stakeholders accountable for their action, pressure on national governments might decrease within such a collaborative setting.

Non-state actors such as Germany's BUND (2019) demand more interaction with government officials when it comes to the development of the NDCs and thus detect a lack of deliberation between states and affected stakeholders despite a strong UNFCCC framework for public communication. Launched at COP 23, the Talanoa Dialogue for Climate Ambition under the UNFCCC provided a platform for a global stocktaking. Not surprisingly, there is a constant growth of admitted non-state actors to the COPs not only in numbers but also in terms of diversity. In 2017, representatives from 2,133 non-governmental organizations and additional 126 intergovernmental organizations attended COP 23 in Bonn, including businesses, youth, and research organizations (Nasiritousi 2019). An example of an event initiated by a subnational actor in dialogue with the UNFCCC secretariat was the 2018 Global Climate Action Summit in San Francisco hosted by the Governor of California, Jerry Brown, and the UN Special Envoy on Climate Change, Michael Bloomberg. The summit brought together states, regions, cities, companies, investors, and citizens to accelerate their pre-2020 commitments to combat climate change and close the emissions gap between required national commitments and current NDC pledges. Similar pledges were made in September 2019 during the Global Climate Action Summit in New York, but not without criticism. While UN Secretary-General António Guterres highlighted that the pledges are not enough to limit the rise of global temperature to less than 1.5 degrees, Swedish climate activist Greta Thunberg criticized the participants for "empty words" with their focus on "money and fairytales of eternal economic growth" (Thunberg 2019). Transparency is widely perceived to be high and a key area for non-state actor involvement due to their role in the monitoring and review process for national commitments as well as the transparency framework of Article 13 (Jacoby et al. 2017).

In 2019, Parties to the UNFCCC acknowledged the important role of non-state actors in supporting Parties' efforts to tackle climate change (UNFCCC 2019b). Parties also agreed to prolong the Marrakech Partnership for Global Climate Action and the system of the High-Level Champions until 2025 (Muñoz and Topping 2020). Entering into a phase of reflection and reviewing, the global stocktaking should consider the contributions of non-state actors alongside those of national governments in an ambition to improve the NDCs (Climate Groundswell 2020). Besides, current forums do not sufficiently acknowledge critical voices or non-technical pledges. Online repositories like the GCP invite non-state actors to submit commitments, but they fail to foster critical reflections between various stakeholders. In contrast, the Global Climate Action Summits offer a more deliberative and flexible mechanism for non-state actors, for example, with a special segment on youth engagement and climate action in 2019 and with a new UN Secretary Envoy of Youth (UNFCCC 2019d).

Non-state actors at the regional level

Regional platforms for climate action have recently emerged under the UN climate change regime to improve the NDCs and their development particularly in the Global South. Initiatives like the African Non-state Climate Action Platform or ActionLAC in Latin America aim to stimulate learning and interaction between local actors, national policymaking, and global climate governance (Chan, Ellinger, and Widerberg 2018). Compared to climate politics at the global and the national level, regional efforts have been less prominent in climate governance debates.

Emerged from the Regional Carbon Forums under the Nairobi Framework Partnership, Regional Climate Weeks are annual meetings in Africa, Latin America and the Caribbean, and Asia-Pacific. In 2019, these events functioned as preparatory meetings to the UN Secretary-General's Climate Action Summit. During these Regional Climate Weeks, regional bodies, as well as each country, receive comments from stakeholders and have the chance to discuss positive examples for climate action by non-state actors. They link the NDCs to the SDGs and other climate-related commitments to kick-start conversations for the annual Climate Action Summit. Two days of the Regional Climate Weeks are dedicated to technical dialogues on NDC implementation and support for countries to advance their NDCs. Their overall aim is to assist countries in these regions to prepare a more ambitious second round of NDCs and enhance capacities to track the NDC implementation progress (Kosolapova 2019). In March 2019, the first in this series, the Africa Climate Week, was held in Accra, Ghana, to better align climate and development priorities (UNDP 2019). Under the theme Climate Action in Africa: A Race We Can Win (IISD 2019), participants discussed technicalities related to the NDCs. In addition, they engaged with topics like energy transitions, nature-based solutions, and local climate action under three parallel tracks on finance, policy, and technology. The event also discussed the role of carbon pricing and markets in enhancing climate action, capacity building for transparency, innovation and investment, and youth-led climate action.

Providing opportunities for participation for a broad set of stakeholders is at the heart of the regional climate weeks. For example, the Regional Dialogue on NDCs for Africa during the African Climate Week brought together 150 participants, including representatives from almost

50 countries, development partners, the private sector, and other institutions involved in NDC implementation. Organized by the United Nations Development Program (UNDP) and the UNFCCC, the Africa NDC Dialogue supports African countries to develop new or update existing NDCs by providing an opportunity to engage a broader group of stakeholders in the NDC process. Particularly sectoral ministries, local actors, and non-state representatives were targeted to get more involved in the NDC development process, ensuring that sectoral policies, private-sector initiatives, and local efforts are fully reflected in national commitments.

In terms of representation, the NDC dialogue involves technical experts, donors, and private sector representatives, but affected stakeholders such as farmers or civil society organizations are underrepresented or even excluded from the discussions among state representatives. Yet, organizations like the Network of Regional Governments for Sustainable Development (2019) welcome the regional climate weeks under the Marrakech Partnership: "They offer those stakeholders, who are normally not able to attend the COPs, valuable opportunities to showcase climate action, to discuss about successful solutions, as well as to share specific challenges and needs" (Network of Regional Governments for Sustainable Development 2019). With its strong focus on finance, technological development, and governance frameworks, the meeting paid relatively little attention to social concerns or questions related to climate justice (UNDP 2019). Run by the Latin American Fundación Avina, ActionLAC aims to provide a more inclusive platform for non-state driven climate action across Latin America. ActionLAC promotes efforts towards sustainable development through multi-stakeholder meetings, design support, finance, and monitoring (Avina 2019).

Although the regional climate weeks aim to foster transparency through reporting and documentation, reports, and presentations given during the events are either limited in scope or not available at all (UNFCCC 2020b). Serious forms of deliberation and public debates around decisions are also limited since the events provide a largely technical setting for knowledge exchange fostered by international organizations and donors and with little room for broader reflections or contestation from civil society. Overall, the Marrakech Partnership's growing emphasis on regional climate weeks is a welcomed complement to climate action at the global, national, and local level, but it also adds complexity to an already fragmented climate governance architecture.

Non-state actors in domestic contexts: the case of Sweden

The national climate plans are considered a mechanism for "ratcheting up the ambition of states over time" (Held and Roger 2018, 534) as governments are required to communicate their post-2020 climate action to the UNFCCC. This dynamic approach intends to foster more progressive NDCs over time.

In Sweden, environmental politics are characterized by broad public and private stakeholder engagement (Lundqvist 2001). Non-state actors and initiatives actively accompany Sweden's NDC process and the country's ultimate goal to become one of the world's first fossil-free welfare states (Government of Sweden 2018). The Swedish Climate Policy Framework (Swedish Ministry of the Environment 2018) underlines the country's ambition to emit zero net greenhouse gas emissions by 2045. However, decarbonization targets are accompanied by significant challenges in a variety of sectors, such as energy-intensive industries, transportation, or agriculture.

The Swedish government's initiative Fossil Free Sweden (FFS), is an example of a nationally orchestrated mechanism and platform for dialogue to enhance collaboration between representatives of more than 450 companies, cities, regions, and civil society. Orchestration occurs when national governments call upon sub-state and non-state actors to increase their action by tapping into nationally convened platforms and resources (Nasiritousi and Grimm 2020). FFS was was announced at the Paris climate summit in 2015 in response to Sweden's commitment to be one of the first fossil-free welfare states in the world (Regeringen 2016; Statens Offentliga Utredningar 2018). FFS is a government-initiated multi-stakeholder platform for dialogue, sharing experiences, and cooperation between the government, non- and sub-state actors such as businesses, municipalities, and civil society organizations to "catalyze climate action" (Governo 2019, 27). It can be conceived as a domestic initiative to scale up climate action and enhance ambition, that was modeled on the LPAA and Marrakech Climate Action (Stenson and Widerberg 2015; Chan et al. 2018). The appointed national coordinator for FFS, Svante Axelsson, was previously head of Sweden's largest environmental NGO – the Swedish Society for Nature Conservation. FFS was initiated to operationalize Sweden's goal to achieve net-zero emissions by 2045, followed by negative emissions. The goal is codified by Sweden's 2017 Climate Policy Framework consisting of long-term climate goals, a Climate Law and a Climate Policy Council, the latter which came into force in January 2018.

FFS was set up to mobilize companies, cities, and regions to contribute to Sweden's plan to become fossil-free by 2045. To this end, FFS is a major effort to encourage businesses to take on targets to formulate their roadmaps to fossil-free competitiveness. Low-carbon and decarbonization plans, roundtables, workshops and seminars, collaborative forums, and voluntary commitments are instruments for engaging actors. FFS was meant to terminate by the end of 2018 but was granted extensions by the Swedish government until December 2024 (Regeringen 2020). FFS involves more than 400 actors such as cities, municipalities, and large- and medium-sized companies, the Swedish church and civil society. Modeled on the GCP, non-state actors can submit their pledges in terms of medium and long-term climate goals.

Concerning the democratic values outlined above, participation at FFS is skewed toward industry actors to enable large-scale industrial decarbonization. FFS's backbone are 21 roadmaps for fossil-free competitiveness in various industrial sectors such as transport, steel, construction, cement, food and retail, mining, aviation, forestry, and maritime industry (FFS 2019). Hence, while all actors are invited to participate in FFS, the primary targets are industrial actors and municipalities. This focus on making business carbon-neutral has paved the way for Sweden to co-chair the Industrial Transition theme of the UN Secretary-General's Global Summit on Climate Action in New York in 2019. This fits well with Sweden's highly eco-modernist and green economy tradition, exemplified by the country's aspiration to be the first in the world to produce fossil-free steel. Sweden's goal to present itself as the first permanent world exhibition to fossil-free technology is another example toward that end (Governo 2019, 11).

While there is broad civil society participation in various national, regional, and local FFS workshops and events, as well as in the formulation of roadmaps, representation by non-state actors such as environmental NGOs, indigenous people (Sami people), and civil society is rather weak. This also fits within the political culture of Sweden's corporatist tradition and the Swedish model, which is built on close collaboration between industry, government, and labor unions. In a review of selected members of FFS, the surveyed participants industry represented 52 percent of respondents, followed by municipalities (21 percent), regional authorities (6 percent), civil society (6 percent), and 15 percent of public agencies, research organizations, and universities (Governo 2019, 14).

On deliberative quality, FFS scores relatively well as it is set up as a mechanism to enhance dialogue, storytelling, and sharing of best practices. A core of the task was to foster and visualize a narrative for all societal stakeholders on the transformation of Sweden into the world's first fossil-free welfare state with the help of newsletters, social media, and outreach (Governo

2019, 11). Both non-state actors that have signed up to the initiative, as well as the general public, are invited to workshops, roundtables, and conferences, where there is ample scope for interaction and dialogue with ministers, companies, businesses, grassroots organizations, and civil society actors. In this sense, FFS epitomizes the Swedish model and political culture of consensus making and deliberation to build public trust and enhance collaboration (Bäckstrand et al. 2010).

Concerning transparency and accountability, FFS has done regular reporting of its activities, e.g. on its roadmaps concerning various industrial sector ranging from concrete to steel (FFS 2018). By 2020, 21 roadmaps for decarbonization have been handed over to the government from industry such as aviation, automobile, shipping, mining, and electricity. Regular reports and reviews of the progress of FFS makes it possible for members and non-members to get information about FFS activities (Governo 2019). However, the bar for joining FFS Sweden is low as no quantitative and measurable targets are required to participate or sign up to the declaration. The voluntary and flexible nature of FFS allows businesses and municipalities to join. Still, neither commitments and goal attainment of individual actors, nor FFS's performance to reduce carbon emissions on an aggregate level are monitored. In other words, accountability is limited as the institutional design does not allow for an evaluation of performance or for third-party organizations to track progress toward greenhouse gas emission reduction targets.

Conclusion

With the institutionalization of the global action agenda, the role of non-state actors in the post-Paris era has largely shifted from antagonists to partners in the UNFCCC (Streck 2020). A closer look at the NDC process under the post-Paris climate governance architecture reveals numerous options for non-state intervention and inclusion. The Paris Agreement proves legitimacy, but also creates new democratic challenges. Non-state actors provide information, shape decision-making processes, foster transparency, hold actors accountable, and make room for deliberation along the NDC formulation and implementation process not only at the global level but also in regional and domestic contexts. The empirical illustrations from the NDC process thus provide an opportunity for a democratic and collaborative climate governance model where greater non-state actor involvement is seen as the beneficiary for stronger and more effective climate policy formulation and implementation.

These experiences underline the diverse and ongoing tensions between climate governance and democratic decision-making which serves as an example for globally reached agreements like the UN Agenda 2030. Implementing the SDGs and translating them into national and local contexts faces similar challenges like the NDCs. The democratic legitimacy of the UN Agenda 2030 can be strengthened by incorporating non-state actor voices at the global, regional, and national level, especially when it comes to knowledge exchange and the operationalization of the SDGs. However, as argued by Ingolfur Blühdorn and Michael Deflorian (2019), the highly formalized system runs into danger to leave out more confrontational voices which articulate resistance and demands in contrast to intergovernmental agreements as well as forms of co-optation where non-state actors are strategically used as a tool for state-driven agendas. The focus on technicalities and the rising imbalances between the Global South and the Global North could eventually leave out issues of broader social and political contestation. If critical non-state actors avoid the official forums for NDC development and implementation, this could delegitimize the whole process, depoliticize climate governance and detach it from local contexts.

We recommend future research to more profoundly engage with at least three issue areas: (1) Instead of focusing on single governance levels, multi-level interlinkages should be investigated more closely. How does decision-making at various levels shape each other and which actors can use the multi-level framework strategically? (2) Researchers should also elaborate on the tensions between formalized, often UN-led, processes and more informal engagement inside and outside the state-led climate negotiations. Particularly interesting are non-state actors who either refuse to be part of a global agreement or struggle to get access to official talks. Which actors dominate the field and which groups are marginalized and struggle to participate? What are the reasons and critical consequences? (3) Finally, we need more substantial studies on the merits and shortcomings of participatory governance innovations. More qualitative and comparative studies on non-state intervention should critically accompany the development of databases like the Global Climate Action portal, or measurements like the SDG indicators to critically assess the political conclusions drawn from them. Echoing Held and Roger (2018), we need to understand better how the pledge-and-review process and other mechanisms work in practice and alter national contexts to grasp their democratic potential. Adding complexity to an already fragmented policy field, the Paris Agreement opens up opportunities for democratic interventions by formerly marginalized actors such as youth organizations. At the same time, tendencies towards cooptation and stronger integration of non-state actors into a system they should critically assess from the outside undermine the democratic legitimacy of climate governance.

Notes

1 We use and define the term "non-state" here in its broadest sense to describe a diverse group of both private and public actors beyond the national governments and the official Parties to the UNFCCC. In the UNFCCC system and the Paris Agreement nine such non-state actor groups ("non-Party stakeholders" or UNFCCC constituencies) are observers to the negotiation: NGOs, business, trade unions, women, youth and children, scientific and technological communities, local governments and cities, indigenous people, and farmers. Also local governments, cities, and municipalities are categorized here as non-state actors despite being governmental stakeholders.
2 While we exclude the local level in this chapter due to length constraints, see Aust (2018), Hsu et al. (2016), or Bansard et al. (2017) for detailed analyses on the role of cities and other local non-state actors in the post-Paris climate regime.
3 Search algorithm: TOPIC: (climate change OR climate governance OR climate politics) AND TOPIC: (non-state OR nonstate OR non-governmental OR nongovernmental OR NGO*) / Databases= WOS, BCI, CCC, DRCI, DIIDW, KJD, MEDLINE, RSCI, SCIELO, ZOOREC / Timespan=1999-2020 (retrieved: December 21, 2020).

References

Abbott, K.W., 2012. The transnational regime complex for climate change. *Environment and planning C. Government and Policy*, 30 (4), 571–590.
Agné, H., Dellmuth, L.M. and Tallberg, J., 2015. Does stakeholder involvement foster democratic legitimacy in international organizations? An empirical assessment of a normative theory. *The Review of International Organizations*, 10(4), 465–488.
Allan, J.I., 2018. Seeking entry: discursive hooks and NGOs in global climate politics. *Global Policy*, 9(4), 560–569.
Allan, J.I., 2019. Dangerous incrementalism of the Paris Agreement. *Global Environmental Politics*, 19(1), 4–11.
Andonova, L.B., Betsill, M.M. and Bulkeley, H., 2009. Transnational climate governance. *Global Environmental Politics*, 9(2), 52–73.
Aust, H.P., 2018. The shifting role of cities in the global climate change regime: from Paris to Pittsburgh and back? *Review of European, Comparative and International Environmental Law*, 1–10.

Avina, F., 2019. *About ActionLAC* [online]. ActionLAC. Available from: <https://actionlac.net/en/about-actionlac>[Accessed 13 March, 2020].
Bäckstrand, K., 2006. Democratizing global environmental governance? Stakeholder democracy after the world summit on sustainable development. *European Journal of International Relations*, 12(4), 467–498.
Bäckstrand, K., 2008. Accountability of networked climate governance: the rise of transnational climate partnerships. *Global Environmental Politics*, 8(3), 74–102.
Bäckstrand, K., 2011. The Democratic Legitimacy of Global Governance after Copenhagen. In J.S. Dryzek, R.B. Norgaard and D. Schlosberg, eds. *The Oxford Handbook of Climate Change and Society*. Oxford: Oxford University Press.
Bäckstrand, K. and Kuyper, J.W., 2017. The democratic legitimacy of orchestration: the UNFCCC, non-state actors, and transnational climate governance. *Environmental Politics*, 26(4), 764–788.
Bäckstrand, K., Kahn, J., Kronsell, A. and Lövbrand, E., 2010. *Environmental Politics and Deliberative Democracy: Examining the Promise of New Modes of Governance*. London: Edward Elgar.
Bäckstrand, K., Kuyper, J.W., Linnér, B.-O. and Lövbrand, E., 2017. Non-state actors in global climate governance: from Copenhagen to Paris and beyond. *Environmental Politics*, 26(4), 561–579.
Bansard, J., Pattberg, P. and Widerberg, O., 2017. Cities to the rescue? Assessing the performance of transnational municipal networks in global climate governance. *Int Environ Agreements*, 17, 229–246.
Bernauer, T. and Betzold, C., 2012. Civil society in global environmental governance. *The Journal of Environment and Development*, 21(1), 62–66.
Betsill, M.M and Bulkeley, H., 2003. *Cities and Climate Change*. London: Routledge.
Betsill, M.M. and Bulkeley, H., 2006. Cities and the multilevel governance of global climate change. *Global Governance*, 12, 141–159.
Betsill, M.M. and Corell, E., 2008. NGO Diplomacy. The Influence of Nongovernmental Organizations in International Environmental Negotiations. In M.M. Betsill and E. Corell, eds. *NGO Diplomacy*. Cambridge MA and London: MIT Press.
Betsill, M.M. and Corell, E., 2014. NGO influence in international environmental negotiations: a framework for analysis. *Global Environmental Politics*, 1(November 2001), 65–85.
Bexell, M., 2014. Global governance, legitimacy and (de)legitimation. *Globalizations*, 11(3), 289–299.
Blühdorn, I. and Deflorian, M., 2019. The collaborative management of sustained unsustainability: on the performance of participatory forms of environmental governance. *Sustainability (Switzerland)*, 11(4), 197–214.
Brühl, T., 2010. Representing the People? NGOs in International Negotiations. In J. Steffek and K. Hahn, eds. *Evaluating Transnational NGOs. Legitimacy, Accountability and Representation*. Basingstoke: Palgrave MacMillan, 181–199.
BUND, 2019. *Civil Society Engagement for Ambitious NDCs*. Bonn.
Burck, J., Hagen, U., Marten, F., Höhne, N. and Bals, C., 2019. *Climate Change Performance Inde: Results 2019*. Bonn.
Chan, S., Asselt, H. Van, Iacobuta, G. and Niles, N., 2019. Promises and risks of nonstate action in climate and sustainability governance. *WIREs Climate Change*, 1–8.
Chan, S., Ellinger, P. and Widerberg, O., 2018. Exploring national and regional orchestration of non-state action for a < 1.5 °C world. *International Environmental Agreements: Politics, Law and Economics*, 18(1), 1–18.
Christoff, P., 2016. The promissory note: COP 21 and the Paris Climate Agreement. *Environmental Politics*, 25(5), 765–787.
Climate Groundswell, 2020. *Building a Vision for Global Climate Action in the UNFCCC after 2020*. Bonn.
Dingwerth, K., 2007. *The New Transnationalism. Transnational Governance and Legitimacy*. London: Palgrave MacMillan.
Dingwerth, K., 2014. Global democracy and the democratic minimum: why a procedural account alone is insufficient. *European Journal of International Relations*, 20(4), 1124–1147.
Dryzek, J.S. and Pickering, J., 2017. Deliberation as a catalyst for reflexive environmental governance. *Ecological Economics*, 131, 353–360.
Engström-Stenson, D. and Widerberg, O., 2016. Linking state, non-state and subnational climate action: the case of Sweden, Policy Brief 2016/11, Fores and the Institute for Environmental Studies (IVM) at Vrije Universiteit Amsterdam, Amsterdam.
Feindt, P.H. and Weiland, S., 2018. Reflexive governance: exploring the concept and assessing its critical potential for sustainable development. Introduction to the special issue. *Journal of Environmental Policy and Planning*, 20(6), 661–674.

FFS, 2018. Roadmap for fossil free competitiveness. Stockholm.
Fisher, D.R. and Galli, A.M., 2015. Civil society. In *Research Handbook on Climate Governance*. London: Edward Elgar, 297–308.
Friedman, R., Oskanian, K. and Pardo, R.P., eds., 2013, *After Liberalism? The Future of Liberalism in International Relations*. London: Palgrave.
Gleckman, H., 2018. *Multistakeholder Governance and Democracy: A Global Challenge*. Routledge: London.
Government of Sweden, 2018. *Sweden tackles climate change* [online]. Available from: <https://sweden.se/nature/sweden-tackles-climate-change/> [Accessed 25 September, 2019].
Governo, 2019. Utvärdering av Fossilfritt Sveriges arbete. Utredning på uppdrag av Fossilfritt Sverige.
Grant, R.W. and Keohane, R.O., 2005. Accountability and Abuses of power in world politics. *American Political Science Review*, 99(1), 29–43.
Green, J.F., 2013. *Rethinking Private Authority*. Princeton: Princeton University Press.
Gupta, A., and van Asselt, H., 2019. Transparency and Accountability in Multilateral Climate Politics. In S. Park and T. Kramarz, eds. *Global Environmental Governance and the Accountability Trap*. Cambridge, MA: MIT Press, 37–62.
Hadden, J., 2015. *Networks in Contention*. Cambridge: Cambridge University Press.
Hale, T., 2016. "All hands on deck": The Paris Agreement and nonstate climate action. *Global Environmental Politics*, 16(3), 12–22.
Hale, T., 2020. Transnational actors and transnational governance in global environmental politics. *Annual Review of Political Science*, 23, 203–220.
Held, D. and Hervey, A., 2011. Democracy, climate change and global governance: democratic agency and the policy menu ahead. *The Governance of Climate Change*, 89–110.
Held, D. and Roger, C., 2018. Three models of global climate governance: from Kyoto to Paris and beyond. *Global Policy*, 9(4), 527–537.
Hermwille, L., 2018. Making initiatives resonate: how can non-state initiatives advance national contributions under the UNFCCC?. *International Environmental Agreements: Politics, Law and Economics*, 18(3), 447–466.
Hoffmann, M.J., 2011. *Climate Governance at the Crossroads*. New York: Oxford University Press.
Hsu, A., Cheng, Y., Xu, K., Weinfurter, A., Yick, C., Ivanenko, M., Nair, S., Hale, T., Guy, B. and Rosengarten, C., 2015. *The Wider World of Non-state and Sub-national Climate Action*. New Haven: Yale School of Forestry and Environmental Studies.
Hsu, A., Cheng, Y., Weinfurter, A., Xu, K. and Yick, C., 2016. Track climate pledges of cities and companies. *Nature*, 532(7599), 303–306.
Hsu, A., Höhne, N., Kuramochi, T., Vilariño, V. and Sovacool, B.K., 2020. Beyond states: harnessing sub-national actors for the deep decarbonisation of cities, regions, and businesses. *Energy Research and Social Science*, 70, 101738.
ICLEI, 2019. *Questions for structuring inputs to the Marrakech Partnership for Global Climate Action. Input by ICLEI – Local Governments for Sustainability* [online]. Available from: <https://unfccc.int/climate-action/marrakech-partnership/invitation-to-provide-feedback-to-the-high-level-champions-on-global-climate-action> [Accessed 3 June, 2019].
IISD, 2019. *Africa Climate Week 2019* [online]. Available from: <https://sdg.iisd.org/events/africa-climate-week-2019/> [Accessed 10 March, 2020].
Jacoby, H.D., Chen, Y.H. and Flannery, B.P., 2017. *Transparency in the Paris Agreement*. Cambridge: MIT Joint Program on the Science and Policy of Global Change.
Jasanoff, S., 2010. A new climate for society theory. *Culture and Society*, 27(2), 233–253.
Keohane, R.O., Macedo, S. and Moravcsik, A., 2009. Democracy-enhancing multilateralism. *International Organization*, 63(1), 1–31.
Kosolapova, E., 2019. *Regional Climate Weeks to Build Momentum Towards UN Climate Summit* [online]. Available from: <http://sdg.iisd.org/news/regional-climate-weeks-to-build-momentum-towards-un-climate-summit/> [Accessed 3 June, 2019].
Kuramochi, T., Roelfsema, M., Hsu, A., Lui, S., Weinfurter, A., Chan, S., Hale, T., Clapper, A., Chang, A. and Höhne, N., 2020. Beyond national climate action: the impact of region, city, and business commitments on global greenhouse gas emissions. *Climate Policy*, 20(3), 275–291.
Kuyper, J.W., Linnér, B.O. and Schroeder, H., 2018. Non-state actors in hybrid global climate governance: justice, legitimacy, and effectiveness in a post-Paris era. *Wiley Interdisciplinary Reviews: Climate Change*, 9(1), 1–18.
Lundqvist, L.J., 2001. Implementation from above: the ecology of power in Swedens environmental governance. *Governance*, 14(3), 319–337.

Macdonald, T., 2008. *Global Stakeholder Democracy: Power and Representation Beyond Liberal States*. Oxford: Oxford University Press.

Machin, A., 2013. *Negotiating Climate Change: Radical Democracy and the Illusion of Consensus*. London: Zed Books.

MacLean, J., 2020. Rethinking the role of nonstate actors in international climate governance. *Loyola University Chicago International Law Review*, 16(1), 21–43.

Marquardt, J. and Nasiritousi, N., 2021. Imaginary lock-ins in climate change politics: the challenge to envision a fossil-free future. *Environmental Politics*, Advance online publication.

Muñoz, G. and Topping, N., 2020. *Letter to parties and non-party stakeholders from the High-level Champions of Global Climate Action*. Bonn: United Nations Framework Convention on Climate Change.

Nasiritousi, N., 2019. NGOs and the Environment. In T. Davies, eds. *Routledge Handbook of NGOs and International Relations*. London: Routledge, 329–342.

Nasiritousi, N. and Grimm, J., 2020. Because there is no plan(et) B: a study of the Fossil Free Sweden initiative and its legitimacy. *Academy of Management Proceedings*, 1, 16636.

Network of Regional Governments for Sustainable Development, 2019. *nrg4SD Feedback to the High-Level Champions on the Marrakech Partnership for Global Climate Action* [online]. Available from: <https://unfccc.int/climate-action/marrakech-partnership/invitation-to-provide-feedback-to-the-high-level-champions-on-global-climate-action> [Accessed 3 June, 2019].

Newell, P., 2000. Environmental NGOs and Globalisation: The Governance of TNCs. In *Global Social Movements*. London: Athlone Press, 117–134.

Obergassel, W., Arens, C., Hermwille, L., Kreibich, N., Mersmann, F., Ott, H.E. and Wang-Helmreich, H., 2016. *Phoenix from the Ashes – An Analysis of the Paris Agreement to the United Nations Framework Convention on Climate Change*. Wuppertal: Wuppertal Institut für Klima, Umwelt, Energie.

Pattberg, P., Chan, S., Sanderink, L. and Widerberg, O., 2018. Linkages. In A. Jordan, D. Huitema, H. van Asselt and J. Forster, eds. *Governing Climate Change: Polycentricity in Action?*. Cambridge: Cambridge University Press, 169–187.

Princen, T. and Finger, M., 1994. *Environmental NGOs in World Politics*. London: Routledge.

Raustiala, K., 1997. States, NGOs, and international environmental institutions. *International Studies Quarterly*, 41(4), 719–740.

Regeringen Sverige. 2016. *Initiativet Fossilfritt Sverige*. Stockholm: Government of Sweden.

Regeringen Sverige. 2020. *Tilläggsdirektiv till Initiativet Fossilfritt Sverige (M 2016:05)*. Stockholm: Government of Sweden.

Scholte, J.A., 2002. Civil society and democracy in global governance. *Global Governance*, 8(3), 281–304.

Scholte, J.A., 2011. *Building Global Democracy. Civil Society and Accountable Global Governance*. Cambridge: Cambridge University Press.

Slaughter, A.M., 2015. *The Paris Approach to Global Governance* [online]. Available from: www.project-syndicate.org/commentary/paris-agreement-model-for-global-governance-by-anne-marie-slaughter-2015-12?barrier=accesspaylog> [Accessed 5 August, 2019].

Statens Offentliga Utredningar, 2018. *Fossil Free Sweden* [online]. Available from: <http://fossilfritt-sverige.se/in-english> [Accessed 25 September, 2019].

Stevenson, H. and Dryzek, J.S., 2014. *Democratizing Global Climate Governance*. Cambridge: Cambridge University Press.

Streck, C., 2020. Filling in for governments? The Role of the private actors in the international climate regime. *Journal for European Environmental and Planning Law*, 17(1), 5–28.

Swedish Ministry of the Environment, 2018. *The Swedish Climate Policy Framework*, Stockholm.

Tallberg, J. and Uhlin, A., 2011. Civil Society and Global Democracy: An Assessment. In D. Archibugi, M. Koenig-Archibugi and R. Marchetti, eds. *Global Democracy: Normative and Empirical Perspectives*. Cambridge: Cambridge University Press, 210–232.

Thunberg, G., 2019. *If world leaders choose to fail us, my generation will never forgive them* [online]. Available from: <www.theguardian.com/commentisfree/2019/sep/23/world-leaders-generation-climate-breakdown-greta-thunberg> [Accessed 10 March, 2020].

Tørstad, V., Sælen, H. and Bøyum, L.S., 2020. The domestic politics of international climate commitments: which factors explain cross-country variation in NDC ambition?. *Environmental Research Letters*, 15(2).

UNDP, 2019. *Africa Climate Week | NDC Dialogues, NDC Support Programme* [online]. Available from: <www.ndcs.undp.org/content/ndc-support-programme/en/home/ndc-events/global-and-regional/2019-africa-climate-week-.html> [Accessed 3 June, 2019].

UNFCCC, 2015. Decision 1/CP.21. Adoption of the Paris Agreement. UN Doc FCCC/CP/2015/ 10/ Add.1, United Nations Framework Convention on Climate Change, Paris.

UNFCCC, 2019a. *Climate Action Pathways, United Nations Climate Change* [online]. Avaible from: <https://unfccc.int/climate-action/marrakech-partnership/reporting-and-tracking/climate_action_pathways> [Accessed 2 April 2020].

UNFCCC, 2019b. Decision 1/CP.25: Chile Madrid Time for Action, Madriid.

UNFCCC, 2019c. United Nations Climate Change Annual Report 2019, Bonn.

UNFCCC, 2019d. Yearbook of Global Climate Action 2019, United Nations Framework Convention on Climate Change, Bonn.

UNFCCC, 2020a. Global Climate Action Platform, NAZCA.

UNFCCC, 2020b. *Regional Climate Weeks, Regional Climate Weeks* [online]. Available from: <www.regionalclimateweeks.org> [Accessed 13 March, 2020].

UNFCCC, 2021. *Full NDC Synthesis Report: Some Progress, but Still a Big Concern* [online]. Available from: <unfccc.int/news/full-ndc-synthesis-report-some-progress-but-still-a-big-concern> [Accessed 2 November, 2021].

UNFCCC High-Level Champions, 2019. Invitation to Provide Feedback to The High-Level Champions on Global Climate Action, UNFCCC website.

United Nations, 2019. Report of the Secretary-General on the 2019 Climate Action Summit and the Way Forward in 2020, New York.

Van Asselt, H. and Bößner, S., 2016. The shape of things to come: global climate governance after Paris. *Carbon and Climate L Rev*, 1(1), 46.

Widerberg, O. and Pattberg, P., 2017. Accountability challenges in the transnational regime complex for climate change. *Review of Policy Research*, 34(1), 68–87.

YOUNGO, 2019. *Feedback from YOUNGO to High-level Champions on the Marrakech Partnership for Global Climate Action Priorities and Focus Areas* [online]. Available from: <https://unfccc.int/climate-action/marrakech-partnership/invitation-to-provide-feedback-to-the-high-level-champions-on-global-climate-action> [Accessed 3 June, 2019].

Zaman, S.T., 2018. The "bottom-up pledge and review" approach of nationally determined contributions (NDCs) in the Paris Agreement: a historical breakthrough or a setback in new climate governance?. *IALS Student Law Review*, 5(2), 3–20.

18
GLOBAL GOVERNANCE AND DEMOCRACY
Aligning procedural and substantive accounts?

Magdalena Bexell

Introduction

Several chapters in this *Handbook* bear witness of the intricate relationship between democracy and sustainability within democratic states. This relationship is, arguably, even more intricate in global and transnational governance where the preconditions for democratic rule in its traditional sense are absent. Such governance is not exercised on the basis of a demarcated demos, an electoral system or effective accountability forms that hold governors to account by those governed. There is no enforcement body capable of ensuring compliance with international political agreements on sustainability. Problems of collective action abound when states are not willing to follow costly sustainability commitments that other states do not respect. Yet the borderless nature of sustainability problems requires effective international cooperation. Moreover, democratic deficits in global governance are interrelated with and reinforced by democratic deficits within states. Despite these circumstances, there are plenty of attempts to democratise governance beyond the state, demanding consideration of what democracy can and should entail in such governance.

This chapter delves into research on the relationship between democracy and sustainability in the context of global and transnational governance. I use "global governance" as the broader term that covers both interstate-based and nonstate-based forms of governance beyond the state (Bexell 2014). There are three subcategories specifying different forms of global governance. Accordingly, "transnational governance" refers specifically to governance interactions crossing national borders at other levels than state-to-state (Hale and Held 2011, 4) whereas "international governance" refers to state-to-state based governance. In turn, "hybrid governance" refers to schemes that involve both state and nonstate actors in cooperative constellations that create new sites of power and regulative authority. The realm of global sustainability governance is by now characterised by a rich diversity of international, transnational and hybrid governance bodies. Transnational and hybrid governance bodies exercise a range of governance functions traditionally belonging to the intergovernmental realm. Key among those functions are rule-setting (e.g. World Commission on Dams, Better Cotton Initiative, UN Global Compact, Forest Stewardship Council), monitoring (Human Rights Watch, Greenpeace,

Global Reporting Initiative) and funding combined with advocacy (Bill and Melinda Gates Foundation, Rockefeller Foundation).

I will begin in section 2 with a review of current normative academic debates on democracy in global and transnational governance, providing the overarching context within which more specific research questions have appeared. Section 3 then looks into examples of recent empirical research on the democratic qualities of global governance in issue areas with bearing on sustainability affairs. Thereafter, I highlight in section 4 that procedural accounts of global democracy have dominated scholarly thinking and I discuss ways in which procedural and substantive accounts of a democratisation of global governance can possibly be reconciled. This feeds into the present Handbook's concern with how ideas of democracy and sustainability support each other – and where tensions remain. In the conclusion I emphasise that global governance is political and that questions on its democratic qualities is a fruitful way of keeping democratic political contestation at the centre of scholarly attention and policy action.

The chapter engages with literature that deals with global or transnational governance domains as part of the research agenda on global governance that has emerged in International Relations since the 1990s. The chapter therefore leaves literature on the green state, domestic deliberative democracy, and experts and democracy, to other chapters in this *Handbook*. Moreover, the chapter is based on an understanding of sustainability as having both economic, social and environmental dimensions which implies that international organizations of several issue realms are relevant study objects. International organizations of global economic governance have as much impact on sustainability as organizations of global environmental governance. For instance, decisions made by the World Trade Organization on global rules that facilitate international trade may lead to an increase in emissions related to long distance transportation of goods. Decisions on agriculture and food systems made by the UN Food and Agriculture Organization have an impact on biodiversity and broader ecosystems. I therefore mainly speak of global governance in general terms rather than seeking to define one issue domain of sustainability per se.

Normative debates on global governance and democracy

What is the state of current normative debates on democracy and global governance? Environmental researchers have long engaged with the fact that environmental problems do not respect political borders, arguing that environmental issues require revisions of both democratic theory and practice. In parallel, questions related to a democratic deficit of international organizations have generated extensive theoretical debates in the fields of International Relations and International Political Theory over the past two decades. This contrasts with prior dominance of Realist thinking in International Relations that focused on interstate relations and the primacy of national interest and state sovereignty as drivers of environmental degradation. Realist scepticism led to a long neglect of the subject of global democracy (Dahl 1999). Early debates mainly revolved around cosmopolitan propositions on global democratic institutions such as a world government (Held 1995). In response, the school of democratic intergovernmentalism emphasises the crucial role of governments as representative of their peoples' interests. It argues intergovernmental negotiations among states should be the primary focus of democratisation attempts, supporting institutional reform through enhanced accountability and transparency (Keohane and Nye 2003). Other critics of global democracy thinking put the emphasis within states. Thus, David Miller (2010) questions whether global governance agencies are at all capable of being democratically accountable in any significant sense, due to the problem of identifying the relevant demos and the constituency to whom those bodies would be accountable. Miller argues that international organisations can deal with global problems but that efforts of moving in the direction of global democracy distract attention from the more urgent task of strengthening democracy within states.

Between a cosmopolitan vision of world government and thinking centred around democratic intergovernmentalism, contemporary scholarly debate on democracy in global governance is much concerned with transnational deliberative democracy and global stakeholder democracy. I now briefly turn to each of those. While not mutually exclusive, accounts of deliberative democracy emphasise discursive contestation whereas stakeholder democracy models pay more attention to participation in decision-making by all affected actors, preferably through institutionalised means. As I return to later, both strands of research also engage in empirical studies, mirroring the actual increase of deliberative forums and stakeholder practices in global governance.

Much recent academic debate has revolved around promises and pitfalls of deliberative democracy in settings beyond the nation state. The promises of deliberative democracy in the global sustainability realm have been explored for instance by John Dryzek and Hayley Stevenson in several publications (e.g. Dryzek and Stevenson 2011; Stevenson and Dryzek 2014) as well as by Karin Bäckstrand and co-authors (e.g. Bäckstrand et al. 2010). They show that deliberative democracy can take many different forms and operates mainly in the informal global public sphere, often centred around civil society. While facing many challenges in a global setting, deliberative practices are expected to nurture more inclusive, participatory policymaking. Examples include the side events running alongside the annual Conference of the Parties to the UN Framework Convention on Climate Change and debates on reform of the Clean Development Mechanism of the global carbon market. Thereby, policymaking is also expected to become more rational by including more perspectives on the common good. Proponents of deliberative democracy argue that deliberation leads to knowledge of a higher quality, on which to base policy decisions. Its proponents are not mainly concerned with establishing or changing formal institutions but rather with deepening public debates in a transnational sphere around and beyond existing institutions. Any democratization of governance in deliberative terms depends on the development of a transnational public sphere, enabling public debate on political proposals (Steffek and Nanz 2008). Deliberation is necessary because, to be effective, internationally adopted policies should reflect needs of people whose circumstances are supposed to be improved. In models of deliberative global governance, political representation is usually understood to be centred on discourses in a global public sphere rather than on actors such as governments, individuals or organisations. In sum, in an ideal form, the model of transnational deliberative democracy entails political representation through reciprocal dialogue where discursive positions rather than the aggregation of interests of different groups are in focus. It is a decentred model of policymaking that profits from including knowledge of the groups intended to benefit from resulting policies.

Global stakeholder democracy, for its part, puts the participation of affected parties in decision-making processes centre stage as well as accountability of decision-makers towards those affected by decisions. It holds greater interest in reform of existing institutions than does the deliberative model. Stakeholder democracy models are underpinned by optimism about the prospects of establishing a pluralist model of democratic representation in the global domain, while acknowledging challenges involved (Macdonald and Macdonald 2010). All parties substantially affected by a decision should have equal opportunity to participate in decision-making and to hold decision-makers accountable for the impact of their decisions. This model invites debate on interpretation of the "all-affected principle", according to which global institutions should be placed more strongly within the political control of their affected stakeholders

(Macdonald 2012). According to this principle, individuals should be allocated a role in collective decision-making based on their degree of affectedness rather than their membership in a political community. Another strand of this research examines the democratic credentials of multi-stakeholder bodies such as public-private partnerships (Bexell and Mörth 2010), a form of hybrid governance that has been prominent in the domain of sustainability (Kramarz 2016). Examples include nonstate-based transnational organizations whose entire design builds on representation of different interests such as the Forest Stewardship Council where decision-making is shared between actors belonging to an environmental, economic or social chamber with an additional weighting of votes between actors from North and South within each chamber. In brief, a model of stakeholder democracy in global politics would in its ideal form subject powerful political agents to democratic control by those affected by their decisions through some form of accountability procedure.

To conclude, debate on what global democratic governance should look like is by now an established part of the field of global governance studies and of International Political Theory more generally. Other normative perspectives are provided by critical theorists who rightly remind global democracy scholars to pay more attention to power relations and politics when exploring governance beyond the state. Feminist perspectives, for instance, highlight power relations that have not been central to climate governance scholarship but that are nevertheless important when the concern is with democracy as a means to inclusion and political equality (Kronsell 2017). For its part, a critical international political economy perspective questions the presumption that there is in any meaningful sense a global "we" on whose behalf global governance is presumed to act. Rather, in critical theory perspective, global governance always contains hegemonic elements such as the presentation of specific interests as universal ones (Katz-Rosene and Paterson 2018, 134). Clearly, a plurality of perspectives ensures that debate on how to think about democracy in global and transnational governance will continue to thrive.

Empirical insights on democracy in global sustainability governance
Models of deliberative and stakeholder democracy

I now turn to examples of empirically-oriented research on democracy in global governance, bearing in mind that many scholars combine normative theoretical engagement with empirical studies. Again, the key normative criteria for deliberative democracy are the qualities of deliberation in terms of depth and openness and the level of inter-discourse debate. In empirical studies of deliberative democracy, Bäckstrand et al. (2010) conclude that new modes of governance have in some instances strengthened the deliberative qualities of environmental politics. The most successful examples, however, are usually not global or even transnational in character but rather nationally or locally based, while engaging with globally set agendas as is the case in local climate governance initiatives. Yet the authors posit that deliberative attempts should best be understood as a piecemeal complement to state-based representative democracy. In further studies of discursive contestation in deliberative democracy, John Dryzek and Hayley Stevenson identify four climate discourses in side events applications for COP-15 in 2009 in Copenhagen (Dryzek and Stevenson 2011) and in non-state summits on climate change related to COP-15 (Stevenson and Dryzek 2012). These range from two discourses that posit sustainability and material growth to be compatible ("Mainstream Sustainability" and "Expansive Sustainability") to discourses that are economically radical. The latter appear in combination with political conservatism ("Limits Discourse") or with political radicalism demanding a redistribution of power ("Green Radicalism"). The authors find the level of inter-discourse engagement to be low. Therefore, the qualities of reflexive capacity envisioned in deliberative democracy theory are not fulfilled in these cases (Dryzek and Stevenson 2011, 1870; Stevenson and Dryzek 2012, 201). Another example of attempts at global deliberation is provided by the consultations conducted by the United Nations on the successor to the Millennium Development Goals that expired in 2015. There was unprecedentedly broad deliberation on the 2030 Agenda for sustainable development and its set of Sustainable Development Goals. In the decision-making phase, the 2030 Agenda was given final shape through traditional intergovernmental political negotiations where contention between high-income countries and low-income countries came to fore and last-minute changes weakened the responsibilities of high-income countries in the final outcome (Cummings et al. 2018, 736; Kamau et al. 2018, 229–236).

In assessments of global stakeholder democracy, central normative criteria are the representation of affected actors and accountability to those of decision-makers. A study by Macdonald and Macdonald (2010, 34) argues that multi-stakeholder systems of supply chain regulations (Fair Labor Association, Common Code for the Coffee Community, Ethical Trading Initiative) have played a part in creating a pluralist system of democratic representation. This was the case at least to the extent such systems allowed workers and producers to identify corporate power being exercised over them, to communicate their demands and increase consumer awareness. Another study of multi-stakeholder partnerships points in a less optimistic direction. In the case of nine global partnerships for biodiversity conservation, funding partners were represented in decision-making bodies of the partnership while partners affected at the local level did not have formal voice in decision-making. Partnership boards that were more inclusive had weaker formal status. This reinforced the underrepresentation of local interests affected by the partnership (Kramarz 2016). A few scholars have evaluated the empirical feasibility of global stakeholder democracy by studying beliefs on such democracy among stakeholders themselves. One study finds that stakeholder beliefs in the democratic legitimacy of intergovernmental organizations are not strengthened as a result of participation opportunities. Rather, the level of democracy in the home country of the stakeholder organizations was decisive for their perceptions of democratic legitimacy of intergovernmental organizations. The level of self-perceived influence over policy outcomes mattered as well (Agné et al. 2015). In other words, empirical studies of global stakeholder democracy have not provided strong evidence of lasting democratic qualities of multi-stakeholder practices, while clearly there may be other benefits from multi-stakeholder cooperation.

Democratic values and democratisation

The two above models are examples of attempts at conceptualising a holistic view of what democracy beyond the state could entail in a desirable end vision. Other researchers put individual democratic values, such as participation, transparency, representation and accountability, at the centre of empirical analysis of efforts at democratising global governance (e.g. Steffek and Nanz 2008; Bexell et al 2010; Marquardt and Bäckstrand, Chapter 17 in this volume). This is a process-oriented perspective where democratisation rather than democracy is in focus. In comparison with the stakeholder model and the deliberative model, the underpinning democratic theory often remains more unclear when individual democratic values are selected as "yardsticks" for assessment. In that vein, accountability has generated much recent research interest in fields related to sustainability, notably global environmental governance (Park and Kramarz 2019) and the 2030 Agenda (Bexell and Jönsson 2019). Given that chains of political accountability become long and complex in global politics, the empirical study of accountability in this context concerns who is able to demand accountability from whom and for what. For instance, how can citizens in one state demand accountability from rulers of other states for the impact of intergovernmental political decisions on their local ecosystems and biodiversity? In a recent study, Gupta and van Asselt (2019) explore the relationship between transparency and accountability in the international climate regime of the UNFCCC, finding that its practices of transparency reflect rather than reduce conflict around who should be held accountable in the climate change realm. Therefore, a positive relationship between transparency and accountability cannot be taken for granted. A volume edited by Jan Aart Scholte (2011) on civil society and accountability explores 13 global regulatory arrangements, concluding that global governance has become more transparent and accountable in some cases. Yet, the volume questions whether this growing openness is effective and who benefits from more information disclosure. In particular, Scholte makes the important observation that civil society involvement does not inherently improve the *democratic* accountability of global governance. It may even detract from it by giving more attention to special interest groups than to democratically elected parliaments (Scholte 2011, 7).

Another democratic value subject to much scholarly interest is participation. Quantitatively grounded research finds a transnational turn in global governance from the 1990s onwards (Tallberg et al. 2013). This takes the form of a steady increase in the openness of intergovernmental organizations to participation by transnational actors. Intergovernmental organizations in the areas of human rights, development and trade are the most open ones while such organizations operating in the realm of security are least open. Moreover, comparisons across the phases of the policy process shows that intergovernmental organizations are most open in the phase of monitoring and enforcement, while decision-making is the least open policy phase. Still, it is the politically most important one where member states are reluctant to share decision-making powers. States primarily open up interstate organizations for broader participation by transnational actors because of the functional benefits obtained (Tallberg et al. 2013). Transnational actor participation can take many different forms, ranging from the right to speak and issue proposals to participating in the implementation of projects, to consultations or information exchange. Participation by nonstate actors has been institutionalised in the Major Groups system of the United Nations. In particular, civil society participation is greater today. This is especially so in the fields of environmental politics and in human rights where civil society organizations operate as transmission belts between international organizations and the wider public (Steffek and Nanz 2008). Chapter 17 in this volume, provides further insights into the participation of non-state actors such as NGOs, business and social movements in multi-level climate governance, confirming the potential for democratising such governance in the case of non-state actor participation in processes related to Nationally Determined Contributions under the post-Paris climate governance framework (Marquardt and Bäckstrand, Chapter 17 in this volume).

Democracy is also an important source of justification in international organizations' self-legitimation attempts. Democratic norms have spread from domestic contexts to interstate governance, affecting through normative pressure the way in which intergovernmental organizations open up to other actors (Grigorescu 2015). Moreover, the democratic narrative has been strong among transnational governance bodies. For those, it serves to justify this comparatively new mode of governance as being more transparent and inclusive than interstate governance. For instance, in the case of the Forest Stewardship Council a norm of democratic governance features strongly in its self-legitimation and in the justification of its multistakeholder design. Yet, Klaus Dingwerth (2017) finds that the democratic narrative has lost its centrality over time in the legitimation claims of transnational governance bodies. The choice of legitimation claims appears to be linked to the presence or absence of state regulation in the field at hand. Transnational regulatory governance bodies rely more on democratic narratives in fields where there is little intergovernmental regulation (sustainable wood, fish). This is because they seek to obtain a mandate for the creation of nonstate rules in the first place. As the field of transnational sustainability regulation has become more established overall, democratic claims have become less central (Dingwerth 2017).

In conclusion, empirical evidence is mixed and scattered with regard to assessments of democratic practices in global governance. Empirical studies have identified islands of deliberative and stakeholder practices. Seen through the process-oriented prism of individual democratic values, there has been examples of democratisation over the past decades in global governance settings, albeit limited in time and space. At the end of the day, to what extent there are democratic qualities in global sustainability governance depends on the yardstick applied (Bexell et al. 2010). Yet, connecting to broader conceptual debates, empirical researchers should be cautious of applying the term (global) democracy in studies on individual democratic values. An increase in one democratic value, say accountability, does not equal more democracy. The reason is that democracy should be understood as a holistic system of political rule building on self-government, political equality and political bindingness (Erman 2010). Such a political system is not at hand in contemporary global governance.

Procedural democratic concerns vs substantive purposes

This chapter has shown thus far that research on democracy and global governance has mainly revolved around procedural aspects of global rule-making with a focus on key institutions and actors rather than on the relationship between democratic processes and substantive policy purposes. Typical research questions in a procedural approach to the study of democracy are: How should we think about the demos beyond the nation state? Who gets to participate in global governance? Who is accountable for decisions with effects on sustainability? In this section I bring forward examples of research that in different ways considers the relationship between procedural democratic concerns and substantive policy issues.

Democratic capacity

Tackling the relationship between procedural and substantive purposes in global governance upfront, Klaus Dingwerth points to the lack of attention in global governance scholarship to the broader structural socio-economic conditions that would allow formal democratic institutions to work as intended. Such structural conditions are "the capacities, resources and skills that enable citizens and their communities to make use of democratic institutions in the first place" (Dingwerth 2014, 1132). For a large part of the global citizenry, those conditions are not met, placing that citizenry below a democratic minimum capacity. For instance, transparency is of little value if illiteracy rates are high, Internet access lacking and language skills and political knowledge low. Because resources are limited, prioritising institutional reform before structural substantive conditions leads to exclusion. The implication for Dingwerth is that if we wish to take global democracy seriously, we should prioritize actions that lift weaker members of the global citizenry above the democratic minimum, rather than creating new institutional practices. Those actions are urgent in areas of basic subsistence, health and education where capabilities are highly unevenly distributed on a global level. We may reasonably add environmental conditions to such a substantive list as well. Food supply, drinking water and shelter are but a few examples that come to mind, impacting the abilities of people to engage effectively in democratic political practices.

The need to combine procedural and substantive accounts when providing direction on democratic transformation is also emphasised by Carol Gould (2018) who considers a modified version of the all-affected principle. This principle was introduced earlier in conjunction with stakeholder democracy. So how does one decide whether someone is sufficiently affected by a decision to merit inclusion in decision-making procedures? In Gould's account, the appropriate indicator of being "importantly affected" by a decision is the degree of impact on human rights (economic and social rights as well as civil and political ones) experienced by individuals and groups. Those who are importantly affected by a decision are those whose possibilities of fulfilling basic human rights are affected. In turn, powerful actors need to make human rights impact assessments and address any negative impact found. This is a proposal on substantive conditions required to be fulfiled for an individual to qualify as being affected. It thereby identifies who is entitled to participate in decision-making procedures. A democratisation of global institutions would require more representation of the interests of those affected, Gould posits (2018). Her argument finds resonance in recent proposals on the environmental domain by Walter F. Baber and Robert V. Bartlett (2020) who argue for the need for both procedural environmental rights and substantive environmental rights as essential for democratic decision-making. For them, the recognition of human rights as a global normative order constitutes the backdrop of the usefulness of thinking of environmental needs in terms of both substantive and procedural rights. This is despite the challenges and setbacks often faced in international human rights protection in practice.

Substantive sources of political legitimacy

Second, employing the prism of legitimacy, global governance researchers challenge the understanding of democracy as belonging only to the procedural input side of political legitimacy. That understanding builds on a strong division between democratic/input legitimacy and problem-solving/output legitimacy that characterises many studies on legitimacy in global governance. In contrast, in Jens Steffek's account (2015), democratic legitimacy is the wider concept, consisting both of output and input elements. What Steffek calls "democratic output legitimacy" refers to the ability of governance bodies to cater to the public interest, keeping majorities and powerful actors in check and to protect human rights. Output legitimacy concerns the democratic quality of governance through the notion of public interest, meaning that a political decision (output) benefits every citizen, not just specific groups. Whenever there is uncertainty or contestation around what the public interest consists in, democratic output legitimacy needs to be complemented with input-based institutional arrangements. At the global level, despite their deficiencies, intergovernmental organizations provide the venue where the global public interest can be debated and decided upon and where government conduct can be exposed to peers (Steffek 2015). These theoretical considerations resonate with empirical research showing that there are both procedural and substantive performance sources of legitimacy beliefs among the general public. Citizens' legitimacy beliefs concerning international organisations are based on a congruence between broader societal values and international organizations' procedures, purposes and performance (Lenz and Viola 2017). Empirical results show that both democratic procedural qualities and performance results matter for the legitimacy beliefs citizens hold on intergovernmental organizations (Dellmuth et al. 2019). Citizens' legitimacy beliefs are moreover not static but shaped through processes of legitimation and delegitimation and the broader social structures (Tallberg et al. 2018; Dingwerth et al. 2019).

Admittedly, a challenge of (technocratic) paternalism arises as soon as substantive notions of political purpose, the public interest or preconditions for democratic rule are proposed. This is a key tension between democracy and sustainability, at least in cases where the latter is understood to be in the public interest or warranted by expert knowledge. Democratic processes cannot and should not predetermine the substance of the decisions made. This creates possible tensions between democracy and sustainability. For instance, voters may not necessarily choose the option most sustainable, neither may democratically elected governments do so in intergovernmental fora. Moreover, sustainability is a contested political concept in any governance realm, embraced in contradictory political and academic discourses. What is it that should be sustained, for whose benefit, and how? In broader perspective, both global environmental governance and global economic governance can be understood as sites of struggle over the future of capitalist development, with great implications for understandings of sustainability (Katz-Rosene and Paterson 2018, 136). Critical political economists rightly emphasise that any outcome deemed "sustainable" have political-economic ramifications of one kind or another (Katz-Rosene and Paterson 2018, 128). From a democratic perspective, the demos is free to decide the content of policy decisions continually made, as long as those decisions do not reduce the possibility of democracy itself. This has led some environmental theorists to the conviction that rather than putting the energy on facilitating representation of mass preferences, it is more important to transform those preferences in sustainable direction (Ellis 2016).

Well aware of this challenge, Steffek (2015) argues that input-oriented attempts to counter possible technocratic paternalism in global governance should be cosmopolitan in nature, such as transnational parliamentary assemblies, other forms of transnational political organization, and broad transnational civil society access. This would serve to enable contestation of definitions of the public interest made by intergovernmental organisations. Most fundamentally, the possibility of (democratic) contestation and opposition is necessary for any substantive notion of, for instance, sustainability to be legitimately proposed in actual governance practice. Democratic politics embodies contestation and public scrutiny which enables politicizication of sustainability, highlighting its political dimension (Knappe et al. 2019). While democratic politics is harder to achieve in global governance, climate change protests have shown that it is not impossible to bring about broad public engagement across national boundaries. Such contestation puts pressure on national politicians to act towards sustainability in intergovernmental bodies.

Cosmopolitan democracy and the environment

A third point of departure for thinking about the relationship between procedural democracy in global governance and sustainability can be found in debates on cosmopolitan democracy and the environment. Political cosmopolitanism advocates the necessity of global political institutions where power is to be distributed at different levels in a system of multi-level governance and a global parliamentary assembly is often considered desirable. The values and practices of cosmopolitanism can be realised by any political institution, including by states (Archibugi and Held 2011). To the extent that cosmopolitan authors engage with environmental issues, those are often framed in terms of environmental justice which is a substantively oriented concept. The idea is that cosmopolitan political institutions will be better at realising environmental goals such as environmental justice. A cosmopolitan theory must, argues one of its proponents, put limits on people's creation of environmental burdens and their use of natural resources in order to create environmental preconditions for justice (Caney 2012, 2016). Cosmopolitanism centres around the individual as bearer of rights and obligations and therefore is less preoccupied with the limits imposed by state boundaries. Yet, it faces challenges related to being too idealistic, not within reach in the foreseeable future.

Substantively, cosmopolitan democracy shares ground with visions on ecological democracy where the territorial boundaries of the nation-state are considered both ecologically and democratically arbitrary and new democratic imaginaries are offered (Eckersley 2020, 218). With regard to the global level, Robyn Eckersley has lately argued that globalisation has not had the effect of making global democracy or ecological democracy more feasible, despite high expectations in this regard a few decades ago (Eckersley 2020, 221). The ideals and institutions of liberal democracy have long been debated in environmental political theory and critiqued for being unresponsive to environmental needs. Recent publications demonstrate that interest in the relationship between the environment and democracy is as central today as in the 1970s (Baber and Bartlett 2020; Pickering et al. 2020). Debates on cosmopolitan thought continue among International Relations scholars and provide a useful resource for those interested in tensions as well as alignments between sustainability and democracy. Cosmopolitanism can take inspiration in accounts of ecological democracy when considering environmental justice and democracy. Countering the charge that ecological democracy seeks to "infect" democratic procedures with ecological norms, Robyn Eckersley argues that there are no perfectly neutral democratic decision-making techniques and that the democratic principle of future revisability is indeed central for democratic contestation around the substance of sustainability. In other words, the tension between democratic processes and substantive notions of political purpose resurfaces from the previous section and needs a defence on cosmopolitan premises as well.

Concluding remarks

This chapter has examined the relationship between democracy and sustainability in light of recent research on global and transnational governance. In particular, I have discussed ways in which procedural and substantive accounts of a democratisation of global governance can be reconciled but also identified tensions of such reconciliation. Normative and empirical debates on global democracy within the field of International Political Theory can fruitfully underpin critical scrutiny of the qualities of global sustainability governance, help in identifying its weaknesses and guide proposals on its improvement. The field of research on democracy and global sustainability governance can make significant contributions to practice. Scholars usefully suggest how to understand problems of democratic deficits and resulting power inequalities as well as possible solutions. Theoretical advances and empirically based ways of justifying democratic governance can contribute to empowering those who seek to advance it in practice with good arguments. Research can also point to the implications of privileging one democratic practice at the expense of another, in order to facilitate policy choice in light of scarce institutional resources. Theoretically derived policy guidance can clarify options and guide policy actors in thinking about norms promoted by choosing one practice rather than another, in the face of many goals these actors wish to promote. Yet, the challenges of democratisation of global governance that this chapter has pointed to imply that equal attention needs to be paid to democratisation within states.

The models and research findings discussed here emphasize different democratic values and pay attention to different arenas of political contestation. Putting the democratic adversarial political process centre stage is important in social scientific sustainability research. This means asking about power relations that shape formal and informal political decisions on global governance as well as its effects and distributive outcomes. Recalling that global governance is political, the possibilities for democratic political contestation beyond the national level should remain a central research consideration. Future research should also critically assess the principle of state sovereignty in relation to external and internal state responsibilities in the sustainability domain. Firm notions of state sovereignty imply that a territorially bounded demos can take democratic decisions that impact sustainable development matters in other countries negatively, without facing penalties. In intergovernmental political negotiations, sovereignty certainly remains a central principle. A possible qualification of the sovereignty principle has hitherto mainly been debated with regard to gross internal human rights violations and humanitarian emergencies. According to the so-called responsibility to protect (R2P) doctrine, International Relations scholars have argued that large scale violations of human rights by a government may render morally illegitimate its claims to non-interference. Similar discussions have appeared in the realm of global health with regard to global disease control governance. It is for future research to consider whether qualifications of sovereignty are warranted in the case of a lack of long-term sustainability actions on the part of governments. While empirical insights provide important components in the continued elaboration of normative theorising, visions of a democratisation of global governance should not be too constrained by contemporary perceptions of what is feasible within a foreseeable future.

References

Agné, H., Dellmuth, L.M. and Tallberg J., 2015. Does stakeholder involvement foster democratic legitimacy in international organizations? An empirical assessment of a normative theory. *Review of International Organizations*, 10 (4), 465–488.

Archibugi, D. and Held, D., 2011. Cosmopolitan democracy: paths and agents. *Ethics & International Affairs*, 25 (4), 433–461.

Baber, W.F., and Bartlett, R.V., 2020. A rights foundation for ecological democracy. *Journal of Environmental Policy & Planning*, 22 (1), 72–83.

Bäckstrand, K., Khan, J., Kronsell, A., and Lövbrand, E., eds., 2010. *Environmental Politics and Deliberative Democracy: Examining the Promise of New Modes of Governance*. Cheltenham: Edward Elgar.

Bexell, M., 2014. Global governance, legitimacy and (de)legitimation. *Globalizations*, 11 (3), 289–299.

Bexell, M. and Jönsson, K., 2019. Country reporting on the sustainable development goals – the politics of performance review at the global-national nexus. *Journal of Human Development and Capabilities*, 20 (4), 403–417.

Bexell, M. and Mörth, U., eds., 2010. *Democracy and Public-Private Partnerships in Global Governance*. Houndmills: Palgrave Macmillan.

Bexell, M., Tallberg, J. and Uhlin, A., 2010. Democracy in global governance: the promises and pitfalls of transnational actors. *Global Governance*, 16 (1), 81–101.

Caney, S., 2012. Just emissions. *Philosophy and Public Affairs*, 40 (4), 255–300.

Caney, S., 2016. Cosmopolitanism and the environment. In T. Gabrielson et al., eds. *The Oxford Handbook of Environmental Political Theory*. Oxford: Oxford University Press, 239–254.

Cummings, S., Regeer, B., Haan, L., Zweekhorst, M. and Bunders, J., 2018. Critical discourse analysis of perspectives on knowledge and the knowledge society within the sustainable development goals. *Development Policy Review*, 36 (6), 727–742.

Dahl, R.A., 1999. Can international organizations be democratic? In I. Shapiro and C. Hacker-Gordon, eds. *Democracy Edges*. Cambridge: Cambridge University Press, 19–36.

Dellmuth, L.M., Scholte, J.A. and Tallberg, J., 2019. Institutional sources of legitimacy for international organisations: beyond procedure versus performance. *Review of International Studies*, 45 (4), 627–646.

Dingwerth, K., 2014. Global democracy and the democratic minimum: why a procedural account alone is insufficient. *European Journal of International Relations*, 20 (4), 1124–1147.

Dingwerth, K., 2017. Field recognition and the state prerogative: why democratic legitimation recedes in private transnational sustainability regulation. *Politics and Governance*, 5 (1), 75–84.

Dingwerth, K., Witt, A., Lehmann, I. Reichel, E. and Weise, T., 2019. *International Organizations under Pressure. Legitimating Global Governance in Challenging Times*. Oxford: Oxford University Press.

Dryzek, J.S. and Stevenson, H., 2011. Global democracy and earth system governance. *Ecological Economics*, 70, 1865–1874.

Eckersley, R., 2020. Ecological democracy and the rise and decline of liberal democracy: looking back, looking forward. *Environmental Politics*, 29 (2), 214–234.

Ellis, E., 2016. Democracy as constraint and possibility for environmental action. In T. Gabrielson et al., eds. *The Oxford Handbook of Environmental Political Theory*. Oxford: Oxford University Press, 506–519.

Erman E., 2010. Why adding democratic values is not enough for global democracy. In E. Erman and A. Uhlin, eds. *Legitimacy Beyond the State? Re-examining the Democratic Credentials of Transnational Actors*. Basingstoke: Palgrave Macmillan, 173–193.

Gould, C., 2018. Democracy and global governance. In C. Brown and R. Eckersley, eds. *The Oxford Handbook of International Political Theory*. Oxford: Oxford University Press, 385–399.

Grigorescu, A., 2015. *Democratic Intergovernmental Organizations? Normative Pressures and Decision-Making Rules*. Cambridge: Cambridge University Press.

Gupta, A. and von Asselt, H., 2019. Transparency in multilateral climate politics: furthering (or distracting from) accountability? *Regulation & Governance,* 13, 18–34.

Hale, T. and Held, D., 2011. Editors' introduction: mapping changes in transnational governance. In T. Hale and D. Held, eds. *Handbook of Transnational Governance. Institutions and Innovations*. Cambridge: Polity Press. 1–36.

Held, D., 1995. *Democracy and the Global Order: From the Modern State to Cosmopolitan Governance*. Stanford: Stanford University Press.

Kamau, M., Chasek, P. and O'Connor, D., 2018. *Transforming Multilateral Diplomacy. The Inside Story of the Sustainable Development Goals*. London and New York: Routledge.

Katz-Rosene, R. and Paterson, M., 2018. *Thinking Ecologically about the Global Political Economy*. London and New York: Routledge.

Keohane, R. and Nye, J., 2003. Redefining accountability for global governance. In M. Kahler and D. Lake, eds. *Governance in the Global Economy. Political Authority in Transition*. Princeton: Princeton University Press, 386–411.

Knappe, H., Holfelder, A.K., Beer, D.L. and Nanz, P., 2019. The politics of making and unmaking (sustainable) futures: introduction to the special feature. *Sustainability Science*, 14, 891–898.

Kramarz, T., 2016. World bank partnerships and the promise of democratic governance. *Environmental Policy and Governance*, 26, 3–15.

Kronsell, A., 2017. The contribution of feminist perspectives to climate governance. In S. Buckingham and V. Le Masson, eds. *Understanding Climate Change Trough Gender Relations*. London and New York: Routledge. 104–120.

Lenz, T. and Viola, L.A., 2017. Legitimacy and institutional change in international organisations: a cognitive approach. *Review of International Studies*, 43 (5), 939–961.

Macdonald, K. and Macdonald, T., 2010. Democracy in a pluralist global order: corporate power and stakeholder representation. *Ethics and International Affairs*, 24 (1), 19–43.

Macdonald, T., 2012. Citizens or stakeholders? Exclusion, equality and legitimacy in global stakeholder democracy. In D. Archibugi, M. Koenig-Archibugi and R. Marchetti, eds. *Global Democracy: Normative and Empirical Perspectives*. Cambridge: Cambridge University Press, 47–68.

Miller, D., 2010. Against Global Democracy. In K. Breen and S. O'Neill, eds. *After the Nation?* Basingstoke: Palgrave Macmillan, 141–160.

Park, S. and Kramarz, T., eds., 2019. *Global Environmental Governance and the Accountability Trap*. Cambridge: MIT Press.

Pickering, J., Bäckstrand, K. and Schlosberg, D., 2020. Between environmental and ecological democracy: theory and practice and the democracy-environment nexus. *Journal of Environmental Policy & Planning*, 22 (1), 1–15.

Scholte, J.A., ed., 2011. *Building Global Democracy? Civil Society and Accountable Global Governance*. Cambridge: Cambridge University Press.

Steffek, J., 2015. The output legitimacy of international organizations and the global public interest. *International Theory*, 7 (2), 263–293.

Steffek, J. and Nanz, P., 2008. Emergent patterns of civil society participation in global and European governance. In J. Steffek, Kissling, C. and Nanz, P., eds. *Civil Society Participation in European and Global Governance. A Cure for the Democratic Deficit?* Basingstoke: Palgrave Macmillan, 1–29.

Stevenson, H. and Dryzek, J.S., 2012. The discursive democratisation of global climate governance. *Environmental Politics,* 21 (2), 189–210.

Stevenson, H. and Dryzek, J.S., 2014. *Democratizing Global Climate Governance.* Cambridge: Cambridge University Press.

Tallberg, J., Bäckstrand, K. and Scholte J.A., eds., 2018. *Legitimacy in Global Governance. Sources, Processes and Consequences.* Oxford: Oxford University Press.

Tallberg, J., Sommerer, T., Squatrito, T. and Jönsson, C., 2013. *The Opening Up of International Organizations: Transnational Access in Global Governance.* Cambridge: Cambridge University Press.

19
URBAN SUSTAINABILITY AND (POST-)DEMOCRACY
Policies, practices and movements

Marit Rosol and Vincent Béal

Introduction[1]

Our societies are increasingly urbanized and the twenty-first century has been heralded as the urban millennium. One reason for such characterization is purely quantitative: according to United Nations demographical data, since 2007 and for the first time in human history the majority of the world's population live in urban areas. More importantly though, and beyond spatial and demographic expansion of city-regions, form, socio-spatial characteristics and nature of urbanization itself have changed. Consequently, Neil Brenner and Christian Schmid have qualified the current global urban condition as "planetary urbanization" (Brenner and Schmid 2014). Furthermore, at a time, when climate change is widely accepted as one of the most important challenges of this century, cities, for a long time seen as sustainability problems, are increasingly portrayed as the arena and actors to bring about progressive visions of a sustainable future. As Angelo and Wachsmuth put it with skepticism, "everyone now thinks cities can save the planet" (Angelo and Wachsmuth 2015, 193). This is despite the fact that the material conditions upon which cities are currently expanding are intensifying global environmental problems, caused by geographically highly uneven resource extraction, production and consumption (Holgersen and Malm 2015).

As societies experience growing tensions between the pursuit of economic growth on the one hand, and the ability to care for their people and for the ecosystems upon which they live on the other, cities increasingly draw on the concept of urban sustainability. The concept of urban sustainability rose to prominence in the 1990s after the publication of the Brundtland Report in 1988 and the organization of the Rio Earth Summit in 1992. Since the late twentieth century, sustainable urban development has been key to current urban planning and policy discourses and cities promote urban sustainability as a way of bringing forward a progressive ecological urban agenda connected to social and economic development. Urban sustainability is now resting upon a wide consensus and broad support from diverse sectors of society. However, urban sustainability appears to be a goal that all parties agree on now precisely because it is devoid of concrete content (Swyngedouw 2009). Contrary to its progressive promise – the goal of an urban ecological transformation, promoted by grassroots urban initiatives since the 1960s, was initially strongly connected to that of strengthening local democracy – it is increasingly used to reinforce local growth dynamics and to foster urban competitiveness at the regional and global level (Krueger and Gibbs 2007). Thus, the concept of urban sustainability is fraught with tension among its ecological, social (including democratic) and economic goals. It soon turned out to be a strategy for greening, modernizing and effectively safeguarding capitalism. As critics point out, sustainability "may not be an obstacle to capitalist accumulation but rather a *constituent* part of it" (Gibbs and Krueger 2007, 103).

In this chapter, we discuss the tension between the progressive and transformative roots of urban sustainability and its current neoliberal and post-democratic shape. More precisely, we ask to what extent current discourses, policies, social practices and movements can be seen as reinforcing this dynamic of depoliticization or, conversely, countering it and providing avenues for the emergence of alternatives debates regarding cities and their role in the global ecological crisis. Besides providing an overview of the literature, we will draw on our own empirical research, conducted primarily in France and Germany, but also to examples from the UK, Canada and the US. We first reflect on the historical trajectory and shifts in discourse around urban environmental governance. Subsequently, we present local initiatives that contest the uneven effects of urban sustainability strategies. Next, we discuss urban food movements as an example of more recent urban environmental movements. We close with some reflections on the recent re-politicization of the debate as well as urban based counter-movements that attest to the unsolved social question within the neoliberal response to the global environmental crisis.

The evolution of urban sustainability

How can the concept of urban sustainability, which aimed to strengthen environmental protection, now be associated with neoliberal urbanization? How could a concept which was at the very beginning considered a radical break with previous urban policymaking, become an emblem of the post-political era? Why did the three pillars – the environment, the economy and the social – which were at the beginning conceptualized together remain separated and unevenly addressed by urban policy making? To answer these questions, we need to first reflect on the history and evolution of urban sustainability, and more generally of urban environmental governance and politics.

Urban sustainability and the question of local democracy: from grassroots movements ...

Although urban environmental strategies in the present are dominated by market discourse and by techno-competitive rationalities, this has not always been the case. In the 1970s and 1980s, early environmental initiatives in Amsterdam, Freiburg, Copenhagen, Nantes, London, San Francisco, Berlin and many other cities evolved from grassroots movements (Castells 1983). These movements demanded better services such as public transport, more urban greenery, and generally better quality of urban life. In doing so they not only strived for more fundamental social and ecological changes, but also demanded a greater say of local residents in urban affairs, thus more local democracy. While some scholars identified "ideological mystification" (Castells 1978, 152) in these early environmental politics, most have considered them as a viable alternative to state-led urban development, which was at that time largely blind to environmental and democratic aspirations (Béal 2012; Rosol 2010; Mössner 2016; Krueger et al. 2019).

In Germany, following the leftist critique of the paternalistic welfare state, new social movements formed in the 1970s (Brand et al. 1986). On the municipal level the most important issues they organized around were the environment and transportation, followed by education (Roth 1999, 6). *Bürgerinitiativen* (citizens' action committees) concerned with municipal policies, mobility and transportation, public service provision, urban planning, and green spaces became part of these new movements. Concerned about the urban environment, urban residents protested, for example, "against the administrative control of urban greenery" (Meissle 1998, 248, translation by author) by starting to "green" patios and backyards of tenement housing blocks, lobbying for more urban green spaces and even publicly squatting existing open spaces in order to protect them from development. But also more radical protest movements emerged, and environmental concerns – closely connected to a critique of the economic growth imperative of the capitalist economy – played a significant role (Roth 1999; Brand 2008; Mayer 2008). Mayer even speaks of the "ecologization of urban protest movements" in the 1970s (Mayer 2008). One of the most important points of reference for the German environmental movement of the 1970s and 1980s was, for example, the massive protest against the expansion of the Frankfurt Airport (Runway 18 West) – despite ultimately not being able to prevent the opening of the new runway in 1984. The protest lasted for more than a decade and combined *Bürgerinitiativen*, mass demonstrations and more radical actions like squatting (Rucht 1984).

At the same time in several French cities, local NGOs and activists challenged mainstream state-led urban interventions. Similar to Germany, they contested the amount of space given to cars in the city, the development of new transport infrastructures (motorways, airports, etc.), or the standardized urbanization advocated by the powerful and *dirigiste* central state (Castells 1983). These struggles played a central role in the emergence of young left-wing elected officials who were the first to integrate – with the help of local NGOs which had been rising around the contestation of nuclear or infrastructural projects – environmental objectives into urban policies. Thus, at the end of the 1970s and beginning of the 1980s, in cities like Nantes and Strasbourg, new urban strategies were developed to promote non-motorized mobility (walking path, public transports, etc.), or to strengthen the role of natural amenities in the urban development (Béal 2015; Blanc et al. 2017). At the time, these strategies were dominated by a restrictive definition of urban ecological transformations which excluded some of the most "urban" issues such as the one of housing construction and renovation. However, the emergence and institutionalization of the concept of urban sustainability in the early 1990s can be seen both as an extension of the original scope of urban environmental transformation and as a success of local environmental movements and their call for strengthened environmental protection, as well as renewed democracy. Indeed, in the 1990s, the elaboration of Local Agenda 21 – the planning tool associated with early urban sustainability initiatives – was strongly connected to the involvement of new, civic actors in urban governance and also to experimental participatory democracy schemes (Hamman 2009).

... to the political mainstream

It was no coincidence that these environmental initiatives emerged and gained significance in the wake of the crisis of Fordism, when the associated accumulation regime and mode of regulation reached its limits (Brenner 2004; Mayer 2006; Heeg and Rosol 2007). Since the 1980s, environmental policies have been selectively institutionalized at the national level. Meanwhile, local authorities have become considerably more entrepreneurial (Harvey 1989), developing new forms of "place marketing" and significantly reducing local welfare measures and public service provision. In this first wave of "roll-back" neoliberalization (Peck and Tickell 2002), environmental concerns were marginalized in urban policies. The environment was considered by most local and national elites as an enemy of the "growth-at-all-cost" approaches of urban management. Yet, during the 1990s, many cities in the Global North became aware of the negative consequences of their entrepreneurial policies and tried to mitigate them by introducing forms of "roll-out" neoliberalism, i.e. a more complex set of approaches with implicit or explicit reminiscences to urban sustainability (While et al. 2004; Raco 2005; Keil and Boudreau 2006). This wave of roll-out neoliberalism also led to new forms of local economy-environment relations that now, if only selectively, also incorporate environmental goals. This embrace of sustainability as "part of the search for a spatio-institutional fix to safeguard growth trajectories in the wake of industrial capitalism's long downturn, the global 'ecological crisis' and the rise of popular environmentalism" (While et al. 2004, 551) has been conceptualized as the "urban sustainability fix" (ibid.).

While the win-win-win ideology of sustainability, i.e. the idea that policies can and must benefit the environment, the economy and the social simultaneously, may have been at least naïve in the first place,[2] it was especially the separation of the idea of urban sustainability from its democratic and social equity potentials that paved the way for growth-compatible ecological modernization policies.[3] Although initiatives that exist under the umbrella of sustainability still cover a wide variety of issues and approaches, urban sustainability or "green" policies are now dominated by entrepreneurial approaches, connecting environmental concerns with growth, competitiveness and attracting capital. Critical urban scholars (While et al. 2004; Rosol 2013; Angelo and Wachsmuth 2015; Angelo 2019) have pointed out major limitations of these new urban environmental regimes (Rosol et al. 2017): they are fueled by techno-market imaginaries, are socially and spatially selective in favour of upper- and middle-class populations living in major city centres, and are based on one dominant "referencescape" (McCann 2017) which limits the imagination and emergence of alternatives.

The democratic dimension of urban sustainability is also questioned by activists and academics. In many cities, the rise of "sustainability" as "discourse of rule" (Eblinghaus and Stickler 1996) favoured decision-making behind closed doors (Béal et al. 2011; Metzger and Lindblad 2020). Some prominent urban scholars even consider urban sustainability policies as emblematic of the post-political era (Swyngedouw 2009).[4] They contend that urban sustainability has become a consensual narrative, which prevents both a proper politicization of environmental problems and more radical approaches to urban changes. As such, environmental politics become de-politicized and excluded from democratic debates. Urban environmental politics thus underwent an evolution, from protest, contestation and struggle towards a consensual mainstreaming in urban policymaking (Krueger and Agyeman 2005; Swyngedouw 2011, 372; Béal 2012; Rosol 2014). In the words of Erik Swyngedouw: "it is a politics reduced to the administration and management of processes whose parameters are defined by consensual socio-scientific knowledges" (Swyngedouw 2009, 602). This results in more than just a political consensus around a certain issue; it aims at a societal unification and standardization in which antagonist interests and perspectives are subordinated and negated. In summary, if the concept of sustainability was, at first, seen by many also as a tool to enhance local democracy, it is now increasingly viewed as an expression of ecological modernization, ecological gentrification and post-democracy.

This trend could be observed in most European countries. In the UK, after timid initiatives put in place by the John Major government, Tony Blair was strongly invested in the issue of urban sustainability. Blair's New Labour government made sustainability one of the pillars of their "urban renaissance" agenda, a political strategy aiming at transforming British city centers and ultimately promoting gentrification processes (Porter and Shaw 2009). Also, the Swedish Government made substantive efforts to brand urban sustainability in order to foster export of clean-tech and urban planning services (Holgersen and Malm 2015; Hult 2017; Rapoport and Hult 2017). In France, it was not until the end of the 2000s that a similar trend occurred. The organization of the 2007 "*Grenelle de l'environnement*" shifted understandings of urban sustainability. This was a multi-party conference about environmental protection initiated by Nicolas Sarkozy and attended by senior government officers, private sector representatives and civil society groups. Following this conference, the objective of the French national government and its agencies now lies in promoting competition between cities, through several calls for projects that reward local "best practices". Ultimately, this strategy aims at stimulating urban innovation that can then be sold to and replicated in other national contexts, particularly in regions of the global South such as the Maghreb in which French governmental agencies have maintained post-colonial relationships (Béal et al. 2018).

At the local level, this trend was even more clear-cut: urban sustainable development became part of roll-out neoliberalization in many European and North American cities (Andersson 2016; McKendry 2017; Champagne 2020). Consultants, architects, urban developers, utility companies, but also local elected officials and bureaucrats, constructed a renewed understanding of urban sustainability in which the environment is considered as an asset for economic growth and place differentiation. By promoting sustainability merely symbolically, or by subsidizing certain sectors like "green building" construction, local authorities were able to present themselves as "green cities" while maintaining the economic status quo (ONeill and Gibbs 2014). The development of environmental planning schemes (While et al. 2004; Kenis and Lievens 2017), the elaboration of climate strategies (North et al. 2017; 2020), the implementation of large scale eco-cities projects (Caprotti 2014; Chang 2017; Rapoport and Hult 2017; Cugurullo 2018) or investment in green infrastructure or landscape (Lang and Rothenberg 2017; Anguelovski et al. 2019), are all good examples of a trend that no longer considers environmental improvement as a goal in itself, but as a way to enhance competitiveness and improve the image and the profitability of (parts of) a city. The consequences of this evolution – particularly the uneven access to environmental goods in cities it has fostered – has spurred critical activism and scholarship to which we turn in the next section.

Contesting and moving beyond urban sustainability

In this section, first, we briefly present examples of radical movements seeking to re-connect ideas of ecological transformation and sustainability to those of equality, justice and democracy. Some voices have pointed to the polarizing effects of urban sustainability policies, while others are more concerned with its consensual and post-political nature, which masks underlying social, economic and political divisions. They share a focus on the links between urban sustainability and neoliberalization processes.

Such critiques have also paved the way for new forms of urban environmental activism that addresses new fields. In the second part, we will present one such field: urban food movements. Besides introducing them as an inspiring example, we also show that while these movements are critical towards the current capitalist agri-food system and try to enable alternatives, they are equally at risk of being co-opted by political or market forces, and often struggle to enact a renewed and democratic vision of urban sustainability.

Contesting urban sustainability: examples from US and French cities

Since the 1990s, cities have been increasingly considered as laboratories to respond to environmental crisis (Angelo and Wachsmuth 2015), as places in which new policies and practices can be envisaged and tested (Acuto 2013). For many grassroots organizations, these policies contribute to the reproduction of social and sometimes ethnic lines of division in the city. They accompany – rather than correct – uneven dynamics of neoliberalization, such as concentration of investments in city centers, gentrification of some neighborhoods (Quastel 2009), while stigmatizing deprived neighborhoods or suburban areas. These criticisms have often been voiced most prominently in the context of urban mega events such as the London Olympics in 2012 or the Rio Olympics in 2016 (Boykoff and Mascarenhas 2016). However, they surface in large, growing metropolitan areas as well as in secondary, declining cities.

In Seattle, for example, in a context of rapid urban growth, local authorities and economic actors promoted a "climate friendly" urban strategy in the early 2010s. This strategy aimed for the city to become carbon neutral by 2050 through initiatives in sectors such as transportation, consumption and the built environment. While strongly supported by retail giant Amazon and connected to the creation of its new headquarters in the South Lake Union neighbourhood, this strategy was denounced by grassroots organizations. These organizations argued that dismissal of suburbanization, support towards IT and creative industries, construction of low-carbon infrastructures, and the promotion of densification policies have increased property values in certain neighbourhoods, facilitating the displacement of low-income residents. These groups thus see the strategy as a lever to deepen the inequalities already affecting this city (Rice et al. 2020). The Seattle example is not isolated. Policies in other growing cities that promote principal objectives of urban sustainability such as densification policies and a "compact city", have also exacerbated social and spatial divisions (Rosol 2013; 2015; Charmes and Keil 2015; Rousseau 2015)

In Nantes, a growing city in western France, activists and resident groups take issue with the city's commitment towards environmental protection, because its consensual vision of the environment mask conflicts and divisions around urban development. The city is considered by the French national government and the EU as a model city; it was awarded "European Green Capital" in 2013 by the European Commission. However, the organization of the European Green Capital event took place in a context of a long-lasting conflict between local authorities and major businesses and economic actors, on the one hand, and activists and environmental groups, on the other hand, over the construction of a new international airport on the fringes of the city (Béal 2015). The struggle included a long-term occupation of the site – called the ZAD ("*Zone à défendre*") – which included experimentation in utopian and alternative modes of living in order to foster socio-ecological transformations (Bulle 2020). This protest thus denounced the contradictory policies of a municipality that was praised as an exemplary case of climate action while supporting the growth of carbon-intensive air transportation. Contrary to the campaign against the Frankfurt runway in the 1980s, this protest proved to be successful, even though the ZAD was partially dismantled by the central government which was looking unfavourably on the radical social and political experiments that took place on the site.

In the different context of declining cities of the American Rust Belt, sustainability policies have also been contested (Safransky 2014). In Cleveland, for example, the greening strategy put in place by the Land Bank – the main agency dealing with urban abandonment after the 2007/2008 subprime crisis – is being challenged by disadvantaged groups. Unlike Seattle or Nantes, the aim of Cleveland's greening strategy is not to support growth by strengthening environmental amenities, but rather to manage urban decline by making mass demolitions acceptable to the populations concerned. As a consequence, while urban sustainability strategies are often publicly presented in declining cities as a means to benefit marginalized areas and residents (by providing new green spaces to remaining inhabitants), in reality, demolition and "green" reuse of spaces have accelerated displacement in low-income black communities and reinforcing racial hierarchies in the city (Akers et al. 2020). Furthermore, in a context of austerity, they are also used as a way to transfer the maintenance of urban services (management of abandoned land, food provision in the face of retail exclusion, etc.) to poor residents, who are increasingly told to organize themselves to deal with political and market "vacancy" (Kinder 2016).

Re-envisioning urban sustainability: the case of urban food movements

One kind of urban sustainability movement that has become particularly visible in the last ten years are urban food movements (Morgan and Santo 2018). Urban residents increasingly wish to consume regional, seasonal and healthier foods that are produced and traded fairly. They are campaigning for an end to food waste, for re-connection with producers, and a renewed relationship with food in general. They are concerned about the damaging ecological, social and economic practices and impacts of the current dominant agri-food systems.[5] These movements not only offer opportunities for advancing long-awaited agri-food related changes but also for greater cooperation between cities and rural areas. Such cooperation may have wider democratic effects given present electoral divisions along urban/rural lines (for an example of emancipatory rural politics and urban-rural cooperation through alternative food networks see Calvário et al. 2019).

With a majority of people now living in cities, and cities being hotspots for intensive resource use, urban actors are increasingly acknowledging the central role of cities in our food systems. Surely, the sustainability of our agri-food systems is not tied to the urban alone – food systems include production, processing, distribution, consumption and waste management, and reach across scales from the global to the local, including urban and rural sites. However, urban demand is playing an increasingly central role and cities are emerging as sites of education about agri-food systems and the need to change them, of re-politicization and protest, and of envisioning and enacting alternatives. Consequently, it is mostly urban initiatives that are currently driving the sustainability agenda. Urban initiatives – mostly civil society actors, but often in partnership with small businesses, farmers and municipal authorities – try to address agri-food sustainability issues through, for example, waste diversion initiatives, local food networks and education efforts. Local governments are also learning that urban food system changes can also have positive impacts on other domains of urban sustainable development, be it transportation and logistics, local economies, waste management or education. They are thus starting to appreciate the wider potentials of food (planning) (Mendes 2017; Sonnino et al. 2019; for early accounts see Koç et al. 1999; Pothukuchi and Kaufman 1999).

There are thus many potentials of these new urban social movements. And yet, there are also important constraints. First, we find an *emphasis on market-based instruments and consumer choice*, often tied to an overemphasis of educating individuals as consumers. This enables the ongoing incorporation of characteristics of "alternative" food by conventional food industries for profit. Aspects of alternative food (e.g., food safety, health, organic, regional and Fair Trade) have been appropriated by conventional producers and retailers, and most sales of organic products are achieved in conventional retailing (Bernzen 2014). Other vital goals, such as living wages, fostering small-scale, sustainable agriculture and improving soil fertility, however, are not pursued to the same extent, leaving problematic and production conditions and other connected socio-economic relations largely ignored (Goodman and Follett 2009; Goodman 2009). This leads to the proliferation of class-based diets and a widening gap between privileged and disadvantaged consumers (Friedmann 2005, 229; see also McMichael 2009, 142). Friedmann (2005) even detects the emergence of a "corporate-environmental food regime". The entry of large companies into now-lucrative organic markets, referred to as the conventionalization of organic agriculture (for California see Guthman 2004; for Austria Grünewald 2015; see also Goodman and Goodman 2007) is testimony to the limits to such individualized consumerist framings, which neglect social and economic conditions of production and consumption.

Second, there is the *local trap*. Local or regional food supplies feature prominently in alternative food networks (AFNs). Short food supply chains (SFSCs) seek to directly connect consumers whose food consumption is guided ethically or ecologically (Clarke 2008), with food producers (see Renting et al. 2003; Kalfagianni and Skordili 2018; Rosol and Strüver 2018; Rosol 2018; 2020). However, such rescaling is not necessarily progressive as local food systems do not preclude industrial agriculture, and can also have exclusionary effects (Jarosz 2008, 233). Privileging the local level may be accompanied by a so-called "defensive localism" (Winter 2003; see also Allen 1999), effectively promoting social and spatial exclusivity (Hinrichs 2003). In their seminal paper, Born and Purcell (2006) call this assumption of the inherent superiority of the local scale the "local trap". They empirically dispel certain positive characteristics attributed to local food.[6] Theoretically, they criticize the equation of a single scale (the local) with certain normative goals (for example, sustainability, health, justice, democracy or trust). They contend that the industrialized food system is not a scalar problem but rather the consequence of a particular economic and political system, shaped by developments at multiple scales. Consequently, they argue, focusing on a single scale also leads to – and this is their third, political, critique – neglecting opportunities for action at other scales (e.g., nation-state or EU regulation of agriculture, food and wages) (see also Guthman 2008; Allen 2010). The local trap critique by no means implies that local production and consumption are wholly problematic, or that local food networks cannot play an important role in structural change. We certainly need to re-localize our food systems (see for a succinct summary of the main arguments De Schutter 2014). The crucial point of the critique is, however, that the achievement of normative goals depends on political struggles which go far beyond the local scale, and there is no scalar solution.

A final constraint is that these movements often *only focus on limited aspects of food systems*. Empirical research in German cities since 2017 by the first author shows that urban food initiatives tend to focus on topics of sustainability and environmental protection (by supporting organic agriculture, limiting food waste etc.). However, there is little discussion of food poverty and unequal social participation in food related developments, which is much more extensively discussed in other countries, such as Canada for example, see Levkoe (2006) or Dachner and Tarasuk (2017). As such, we often find a narrow focus on sustainability at the expense of questions of justice and equity – or democracy more general.

The term "food democracy" was coined by Lang (1999) and Hassanein (2003, 2008) to oppose current agri-food systems dominated by corporate interests, but also to oppose the idea of political consumerism (or "voting with your fork") as way forward (see also the recent special issue edited by Bornemann and Weiland 2019). It is linked to, yet distinct from perhaps the more radical terms (according to Tilzey 2019; and Holt-Giménez and Shattuck 2011) "food justice" (which combines the demand for access to good food for all – regardless of income, origin and education – with democratic participation and fair labour conditions across the food system (Allen 2010; Alkon and Agyeman 2011; Gottlieb and Joshi 2013; Alkon and Guthman 2017)), and "food sovereignty" ("the right of peoples to healthy and culturally appropriate food produced through ecologically sound and sustainable methods, and their right to define their own food and agriculture systems" – La Via Campesina, Declaration of Nyéléni in 2007) (Wittman et al. 2010).

One interesting laboratory for enacting food democracy and bridging environmental, democracy and social justice concerns are Food Policy Councils (FPCs). And indeed, the first meeting of all German speaking FPCs took place in 2017 under the motto of "Food Democracy Now!" FPCs have been established in Germany since 2016, following North American models emerging since the 1990s (Doernberg et al. 2019; Hoffmann et al. 2019). Most FPCs are strongly civil society driven, some with the formal participation of government officials and (small) business representatives. As the food policy council movement in Germany is still in its infancy, it remains to be seen how such a call for food democracy will play out in action and also how attentive Food Policy Councils will be to the needs of marginalized urban populations.

Outlook

In this chapter we followed the trajectory of urban sustainability through an analysis of discourses, policies, practices and movements in different urban and national contexts. We pointed out its links to ecological modernization theory and its shortcomings regarding equity, justice and democracy. As the example of food illustrates, a successful socio-ecological transformation cannot do without understanding capitalism (Holt-Giménez 2017), nor without addressing questions of justice (Blue et al. 2019; Gumbert 2019). More generally, if we want to address and overcome the environmental crisis in a meaningful and substantive way, we cannot ignore capitalism – the economic underpinnings of our current societies – and our actions have to be guided by justice considerations – questions of distribution of resources, cultural recognition and political representation – (see Fraser 2013). Cities have to play an important role in any successful socio-ecological transformation, particularly nowadays with the rapid extension of the various spaces that constitute their operational landscapes of extraction, production, distribution and power (Brenner and Schmid 2014).

2019 has brought new hopes into the continual reshaping of sustainability issues. The rise of mass climate protest – mainly but not only organized by young people and most visible in major cities – could be considered as a rupture of the consensual trajectory of urban sustainability. Ten years after the financial crisis which highlighted close links between neoliberal capitalism and social, territorial and environmental inequalities and degradation, new forms of politicization have emerged that challenge the structural roots of socio-ecological problems. These new movements are diverse in their ideologies and objectives. Some protesters take to the streets to demand government action to fight climate change, currently most notably with the "Fridays for Future" school strikes for climate action, or use forms of civil disobedience such as Extinction Rebellion. Other groups, inspired by degrowth ideas are trying to set up self-organized communities promoting alternative ways of living in the here and now (Demaria et al. 2019; Bulle 2020).

However, those new movements are only one dimension of the current reshaping of the environmental question. In some part of the world, climate-change-denialism and (sometimes right-wing) populist movements are also gaining visibility. For example, in Alberta, Canada, where one of the authors lives, despite attempts of the previous government to reconcile climate and growth policies in the name of sustainability, the notion of sustainability still evokes opposition, protest, fear and anger. People rally for more pipelines, a proxy for expanded tar sands production, and against a provincial or national carbon tax. Cars bear stickers proclaiming "I love Canadian Oil & Gas", and many demand more government action to support fossil fuel extraction. Surely, not the whole of Alberta thinks this way, but a majority does – the 2019 election with an overwhelming majority of a new provincial government that is aggressively and unapologetically supporting the fossil fuel industry, through cuts to environmental regulation and to corporate taxes amongst other, being the most visible testament to this. An important reason for such strong support for an economy mainly based on fossil fuel extractivism is that a majority of livelihoods are tied directly or indirectly to precisely this industry, and the socio-economic question of how to achieve a just energy and economic transition at the necessary scale is scarcely addressed and yet to be solved (Rosol 2019; Lawhon and McCreary 2020, also for an proposal on how to overcome the jobs vs. environment divide; see also Daggett 2018).

Meanwhile, the "Yellow Vest" movement in France, home of the second author, has been protesting against carbon taxes proposed by the national government. This movement – which began in November 2018 and involved several months of road blockage, roundabout occupation and mass demonstration in several French cities – differs significantly from pro-oil and anti-carbon tax street protest in Alberta. The rejection of carbon tax was based on a larger criticism of national government policies which were considered as authoritarian, on the one hand, and socially and territorially uneven, on the other hand. As a consequence, some of the protesters called for the creation of democratic schemes such as citizens' initiatives referendum and for the implementation of new social policies (solidarity tax, minimum-wage increase). In the end, this movement was not contesting environmental policies per se, but more the way this question has been framed under the name of sustainability – and thus also, in essence, democracy and justice. If these two political movements can be portrayed – for different reasons – as threats for the environment, they also reflect thirty years of neoliberalization which has increased socio-economic inequalities and limited our collective capacity to link the ecological crisis to its economic roots and thus find transformative solutions.

The concept of urban sustainability has failed to connect the environmental question with those of the social and of the economy in a progressive and democratic way. By promoting city-centric and pro-market policies which favors the most advantaged groups, it has obscured other approaches, spaces and social interests. It remains the task for (urban) environmental movements and critical scholars to challenge the underlying assumptions of current urban and environmental politics, asking "the politically sensitive, but vital, question as to what kind of socio-ecological arrangements and assemblages we wish to produce, how this can be achieved, and what sort of environments we wish to inhabit" (Swyngedouw 2018, 84) and work collectively for the "egalitarian and democratic production of socio-ecological commons" (Swyngedouw 2018, 164), connecting the environmental question with those of democracy, of the social, and the economy in a meaningful way.

Notes

1 Some of the ideas that informed this chapter stem from previous discussion published as ROSOL, Marit/ BÉAL, Vincent /MOESSNER, Samuel (2017): Greenest cities? The (post-)politics of new environmental regimes. In: Environment and Planning A 49(8): 1710–1718. We are grateful to Charlie Spring for her constructive comments on an earlier version of the manuscript.
2 The initial idea of promoting responsible development, and of economic growth, social welfare and environmental values supporting each other, increasingly turned into economic growth being the crucial driver (Lidskog and Elander 2012) and thus the mantra that what benefits the economy, benefits the social, and benefits the environment.
3 The theory of ecological modernization is based in the belief that economic growth can be de-coupled from its detrimental environmental impacts. It thus rests on the assumption that economic growth and environmental protection are compatible and can take place simultaneously, and thus systemic changes can be avoided (Foster 2012; Keil 2007). It is thus a strategy to "sustain (…) what is known to be unstainable" (Hult 2017, 30; referencing Lidskog and Elander 2012) and that is preventing much needed socio-ecological transformations.
4 The concept of the *post-political city* was mainly introduced into geography by Erik Swyngedouw, drawing on works of political philosophy and theory on post-democracy by Slavoj Žižek, Jacques Rancière and Chantal Mouffe (amongst other Swyngedouw 2009; 2011). It identifies a replacement of debate, disagreement and dissent in current urban governance with "a series of technologies of

ment." (Swyngedouw 2009, 604).
5 Our current agri-food systems cause severe environmental, economic, health and social problems (for an overview see Friedmann 1993; McMichael 2009; Wiskerke 2009; Galt 2013; De Schutter 2014; Holt-Giménez 2017). They are not only a leading cause of severe environmental degradation and climate change, they are also already tremendously impacted by it (IPCC 2019; Rockström et al. 2020). As the 2008 UN world agricultural report (IAASTD 2009; Beck et al. 2016) concluded: "Business as usual is not an option".
6 Local production is not necessarily more environmentally friendly (as the sole focus on transport routes ignores other environmental costs, local cultivation is not necessarily organic, and bulk shipping across longer distances may consume less fuel than individual pick-ups), foods are not per se of higher quality and fresher (as freshness depends above all on fast transport and an uninterrupted cold chain, which may be better organized by larger companies), and working conditions are not automatically fair.

References

Acuto, M., 2013. *Global Cities, Governance and Diplomacy: The Urban Link*. London and New York: Routledge.
Akers, J., Béal, V. and Rousseau, M., 2020. Redefining the city and demolishing the rest: the techno-green fix in postcrash Cleveland, Ohio. *Environment and Planning E: Nature and Space*, 3 (1), 207–227.
Alkon, A. and Agyeman, J., eds., 2011. *Cultivating Food Justice: Race, Class, and Sustainability*. Cambridge: MIT Press.
Alkon, A.H. and Guthman, J., eds., 2017. *The New Food Activism. Opposition, Cooperation, and Collective Action*. Oakland: UC Press.
Allen, P., 1999. Reweaving the food security safety net: Mediating entitlement and entrepreneurship. *Agriculture and Human Values*, 16 (2), 117–129.
Allen, P., 2010. Realizing justice in local food systems. *Cambridge Journal of Regions, Economy and Society*, 3 (2), 295–308.
Andersson, I., 2016. 'Green cities' going greener? Local environmental policymaking and place branding in the 'greenest city in Europe'. *European Planning Studies*, 24 (6), 1197–1215.
Angelo, H., 2019. Added value? Denaturalizing the "good" of urban greening. *Geography Compass*, 13 (8), e12459.
Angelo, H., 2020. Why does everyone think cities can save the planet? In J. Hoff, G. Quentin and L. Simon, eds. *The Role of Non-State Actors in the Green Transition: Building a Sustainable Future*. London and New York: Routledge, 193–209.
Angelo, H. and Wachsmuth, D., 2015. Urbanizing urban political ecology: a critique of methodological cityism. *International Journal of Urban and Regional Research*, 39 (1), 16–27.
Anguelovski, I., Connolly, J.J., Garcia-Lamarca, M., Cole, H. and Pearsall, H., 2019. New scholarly pathways on green gentrification: what does the urban 'green turn' mean and where is it going? *Progress in Human Geography*, 43 (6), 1064–1086.
Béal, V., 2012. Urban governance, sustainability and environmental movements: post-democracy in French and British cities. *European Urban and Regional Studies*, 19 (4), 404–419.
Béal, V., 2015. Selective public policies: sustainability and neoliberal urban restructuring. *Environment and Urbanization*, 27 (1), 303–316.
Béal, V., Epstein, R. and Pinson, G., 2018. Networked cities and steering states: urban policy circulations and the reshaping of state–cities relationships in France. *Environment and Planning C: Politics and Space*, 36 (5), 796–815.
Béal, V., Gauthier, M., and Pinson, G., eds., 2011. *Le développement durable changera-t-il la ville? Le regard des sciences sociales*. Saint-Etienne: Publications de l'Université de Saint-Etienne.
Beck, A., Haerlin, B. and Richter, L., 2016. *Agriculture at a Crossroads. IAASTD findings and recommendations for future farming*. 56. Berlin: Foundation on Future Farming (Zukunftsstiftung Landwirtschaft)
Bernzen, A., 2014. Reassessing supplier reputation in international trade coordination – a German and Australian perspective of global organic food networks. *Die Erde*, 145 (3), 162–174.
Blanc, N., Glatron, S., Lamarche, T., Rankovic, A. and Sourdril, A., 2017. Governance of urban nature. *Articulo – Journal of Urban Research, Briefings*.

Blok, A., 2020. Urban green gentrification in an unequal world of climate change. *Urban Studies*, 57 (14), 2803–2816.

Blue, G., Rosol, M. and Fast, V., 2019. Justice as parity of participation. Enhancing Arnstein's ladder through Fraser's justice framework. *Journal of the American Planning Association*, 85 (3. Special Issue: 50 Years Since Arnstein's Ladder), 363–376.

Born, B. and Purcell, M., 2006. Avoiding the Local trap: scale and food systems in planning research. *Journal of Planning Education and Research*, 26 (2), 195–207.

Bornemann, B. and Weiland, S., 2019. Special issue: new perspectives on food democracy. *Politics and Governance*, 7 (4).

Boykoff, J. and Mascarenhas, G., 2016. The Olympics, sustainability, and greenwashing: the Rio 2016 summer games. *Capitalism Nature Socialism*, 27 (2), 1–11.

Brand, K.W., 2008. Umweltbewegung (inkl. Tierschutz). In R. Roth and D. Rucht, eds. *Die Sozialen Bewegungen in Deutschland seit 1945. Ein Handbuch,* Frankfurt and New York: Campus, 219–244.

Brand, K.W., Büsser, D., amd Rucht, D., 1986. *Aufbruch in eine andere Gesellschaft. Neue soziale Bewegungen in der Bundesrepublik.* Frankfurt/Main: Campus.

Brenner, N., 2004. *New State Spaces. Urban Governance and the Rescaling of Statehood*. Oxford and New York: Oxford University Press.

Brenner, N. and Schmid, C., 2014. The 'urban age' in question. *International Journal of Urban and Regional Research*, 38 (3), 731–755.

Bulle, S., 2020. A zone to defend: the utopian territorial experiment of Notre Dame Des Landes. In B. Frère and M. Jacquemain, eds. *Everyday Resistance: French Activism in the 21st Century*. Cham: Springer International Publishing, 205–228.

Calvário, R., Desmarais, A.A. and Azkarraga, J., 2020. Solidarities from below in the making of emancipatory rural politics: insights from food sovereignty struggles in the Basque Country. *Sociologia Ruralis*, 60 (4), 857–879.

Caprotti, F., 2014. Eco-urbanism and the eco-city, or, denying the right to the city? *Antipode*, 46 (5), 1285–1303.

Castells, M., 1978. *City, Class and Power*. London: Macmillan.

Castells, M., 1983. *The City and the Grassroots. A Cross-Cultural Theory of Urban Social Movements*. London: Edward Arnold.

Champagne, D., 2020. Urban sustainability policies in neoliberal Canada: room for social equity? *Current Sociology*, 68 (6), 761–779.

Chang, I.C.C., 2017. Failure matters: reassembling eco-urbanism in a globalizing China. *Environment and Planning A: Economy and Space*, 49 (8), 1719–1742.

Charmes, E. and Keil, R., 2015. The politics of post-suburban densification in Canada and France. *International Journal of Urban and Regional Research*, 39 (3), 581–602.

Clarke, N., 2008. From ethical consumerism to political consumption. *Geography Compass*, 2 (6), 1870–1884.

Cugurullo, F., 2018. Exposing smart cities and eco-cities: Frankenstein urbanism and the sustainability challenges of the experimental city. *Environment and Planning A: Economy and Space*, 50 (1), 73–92.

Dachner, N. and Tarasuk, V., 2017. Origins and consequences of and responses to food insecurity in Canada. In M. Koç, J. Sumner and A. Winson, eds. *Critical Perspectives in Food Studies*. Don Mills: Oxford University Press, 221–236.

Daggett, C., 2018. Petro-masculinity: fossil fuels and authoritarian desire. *Millennium*, 47 (1), 25–44.

De Schutter, O., 2014. *Report of the Special Rapporteur on the right to food. Final report: The transformative potential of the right to food.* 28. United Nations General Assembly.

Demaria, F., Kallis, G. and Bakker, K., 2019. Geographies of degrowth: nowtopias, resurgences and the decolonization of imaginaries and places. *Environment and Planning E: Nature and Space*, 2 (3), 431–450.

Doernberg, A., Horn, P., Zasada, I. and Piorr, A., 2019. Urban food policies in German city regions: an overview of key players and policy instruments. *Food Policy*, 89, 101782.

Eblinghaus, H. and Stickler, A., 1996. *Nachhaltigkeit und Macht. Zur Kritik von Sustainable Development*. Frankfurt/Main: IKO-Verlag.

Follett, J., 2009. Choosing a food future: differentiating among alternative food options. *Journal of Agriculture and Environmental Ethics*, 22 (1), 31–51.

Foster, J.B., 2012. The planetary rift and the new human exemptionalism: a political-economic critique of ecological modernization theory. *Organization & Environment*, 25 (3), 211–237.

Fraser, N., 2013. *Fortunes of Feminism. From State-Managed Capitalism to Neoliberal Crisis*. London and New York: Verso.

Friedmann, H., 1993. The political economy of food: a global crisis. *New Left Review*, (I/197), 29–57.

Friedmann, H., 2005. From colonialism to green capitalism: social movements and the emergence of food regimes. In F. H. Buttel and P. McMichael, eds. *New directions in the sociology of global development. Research in rural sociology and development*. Amsterdam: Elsevier, 229–267.

Galt, R. E., 2013. Placing food systems in first world political ecology: a review and research agenda. *Geography Compass*, 7 (9), 637–658.

Gibbs, D. and Krueger, R., 2007. Containing the contradictions of rapid development?: New economy spaces and sustainable urban development. In R. Krueger and D. Gibbs, eds. *The Sustainable Development Paradox – Urban Political Economy in the United States and Europe*. New York: The Guilford Press, 95–122.

Goodman, D., 2009. Food networks, alternative. In R. Kitchin and N. Thrift, eds. *International Encyclopedia of Human Geography*. Oxford: Elsevier, 208–220.

Goodman, D. and Goodman, M., 2007. Localism, livelihoods and the 'post-organic': changing perspectives on alternative food networks in the United States. In D. Maye, L. Holloway and M. Kneafsey, eds. *Alternative Food Geographies: Representation and Practice*. Linacre, JH: Elsevier, 23–28.

Gottlieb, R. and Joshi, A., 2013. *Food Justice*. Cambridge: MIT Press.

Grünewald, A., 2015. Zwischen Selbstermächtigung und neuen Abhängigkeiten: Die Standardisierung des Biolandbaus in Österreich. In C. Reiher and S. R. Sippel, eds. *Umkämpftes Essen. Produktion, Handel und Konsum von Lebensmitteln in globalen Kontexten*. Göttingen: Vandenhoeck & Ruprecht, 143–171.

Gumbert, T., 2019. Anti-democratic tenets? Behavioural-economic imaginaries of a future food system. *Politics and Governance*, 7 (4), 11.

Guthman, J., 2004. *Agrarian Dreams. The Paradox of Organic Farming in California*. Berkeley: University of California Press.

Guthman, J., 2008. Neoliberalism and the making of food politics in California. *Geoforum*, 39 (3), 1171–1183.

Hamman, P., 2009. Urban sustainable development and the challenge of French metropolitan strategies. *Urban Research & Practice*, 2 (2), 138–157.

Harvey, D., 1989. From managerialism to entrepreneurialism: the transformation in urban governance in late capitalism. *Geografiska Annaler Series B*, 71 (1), 3–17.

Hassanein, N., 2003. Practicing food democracy: a pragmatic politics of transformation. *Journal of Rural Studies*, 19 (1), 77–86.

Hassanein, N., 2008. Locating food democracy: theoretical and practical ingredients. *Journal of Hunger & Environmental Nutrition*, 3 (2–3), 286–308.

Heeg, S. and Rosol, M., 2007. Neoliberale Stadtpolitik im globalen Kontext – Ein Überblick. *Prokla – Zeitschrift für kritische Sozialwissenschaft, Heft 149*, 37 (4), 491–509.

Hinrichs, C. C., 2003. The practice and politics of food system localization. *Journal of Rural Studies*, 19 (1), 33–45.

Hoffmann, D., Morrow, O. and Pohl, C., 2019. What's cooking in Berlin's Food Policy Kitchen? *RUAF Urban Agriculture Magazine* (36 – Food Policy Councils), 37–39.

Holgersen, S. and Malm, A., 2015. "Green Fix" as crisis management. Or, in which world is Malmö the worl's greenest city? *Geografiska Annaler: Series B, Human Geography*, 97 (4), 275–290.

Holt-Giménez, E., 2017. *A Foodie's Guide to Capitalism: Understanding the Political Economy of What We Eat*. New York: Monthly Review Press.

Holt-Giménez, E. and Shattuck, A., 2011. Food crises, food regimes and food movements: rumblings of reform or tides of transformation? *The Journal of Peasant Studies*, 38 (1), 109–144.

Hult, A., 2017. Unpacking Swedish Sustainability. The promotion and circulation of sustainable urbanism. In *School of Architecture and the Built Environment*, 164. Stockholm: KTH Royal Institute of Technology.

IAASTD, 2009. *Agriculture at a crossroads. The Global Report*. 608 pages. Washington: International Assessment of Agricultural Knowledge, Science and Technology for Development

IPCC, 2019. *Climate Change and Land. An IPCC Special Report on climate change, desertification, land degradation, sustainable land management, food security, and greenhouse gas fluxes in terrestrial ecosystems. Summary for Policymakers*. Intergovernmental Panel on Climate Change.

Jarosz, L., 2008. The city in the country: growing alternative food networks in Metropolitan areas. *Journal of Rural Studies*, 24 (3), 231–244.

Kalfagianni, A. and Skordili, S., 2018. *Localizing Global Food: Short Food Supply Chains as Responses to Agri-food System Challenges*. London: Routledge.

Keil, R., 2007. Sustaining modernity, modernizing nature: the environmental crisis and the survival of capitalism. In R. Krueger and D. Gibbs, eds. *The Sustainable Development Paradox – Urban Political Economy in the United States and Europe*, New York: Guilford Press, 41–65.

Keil, R. and Boudreau, J.A., 2006. Metropolitics and metabolics. Rolling out environmentalism in Toronto. In N. Heynen, M. Kaika and E. Swyngedouw, eds. *In the Nature of Cities. Urban Political Ecology and the Politics of Urban Metabolism*, London: Routledge, 40–61.

Kenis, A. and Lievens, M., 2017. Imagining the carbon neutral city: the (post)politics of time and space. *Environment and Planning A: Economy and Space*, 49 (8), 1762–1778.

Kinder, K., 2016. *DIY Detroit: Making do in a City Without Services*. Minneapolis: University of Minnesota Press.

Koç, M., McRae, R., Mougeot, L.J.A., and Welsh, J., 1999. *For Hunger Proof Cities: Sustainable Urban Food Systems*. Ottawa: International Development Research Centre.

Krueger, R. and Agyeman, J., 2005. Sustainability schizophrenia or "actually existing sustainabilities?" toward a broader understanding of the politics and promise of local sustainability in the US. *Geoforum*, 36 (4), 410–417.

Krueger, R., Freytag, T., and Mössner, S., eds., 2019. *Adventures in Sustainable Urbanism*. Albany: State University of New York Press.

Krueger, R. and Gibbs, D., eds., 2007. *The Sustainable Development Paradox – Urban Political Economy in the United States and Europe*. New York: The Guilford Press.

Lang, S. and Rothenberg, J., 2017. Neoliberal urbanism, public space, and the greening of the growth machine: New York City's High Line park. *Environment and Planning A: Economy and Space*, 49 (8), 1743–1761.

Lang, T., 1999. Food policy for the 21st century: can it be both radical and reasonable? In M. Koç, R. MacRae, L. J. A. Mougeout, and J. Welsh, eds. *For Hunger-proof Cities: Sustainable Urban Food Systems*, Ottawa: International Development Research Centre Books, 216–224.

Lawhon, M. and McCreary, T., 2020. Beyond jobs vs environment: On the potential of universal basic income to reconfigure environmental politics. *Antipode*, 52 (2), 452–474.

Levkoe, C. Z., 2006. Learning democracy through food justice movements. *Agriculture and Human Values*, 23 (1), 89–98.

Lidskog, R. and Elander, I., 2012. Ecological modernization in practice? The case of sustainable development in Sweden. *Journal of Environmental Policy & Planning*, 14 (4), 411–427.

Mayer, M., 2006. Urban social movements in an era of globalization. In N. Brenner and R. Keil, eds. *The Global Cities Reader*, London and New York: Routledge (first published in: P. Hamel, H. Lustiger-Thaler and M. Mayer (eds., 2000): Urban Movements in a Globalizing World.), 296–303.

Mayer, M., 2008. Städtische soziale Bewegungen. In R. Roth and D. Rucht, eds. *Die Sozialen Bewegungen in Deutschland seit 1945. Ein Handbuch*, Frankfurt / New York: Campus, 293–318.

McCann, E., 2017. Mobilities, politics, and the future: critical geographies of green urbanism. *Environment and Planning A*, 49 (8), 1816–1823.

McKendry, C., 2017. *Greening Post-industrial Cities: Growth, Equity, and Environmental Governance*. New York: Routledge.

McMichael, P., 2009. A food regime genealogy. *The Journal of Peasant Studies*, 36 (1), 139–169.

Meissle, K., 1998. Brachland in Berlin. Zur Bedeutung transitorischer Räume in der Stadt. *Stadt und Grün* (4/1998), 247–251.

Mendes, W., 2017. Municipal governance and urban food systems. In M. Koç, J. Sumner, and A. Winson, eds. *Critical Perspectives in Food Studies*, Don Mills: Oxford University Press, 286–304.

Metzger, J. and Lindblad, J., eds., 2020. *Dilemmas of Sustainable Urban Development: A View from Practice*. New York: Routledge.

Morgan, K. and Santo, R., 2018. The rise of municipal food movements. In S. Skordili and A. Kalfagianni, eds., *Localizing Global Food: Short Food Supply Chains as Responses to Agri-Food System Challenges*, London: Routledge, 27–40.

Mössner, S., 2016. Sustainable urban development as consensual practice: post-politics in Freiburg, Germany. *Regional Studies*, 50 (6), 971–982.

North, P., Nurse, A. and Barker, T., 2017. The neoliberalisation of climate? Progressing climate policy under austerity urbanism. *Environment and Planning A*, 49 (8), 1797–1815.

O'Neill, K. J. and Gibbs, D.C., 2014. Towards a sustainable economy? Socio-technical transitions in the green building sector. *Local Environment*, 19 (6), 572–590.

Peck, J. and Tickell, A., 2002. Neoliberalizing space. *Antipode*, 34 (3), 380–404.
Porter, L. and Shaw, A., eds., 2009. *Whose Urban Renaissance? An International Comparison of Urban Regeneration Strategies*. London: Routledge.
Pothukuchi, K. and Kaufman, J., 1999. Placing the food system on the urban agenda: the role of municipal institutions in food systems planning. *Agriculture and Human Values*, 16 (2), 213–224.
Quastel, N., 2009. Political ecologies of gentrification. *Urban Geography*, 30 (7), 694–725.
Raco, M., 2005. Sustainable development, rolled-out neoliberalism and sustainable communities. *Antipode*, 37 (2), 324–347.
Rapoport, E. and Hult, A., 2017. The travelling business of sustainable urbanism: international consultants as norm-setters. *Environment and Planning A: Economy and Space*, 49 (8), 1779–1796.
Renting, H., Marsden, T.K., and Banks, J., 2003. Understanding alternative food networks: exploring the role of short food supply chains in rural development. *Environment and Planning A*, 35 (3), 393–411.
Rice, J.L., Cohen, D.A. Long, J., and Jurjevich, J.R., 2020. Contradictions of the climate-friendly city: new perspectives on eco-gentrification and housing justice. *International Journal of Urban and Regional Research*, 44 (1), 145–165.
Rockström, J., Edenhofer, O., Gaertner, J., and DeClerck, F., 2020. Planet-proofing the global food system. *Nature Food*, 1 (1), 3–5.
Rosol, M., 2010. Public participation in post-Fordist urban green space governance: the case of community gardens in Berlin. *International Journal of Urban and Regional Research*, 34 (3), 548–563.
Rosol, M., 2013. Vancouver's "EcoDensity" Planning Initiative: A Struggle over Hegemony? *Urban Studies*, 50 (11), 2238–2255.
Rosol, M., 2014. On resistance in the post-political city: conduct and counter-conduct in Vancouver. *Space and Polity*, 18 (1), 70–84.
Rosol, M., 2015. Social mixing through densification? The struggle over the Little Mountain public housing complex in Vancouver. *Die Erde*, 146 (2–3), 151–164.
Rosol, M., 2018. Alternative Ernährungsnetzwerke als Alternative Ökonomien. *Zeitschrift für Wirtschaftsgeographie*, 62 (3–4), 174–186.
Rosol, M., 2019. On crisis, protest, and hope. Commentary on Erik Swyngedouw's 'Promises of the political'. Part of: Penny, Joe/Barnett, Clive/Legacy, Crystal/Dikec, Mustafa/Rosol, Marit/Featherstone, David and Swyngedouw, Erik. Urban Geography Review Symposium on: Promises of the political. Insurgent cities in a post-political environment, by Erik Swyngedouw, 2018. *Urban Geography*, early view.
Rosol, M., 2020. On the significance of alternative economic practices – reconceptualizing alterity in alternative food networks. *Economic Geography*, 96 (1), 52–76.
Rosol, M., Béal, V. and Mössner, S., 2017. Greenest cities? The (post-)politics of new urban environmental regimes. *Environment and Planning A*, 49 (8), 1710–1718.
Rosol, M. and Strüver, A., 2018. (Wirtschafts-)Geographien des Essens: transformatives Wirtschaften und alternative Ernährungspraktiken. *Zeitschrift für Wirtschaftsgeographie*, 62 (3–4), 169–173.
Roth, R., 1999. Lokale Demokratie "von unten". Bürgerinitiativen, städtischer Protest, Bürgerbewegungen und neue soziale Bewegungen in der Kommunalpolitik. In H. Wollmann and R. Roth, eds. *Kommunalpolitik*, Opladen: Leske+Budrich, 2–22.
Rousseau, M., 2015. 'Many rivers to cross': suburban densification and the social status quo in Greater Lyon. *International Journal of Urban and Regional Research*, 39 (3), 622–632.
Rucht, D., eds., 1984. *Flughafenprojekte als Politikum. Die Konflikte in Stuttgart, München und Frankfurt*. Frankfurt/New York: Campus.
Safransky, S., 2014. Greening the urban frontier: race, property, and resettlement in Detroit. *Geoforum*, 56 237–248.
Sonnino, R., Tegoni, C.L.S., and De Cunto, A., 2019. The challenge of systemic food change: insights from cities. *Cities*, 85 110–116.
Swyngedouw, E., 2009. The antinomies of the postpolitical city: in search of a democratic politics of environmental production. *International Journal of Urban and Regional Research*, 33 (3), 601–620.
Swyngedouw, E., 2011. Interrogating post-democratization: reclaiming egalitarian political spaces. *Political Geography*, 30 (7), 370–380.
Swyngedouw, E., 2018. *Promises of the Political. Insurgent Cities in a Post-Political Environment*. Cambridge: MIT Press.
Tilzey, M., 2019. Food democracy as 'radical' food sovereignty: agrarian democracy and counter-hegemonic resistance to the neo-imperial food regime. *Politics and Governance*, 7 (4), 203–213.

While, A., Jonas, A.E.G., and Gibbs, D., 2004. The environment and the entrepreneurial city: searching for the urban 'sustainability fix' in Manchester and Leeds. *International Journal of Urban and Regional Research*, 28 (3), 549–569.

Winter, M., 2003. Embeddedness, the new food economy and defensive localism. *Journal of Rural Studies*, 19 (1), 23–32.

Wiskerke, J.S.C., 2009. On places lost and places regained: reflections on the alternative food geography and sustainable regional development. *International Planning Studies*, 14 (4), 369–387.

Wittman, H., Desmarais, A.A., and Wiebe, N., eds., 2010. *Food Sovereignty: Reconnecting Food, Nature and Community*. Halifax and Oakland: Fernwood Publishing and FoodFirst Books.

20
SCIENCE AND DEMOCRACY
Partners for sustainability?

Jennifer S. Bansard and Sandra van der Hel

Acknowledgments: We thank Henrike Knappe, Ina Möller, and Carole-Anne Sénit for valuable comments on an earlier draft of this chapter.

Introduction

On April 22, 2017, scientists and their supporters turned to the streets in cities across the world to defend the role of science in democracy. They carried signs that read "science not silence" and "pursuing truth, saving the world." The movement grew out of US scientists' frustration over repeated "attacks on science" by the country's newly elected president, Donald J. Trump. The organizers emphasized the common good orientation of science as one of the movement's core principles (MfS 2017). "I'm not in science for money, I'm in science for *us*" read a protest sign (St Fleur 2017b), underscoring the holder's perspective on the societal role of science. Protesters saw it as their responsibility to defend science from increasingly frequent and loud attacks on scientific evidence. "Evidence-based policy making" became the mantra of the movement, which rapidly spread across the world, connecting citizens concerned about the increasing prevalence of science denial and "alternative facts."

The marches took place on Earth Day – an annual event launched in the 1970s to demonstrate support for environmental protection – and the timing was no coincidence. In the US, President Trump had repeatedly called climate change a hoax. Within its first months in office, his administration changed the US Environmental Protection Agency's mission statement, replacing a reference to developing "science-based" standards with "economically and technologically achievable" standards (Atkin 2017). This set the tone for Trump's entire presidency. Jair Bolsonaro's presidency in Brazil is similar in many aspects: both presidents reversed course on the protection of minority rights, dismantled decades-old environmental regulations, and restaffed environmental agencies with industry lobbyists. While these are blatant examples, an increasing number of high-level policy makers around the world appear to share this denial of scientific evidence and contribute to both the unraveling of democratic norms and the crumbling environmental protection measures.

Amid rising populist tendencies, the March for Science positions science as a key bastion for upholding democratic integrity. As its initiators wrote: "Science is a vital feature of a working democracy, spurring innovation, critical thinking, increased understanding, and better, healthier lives for all people" (MfS 2017). The March meant to defend these values of science in democracy.

Yet, the March for Science was not welcomed by all scientists. Specifically, the political nature of the March was a topic of contention. Some scientists expressed discomfort at seeing their colleagues take what they consider to be an affirmative stand in the political discourse, arguing it would threaten trust in the impartiality of science. "A march by scientists, while well intentioned, will serve only to trivialize and politicize the science we care so much about, turn scientists into another group caught up in the culture wars and further drive the wedge between scientists and a certain segment of the American electorate" wrote Young (2017) in an op-ed ahead of the March. Surely, US scientists are more cautions than others in this regard, seeing how just about anything can be painted a partisan issue in their country – as was for example the case of "wearing masks" during the COVID-19 pandemic. The fundamental premise is however shared by others: they cherish a view of science as an independent system that feeds on objectivity and produces ultimate facts. From this perspective, opening up science to societal issues and debates threatens the foundations of scientific institutions.

Trying to assuage these fears, March organizers such as Jonathan Berman argued that "[y]es, this is a protest, but it's not a political protest" (St Fleur 2017a). Other researchers in turn criticized such statements and the underlying discourse that portrays science as a-political. "History has shown us again and again [...] that science does not exist in a vacuum, but will be exactly used – as a constructive tool or a weapon – to impact ideological, political, and socio-economic goals" emphasized Prescod-Weinstein et al. (2017). This perspective is grounded in the recognition that science is embedded in the societal tissue, not only with regard to the societal repercussions of scientific research, but also for the simple fact that science is done by *people*. Scientists are not a special breed of humans: they hold worldviews just like anyone else. On top of their socialization as citizens, they undergo a process of disciplinary socialization over the course of their academic careers. These worldviews – much like the worldviews held by the people deciding over the allocation of research funding – affect science. Research priorities do not divinely manifest, they are the result of peoples' pondering over what is important – and such judgements are inherently value-laden. As Zevallos (2017) notes in a reflection on the debate surrounding the March for Science "[t]he idea that a protest can be 'not political' and that science can be separated from scientists are both political ideas."

A further point of contention related to the movement's stand on diversity. Researchers sympathetic to the March's goals denounced a lack of inclusivity and emphasized that the organizers' communication strategy obscures the role of women and people of color in science, reinforcing existing biases in academia. Others then countered that such "identity politics" (Pinker 2017b) are compromising the March's goals and that diversity questions are "a distraction" (Pinker 2017a). Yet, we can also see this argument as displaying stereotypical gatekeeping behavior that reinforces the status quo in science by, as Zevallos (2017) underscores, "centering the politics, identities and values of White scientists, especially White cisgender, able-bodied men."

The story of the March for Science illustrates the contentious relationship between science and democracy. While the position that science has an important role to play in democratic societies is widely shared, different views exist among scientists, citizens, and decision-makers about how societal decision-making should relate to science, the extent to which science and scientists should be involved in societal debates or can and should keep a distance from value-laden decisions, what can be considered a scientific fact, and whether it matters by whom scientific knowledge is produced.

In this chapter, we further unpack different perspectives on the desired relationship between science and democracy. We focus specifically on issues of sustainability, which are often complex, contested, and pervaded by inequalities. As we will see, people hold different perspectives on the ways in which scientific knowledge and societal decision-making on sustainability (should) relate. First, we turn our focus to the role of science in decision-making. Scientists and policy-makers alike emphasize the important role of science in addressing sustainability challenges. Yet, as we also highlight, the road from science to decision-making is not a simple one-way street, but involves value-laden decisions about the kind of knowledge that is appropriate for guiding society towards desirable sustainable futures. Second, we turn to the question of democracy in science. We argue that participation, representation, and recognition matter for the kind of knowledge that gets produced and becomes authoritative in decision-making on sustainability. For democratic decision-making on sustainability, it is important that those affected not only have a say in decision-making, but also in the development of knowledge on which these decisions are based.

Science in democracy

Decades of advances in science have provided an in-depth understanding of the sustainability challenges societies worldwide face today. Within recent years, sustainability challenges are increasingly framed in terms of emergency. Scientists and scientific organizations step up and speak out about the urgent need for action to address sustainability challenges. They warn that the window to limit global temperature increase to below 2°C is closing (IPCC 2018); that animal and plant species are threatened with extinction at unprecedented rates (IPBES 2019); that plastic pollution sprawls into the deep sea (Chiba et al. 2018); and that air pollution threatens human health (Kampa and Castanas 2008). They show that urgent action is needed, and that time is running out (van der Leeuw et al. 2012).

And yet, responses to these urgent calls for action have been limited. Intergovernmental negotiations have not resulted in the ambitious agreements that many deem necessary to counter the climate or biodiversity crisis. Decision-making from local to global scales more often than not balances environmental concerns against economic ones and prioritizes the latter. Considerations of environmental justice are persistently ignored around the world. Clearly, more and better scientific knowledge has not been sufficient to ignite a fitting societal response to today's sustainability crisis. What can or should researchers and their organizations do differently to increase their impact? What is the responsibility of science in supporting sustainability?

Beyond uncovering causes and potential impacts of sustainability challenges, science is increasingly expected to "help guide humanity's path towards plausible, desirable and novel futures" (Bai et al. 2016, 360). Unpacking the problems of environmental change is no longer enough. Instead, science is expected to support society in developing responses and solutions and seeking pathways towards global sustainability. This expectation for science to respond to urgent challenges of sustainability echoes across policy spheres. Policymakers call on science to take responsibility in steering society away from a dark and desolate future and towards global sustainability. The UN agenda 2030 for sustainable development, for example, stresses the important role of science as a driver and enabler of sustainable development (Schneider et al. 2019). At the local level, scientists find increasing opportunities to engage with political and social actors in decision-making processes (Bansard et al. 2019). At the global level, decision makers' appetite for state of the art knowledge is such that the Intergovernmental Panel on Climate Change (IPCC) and the Intergovernmental Science-Policy Platform on Biodiversity and Ecosystem Services (IPBES) are struggling to keep up with the increasing workload (IISD 2019).

And yet, the relationship between science and decision-making on sustainability is fraught with controversy. To what extent can scientific findings inform decisions over sustainable practices and help resolve conflict over different possible courses of action? Questions of sustainable futures are intertwined with contested values, interests, and trade-offs, which are not the kind of issues that science can easily resolve. Think for example of thorny questions surrounding the expansion of protected area coverage or the reliance on bioenergy with carbon capture and storage (BECCS), which both bear negative effects, notably in terms of local community displacement and threatened livelihoods (Schleicher et al. 2019; Creutzig et al. 2021). Who is to say just how much "lesser evil" is acceptable in order to secure "greater goods" such as biodiversity or a stable climate? "The risk of not doing research on [stratospheric aerosol injection, SAI] outweighs the risk of doing this research" considers Frank Keutsch (cited in Greenfield 2021); but with what legitimacy can US-based Harvard researchers such as Keutsch plan test flights for SAI in northern Sweden and deem risks acceptable without ever engaging with the Saami people over whose lands the experiment is supposed to take place?

To further unpack different positions on science's role in democratic decision-making, we turn to the discourse surrounding the notion of Planetary Boundaries. The Planetary Boundaries framework, initially published in *Nature* in 2009, puts forward a strong message about limits to human exploitation of earth system services. The framework identifies nine areas of biophysical risk where human development threatens Earth system stability, including the climate system, biodiversity loss, and the nitrogen cycle. Crossing the threshold in one or multiple of these areas would move societies out of the Holocene conditions in which humanity has flourished for thousands of years. But "as long as the thresholds are not crossed, humanity has the freedom to pursue long-term social and economic development" (Rockström et al. 2009b, 474).

Based on the concept of Planetary Boundaries, Earth system scientist Johan Rockström makes a clear distinction between what can and what can't be subject to democratic deliberation by arguing that "there is no negotiating with the Earth system" (quoted in Haider 2014). The boundaries are understood as immutable reality of the Earth system, as "non-negotiable planetary preconditions" (Rockström et al. 2009b, 2). Societal decision-making, then, should be about "how to maneuver within the safe operating space" (Steffen et al. 2015, 1259855–8). In this respect, the scientists are not setting thresholds but *identifying* and *finding* them, "[t]he thresholds in key Earth System processes exist irrespective of peoples' preferences, values, or compromises" (ibid., 5). The underlying argument is one of a division of labor between science and democracy: science demarcates a safe operating space for humanity, and within that operating space, democratic deliberation over questions of values, interests, and direction can take place.

This perspective drew a fair share of criticism with regard to the lack of democratic legitimacy of such an expert-driven and technocratic approach. As one firm critic notes: "[t]he framing of planetary boundaries as being scientifically derived non-negotiable limits, obscures the inherent normativity of deciding how to react to environmental change" (Raynor 2013). Where the authors of the Planetary Boundaries framework have been at pains to show the detailed and elaborate scientific work that went into identifying and measuring the boundaries, Raynor, among others, accuses them of shutting down democratic debate by presenting the boundaries as facts of nature.

Though they don't address the question of intent, Beck and Mahoney (2017) make an important, related point with regard to the climate pathways developed by the IPCC, specifically their reliance on negative emission technologies (NETs). The pathways address negative emission technologies (such as BECCS) from the perspective of technical feasibility, while implications in terms of displacement or food security, among others, were neither adequately assessed nor communicated (Anderson and Peters 2016). Yet, seeing as the IPCC is "widely accepted as the authoritative voice of scientific knowledge on climate change" (Corbera et al.

2016, 94), the pathways, and through them the use of NETs, "quickly became a fact that mattered" (Beck and Mahoney 2017, 312) in the policy discourse. In that sense, the pathways contributed to normalizing the idea of NETs. The existence of these pathways, put forward by the authoritative voice of the IPCC, can be used to "legitimize the deployment of technologies without broader societal assent, and without democratic discussion of alternatives" (ibid.). More than mere research outputs, these pathways then constitute mechanisms of *de facto* governance (Gupta and Möller 2019). Beck and Mahoney emphasize the performative nature of (anticipatory) research, especially in the context of the increased expectation for solution-oriented sustainability science, which we described earlier. In this regard, they underscore the "responsibility of knowledge-makers to engage with the consequences of their work" (p. 312) and argue that "questions about societal values and political feasibility need to be engaged with earlier in the scenario-production and assessment process" (ibid.).

This shows how scientific concepts can effectively "lock-in" certain worldviews which then come to shape societal decision-making. Against this background, some scholars behind the Planetary Boundaries framework did recognize that "the position of the boundary is a normative judgment, informed by science but largely based on human perceptions of risk" (Steffen et al. 2011, 61). In an attempt to reconcile the framework with the aspiration for democratic legitimacy and avoid the trap of linear perspective on the relation between science and decision-making, Pickering and Persson (2020) offer a more nuanced understanding of the Planetary Boundaries framework. Their proposition builds on and advances Bäckstrand (2017)'s distinction between "critical" loads of air pollution identified primarily by experts, and "target" loads, which represent air pollution levels that policy makers view as acceptable. Pickering and Persson propose to complement the planetary boundaries with planetary targets and emphasize that both need to be defined through iterative processes of deliberation. They situate both tasks "on a spectrum that involves varying mixtures of knowledge about biophysical processes on the one hand and normative or political judgements on the other" (p. 67) and note "both tasks require iterative dialogue between experts, policy-makers and civil society" (ibid.).

This perspective on the entanglement of scientific facts and normative judgement breaks with the idea that science and societal deliberation lie in a linear sequence. It speaks to the recognition that neatly demarcating between science and politics is perilous, especially when it comes to complex and contested issues such as sustainability transformations. Sustainability questions are always about facts and values simultaneously, as they concern questions of what desirable futures look like and how we can reach them. "The idea, then, that we can rid values from environmental science is not only unlikely but absurd" (Carolan 2006, 230), the point rather is to be transparent about normative assumptions. As Carolan contends, this might be a fruitful avenue to develop environmental policies while also "having an eye toward issues of social justice" (p. 236). This perspective has increasingly been gaining ground and opened up momentum for critical introspection into the practice and organization of science itself, which we address in the next section.

Democracy in science

As scholars increasingly have to position their role in complex decision-making on sustainability and contested societal change processes, there is an overall reckoning that science is not free of power dynamics and that there is thus a need for "opening up" the process of authoritative knowledge production to greater scrutiny. Against this background, in this section, we first unpack who presently has a voice in science and which perspectives shape science, before expanding further on rationales for broadening participation, representation, and recognition in science for sustainability.

Over two decades ago, at the 1999 World Conference on Science, member states of the United Nations Educational, Scientific, and Cultural Organization (UNESCO) already noted that "whilst unprecedented advances in the sciences are foreseen, there is a need for a vigorous and informed democratic debate on the production and use of scientific knowledge" (UNESCO 1999, 8). The Declaration on Science and the Use of Scientific Knowledge adopted at the conference provides a good overview of the many tenets of this ongoing debate. The Declaration highlights the importance of education for all, without discrimination, in creating scientific capacity, and underscores socio-economic disparities in access to science, especially between developing and developed countries. It speaks to the potential for detrimental applications of science, to research funding, to open access to data and the free flow of knowledge, and calls for curricula to address science ethics and the history of science. Crucially, the Declaration underscores the historical imbalance in the participation of men and women in science, and that barriers have precluded the full participation of disabled people, Indigenous Peoples, and ethnic minorities, among other disadvantaged groups. It recognizes that "traditional and local knowledge systems [...] can make, and historically have made, a valuable contribution to science" (ibid., 9), and emphasizes that "a new relationship between science and society is necessary to cope with pressing global challenges" (ibid., 10).

When it comes to sustainability science, one aspect is especially key to the democratization of science: ensuring that those affected have a say in the direction that is taken (Eckersley 2004; Dryzek 2010; Smith and Stirling 2016). As delineated in the previous section, pathways for sustainability charted out by science effectively carry certain values and interests about desirable futures and there is no objective way to manage inevitable trade-offs. Therefore, to enhance the democratic quality of decisions on sustainability, equal and fair participation is not only important for political decision-making, but should also be considered as part of scientific knowledge production.

Despite some progress, the status quo of participation in science remains unbalanced. Science remains far from inclusive and representative of the heterogeneous voices in society. While this is the case all around the world,[1] it becomes quite evident looking at US statistics, which importantly grant an intersectional perspective. They show that, in 2015, 56 percent of US Full Professors were white men and only 1 percent were Black women, despite respectively representing about 30 percent and 6.5 percent of the general population (McFarland et al. 2017; US Census 2019). Further, the percentage of American Indian/Alaska Natives across all academic ranks in the US "rounds to zero" (McFarland et al. 2017, 151). It is shocking to realize that when it comes to diversity in science, we are still at the stage of a sequence of firsts (Amâncio 2005: 26). The scientific landscape is so skewed toward white men, that we celebrate nominations such as those, in 2016, of Ingrid Burke as the first female dean of the 116-year old Yale School of Forestry and Environmental Studies or of Jacinta Ruru as the first Māori law Professor in Aotearoa New Zealand. As of 2020, women and people of color remain vastly underrepresented in science.

The picture becomes even more skewed when we consider not just who participates in science, but which voices are represented and carry authority to shape societal debates and decision-making. One example are high profile science assessments, such as those of the IPCC. Looking at authorship of IPCC assessment reports, there is mounting evidence that this authoritative voice is predominantly shaped by scholars that are male, from the Global North, and from natural science disciplines (Hulme and Mahony 2010; Corbera et al. 2016). While this point is often raised and, indeed, perceived as a risk for the legitimacy of the IPCC to inform decision-making, efforts to counter the bias in authorship and become more inclusive have been of limited success thus far. One possible reason for this, as Corbera and colleagues note, is that the IPCC is organized as a consensus seeking organization: with the overall aim to speak "on behalf of science with one voice," there is little room for multiplicity of perspectives coming, for example, from critical social sciences or Indigenous scholars. Nevertheless, broadening participation in the IPCC may:

> help unearth the key conflicts and choices to be made in climate change mitigation policy, between different values and interests. This might in turn enable the IPCC to increase its policy usefulness by emphasizing the important political choices societies confront as they respond to climate change.
>
> *Corbera et al. 2016, 99*

Díaz-Reviriego et al. (2019) show that this assessment also holds true for IPBES, which, despite its widely recognized efforts to be inclusive of a wider spectrum of voices, still presents a significant authorship bias.

That the problem of unequal representation is not restricted to international scientific assessments but is in fact deeply embedded in scientific organization and practices can aptly be illustrated by turning our focus to teaching, as one of the core tasks of the university. Take syllabi as an example. Readings assigned as part of the university curriculum shape students' perception of authoritative knowledge and introduce the next generation of scientists to the voices that matter. Yet, university curricula (often unwittingly) reify old power structures. As Qureshi (2018) notes, "[p]resent curricula assume that white men write about universal truths, while people of color are only expert in a narrow field – usually to do with questions of their identity and heritage." While certain perspectives and topics are posited as the mainstream, others are deemed radical and are fenced off. For example, introductions courses to International Relations (IR), as a discipline that feeds into sustainability science, generally follow a paradigmatic structure whereby everything from feminist to post-colonial perspectives gets mingled into a single "critical theory" session, positioning these perspectives as *other* and *radical*. Newell (2020) further highlights that although we need bolder visions to deal with sustainability challenges, mainstream IR approaches treat capitalism (or industrialism) and militarism as givens. In this regard, Lundegård (2008) emphasizes that "the actual basis of the environmental problems that we are facing today are built into modern society's meta-narratives and structures" (p. 125) and that "future issues can only be solved when we have learned to see beyond the basic power structures that Western culture is built on" (ibid.). Much scholarship confirms that past and present power dynamics carry great effect over sustainability issues – see e.g. Newell (2021) and Deitz and Meehan (2019) on the racialized politics of energy, respectively water governance. Yet, many educators tend to avoid topics that can trigger emotional discomfort altogether and thus glance over topics such as settler colonial history and how these shape the current state of play (Korteweg and Root 2016).

Discussions of participation and representation are deeply entangled with the question of recognition in science. Though far from the formal entry barriers and blatant discrimination that once saw Marie Curie being denied membership in the French Academy of Sciences (even though she already held a Nobel Prize!), recognition in academia is still imprinted with bias that favors some segments of the population over others. Mechanisms of recognition tend to reinforce the status quo of unequal representation in science and lead to the prevalence of what Thomas (2017) calls the norm of the white male template in science. As Carlone and Johnson (2007) highlight, "[i]t is much easier to get recognized as a scientist if your ways of talking, looking, acting, and interacting align with historical and prototypical notions of scientist" (p. 1207). Joubert and Guenther (2017)'s research on public visibility of South African scientists give further credence to this mechanism. They find an over-representation of white scientists in South Africa's public media. Although only 8% percent of South Africans are white, white scientists constitute 59 percent of the scientific workforce. This historically developed inequity is reinforced by the representation of white scientists in the media: 78 percent of the country's group of visible scientists are white. Joubert and Guenther point to the fact that the panel of science-media experts they relied on in their study was predominantly white, noting this poses a limitation to their findings. Yet, one could also argue that this rather underscores the similarity in power dynamics affecting science and society at large, and the need to address these with intent.

Now, why are participation, representation, and recognition such central topics of discussion in a chapter on science for sustainability? Let us return to the UNESCO declaration by which we started this section. The Declaration states that "[e]qual access to science is not only a social and ethical requirement for human development, but also essential for realizing the full potential of scientific communities worldwide and for orienting scientific progress towards meeting the needs of humankind" (p. 13).

As a social and ethical requirement, consideration of participation, representation, and recognition speak to the principle of equal opportunities for all. Today, women, people of color, people with disabilities, or children of parents with limited educational attainment can, in principle, all go to university and eventually enter the academe. In practice however, they have many more rocks and hurdles to overcome than affluent white men. These hurdles are manifold and well documented.[2] To highlight just one study, Milkman et al. (2015) found, by means of a field experiment in the US, that when considering requests from prospective students seeking mentoring ahead of entering a doctoral program, faculty were significantly more responsive to white males than to all other considered categories of students combined (white women, and Black, Hispanic, Chinese, and Indian students). This held true across disciplines, except the fine arts, and was especially pronounced in higher-paid professional environments. There is not merely a "leak" in the pipeline leading to scientific careers, but a multi-layered filter (Blickenstaff 2005). The ideal of equal opportunities for all is not upheld in practice and it is morally warranted to address this. At a time of increased disenfranchisement from decision-making elites and science denial it is also key for upholding legitimacy.

In terms of orienting scientific progress towards meeting the needs of humankind, biases in participation, representation, and recognition are particularly problematic with regard to sustainability science, because those that are marginalized from knowledge production are also those most vulnerable to sustainability challenges. Research on sustainability issues has a strong geographical bias (Karlsson et al. 2007; Pasgaard et al. 2015). Karlsson and colleagues show that environmental science is not only dominated by scholars from the Global North, but also predominantly focuses on moderate or cold eco-climatic zones, which are prominent in the Global North, whereas less research covers dry subtropical and tropical zones more prevalent in the Global South (Karlsson et al. 2007). This global knowledge divide has not diminished since the publication of the study by Karlsson et al. (2007). In their 2015 article, Pasgaard and colleagues, focusing specifically on climate science, show that "production of climate change knowledge is biased away from developing, more vulnerable regions of the world with warmer climates and low climate footprints, and that in these regions, relatively few authors are based in the country being studied" (Pasgaard et al. 2015, 280). They advocate for strengthening local research capacity and supporting collaboration across national and geographical boundaries, for example through international research networks, as had already been called for in the 1999 UNESCO Declaration. Yet, international research networks so far do not succeed in meeting the objective of equal participation of scholars from the Global South, even though this objective has been on the agenda for decades (van der Hel 2019).

The argument in this regard is that broadening and diversifying participation will enhance the effectiveness of responses to complex sustainability challenges. Demonstrating the structural bias in urban sustainability science, Nagendra et al. (2018) for example highlight the importance of contextual knowledge to address the *distinct* challenges of cities in the Global South. As there is increasing awakening to the perils of centering medical research and, more broadly, design, on the male body (see e.g. Criado-Perez 2019), it is key to expand the knowledge base that informs global sustainability policy to ensure it is not molded on the reality of only part of humanity and to minimize adverse impacts of response measures. Although the onus to shift the balance on under-researched subjects should not fall on researchers from marginalized communities but rather be collectively shouldered, broadening participation in knowledge production is seen as key to avoid blind spots. Who gets to participate in science does matter, not only because it affects what questions are asked but also what evidence and perspectives are brought to the table. In his piece *The Imperial Scholar*, Delgado (1984) reflects on what difference it makes if the scholarship about the rights of group A is written by members of group B. He highlights that "members of group B may be ineffective advocates of the rights and interests of persons in group A. They may lack information; more important, perhaps, they may lack passion, or that passion may be misdirected" (p. 567) and he adds that "while the B's might advocate effectively, they might advocate the wrong things" (ibid.). Crucially, he says such scholarship can – in addition to factual ignorance or naiveté – suffer from "a failure of empathy, an inability to share the values, desires, and perspectives of the population whose rights are under consideration" (p. 568). Though centered on civil rights scholarship, Delgado's reflection is very fitting with regard to sustainability science as well. As we have to deal with complex sustainability challenges that affect people in different ways, it is crucial that different perspectives, and especially those of people concerned by the specific matter, inform the research on these subjects.

Conclusion

Sustainability science has expanded our understanding of the complex sustainability challenges that the world is facing. Increasingly, discussions on the transformation towards sustainability are marked by a discourse of urgency and by calls for a stronger role of science in supporting societal transformations to sustainability. We showed that views differ significantly over what this role should be. Should science be in a steering role, charting out the space for democratic deliberation over the course of action? Or should science stay put until society identifies the course of action and then jump in to support the chosen pathway? The main take away from the chapter is that such a linear perspective of the relation between science and society and such a separation of knowledge production and value considerations does not stand the test of reality. It is important to recognize that upon closer inspection, the veneer of objective and neutral science crumbles. Even the identification of what constitutes tipping points in the Earth system is, though informed by the scientific understanding of biophysical mechanisms, subject to "human perceptions of risk" (Steffen et al. 2011, 61) and thus a normative judgment of what is deemed acceptable. Acknowledging the effect of individual perspectives on the construction of concepts such as planetary boundaries or NETs, which carry governance effects, then calls for ensuring that a diversity of perspectives feed into the production of authoritative knowledge claims. In this respect, the chapter has shown that, despite the decades-old recognition of structural imbalances in science, those most vulnerable to sustainability challenges remain marginalized. Science still carries the voice of those privileged by past developmental pathways rather than reflecting our world's heterogeneous society.

This does not mean, however, that there has been no progress. The March for Science, which we used in the beginning of the chapter to illustrate the persistent contention over the tryptic relation between science, democracy, and sustainability, has come a long way since its inception in early 2017. After several (clumsy) revisions, the March's website now quotes Rosalin Franklin saying that "science and everyday life cannot and should not be separated" (MfS 2020). Crucially, it recognizes that "science can be exploited to perpetuate harms and reinforce oppression" and advocates for an "application of science that strengthens human rights, addresses injustices, and improves conditions for all species to thrive" (ibid.). The movement now highlights a commitment to "challenging power structures within science communities that cause harm." Underscoring the realization of "how privilege works," it stipulates to strive to "ensure that the voices of people hit the hardest are heard" and to "dismantle hierarchies of power while intentionally constructing spaces for more equitable participation in movement work" (ibid.).

Since the adoption of the 1999 UNESCO Declaration, the reflexive movement geared at a democratization of science has deepened and broadened. It has – especially in the last five years – taken up speed and is sweeping across the academe. Social media is bustling with scholars speaking up and rallying against bias in academia, giving backlash against all-male panels, and calling for decolonizing the classroom (see e.g. @womenalsoknow and #BlackInTheIvory on Twitter). Some universities are experimenting with opening women only positions. The Dutch Academy of Sciences proposes an overhaul of funding schemes towards a guaranteed baseline funding for staff in professorial positions. Entire editorial boards join in mass resignation over publishers' open access policies.

This movement not only pertains to the question of who gets to *be a scientist* but also about how to *do science*. The European Commission recently took an important step in this regard: grant recipients will now be required to incorporate sex and gender analyses in the design of research studies, with the only exception for topics (e.g. in theoretical mathematics) for which the Commission itself indicates that it may not be relevant. And researchers will also be expected to take into account intersecting aspects like ethnicity, disability, or sexual orientation (EC 2020). Such measures contribute to de-centering the perspective of those historically privileged by and in science and ultimately foster more inclusive policy development.

Two other interlinked developments stand out in the context of "opening up" science: the increasing attention for knowledge co-production and efforts to mobilize local and Indigenous knowledge. Knowledge co-production is a response to the call for science to "have closer and different relations with practice […] where science not only informs practice but also learns from practice" (Bai et al. 2016, 360). It also responds to the recognition that "scientific knowledge can be conceived as a global public good in which the citizens have a stake" (Bäckstrand 2003, 25) and that "[t]he citizen is not just the recipient of policy but an actor in the science-policy nexus" (ibid.). Though scientists retain the power to offer other knowledge holders a platform for sharing their views, there is a notable normative shift towards recognizing the importance of having multiple voices at the table (Milkoreit et al. 2020). It is a move towards bringing those affected by research outcomes into the research process, bringing in value discussions and making the research process more iterative. As such it is distinct from forms of citizen science where non-scientists merely contribute data.

This opening-up is evidently not challenge-free. For one, structured training on how to conduct co-productive research is significantly lagging behind its increased momentum, leaving many scholars to fend for themselves if they want to pursue it. Further, this type of research typically takes time, and time is a luxury many academics do not have. Speaking from her experience working with Indigenous communities, Otakuye Conroy-Ben underscores that "it can take a year or two to receive tribal approvals, which means there is often not enough time for someone at a pre-tenure stage" who needs to publish to advance their career (Gewin 2021). Co-productive research, of course, also generates frictions with those who fear a "politicization" of science and deny the "science" attribute to anything that comes close to action research. Opening-up science requires us to rethink how we *do science* in many ways, notably challenging the publish-or-perish system that governs today's academic employment and rethinking notions of impact and quality science (van der Hel 2020).

Another noteworthy point is that the increasing mobilization of local and Indigenous knowledge contributes to challenging the pervasive assumption that western science "is a form of knowledge that lacks the cultural finger-prints that seem much more conspicuous in knowledge systems that have retained their ties to specific localities" (Gough 2002, 1223). It helps challenging "unmarked" categories and positions (see e.g. Haraway 1988, Hawthorne 1999), notably the human/nature divide emblematic of western ways of knowing which is at odds with the lived reality of many people around the world (Breidlid 2009; Bang et al. 2014; Engel-Di Mauro and Carroll 2014). Slowly, other perspectives on the relationship between humans and nature gain ground. Something to look out for in that regard is the IPBES assessment report on diverse conceptualization of values of nature and its benefits. Brigitte Baptiste, one of the co-chairs of the assessment process, highlights that "[o]ne of the key elements of the assessment will be to empower individuals and groups whose voices are typically not heard" (IPBES 2018), with Patricia Balvanera, another co-chair, adding that "assessing this diversity of values and how they are incorporated into decision making will contribute to addressing conflicts over nature and promoting more equitable decisions" (ibid.).

As science plays a key role in supporting societal transformations to sustainability, it is crucial to continue this introspective movement and ensure scientific knowledge is produced in an inclusive manner. The voice of the scientific community carries authority in societal debates. This voice should not cement the status quo, it should challenge power differentials and truly support transformative change both inward and outward.

Notes

1 Although the European Union is for example close to reaching gender balance in doctoral programs, disciplinary imbalances remain, and crucially, the gender gap widens at higher employment levels (EC 2019). Similarly, in India, women represented 41 percent of PhD level degree awardees in 2017 but only 27.3 percent of Full Professors (AISHE 2018) and while Canada achieves gender parity at the level of Assistant Professors, it only has 28 perecent female Full Professors (Statistic Canada 2019). In India, the Muslim minority group further makes up only 5.3 percent of higher education teaching staff as opposed to 14.2 percent of the population (AISHE 2018; CCI 2011).
2 Hurdles to equal participation, representation, and recognition in science relate to fundamental notions such as economic, social, and cultural capital (Bourdieu 1986). They relate to the difficulty for individuals deviating from the template of "the scientist" along white, masculine values and behavioral norms to develop an identification with science (Carlone and Johnson 2007; Archer et al. 2015; Wong 2015); and to the difficulty for "first generation" students to navigate an academic landscape full of unspoken norms (Schwartz et al. 2018). They also relate to the fact that many supposedly "objective" performance measures used in academic recruitment and promotion processes are effectively biased, as research for example shows with regard to student evaluations or citation practices (see e.g. MacNell et al. 2015; Dion et al. 2018; Fan et al. 2019).

References

AISHE, 2018. *All India Survey on Higher Education 2017–18* [online]. Available from: http://aishe.nic.in/aishe/viewDocument.action?documentId=245.

Amâncio, L., 2005. Reflections on science as a gendered endeavour: changes and continuities. *Social Science Information*, 44(1), 65–83.

Anderson, K. and Peters, G., 2016. The trouble with negative emissions. *Science*, 354(6309), 182–183.

Archer, L., Dewitt, J. and Osborne, J., 2015. Is science for us? Black students' and parents' views of science and science careers. *Science Education*, 99(2), 199–237.

Atkin, E., 2017, *The EPA's Science Office Removed "Science" From Its Mission Statement* [online]. Available from: https://newrepublic.com/article/141174/epas-science-office-removed-science-mission-statement.

Bäckstrand, K., 2003. Civic science for sustainability: reframing the role of experts, policy-makers and citizens in environmental governance. *Global Environmental Politics*, 3(4), 24–41.

Bäckstrand, K., 2017. Critical loads: negotiating what nature can withstand. *Conceptual Innovation in Environmental Policy*, 129–154.

Bai, X. et al., 2016. Plausible and desirable futures in the Anthropocene: a new research agenda. *Global Environmental Change*, 39, 351–362.

Bang, M. et al., 2014. Muskrat theories, tobacco in the streets, and living Chicago as Indigenous land. *Environmental Education Research*, 20(1), 37–55.

Bansard, J.S., Hickmann, T. and Kern, K., 2019. Pathways to urban sustainability: how science can contribute to sustainable development in cities. *GAIA-Ecological Perspectives for Science and Society*, 28(2), 112–118.

Beck, S. and Mahony, M., 2017, The IPCC and the politics of anticipation. *Nature Climate Change*, 7(5), 311–313.

Blickenstaff, J.C., 2005. Women and science careers: leaky pipeline or gender filter? *Gender and Education*, 17(4), 369–386.

Bourdieu, P., 1986. The forms of capital. In J. Richardson, eds. *Handbook of theory and research for the sociology of education*. New York: Greenwood, 241–258.

Breidlid, A., 2009. Culture, indigenous knowledge systems and sustainable development: a critical view of education in an African context. *International Journal of Educational Development*, 29(2), 140–148.

Carlone, H.B. and Johnson, A., 2007. Understanding the science experiences of successful women of color: science identity as an analytic lens. *Journal of Research in Science Teaching: The Official Journal of the National Association for Research in Science Teaching*, 44(8), 1187–1218.

Carolan, M.S., 2006. Scientific knowledge and environmental policy: why science needs values. *Environmental Sciences*, 3(4), 229–237.

Chiba, S. et al., 2018. Human footprint in the abyss: 30 year records of deep-sea plastic debris. *Marine Policy*, 96, 204–212.

Corbera, E., Calvet-Mir, L., Hughes, H. and Paterson, M., 2016. Patterns of authorship in the IPCC Working Group III report. *Nature Climate Change*, 6(1), 94–99.

Creutzig, F., Erb, K.H., Haberl, H., Hof, C., Hunsberger, C. and Roe, S., 2021. Considering sustainability thresholds for BECCS in IPCC and biodiversity assessments. *GCB-Bioenergy*. Early View.

Criado-Perez, C., 2019. *The deadly truth about a world built for men – from stab vests to car crashes* [online]. Available from: www.theguardian.com/lifeandstyle/2019/feb/23/truth-world-built-for-men-car-crashes.

Deitz, S. and Meehan, K., 2019. Plumbing poverty: mapping hot spots of racial and geographic inequality in U.S. household water insecurity. *Annals of the American Association of Geographers*, 109(4), 1092–1109. https://doi.org/10.1080/24694452.2018.1530587

Delgado, R., 1984. The imperial scholar: Reflections on a review of civil rights literature. *University of Pennsylvania Law Review*, 132(3), 561–578.

Díaz-Reviriego, I., Turnhout, E. and Beck, S., 2019. Participation and inclusiveness in the intergovernmental science–policy platform on biodiversity and ecosystem services. *Nature Sustainability*, 2(6), 457–464.

Dion, M.L., Sumner, J.L. and Mitchell, S.M., 2018. Gendered citation patterns across political science and social science methodology fields. *Political Analysis*, 26(3), 312–327.

Dryzek, J.S., 2010. Rhetoric in democracy: a systemic appreciation. *Political Theory*, 38(3), 319–339.

Eckersley, R., 2004. *The Green State: Rethinking Democracy and Sovereignty*. Cambridge: MIT Press.

Engel-Di Mauro, S. and Carroll, K.K., 2014. An African-centred approach to land education. *Environmental Education Research*, 20(1), 70–81.

European Commission, 2020. *Accounting for sex and gender makes for better science – The European Commission is set to insist on steps that will make research design more inclusive* [online]. Available from: https://ec.europa.eu/info/news/accounting-sex-and-gender-makes-better-science-european-commission-set-insist-steps-will-make-research-design-more-inclusive-2020-dec-11_en.

European Commission, 2019. *She Figures 2018* [online]. Available from: https://op.europa.eu/en/publication-detail/-/publication/9540ffa1-4478-11e9-a8ed-01aa75ed71a1.

Fan, Y., Shepherd, L.J., Slavich, E., Waters, D., Stone, M., Abel, R. and Johnston, E.L., 2019. Gender and cultural bias in student evaluations: why representation matters. *PloS one*, 14(2), e0209749.

Gewin, V., 2021. *How to include Indigenous researchers and their knowledge* [online]. Available from: www.nature.com/articles/d41586-021-00022-1.

Gough, N., 2002. Thinking/acting locally/globally: Western science and environmental education in a global knowledge economy. *International Journal of Science Education*, 24(11), 1217–1237.

Greenfield, P., 2021. 8 February. *Balloon test flight plan under fire over solar geoengineering fears* [online]. Available from: www.theguardian.com/environment/2021/feb/08/solar-geoengineering-test-flight-plan-under-fire-over-environmental-concerns-aoe.

Gupta, A. and Möller, I., 2019. De facto governance: how authoritative assessments construct climate engineering as an object of governance. *Environmental Politics*, 28(3), 480–501.

Haider, J., 2014. *More great quotes from #PBMOOC coming soon…. sign up today!* [online]. Available from: www.youtube.com/watch?v=-CiAt_ZjR74&list=UUG0QUKa0MTBzBKiW18AZfTg" [Tweet]. https://twitter.com/JamilaHaider/status/534331552076169216.

Haraway, D., 1988. Situated knowledges: the science question in feminism and the privilege of partial perspective. *Feminist Studies*, 14(3), 575–599.

Hawthorne, S., 1999. Cyborgs, virtual bodies and organic bodies: theoretical feminist responses. *Cyberfeminism: Connectivity, Critique and Creativity*, 213–249.

Hulme, M. and Mahony, M., 2010. Climate change: what do we know about the IPCC? *Progress in Physical Geography*, 34(5), 705–718.

International Institute for Sustainable Development, 2019. Summary of the Seventh Session of the Plenary of the Intergovernmental Science-Policy Platform on Biodiversity and Ecosystem Services. *Earth Negotiations Bulletin*, 31(49).

IPBES, 2018. *New IPBES Assessment Begins: Making the Many Values of Nature Count* [online]. Available from: https://ipbes.net/news/new-ipbes-assessment-begins-making-many-values-nature-count.

IPBES, 2019. *Global assessment report on biodiversity and ecosystem services of the Intergovernmental Science-Policy Platform on Biodiversity and Ecosystem Services*. Bonn, Germany.

IPCC, 2018. Global Warming of 1.5°C. An IPCC Special Report on the impacts of global warming of 1.5°C above pre-industrial levels and related global greenhouse gas emission pathways, in the context of strengthening the global response to the threat of climate change, sustainable development, and efforts to eradicate poverty.

Joubert, M. and Guenther, L., 2017. In the footsteps of Einstein, Sagan and Barnard: identifying South Africa's most visible scientists. *South African Journal of Science*, 113(11–12), 1–9.

Kampa, M. and Castanas, E., 2008. Human health effects of air pollution. *Environmental Pollution*, 151(2), 362–367.

Karlsson, S., Srebotnjak, T. and Gonzales, P., 2007. Understanding the North–South knowledge divide and its implications for policy: a quantitative analysis of the generation of scientific knowledge in the environmental sciences. *Environmental Science and Policy*, 10(7–8), 668–684.

Korteweg, L. and Root, E., 2016. Witnessing Kitchenuhmaykoosib Inninuwug's strength and struggle: the affective education of reconciliation in environmental education. *Canadian Journal of Environmental Education (CJEE)*, 21, 178–197.

Lundegård, I., 2008. Self, values and the world – young people in dialogue on sustainable development. *Values and Democracy in Education for Sustainable Development – Contributions from Swedish Research*, 123–144.

MacNell, L., Driscoll, A. and Hunt, A.N., 2015. What's in a name: exposing gender bias in student ratings of teaching. *Innovative Higher Education*, 40(4), 291–303.

March for Science, 2017. *Principles and Goals. Archived from the original on 16 February, 2017* [online]. Available from: https://web.archive.org/web/20170216072446/www.marchforscience.com/mission-and-vision/.

March for Science, 2020. *Our Mission* [online]. Available online from: https://marchforscience.org/our-mission/.

McFarland, J., Hussar, B., de Brey, C., Snyder, T., Wang, X., Wilkinson-Flicker, S., Gebrekristos, S., Zhang, J., Rathbun, A., Barmer, A., Bullock Mann, F., and Hinz, S., 2017. *The Condition of Education 2017 (NCES 2017-144)* [online]. Available from: https://nces.ed.gov/pubsearch/pubsinfo.asp?pubid=2017144.

Milkman, K.L., Akinola, M. and Chugh, D., 2015. What happens before? A field experiment exploring how pay and representation differentially shape bias on the pathway into organizations. *Journal of Applied Psychology*, 100(6), 1678.

Milkoreit, M., Bansard, J.S., and van der Hel, S., 2020. Agency and knowledge in environmental governance: a thematic review. In M. Betsill, T.M. Benney, and A.K. Gerlak, eds., *Agency in Earth System Governance*. Cambridge: Cambridge University Press, 86–96.

Nagendra, H., Bai, X., Brondizio, E.S. and Lwasa, S., 2018. The urban south and the predicament of global sustainability. *Nature Sustainability*, 1(7), 341–349.

Newell, P., 2021. Race and the politics of energy transitions. *Energy Research & Social Science*, 71, 101839.

Newell, P., 2020. Global green politics in a time of crisis. *Green European Journal*. www.greeneuropeanjournal.eu/global-green-politics-in-a-time-of-crisis accessed 18 August 2020.

Pasgaard, M., Dalsgaard, B., Maruyama, P.K., Sandel, B. and Strange, N., 2015. Geographical imbalances and divides in the scientific production of climate change knowledge. *Global Environmental Change*, 35, 279–288.

Pickering, J. and Persson, Å., 2020. Democratising planetary boundaries: experts, social values and deliberative risk evaluation in Earth system governance. *Journal of Environmental Policy and Planning*, 22(1), 59–71.

Pinker, S., 2017a, *Glad to see that the March for Science Web site has removed the distractions. It's an important event* [online]. Available from: https://marchforscience.com." [Tweet]. https://twitter.com/sapinker/status/826113252585250816.

Pinker, S., 2017b, *Scientists' March on Washington plan compromises its goals with anti-science PC/identity politics/hard-left rhetoric* [online]. Available from: https://goo.gl/AVB7mR." [Tweet]. https://twitter.com/sapinker/status/825769152627482624.

Prescod-Weinstein, C., Tuttle, S. and Osmundson, J., 2017. *We Are The Scientists Against A Fascist Government* [online]. Available from: https://medium.com/the-establishment/we-are-the-scientists-against-a-fascist-government-d44043da274e.

Qureshi, S., 2018. Short cuts: black history. *London Review of Books*, 40(22).

Raynor, S., 2013. *Planetary Boundaries as Millenarian Prophecies Malthusian Echoes*. Oakland: The Breakthrough Institute.

Rockström, J., Steffen, W., Noone, K. Persson, Å., Chapin, F. Stuart III, Lambin, E., ... Foley, J., 2009a. Planetary boundaries: a safe operating space for humanity. *Nature*, 461(24), 472–475.

Rockström, J., Steffen, W., Noone, K., Persson, Å., Chapin, F. Stuart III, ... and Nykvist, B., 2009b. Planetary boundaries: exploring the safe operating space for humanity. *Ecology and Society*, 14(2).

Schleicher, J., Zaehringer, J.G., Fastré, C., Vira, B., Visconti, P. and Sandbrook, C., 2019. Protecting half of the planet could directly affect over one billion people. *Nature Sustainability*, 2(12), 1094–1096.

Schneider, F., Kläy, A., Zimmermann, A.B., Buser, T., Ingalls, M., and Messerli, P., 2019. How can science support the 2030 Agenda for Sustainable Development? Four tasks to tackle the normative dimension of sustainability. *Sustainability Science* (0123456789).

Schwartz, Sarah E., Kanchewa, Stella S., Rhodes, Jean E., Gowdy, Grace, Stark, Abigail M., Horn, John P., McKenna, Parnes, and Spencer, Renée, 2018. "I'm Having a Little Struggle With This, Can You Help Me Out?": Examining Impacts and Processes of a Social Capital Intervention for First-Generation College Students. *American Journal of Community Psychology*, 61(1–2), 166–178.

Smith, A. and Stirling, A., 2016. Grassroots Innovation and Innovation Democracy, STEPS Working Paper 89, Brighton: STEPS Centre.

St Fleur, N., 2017a. *'Listen to Evidence': March for Science Plans Washington Rally on Earth Day* [online]. Available from: www.nytimes.com/2017/02/01/science/march-for-science-washington-date.html.

St Fleur, N., 2017b. *Scientists, Feeling Under Siege, March Against Trump Policies* [online]. Available from: www.nytimes.com/2017/04/22/science/march-for-science.html.

Statistics Canada, 2019. *Number and Salaries of Full-time Teaching Staff at Canadian Universities (final), 2018/2019*. Available from: https://www150.statcan.gc.ca/n1/daily-quotidien/191125/dq191125b-eng.htm.

Steffen, W.L., Rockström, J. and Costanza, R., 2011. How defining planetary boundaries can transform our approach to growth. *Solutions: For A Sustainable & Desirable Future*, 2(3), 59–65.

Steffen, W., Richardson, K., Rockström, J., Cornell, S.E., Fetzer, I., Bennett, E.M., ... and Sörlin, S., 2015. Planetary boundaries: guiding human development on a changing planet. *Science*, 347(6223).

Thomas, P., 2017, 27 May. *Power, Responsibility, and the White Men of Academia* [online]. Available from: https://plthomasedd.medium.com/power-responsibility-and-the-white-men-of-academia-c9eca01d48c6.

U.S. Census Bureau, 2019. *Population by Sex, Race, and Ethnicity for the United States and Regions: 2018* [online]. Available from: www.census.gov/content/dam/Census/newsroom/press-kits/2019/v2018_table2.xlsx.

UNESCO, 1999. *Declaration on Science and the Use of Scientific Knowledge and the Science Agenda: Framework for Action* [online]. Available from: https://unesdoc.unesco.org/ark:/48223/pf0000116994/PDF/116994eng.pdf.multi.

van der Hel, S., 2018. Science for change: a survey on the normative and political dimensions of global sustainability research. *Global Environmental Change*, 52, 248–258.

van der Hel, S., 2019. Research programmes in global change and sustainability research: what does coordination achieve? *Current Opinion in Environmental Sustainability*, 39, 135–146.

van der Hel, S., 2020. *New Science Institutions for Global Sustainability*. Utrecht: Utrecht University.

van der Leeuw, S., Wiek, A., Harlow, J. and Buizer, J., 2012. How much time do we have? Urgency and rhetoric in sustainability science. *Sustainability Science*, 7(1), 115–120.

Wong, B., 2015. Careers "From" but not "in" science: why are aspirations to be a scientist challenging for minority ethnic students? *Journal of Research in Science Teaching*, 52(7), 979–1002.

Young, R.S., 2017, *A Scientists' March on Washington Is a Bad Idea* [online]. Available from: www.nytimes.com/2017/01/31/opinion/a-scientists-march-on-washington-is-a-bad-idea.html.

Zevallos, Z., 2017. *The March for Science Can't Figure Out How to Handle Diversity. Latino Rebels* [online]. Available from: www.latinorebels.com/2017/03/14/the-march-for-science-cant-figure-out-how-to-handle-diversity/.

PART V

Issues and policy areas

21
CLIMATE CHANGE AND GREEN DEMOCRATIC TRANSFORMATIONS

Amanda Machin

Introduction

As the concentration of carbon dioxide in the atmosphere increases, so does the pressure on political structures. The 'enhanced greenhouse effect' will have a drastic, if differentiated effect, on socio-ecological systems around the world, threatening agriculture, livelihoods, biodiversity and generating uncertainty and risk (Stehr and Machin 2019). Yet despite growing awareness of the problem, an escalating volume of greenhouse gases are emitted, by some countries more than others, and efforts to reverse this trend are clearly insufficient (Wendling et al. 2020: 124). International treaties, new technologies, carbon markets and shifts in consumer behaviour do not appear, so far, to have had much impact. Part of the reason for this is that climate change is a global 'wicked' problem that has no obvious straightforward solution that can be implemented smoothly.

It might seem appropriate to blame the democratic institutions and processes that seem unable to respond urgently and adequately to environmental issues and hazards. Held hostage to corporate interests, public ignorance, short-term electoral cycles and outdated conceptions of agency and sovereignty, democracy appears to be part of the problem rather than part of the solution. Environmental philosopher Dale Jamieson, for example, highlights the limitations of democracies in which 'expertise is subservient to the voice of the people' and raises doubts that democracies are necessarily any better than theocratic autocracies in the fight against climate change (Jamieson 2020). This raises the problem of the 'democracy-environment nexus' (Pickering et al. 2020, 1) that is particularly acute in the case of climate change, for it is perhaps this issue more than any other that exposes the problem of 'democratic myopia' (Smith 2021, 8). I argue, however, that the validity of this scepticism about democracy really hinges upon the particular form of democracy in question. Perhaps it is no coincidence that we puzzle over the 'democratic crisis' while lamenting the onset of the 'climate crisis'. Perhaps the problem with contemporary political structures is not that they are too democratic, but that have been corrupted, abused and maligned and have been depleted of genuine democracy. Perhaps this moment of crisis opens the space to reconsider not only what is wrong with democracy, but also how it could be put right.

DOI: 10.4324/9780429024085-26

So, if climate change is a challenge for democracy, then it also poses the possibility of revising prevailing theories, models and practices of democratic politics and of precipitating a transformation that not only enfolds environmental aims but also a democratic renewal. Democracy has never been a static arrangement but takes myriad forms (Dean et al. 2019, v). Revisiting and revising democracy is crucial because without being bolstered by democratic legitimacy, environmental policy is likely to fail while at the same time, the future of democracy hinges on how it responds to a warming planet. As Frank Fischer writes "the future of democratic governance itself will depend on our ability to meet the ecological challenge by imagining ways to construct and practice new forms of democracy" (2017, 3). In other words, the future of political democracy and ecological sustainability are intertwined.

This chapter asks, then, how might contemporary democracy be revised in the face of a changing climate? Can it be made both 'greener' and more democratic? Numerous scholars have asked this question (see for example the collection edited by Doherty and De Geus 1996). The chapter engages with some of their answers. It outlines five different 'pathways' for a 'greening' of democracy in the face of climate change: green representation, green deliberation, green cosmopolitanism, green localism and green agonism. Drawing on the work of Leach, Scoones and Stirling (2010) I use the term 'pathways' here to emphasise that 'democracy' should not be understood as a fixed arrangement of institutions, but rather involves continual revision in a dynamic socio-ecological context. 'Pathways' are 'alternative possible trajectories' with distinct 'goals, values and functions' (Leach et al. 2010). In the context of uncertainty and risk posed by climate change the negotiation and contestation between alternative pathways of 'greening democracy' is not only inevitable but also valuable for opening up new options not only for tackling climate change, but for reviving democracy too. As we will see, the five pathways I critically describe below have different priorities and distinct conceptions of human beings and their political interaction.

Green representative democracy

The dominant form of democracy, in many parts of the world, is liberal representative democracy, in which the democratic principle of equality works in tension with the liberal emphasis on individual rights and freedom. Representation in a liberal democracy hinges on the idea that equal political rights should be granted to *all* citizens to select and challenge their representatives in free and fair elections (Held 1996, 120). The struggles of the nineteenth and twentieth centuries over the meaning and allocation of citizen rights led to enfranchisement of various previously excluded groups and the establishment of 'universal suffrage' (Held 1996, 119).

Environmental issues, however, have put this claim of universal suffrage under the spotlight. For it is clear that the policies of a particular state can have drastic environmental implications for groups who are not currently allocated full citizen rights by that polity. As Andrew Dobson writes: 'Environmental concern has put new (but contested) constituencies on the political agenda – constituencies that render problematic current understandings of the way representative democracies should function' (Dobson 1996, 124).

For instance, air and water pollution are not confined to the boundaries of the state that produced it, but those populations living outside those boundaries and who suffer from such pollution have no political rights in that state.[1] The issue becomes particularly acute in the case of climate change. The climate policy of a state will affect people living on the other side of the planet, to whom the governments of those states are not accountable. As one well documented example, the historical and current carbon emissions of the global north that drive climate change, contribute to the dangers of rising sea levels for small island developing states. Scholars point out that an adequate response does not simply consist of a greater emphasis on the vulnerabilities of these countries, but would rather demand the political empowerment of their populations (Barnett and Campbell 2010).

We see later in the chapter how the 'green cosmopolitan pathway' exposes and engages with this particular concern. But there are other groups who are excluded from current mechanisms of democratic representation too. Future generations and non-human nature will be affected by a changing climate but have neither vote nor voice in climate policy. Researchers have long been interested in the rights of 'animals and unborn generations' (see for example Feinberg 1974).

Robyn Eckersley recommends the 'ecological extension' of the demos to all those potentially affected by a particular proposal (2004, 112) an extension which 'does not regard the boundaries of the nation-state as necessarily coterminous with the community of morally considerate beings' (2004, 114). Similarly, Terence Ball promotes a 'greatly expanded democracy' or what he calls 'biocracy' (2006, 139). In this 'democracy of the affected' human interests are no longer placed 'at the apex of a hierarchical pyramid of moral considerability' (2006, 135) and the boundaries of the community are extended to include animals, ecosystems and future generations who together constitute the 'biotic community' (2006, 138; see also Eckersley 2004, 10).

The claim here is that the political representation of non-human nature and future generations would inevitably produce climate policy that is not only more democratic but more ecologically sensitive. But how might these constituents be politically represented? These theorists suggest that the interests of future generations and non-human nature could be represented by proxies (Dobson 1996, 132) spokespersons, ombudsmen (Ball 2006, 144; see also Beckman and Uggla 2016) or an 'environmental defenders office' (Eckersley 2004, 134). Various governments – Hungary, Israel and Wales for example – have attempted to introduce some form of political representation for future generations (see Beckman and Uggla 2016; Karnein 2016).[2] And yet Anja Karnein observes the 'formidable obstacles' in attempting to represent future generations; she refers to 'inherent problems of trying to represent those who are categorically unable to speak for themselves' (2016, 84).

One obvious objection is that it is impossible to know the interests of these constituents who are unable to speak for themselves. Dobson's response here is to point out that: "while it is obviously true that we cannot know what the interests of future will be exactly, we can be fairly sure that they will want both viable environment in which to live and the possibility of satisfying their basic needs' (1996, 132). Ball explains that it is not that these new members are given voting rights, but rather that their *interests* are represented and 'they need not know about or be able to articulate these interests in order for us to recognise, respect and protect them' (2006, 142). He therefore recommends not listening *to* but 'listening *for*' 'nature's cries of distress', since 'listening need not be coextensive with hearing human speech' (Ball 2006, 142).

Yet, as Eckersley highlights, there are dangers with assuming that a political actor, however well-meaning and sensitive, can adequately grasp the outlook of an embodied creature who resides in a different time or place: 'political representatives may find it difficult or impossible to understand or imagine the perspectives of all differently situated others in order to formulate norms that may be acceptable to those others' (2004, 132). And as Karnein points out 'future generations are likely to be composed of an infinite plurality of different persons with dissimilar perspectives' (2016, 87). She therefore challenges the reductive assumption that any future generation would share a single perspective or set of interests (2016, 87). Karneim advises there should not only be *one* representative for future generations (2016, 94) and Beckman and Uggla specifically recommend an ombudsman who is not given formal powers of obligation or sanction (2016, 118). We might prefer therefore Eckersley's alternative suggestion that 'political representation be as diverse as possible' (2004, 132).

The question of how democracy might be transformed in an era of climate change can be framed in terms of the further expansion of rights of representation to these new, yet tricky, constituents. The strategy of this pathway of 'green representation' to extend and enrich political rights and the introduction of new institutions and mechanisms to re-present the interests of future generations and non-human nature will be neither straightforward or uncontested. In order to be legitimate, the radical revising of the institutional framework of liberal democracies this would involve would itself need to be democratic. Perhaps this pathway should start out by attending to the political representation of new *existing* generations, the young citizens of the *Fridays for Future* generation who, as Bronwyn Hayward writes, 'must confront not only the risks of chaotic climate change but also work to transform the diverse social and economic drivers of injustice and suffering' (Hayward 2020, 2).

Sensitive to the dangers of claims to represent future generations, Karnein suggests that present day political decisions are subject to public discussion about the impact of those decisions on the future and she recommends 'deliberative bodies or assemblies' to specifically address this issue (2016, 96). The next pathway I describe emphasises the importance of deliberation in tackling climate change. This pathway, as we will see, extends deliberation more generally across the political arena.

Green deliberative democracy

An alternative pathway to green democracy is mapped out by political thinkers who suggest that the problem with contemporary liberal representative democracies is that it has encouraged the notion that political interaction consists of the bargaining between self-preoccupied strategic parties and compromises between their competing interests (Habermas 1994, 6). Their claim is that democracy should not be reduced to the aggregation of the preferences of individuals, regarded mainly as *consumers*. Rather it should be understood as the collective endeavour of *citizens* working together to contemplate the common good. The important starting point here is that political preferences are not an expression of interests that are fully formed prior to social interaction, but that preferences can change through that interaction. It is the quality of that interaction that is the focus of those proposing a 'deliberative' or 'discursive' form of democracy. These theorists advocate deliberative discussion between all members of society such that 'all have the opportunity to participate in influencing the process of discussion and the interests of all are properly taken into account' (Christiano 2012, 27). As Jon Elster argues, political deliberation requires citizens to go beyond the private self-interest of the market and orientate themselves to the public interests of the forum (1986). Thus, the pathway of green deliberative democracy, in contrast to green representative democracy, is not focused on *expanding* political rights, but rather emphasises the *deepening* of political participation

Deliberative democracy, rooted in the work of Jürgen Habermas and John Rawls, aims to base decisions on what Habermas refers to as 'a public use of reason jointly exercise by autonomous citizens' (1994, 3). The claim here is that fair, inclusive, equal and careful discussion between citizens, stakeholders, politicians and experts can generate better-informed policy decisions and recommendations. Participants are called to justify their own perspectives and to listen to others. Some recommend that deliberation between representatives is made more deliberative (Lidskog and Elander 2007, 88) but more commonly the emphasis is placed on a more widespread change in democracy participation beyond voting in elections: individuals should not only be represented but be active political participants in determining and implementing the common good.

This is seen as an important pathway to a green democracy that can better tackle climate change because the decisions and recommendations generated through collective deliberation, it is claimed, are more likely to be better informed about environmental issues and more orientated towards ecological ends. Numerous political thinkers and environmental activists recommend deliberative democracy as the pathway towards greening democracy and tackling climate change (Barry 1999; Smith 2003; Eckersley 2004; Baber and Bartlett 2005; Christiano 2012; Niemeyer 2013; Dryzek 2000, 2015; Hammond 2020; Smith 2021). They provide both ethical and epistemological justifications. Deliberation is seen first of all as *ethically* important, because it is supposed encourage individuals to transcend their self-interest and become 'other regarding'. By engaging in face-to-face discussions with their fellow citizens, deliberative democracy is expected to broaden perspectives and to encourage a sense of community and consideration of others. David Miller refers to the 'moralising effect of public discussion' narrow self-interest is difficult to defend in the public sphere (Miller 1992, 61). Deliberation therefore encourages an awareness of the dangers of climate change that are distributed unevenly around the world. It also allows the public scrutinizing of environmentally unsustainable practices. For Eckersley, deliberative democracy 'privileges generalizable interests over private, sectional, or vested interests, thereby making public interest environmental advocacy a virtue rather than a heroic aberration in a world of self-regarding rational actors' (2004, 117).

Second, and relatedly, deliberation is justified on the *epistemological* basis that it educates citizens and generates better-informed policy recommendations. Grasping the implications and mechanisms of climate change demands a basic grasp of the science, therefore it is claimed that a sustained exchange between various types of experts and lay people from different backgrounds has the salutary effect of fomenting mutual learning: 'In the process of exchanging evidence related to proposed solutions, individuals discover information they did not previously have … deliberation is in itself a procedure for becoming informed' (Manin 1987, 349). Deliberative democrats believe that under ideal conditions, in which participants can engage in free, fair and transparent discussion with full information and no time constraints, the decisions reached would be rational, fair and acceptable to all (Bohman 1998, 402). Deliberation 'makes the realization of reasonable results more likely' (Manin 1987, 362).

John Dryzek therefore claims that deliberation will make policy making more 'ecologically rational'. As he writes: 'discursive democracy can be extended in a direction that overcomes anthropocentric arrogance and that can cope more effectively with the ecological challenge' (Dryzek 2000, 160). Similarly, Eckersley argues that deliberative democracy is particularly appropriate in the case of complex ecological problems and that it makes it possible to expose the policies and interests of social, political and economic elites to public scrutiny and that 'a case can be made that deliberative democracy is especially suited to making collective decisions about long-range, generalizable interests, such as environmental protection and sustainable development' (Eckersley 2004, 118).

Many deliberative democrats recommend the introduction of deliberative forums on climate policy into the political system. They assess and promote the effectiveness of deliberative forums or mini-publics such as citizen assemblies, citizen juries, citizen councils, town meetings and consensus conferences (Hammond and Smith 2017, 14; Dryzek et al. 2019). In his research Simon Niemeyer writes that deliberation in a mini-public in the Australian Capital Region 'improved the ability of citizens to better deal with the kind of complexity associated with climate change' (2013, 442). He concludes that 'deliberative democracy … has the ability to transform the public response to climate change' (2013, 448). Others repudiate 'quick fixes' and are more concerned with precipitating a broader 'cultural' change (Hammond and Smith 2017, 23). Marit Hammond therefore argues for the promotion of 'socio-political spaces of inclusive critical engagement' that foster a vibrant deliberative culture (2020, 188).

In summary, the strategy of this pathway is that by introducing real opportunities for deliberation, citizens will come to formulate socially and environmentally responsible opinions and articulate strong policy recommendations so that climate change can be tackled more creatively, effectively and legitimately. There are several important criticisms of deliberative pathway, however. The suggestion that rational deliberation can eradicate difference and reach consensus on a highly contested issue such as climate change is highly suspicious (Machin 2013). The very orientation towards agreement can disguise the persistent inequalities and hierarchies in deliberative forums (Sanders 1997; Ruser and Machin 2017, 37). Deliberatives today concede that differences cannot always be overcome and are aware of problems of power relations, yet there is also a concern that deliberative democracy is preoccupied with the creation of 'spaces' for careful, rational reflection and exchange and that it forgets the important passionate, spontaneous and unruly interaction that constitutes lively democratic politics. Emotions cannot be so easily bracketed off from political deliberation and 'the issues that most people want to talk about are not always easy to articulate in the format of rational reasoned argument' (Hayward 2020, 123; see also Hall 2007). Those advocating a 'green agonistic' pathway, as we will see, view disruptive and impassioned political disagreements as concomitant to democratic politics. This criticism also applies to some accounts of 'cosmopolitanism' which also attempt to install deliberative 'spaces' of democracy. It is the cosmopolitan pathway to green democracy which I consider next.

Green cosmopolitan democracy

Since both the causes and consequences of a changing climate are distributed around the planet, environmental political scientists and theorists are interested in how climate governance operates beyond the state. As we saw above, one of the political problems posed by climate change is that the populations that are the least responsible for driving climate change will be those that are most affected by it. John Barnett and John Campbell point out the terrible irony in their work on small island states in the South Pacific: 'the societies that are most responsible for the emissions of greenhouse gases are those that are least vulnerable because of the adaptive capacity conferred by the wealth they have generated largely through polluting forms of development' (Barnett and Campbell 2010, 10).

But if states are unlikely to tackle any complex ecological problem unilaterally, they are also unable to do so. This is the starting point of this third pathway. Climate change clearly exceeds conventional political borders, which makes it notoriously difficult for a solitary sovereign state to govern (Holden 2002, 123). According to David Held and Angus Hervey, what can be seen as 'the paradox of our times' consists in the reality that 'the collective issues we must grapple with are of growing cross-border extensity and intensity, but the means of addressing these are state-based, weak and incomplete' (Held and Hervey 2011, 95). Therefore 'it is widely recognised' writes Robert Garner 'that the most critical environmental problems can only be tackled internationally' (2011 84; see also Lidskog and Elander 2007, 77).

But democrats are wary of the tendency to assume that climate governance beyond the state should be placed in the hands of 'a cosmopolitan epistemic community' who generate a climate science that is somehow 'uncontaminated by politics and disagreement' (Eckersley 2017, 4). As Alexander Ruser explains, this approach to global climate politics 'overlooks the complicated and problematic relations between expertise and decision-making' in which scientific experts are not free either from political motivation nor public distrust (2018, 2). The cosmopolitan pathway to green democracy therefore involves the search for ways in which to democratise the governance of climate change, by ensuring that international treaties and institutions are exposed to democratic critique and by encouraging the formation of a democratic culture (Eckersley 2017). As mentioned above, the 'all-affected principle' demands that those affected by an issue should have their voice heard. Barry Holden argues, therefore, that 'it is perhaps in respect of global warming, that the case for democratisation at a transnational level becomes most compelling' (2002, 119).

Deliberative democrats concerned about climate change have enquired into the possibility that deliberation could be 'scaled up' to a global level in order to democratise global climate governance. As Hayley Stevenson and John Dryzek explain, traditional electoral democracy clearly does not currently function at a global level (2014, 190). Instead they follow recent literature on deliberative democracy, in which the idea has been developed that deliberation does not take place at a single place or level but rather is spread out through a 'deliberative system' (Parkinson and Mansbridge 2012). For Stevenson and Dryzek define it: 'a deliberative system is generally composed of multiple locations and practices that can be interpreted as together enabling the achievement of qualities we might seek in a more deliberative democracy' (Stevenson and Dryzek 2014, 7). Instead of focusing on the formal institutions of global governance they instead investigate global climate governance as an informal polycentric *system*. They assess how deliberation appears across various arenas, summits and practices – 'empowered spaces' – of a decentred global governance system and they suggest that by connecting these 'spaces' up it might be possible to develop 'inclusive, competent, and dispersed reflexive capacity' (2012, 203). Perhaps this might include a global citizens' assembly, as recommended by Michael Vlerick (2020).

The aim of Stevenson and Dryzek is to create an engagement between and across different discourses of climate change within 'organised spaces for discussion' (2014, 194). Missing from this account, however, is an acknowledgement that these spaces are not neutral arenas to which all political differences are given equal access. Although it is acknowledged that there are structural inequalities in the international system (2014, 192), these inequalities are supposed to disappear in the spaces they promote. There are also restrictions placed on the form of interaction permitted by their understanding of democracy. For although they believe that all discourses should be exposed to "critique and challenge" (2014, 202) this should be a critique that stimulates "reflective capacity". Impassioned disagreement between different approaches is definitely seen as an unhelpful obstruction for climate governance. So, while Stevenson and Dryzek point out that political engagement can take the form of contestation, they claim that "when it comes to climate change, contestation is not necessarily productive" (2014, 203).

This pathway leads to the 'scaling up' of democratic discussion and decision making, in an attempt to make climate change policy more inclusive, just and legitimate. The danger here however is that the attempt to do so simply covers over the exclusions and inequalities that currently exist. Actually, cosmopolitan democracy is understood by many of its proponents as 'an attempt to generate democratic governance at a variety of levels, including the global level' (Archibugi and Held 2011, 434). Next I consider the pathway that takes us back down to a democracy operating at a local level.

Green local democracy

Although climate politics is often presented as unfolding at the global level, this underplays the relevance of the specific regional and local context in which climate change is framed and negotiated, particularly in low- and middle-income countries; local politics is highly relevant to tackling global climate change (Dodman and Mitlin 2015). As Thomas Bernauer points out: 'Stalemate at the global level has not prevented some states and/or subnational units from pushing ahead with more ambitious climate policies' (Bernauer 2013, 434)

Turning the cosmopolitan approach on its head is the 'turn to the local' proposed by Frank Fischer who claims that in the face of climate change 'we can no longer rely on global agreements or national strategies' (2017, 13). He suggests not only are strategies for sustainability most effectively carried out at the local level but that democracy also flourishes best at that level (Fischer 2017, 14). It is at the grassroots that it is possible 'to experiment and act inventively and exuberantly' (Fischer 2017, 13). He therefore promotes through a re-orientation away from 'larger political-institutional structures' and towards 'specific local environmental projects' (2017, 90).

According to Fischer, this eco-localism does not need to be invented, it just needs to be (re)discovered: 'eco-localism is in fact thriving around the globe, even if operating under the conventional radar' (2017, 281). Transition Towns and 'ecovillages' he says are examples of this thriving localism that are already 'producing valuable participatory insights and practices that will likely be useful in the future' (2017, 282). Karen Litfin agrees that ecovillages are 'living laboratories' (2014). In her extensive research into various different examples of these 'self-contained communities' around the world she concludes that 'ecovillagers are like applied scientists, running collective experiments in ever realm of life: building, farming, waste management, decision making, communication, child rearing, finance, ownership, ageing and death' (2014, 18).

Environmentalism has long been associated with an emphasis on decentralisation and localism. As Alan Carter writes 'many environmentalists argue on straightforward environmental grounds that moving from large-scale, urban communities to small-scale decentralised ones is essential if we are to reduce our environmental impact' (Carter 1999, 239). But there is also an impetus to decentralise political decision making too, and therefore localism coincides with an emphasis on participatory democracy in which negotiations and decision-making also takes place at a local 'grassroots' level (Carter 1999, 241). Face-to-face interaction is expected to generated trust between citizens (Kenis and Mathijs 2014, 174).

However, as Anneleen Kenis and Erik Mathijs notice in their analysis of localisation movements such as Transition Towns, there is a danger that localisation is often idealised as a strategy for sustainability: 'the local is depicted as an intrinsic site of opposition and resistance to what are called the "destructive forces of globalization"' (2014, 174). The danger, they argue, is that this strategy is too often *depoliticised*, so that power, exclusion and conflict that occur at all levels of politics are glossed over (Kenis and Mathijs 2014, 175). They point out interactions at a local level can potentially be undemocratic and unrepresentative: 'while the local can be empowering for certain local actors, it can in the same way be disempowering for others' (2014, 175).

Kenis and Mathijs therefore call for 'politicising the local' (2014, 182). They do not reject the idea of the local as a starting point for movement building, but they do suggest that any movement that is built should make visible 'the disagreements and powers that permeate and surround it' (2014, 182). The danger of depoliticizing climate change, of overlooking the operation of power relations and political marginalization, exclusion and inequality, is manifested also in a persistent tendency to see passionate contestation as something that should be expunged from climate politics (Machin 2013). As we have seen, this overshadows some of the other pathways above. This tendency is challenged by the call for (re)politisiation of climate change that informs the final pathway of green agonism I turn to now.

Green agonistic democracy

Political disagreement over climate change can be viewed not only as inevitable but also as valuable. This is the starting point of the fifth pathway to green democracy – the 'agonistic' approach, which I have elsewhere called 'ecological agonism' (Machin 2020). The aim of green agonists is not to find a consensus on climate change but rather to celebrate the *agonistic* disagreements around it, while aiming to prevent those disagreements from becoming *antagonistic*.

There are various theorists who promote an 'agonistic' politics (Honig 1993; 2009; Tully 2001; Mouffe 2000, 2005, 2013; Connolly 2013). Although there are some important differences between them, in general agonists 'coalesce around an acknowledgement of pluralism, tragedy and the value of conflict' (Wenman 2013). Disagreements are integral to democratic politics. As Chantal Mouffe asserts most strongly, 'conflict and division are inherent to politics' (2000, 14). For agonists, political disagreements are not (only) salutary expressions of difference that are likely to emerge within political negotiations, but also come from outside the already counted political order, and that offer to disrupt the status quo and enliven politics.

Climate change seems to be particularly liable to disagreement (Smith 2003; Hulme 2009; Machin 2013; Machin and Smith 2014). But disagreement about the interpretations and implications of climate change is not necessarily rooted in irrationality, immorality or ignorance; it can, on the contrary, be entirely reasonable. As James Tully notices: "in any agreement we reach on procedures, principles, ethics, scientific studies or policies with respect to the environment … there will always be an element of reasonable disagreement, and thus the possibility of raising a reasonable doubt and dissention" (2001, 162). Disagreement over environmental issues may not be a clash of interests but rather a conflict between different of ways of being and living (Connolly 2013, 49). Climate change might make us think differently about ourselves and our environment. But it is unlikely that we will all think the same way.

The insight of 'green agonism', then, is that climate change might well be better served through the acknowledgement of the existence of political disagreement and at the same time, democratic institutions and practices might be enriched through the clash of perspectives over environmental issues. There are three central claims of the green agonist pathway (for a more detailed account see Machin 2020). First, it is suggested, if democratic disagreement is respected and celebrated rather than repressed, it becomes more likely, although certainly not guaranteed, that new ideas emerge for tackling climate change. Second, democratic disagreement allows legitimate challenges to be made prevailing assumptions, allowing the radical disruption of unsustainable institutions and conventions and the divergence onto a different path. Third, disagreement over environmental issues between political groups enlivens democratic politics, for it is only with real political differences that passionate identifications are made and strong coalitions are formed. In contrast to the 'deliberative spaces' called for by Stevenson and Dryzek, for example, this approach calls for disruptive moments.

But for green agonism it is crucial that political disagreement is expressed as legitimate disagreement between adversaries or 'friendly enemies' rather than violent antagonism between enemies that threatens the destruction of the political realm (2000, 13). According to Mouffe it is precisely by allowing the expression of difference that the emergence of antagonistic conflicts is kept in check (Mouffe 2005, 21). Therefore in order to protect and nurture democracy, political institutions, though themselves not immune from contestation, must facilitate the expression of political differences, while preventing that such expression from becoming antagonistic. The challenge for 'green agonism' is that in the current polarised and populist political climate, disagreement is often disrespectful on the one hand while it is disavowed on the other.

Conclusion

No longer the marginal concern of green activists, climate change has moved onto the political centre stage. In climate protests over the last few years, eco-warriors have been joined on the streets by children and their grandparents, scientists, farmers and 'yellow vests', rallying to demand or resist climate policy change. In September 2019, millions of people from 150 countries reportedly gathered for a 'global climate strike', drawing citizens into active political participation.[3] This indicates not only that there is a growing politicisation of the issue of a changing climate but that this issue is stirring political activism, discussion and contestation. I have argued in this chapter that the politics around climate change has the potential to enliven democracy. I have suggested that we might consider how a transforming climate might provoke the transformation of the political landscape, by cutting out new pathways towards green democracy.

These five 'pathways' I have emphasised all consist what Andrew Stirling would call a 'transformation', in contrast to a 'transition' (Stirling 2014). They do not all lead in the same direction and it is unlikely that all of them can be travelled at the same time. But it might be that there are junctions at which the productive tensions between them can be assessed.

While all of these pathways contain important insights, I suggest that the fifth pathway of green agonism is particularly worth heeding. If we want to tackle climate change without giving up on democracy, we need strong political alternatives that engage citizens, revive the public realm and disrupt the socio-economic structures that impede both democracy and sustainability.

Notes

1 The violation of the 'all-affected principle'.
2 In 2016, Wales established a Future Generations Commissioner as part of the Well-being of Future Generations Act See www.futuregenerations.wales/about-us/future-generations-act/
3 www.theguardian.com/environment/2019/sep/27/climate-crisis-6-million-people-join-latest-wave-of-worldwide-protests

References

Archibugi, D. and Held D., 2011. Cosmopolitan Democracy: Paths and Agents. *Ethics & International Affairs*, 25(4), 433–461.
Baber, W.F. and Barlett R.V., 2005. *Deliberative Environmental Politics: Democracy and Ecological Rationality*. Cambridge, MA: MIT Press.
Ball, T., 2006. Democracy. In A. Dobson and R. Eckersely, eds. *Political Theory and the Ecological Challenge*. Cambridge and New York: Cambridge University Press.
Barry, J., 1999. *Rethinking Green Politics: Nature, Virtue and Progress*. London, Thousand Oaks and New Delhi: Sage.
Barnett, J. and Campbell J., 2010. *Climate Change and Small Island States: Power, Knowledge and the South Pacific*. London and Washington: Earthscan.
Beckman, L. and Uggla F., 2016. An Ombudsman for Future Generations. In I. González-Ricoy and A. Gosseries, eds. *Institutions For Future Generations*. Oxford: Oxford University Press, 117–134.
Bernauer, T., 2013. Climate Change Politics. *Annual Review of Political Science*, 16, 421–448.
Bohman, J., 1998. The Coming of Age of Deliberative Democracy. *The Journal of Political Philosophy*, 6(4), 400–425.
Christiano, T., 2012. Rational Deliberation between Citizens. In J. Parkinson and J. Mansbridge, eds. *Deliberative Systems: Deliberative Democracy at the Large Scale*. New York: Cambridge University Press, 27–51.

Connolly, W., 2013. *The Fragility of Things: Self-organizing Processes, Neoliberal Fantasies and Democratic Activism*. Durham and London: Duke University Press.
Doherty, B. and de Geus, M., 1996. *Democracy and Green Political Thought: Sustainability, Rights and Citizenship*. London and New York: Routledge.
Carter, A., 1999. *A Radical Green Political Theory*. London and NY: Routledge.
Dean, R., Gagnon, J.P. and Asenbaum, H., 2019. What is Democratic Theory? *Democratic Theory*, 6 (2), v–xx.
Dodman, D. and Mitlin, D., 2015. The National and Local Politics of Climate Change Adaptation in Zimbabwe. *Climate and Development*, 7(3), 223–234.
Dobson, A., 1996. Representative Democracy and the Environment. In W. Lafferty and J. Meadowcroft, eds. *Democracy and the Environment*. Edward Elgar, 124–139.
Dryzek, J., 2000. *Deliberative Democracy and Beyond: Liberals, Critics, Contestations*. Oxford: Oxford University Press.
Dryzek, J., 2015. Global Deliberative Democracy. In J.F. Morin and A. Orsini, eds. *Essential Concepts of Global Environmental Governance*. Abingdon and New York: Routledge, 76–78.
Dryzek, J.S., et al., 2019. The crisis of democracy and the science of deliberation. *Science*, 363(6432), 1144–1146. https://doi.org/10.1126/science.aaw269
Eckersley, R., 2004. *The Green State: Rethinking Democracy and Sovereignty*. Cambridge and London: MIT Press.
Eckersley, R., 2017. Geopolitan Democracy in the Anthropocene. *Political Studies*, 65(4), 983–999.
Elster, J., 1986. The Market and the Forum: Three Varieties of Political Theory. In J. Elster and A. Hylland, eds. *Foundations of Social Choice Theory*. Cambridge: Cambridge University Press, 104–132.
Feinberg, J., 1974. The Rights of Animals and Unborn Generations. In W.T. Blackstone, eds. *Philosophy & Environmental Crisis*, University of Georgia Press, 43–68.
Fischer, F., 2017. *Climate Crisis and the Democratic Prospect: Participatory Governance in Sustainable Communities*. Oxford: Oxford University Press.
Garner, R., 2011. *Environmental Politics: The Age of Climate Change*. Hampshire and New York: Palgrave Macmillan.
Habermas, J., 1994. Three Normative Models of Democracy. *Constellations*, I(I), 1–10.
Hall, C., 2007. Recognizing the Passion in Deliberation: Toward a More Democratic Theory of Deliberative Democracy. *Hypatia*, 22(4), 81–95.
Hammond, M., 2020. Sustainability as a Cultural Transformation: The Role of Deliberative Democracy. *Environmental Politics*, 29(1), 173–192.
Hammond, M. and Smith, G., 2017. *Sustainable Prosperity and Democracy: A Research Agenda* [online]. Available from: https://core.ac.uk/download/pdf/161103463.pdf.
Hayward, B., 2020. *Children, Citizenship and Environment*. London and New York: Routledge.
Held, D., 1996. *Models of Democracy*. Cambridge and Oxford: Polity.
Held, D. and Fane-Hervey, A., 2011. Democracy, Climate Change and Global Governance: Democratic Agency and the Policy Menu Ahead. In D. Held, A. Fane-Hervey and M. Theros, eds. *The Governance of Climate Change*. Cambridge: Polity, 89–110.
Holden, B., 2002. *Democracy and Global Warming*. London and New York: Continuum.
Honig, B., 1993. *Political Theory and the Displacement of Politics*. Ithaca and London: Cornell University Press.
Honig, B., 2009. *Emergency Politics: Paradox, Law, Democracy*. Princeton and Oxford: Princeton University Press.
Hulme, M., 2009. *Why We Disagree About Climate Change: Understanding Controversy, Inaction and Opportunity*. Cambridge: Cambridge University Press.
Jamieson, D., 2020. Can democracies beat climate change? [online]. Available from: www.politico.eu/article/can-democracies-beat-climate-change/ [accessed 8 November 2020].
Karnein, A., 2016. Can we Represent Future Generations. In I. González-Ricoy and A. Gosseries, eds. *Institutions For Future Generations*. Oxford University Press, 83–97.
Kenis, A. and Mathij, E., 2014. (De)politicising the Local: The Case of the Transition Towns Movement in Flanders (Belgium). *Journal of Rural Studies*, 34, 172–183.
Leach, M., Scoones, I. and Stirling, A., 2010. *Dynamic Sustainabilities Technology, Environment, Social Justice*. London and New York: Earthscan.
Lidskog, R. and Elander, I., 2007. Representation, Participation or Deliberation? Democratic Responses to the Environmental Challenge. *Space and Polity*, 11(1), 75–94.
Litfin, K.T., 2014. *Ecovillages: Lessons for Sustainable Community*. Cambridge, Malden: Polity.

Machin, A., 2013. *Negotiating Climate Change: Radical Democracy and the Illusion of Consensus*. London: Zed Books.

Machin, A., 2020. Democracy, Disagreement, Disruption: Agonism and the Environmental State. *Environmental Politics*, 29(1), 155–172.

Machin, A. and Smith, G., 2014. Means, Ends, Beginnings: Environmental Technocracy, Ecological Deliberation or Embodied Democracy? *Ethical Perspectives*, 21(1), 47–72.

Manin, B., 1987. On Legitimacy and Political Deliberation. *Political Theory*, 15(3), 338–368.

Miller, D., 1992. Deliberative Democracy and Social Choice. *Political Studies*, 40, 54–67.

Mouffe, C., 2000. *The Democratic Paradox*. London and New York: Verso.

Mouffe, C., 2005. *On the Political*. London and New York: Routledge.

Mouffe, C., 2013. *Agonistics: Thinking the World Politically*. London: Verso.

Niemeyer, S., 2013. Democracy and Climate Change: What Can Deliberative Democracy Contribute. *Australian Journal of Politics and History*, 59(3), 429–448.

Parkinson, J. and Jane M., 2012. *Deliberative Systems: Deliberative Democracy at the Large Scale*. Cambridge: Cambridge University Press.

Pickering, J., Bäckstrand, K. and Schlosberg, D., 2020. Between Environmental and Ecological Democracy: Theory and Practice at the Democracy-Environment nexus. *Journal of Environmental Policy & Planning*, 22(1), 1–15.

Ruser, A., 2018. *Climate Politics and the Impact of Think Tanks: Scientific Expertise in Germany and the US*. Cham: Palgrave Macmillan.

Ruser, A. and Machin, A., 2017. *Against Political Compromise: Sustaining Democratic Debate*. Abingdon and New York: Routledge.

Sanders, L.M., 1997. Against Deliberation. *Political Theory*, 25(3), 347–376.

Smith, G., 2003. *Deliberative Democracy and the Environment*. London and New York: Routledge.

Smith, G., 2021. *Can Democracy Safeguard the Future?* Cambridge, Medford: Polity Press.

Stevenson, H., and Dryzek, J., 2014. *Democratizing Global Climate Governance*. New York: Cambridge University Press.

Stehr, N. and Machin, A., 2019. *Society and Climate: Transformations and Challenges*. Singapore: World Scientific.

Stirling, A., 2014. *Emancipating Transformations: From Controlling 'the Transition' to Culturing Plural Radical Progress* [online]. Available from: https://steps-centre.org/wp-content/uploads/Transformations.pdf.

Tully, J., 2001. An Ecological Ethics for the Present. In B. Gleeson and N. Low, eds. *Governing for the Environment: Global Problems, Ethics and Democracy*. New York: Palgrave, 147–164.

Vlerick, M., 2020. Towards Global Cooperation: The Case for a Deliberative Global Citizens' Assembly. *Global Policy*, 11(3), 305–314.

Wendling, Z. A., Emerson, J. W., de Sherbinin, A., Esty, D. C., et al. 2020. *Environmental Performance Index*. New Haven, CT: Yale Center for Environmental Law & Policy.

Wenman, M., 2013. *Agonistic Democracy: Constituent Power in the Era of Globalisation*. Cambridge: Cambridge University Press.

22
BIODIVERSITY CONSERVATION AND THE ROLE OF DEMOCRACY

Stefan Ewert and Susanne Stoll-Kleemann

Introduction

Securing biodiversity is one of the most important environmental challenges facing the world today. Biosphere integrity is one out of four of the overall nine planetary boundaries that have already been exceeded (Steffen et al. 2015). The loss of species 'affect[s] the functioning of a wide variety of organisms and ecosystems' (Cardinale et al. 2006, 989). Biodiversity experiments show that greater diversity leads to higher productivity and stability of ecosystems (Tilman 2000). Thus, biodiversity loss threatens the livelihood of humans through unpredictable effects, e.g., on food production or health. Next to the physical functional reasons, other authors emphasize that a species-rich nature is linked to the intellectual and spiritual needs of humans (Angermeier 2000) or argue with the intrinsic value of nature in order to justify nature conservation (Gorke 2003). Therefore, it is obvious that there is a strong relationship between the discourses on biodiversity and sustainable development (e.g., Perrings et al. 1992; Secretariat of the Convention on Biological Diversity 2001). Biodiversity loss can be seen as a core problem of sustainability. With the designation of the UN Decade for Biodiversity (2011–2020), the United Nations underlined the central importance of the variability among life on Earth for sustainable development.

Research over the past 20 years has identified a number of drivers whose interaction causes a decline in biodiversity far beyond the natural rate of extinction. These include climate change, habitat loss and fragmentation, overexploitation of natural resources and eutrophication, and the emergence of invasive species (Brook et al. 2008). From a social science perspective, Wood et al. (2013) identify several socioeconomic factors as 'root causes' for the loss of biodiversity that have an effect on these drivers. Amongst others, they describe international market pressure and trade liberalization as the main 'root cause' of species extinctions (Wood et al. 2013). Over the last ten years, a lot of empirical examinations have been carried out on the question of the relationship between such economic factors and biodiversity. Often, economic development is associated with the ecological hope that an increasing gross domestic product of a country will also lead to improved environmental protection. However, most research shows that the assumption of a U-shaped relationship between economic prosperity and environment protection (the so-called 'environmental Kuznets curve') holds rather not true for species conservation (Dietz and Adger 2003; Mills and Waite 2009). Growing prosperity leads to a growing number of threatened species, irrespective of the economic starting level. 'There is reason to expect, as with other global problems, that it is not possible to "grow out of" the problem of biodiversity decline' (Dietz and Adger 2003, 23).

But, might democracy help out of the problem? While Wood et al. (2013) do not refer to democracy in their study on socioeconomic factors of biodiversity loss, the role of democratic governance is part of several theoretical reflections and empirical studies on nature conservation and biodiversity protection. In this chapter, we summarize this research and ask if a certain form of democracy and democratic legitimacy might have a positive influence on nature conservation. In other words: Is it possible to 'participate out of' the problem? Before we do so, we start with the definition of nature conservation and biodiversity and an outline of the history of the concepts. At the end of our contribution, we look at the role of democracy in the management of protected areas, especially Biosphere Reserves, and outline the complexity of biodiversity protection in human land use outside protected areas.

Nature conservation and biodiversity

Environmental historians date the impact of humans on the extinction of species back to the late Pleistocene, some 50,000 years ago (McNeill 2012). Human activities and provisions by authorities in order to save nature and to avoid extinctions are known for a lot of ancient cultures. Hambler and Canney (2013, 3) list examples for the protection of species from past societies in different world regions dating back more than 2,500 years ago. However, in the context of humans' relationship with nature, the term 'conservation' is relatively new. It has been used for about 100 years and can be defined as:

> protection of wildlife from irreversible harm. Wildlife includes all non-domestic species and populations of plants, microorganisms and animals, and their habitats. By 'harm', we mean damage or decline due to people.
>
> *Hambler and Canney 2013, 2*

While the diversity of species or certain habitats has long been the focus of biological and ecological research, *biodiversity* is a relatively new term. It has only been used in public discourse for almost 40 years. A number of scientists – amongst others the famous biologist Edward O. Wilson – introduced the term in the 1980s in order to raise public awareness for the growing rates of species extinction and the human impact on this development (Maclaurin and Sterelny 2008). Thus, the term had a political dimension from the very beginning of its use by scientists. Biodiversity gained worldwide attention with the establishment of the Convention on Biological Diversity (CBD) at the beginning of the 1990s. The multilateral treaty was opened for signature in 1992 at the United Nations Conference on Environment and Development (UNCED) in Rio de Janeiro and demonstrates the close links between biodiversity protection and sustainable development. The Convention defines in article 2:

> 'Biological diversity' means the variability among living organisms from all sources including, *inter alia*, terrestrial, marine and other aquatic ecosystems and the ecological complexes of which they are a part: this includes diversity within species, between species and of ecosystems.
>
> *United Nations 1992, 3*

Even if the estimation of the current species extinction rate is highly controversial amongst biologists, most scientists agree that we experience the sixth mass extinction period in Earth's history at the moment. There is a consensus that mankind is responsible for most of the extinctions. The 'background' extinction rate (i.e., the extinction rate in 'normal' times between mass extinction events) is estimated to be 'somewhere between 0.1 and 1 species extinction per 10,000 species per 100 years' (Ceballos et al. 2015, 1). In contrast, the extinction rate today is somewhere between 100 and 1,000 times higher than the background rate (Pimm et al. 1995; Mace et al. 2005). Given the importance of all species for ecosystem functioning and stability, biodiversity loss is one of the major threats to the future of mankind and the life on Earth. In their highly influential definition of planetary boundaries, Rockström et al. (2009) describe the loss of biodiversity as one of the boundaries which are already exceeded substantially.

Democracy and biodiversity

As outlined in the introduction, research has identified different reasons for biodiversity loss. These reasons can be differentiated in drivers like climate change, eutrophication, or the emergence of invasive species and 'root causes' as socioeconomic factors (like trade liberalization) behind (Brook et al. 2008; Wood et al. 2013). Political factors have an impact on these drivers and causes of biodiversity loss. Basically, policy instruments like the protection of certain species or the designation of protected areas are used in all political systems. Thus, the question arises: Do democracies perform better in biodiversity protection?

At the theoretical level, the debate can be closely linked to the debate on the relationship between democracy and environmental protection in general. First, democracy is more open to new insights and arguments since freedom of information should be guaranteed here. Following this argument, a political decision to protect a species or habitat and its effective implementation is more likely in a democracy, as scientists and conservation associations can freely articulate their knowledge and beliefs. In addition, one might assume a positive effect on the environment due to secured property rights and flourishing environmental activism (Dietz and Adger 2003). The second assumption is that democracies create more public goods because the entire population, not just the elite, controls the political process (Scruggs 2009). In the logic of this argument, the establishment of a new protected area is more likely in a democracy since the population demands the protection as a public good. Third, the duration and structure of the democratic process lead to improved outcomes. In the case of biodiversity conservation, the democratic political process of, e.g., the designation of a new protected area, opens the time and space for weighing different arguments and thus leads to a better implementation (Scruggs 2009). DeCaro and Stokes (2008) extend the debate to a socio-psychological argument. From the point of view of different social-psychological theories, they explain why democratic engagement might increase the conservation success: An autonomous, non-coercive motivation (rather than motivation imposed autocratically from outside) makes conservation part of an individual's self-identity and thus facilitates effective conservation projects.

Another argument refers to the role of science. Scientific integrity is a crucial precondition for effective nature conservation and biodiversity protection. For example, a national list of species protected by law has to be compiled and updated with scientific support. The coverage of species in a certain area or whole country and the assessment of its development need scientific knowledge. The freedom to conduct research and to publish free from censorship is a pivotal element of liberal democracies. Carroll et al. (2017) show that the selection of scientific reviewers for the compilation of lists of endangered species is highly politicized. They demonstrate that scientific integrity is in danger also in established democracies. Nevertheless, the open, democratic society is still most appropriate to make this process public and to find the most suitable researchers for scientific support.

However, a lot of the theoretical arguments might also hold true for political decisions that are in line with people's will but not with conservation aims. Most of these arguments 'are more or less procedural and hence non-directional' (Rydén et al. 2020, 420). In addition, the literature on the relationship between democracy and sustainability in general also presents theoretical arguments for a negative impact of democracy, which can be transferred to the question of the impact on biodiversity in particular. Mitchell (2006) identifies several factors in liberal democracies that might hinder effective nature conservation. For example, periodic elections force political activities into short- and medium-term time frames, while biodiversity protection needs long-term engagement and often only shows long-term effects. Liberal democracies are acting in a global political economy, which favors powerful interests and hamper nature conservation (Mitchell 2006). In addition, the performance of democracies in the field of lobby control and the fight against corruption is ambivalent (Winslow 2005).

To find empirical evidence, Rydén et al. (2020) evaluated 58 macro-quantitative studies dealing with the correlation between democracy and biodiversity. Most of these studies used deforestation as a proxy for biodiversity, other proxies like the proportion of protected areas or the red list threat are rarely used. A direct assessment of biodiversity on the national level (e.g., on the basis of DNA sequencing) is almost impossible at the moment due to data availability. In almost all studies investigated, democracy was only one of several independent variables tested.

As a result, the empirical findings are mixed. Some studies (e.g., Li and Reuveny 2006) find a positive correlation between democracy and biodiversity, while others identify a negative correlation (e.g., Marquart-Pyatt 2004). Most studies find out a mixed relationship between both variables. Due to the lack of adequate data for both the dependent and the independent variable and poor model specifications on the theoretical level, Rydén et al. (2020) conclude that 'the existing literature on the empirical link between biodiversity conservation and political regimes is ambiguous and important facets for a synthetic understanding are missing' (Rydén et al. 2020, 429).

This conclusion is also true for the political level above and below the nation-state. On the global level, the Convention on Biological Diversity (CBD) sets the legal framework, while the financial framework is given by the Global Environment Facility (Wood et al. 2013). There is a lot of literature that evaluates the success of the CBD (e.g., Wood et al. 2013; Borrini-Feyerabend and Hill 2015), most of them conclude that the success is rather limited. Most of the political science analyses in the field are theoretical or conceptual (cf. Agrawal and Ostrom 2006). For example, Rask and Worthington (2015) ask how deliberation can increase biodiversity protection success also on the global level. However, empirical evidence for the impact of the democratic quality of international institutions on conservation success is even more difficult to provide here than in a comparative analysis of national policies.

Between the global level and the nation-states, powerful regional agreements for nature conservation exist in some regions of the world. This is particularly the case in the European Union, where the Natura 2000 network is the main legal framework for species and habitat protection. Studies on this regional level often deal with the question of democratic legitimacy. Engelen et al. (2007) show that at the beginning of the EU nature conservation policy, legitimacy was to be generated above all by scientific evidence. But clashes with local interests created a legitimacy deficit. Different case studies examine how European nation-states shifted from substantive to more procedural sources of legitimacy within the Natura 2000 framework (see, e.g., the different contributions in Keulartz and Leistra 2007). These studies argue that participatory forms of democratic decision-making create legitimacy and that the acceptance for collectively binding decisions has a positive impact on nature protection projects.

The example of Natura 2000 shows how strongly the various political levels are interwoven in the field of nature conservation. The EU's Natura 2000 network as the legal frame refers to the global aims in biodiversity protection, and the nation-states try to adjust the European frame in order to create legitimacy on the local level. In conservation science, the strengthening of the participation of the local level has been and is being promoted in order to increase the effectiveness of conservation policy (cf. summarizing Brosius et al. 2005). Sustainable use and effective nature conservation should be implemented via community-based natural resource management. This idea

> is based on several premises: that local populations have a greater interest in the sustainable use of resources than does the state or distant corporate managers, that local communities are more cognizant of the intricacies of local ecological processes and practices, and that communities are more able to effectively manage those resources through local or traditional forms of access.
>
> *Tsing et al. 2005, 1*

However, the understanding of the role of the community in the conservation process follows still different approaches (community as a small spatial unit, as a homogeneous social structure, or as shared norms, cf. Agrawal and Gibson 1999) and often remains vague. A lot of scholars take a policy-advising, rather normative perspective and recommend the reinforcement and democratization of the local level. For example, Bawa et al. (2011) call for more democratic involvement of the local communities, especially in developing countries, in order to 'allow local institutions to seek more equal returns on the global benefits accrued from conservation of biological diversity that are currently being captured by state agencies and conservation groups' (Bawa et al. 2011, 640). Democratic governance of natural resources should not only empower the local people but also help to implement effective protection of species and ecosystems due to increased legitimacy.

There is some empirical evidence that supports these theoretical assumptions, but the evidence relates mainly to case studies (Cetas and Yasué 2017). For example, Ranger et al. (2016) show with a case study on marine protected areas in the southeast of England that certain forms of local participation boost the acceptance of conservation management and contribute to conservation success in that way. Others warn against too much participation at the local level, and too strong emphasis on consensus, as this underpins the status quo and at least delays protection efforts (Peterson et al. 2005). Here again, the question is not whether democracy might impact conservation success, but *what form* of democracy could do this best. Therefore, we outline the discourse on different types of democracy and biodiversity protection in the next section.

Which kind of democracy is best? The question of democratic legitimacy

As the previous section has outlined, democracies are not necessarily better than non-democracies in nature conservation. There are theoretical and empirical arguments in favor of a positive relationship between democracy and biodiversity protection, but also some arguments against it. It also seems to be the case that within democracies, various conditions must be met in order to effectively protect biodiversity. There is a whole range of research to identify these conditions, to clarify the underlying causalities, and to recommend a certain policy or institutional design on that basis.

One crucial question in this field is the construction of democratic legitimacy (Engelen et al. 2007). The main criterion for democratic legitimacy is mutual justification (Lafont 2015). This requires that decision-making in the field of biodiversity protection has to 'track [...] the interests and the ideas of those citizens whom it affects' (Pettit 1997, 184). For several decades, democratic conservation policy can be interpreted to have emphasized the output legitimacy. Following this approach, decisions by the government, the parliament and/or the administration were based on expert judgments in order to gain acceptance. Ecologists defined the good ecological status and measures to achieve it. This is especially true for the European nature protection policy. In the first time of the Natura 2000 policy, the direct consultations were conducted only with scientists (Turnhout et al. 2015), even if the decision to be taken was always influenced by power, values and beliefs, emotions and history (Peterson et al. 2013). But scientists were the only group consulted in the decision-making process during that time. Keulartz (2009) shows that this expertocratic policy provoked a lot of resistance amongst landowners and land users. As an answer to this, new forms of participatory governance were introduced in a lot of countries in the 1990s. Peterson et al. (2005) show how the sustainability discourse in the late 1980s brought the idea of participative, consensual decision-making in nature conservation policies. These new approaches were rather input-oriented. Stakeholder consultation and participation in decision making were the new concepts for legitimacy building. The overarching objective was a consensus (Peterson et al. 2005). The procedural approach of input legitimacy generation has been added to the approach of substantial legitimacy creation through scientific consultations (cf. Keulartz and Leistra 2007). Not surprisingly, both approaches came into conflict. The scientific debate for and against more participation and the appropriate forms of public involvement is still ongoing. The debate can be linked to the observation of an ongoing shift from input to output legitimacy in theories of democracy in general (Buchstein and Jörke 2007). The discourse on the deliberative approaches (cf. Rosenberg 2007) revealed the tensions between the quality of deliberation in the decision-making process and the requirement of broad participation.

Proponents of participatory approaches argue that scientific input can define the best possible ecological status, but at the same time creates resistance on the ground that hinders implementation. Participation, on the other hand, brings new knowledge into the conservation process and increases the identification of (local) participants with conservation projects (see above). Therefore, these authors consider citizen participation as the key to transform democracies into ecological democracies (Mitchell 2006). Critics, on the other hand, point to several problems: A broad participation is costly and time-intensive and might delay urgent conservation projects; it might dilute conservation aims and the scientific input (Keulartz 2009). '[T]he attempt to placate everyone risks the attenuation of any impetus for change and reifies the status quo' (Peterson et al. 2005, 764).

Proponents and opponents give anecdotic empirical evidence for their respective assertions. For example, Leach (2006) suggests that from the point of view of ecological restoration, a lot of consensus-based projects have been successful in the past. Redpath et al. (2017) argue that for the protection of large carnivores, coercive top-down forms of conservation governance help best when the population is very low, while more participative forms of governance and active stakeholder involvement are more suitable when the populations recover. However, systematic empirical evidence for the question of which type of democracy is better for the effective protection of endangered species is scarce. Empirical research on that question has to deal with a lot of uncertainties (Redpath et al. 2017) and external effects. Some case studies point out methods that successfully combined participation and effective conservation. Ranger et al. (2016, see above) tested innovative forms of stakeholder participation, e.g., film production, in order to document interviews and workshops with 'management option carousels' and could increase the success in the management of marine protected areas in that way.

One can conclude from these case studies that participation in conservation policy is not the solution per se but must meet certain criteria. Non-transparent participation processes and unrepresentative participation institutions do neither protect biodiversity nor can they create legitimacy (López-Bao et al. 2017), but innovative forms of participation can meet both objectives. However, the democratic question then is: Who defines these participation models and who decides in a particular conservation project about the form of participation and the participants to invite? From the perspective of democracy, this is still an open question in nature conservation projects.

With the shift from the expertocratic approach of nature conservation to more participatory approaches, science lost its privileged position in the consultation process. Since that, conservation scientists discuss their role in conservation policy. Most conservation biologists see themselves as the scientific experts for biodiversity and conclude from this the obligation for political activities and public commitment (Robertson and Hull 2001; Rose 2015). Paul Angermeier defined as a task for the scientific community:

> To be effective, conservation biologists will need to frankly acknowledge crucial values, consistently incorporate those values into management actions, and, ultimately, persuade many people outside the discipline to adopt these values.
>
> Angermeier 2000, 374

The complexity and often uncertainty of ecological phenomena make it difficult to contribute to public deliberations and decision making, but necessary at the same time (Lackey 2007). To be noticed, conservation scientists should know the mechanisms of the democratic policy-making process and use this knowledge in order to place the scientific evidence in the decision-making (Rose 2015).

Biodiversity protection in protected areas and biosphere reserves

Establishing and managing protected areas is still a common strategy for reducing biodiversity loss and ecosystem services. Recent studies on the global level show that, on average, protected areas have a positive effect on biodiversity (Gray et al. 2016). Unfortunately, the destructive activities of human beings can become so overwhelming that the status 'protected' is no longer a safeguard for a species-rich area. Watson et al. (2014) have argued that protected areas are becoming ripe for declassification and vulnerable to resource extraction because governments have heavily reduced their support towards protected areas 'through disproportionate funding cuts, reductions in professional staff and by ignoring their own policies' (Watson et al. 2014, 70). This holds true not only for countries in the Global South but for established democracies (such as Australia, the United States and Canada) as well.

> This practice has been labelled protected area downgrading, downsizing and degazettement (PADDD), where downgrading is the legal authorization of an increase in the number, magnitude or extent of human activities within a protected area; downsizing is the decrease in size of a protected area through a legal boundary change; and degazettement is the loss of legal protection for an entire protected area.
>
> Watson et al. 2014, 70

All three forms of PADDD are increasing. Mascia et al. (2014) show that PADDD is mainly caused by access to and use of land in the protected areas, in particular for industrial-scale resource extraction. Here, the clear contradiction between sustainability and economic growth becomes evident. Therefore, degrowth is discussed as a strategy for sustainability in the field of biodiversity protection, too. The 'pathway towards a sustainable future is to be found in a democratic and redistributive downscaling of the biophysical size of the global economy' (Asara et al. 2015, 375). In these approaches, democracy is mostly understood as broad and deep citizen participation.

Globally, there is a massive expansion of agricultural land use due to the sharp increase in meat and dairy product consumption and the concomitant demand for huge swathes of terrain devoted to livestock feed cultivation, especially soya and maize (Godfray et al. 2010; Foley et al. 2011; Garnett et al. 2013). This has not spared Protected Areas and Biosphere Reserves (see below) from the land-grab that now affects protected areas around the world (Watson et al. 2014; Lahsen et al. 2016). Next to the expansion of agricultural land use, we see an intensification of agricultural practices on the global scale (Foley et al. 2011). The negative consequences of non-sustainable intensive land use are extending into protected areas and biosphere reserves (see text and maps for Europe and Germany in Levers et al. (2016); cf. Garnett et al. (2013) and Stoll-Kleemann and Kettner (2016)). One approach here would be to create landscapes that took care of both the needs of humans and the natural environment coupled with responsible cooperation. Such lived-in landscapes would correspond to large tracts of land where biodiversity conservation is practiced in coherence with people living and working in the area and striving for sustainable livelihoods. Different models of living landscapes already exist, of which the Biosphere Reserve model is the best known (UNESCO 1996; Batisse 1997; Ishwaran et al. 2008; Coetzer et al. 2014; Bridgewater 2016; Reed 2016).

While one part of the Biosphere Reserve concept still seeks to focus on managing core zones for biodiversity conservation, it also tries to respond creatively to the underlying causes of biodiversity loss and ecosystem destruction by piloting more sustainable land use and living options in all realms of life. Biosphere Reserves, launched by the Man and the Biosphere (MAB) Programme of UNESCO in 1970, form a worldwide network of representative landscapes, with 669 sites across 120 countries. Their primary goal is to serve as learning sites for information exchange on environmental policy, sustainable development and appropriate management practices (UNESCO 1996). Furthermore, they were explicitly designed to be experimental where environmental change could be monitored and remediative policies or practices could be 'tested' (UNESCO 1996; Batisse 1997; Price et al. 2010; Reed 2016; Köck and Arnberger 2017).

According to the Statutory Framework (UNESCO 1996), Biosphere Reserves are expected to fulfill three main complementary functions: the conservation function of in situ conservation of natural and semi-natural ecosystems and landscapes; a development function to foster sustainable economic and human development; and the logistic function to support research, monitoring, environmental education and training. Coetzer et al. (2014, 83) warn that 'conceptually the Biosphere Reserve model is attractive, yet the practical reality is likely to be challenging'. One reason is that Biosphere Reserves remain under the sovereignty and legislation of the country in which they are designated. Thus, the state can ignore the requirements of any designation, as well as the management objectives of the individual protected areas contained within the Biosphere Reserve. A further reason is that the implementation of the MAB Programme is struggling with horizontal integration at the local level, as well as vertical integration with national authorities (Pool-Stanvliet 2014). The result is a considerable gap between the Biosphere Reserve concept and reality worldwide (Price 2002; Ishwaran et al. 2008; Stoll-Kleemann and Welp 2008; Bridgewater 2016; Reed 2016; van Cuong et al. 2017a).

Generally, one of the most important purposes of Biosphere Reserves is to develop and initiate cooperation among authorities and other involved parties (UNESCO 1996; Bouamrane 2007; Schultz et al. 2011; UNESCO 2015). Thus, considerations on democracy and especially the participation of inhabitants are crucial in the concept of Biosphere Reserves. Strengthening Biosphere Reserves' advisory bodies to serve better management boards by adding representatives from different interest groups and agencies is one way to institute better overall cooperation (UNESCO 2015; Köck and Arnberger 2017). In cases where a Biosphere Reserve administration does not have a strong regulatory role, it could nevertheless become an initiator and mediator of efforts towards improved democratic participation. This would also bundle limited resources, which has been mentioned previously as an obstacle to effective participation (Stoll-Kleemann and Welp 2008; Schultz et al. 2011; Pool-Stanvliet 2014).

The task of effectively engaging communities in the governance and management of Biosphere Reserves is a complex one that involves many hurdles. Substantial long-term commitments of financial and human resources are needed to establish continuity, competence and trust. Power asymmetries between conservation institutions and local populations as well as among local actors themselves need to be better related and resolved. Parties capable of and willing to work for common conservation compromises need to be found, championed and negotiated with (Pimm et al. 1995; Stoll-Kleemann and Welp 2008; Stoll-Kleemann et al. 2010; Pool-Stanvliet 2014; van Cuong et al. 2017b). These ideal conditions are rarely in place. In addition, factors beyond the control of the Biosphere Reserve communities and their management, such as structural poverty, corruption and weak governance may overwhelm even the best-designed programs, with degradation and destruction of biodiversity as the final output of these failures (Stoll-Kleemann et al. 2010; van Cuong et al. 2017b). In cases where the Biosphere Reserve administration has a strong regulatory function in regard to land use and construction activities, such as in some areas of Germany, the administration might be too involved in promoting nature and landscape-protection interests to be acknowledged by all actors as a legitimate 'neutral' governing partner (Stoll-Kleemann and Welp 2008) and not as an expertocratic top-down-institution. In most Biosphere Reserves, a number of agencies are involved in management, requiring messy negotiation strategies. Many bodies still perceive the typical Biosphere Reserve administration primarily as an authority for promoting nature conservation to the point of single-mindedness (Stoll-Kleemann and Welp 2008). The many advantages of the special status of Biosphere Reserves as model regions, as stated in the Statutory Framework and the Seville Strategy, should be better acknowledged and tested.

Democratic biodiversity protection outside protected areas

For the effective implementation of biodiversity protection measures, activities outside protected areas are necessary (Angermeier 2000). Thus, biodiversity protection is closely connected to all policies with an impact on agriculture, forestry and fishery. Several drivers of biodiversity loss like habitat fragmentation, overexploitation of natural resources and eutrophication are closely connected to agricultural practices. While the expansion of agriculture endangers biodiversity in protected areas (see above), the intensification of agriculture as global trend threatens biodiversity in general (Foley et al. 2011). Although sustainable farm practices have a positive influence on biodiversity, most practices – especially within the agricultural subsidy systems of the global north – foster biodiversity loss (Butler et al. 2007; Henle et al. 2008).

One example might illustrate this complex situation. Mires and peatlands are ecosystems with many highly specialized species (Joosten and Clarke 2002, 87–90). There is clear empirical evidence that conventional farming on organic soils – mainly on drained peatlands – not only leads to heavy greenhouse gas emissions, but also has negative consequences for biodiversity (van Diggelen et al. 2006). The only way to stop both the emissions and the loss of biodiversity is to rewet the peatlands. These rewetting might take place in protected areas, where the corresponding farmlands are taken out of use. But especially in densely populated regions, not all organic soils can be taken out of agricultural production. Therefore, sustainable use of peatlands outside of protected areas is necessary for the protection of species adapted to life in the mires. With paludiculture – the use of wet peatlands in a productive way – a concept for such a sustainable use has been developed and successfully tested (Wichtmann et al. 2016). However, in the case of Europe, agricultural subsidies are paid for agriculture on drained peatlands, but not on wet peatlands (Wichmann 2018). Thus, the incentives for farming on peatlands strongly support the unsustainable use. Additionally, next to the agricultural policy in the narrow sense, legislation in the fields of nature conservation, water use and climate protection has an influence on farming on peatlands (cf. Paavola et al. 2009). In the case of Europe, several inherent conflicts of objectives are examined in these fields that explain the weak regulatory effectiveness (Peters and von Unger 2019). This is an example of the challenge for multilevel democratic legislation: A coherent policy needs scientific expertise and policy integration, but has to integrate citizen participation in order to create input legitimacy simultaneously.

Conclusion

During the last years, much research has been done in order to investigate the relationship between democracy and biodiversity conservation. Overall, the examinations show that the evidence for the influence of democracy on biodiversity protection is contested. Furthermore, there is no consensus on which form of democratic legitimacy is best for nature conservation.

What does it mean for further research? To our understanding, there is a need for more academic studies in at least three very different analytical fields:

1. On the level of empirical studies, further research should investigate the interplay between the different factors that have an effect on biodiversity: How do (the quality of) democracy, the economic status, the demographic situation and other socioeconomic factors interact in their effect on nature conservation? And, looking at the different pilot projects on participatory nature conservation: Which form performs best in terms of biodiversity protection? Furthermore, the role of interest groups in nature conservation decision-making has to be analyzed more comprehensively. Many examples show that widespread lobbying efforts enjoy continuous significant success in shaping laws and weakening regulations in ways that work against not only climate but also biodiversity protection (Stengel 2011; Klein 2015). The activities of agribusiness lobby groups are obvious in the policy field and have strong impacts on biodiversity. However, evidence for this often comes from journalist analyzes (e.g., Balser and Bauchmüller 2019). As in other policy fields, it is still a challenge for empirical social science analyzes to investigate this influence systematically.
2. On the level of normative research on democracy, there is the need to adopt the discussion of democratic innovations to nature conservation. As we have worked out in the previous sections, the strengthening of the local democracy and participatory approaches are discussed manifold as a solution to biodiversity losses. Yet, the crucial questions of the democratic procedure remain unsolved so far: Who defines the local stakeholders and legitimate

interest groups? Who decides the form of participation and the final form of decision-making? Current research in the theories of democracy offers possible answers to these questions. For example, it might be promising to adopt the ideas of aleatory democracy to nature conservation projects (Buchstein 2010). Following this approach, it could be reasonable to draw the local stakeholders in participation processes by lot. As demonstrated in different experiments, the random sampling of participants in participation forums is crucial for deliberation (Fishkin and Luskin 2005) and might help to combat corruption.

3. Finally, the questions of the relationship between democracy and biodiversity might be traced back to the fundamental question if human existence within the planetary boundaries is compatible with continued economic growth. The ongoing question of the role and form of economic growth for sustainable development (cf. already Lélé 1991) has still to be investigated in the light of biodiversity loss. Generally, it remains very difficult in an environment driven primarily by the fortress mindsets promoting economic growth to meet all the criteria for real sustainability. Present patterns of growth are contradictory to all three dimensions of sustainability (Hueting 2010; Muraca 2012; Kallis et al. 2014; Kothari et al. 2014; Asara et al. 2015). Hueting (2010, 525) asserts, 'our planet is threatened by a wrong belief in a wrongly formulated growth'. The question of whether concepts such as 'green growth' are suitable with the aim of sustainability has to be answered in the light of biodiversity as well.

Sustainability research has often been described as multi-, inter-, and transdisciplinary (e.g., Stock and Burton 2011; Lang et al. 2012). The complexity of the research field requires an exchange across disciplinary boundaries, and the high urgency of the real-world problems also requires the involvement of actors beyond science (Lang et al. 2012). Furthermore, science must find its place in public decision-making. As outlined above, a discourse on this issue is taking place among biodiversity researchers. Our contribution has shown in which fields social scientists can contribute to inter- and transdisciplinary research for the protection of biodiversity. In this way, they can not only help to understand the social conditions of effective biodiversity protection. This research can also be a contribution to making democratic constellations more effective in reducing the loss of biodiversity and thus contribute to sustainable development.

References

Agrawal, A. and Gibson, C.C., 1999. Enchantment and disenchantment: the role of community in natural resource conservation. *World Development*, 27 (4), 629–649.

Agrawal, A. and Ostrom, E., 2006. Political science and conservation biology: a dialog of the deaf. *Conservation Biology*, 20 (3), 681–682.

Angermeier, P.L., 2000. The natural imperative for biological conservation. *Conservation Biology*, 14 (2), 373–381.

Asara, V., et al., 2015. Socially sustainable degrowth as a social–ecological transformation: repoliticizing sustainability. *Sustainability Science*, 10 (3), 375–384.

Balser, M. and Bauchmüller, M., 2019. Streit um Glyphosat-Zulassung Wie Lobbyisten Ministerien und Kanzleramt bearbeiteten. *Süddeutsche Zeitung*, 8 Jul.

Batisse, M., 1997. Biosphere reserves: a challenge for biodiversity conservation & regional development. *Environment: Science and Policy for Sustainable Development*, 39 (5), 6–33.

Bawa, K.S., Rai, N.D., and Sodhi, N.S., 2011. Rights, governance, and conservation of biological diversity. *Conservation Biology*, 25 (3), 639–641.

Borrini-Feyerabend, G. and Hill, R., 2015. Governance for the conservation of nature. In G.L. Worboys, et al., eds. *Protected area governance and management*. Canberra: ANU Press, 169–206.

Bouamrane, M., ed., 2007. *Dialogue in Biosphere Reserves: References, Practices and Experiences*. Paris: UNESCO.

Bridgewater, P., 2016. The Man and Biosphere programme of UNESCO: rambunctious child of the sixties, but was the promise fulfilled? *Current Opinion in Environmental Sustainability*, 19, 1–6.

Brook, B.W., Sodhi, N.S., and Bradshaw, C.J.A., 2008. Synergies among extinction drivers under global change. *Trends in Ecology & Evolution*, 23 (8), 453–460.

Brosius, P.J., Tsing, A.L., and Zerner, C., eds., 2005. *Communities and Conservation: Histories and Politics of Community-based Natural Resource Management*. Walnut Creek, CA: Rowman Altamira.

Buchstein, H., 2010. Reviving randomness for political rationality: elements of a theory of aleatory democracy. *Constellations*, 17 (3), 435–454.

Buchstein, H. and Jörke, D., 2007. Redescribing democracy. *Redescriptions: Political Thought, Conceptual History and Feminist Theory*, 11 (1), 178–200.

Butler, S.J., Vickery, J.A., and Norris, K., 2007. Farmland biodiversity and the footprint of agriculture. *Science*, 315 (5810), 381–384.

Cardinale, B.J., et al., 2006. Effects of biodiversity on the functioning of trophic groups and ecosystems. *Nature*, 443 (7114), 989.

Carroll, C., et al., 2017. Defending the scientific integrity of conservation-policy processes. *Conservation Biology*, 31 (5), 967–975.

Ceballos, G., et al., 2015. Accelerated modern human–induced species losses: Entering the sixth mass extinction. *Science Advances*, 1 (5), e1400253.

Cetas, E.R. and Yasué, M., 2017. A systematic review of motivational values and conservation success in and around protected areas. *0888–8892*, 31 (1), 203–212.

Coetzer, K.L., Witkowski, E.T.F., and Erasmus, B.F.N., 2014. Reviewing biosphere reserves globally: effective conservation action or bureaucratic label? *Biological Reviews*, 89 (1), 82–104.

DeCaro, D. and Stokes, M., 2008. Social-psychological principles of community-based conservation and conservancy motivation: attaining goals within an autonomy-supportive environment. *Conservation Biology*, 22 (6), 1443–1451.

Dietz, S. and Adger, W.N., 2003. Economic growth, biodiversity loss and conservation effort. *Journal of environmental management*, 68 (1), 23–35.

Engelen, E., Keulartz, J., and Leistra, G., 2007. European nature conservation policy making. In J. Keulartz and G. Leistra, eds. *Legitimacy in European Nature Conservation Policy: Case Studies in Multilevel Governance*. Dordrecht: Springer, 3–21.

Fishkin, J.S. and Luskin, R.C., 2005. Experimenting with a democratic ideal: deliberative polling and public opinion. *Acta Politica*, 40 (3), 284–298.

Foley, J.A., et al., 2011. Solutions for a cultivated planet. *Nature*, 478 (7369), 337.

Garnett, T., et al., 2013. Sustainable intensification in agriculture: premises and policies. *Science*, 341 (6141), 33–34.

Godfray, H.C.J., et al., 2010. Food security: the challenge of feeding 9 billion people. *Science*, 327 (5967), 812–818.

Gorke, M., 2003. *The Death of our Planet's Species: A Challenge to Ecology and Ethics*. London: Island Press.

Gray, C.L., et al., 2016. Local biodiversity is higher inside than outside terrestrial protected areas worldwide. *Nature Communications*, 7, 12306.

Hambler, C. and Canney, S.M., 2013. *Conservation*. Cambridge: Cambridge University Press.

Henle, K., et al., 2008. Identifying and managing the conflicts between agriculture and biodiversity conservation in Europe – a review. *Agriculture, Ecosystems & Environment*, 124 (1–2), 60–71.

Hueting, R., 2010. Why environmental sustainability can most probably not be attained with growing production. *Journal of Cleaner Production*, 18 (6), 525–530.

Ishwaran, N., Persic, A., and Tri, N.H., 2008. Concept and practice: the case of UNESCO biosphere reserves. *International Journal of Environment and Sustainable Development*, 7 (2), 118–131.

Joosten, H. and Clarke, D., 2002. *Wise Use of Mires and Peatlands*. Devon: International Mire Conservation Group and International Peat Society.

Kallis, G., Demaria, F., and D'Alisa, G., 2014. Introduction: degrowth. In G. D'Alisa, F. Demaria, and G. Kallis, eds. *Degrowth: A Vocabulary for a New Era*. London: Routledge, 1–17.

Keulartz, J., 2009. European nature conservation and restoration policy – problems and perspectives. *Restoration Ecology*, 17 (4), 446–450.

Keulartz, J. and Leistra, G., eds., 2007. *Legitimacy in European Nature Conservation Policy: Case Studies in Multilevel Governance*. Dordrecht: Springer.

Klein, N., 2015. *This Changes Everything: Capitalism vs. The Climate*. New York: Simon and Schuster.

Köck, G. and Arnberger, A., 2017. The Austrian Biosphere Reserves in the light of changing MAB strategies. *Eco. Mont-Journal on Protected Mountain Areas Research*, 9, 85–92.

Kothari, A., Demaria, F., and Acosta, A., 2014. Buen Vivir, degrowth and ecological Swaraj: alternatives to sustainable development and the green economy. *Development*, 57 (3–4), 362–375.

Lackey, R.T., 2007. Science, scientists, and policy advocacy. *Conservation Biology*, 21 (1), 12–17.

Lafont, C., 2015. Deliberation, participation, and democratic legitimacy: should deliberative mini-publics shape public policy? *Journal of Political Philosophy*, 23 (1), 40–63.

Lahsen, M., Bustamante, M.M.C., and Dalla-Nora, E.L., 2016. Undervaluing and overexploiting the Brazilian Cerrado at our peril. *Environment: Science and Policy for Sustainable Development*, 58 (6), 4–15.

Lang, D.J., et al., 2012. Transdisciplinary research in sustainability science: practice, principles, and challenges. *Sustainability Science*, 7 (1), 25–43.

Leach, W.D., 2006. Theories about consensus-based conservation. *Conservation Biology*, 20 (2), 573–575.

Lélé, S.M., 1991. Sustainable development: a critical review. *World Development*, 19 (6), 607–621.

Levers, C., et al., 2016. Drivers of changes in agricultural intensity in Europe. *Land Use Policy*, 58, 380–393.

Li, Q. and Reuveny, R., 2006. Democracy and environmental degradation. *International Studies Quarterly*, 50 (4), 935–956.

López-Bao, J.V., Chapron, G., and Treves, A., 2017. The Achilles heel of participatory conservation. *Biological Conservation*, 212, 139–143.

Mace, G.M., Masundire, H., and Baillie, J.E., 2005. Biodiversity. In R. Hassan, R. Scholes, and N. Ash, eds. *Ecosystems and Human Well-being: Current State and Trends*. Washington: Island Press, 79–115.

Maclaurin, J. and Sterelny, K., 2008. *What is Biodiversity?* Chicago: University of Chicago Press.

Marquart-Pyatt, S., 2004. A cross-national investigation of deforestation, debt, state fiscal capacity, and the environmental Kuznets Curve. *International Journal of Sociology*, 34 (1), 33–51.

Mascia, M.B., et al., 2014. Protected area downgrading, downsizing, and degazettement (PADDD) in Africa, Asia, and Latin America and the Caribbean, 1900–2010. *Biological Conservation*, 169, 355–361.

McNeill, J.R., 2012. Global environmental history: the first 150,000 years. In J.R. McNeill, E.S. Mauldin, and J. Wiley, eds. *A Companion to Global Environmental History*. Chichester [et al.]: Wiley Blackwell, 3–17.

Mills, J.H. and Waite, T.A., 2009. Economic prosperity, biodiversity conservation, and the environmental Kuznets curve. *Ecological Economics*, 68 (7), 2087–2095.

Mitchell, R.E., 2006. Green politics or environmental blues? Analyzing ecological democracy. *Public Understanding of Science*, 15 (4), 459–480.

Muraca, B., 2012. Towards a fair degrowth-society: justice and the right to a 'good life'beyond growth. *Futures*, 44 (6), 535–545.

Paavola, J., Gouldson, A., and Kluvánková-Oravská, T., 2009. Interplay of actors, scales, frameworks and regimes in the governance of biodiversity. *Environmental Policy and Governance*, 19 (3), 148–158.

Perrings, C., Folke, C., and Mäler, K.-G., 1992. The ecology and economics of biodiversity loss: the research agenda. *Ambio*, 201–211.

Peters, J. and von Unger, M., 2019. Moore im Rechtssystem der Europäischen Union. Eine Analyse anhand ausgewählter Mitgliedsstaaten. *Natur und Landschaft*, 94 (2), 45–51.

Peterson, M.N., et al., 2013. Why transforming biodiversity conservation conflict is essential and how to begin. *Pacific Conservation Biology*, 19 (2), 94–103.

Peterson, M.N., Peterson, M.J., and Peterson, T.R., 2005. Conservation and the myth of consensus. *Conservation Biology*, 19 (3), 762–767.

Pettit, P., 1997. *Republicanism: A Theory of Freedom and Government*. Oxford: Clarendon Press.

Pimm, S.L., et al., 1995. The future of biodiversity. *Science*, 269 (5222), 347–350.

Pool-Stanvliet, R., 2014. *The UNESCO MAB Programme in South Africa: current challenges and future options relating to the implementation of biosphere reserves*. Greifswald.

Price, M.F., 2002. The periodic review of biosphere reserves: a mechanism to foster sites of excellence for conservation and sustainable development. *Environmental Science & Policy*, 5 (1), 13–18.

Price, M.F., Park, J.J., and Bouamrane, M., 2010. Reporting progress on internationally designated sites: the periodic review of biosphere reserves. *Environmental Science & Policy*, 13 (6), 549–557.

Ranger, S., et al., 2016. Forming shared values in conservation management: an interpretive-deliberative-democratic approach to including community voices. *Ecosystem Services*, 21, 344–357.

Rask, M. and Worthington, R., 2015. *Governing Biodiversity Through Democratic Deliberation*. Abingdon: Routledge.

Redpath, S.M., et al., 2017. Don't forget to look down–collaborative approaches to predator conservation. *Biological Reviews*, 92 (4), 2157–2163.

Reed, M.G., 2016. Conservation (in) action: renewing the relevance of UNESCO biosphere reserves. *Conservation Letters*, 9 (6), 448–456.

Robertson, D.P. and Hull, R.B., 2001. Beyond biology: toward a more public ecology for conservation. *Conservation Biology*, 15 (4), 970–979.

Rockström, J., et al., 2009. Planetary boundaries: exploring the safe operating space for humanity. *Ecology and Society*, 14 (2).

Rose, D.C., 2015. The case for policy-relevant conservation science. *Conservation Biology*, 29 (3), 748-754.

Rosenberg, S.W., 2007. An introduction: theoretical perspectives and empirical research on deliberative democracy. In S.W. Rosenberg, ed. *Deliberation, Participation and Democracy: Can the People Govern?* London: Palgrave Macmillan, 1–22.

Rydén, O., et al., 2020. Linking democracy and biodiversity conservation: empirical evidence and research gaps. *Ambio* [online], 49 (2), 419–433. Available from: https://doi.org/10.1007/s13280-019-01210-0.

Schultz, L., Duit, A., and Folke, C., 2011. Participation, adaptive co-management, and management performance in the world network of biosphere reserves. *World Development*, 39 (4), 662–671.

Scruggs, L., ed., 2009. *Democracy and Environmental Protection: An Empirical Analysis*. Citeseer. http://citeseerx.ist.psu.edu/viewdoc/download?doi=10.1.1.516.2802&rep=rep1&type=pdf

Secretariat of the Convention on Biological Diversity, 2001. *Handbook of the Convention on Biological Diversity*. London: Earthscan/James & James.

Steffen, W., et al., 2015. Planetary boundaries: guiding human development on a changing planet. *Science*, 347 (6223), 1259855.

Stengel, O., 2011. Weniger ist schwer: Barrieren in der Umsetzung suffizienter Lebensstile; und wie wir sie überwinden können. *GAIA-Ecological Perspectives for Science and Society*, 20 (1), 26–30.

Stock, P. and Burton, R.J.F., 2011. Defining terms for integrated (multi-inter-trans-disciplinary) sustainability research. *Sustainability*, 3 (8), 1090–1113.

Stoll-Kleemann, S., de la Vega-Leinert, A Cristina, and Schultz, L., 2010. The role of community participation in the effectiveness of UNESCO Biosphere Reserve management: evidence and reflections from two parallel global surveys. *Environmental Conservation*, 37 (3), 227–238.

Stoll-Kleemann, S. and Kettner, A., 2016. Schutzgebiete. In K. Ott, J. Dierks, and L. Voget-Kleschin, eds. *Handbuch Umweltethik*. Stuttgart: Metzler Verlag, 305–311.

Stoll-Kleemann, S. and Welp, M., 2008. Participatory and integrated management of biosphere reserves: lessons from case studies and a global survey. *GAIA-Ecological Perspectives for Science and Society*, 17 (1), 161–168.

Tilman, D., 2000. Causes, consequences and ethics of biodiversity. *Nature*, 405 (6783), 208.

Tsing, A.L., Brosius, J.P., and Zerner, C., 2005. Introduction: raising questions about communities and conservation. In P.J. Brosius, A.L. Tsing, and C. Zerner, eds. *Communities and Conservation: Histories and Politics of Community-based Natural Resource Management*. Walnut Creek: Rowman Altamira, 1–34.

Turnhout, E., et al., 2015. The construction of legitimacy in European nature policy: expertise and participation in the service of cost-effectiveness. *Environmental Politics*, 24 (3), 461–480.

UNESCO, 1996. *Biosphere reserves: The Seville Strategy and the Statutory Framework of the World Network*.

UNESCO, 2015. *MAB Strategy*.

United Nations, 1992. *Convention on Biological Diversity*.

van Cuong, C., et al., 2017a. Factors influencing successful implementation of Biosphere Reserves in Vietnam: challenges, opportunities and lessons learnt. *Environmental Science & Policy*, 67, 16–26.

van Cuong, C., Dart, P., and Hockings, M., 2017b. Biosphere reserves: attributes for success. *Journal of Environmental Management*, 188, 9–17.

van Diggelen, R., et al., 2006. Fens and floodplains of the temperate zone: present status, threats, conservation and restoration. *Applied Vegetation Science*, 9 (2), 157–162.

Watson, J.E.M., et al., 2014. The performance and potential of protected areas. *Nature*, 515 (7525), 67.

Wichmann, S., 2018. *Economic incentives for climate smart agriculture on peatlands in the EU*: Report, CINDERELLA project, University of Greifswald/Greifswald Mire Centre.

Wichtmann, W., Schröder, C., and Joosten, H., eds., 2016. *Paludiculture-productive use of wet peatlands.* Stuttgart: Schweizerbart'sche Verlagsbuchhandlung.

Winslow, M., 2005. Is democracy good for the environment? *Journal of Environmental Planning and Management*, 48 (5), 771–783.

Wood, A., Stedman-Edwards, P., and Mang, J., 2013. *The Root Causes of Biodiversity Loss.* Hoboken: Taylor and Francis.

23
GENDERED PATHWAYS OF DEMOCRACY TO SUSTAINABILITY

Philippe Doneys and Bernadette P. Resurrección

Introduction

We argue in this chapter that gender is key to understanding ways democratic governance can more effectively generate sustainable solutions to current global challenges. We begin by asserting that sustainability has to be understood beyond simple environmental protection and mitigation of degradation in biophysical or technical terms and fixes – or even environmentally-protected economic development. Sustainability also entails a process that requires greater equity both between different groups and individuals at any particular moment, and between generations over time, and greater equity of, or over, different resources, rights and capacities. This is a wider view of sustainability that places democratic and equitable practices at its core (Leach et al. 2018; Nightingale et al. 2020). It is in this context that we position gender equality in any effort to advance sustainable development.

To put it in starker terms, in this chapter, we suggest that a lack of gender sensitive democratic governance will most likely lead to unsustainable forms of development: in a social sense, where members of current and future generations are not enjoying the same opportunities and benefits from sustainable development; and in an environmental sense, since the capacity of democratic systems to produce environment-friendly solutions are undermined by deeply patriarchal governance systems that fail to recognize women's and other socially-marginalized groups' environmental knowledge and practices. Altogether, these reduce their ability to benefit from sustainable resource management, and in the process also undermine their contribution to long term environmental solutions for all. That gender equality is essential to sustainable development is not new as such, in fact it is the basis of Sustainable Development Goal 5 (SDG 5) on gender equality. As UN Women argues, gender equality is 'also integral to all dimensions of inclusive and sustainable development,' which is fundamentally based on the norm and spirit of 'Leave No One Behind' that is core to the SDGs and Agenda 2030. 'In short, all the SDGs depend on the achievement of Goal 5' (UN Women 2020).

In this chapter, we break down this argument further to show dependencies and pathways between gender equality in democratic governance and the achievement of sustainable policy outcomes. To do this, we begin our discussion by re-visiting gender dimensions of democratic governance in formal political and liberal democratic regimes. Through our re-visit, we aim to highlight the trend of gender-related exclusions that, in turn, also define sustainable development policy realms. Drawing on this discussion, we shift to sustainable development to show how this is as much a politicized space where resources and knowledge are also often politically contested in gender- and social terms, despite the propensity of their proponents to rely on scientific knowledge to search for technical solutions. Overall, this chapter will then draw from aspects of both feminist political theory and feminist political ecology to show how sidestepping a gender lens is particularly short-sighted if we want democratic governance systems to create promising pathways towards sustainability.

Gender, democracy and politics

Feminist political theory has long seen a paradox in governance systems to deliver equitable benefits when their power structures are so enmeshed and infused with patriarchal values. This is the case both in terms of what these systems ignore (i.e. the personal is political has been a key motto of feminists condemning the lack of government intervention in the private or domestic sphere) and what they focus on (priorities such as infrastructure, military power or trade, often seen as benefiting men as they were until recently dominating these fields), hence explaining the claim by Catharine Mackinnon that 'the state is male in a feminist sense: the law sees and treats women the way men see and treat women' (MacKinnon 1989, 161–162). Here, we refer to 'politics' as formal political systems of governance and representation as a site of contestation and power relations. One can see this realm of politics as the one remaining sphere that is still almost completely dominated by men. Women have entered the labor market in great numbers around the world in the last few decades, and although women's labor participation rate in developed countries is at 52.4 percent, in developing countries it stood at 69.3 percent by 2018 (ILO 2018). This growing number alone does not indicate transformation in gender equality as many forms of employment are exploitative and can reinforce gender and social inequality. Still, the rapid increase after World War II suggests that labor markets in the early part of the twentieth century, which were entirely dominated by male workers, have been replaced with a more gender balanced labor force. In contrast, the realm of politics remains elusive for women in most parts of the world. Even high-income democracies, which tend to rank high in indexes of gender empowerment, are barely able to push their percentages of women representatives above 20 percent to 30 percent of their assemblies, thus only just achieving or remaining below a 'critical mass' (when female representatives champion women's needs and interests), usually described as being between 20 percent (Thomas 1994) and 30 percent (Stokes 2005). The five largest democracies in the world do not fare much better with Japan at 10 percent, Brazil at 15 percent, Indonesia at 20 percent, the US at 23 percent, and India, the largest democracy, having just reached its highest number of women MPs with 14 percent (IPU 2020). Moreover, considering that some of the oldest democracies, such as the US and India, have a relatively low number of women representatives in their assemblies, it would seem that democracy is not enough in and of itself to address gender imbalance in a short timeframe (another old democracy, France, however, improved its percentage significantly in the 2017 election with 38 percent female parliamentarians).

Many governments no longer prevent women from engaging or participating in the political process on a legal or policy basis, in fact one could argue that the electoral process is essentially gender neutral, unlike governance structures and norms in countries where women face either strict cultural or normative barriers (lack of mobility, certain schools or professional positions being closed to women, etc.). This however fails to recognize that the sphere of politics, being a male-dominated domain in most countries, has long excluded and continue to exclude women in more informal or indirect ways (it is in fact Mackinnon's argument that the liberal state is designed to be judicially neutral in order to keep an unequal societal status quo, see Mackinnon 1989, 157–170). Beyond the obvious barriers of being the first women in a male dominated sphere in terms of recognition of competence and general inclusion, women also face indirect discriminatory practices that are often excused based on political expedience (for instance based on the need to put a male candidate to ensure a party's win in a close-call election). Gender-responsive policies are needed yet much of the affirmative action measures in place are ineffective. For instance, we know that positive or affirmation action policies, as opposed to hard quotas, are often skirted by political parties by assigning female candidates to unwinnable electoral districts, thereby meeting their target number of female candidates yet getting very few of them elected (Dahlerup 2006; Ryan et al. 2010). Affirmative action policies also have unintended effects as Bos argues, since they can reinforce a bias of party delegates for male candidates by inflating their views of a female candidate's male opponent (Bos 2015). The influence of political parties on women's representation, since they are gatekeepers of the electoral system, was highlighted by Tremblay who called them the 'true masters of the parliamentary representation of women' (Tremblay 2007, 537). Therefore, addressing inequalities in representation calls in part for reform of political parties and the process of candidate selection.

It is noted that democracies often have more positive indicators of gender equality. In addition, some remark that we need to take note of time for democracy to lead to greater political inclusion and therefore gender equality (Beer 2009). Yet, often such assessment of success by democracies in terms of gender equality is done by looking at the relationship between democracy and various gender equality indicators, such as income, schooling, fertility rates or life expectancy (see Tremblay 2007), rarely so between democracy and indicators of women's political engagement. We would argue that this tends to hide the slow propensity of democracies to generate gender equality in the political sphere, and the fact that Western and/or high-income countries with long existing democratic governance, except for Scandinavia, do not have particularly outstanding success in this area. In fact in the latest IPU data, from the top ten list of countries with the highest number of women in political assemblies, only one, Sweden, comes from either North America or Europe, Rwanda being at the top with 61 percent of members in the lower house who are women (Chamber of Deputies) and 38.5 percent in the upper house (Senate) (IPU 2020). This does not mean that democracy is not associated with greater political engagement by women but that democracy, left on its own, in a gender neutral normative or regulatory context, is not particularly effective in bringing changes towards a gender-balanced political sphere.

In fact, an expansion of participation, without a clear gender approach, can even lead to a decrease in women's decision-making power. For instance, decentralization is often suggested as a means to strengthen gender equality by opening 'up more access points for new political actors' (Slack et al. 2014, 7). The argument is that governance needs to be decentralized in order to be truly democratic (through its equality dimension) since those who would benefit directly from policies would also be more directly in charge of the policy process. Yet this form of local level decision-making in more gender conservative socio-cultural contexts has often led not only to diminishing women's voices in the policy process, but to a tightening of elite capture and patriarchal control (Siahaan 2003; Beall 2005). In Indonesia, for instance, decentralization has led local communities passing regulations restricting women's movement or forcing them to wear *jilbab* (Siahaan 2003). We are not rejecting decentralization as a way to enhance democracy. We argue, however, that expanding participation into local decision-making, a key aspect of democracy, can in some contexts, and if done without implementing gender-responsive measures, reinforce inequalities and undermine both women's freedoms and their contribution to political decision-making. This further reinforces the argument that democratic progress alone may not necessarily lead to an increase in political power by women.

In this context, it is hardly surprising that women have limited influence on policy matters generally, and on environmental policies more specifically, and this raises the question of the need for governance to be inclusive and socially responsive to address sustainability. This of course has important implications for sustainability, especially considering the need for urgent actions in the context of climate change. This is particularly problematic as women have been shown in many studies to hold more pro-environmental views or have higher perceived vulnerability to risk in a number of contexts, although not uniformly (Mohai 1992; Zelezny et al. 2000; Xiao and McCright 2017; Ramstetter and Habersack 2019). In a study about Members of the European parliament, although both women and men had similar concerns for the environment, women were more likely to support environmental legislation but their underrepresentation meant that policies were largely decided by men (Ramstetter and Habersack 2019). A similar effect is found with regards to environmental activism where women's environmentally friendly behavior (EFB) is reported to be higher than men, yet their activism is hampered by barriers to participation, including a division of labor that places an undue burden of paid and domestic work on women (Tindall et al. 2003). Studies across developing regions demonstrate how embedded power relations defined by patriarchal attitudes and norms constrain women's political voices, participation and activism (Tadros 2014). This patriarchal control of political institutions overlaps with elite and majoritarian capture of power which leaves indigenous people and minorities (ethnic, racial, SOGIE, etc.) with little influence over environmental decision-making. This intersectional lack of influence based on gender and social differentiation needs to be addressed to achieve sustainability because these groups are often most affected by the impacts of environmental stresses and climate change (Chambers 2007).

Despite the drivers and uneven patterns of women's weak representation in democratic political regimes highlighted above, governments are nevertheless increasingly attentive to gender equality agendas. This has opened up more unprecedented spaces for deliberative engagement; for example, the women's constituencies in various UN landmark platforms such as during the formulation of the Post-2015 Development SDGs and the Paris Agreement on Climate Change in 2015 (Esquivel and Sweetman 2016; Dhar 2018). At various historical junctures, states have also adopted gender mainstreaming programs and created national gender machineries in large part in response to the Beijing Platform for Action, a consensual agreement among states during the World Conference of Women in Beijing in 1995. These, apart from the growing global momentum of feminist and environmental movements, have placed gender and social equity issues increasingly at the center of sustainable development efforts. At no other time has gender, equity and sustainability issues become so prominent as policy agenda flashpoints (Arora-Jonsson and Sijapati 2017). However, a number of barriers persist, and these are especially palpable in the lack of equity in the distribution of resource assets as well as contested knowledge claims in the field of sustainable development. They also persist through the exclusions made in important deliberations and decisions around environment and development, as similarly described in political arenas above. The next sections will draw from the gender and environment literature, and especially from feminist political ecology and environmental justice to explain how such political power is a pre-requisite, not only to advance equitable access to and a fair distribution of environmental resources and benefits derived from them, but also to long term sustainability.

Social nature, justice and equity in sustainable development

Sustainable development has been a phrase that has emerged prominently as a response to the environmental crises in the late 1980s and articulated as a global vision during the UN Conference on Environment and Development (UNCED) in Rio de Janeiro in 1992. Over the years, the normative dimensions of sustainable development – however diversely defined by various groups – coalesced civil society, governments, academia and even the private sector around the mandate to protect and save the environment while advancing economic growth. Growing interest in sustainable development has also gradually led to the recognition that there are winners and losers as environments degrade and disrupt human lives and livelihoods, when many of those losing out were not responsible for these disruptions in a fundamental sense. Noting the evolution of debates on climate change as an example, Scoones (2007, 593) points out that these debates have become more political as they are no longer about 'the arcane specifics of global climate models, but a real political and economic issue, to which people and governments had to pay attention.' This point leads us to a brief discussion on the relationship between nature and society, highlighting that politics, society and nature are tightly interconnected.

Critical scholars have long argued that we cannot separate nature from the social world, putting forward the idea that there are co-constitutive ties between society and nature, thus referring to this nexus as 'social nature' or 'socionatures' (Castree and Braun 2001; Swyngedouw 1999). First, 'social nature' is reflected in how nature is socially understood and then acted upon by experts and planners. From the Enlightenment period in Western civilization, nature has been largely understood as a phenomenon standing 'out there' to be studied, fixed, extracted and controlled through objective and value-free scientific and disciplinary practices for economic ends. These Enlightenment ontologies of nature recur in a great deal of policymaking on the environment until today (Arora-Jonsson and Ågren 2019). For instance, they are found in the dominant discourses of sustainable development, especially in its original view of overcoming the limits to (economic) growth by realizing a pathway of 'green' economic initiatives and programs. It is this same dichotomized view of nature and society that deploys technical solutions to adverse environmental problems without addressing the deeper social and political causes of such problems in the first place. In relation with this, there is growing blindness to the inequitable power system that can account for both unsustainable environmental practices and the unequal distribution of benefits and disproportionate costs by vulnerable communities that result from the exploitative use of environmental resources. For instance, forms of accumulation through massive natural resource extraction, fossil fuel-dependent industrialization, and dramatic agrarian change processes are largely sidestepped and remain hidden in favor of technical and managerialist solutions to stave off and manage 'unruly nature' and disasters (MacGregor 2010; Taylor 2014; Nightingale et al. 2020).

Second, 'social nature' is also reflected in nature's dynamic physical characteristics that are contingent on social practices (Castree and Braun 2001). A forest, for example, will have different physical attributes and implications for societies, depending on how those societies use it. In this sense, the physical characteristics of nature are contingent upon social practices of resource use. Mediating these social practices on nature are people's access to resources, skills and vulnerabilities to environmental degradation which are often shaped by social and political differences based on gender, class, ethnicity, race or age. The use of and access to local resources by poor communities also depends on wider economic, political and social factors.

It is in this politicized understanding of 'social nature' that we situate the relevance of recognizing the need for norms and practices of equity and gender justice. And for this, we turn to Nancy Fraser's conceptualization of justice, which she refers to as institutional and social in nature, as she poses questions that describe the workings of justice:

> How fair or unfair are the terms of interaction that are institutionalized in the society? Does the society's structural-institutional framework, which sets the ground rules for social interaction, permit all to participate as peers in social interaction? Or does it institutionalize patterns of advantage and disadvantage that systematically prevent some people from participating on terms of parity? Do the society's institutionalized patterns of cultural value create status hierarchies, which impede parity of participation? Does its economic structure create class stratification, which also forecloses the possibility of parity?
>
> Dahl et al. 2004, 379

In summary, Fraser underscores the intrinsic links of justice to distribution (equity of economic and resource assets), recognition (of cultural status and subjectivities of marginal groups) and representation (democratic participation and parity in deliberation).

In the context of sustainability, justice needs to be understood further in the *longue durée*, not only in terms of relations with other individuals or groups, but in terms of the next generation. This informs the notion of equity of 'what' and, especially, 'between whom' through generations to come (Leach et al. 2018). This equity through dependencies over time also raises the issue of what sustainability's endpoint is envisaged to be, which Matson, Clarck and Andersson argue is human well-being (Matson et al. 2016). They propose to think of well-being inclusively, that is 'assuring the well-being of a few people today should not be achieved by degrading the well-being of their neighbors or their grandchildren' (p. 12). They add further that determinants of inclusive well-being are 'the stocks of assets' that people need which are based on a set of capitals (natural, social, human, manufactured and knowledge). This suggests that the outcome of sustainability depends on the fulfillment of needs (which was how the 1987 Brundtland report defined sustainable development), and that this fulfillment cannot be achieved at the expense of others.

This generational understanding of equity however raises not only differences between subsequent groups but how needs are redefined over time, and increasingly linked to the concept of justice in their formulation. Matson, Clarck and Andersson's view of human well-being as an outcome of sustainability echoes to some extent what Simon, Steel and Lovrich (2011) argue is substantial value change that support an expanded view of needs away from being purely subsistence-based to what they argue, borrowing from Abraham Maslow, are 'higher order' needs; needs about quality of life that combines environmental protection with greater gender equality and social justice (Simon et al. 2011, 12). In the context of sustainable development efforts, these higher order needs make clear that sustainability has to be understood in political and power-laden terms that call for greater justice and a fair distribution of decision-making power, democratic representation, and resources and benefits, with gender equality as a key component as the following two sections will argue.

Gender equity and sustainability: the access to resource assets, knowledge and intersectionality

As briefly discussed above, sustainability has to be understood beyond simple environmental protection and mitigation of degradation in biophysical or technical terms and fixes. The notion of 'social nature' instead enables us to highlight the linkages between gender equity and sustainability through social practices such as the rights to resource assets, the production of knowledge and intersecting subjectivities prevalent in gender and environment research.

Roughly three decades of research on gender, environment and natural resource management, in particular in managing forest, land and water systems have clearly shown that rights to access and control of resources are gender- and socially differentiated. Gender-responsive action requires addressing socio-economic disadvantage in productive livelihoods and disproportionate obligations for reproductive care, well-being and access to resources: equal access to and control over ecosystem-based resources and their benefits (Leach 2015).

Gender and environment scholars have also argued that in order for equity to be recognized and addressed, we need to take into account women's and marginal groups' differentiated needs, embodied experiences and capacities. To realize this, methodologies have to be more inclusive, bottom up and contextualized. From Donna Haraway's situated knowledges (Haraway 1988) to standpoint feminism and Sandra Harding's 'sciences from below' (Harding 2008), feminist scholars have shown that real equity cannot be achieved without understanding women's experiences as well as those of marginal groups as part of the knowledge being produced about environment and sustainability. This circles back to and aligns with the idea of 'social nature' earlier that posits objective and value-free knowledge as serving the interests of powerful actors rather than the grounded practices and conditions of resource use and environmental change.

The gender and development literature has argued that the Women in Development approach was too 'women focused' and unable to address power imbalances at the root of gender inequalities. Similarly, studies of gender and the environment in the last two or three decades questioned the 'addition of women' approach to environmental protection and management without a real analysis of gender power relations and social structures (Bretherton 1998; Resurrección and Elmhirst 2008; MacGregor 2017) that could give way to de-centering women and instead, highlight how gender intersects with other axes of power (Crenshaw 1991; Cho et al. 2013). It would be too long to give a history of this development here, however, we can better understand how a gender-responsive democratization of power structures and decision-making processes is viewed as key to sustainability through both the literature on feminist political ecology and feminist environmental justice.

Democratizing sustainable development: views from feminist political ecology and feminist environmental justice

In the need to realize equity that is germane to sustainability, the exclusion of women and other socially marginalized groups in political systems should highlight the large gap between the objectives of sustainability and the necessary gender-responsive democratic process or means required to get there. Gender equality requires the realization of human rights. It also means enhancing equal participation in decision-making at multiple levels. This includes supporting agency, power and voice in institutions and decision-making; building deliberative forms of democracy that can debate sustainability goals and values in inclusive ways; and assuring space for feminist collective action (Leach 2015, 7).

Feminist Political Ecology (FPE), as a subfield of political ecology, is an analytical approach that examines how governance and political economic structures are suffused with gender power relations that dictate the different access to and control over resources that women and men have, and the positions they embody that either reproduce or contest these structures (for a discussion of the evolution of FPE see Resurrección 2017). As such, FPE goes beyond a women-centric view to a deeper understanding of the intersectional gender order that creates environmental and livelihood vulnerabilities and yet at the same time attributes a social positioning that gives women – in varying degrees – specific and relevant knowledge of environmental change and resources, as well as the adaptation needed to respond to climate and other environmental challenges. FPE however goes beyond an analysis of power relations between women and men and also addresses inter-group inequalities and intersectional processes at play where gender overlaps or compounds (or is compounded by) other forms of marginalization and discrimination based on social differentiations (such as race, caste, ethnicity, religion or class) (Mollett 2017). This can be seen when women from lower castes and racialized groups are discriminated against and hence become more vulnerable (Buchy and Rai 2008). A key approach of FPE is to highlight the connections between gender and society's ability to manage and benefit from environmental resources in an equitable way, by focusing more specifically on gender power dynamics around decision-making. With climate change and other environmental challenges such as natural disasters, feminist scholars have shown how power systems not only limit women's ability to participate and engage in decision-making related to the environment, but undermine their ability to adapt as well as contribute to sustainable solutions for all (Dankelman 2010; Pham et al. 2016).

Yet gender is not just an analytical lens used to understand vulnerabilities in FPE. It is also a lens used to understand ways women's and men's positionalities in the gender order give them specific and differentiated knowledge of environmental change, and at the same time enable them to engage in environmental struggles and resistance against forces that undermine their environmental capital using different ways of responding to those challenges (Agarwal 1994; Dey et al. 2014).

The body of work of feminist environmental justice scholars focuses on the ways in which political activism and engagement is key to a better and more effective relationship between nature and culture. Di Chiro for instance argues that 'Far from conceiving of nature as an abstracted disembodied "elsewhere", environmental justice activists show that the health of their communities and the health of the environment are inseparable' (Di Chiro 2015, 213). Feminist environmental justice further disrupts the nature/culture binary discussed in an earlier section. The discussion on environmental justice is particularly salient to our discussion of democracy and sustainability since the increasing threats posed by climate change will create future conflicts and call for greater climate justice (Walker 2012; Sze 2017). However, if we accept that environmental justice is especially important because those who require it the most, namely the poor and disenfranchised as they face high risk exposure and may lack the capacity or resources to adapt, are also those who are least likely to be protected or to have the means to fight for environmental justice, then it is also paradoxical that the environmental justice literature tend to be gender blind, especially as Sze argues that 'gender also plays a significant part in causing and sustaining environmental injustice' (Sze 2017, 159).

It is indeed a paradox that on the one hand women tend to be given less decision-making power and on the other hand they tend to be made vulnerable by climate and other environmental changes caused by a mostly male-driven industrialization process. Combined with their differentiated knowledge and experience of the environment, we can identify a gap between the needed equity in democratic governance and the growing environmental threats against those most marginalized, that will need to be reduced or resolved if we are to achieve or progress towards the goal of sustainability.

Finally, the politics of sustainable development also highlights whose voices and knowledge most count. Postcolonial thinking highlights how gender is also embedded in current neoliberal globalization involving North-South relations. Feminist postcolonial scholars draw attention to the power dynamics of gender and race, situated knowledges and alternative knowledges that have been generally marginalized through colonialism, imperialism, inequality, unequal power relations, and the domination of Eurocentric science (Harding 2011). By questioning the universality of models of the 'modern' and 'developed,' we come to see how knowledge and decisions are being shaped within the realm of sustainable development programs and climate change models (see for example, Tuana 2013). The question of whose voice counts thus also raises issues of what Gayatri Spivak refers to as the discursive production of the subaltern, poor 'Third World' woman as a way of asserting the superiority of the West over the non-West (Mendoza 2016), leading thus to their persistent silencing (Spivak 1988). A more democratic sustainable development agenda requires parity in representation and an openness to a plurality in situated knowledges.

Conclusion

The purpose of this chapter was to argue that democratic governance practices can lead to sustainable development. It does this by first arguing that political participation in democracies is key to ensuring equity, an important ingredient of sustainability in terms of ensuring equitable distribution of resources and assets at any one period, and over time. Yet it also proposes that it is in fact political and governance systems that are often those least likely to achieve gender parity. The unequal power and ability to influence the policy process that women experience (contributing to social unsustainability) undermine society's ability to respond equitably to, and address, environmental unsustainability, which in turn hampers our ability to generate sustainable solutions that benefit both society and the environment. Using a feminist political ecology approach, it suggests that sustainable solutions cannot be achieved without a concomitant effort to address gender inequalities, and especially gaps in representation, that is, political and decision-making power. This will also ensure that women and other socially marginalized groups advance environmental justice addressing the growing threat of climate change and pandemic outbreaks such as COVID-19.

Furthermore, eliminating gender inequalities in political power would also address to some extent the conflict between the short-term electoral cycles and needs of democratic governance and the required long-term vision and planning needed for sustainable development to take place. If equity is key to sustainability, as we have argued here, then a more accountable and responsive political system, with gender equality properly built in, would ensure that sustainability is not built on a zero-sum political game that produces environment 'winners' and 'losers.' And since women, as research indicates, tend to show more pro-environmental views and support comparatively more environmental legislation, then it follows that a more gender-responsive political system will generate more long-term sustainable solutions. It is therefore our argument in this chapter that advancing gender equality is key to ensuring better democratic governance pathways towards more sustainable solutions in an uncertain environmental future.

References

Arora-Jonsson, S. and Ågren, M., 2019. Bringing diversity to nature: politicizing gender, race and class in environmental organizations? *Environment and Planning E: Nature and Space*, 2(4), 874–898.

Beer, C., 2009. Democracy and gender equality. *Studies in Comparative International Development*, 44, 212–227.

Agarwal, B., 1994. Gender, resistance and land: interlinked struggles over resources and meanings in South Asia. *Journal of Peasant Studies*, 22(1), 81–125.

Arora-Jonsson, S. and Sijapati, B., 2017. Disciplining gender in environmental organizations: the texts and practices of gender mainstreaming. *Gender, Work and Organization,* 25(3), 309–325.

Beall, J., 2005. Decentralizing government and decentering gender: lessons from local government reform in South Africa. *Politics & Society,* 33(2), 253–276.

Bos, A.L., 2015. The unintended effects of political party affirmative action policies on female candidates' nomination chances. *Politics, Groups, and Identities,* 3(1), 73–93.

Bretherton, C., 1998. Global environmental politics: putting gender on the agenda? *Review of International Studies,* 24, 85–100.

Buchy, M. and Rai, B., 2008. Do Women-Only Approaches to Natural Resource Management Help Women? The Case of Community Forestry in Nepal. In B.P. Resurrección and R. Elmhirst, eds. *Gender and Natural Resource Management: Livelihoods, Mobility and Interventions.* London: Earthscan, 127–149.

Castree, N., and Braun, B., 2001. *Social Nature: Theory, Practice and Politics.* Malden: Blackwell Publishing.

Chambers, S., 2007. Minority empowerment and environmental justice. *Urban Affairs Review,* 43(1), 28–54.

Cho, S., Crenshaw, K.W. and McCall, L., 2013. Toward a field of intersectionality studies: theory, applications, and praxis. *Sign: Journal of Women in Culture and Society,* 38(4).

Crenshaw, K., 1991. Mapping the margins: intersectionality, identity politics, and violence against women of color. *Stanford Law Review,* 1241–1299.

Dahl, H.M., Stoltz, P. and Willig, R., 2004. Recognition, redistribution and representation in capitalist global society: an interview with Nancy Fraser. *Acta Sociologica,* 47(4), 374–382.

Dahlerup, D., 2006. Introduction. In D. Dahlerup, eds. *Women, Quotas and Politics.* Abingdon: Routledge, 3–31.

Dankelman, I., 2010. *Gender and Climate Change: An Introduction.* London: Earthscan.

Dey, S., Resurrección, B.P. and Doneys, P., 2014. Gender and environmental struggles: voices from Adivasi Garo Community in Bangladesh. *Gender, Place and Culture,* 21(8).

Dhar, S., 2018. Gender and Sustainable Development Goals (SDGs). *Indian Journal of Gender Studies,* 25(1), 47–78.

Di Chiro, G., 2015. A New Spelling of Sustainability: Engaging Feminist-Environmental Justice Theory and Practice. In W. Harcourt and I. L. Nelson, eds. *Practising Feminist Political Ecologies Moving Beyond the 'Green Economy'.* London: Zed Books, 211–237.

Esquivel, V. and Sweetman, C., 2016. Gender and the sustainable development goals. *Gender & Development,* 24(1), 1–8.

Haraway, D., 1988. The science question in feminism and the privilege of partial perspective. *Feminist Studies,* 14(3), 575–599.

Harding, S., 2008. *Sciences from Below: Feminisms, Postcolonialities, and Modernities.* Durham: Duke University press.

Harding, S. G., eds., 2011. *The Postcolonial Science and Technology Studies Reader.* Durham: Duke University Press.

ILO., 2018. *World Employment and Social Outlook: Trends for Women 2018 – Global Snapshot.* Geneva: ILO.

IPU., 2020. *Women in national parliaments* [online]. Available from: ipu.org.

Leach, M., 2015. *Gender Equality and Sustainable Development.* London: Routledge – Earthscan.

Leach, M., Reyers, B., Bai, X., Brondizio, E.S., Cook, C., Díaz, S., … Subramanian, S. M., 2018. Equity and sustainability in the Anthropocene: a social–ecological systems perspective on their intertwined futures. *Global Sustainability,* 1(e13), 1–13.

MacGregor, S., 2010. Gender and climate change: from impacts to discourses. *Journal of the Indian Ocean Region,* 6(2), 223–238.

MacGregor, S., 2017. *Routledge Handbook of Gender and Environment.* London: Routledge.

MacKinnon, C.A., 1989. *Toward a Feminist Theory of the State.* Cambridge: Harvard University Press.

Matson, P., Clarck, W.C. and Andersson, K., 2016. *Pursuing Sustainability: A Guide to the Science and Practice.* New Jersey: Princeton University Press.

Mendoza, B., 2016. Coloniality of gender and power: from postcoloniality to decoloniality. In L. Disch and M. Hawkesworth, eds. *The Oxford Handbook of Feminist Theory.* Oxford University Press, 100–121.

Mohai, P., 1992. Men, women, and the environment: an examination of the gender gap in environmental concern and activism. *Society & Natural Resources,* 5(1), 1–19.

Mollett, S., 2017. Gender's Critical Edge: Feminist Political Ecology, Postcolonial Intersectionality, and the Coupling of Race and Gender. In S. MacGregor, eds. *Routledge Handbook of Gender and Environment.* London: Routledge, 146–158.

Nightingale, A.J., Eriksen, S., Taylor, M., Forsyth, T., Pelling, M., Newsham, A., ... Whitfield, S., 2020. Beyond technical fixes: climate solutions and the great derangement. *Climate and Development*, 12(4), 343–352.

Pham, P., Doneys, P. and Doane, D.L., 2016. Changing livelihoods, gender roles and gender hierarchies: the impact of climate, regulatory and socio-economic changes on women and men in a Co Tu Community in Vietnam. *Women's Studies International Forum*, 54, 48–56.

Ramstetter, L. and Habersack, F., 2019. Do women make a difference? Analysing environmental attitudes and actions of Members of the European Parliament. *Environmental Politics*, 29(6), 1063–1084. https://doi.org/10.1080/09644016.2019.160915.

Resurrección, B.P., 2017. Gender and Environment in the Global South: From 'Women, Environment and Development' to Feminist Political Ecology. In S. MacGregor, eds. *Routledge Handbook of Gender and Environment*. London: Routledge, 71–85.

Resurrección, B.P., and Elmhirst, R., 2008. *Gender and Natural Resource Management: Livelihoods, Mobility and Interventions*. London: Earthscan.

Ryan, M.K., Haslam, S.A. and Kulich, C., 2010. Politics and the glass cliff: evidence that women are preferentially selected to contest hard-to-win seats. *Psychology of Women Quarterly*, 34, 56–64.

Scoones, I., 2007. Sustainability. *Development in Practice*, 17(4–5), 589–596.

Siahaan, A.Y., 2003. *The Politics of Gender and Decentralization in Indonesia*. Budapest: Center for Policy Studies, Central European University, and the Open Society Institute.

Simon, C.A., Steel, B.S., and Lovrich, N.P., 2011. *State and Local Government: Sustainability in the 21st Century*. New York: Oxford University Press.

Slack, E., Spicer, Z., and Montacer, M., 2014. *Decentralization and Gender Equity*. Ottawa: Forum of Federations: The Global Network on Federalism and Devolved Governance.

Spivak, G., 1988. Can the Subaltern Speak? In C. Nelson and L. Grossber, *In Marxism and the Interpretation of Culture*. London: Macmillan, 271–313.

Stokes, W., 2005. *Women in Contemporary Politics*. Cambridge: Polity.

Swyngedouw, E., 1999. Modernity and hybridity: nature, regeneracionismo, and the production of the spanish waterscape, 1890–1930. *Annals of the Association of American Geographers*, 89(3), 443–465.

Sze, J., 2017. Gender and Environmental Justice. In MacGregor, *Routledge Handbook of Gender and Environment*. London: Routledge, 159–168.

Tadros, M., 2014. *Women in Politics: Gender, Power and Development*. London: Zed Books.

Taylor, M., 2014. *The Political Ecology of Climate Change Adaptation: Livelihoods, Agrarian Change and the Conflicts of Development*. London: Routledge.

Thomas, S., 1994. *How Women Legislate*. New York: Oxford University Press.

Tindall, T.B., Davies, S., and Mauboulès, C., 2003. Activism and conservation behavior in an environmental movement: the contradictory effects of gender. *Society & Natural Resources*, 16(10), 909–932.

Tremblay, M., 2007. Democracy, representation, and women: a comparative analysis. *Democratization*, 14(4), 533–553.

Tuana, N., 2013. Gendering Climate Knowledge for Justice: Catalyzing a New Research Agenda. In M. Alston and K. Whittenbury, *Research, Action and Policy: Addressing the Gendered Impacts of Climate Change*. Springer Netherlands, 17–31.

UN Women, 2020. *Women and the Sustainable Development Goals (SDGs)* [online]. Available from: www.unwomen.org/en/news/in-focus/women-and-the-sdgs [Accessed 2019].

Walker, G., 2012. *Environmental Justice: Concepts, Evidence and Politics*. London: Routledge.

Xiao, C., and McCright, A.M., 2017. Gender Differences in Environmental Concern: Sociological Explanations. In S. MacGregor, *Routledge Handbook of Gender and Environment*. London: Routledge, 169–185.

Zelezny, L.C., Chua, P.P. and Aldrich, C., 2000. Elaborating on gender differences in environmentalism. *Journal of Social Issues*, 56(3), 443–457.

24
MIGRATION AND MOBILITY
Environmental, social and political dimensions

Katrin Sontag

Introduction[1]

This chapter presents an introduction to how sustainability and democracy interconnect with human movement. These topics form a complex nexus, of which three issues are presented in this chapter: effects of climate change on human movement, processes and outcomes of migration in terms of social inclusion and the question of political inclusion in democratic countries of arrival in Europe. The chapter critically questions simple explanations and predictions, introduces current debates and provides concrete examples.

To lay the ground, the chapter starts by discussing the concept of migration as limited to a specific kind of movement and argues that a broader understanding is useful in this context. Thus, section 2 presents differences between approaches of "migration" and "mobility". Depending on the concept, the "lens", that is used, different phenomena of movement become visible and can be understood in different ways.

Section 3 deals with the consequences of climate change and their relations to human movement. It shows the complexity of these relations and argues that the idea of general "climate migration" to the "Global North" is too simple. Rather, climate change has various effects, which can connect with other phenomena, such as political conflict and economic issues, and can lead to different kinds of short- or long-distance, and short- or long-term mobilities – and also im-mobilities.

Section 4 addresses social sustainability and inclusion in terms of controversial migration and integration practices and policies in the "Global North" that may limit migrants' access to local life, social inclusion and future prospects. An important topic when it comes to inclusion are political rights and the migrants' participation in democratic systems. In fact, when more people move more frequently, the number of residents in democratic countries who cannot participate in the democracy increases and questions arise as to who should have the right to vote where and when.

Section 5 focuses on this intersection between migration and democracy and presents discussions about more inclusive understandings of political participation, voting rights and citizenship.

The predominant focus on Europe in this chapter contributes to the discussion in this particular area, however, it should not detract from pressing and important challenges in other areas

DOI: 10.4324/9780429024085-29

of the world, such as issues of migration, mobility and democracy in countries of the "Global South".

Migration and mobility

Migration is a phenomenon that has been and is being understood in different ways depending on the perspective and worldview from which one looks at it. The general definition is a definition from a state perspective. From this perspective it can be defined as a move across a national border resulting in several years of residence (see e.g. UNESCO 2019). This view of migration has its roots in the context of nation building and nationalism in the nineteenth century, when national citizenship and fixed home addresses – the "double container perspective" – became a dominant issue (Duchêne-Lacroix et al. 2013). It led to the perspective that "immigrants appear as natural enemies of a political world divided into culturally homogenous and territorially bounded nations each represented by a sovereign state" (Wimmer and Glick Schiller 2002, 217).

Criticism of methodological nationalism (Wimmer and Glick Schiller 2002) has pointed out how this prevalent national perspective has traditionally been largely unquestioned, not only in politics but also in social sciences, because official migration data, statistical knowledge production and funding for research is most often based on the parameters of the nation state. As a result, the focus for many years was on immigrants/foreigners (of particular groups, constructed as ethnic) in a particular nation state and their assimilation or integration (Wimmer and Glick Schiller 2002). Other aspects of migration and mobility, such as trajectories of movements, mobile lifestyles or indeed emigration were largely ignored. Being sedentary was taken as "the normal" and being mobile as "the other" or less normal way of living. The most extreme expression of this ideology can be seen in the discrimination, incarceration or suppression of nomadic or mobile peoples in different countries of the world.

Recent migration research in cultural anthropology and other social sciences has challenged this perspective and has started to analyze migration as "the norm", the "autonomy of migration", by taking a post-migrant perspective on society (Bojadžijev and Karakayali 2007; Hess 2010; Römhild 2015), or by looking at trajectories of migrants (Schapendonk 2012). It has also focused on transnational social fields and the different connections that migrants might have to different places at any given time (Levitt and Glick Schiller 2004). It is now understood that people can have parallel places of living (multilocalism) or move in various patterns that do not necessarily match the definition of a one-time, one-way move across national borders (Sontag 2018b).

Meanwhile, research associated with mobility studies or the "mobility turn" has investigated the many different ways of being mobile (Urry 2000; Rolshoven 2011) and thus opened up a range of new ways of understanding and analysing movements. These include human movements, but also movements of, e.g., ideas or objects. Migration then can be one form of mobility. The connections between migration and mobility, the "migration-mobility nexus" has also been depicted as a scale ranging from permanent to less permanent movements (D'Amato et al. 2019). When studying movement, it is thus helpful to take into account not only concepts of migration, but other approaches such as transnationalism or mobility. Human movement is not restricted to the traditional concept of migration understood as an international, long-term move. Rather, mobilities can be complex, internal, short-term and un-monitored. In fact, scholars have called for using "climate mobilities" instead of "climate migration" to encompass the variety of forms of movement in the context of climate change (Boas et al. 2019, 902).

In terms of numbers, international migration increased by 49 percent (in numerical terms) between 2000 and 2017, as estimated by the UN. The percentage of the world's population that is migrating is still only around 3 percent (United Nations 2017). In 2000 it was 2.8 percent, in 2019 3.5 percent (United Nations DESA 2019). While these numbers can be criticized, it is nonetheless clear that international migration involves only a small percentage of the world's population at a given time.

More movement takes place within countries and regions than between them, even if these movements are often ignored in Western discourse. The UN estimates that there were 272 million international migrants in 2019 (United Nations 2019), and 740 million internal migrants were estimated in 2009 (International Organization for Migration 2018, 2). Moreover, there were 25.9 million refugees and asylum seekers (United Nations 2017) and 40.3 million internally displaced persons in 2016 (International Organization for Migration 2018, 2). In fact, the next section shows that movement that takes place in connection with environmental degradation mostly leads to the internal displacement of people.

Migration and climate change

The most salient topic in the context of sustainability and migration is the migration caused by environmental transformation, such as through human-induced climate change. It goes without saying that climate change has already affected how and where humans can live – and will have an even greater impact in the future. The International Organization for Migration (IOM) estimates between 25 million and 1 billion "environmental migrants"[2] by 2050 (IOM 2019). Most of these are predicted to be displaced within countries or geographical regions – in contrast to the notions in Western countries that focus on and promote fear of migration into Western countries or that frame the topic as a security issue (Boas et al. 2019).

The Internal Displacement Monitoring Center states for the last ten years that environmental disasters have been causing significantly more internal displacement than conflicts or violence.[3] However, precise numbers are difficult to come by, and the general understanding is that there is still too little knowledge about these processes, their complexities and future developments. The issues of migration, local conflicts, economic downturn and environmental degradation are often interconnected. Moreover, climate change can have many different effects and create different vulnerabilities and some of the slower developments are difficult to depict. In addition to such effects as flooding, droughts and the rise in sea levels, there are others that are more difficult to determine like the spreading of disease, scarcity of resources, saltwater intrusion, consequences of water shortages or the death of insects.

As discussed above, migration and mobility, too, can have various causes and take different forms (Warner et al. 2010; Piguet et al. 2011; Migration Data Portal 2019). It is in fact often the poorest and most vulnerable people who move within their proximity, within rural spaces (and not into cities) or who cannot afford to move at all (Tacoli 2009). Black et al. have called these "trapped populations", as they face a double set of risks: "They are unable to move away from environmental threats, and their lack of capital makes them especially vulnerable to environmental changes" (Black et al. 2011). This term has in turn been criticized for under-playing the agency of the people (Ayeb-Karlsson et al. 2018). In addition, factors other than poverty, e.g., gender, play a role in possibilities to be mobile.

The very notions of "environmental migrants", "environmental refugees" (El-Hinnawi 1985) or even "climate refugees" have been criticized for overlooking the complexity of social, political and economic factors that affect migration (Castles 2002, 5; Piguet et al. 2011, 17).

Migration decisions also have to do with political and economic power structures. Governance and local infrastructure can play a major role in tackling effects of environmental transformation. Richer countries bear a greater responsibility for causing climate change and are also better equipped to react to climate change and environmental degradation. Concepts in social sciences that relate to power relations and possibilities of movement, such as motility, the potential to move (Kaufmann et al. 2004), regimes of mobility (Glick Schiller and Salazar 2012) or mobility justice (Sheller 2018) are useful in order to assess the multiple facets of migration and mobility and their relation to power structures.

More specifically, the term "refugee" has been discussed in this context. As defined by the Geneva Convention of 1951, the term "refugee" does not include people displaced by environmental factors, and critics fear that the term might be weakened if the definition is widened to apply also to those who are not directly persecuted (Piguet et al. 2011, 17). On the other hand, if the alternative term "migrant" is used to refer to people who are displaced as a consequence of worsening environmental conditions and natural hazards, this could wrongly imply a certain degree of voluntariness.[4]

Biermann and Boas (2010) argue for establishing the term "climate refugees" specifically for "victims of a set of three direct, largely undisputed climate change impacts: sea-level rise, extreme weather events, and drought and water scarcity" (p. 11). However, they propose that it should not become an extension of the Geneva Convention, but rather call for a new instrument, "a Protocol on Recognition, Protection, and Resettlement of Climate Refugees to the United Nations Framework Convention on Climate Change", and also demand an additional fund (p. 83). The authors point out that it is time for "global adaptation governance" (p. 60) to plan adaptation strategies to climate change now instead of waiting for more emergencies to happen. Biermann and Boas propose specific principles and settings for this, taking into account the specificities of the situation of climate refugees, for example, when compared to other situations of forced migration.

In fact, the terms "environmental migrants" or "environmental refugees" suggest that migration is the forced or even sudden effect of environmental change. But scholars have pointed out that there are also other perspectives. Instead of looking at migration as the worst outcome, it could in fact also be a planned and supported adaptation strategy (Tacoli 2009; Black et al. 2011; Piguet et al. 2011, 15). Again, others point to the effect of migration on nature (e.g., when humans leave landscapes or come to new places), or to the fact that nature can also support people in adapting to climate change.[5] If only a few people migrate and send back remittances, these can support those who stayed behind. However, remittances can also have different effects on the environment of the countries of origin. Moran-Taylor and Taylor (2010) find for Guatemala, for example, that migrant remittances lead to the purchase of land to build bigger houses and to perform a different kind of agriculture, moving away from traditional maize and its cultural rituals to other crops, and a more extensive use of fertilizers and other chemicals that lead to pollution of water. Both, the places of arrival and of departure are thus far from being homogenous, static, collective entities.

An aspect that should not be overlooked is that frequent mobility, taken with the building and usage of associated infrastructures, generates greenhouse gas emissions and thus itself contributes to climate change. On a continuous scale that ranges from long-term, permanent migration at one end to more frequent mobility at the other (D'Amato et al. 2019), it is the latter end that has a higher impact in terms of greenhouse gas emissions when it comes to air travel. The European Commission estimates that international aviation emissions (that already make up 2 percent of global emissions) increased by 70 percent between 2005 and 2018 (European Commission 2018), to which one should add emissions caused by the infrastructure that supports mobility and air travel, as well as the industry of mass tourism. Thus, migration and mobility are not only an effect of environmental issues, but in turn also contribute to climate change.

There are thus a variety of causes, effects and forms of migration and mobility. History also shows us that migration has always taken place, regardless of attempts to confine it. And one might well argue that the migration policies of nation states hinder the kind of migration that has always taken place and is now taking on new forms and dynamics in the face of environmental transformations.

Migration policies and social inclusion

Alongside environmental issues, social inclusion is central to the debate on sustainability and migration. Sachs uses the term "social inclusion" to subsume aspects of sustainable development such as:

> the end of extreme poverty; the reduction of glaring gaps of wealth and poverty; a high degree of social mobility (…); the absence of discrimination including by gender, race, religion, or ethnicity; and the fostering of social trust, mutual support, moral values, and cohesion.
>
> Sachs 2015, 12

The UN expresses the demand for social inclusion not least in the slogan to "leave no one behind" in connection with the Sustainable Development Goals.

This section deals specifically with social inclusion in view of migration policies towards and in countries of the "Global North". Migration policies are addressed in Sustainable Development Goal 10.7 of the UN (n.d.): "Facilitate orderly, safe, regular and responsible migration and mobility of people, including through the implementation of planned and well-managed migration policies."

The reality, especially for those who move towards the "Global North" and do not hold visas as (highly skilled) employees, family members or to study, but try to apply for asylum is of course often very difficult. Migration routes across the Mediterranean and in many other areas of the world used by refugees and migrants are dramatic examples of the failure of migration policies. In 2018 the UNHCR counted 2,262 deaths in the Mediterranean (UNHCR 2019) and people who manage to arrive in Europe under these circumstances may then be faced with inhumane conditions in overcrowded camps, e.g. on the Greek islands. Sometimes even the basic principle of non-refoulement – that people who have come to seek asylum should not be turned away – is not observed by European countries.

Migration policies that hinder social inclusion and access are also an issue in the further process of migration within countries of arrival. Depending on the visa type, bureaucratic "channel" (Sandoz 2018), and supporting infrastructure (e.g., from employers or family), people can have very different migration experiences and opportunities.

The topic of social inclusion is especially relevant in the case of asylum seekers. One of the debates of the last years concerned the long waiting times for the decision on an asylum application, which can be followed by an appeal in court or a temporary admission in some countries. Governments of Switzerland and Germany have recently sped up the procedures. However, this time of waiting in uncertainty, sometimes in remote places, in some cases without access to language courses, the job market or social life could add to the pressure and uncertainty that people have already experienced in their home countries or during their journeys.

To name an example, we looked at the situation of students with refugee backgrounds in different European countries, who wanted to join a local university. They met a number of difficulties, e.g., in navigating rules and information, but also the recognition of previous diplomas and problems with their bureaucratic situation between the asylum, education and funding sector (Sontag 2018a, 2019).

Taking the case of Switzerland, also non-EU nationals who come with a student visa and graduate in Switzerland, experience challenges if they choose to stay in the country and look for a job. They fall under the yearly quota of non-EU migrants and may only stay for six months, which can be too short a time to find a job. Other obstacles include the selection of preferred disciplines, and the difficulty in accessing relevant information (Riaño and Piguet 2018). There are thus a number of formal or semi-formal mechanisms in different migration processes that make inclusion difficult.

These add to the informal dynamics of exclusion and discrimination that exist, for example, in the labor market. A current study in Switzerland shows "that children of immigrants holding Swiss qualifications and dual nationality need to send 30% more applications to receive a callback for an interview when applying for apprenticeship level occupations" (Zschirnt and Fibbi 2019).

Undocumented migrants are in an especially precarious situation with regard to social inclusion, and this has given rise, in the US for example, to initiatives like "sanctuary cities" that do not cooperate with national immigration agencies, or to other "urban citizenship" schemes in other countries (Schilliger and Ataç 2017). Some urban citizenship initiatives demand, for example, that all the inhabitants in a city have a city ID card, which gives undocumented migrants access to official institutions, hospitals, social services, the police, different kinds of contracts and cultural facilities. Such schemes can benefit all the inhabitants, not only the migrants. Such a city ID card is already in operation in New York City, but there are discussions also in other countries about the introduction of city ID cards. The group of undocumented people is diverse and includes those who have overstayed a visa, those whose residence permit has expired, whose asylum claim has been denied, or refugees who travelled through Italy or Greece to other European countries. Afraid of being sent back to their country of origin or the countries of arrival in the EU within the framework of the Dublin Agreement, some refugees are living undocumented and homeless in Europe. This is evident in many cities such as Calais, Paris, Bihac or Brussels. A number of local and international initiatives have, off their own bat, set up supporting infrastructures to help with food, clothes or shelter to show solidarity and humanity (e.g. in Brussels BXLRefugees n.d.).

Some scholars have developed the concept of "sustainable migration" – a term with scope for controversy, because it begs the question as to which actors and policies should be taken into account. Betts and Collier, for example, define sustainable migration as "migration that has the democratic support of the receiving society, meets the long-term interests of the receiving state, sending society, and migrant themselves, and fulfils basic ethical obligations" (2018, 9). They take, amongst other factors, the perspectives of local citizens, anti-immigrant attitudes and political effects into consideration, for instance the growth of right-wing parties in many European countries and argue that sustainable migration policies should avoid "politics of panic", "tipping points" and backlashes against migration in receiving countries. This is a controversial approach, not least because the roots of anti-migrant attitudes are complex, and it is important not to draw direct conclusions between the arrival of migrants and anti-migrant attitudes. The authors themselves mention economic and context factors. Moreover, it is arguable that the concept of sustainable migration should give more weight to stakeholders such as places of transit or departure. In a parallel report on sustainable migration, Erdal et al. elaborated the following, more encompassing definition of sustainable migration: "migration that ensures a well-balanced distribution of costs and benefits for the individuals, societies and states affected, today and in the future" (2018, 9).

Migration and political participation

Political participation is another important dimension of social inclusion, which also refers to the link between migration and democracy. In fact, migration and mobility lay bare some of the problems in the organization of democratic participation. Migrants may have no – or limited – voting rights in their country of arrival, while still having voting rights in the countries they left. In Switzerland, for example, around 25 percent of adult residents are not Swiss citizens and thus have no voting rights on the national level (Blatter et al. 2016, 40). Yet Swiss citizens who live abroad can vote in Switzerland. So, who should have the right to vote and decide where? And how will democratic inclusion develop with increasing migration?

Marshall (1950) differentiated between social, civic and political rights. Migrants often gain social and civic rights before they gain political rights and can participate in official elections. One way to gain political rights is through naturalization. The idea of naturalization also springs both from a traditional understanding of homogenous societies, and from the idea of migration as consisting of one permanent move. In fact, citizenship has been described as a "device for sorting out desirable and undesirable immigrants" (Bauböck 2006, 18). Naturalizing requires different periods of (continuous) residence. Switzerland, for example, is comparatively strict, requiring 10–12 years of residence. Before that, migrants are excluded from voting rights, except in several communes and two cantons. But while migrants are denied the right to vote, they are at the same time expected to integrate quickly. Leimgruber argues that citizens have to be "formed" and that it is not realistic to expect migrants to be able automatically to participate politically after obtaining citizenship if they have been excluded from political participation for many years (Leimgruber 2016, 26). Current proposals suggest five years of residence before migrants may receive voting rights, which, as Blatter, Schmid and Blättler argue, ties in with legislative periods, leaves time to become familiar with the system, and excludes those who are only staying for short periods (Blatter et al. 2017, 452–453).

People who do not have full citizenship rights are referred to as denizens (Hammar 1990). They include people who are very mobile and keep moving on, or who have other reasons for not changing their nationality (e.g., as EU citizens, or because of barriers in home countries). These groups find themselves excluded from democratic processes based on the nationality of the electors, even if they want to engage. In some cities such as Brussels, Vienna or Basel, the rate of residents without voting rights is above 30 percent. In Brussels, a hub for highly skilled, highly mobile professionals, 39 percent of the population is not allowed to vote at the level of the region (which encompasses the city of Brussels) – an issue that the non-partisan initiative "1bru1vote" has taken up in their campaign for voting rights for all Brussels residents (1bru1vote n.d.). Within the EU, citizens from one EU country can vote in other EU countries at the communal and EU levels, but not at regional (e.g., bigger cities that are composed of different communes) or national levels. The result is a complex multi-layered citizenship regime in which different people have different combinations of voting rights depending on their nationality. Initiatives demanding voting rights for non-nationals at local levels are also active in other European countries and cities, such as Basel, Geneva, Vienna, Freiburg, Bari or Paris.

In terms of sustainable development, lacking voting rights can be seen as a hindering factor to full social inclusion and the situation raises the question as to the future of democracies when the percentage of residents who do not have a say is increasing. Moreover, the situation that residents of the same place do not share the same citizenship rights runs contrary to ideas of a general "environmental citizenship" in terms of pro-environmental behavior and responsibility for the greater good across national boundaries (Dobson 2007, 280–282).

Many people are also citizens of more than one country and hold dual citizenship. In fact, more than 73 percent of the Swiss who live abroad have dual citizenships (Schlenker et al. 2017). However, it is not always possible to obtain dual citizenship. Dual citizenship can be an illustration of how people move and live in different places at the same time in what has been called "transnational social spaces" (Levitt and Glick Schiller 2004; Schlenker et al. 2017).

Scholars point to the fact that citizenship has always been a matter of negotiation and development, as can be seen in the gradual granting of voting rights to different groups of the population, as Leimgruber (2016) illustrates. In Switzerland, the right to vote, first restricted to men with residence rights and assets, was extended to men without these, then (in 1866) to non-Christian men, and finally (in 1971) to women. In 1975 Swiss living abroad were included (Leimgruber 2016, 29–30). In 1991 the age limit was reduced from 20 to 18 years. Leimgruber sees parallels in the arguments against extending voting rights to women and extending the same rights to foreigners today (2016, 31).

Seen in this light, citizenship has been discussed as a process, an act (Isin and Nilsen 2008) or as insurgent (Holston 2009). Current examples of such processes are the campaigns for extending voting rights to migrants, or schemes such as sanctuary cities and urban citizenship, referred to in the previous section.

While there is a struggle for and against extending voting rights to non-nationals in democratic countries of arrival, migration and mobility are also posing questions to countries of origin. External political rights and engagements of citizens who live abroad have been analyzed under the term "political transnationalism" (Bauböck 2003; Østergaard-Nielsen 2003).

Moreover, there is some discussion as to what kind of effects emigration can have on less democratic countries of origin. Pérez-Armendáriz and Crow (2010) come to the conclusion that migrants from Mexico who go to the US and Canada are "agents of democratic diffusion". In their quantitative survey in Mexico, they find that democratic attitudes and behavior in a less democratic home country are strengthened through migration in three ways: through migrants who return, through individual contact with migrants who are abroad and through broader networks. This kind of diffusion thus does not only affect migrants themselves and their immediate contacts but can have an effect on a larger community.

Not only migrants, but also migration policies shape these dynamics. Miller and Peters (2018) found with regard to autocracies that migration policies become stricter when a larger number of people emigrate to democracies, to hinder democratic diffusion. For economic emigration that leads to remittances and possible emigration of opponents on the other hand, migration policies become liberal as this kind of movement can stabilize autocracies (Miller and Peters 2018).

Conclusion

Migration and mobility are interconnected with sustainable development and democracy in a number of ways. This chapter focused on three such connections: the complex situation around climate change and how environmental degradation can lead to human movement, challenges of social inclusion in terms of migration policies and identities of liberal democracies and the challenges of democratic participation, its negotiation and demands to participate politically in countries of arrival in Europe.

These topics are connected, as environmental degradation and climate change affect those living in poorer countries more severely. Industrialized countries, in turn, are largely responsible for climate change and need to rethink how they position themselves with respect to climate change and displacement. They also need to rethink values and mechanisms of social inclusion in different fields and levels, such as who can move where, and how, who can access which resources and who can have a say, to better adjust to current and future movements of people. Finding sustainable and inclusive approaches, solutions and actions is important now and will become even more pressing in the future.

Notes

1 This research was supported by the National Center of Competence in Research nccr – on the move funded by the Swiss National Science Foundation. I would like to thank Basil Bornemann, two anonymous reviewers, Silva Lässer and Rasmus Priess for comments.
2 The IOM defines environmental migrants as: "Environmental migrants are persons or groups of persons who, for reasons of sudden or progressive changes in the environment that adversely affect their lives or living conditions, are obliged to have to leave their habitual homes, or choose to do so, either temporarily or permanently, and who move either within their territory or abroad" (IOM 2019b).
3 The Internal Displacement Monitoring Centre estimates for 2017, that there were 18,700,000 new internal displacements because of disasters and 11,774,000 because of conflicts. In 2010, the numbers differed as much as 42,350,000 against 2,900,000 (IDMC 2019).
4 See for example the broad UNESCO approach quoting the Commission on Human Rights: "The term 'migrant' in article 1.1 (a) should be understood as covering all cases where the decision to migrate is taken freely by the individual concerned, for reasons of 'personal convenience' and without intervention of an external compelling factor" (UNESCO 2019).
5 Presentation by Giacomo Fedele at the CLISEL conference Ascona, March 3–6, 2019.

References

1bru1vote, n.d. *The #1bru1vote Manifesto* [online]. Available from: www.1bru1vote.be/#manifest [Accessed 15 Dec 2020].
Ayeb-Karlsson, S., Smith, S.D. and Kniveton, D., 2018. *The Conceptual Birth of Trapped Populations and the Danger of Using it as a Policy Tool* [online]. Available from: http://transre.uni-bonn.de/en/blog/conceptual-birth-trapped-populations-and-danger-policy-tool/ [Accessed 2 Dec 2019].
Bauböck, R., 2003. Towards a political theory of migrant transnationalism. *International Migration Review*, 37 (3), 700–723.
Bauböck, R., 2006. *Migration and Citizenship: Legal Status, Rights and Political Participation*. Amsterdam: University Press.
Betts, A. and Collier, P., 2018. *Sustainable Migration: A Framework for Responding to Movement from Poor to Rich Countries*. EMN Norway Occasional Papers, European Migration Network National Contact Point Norway.
Biermann, F. and Boas, I., 2010. Preparing for a Warmer World: Towards a Global Governance System to Protect Climate Refugees. *Global Environmental Politics*, 10 (1), 60–88.
Black, R., et al., 2011. Migration as adaptation. *Nature*, 478, 447–449.
Blatter, J., Hauser, C., and Wyrsch, S., 2016. Kein Stimmrecht – trotzdem mitstimmen. In C. Abbt and J. Rochel, eds. *Migrationsland Schweiz. Vorschläge für eine Politik der Öffnung*. Baden: Hier und Jetzt, 39–54.
Blatter, J., Schmid, S., and Blättler, A., 2017. Democratic deficits in Europe: the overlooked exclusiveness of nation-states and the positive role of the European Union. *Journal of Common Market Studies*, 55 (3), 449–467.
Boas, I., Farbotko, C., Adams, H. et al., 2019. Climate migration myths. *Nature Climate Change*, 9, 901–903.
Bojadžijev, M. and Karakayali, S., 2007. Autonomie der Migration: 10 Thesen zu einer Methode. In Transit Migration Forschungsgruppe, eds. *Turbulente Ränder: Neue Perspektiven auf Migration an den Grenzen Europas*. Bielefeld: Transcript, 203–210.

BXLRefugees, n.d. *About us* [online]. Available from: www.bxlrefugees.be/en/ [Accessed 15 Dec 2020].
Castles, S., 2002. Environmental Change and Forced Migration: Making Sense of the Debate. New Issues in Refugee Research, Research Paper No. 70. Geneva: UNHCR.
D'Amato, G., Wanner, P., and Steiner, I., 2019. Today's Migration-Mobility Nexus in Switzerland. In I. Steiner, and P. Wanner, eds. *Migrants and Expats: The Swiss Migration and Mobility Nexus*. Switzerland: IMISCOE Springer Open.
Dobson, A., 2007. Environmental citizenship: towards sustainable development. *Sustainable Development*, 15 (5), 276–285.
Duchêne-Lacroix, C., Hilti, N., and Schad, H., 2013. L'habiter multilocal: discussion d'un concept émergent et aperçu de sa traduction empirique en Suisse. *Revue Quetelet*, 1 (1), 63–89.
El-Hinnawi, E., 1985. *Environmental Refugees*. Nairobi: UNEP
Erdal, M.B., *et al.*, 2018. Defining Sustainable Migration. EMN Norway Occasional Papers, EMN, PRIO, Norwegian Ministry of Justice and Public Security, Norwegian Directorate of Immigration.
European Commission, 2018. *Reducing emissions from aviation* [online]. Available from: https://ec.europa.eu/clima/policies/transport/aviation_en [Accessed 2 Dec 2019].
Glick Schiller, N. and Salazar, N.B., 2012. Regimes of mobility across the globe. *Journal of Ethnic and Migration Studies*, 39 (2), 183–200.
Hammar, T., 1990. *Democracy and the Nation State. Aliens, Denizens and Citizens in a World of International Migration*. Avebury: Aldershot.
Hess, S., 2010. Aus der Perspektive der Migration forschen. In S. Hess and M. Schwertl, eds. *München migrantisch: migrantisches München: Ethnographische Erkundungen in globalisierten Lebenswelten*. München: Herbert Utz, 9–25.
Holston, J., 2009. *Insurgent Citizenship: Disjunctions of Democracy and Modernity in Brazil*. Princeton: Princeton University Press.
IDMC, 2019. *Displacement Data* [online]. Available from: www.internal-displacement.org/database/displacement-data [Accessed 2 Dec 2019].
International Organization for Migration IOM, 2018. *World Migration Report 2018*. Geneva: International Organization for Migration.
IOM, 2019. *Migration and Climate Change* [online]. Available from: www.iom.int/migration-and-climate-change-0 [Accessed 2 Dec 2019].
IOM, 2019b. *Definitional Issues* [online]. Available from: www.iom.int/definitional-issues [Accessed 2 Dec 2019].
Isin, E. F. and Nilsen, G.M., 2008. *Acts of Citizenship*. Berkeley: University of Chicago Press.
Kaufmann, V., Bergman, M. M., and Joye, D., 2004. Mobility: mobility as capital. *International Journal of Urban and Regional Research*, 28 (4), 745–756.
Leimgruber, W., 2016. Demokratische Reche auf Nicht-Staatsbürger ausweiten. In C. Abbt and J. Rochel, eds. *Migrationsland Schweiz. Vorschläge für eine Politik der Öffnung*. Baden: Hier und Jetzt, 21–37.
Levitt, P. and Glick Schiller, N., 2004. Conceptualizing simultaneity: a transnational social field perspective on society. *International Migration Review*, 38 (3), 1002–1039.
Marshall, T. H., 1950. *Citizenship and Class and Other Essays*. New York: Cambridge University Press.
Migration Data Portal, 2019. *Environmental Migration* [online]. Available from: https://migrationdataportal.org/themes/environmental_migration [Accessed 2 Dec 2019].
Miller, M. K. and Peters, M. E., 2018. Restraining the huddled masses: migration policy and autocratic survival. *British Journal of Political Science*, 50 (2), 403–433.
Moran-Taylor, M. J. and Taylor, M.J., 2010. Land and leña: linking transnational migration, natural resources, and the environment in Guatemala. *Population and Environment*, 32 (2–3), 198–215.
Østergaard-Nielsen, E., 2003. The politics of migrants' transnational political practices. *International Migration Review*, 37 (3), 760–786.
Pérez-Armendáriz, C. and Crow, D., 2010. Do migrants remit democracy? International migration, political beliefs, and behavior in Mexico. *Comparative Political Studies*, 42 (1), 119–148.
Piguet, E., Pécoud, A., and de Guchteneire, P., 2011. Migration and climate change: an overview. *Refugee Survey Quarterly*, 33 (3), 1–23.
Rolshoven, J., 2011. Mobilitätskulturen im Parkour: Überlegungen zu einer kulturwissenschaftlichen Mobilitätsforschung. In R. Johler, M. Matter, and S. Zinn-Thomas, eds. *Mobilitäten: Europa in Bewegung als Herausforderung kulturanalytischer Forschung*. Münster: Waxmann, 52–60.

Römhild, R., 2015. Jenseits ethnischer Grenzen. Für eine postmigrantische Kultur- und Gesellschaftsforschung. In E. Yildiz and M. Hill, eds. *Nach der Migration. Postmigrantische Perspektiven jenseits der Parallelgesellschaft*. Bielefeld: transcript, 37–48.

Sachs, J. D., 2015. *The Age of Sustainable Development*. New York: Columbia University Press.

Schapendonk, J., 2012. Turbulent trajectories. *Societies*, 2 (2), 27–41.

Schilliger, S. and Ataç, I., 2017. Urban Citizenship – Stadt für alle. In Stadtentwicklung Wien, eds. *Gutes Leben für alle braucht eine andere Globalisierung. Herausforderungen und Gestaltungsräume für Städte und Regionen*. Wien: Stadtentwicklung und Stadtplanung Wien, 69–71.

Schlenker, A., Blatter, J., and Birka, I., 2017. Practising transnational citizenship: dual nationality and simultaneous political involvement among emigrants. *Journal of Ethnic and Migration Studies*, 43 (3), 418–440.

Sheller, M., 2018. *Mobility Justice: The Politics of Movement in an Age of Extremes*. New York: Verso.

Sontag, K., 2018a. Highly skilled asylum seekers: case studies of refugee students at a Swiss university. *Migration Letters*, 15 (4), S. 533–544.

Sontag, K., 2018b. *Mobile Entrepreneurs. An Ethnographic Study of the Migration of the Highly Skilled*. Opladen: Budrich UniPress.

Sontag, K., 2019. Refugee students' access to three European universities: an ethnographic study. *Social Inclusion*, 7 (1), 71–79.

Tacoli, C., 2009. Crisis or adaptation? Migration and climate change in a context of high mobility. *Environment & Urbanization*, 21 (2), 513–525.

UNESCO, 2019. *Migrant/Migration* [online]. Available from: www.unesco.org/new/en/social-and-human-sciences/themes/international migration/glossary/migrant/ [Accessed 2 Dec 2019].

UNHCR, 2019. *UNHCR appalled at news of refugee and migrant deaths on Mediterranean Sea*. Available from: www.unhcr.org/news/press/2019/1/5c41e8a04/unhcr-appalled-news-refugee-migrant-deaths-mediterranean-sea.html [Accessed 2 Dec 2019].

United Nations, Department of Economic and Social Affairs, Population Division, 2017. *International Migration Report 2017: Highlights* (ST/ESA/SER.A/404).

United Nations, Department of Economic and Social Affairs, Population Division, 2019. *International Migrant Stock 2019* [online]. Available from: www.un.org/en/development/desa/population/migration/publications/migrationreport/docs/MigrationStock2019_TenKeyFindings.pdf [Accessed 2 Dec 2019].

United Nations, Department of Economic and Social Affairs, n.d. Transforming our world: the 2030 Agenda for Sustainable Development [online]. Available from: https://sdgs.un.org/2030agenda [Accessed 15 Dec 2020].

Urry, J., 2000. *Sociology BEYOND SOCIETIES: Mobilities for the Twenty-first Century*. London: Routledge.

Warner, K., et al., 2010. Climate change, environmental degradation and migration. *Natural Hazards*, 55 (3), 689–715.

Wimmer, A. and Glick Schiller, N., 2002. Methodological nationalism and the study of migration. *Archives of European Sociology*, 43 (2), 217–240.

Zschirnt, E. and Fibbi, R., 2019. Do Swiss Citizens of Immigrant Origin Face Hiring Discrimination the Labour Market? *Working Paper#20, nccr – on the move* [online]. Available from: https://nccr-onthemove.ch/publications/do-swiss-citizens-of-immigrant-origin-face-hiring-discrimination-in-the-labour-market/ [Accessed 2 Dec 2019].

25
FOOD SUSTAINABILITY AND FOOD DEMOCRACY
Exploring the links

Basil Bornemann

Introduction

There was a time when the food question seemed to be solved, at least for the Global North (considered "developed countries" at the time). Driven by massive, state-subsidized technological innovation and industrialization, a food regime producing ever more and cheaper food to satisfy the increasing consumption demands of a growing and ever more affluent population dominated. Food was hardly a relevant topic on the political agenda. It was an object dealt with by experts, administrators, and lobbyists in relatively closed circles that were fenced off the realm of politics, let alone the broader public. In recent years, however, this picture has substantially changed. Food issues have become considerably politicized in numerous ways. Scientists, social movements, citizens, and consumers increasingly question the adequacy of current food production and consumption patterns (Lang, Barling, and Caraher 2009). Although there are certainly many sources and forms of food politicization, two developments and related strands of academic discussion are particularly relevant in the context of this volume's overall theme: sustainable food and food democracy.

First, in recent years, food has become a core topic of sustainability politics and governance and related research (Hinrichs 2010; 2014). Driven by mounting scientific insights and a rising concern for the risks induced by modernization, the consequences of the industrialized agricultural production system for the environment and human beings have become increasingly problematized by social movements and (predominantly) green political parties. As a result, a broad debate about more sustainable forms of food supply has emerged, rapidly developing over the past decade. Whereas the initial focus was on sustainable agriculture (Obach 2015), the debate and politics of sustainable food today extend to other parts of the food system, such as trade and distribution, consumption and dietary patterns, and disposal of food (Garnett 2013; Reisch, Eberle, and Lorek 2013).

Second, and certainly to a much lesser degree, food has become an object of democratic practice and reflection. As in the debate surrounding sustainable food, the starting point of food democracy calls have been the increasingly industrialized and globalized food supply. However, the primary concern here is not the substantial social and environmental impacts of the food system, but the experience of increasing alienation of people from their food base and limited opportunities to take part in food-related decisions. Modern food systems, which are characterized by industrial mass production, are beyond people's control; they are dominated by powerful multinational corporations, while people are increasingly forced into the role of passive consumers, who can, at best, articulate their interests and ideas in the form of a demand mediated by anonymous market mechanisms (with some observers considering the resulting power of consumers to be no more than a simulation) (Lang 1999; 2003). As a reaction to the prevailing power concentration in the food system, numerous counter-movements have formed over the last 20 years, demanding equal access to food ("food justice"), more autonomous food production ("food sovereignty"), or increased possibilities to take part in food-related decisions, that is, "food democracy" (Lang 2005; Hassanein 2008; Booth and Coveney 2015;).

The two debates around "sustainable food" and "food democracy" partly overlap and are interrelated in multiple ways. For example, calls for more food democracy are sometimes made with reference to the expected positive sustainability effects (Dahlberg 2001; Hassanein 2003; Lang 2005; Blay-Palmer 2010; Booth and Coveney 2015; Petetin 2016). In democratically organized food systems, people are more aware of the ecological and social impacts and are more capable of responding collectively. Some consider sustainable food systems as requiring the democratization of food production and consumption in the first place. However, there are also doubts that sustainable food systems can be organized in a democratic manner, at least if food democracy is being understood as involving increased local practices of organic farming (see Trewavas 2001). To feed the planet's growing population in a sustainable way, the conventional mass production system backed by large corporations, who cannot be controlled in a democratic manner, is essential (see Harriss and Stewart 2015).

Considering the lively and sometimes interrelated debates on sustainable and democratic food systems, this chapter aims to provide an overview of the two concepts and their complex relationships. By asking how sustainability and democracy are related in contemporary food systems and their governance, this chapter seeks to explore whether – and to what extent and how – it is possible to have "sustainable food" and "democratic food" at the same time.

In the next section, I recapitulate the sustainability implications of contemporary food systems and open up various interpretations of sustainable food (section 2). I then focus on the debate about food democracy by outlining established and more recent critical accounts (section 3). I pull together the two strands of discussion and identify both productive and dysfunctional relations between sustainable food and food democracy (section 4). To further discuss democratic and sustainable food systems, I propose a scheme that can guide more systematic considerations on the relationship between sustainability and democracy within the food system (section 5). In the conclusion, future research perspectives are pointed out (section 6).

Sustainable food

There is widespread agreement that current food production and consumption patterns are "unsustainable" in many respects (Weis 2007; Blay-Palmer 2010; McMichael 2011; Lang and Barling 2012; Reisch, Eberle, and Lorek 2013). To ensure the long-term supply of sufficient healthy food for the world's growing population while respecting the earth's ecological carrying capacities, a fundamental sustainability-oriented transformation of the food system is required. And indeed, there is growing evidence that food-related practices are shifting toward sustainability (Spaargaren, Oosterveer, and Loeber 2012; Eakin et al. 2017). In the following, I briefly shed light on how food contributes to sustainability problems. Subsequently, the formation of the sustainable food policy discourse is discussed, and different understandings of sustainable food are summarized and related to each other.

Food-based sustainability problems

Food production and consumption patterns in contemporary societies are widely recognized as contributing to the emergence of numerous local and global sustainability problems (Garnett 2013; Lawrence, Lyons, and Wallington 2010). For example, food production is largely responsible for the generation of climate-damaging gases. In particular, the production of animal products is a major driver of global climate change – directly through the production of methane in livestock farming and indirectly through the deforestation of carbon-storing forests for feed crop production. The loss of biodiversity, as well as the exploitation and consumption of land and soil, can be significantly attributed to industrialized agriculture. This is true, as well, for the depletion of freshwater resources through the use of irrigation. The ecological footprint of food production that is generated by industrialized and intensive agriculture and factory farming is amplified on the consumption side by a dietary transition toward a meat-based diet but also by food waste (Reisch, Eberle, and Lorek 2013). At the same time, the ecological footprint of the food system along with that of other societal sectors poses an increasing challenge to food production. Climate change or the destruction of soils and genetic diversity threaten food production capacities in the medium or even short term (Godfray et al. 2010; Garnett 2013).

In addition to these ecological effects, food systems have numerous social consequences. Climate-damaged or otherwise ecologically overburdened agricultural production systems contribute to impoverishment, conflict and migration, which can also trigger social conflicts elsewhere (Maharatna 2014). The reliance of smallholder farms on the provision of production inputs (land, seeds, pesticides, and fertilizers) by agrochemical corporations leads to neofeudal dependency structures and related social vulnerability (Weis 2007). The exploitation of workers (many of them with a migration background) in agricultural production in the countries of the Global North and the sometimes precarious working conditions in the trade and distribution of food are further examples of the negative social impacts of the current food system (Davies 2019). In addition, there are significant social distortions and inequalities on the consumption side; these range from dramatic food shortages and acute hunger of a large part of the world population – no longer only in Global South countries – to considerable inequalities in access to good/healthy food (e.g., "food deserts") with the corresponding health consequences (Alkon and Agyeman 2011). The undernourishment that is still widespread in the Global South and the over- and malnutrition prevalent in the Global North are two sides of the same coin of a globalized food system that is characterized by considerable inequalities (Béné et al. 2019).

Food production and trade are significant economic factors at both the global and local levels and are responsible for the livelihoods of a large proportion of the world's population. Indeed, food security in the Global South has steadily improved over the years, which has driven economic development in other sectors (Timmer 2005). In many countries of the Global North, relative declines in food prices have triggered consumption dynamics and fueled economic growth in other sectors. (The fact that this has also increased the ecological footprint in other consumption sectors – fashion, mobility, and consumer electronics – is another matter.) In this respect, today's globalized and corporate-controlled food system can be seen as a success story that has spurred socioeconomic development.

Nevertheless, economic dislocations have also become increasingly visible, particularly in the wake of the food crises of 2007/2008 and 2011/2012. These crises were the result of the emergence of food as a source of international speculative investment, which was driven by increased financialization and that led to significant price dynamics with massive consequences for global and local food markets (Field 2016). Economic dislocations also include the large-scale exploitation of agricultural production land through intensive farming practices, which have led to medium-term productivity degradation in ever more climate-challenged regions. Furthermore, the destruction of local food markets by flooding them with industrially produced and increasingly "standardized" mass products of globally operating large corporations and state-subsidized production surpluses in the Global North undermines local economies in the Global South. In the Global North, too, considerable negative economic effects of the corporate food regime can be observed, such as the destruction of smallholder structures or the macroeconomic follow-up costs of profit-driven supply of cheap and unhealthy food for public budgets and social security systems (subsidies and health care costs) (Lang, Barling, and Caraher 2009).

The sustainability impacts of today's food production and consumption are contextualized in that they manifest in different ways in local settings (e.g., undernutrition in the Global South and overnutrition in the Global North as two forms of malnutrition). However, they are all together (and on a global scale) related to a certain historically evolved and politically shaped formation of the current food system, which is based on a combination of industrialized mass production, globalized markets, and expanding consumption dynamics. Although this regime has been relatively successful in addressing food insecurity over many years, the numerous negative side effects of this temporary success model point to its limitations and the need for transformation (Blay-Palmer 2010).

Sustainability-oriented food politics and policy

Issues such as the ecological consequences of industrialized agriculture or global inequality had been addressed long before the emergence of the sustainability debate (albeit predominantly in narrowly defined scientific and activist circles). However, the emergence of the sustainability idea has raised awareness of the numerous interactions between individual problems, promoting an integrated view of individual problem dimensions (Hinrichs 2010; 2014; Eakin et al. 2017). From the early years of the sustainability debate, food was a relevant topic, as evidenced, for example, by the corresponding thematic chapters in the Brundtland Report and Agenda 21 (Allen 1993). However, at the beginning of the sustainability discussion, especially in the Global North, other topics, such as energy and climate policy or the loss of biodiversity initially dominated. It is only in recent years that the relationship between food and sustainability has come more clearly to the center of public and political attention.

In addition to a general turn to food and nutrition issues (also driven by increased health awareness), science has been an important driver for linking food with sustainability. Thus, research has repeatedly pointed out the complex interactions between food systems and social-ecological systems and has made comprehensive proposals for shaping sustainability-oriented transformation processes (Godfray et al. 2010). Social food movements or non-governmental organizations (NGOs) also play an important role in the sustainability-oriented politicization of the current food regime. Thus, numerous food initiatives and movements have emerged at different levels, sometimes more and sometimes less explicitly pointing to sustainability problems and the need for sustainability-oriented transformation of the food system (Holt-Giménez 2011). Examples include "organic farming," "fair trade," "food sharing," and "plant-based diets" movements. In addition to their attempts at shaping the political agenda toward sustainability, many of these groups establish their own alternative approaches and practices to address sustainability problems.

The key role of food system transformations for sustainable development is also being recognized more often in "official" politics and policy making. With the 2030 Agenda and the 17 SDGs, food has finally been recognized as a central topic of the sustainability debate and research. Apart from a separate global goal on food (SDG2, Zero hunger: end hunger, achieve food security and improved nutrition, and promote sustainable agriculture), direct or indirect references to food and nutrition issues can be found in numerous other goals. Conversely, food also affects the realization of multiple other SDGs (Valentini et al. 2019). Because of its numerous references to various sustainability issues and goals, food is considered an important transformation lever for sustainability transformations (Blay-Palmer 2010; Hinrichs 2014).

In addition to sustainability strategists discovering food as an important vehicle for a sustainability-oriented transformation of society, we can also observe an increasing "sustainabilization" of food policy. Thus, the idea of sustainable development, which has spread to almost all sectors of society and policy areas since the early 1990s, has also penetrated food policy at various levels. For example, it has become an important normative reference point for international food security governance (Berry et al. 2015). Sustainability also plays an increasingly important principle of European agricultural policy (Rayner, Barling, and Lang 2008). Previously, agricultural policy in the European context was dominated by the paradigm of industrial, export-oriented agriculture, which was considered in need of special protection because of its potential vulnerability in the global markets and, therefore, was treated as an "exceptional policy." This belief system has been increasingly challenged over time and has gradually become fragile despite significant forces of persistence (Daugbjerg and Feindt 2020). Especially in the wake of various food safety crises (such as the "mad cow disease"), industrialized agriculture's limits, and side effects – and the agricultural policies that support it – have become visible and politicized. In the reform processes beginning in the early 2000s, sustainability was certainly neither the only nor an undisputed paradigm of reorientation. Instead, several guiding principles, such as "competitive agriculture" or "multifunctional agriculture," have been competing for relative supremacy ever since (Feindt et al. 2008). However, the notion of a "sustainable agriculture" has now become established as an almost indispensable conceptual and normative reference in the EU's food policy discourse.

This "sustainabilization of agricultural policy" is evidenced not only by the symbolic reference to sustainability in food policies, but also by a number of concrete political measures. These include, for example, programs to promote organic farming or the greening of agriculture by changed incentive systems, such as the linking of subsidies to compliance with ecological criteria, but also new regulations regarding the use of certain pesticides and fertilization methods, or in the area of animal welfare (Rayner, Barling, and Lang 2008; Daugbjerg and Swinbank 2016; Buller et al. 2018).

Apart from these agricultural policy reforms, the emergence of sustainability has increasingly broadened the frame of reference for food policymaking. For a long time, a production-centered interpretation of food dominated. Yet informed by the systemic view of sustainability, other sectors and spheres of food-related activities ("from field to fork," as it has been recently called in the European Green Deal) and with them other actors are increasingly coming into the focus of design efforts: the role of large corporations in globalized trade relations, but also the role of consumers as relevant market forces, whose behavior can be influenced by approaches of consumer information. In contrast to agricultural policy focused on production issues, today's food governance presents itself as a comprehensive, cross-sectoral policy that spans different sectors and levels of the food system (Reisch, Eberle, and Lorek 2013).

Perspectives on sustainable food (systems)

At the nexus of food and sustainability policy, a diverse discourse on sustainable food has emerged, including numerous approaches to clarifying the meaning of the term (Garnett 2013; Béné et al. 2019). These approaches are policy relevant in that they guide thinking about sustainability-oriented transformations of the food system and the design of corresponding food governance arrangements. In doing so, the discourse feeds on the narratives of different "communities of practice" that, while agreeing on the unsustainability of the current state, each is based on specific ontological, epistemological, and normative assumptions that translate into different understandings of sustainable food system transformation (Hinrichs 2010; Eakin et al. 2017; Béné et al. 2019).

For example, the narratives differ regarding the problem drivers and leverage points for sustainability-oriented change (Garnett 2013). For one, they emphasize the importance of food production as the key to sustainable food, accordingly calling for a shift toward sustainable agriculture (Velten et al. 2015). Related ideas vary between high-tech efficiency-enhanced production, such as precision farming and sustainable intensification (Godfray 2015) and more alternative practices of organic farming. On the other hand, consumption is identified as a driver and key for transformation (Reisch, Eberle, and Lorek 2013). Accordingly, the focus is on shaping food systems through transitions to sustainable diets (Auestad and Fulgoni 2015). Finally, there are approaches that emphasize the systemic interplay of production and consumption in complex food systems shaped by social and economic power relations and political governance arrangements (Garnett 2013; Eakin et al. 2017). Consequently, they see multiple entry points for sustainability-oriented transformations of the food system.

Across the various approaches to problematizing and shaping sustainable food, the discourse varies in terms of normative orientations, that is, the explicit or implicit objectives envisioned in terms of sustainable development. Three basic perspectives can be identified that largely correspond to the three basic normative orientations that are characteristic of the general sustainability discourse. These normative perspectives hardly appear in a pure form but instead are combined in different ways in concrete approaches (Garnett 2013; Béné et al. 2019).

First, there are approaches that, with different emphases, direct the normative focus toward ensuring a sufficient supply of food for all people worldwide. The starting point here is an understanding of sustainability that focuses on the just provision of the basic human needs of all people living now and in the future. Accordingly, the aim is to satisfy the growing demand for food because of population growth and increasing prosperity under increasingly difficult production conditions (e.g., climate change) through a more efficient food supply. Although this debate has long been characterized by a productionist orientation that focuses solely on "closing the yield gap" (Godfray et al. 2010), there are an increasing number of positions that accentuate the issues of distributive justice and equitable access to food.

A second perspective is clearly characterized by an ecological interpretation of sustainable food. The focus is on the negative ecological consequences of the current food system or, more precisely, on their effects on the functioning of ecological systems (including the repercussions of disturbed ecological systems on the food system itself). Accordingly, the normative focus is on maintaining the ecological carrying capacities and preserving the resilience of ecological systems – thus maintaining the functioning of the food system itself. The central objective underlying this interpretation of sustainable food is the reduction of the "food print" (i.e., the ecological footprint of food) at all stages of the food system, from production to distribution, trade, consumption, and disposal.

A third normative orientation in the sustainable food discourse is based on the proposition of an inescapable indeterminacy and contestedness of notions of sustainable food. It argues for a particularized, contextualized, and proceduralized interpretation of the ideas and practices that are supposed to inform a sustainability-oriented transformation of the food system (Hinrichs 2010). For example, the sustainability-related impacts of certain production practices, as well as of consumption patterns or diets, are likely to vary locally; therefore, they can only be assessed "on the ground." Apart from the material effects of food practices, the evaluation basis, that is, the respective understandings of "good" or "just food" and of valuable ecological limits, also vary. This is reflected in the idea of "cultural food adequacy," which has become a central orientation of sustainable food discourse. Because our relation to food is primarily cultural, the aspect of local-specificity is central to sustainable food systems (Béné et al. 2019). Therefore, sustainability in food systems is unlikely to result from "one blue ribbon recipe, publicized, circulated, and followed to the letter. Instead, multiple recipes need to be located, tested, perused, adapted and shared" (Hinrichs 2010, p. 19). Sustainable food systems "emerge from participation in everyday practice. They must involve a collaborative and inevitably political process of inquiry and adjustment. This means incremental and collective tinkering" (Hinrichs 2010, p. 26).

In sum, the three perspectives on sustainable food reflect the three basic normative understandings of the sustainability discourse more generally, with "justice" representing a moral understanding, "resilience" pointing to a functional conception, and "deliberation" forming a procedural interpretation (Bornemann and Burger 2019). Taken together, these understandings can be considered a comprehensive normative basis for sustainable development and sustainable food in particular. Sustainable food then becomes a deliberative process of context-specific clarification of the appropriate forms of food production, distribution, and consumption that takes into account a complex idea of justice, on the one hand, and ecological resilience, on the other hand.

Food democracy

At first glance, food and democracy seem to have a mutually productive relationship. Comparative historical analyses show that democratic regimes tend to be better able to supply their populations with food and avert hunger crises (Sen 1982; Rossignoli and Balestri 2018). Conversely, sufficient availability of food can be seen as a prerequisite for the functioning and stability of democracy. People whose basic material needs are sufficiently satisfied are more inclined to develop emancipative value orientations and pursue them democratically (Inglehart and Welzel 2005). In this respect, today's prevailing system of industrialized mass production of food could be interpreted as a contribution to the democratization or stabilization of today's democratic political systems. On a global historical scale, one could argue that the model of industrialized agricultural mass production is at least partly responsible for the triumph of democracies. However, it is precisely this model that has been criticized for some years – not only from the perspective of sustainability, but also from the perspective of democracy. In the following section, the democratic critique of the food system will be briefly outlined before conceptual perspectives on food democracy are presented.

Democratizing the food system: problems and movements

First introduced by food academic and former farmer Tim Lang in 1999 (Lang 1999), the term food democracy has been used ever since to criticize the state of the current food system and its governance (Hassanein 2003; 2008; Booth and Coveney 2015; Bornemann and Weiland 2019a). While the general object of this criticism, "the current food system," corresponds to that of the sustainability critique presented in the previous section, the democratic critique sets other emphases. Its focus is less on the material effects of the food system (although the democratic implications of these consequences are problematized as well). Instead, the normative qualities of the practices of food production, distribution, and consumption that make up for the current food system as well as the governance arrangements and power relations that have produced and continue to shape this system are at the center of concern: many food practices are incompatible with the idea of democratic self-determination as they promote the disenfranchisement of people in terms of choosing and organizing their food supply. In a system of industrial mass food production run by a few global corporations, people are disconnected, if not alienated, from their food base and thus from the very conditions of their survival (Lang 1999; Booth and Coveney 2015; Petetin 2016). Power is concentrated in the hands of a few corporate actors, and there are few opportunities for the people to participate in shaping the food system (Lang 1999; 2003; Hassanein 2003; 2008). The multinational corporations and institutions of "Big Food" that dominate the global food value chains can largely escape democratic control (Booth and Coveney 2015, 3–9; Hamilton 2004). In part, they are proactively trying to maintain control over the design and values of the food system by fighting the use of consumer information and alternative products and markets (Petetin 2016). Even within national and supranational democratic contexts, agricultural policy has been made mainly by a relatively closed circle of political-administrative actors and lobbyists who exclude the broader public from decision making (Tangermann and von Cramon-Taubadel 2013; Daugbjerg and Feindt 2020).

For some time now, however, a fracturing of this regime can be observed, not least as a result of the general politicization of food, but, above all, in the wake of the food safety crises that emerged at the beginning of the 2000s. Thus, in the European context, the role of parliaments in shaping food policy has been strengthened. Increasingly, important agricultural policy decisions have also been debated and voted on in the parliamentary arena (Tangermann and von Cramon-Taubadel 2013). In this respect, especially in the European context, certain tendencies toward the pluralization of actor constellations and processes are evident, which can be interpreted as a democratization of the food policy system.

However, the term "food democracy" proper is used to refer to democratization movements and governance arrangements located more at the periphery of the institutional system of liberal democracies. A prototypical example of this are food policy councils. These are pluralistically composed, more or less formalized, and organized governance networks that are usually formed at the local or regional level to deal with food-related issues (Harper et al. 2009). Food policy councils often originate from civil society initiatives, but sometimes, they are also launched, established, and supported by local or regional governments. Food policy councils aim at creating or strengthening networks between local or regional actors in the food sector. Furthermore, they seek to influence food policy by acting as agenda setters for food issues and making recommendations on current food-related policy processes (Bassarab et al. 2019). To the extent that they challenge entrenched food systems and confront them with alternative ideas and interests, food policy councils contribute to the democratization of food systems (Bornemann and Weiland 2019b).

In addition to the emergence of (semiofficial) food policy councils, the rise of food democracy is associated with a growing number of other, mainly local, governance arrangements and practices that are aimed at changed producer-consumer relations. These "civic food networks" include local food markets, community supported agriculture schemes, urban gardening projects, food-sharing initiatives, consumer cooperatives, and so on (Lyson 2004; Renting, Schermer, and Rossi 2012; A. R. Davies, Cretella, and Franck 2019). Notwithstanding the numerous differences between these various forms and their local manifestations, the normative–political self-understanding of many of these initiatives is to reclaim individual and collective autonomy in relation to the production, distribution, and consumption of food, and to remake the food system in a way that reconnects people with their food base and related decision-making (Booth and Coveney 2015; Bornemann and Weiland 2019b).

From a historical perspective, the emergence of these alternative approaches and practices of food democracy can be seen in the context of democratizing tendencies in society as a whole (Dahlberg 2001). Hence, democracy becomes the guiding idea for shaping collective action in different spheres of society beyond institutionalized forms of (strictly speaking, political) governance and policymaking. Food democracy lines up with other forms of democratization in various societal sectors, such as the economy and the workplace (Frega, Herzog, and Neuhäuser 2019) or the energy system (Szulecki and Overland 2020). Their common denominator is the diagnosis of a democratic deficit in the respective socio-economic fields that requires, therapywise, a re-shaping of corresponding governance arrangements along democratic principles (Warren 2009).

Perspectives on food democracy

At the heart of many definitions of food democracy is the notion that people can exert power, remodel, and improve the existing food system (Booth and Coveney 2015, 14). It refers to increased abilities of the public to actively participate in the development of their food systems and to create alternative outlooks on what food is and how it should be produced and consumed (Petetin 2016). Self-understandings and analyses of food democracy, therefore, often make reference to comprehensive, direct, and active opportunities for "food citizens" to participate in and shape the collective decisions regarding food-related production, distribution, and consumption practices in specific local food systems on the ground. Based on the notion "that all people actively and meaningfully participate in the shaping of food systems," Neva Hassanein (2008, p. 289), for example, conceptualizes food democracy in terms of five dimensions (though they take the form of postulates rather than argumentatively derived conceptual elements). The basic premise is that food democracy is based on the combination of collective action by various food actors and organizations, on the one hand (the "Collaborating Toward Food System Sustainability" dimension), and meaningful participation by individual actors, on the other hand. The latter is conceptualized along four additional dimensions. Participation is meaningful when it enables people to "gain knowledge about food and the food system" and "share ideas about the food system with others." Further, participation should enable people to develop "efficacy with respect to food and the food system" and "acquiring an orientation toward the community good."

That this understanding of food democracy is linked to a notion of strong participatory democracy is not only conceptually evident but also becomes clear when considering the references Hassanein herself cites in developing her approach. Central here is Benjamin Barber and his theory of strong democracy (Barber 2003). References to strong, participatory democracy can be found in numerous other passages in the debate about food democracy – not least because Hassanein's text itself has become an important point of reference for corresponding analyses. In this respect, it is not surprising that the thematization and analysis of food democracy refer quite significantly to the practices of collaboration and participation in local settings.

References to other regional, national, and global governance contexts that have been alluded to in Hassanein's original text remain rather underexposed.

From a critical perspective, a certain narrowing of the focus can be noted, which has been described as a "local bias" or even a "local trap" (Hinrichs 2003; Born and Purcell 2006). These terms refer to an a priori attribution of positive qualities to the local level, meaning that the local level is associated with the hope and expectation not only of a better (e.g., more sustainable) food system but also of a better democracy. Even if one does not follow the critique of the "local trap" in all its implications, the dominant conceptualization of food democracy as a strong and participatory local democracy is at least accompanied with a particular focus on one aspect of democracy (participation) in a specific governance context (local governance). Here, the question arises whether and to what extent the emphatic appeal to local participatory practices obscures particular alternative possibilities for thinking about and practicing food democracy.

Taking up this criticism, attention has recently been drawn to alternative interpretations of food democracy beyond strong participatory democracy, which are particularly relevant in governance contexts beyond the local level (Behringer and Feindt 2019; Bornemann and Weiland 2019b). The conceptual starting point of the corresponding contributions is an understanding of complex democracy, within which participation is only one element among others. According to the concept of complex democracy, the democratic quality of governance arrangements at different levels is determined by three dimensions of democratic legitimacy (Schmidt 2013). The input dimension refers to the possibilities of articulating interests and ideas and, thus, to democratic principles such as participation and representation. Output legitimacy is measured by the ability of a governance arrangement to deal with problems effectively and efficiently. Finally, throughput legitimacy refers to procedural quality, including aspects such as transparency and the deliberative capacity of democratic procedures.

Such a complex understanding of democracy underlines that increasing the possibilities and capacities of people to take part in food-related decision making is only one way, among others, to enhance the democratic quality of food governance. Apart from expanding participation opportunities, the democratization of the food system can be achieved through more deliberative processes or improved (more efficient and effective) government policies. This broadening of perspective opens a new view for a broad set of additional conceptual starting points for the analysis and design of democratic food governance. In particular, a perspective of complex democracy also opens for the view for different practices of input-, throughput-, and output-oriented democratization of food governance and their interactions (Bornemann and Weiland 2019b). For example, a particular practice of relying on food policy councils, which increases input and throughput legitimacy, might be combined with food-related education policies that can contribute to output legitimacy.

Linking sustainable food and food democracy

The preceding sections show how the current food system has been politicized from and in different directions. On the one hand, the discourse on sustainable food problematizes the existing patterns of food production, processing, distribution, and consumption from a sustainability perspective, pointing to the perverse social, economic, and ecological side effects of a largely industrialized food system, hence calling for a sustainable transformation of the food system. On the other hand, food democracy critically addresses power concentration in the existing food regime (and its social consequences), hence calling for more inclusive and participative food governance arrangements. This section highlights some general propositions and findings on the relationship between sustainability and democracy in the context of food systems. In so doing, I point out four types of possible relationships, two of them being synergistic and two others being of a conflictual nature.

The first, almost classical, perspective is that food democracy serves as a driver of sustainable development. Underlying this is the assumption of a positive impact of food system democratization on its sustainability: the democratization of the food system can trigger sustainability-oriented transformations of food systems and beyond (Petetin 2016). In line with the long-standing notion that sustainable development requires participation, the argument is that involving people in decisions about the food system will lead to its improved sustainability. Two specific reasons are given: first, at the level of individual action, democracy has an educative function. By actively addressing food issues within the framework of a democratic process, people are encouraged to broaden their food knowledge and reflect on the consequences of their food-related behavior, not to mention the negative consequences of the current food system more generally. Their insights will lead to behavioral changes toward more sustainable food practices. People who are actively involved in shaping food systems "on the ground" tend to be more inclined to follow sustainable consumption patterns (Hassanein 2003). The second reason is located at the level of collective action and concerns the function of democratic processes to create collectively binding decisions. Democratic food governance that relies on the representation, participation, and deliberation of actors with different ideas, interests, and identities is more likely to consider and address the variety of environmental and social consequences of certain production and consumption patterns and the associated concerns of different actors (Lang 2005). Unsustainable food systems, on the other hand, reflect the failure of governance systems to consider the negative impacts of food production and consumption on people and nature in food-related decision-making and design processes (Dahlberg 2001).

Second, arguments can be made that food sustainability is a driver of the democratization of the food system. Sustainable food, including its components such as food justice, has become a relevant objective for social and political actors to engage in politics and policymaking (Levkoe 2006; Alkon and Agyeman 2011). The rise of food politics – the problematization of the unsustainable impacts of food production and consumption and our relationship with food more generally – can be interpreted in terms of democratization: actors organize their interests and bring together their ideas to challenge the existing status quo of the food systems, push for food policy change, and, sometimes, aim for change of the political conditions more generally (Wekerle and Classens 2015). Driven by concerns about the unsustainability of the current food system and motivated by its potential to trigger and shape a sustainability-oriented transformation, people empower themselves or are empowered to take food-related decisions into their own hands (Bornemann and Weiland 2019b). They initiate food policy councils and engage in democratic practices on the ground, with which they seek not only to express their ideas and interests, but also to develop more sustainability-oriented food governance.

Besides these productive relationships, there are also a number of trade-offs and tensions between concepts and practices of food democracy on the one hand, and sustainable food (systems), on the other. For one, strengthening food democracy may have negative sustainability effects. There are, at least, potential tensions between decidedly local approaches to food democracy and the sustainability performance of local food systems. Classical understandings of food democracy are based on the idea of a food system that is characterized by largely local production, distribution, and consumption practices that are shaped by people "on the ground." However, critics argue that a localized food system is by no means a guarantee of a sustainable food system (Born and Purcell 2006). Even local food systems can bring unsustainable impacts locally or elsewhere, which can accumulate into supralocal problems. In any case, numerous analyses show that locally produced food is not always the most resource- and emissions-efficient alternative. In addition to potentially negative economic effects (inefficiencies in production and distribution), negative social effects of local food democracy can also be observed, such as the exclusion of certain social groups or milieus from participation in local food consumption practices as well as political participation in local food governance (Hinrichs 2003). These concrete tensions between local food democracy and sustainable food point to a more fundamental conflict between the procedural openness of democratic processes, on the one hand, and the substantial values and claims related to sustainability, that is, the appeal to justice and consideration of boundaries, on the other hand.

Conversely, the approaches and practices of sustainability-oriented governance of food systems can come into conflict with, or even obstruct, food democracy. For example, technocratic tendencies as expressed in rationalistic, goal-fixated, and science-based sustainability assessment frameworks for food (Slätmo, Fischer, and Röös 2017) stand in conflict with democratic norms of participation and deliberation. Tensions can also arise regarding governance practices that, at first glance, are democracy-enhancing. For example, calls for participation in sustainable food discourse often refer to the involvement of organized stakeholder and build less on an emphatic notion of citizen participation (Wezel et al. 2020). The hope for participation is driven by more instrumental–functional considerations of whether the state alone would be able to provide sufficient resources to initiate and shape a sustainability-oriented transformation of society. This instrumental idea of stakeholder participation, which dominates much of the broader literature on sustainability (Meadowcroft 2004), stands in marked contrast to the radical democratic notions of participation inherent in classical concepts of food democracy, which emphasize the intrinsic value of participation as an expression of equality and autonomy.

Toward an integrated understanding of sustainability-oriented food democracy

The previous section mapped out some synergistic and conflictual relationships between sustainable food and food democracy that are present in the literature. In this last section, I seek to further develop the existing discussion in conceptual respects. I do so by proposing a scheme that relates the considerations of democracy and sustainability in the field of food in a more systematic manner. Thereby, I provide a simple framework for imagining approaches and practices of sustainability-oriented democratic food governance and for guiding corresponding empirical research and practical design efforts.

This framework combines a broad understanding of food democracy with a comprehensive understanding of sustainable development. Following the considerations about a three-dimensional understanding of food democracy introduced above, I distinguish among the input, throughput, and output dimensions of democratic legitimacy. Likewise, I conceptualize sustainable development through the three perspectives highlighting the different dimensions of sustainable food, namely a moral dimension of justice, a functional dimension of resilience, and a procedural dimension of deliberation. The cross-tabulation of the concepts opens an interpretive space for mapping and assessing the democratic and sustainability-related potential of food governance ideas and practices (see Table 25.1). Doing this reminds us that democratization does not necessarily lead to sustainable development and vice versa. In addition, it opens up opportunities to address the potential tensions and contradictions between sustainability and democracy and to think about how food governance practices can be conceived of and designed to meet both democratic standards and sustainability criteria.

For example, a practice of strengthening democratic input legitimacy (e.g., a practice of participation) is only a contribution to food system sustainability insofar as it also contributes to the achievement of intertemporal equity, the adherence to systemic boundaries, or deliberative clarification of the meaning of sustainable food in a specific context. Conversely, practices of aligning food systems with ecological boundaries (e.g., setting rules that restrain certain food production and consumption practices such that certain limits are respected) are democratic only to the extent that they also contribute to input, throughput, or output legitimacy. This is the case, for example, when people are involved in setting appropriate limits, when the definition of these limits is embedded in deliberative processes, or when people are empowered to accept limits (e.g., through information and education).

As a theoretical framework for reflection, the scheme confirms a number of potentially tense or, at least, ambivalent relationships between food democracy and sustainable food. These occur, for example, when the processual nature of democracy meets the substantive requirements of sustainable food. The expansion of opportunities for participation in food-related decision-making processes does not yet guarantee that these opportunities for participation will be used for redistributive or limiting policies. Rather, in view of the utility calculations of real actors, there are justifiable doubts about precisely this. Other connections are challenging, but certainly conceivable in terms of creating positive relationships, some of which have been realized in practice. The democratic governance of intra- and intertemporal justice, for example, is associated with considerable challenges, but there are numerous conceptual

Table 25.1 Relating dimensions of democratic legitimacy with sustainability dimensions

	Normative sustainability JUSTICE / CAPABILITIES	*Functional sustainability* RESILIENCE / LIMITS	*Procedural sustainability* DELIBERATION
Input legitimacy *participation*	! Providing capabilities that empower people to voice food-related concerns and take part in food governance	? Governance that enables people to voice concerns for ecological boundaries of food systems	? Governance that empowers people to initiate and take part in discourses about sustainable food
Throughput legitimacy *deliberation*	? Governance that fosters the deliberation of food-related issues with reference to (intertemporal) justice considerations	? Processes that allow for the common consideration of food-related boundaries/food system resilience	! Deliberative processes about the meaning and implications of sustainable food in a particular context
Output legitimacy *effectiveness*	? Effective implementation of collectively binding decisions to address food-related inequalities within and between generations	! Effective institutions for implementing policies that keep food systems within limits	? Effective (meta-)governance of deliberation by providing supportive conditions for deliberative decision making

Note: Acclamation marks (!) indicate a stable positive relation between dimensions of food democracy and food sustainability; question marks (?) stand for ambivalent or conflictual relations.

proposals and governance practices geared toward taking into account the interests of future generations (González-Ricoy and Gosseries 2016).

Apart from these contradictory or ambivalent relationships, three links between sustainable nutrition and food democracy can be identified that seem productive in a stable way and could therefore serve as starting points for a closer integration of food democracy and sustainable food in theory and practice:

1. First, a systematic link can be identified between input-oriented legitimacy and the justice-oriented dimension of sustainable food, at least if justice is understood in terms of the provision of the capabilities for autonomous agency. Thus, strengthening people's opportunities and capabilities to participate potentially goes hand-in-hand with broadening normative and empirical consideration horizons in food-related decision-making processes. Conversely, the promotion of food-related reflection capabilities also represents a moment of political empowerment in terms of strengthening the opportunities and capabilities for participation.
2. There is also a systematic link between democratic throughput legitimacy and procedural sustainability. To the extent that the practices to strengthen the deliberative quality of food governance also relate to the clarification of understandings of sustainability (taking into account equity and ecological limits), they also contribute to the sustainabilization of the corresponding food governance.
3. Finally, a link can be drawn between democratic output legitimacy and the resilience dimension of sustainable food. Sustainability-oriented food governance is based on the consideration of (deliberatively clarified) ecological boundaries to ensure the reproductive capacity of ecological systems. Although democratic systems certainly face significant challenges in setting and enforcing boundaries, they are also demonstrably capable of producing governance arrangements that can set and enforce boundaries in highly effective (and hence legitimate) ways. Democratic systems have considerable potential for self-restraint, suggesting that they are – at least in principle – capable of implementing constraining policies in a legitimate way. In doing so, they also generate output legitimacy through the productive, freedom-expanding, and innovation-driving effects of policies of limitation.

These proposed relationships are theoretical, and they can serve to imagine food-related governance practices that are both democratic and sustainable. In the future, the framework should be used for empirical research on the democratic effects of sustainability-oriented governance practices, on the one hand, and the sustainability-related consequences of democracy-promoting governance practices, on the other. In addition, the framework may serve practical purposes: as a guiding framework for designing or shaping food governance practices oriented toward sustainability and democratic legitimacy.

Conclusions and outlook

In its everyday ubiquity, food opens up the possibility to question, rethink, and collectively reshape our relationships to each other and to the earth. In this respect, food appears to be a particularly promising field for imagining social transformation processes and initiating them in practice. Therefore, it is not surprising that food has become an important subject area and field of experimentation for sustainability-oriented and democratic transformations in recent years.

Sustainable food and food democracy are two recently evolving concepts that refer to the problems of current food systems and that provide normative orientations and proposals to deal with them. Although with different emphases, both discourses address the problematic implications of the current globalized food system, which is dominated by industrialized mass production. The sustainable food discourse refers to the negative material consequences of the food system in ecological, social, and economic terms. Food democracy, on the other hand, problematizes the existing power structures and the lack of opportunities for participation in food-related decisions. Based on a reconstruction of the problematizations and orientations associated with the discourses, this chapter has pointed out productive relations but also tensions between food democracy and sustainable food. An integrative scheme was outlined to identify the starting points for relating the two concepts in more systematic ways.

This scheme can be used to highlight the democratic and sustainability potential of food governance practices. As such, it can provide a basis for future theoretical considerations and empirical analyses of the relationships between the two concepts and related practices in a variety of contexts. For example, it may help highlight the specific sustainability implications of certain concrete efforts to democratize food governance (e.g., through food councils): to what extent do the approaches and practices of democratization promote or hinder sustainability-oriented transformations? Conversely, the question of the democratic implications of concrete attempts to make food governance more sustainable arises. For example, how do the approaches and practices of sustainability-oriented assessment of food systems affect the democratic quality of corresponding governance arrangements? Ultimately, based on this, it can be clarified which practices of food governance or combinations have both sustainability-promoting and democratizing potential. In this way, the framework can help advance transformations of the food system that are both democratic and sustainable.

References

Alkon, Alison Hope, and Julian Agyeman, eds. 2011. *Cultivating Food Justice: Race, Class, and Sustainability*. Food, Health, and the Environment. Cambridge: MIT Press.

Allen, Patricia, ed. 1993. *Food for the Future: Conditions and Contradictions of Sustainability*. New York: Wiley.

Auestad, N., and V. L. Fulgoni. 2015. "What Current Literature Tells Us about Sustainable Diets: Emerging Research Linking Dietary Patterns, Environmental Sustainability, and Economics." *Advances in Nutrition: An International Review Journal* 6 (1): 19–36. https://doi.org/10.3945/an.114.005694.

Barber, Benjamin. 2003. *Strong Democracy: Participatory Politics for a New Age*. Berkeley: University of California Press.

Bassarab, Karen, Jill K. Clark, Raychel Santo, and Anne Palmer. 2019. "Finding Our Way to Food Democracy: Lessons from US Food Policy Council Governance." *Politics and Governance* 7 (4): 32–47. https://doi.org/10.17645/pag.v7i4.2092.

Behringer, Julia, and Peter H. Feindt. 2019. "How Shall We Judge Agri-Food Governance? Legitimacy Constructions in Food Democracy and Co-Regulation Discourses." *Politics and Governance* 7 (4): 119–130. https://doi.org/10.17645/pag.v7i4.2087.

Béné, Christophe, Peter Oosterveer, Lea Lamotte, Inge D. Brouwer, Stef de Haan, Steve D. Prager, Elise F. Talsma, and Colin K. Khoury. 2019. "When Food Systems Meet Sustainability – Current Narratives and Implications for Actions." *World Development* 113 (January): 116–130. https://doi.org/10.1016/j.worlddev.2018.08.011.

Berry, Elliot M, Sandro Dernini, Barbara Burlingame, Alexandre Meybeck, and Piero Conforti. 2015. "Food Security and Sustainability: Can One Exist without the Other?" *Public Health Nutrition* 18 (13): 2293–2302. https://doi.org/10.1017/S136898001500021X.

Blay-Palmer, Alison. 2010. "Imagining Sustainable Food Systems." In *Imagining Sustainable Food Systems*, edited by Alison Blay-Palmer, 3–15. Farnham and Burlington: Ashgate.

Booth, Sue, and John Coveney. 2015. *Food Democracy*. New York: Springer Berlin Heidelberg.

Born, Branden, and Mark Purcell. 2006. "Avoiding the Local Trap: Scale and Food Systems in Planning Research." *Journal of Planning Education and Research* 26 (2): 195–207. https://doi.org/10.1177/0739456X06291389.

Bornemann, Basil, and Paul Burger. 2019. "Nudging to Sustainability? Critical Reflections on Nudging from a Theoretically Informed Sustainability Perspective." In *Handbook of Behavioural Change and Public Policy*, by Holger Straßheim and Silke Beck, 209–226. London: Edward Elgar. https://doi.org/10.4337/9781785367854.00022.

Bornemann, Basil, and Sabine Weiland. 2019a. "Editorial: New Perspectives on Food Democracy." *Politics and Governance* 7 (4): 1–7. https://doi.org/10.17645/pag.v7i4.2570.

Bornemann, Basil, and Sabine Weiland. 2019b. "Empowering People – Democratising the Food System? Exploring the Democratic Potential of Food-Related Empowerment Forms." *Politics and Governance* 7 (4): 105–118. https://doi.org/10.17645/pag.v7i4.2190.

Buller, Henry, Harry Blokhuis, Per Jensen, and Linda Keeling. 2018. "Towards Farm Animal Welfare and Sustainability." *Animals* 8 (6): 81. https://doi.org/10.3390/ani8060081.

Dahlberg, Kenneth A. 2001. "Democratizing Society and Food Systems: Or How Do We Transform Modern Structures of Power?" *Agriculture and Human Values* 18 (2): 135–151. https://doi.org/10.1023/A:1011175626010.

Daugbjerg, Carsten, and Peter H. Feindt, eds. 2020. Transforming Food and Agricultural Policy: Post-Exceptionalism in Public Policy. London: Routledge.

Daugbjerg, Carsten, and Alan Swinbank. 2016. "Three Decades of Policy Layering and Politically Sustainable Reform in the European Union's Agricultural Policy." *Governance* 29 (2): 265–280. https://doi.org/10.1111/gove.12171.

Davies, Anna R., Agnese Cretella, and Vivien Franck. 2019. "Food Sharing Initiatives and Food Democracy: Practice and Policy in Three European Cities." *Politics and Governance* 7 (4): 8–20. https://doi.org/10.17645/pag.v7i4.2090.

Davies, Jon. 2019. "From Severe to Routine Labour Exploitation: The Case of Migrant Workers in the UK Food Industry." *Criminology & Criminal Justice* 19 (3): 294–310. https://doi.org/10.1177/1748895818762264.

Eakin, Hallie, John Patrick Connors, Christopher Wharton, Farryl Bertmann, Angela Xiong, and Jared Stoltzfus. 2017. "Identifying Attributes of Food System Sustainability: Emerging Themes and Consensus." *Agriculture and Human Values* 34 (3): 757–773. https://doi.org/10.1007/s10460-016-9754-8.

Feindt, Peter H., Manuel Gottschick, Tanja Mölders, Franziska Müller, Rainer Sodtke, and Sabine Weiland, eds. 2008. *Nachhaltige Agrarpolitik Als Reflexive Politik: Plädoyer Für Einen Neuen Diskurs Zwischen Politik Und Wissenschaft*. Berlin: Edition Sigma.

Field, Sean. 2016. "The Financialization of Food and the 2008–2011 Food Price Spikes." *Environment and Planning A: Economy and Space* 48 (11): 2272–2290. https://doi.org/10.1177/0308518X16658476.

Frega, Roberto, Lisa Herzog, and Christian Neuhäuser. 2019. "Workplace Democracy – The Recent Debate." *Philosophy Compass* 14 (4): e12574. https://doi.org/10.1111/phc3.12574.

Garnett, Tara. 2013. "Food Sustainability: Problems, Perspectives and Solutions." *Proceedings of the Nutrition Society* 72 (01): 29–39. https://doi.org/10.1017/S0029665112002947.

Godfray, H. Charles J. 2015. "The Debate over Sustainable Intensification." *Food Security* 7 (2): 199–208. https://doi.org/10.1007/s12571-015-0424-2.

Godfray, H. Charles J., J. R. Beddington, I. R. Crute, L. Haddad, D. Lawrence, J. F. Muir, J. Pretty, S. Robinson, S. M. Thomas, and C. Toulmin. 2010. "Food Security: The Challenge of Feeding 9 Billion People." *Science* 327 (5967): 812–818. https://doi.org/10.1126/science.1185383.

González-Ricoy, Iñigo, and Axel Gosseries, eds. 2016. Institutions For Future Generations. Oxford: Oxford University Press. https://doi.org/10.1093/acprof:oso/9780198746959.001.0001.

Hamilton, Neil. 2004. "Essay – Food Democracy and the Future of American Values." *Drake Journal of Agricultural Law* 9: 9–31.

Harper, Alethea, Annie Shattuck, Eric Holt-Giménez, Alison Alkon, and Frances Lambrick. 2009. *Food Policy Councils: Lessons Learned*. Food First/Institute for Food and Development Policy Oakland, California.

Harriss, John, and Drew Stewart. 2015. "Science, Politics, and the Framing of Modern Agricultural Technologies." In *The Oxford Handbook of Food, Politics, and Society*, edited by Ronald J. Herring, 43–64. Oxford Handbooks. New York: Oxford University Press.

Hassanein, Neva. 2003. "Practicing Food Democracy: A Pragmatic Politics of Transformation." *Journal of Rural Studies* 19 (1): 77–86. https://doi.org/10.1016/S0743-0167(02)00041-4.

Hassanein, Neva. 2008. "Locating Food Democracy: Theoretical and Practical Ingredients." *Journal of Hunger & Environmental Nutrition* 3 (2–3): 286–308. https://doi.org/10.1080/19320240802244215.

Hinrichs, Clare. 2003. "The Practice and Politics of Food System Localization." *Journal of Rural Studies*, International Perspectives on Alternative Agro-Food Networks: Quality, Embeddedness, Bio-Politics, 19 (1): 33–45. https://doi.org/10.1016/S0743-0167(02)00040-2.

Hinrichs, Clare. 2010. "Conceptualizing and Creating Sustainable Food Systems: How Interdisciplinarity Can Help." In *Imagining Sustainable Food Systems*, edited by Alison Blay-Palmer, 17–35. Farnham and Burlington: Ashgate.

Hinrichs, Clare. 2014. "Transitions to Sustainability: A Change in Thinking about Food Systems Change?" *Agriculture and Human Values* 31 (1): 143–155. https://doi.org/10.1007/s10460-014-9479-5.

Holt-Giménez, Eric, ed. 2011. *Food Movements Unite! Strategies to Transform Our Food Systems*. Oakland: Food First Books.

Inglehart, Ronald, and Christian Welzel. 2005. *Modernization, Cultural Change, and Democracy: The Human Development Sequence*. Cambridge and New York: Cambridge University Press.

Lang, Tim. 1999. "Food Policy for the 21st Century: Can It Be Both Radical and Reasonable?" In *For Hunger-Proof Cities: Sustainable Urban Food Systems*, edited by Mustafa Koç, Rod MacRae, Luc J.A. Mougeot, and Jennifer Welsh. London: Earthscan, 216–224.

Lang, Tim. 2003. "Food Industrialisation and Food Power: Implications for Food Governance." *Development Policy Review* 21 (5–6): 555–568. https://doi.org/10.1111/j.1467-8659.2003.00223.x.

Lang, Tim. 2005. "Food Control or Food Democracy? Re-Engaging Nutrition with Society and the Environment." *Public Health Nutrition* 8 (6a): 730–737. https://doi.org/10.1079/PHN2005772.

Lang, Tim, and David Barling. 2012. "Food Security and Food Sustainability: Reformulating the Debate." *The Geographical Journal* 178 (4): 313–326. https://doi.org/10.1111/j.1475-4959.2012.00480.x.

Lang, Tim, David Barling, and Martin Caraher. 2009. *Food Policy: Integrating Health, Environment and Society*. Oxford and New York: Oxford University Press.

Lawrence, Geoffrey, Kristen Lyons, and Tabatha Wallington. 2010. "Introduction: Food Security, Nutrition and Sustainability in a Globalized World." In *Food Security, Nutrition and Sustainability*, edited by Geoffrey Lawrence, Kristen Lyons, and Tabatha Wallington. Sterling, VA: Earthscan, 1–2.

Levkoe, Charles Z. 2006. "Learning Democracy Through Food Justice Movements." *Agriculture and Human Values* 23 (1): 89–98. https://doi.org/10.1007/s10460-005-5871-5.

Lyson, Thomas A. 2004. *Civic Agriculture: Reconnecting Farm, Food, and Community*. Civil Society. Medford, Mass.: Lebanon: Tufts University Press; University Press of New England.

Maharatna, Arup. 2014. "Food Scarcity and Migration: An Overview." *Social Research* 81 (2): 277–298.

McMichael, Philip. 2011. "Food System Sustainability: Questions of Environmental Governance in the New World (Dis)Order." *Global Environmental Change* 21 (3): 804–812. https://doi.org/10.1016/j.gloenvcha.2011.03.016.

Meadowcroft, James. 2004. "Participation and Sustainable Development: Modes of Citizen, Community and Organisational Involvement." In *Governance for Sustainable Development: The Challenge of Adapting Form to Function*, edited by William M. Lafferty, 162–190. Cheltenham and Northampto: Edward Elgar.

Obach, Brian K. 2015. *Organic Struggle. The Movement for Sustainable Agriculture in the United States*. Cambridge: MIT Press.

Petetin, Ludivine. 2016. "Food Democracy in Food Systems." In *Encyclopedia of Food and Agricultural Ethics*, edited by Paul B. Thompson and David M. Kaplan, 1–7. Dordrecht: Springer Netherlands. https://doi.org/10.1007/978-94-007-6167-4_548-1.

Rayner, Geof, David Barling, and Tim Lang. 2008. "Sustainable Food Systems in Europe: Policies, Realities and Futures." *Journal of Hunger & Environmental Nutrition* 3 (2/3): 145–168. https://doi.org/10.1080/19320240802243209.

Reisch, Lucia, Ulrike Eberle, and Sylvia Lorek. 2013. "Sustainable Food Consumption: An Overview of Contemporary Issues and Policies." *Sustainability: Science, Practice, & Policy* 9 (2): 7–25.

Renting, H., M. Schermer, and A. Rossi. 2012. "Building Food Democracy: Exploring Civic Food Networks and Newly Emerging Forms of Food Citizenship." *International Journal of Sociology of Agriculture and Food* 19 (3): 289–307.

Rossignoli, Domenico, and Sara Balestri. 2018. "Food Security and Democracy: Do Inclusive Institutions Matter?" *Canadian Journal of Development Studies / Revue Canadienne d'études Du Développement* 39 (2): 215–233. https://doi.org/10.1080/02255189.2017.1382335.

Schmidt, V.A. 2013. "Democracy and Legitimacy in the European Union Revisited: Input, Output and 'Throughput.'" *Political Studies*, 61 (1), 2–22. https://doi.org/10.1111/j.1467-9248.2012.00962.x.

Sen, Amartya. 1982. *Poverty and Famines: An Essay on Entitlement and Deprivation*. Oxford: Oxford University Press.

Slätmo, Elin, Klara Fischer, and Elin Röös. 2017. "The Framing of Sustainability in Sustainability Assessment Frameworks for Agriculture." *Sociologia Ruralis* 57 (3): 378–395. https://doi.org/10.1111/soru.12156.

Spaargaren, Gert, Peter Oosterveer, and Anne Loeber, eds. 2012. *Food Practices in Transition: Changing Food Consumption, Retail and Production in the Age of Reflexive Modernity*. Routledge Studies in Sustainability Transitions 3. New York: Routledge.

Szulecki, Kacper, and Indra Overland. 2020. "Energy Democracy as a Process, an Outcome and a Goal: A Conceptual Review." *Energy Research & Social Science* 69 (November): 101768. https://doi.org/10.1016/j.erss.2020.101768.

Tangermann, Stefan, and Stephan von Cramon-Taubadel. 2013. "Agricultural Policy in the European Union. An Overview." Discussion contribution No. 1302. Goettingen: Department for Agricultural Economics and Rural Development, University of Goettingen.

Timmer, C. Peter. 2005. "Food Security and Economic Growth: An Asian Perspective." *Asian-Pacific Economic Literature* 19 (1): 1–17. https://doi.org/10.1111/j.1467-8411.2005.00155.x.

Trewavas, Anthony. 2001. "Urban Myths of Organic Farming." *Nature* 410 (6827): 409–410. https://doi.org/10.1038/35068639.

Valentini, Riccardo, John L. Sievenpiper, Marta Antonelli, and Katarzyna Dembska, eds. 2019. *Achieving the Sustainable Development Goals Through Sustainable Food Systems*. Cham: Springer International Publishing. https://doi.org/10.1007/978-3-030-23969-5.

Velten, Sarah, Julia Leventon, Nicolas Jager, and Jens Newig. 2015. "What Is Sustainable Agriculture? A Systematic Review." *Sustainability* 7 (6): 7833–7865. https://doi.org/10.3390/su7067833.

Warren, Mark E. 2009. "Governance-Driven Democratization." *Critical Policy Studies* 3 (1): 3–13. https://doi.org/10.1080/19460170903158040.

Weis, Tony. 2007. *The Global Food Economy: The Battle for the Future of Farming*. London and New York: Zed Books Ltd.

Wekerle, Gerda R., and Michael Classens. 2015. "Food Production in the City: (Re)Negotiating Land, Food and Property." *Local Environment* 20 (10): 1175–1193. https://doi.org/10.1080/13549839.2015.1007121.

Wezel, Alexander, Barbara Gemmill Herren, Rachel Bezner Kerr, Edmundo Barrios, André Luiz Rodrigues Gonçalves, and Fergus Sinclair. 2020. "Agroecological Principles and Elements and Their Implications for Transitioning to Sustainable Food Systems. A Review." *Agronomy for Sustainable Development* 40 (6): 40. https://doi.org/10.1007/s13593-020-00646-z.

26
HEALTH AND HUMAN RIGHTS

Markus Sperl, Anna Holzscheiter and Thurid Bahr

Introduction[1]

In the context of contemporary debates on sustainability and democracy, the nexus between health and human rights constitutes a field of inquiry rich in pertinent issues and questions. To start with, there is a bedazzling array of past and present themes regarding health and human rights that this chapter can draw upon, starting with the vibrant discussion on Universal Health Coverage (UHC) as a realization of the human right to health, the link between health and climate change, or the contentious politics of reproductive health in the context of the rise of authoritarian and populist governments and their growing authority in international organizations. The two core concepts of this handbook – sustainability and democracy – offer an excellent starting-point for the analysis of health and human rights. They provide the means to address a wide range of determinants, most notably economic, social and ecological factors influencing the health and well-being of populations and people around the world. There is by no means a singular, universal understanding of what 'being well and healthy' entails, to what extent states are obliged to undertake measures to provide care, who is supposed to legitimately enjoy it, or what the most sustainable means of managing health are. Additionally, achieving universal health is an essentially cross-sectoral and boundary-crossing endeavor, making it even more difficult to design policies democratically and sustainably in all dimensions of the term. Without doubt, the adoption of the Sustainable Development Goals – specifically SDG 3 – and the Agenda 2030 has marked a new avenue in thinking about the nexus between health and human rights. At least rhetorically, this constitutes a 'paradigm shift' (Buse and Hawkes 2015) towards a greater recognition of the structural drivers of health, including social inequality, as well as rights-based approaches, including more civic engagement and accountability.

Linking health and human rights in the year 2021 inevitably necessitates addressing questions of sustainability and democracy on different levels. As we will show in this chapter, the broad acceptance of human rights has changed our way of thinking about health policy making, culminating in the contemporary prominence of universal access to health care in global health governance. The acceptance of a universal 'human right to health', thus, has enabled addressing questions of equity and sustainability in health policy. Going beyond a narrow focus on the 'human right to health', though, our chapter will discuss the implications of civil and political human rights for health-policy making, most notably the right to participation, and their catalytic effect on demands for inclusion and diversity in global health institutions.

In our exploration of how policymaking in domestic and international health institutions shapes action on the 'human right to health' as well as on other human rights dimensions of health policymaking, both sustainability and democracy are important concepts. First, sustainability encompasses not only questions of continuity over time, but also the balancing of social, economic and ecological determinants of health. Second, sustainability and democracy are fundamental criteria in the assessment of effectiveness and legitimacy of health policies and programs. Democracy not only serves as a yardstick to interrogate possibilities of access and participation of a diverse set of actors to sites where health policies are negotiated, crafted and assessed, but also shapes good practices such as 'participatory budgeting' in health (Campbell et al. 2018). Sustainability, in turn, is a strong normative referent when it comes to addressing funding institutions' long-time financial commitments or recent attempts to consider principles of affectedness and community involvement by establishing country ownership in development cooperation (Goldberg and Bryant 2012). Third, the prominence of human rights has doubtlessly been a major driver behind a health perspective focusing on sustainability and democracy; the 'human right to health' has motivated a number of social movements rallying for universal access to health services and medicines and has led to a shift in global health priorities away from vertical, disease-specific programs towards strengthening health-systems and universal health coverage. On a more general level, civil and political rights have been extended towards health to the effect that claims for more participation and access for people affected by health issues and policies have become increasingly vocal. It is thus possible to differentiate between two understandings of the nexus between health and human rights: a) the human right to health; and b) the recognition, protection and realization of a broad range of human rights in health policy. As our chapter will evidence, however, there is neither a fixed understanding of the 'human right to health' nor a definite answer to how a broader human rights catalogue should shape health policymaking and implementation. Rather, the nexus between health and human rights constitutes a field marked by contestation and historical transformation, an observation seen even more clearly since questions of sustainability came to be negotiated on a global scale.

Our chapter is structured as follows. In a first step, we will give an overview of how health is defined and regulated in human rights (HR) instruments and the World Health Organization's (WHO) constitution. Second, we introduce a commonly used interpretation of the 'right to health' by a treaty monitoring body: the Committee of Economic, Social and Cultural Rights (CESCR). Putting that interpretation in perspective, we explore different understandings of the right to health in section two. We point to a number of historical milestones in rights-based thinking on health and identify the most relevant actors advocating for specific health understandings. In a next step, we address those dimensions of the discussion on health and human rights that bear most directly on questions of sustainability and democracy, seeking to illustrate the complex interplay between the various aspects. In the final section of this chapter, we briefly discuss four contemporary themes, with the aim to highlight health issues that speak to the nexus of democracy and sustainability: first, universal health coverage as the most recent right-to-health approach; second, questions of democracy and political representation in global health institutions; third, sexual and reproductive health and rights as one of the most contentious, politicized areas of health-policy making; and lastly, holistic health concepts including terrestrial ecosystems at the nexus of ecological sustainability and health.

The human right to health as a codified norm and its interpretation(s)

In principle, the concept of human rights describes norms that have developed historically and, for the most part, specify individual rights. In their modern interpretation, they theoretically apply to all people unconditionally and without differentiation (United Nations General Assembly 1948, § 2; Bielefeldt et al. 2017). Under the human rights regime, states primarily have duties to people who possess rights. This relationship exists not only between a state and its citizens, but depending on the right in question, can also apply to the relationship between a state and those who are inside its sovereign territory. This also applies to the right to health (Bielefeldt et al. 2017; Krennerich 2017). The fundamental features of the right to health will be explained in the following paragraphs.

Reference to the right to health as a human right first appeared in the 1946 Constitution of the World Health Organization. Here, health is determined as 'a state of complete physical, mental and social well-being and not merely the absence of disease or infirmity' and designated a fundamental right for all people (International Health Conference 1946). The right to health is indirectly touched upon in the Universal Declaration of Human Rights, where it is presented as part of the right to an adequate standard of living which guarantees the health and well-being of all people (United Nations General Assembly 1948), and appears as a stand-alone article in the International Covenant on Economic, Social and Cultural Rights (ICESCR; United Nations General Assembly 1966), where it is embedded as the right of every person to the highest attainable standard of health for him- or herself. Additionally, the article includes a definition of health (with a physical and a mental component) and makes it clear that the condition of health is subjective. Furthermore, according to the ICESCR there is a right to health, but not a right to be healthy (Krennerich 2017). The ICESCR has been in force since 1973 and binds the majority of UN member states (Office of the High Commissioner for Human Rights, n.d.).

The right to health is taken up in other UN conventions, for example in the Convention on the Rights of Persons with Disabilities, the Convention on the Elimination of all Forms of Discrimination Against Women (CEDAW), the International Convention on the Elimination of All Forms of Racial Discrimination (ICERD) and the Convention on the Rights of the Child (CRC). Common to these conventions is an understanding that the access of particular groups to healthcare and health information requires special protection and support and that the social status of these groups can impact the state of their health. The right to health can also be found in regional human rights instruments. In the European Social Charter (ESC) it is defined as follows: 'Everyone has the right to benefit from any measures enabling him to enjoy the highest possible standard of health attainable' (Council of Europe 1961, I/11). The Charter guaranteeing social and economic rights has been in force since 1965 and compliance is periodically reviewed by signatory states. The right to health can also be found in Article 35 of the Charter of Fundamental Rights of the European Union (European Union 2012), which has been binding for European member states since the Lisbon Treaty came into force (Trilsch 2012). The African Charter of Human and People's Rights (Organization of African Unity 1981) enshrines the 'best attainable standard of physical and mental health' (Article 16), while the respective American Human Rights Convention in its supplementary protocol (Organization of American States 1999) calls for the highest level of physical, mental and social well-being (Article 10, §1).

The right to health in Article 12 of the ICESCR is more closely defined in General Comment 14 of the United Nations Committee on Economic, Social and Cultural Rights. Issued by the ICESCR treaty-monitoring institution, the General Comment is a useful tool for interpreting the right to health, as human rights experts lay out the content of the right to health and the associated duties of states. According to the General Comment, states must respect and protect health-related freedoms and rights and guarantee the right to healthcare. A person has the right to 'control one's health and body, including sexual and reproductive freedom, and the right to be free from interference, such as the right to be free from torture, non-consensual medical treatment and experimentation' (United Nations Committee on Economic Social and Cultural Rights 2000). The General Comment equally stresses the access-dimension of the right to health when mentioning 'the right to a system of health protection which provides equality of opportunity for people to enjoy the highest attainable level of health' (United Nations Committee on Economic Social and Cultural Rights 2000). In addition, adequate social conditions, or 'the underlying determinants of health', must exist in order to lay the basis for a healthy life (United Nations Committee on Economic Social and Cultural Rights 2000, paragraphs 4 and 11; Krennerich 2017), for example through occupational safety or a clean environment. More broadly, the social determinants of health also indicate the impact of socio-economic and living circumstances on the health of persons and groups. At worst, these are social conditions that damage health, such as malnutrition or loss of prospects (for similar interpretation see World Health Organization 2008); at best, good education and working conditions, adequate accommodation and access to healthcare and medication positively reinforce each other and, according to WHO, contribute to physical, social and mental well-being (World Health Organization 2008). As such the realization of the right to health closely depends on that of other human rights. It can also be taken as a precondition for the exertion of other rights, such as the right of equal access to public service in one's country or participation in elections.

The right to health is at times perceived as too challenging for an effective implementation at a national level, even in some cases as weakening the legal force of Human Rights in general by being too ambitious and dependent on material resources (Wolff 2012). The case of South Africa, where the right to health is constitutionally enshrined and actionable, indicates that this is not necessarily the case and that opposition to economic, social and cultural human rights is also politically and not merely legally based.

Health and human rights: contestations of an intersectoral issue

As illustrated above, there are numerous treaties of international law binding member-states to commit to the right to health. However, how this is translated into political practice is dependent on a further set of variables including power, changing discourses on health and development and resource mobilization by influential actors. Unsurprisingly, democratic and sustainable programmes on achieving health for all are especially difficult to design, establish and legitimize – they are politically complex, as they set contestable priorities.

Health is situated within a sphere of multiple overlapping social and political tensions. International organizations (IO), governments and non-state actors compete for funding by donors and philanthropies, spend limited resources which might be urgently needed elsewhere, promote focus either on eliminating specific diseases with direct impact on mortality rates or on broadly investing in health infrastructure, financing and workforce (mostly summarized as 'health systems strengthening'), while staying vigilant and responsive to epidemic emergencies. As our following discussion of the history of global health policy evidences, the power and transformation of specific health policy paradigms has depended on measurement and evaluation methods, questions of power and reputation and geopolitical constellations. Issues of controversy in health-policy making range from culturally specific definitions of health and wellbeing and the question of which populations need special attention or protection, up to the right means and instruments of achieving access (to medicines or infrastructure), treatment, prevention, and sound financing, as well as variants of measuring and evaluating success. Paradigm shifts result from academic innovation, effective advocacy and mobilization of human-rights-frameworks, and leadership or mere financial weight of specific actors changing the organizational architecture and health agenda (Youde 2012).

In the HR conventions and declarations, the underlying understanding of the concept of health varies from a social understanding of health in the WHO Constitution, to an indirect mention as part of the right to an adequate standard of living in the Universal Declaration, to a bio-medical understanding of health (focusing on bodily and mental health) in the ICESCR (Krennerich 2017). This period in Global Health was nevertheless characterized by 'vertical' disease-specific approaches and costly technology transfers (Cueto 2004). In contrast, a broad understanding of health and its underlying factors can be found in the Declaration of Alma Ata (UNICEF and World Health Organization 1978). The realization of the right to health is interpreted here as a matter of concern for society, which requires more than medical intervention (World Health Organization and UNICEF 1978; Mason Meier, 2013). The emerging concept of Primary Health Care (PHC) was the first global attempt to push global health cooperation beyond containing disease outbreaks that put trade and the global economy at risk (Hall and Taylor 2003). It aimed to build a functioning health infrastructure ensuring provision of care in resource-poor areas of e.g. decolonized states, rooted in local contexts. This WHO move was perceived as a step towards politicized realms in which the predominantly technical organization was not readily welcomed. Alma Ata's widely-known title 'Health For All' in the aftermath gradually turned into a rudimentary program of 'Selective Primary Health Care for Children up to 5' (Hall and Taylor 2003). A more comprehensive implementation in the follow-up years lacked political support and lost traction, accompanied by a major setback in WHO's relevance due to lack of funding and leadership (Youde 2012). Nonetheless, the General Comment on Article 12 of the ICESCR draws on the Alma Ata Declaration in its summary of the core obligations of states. In addition, prominent civil society campaigns such as the People's Health Movement continue to use a PHC approach and the declaration's 'Health For All' slogan (see People's Health Movement, n.d.). Its core demands against gross health inequity have unfortunately remained relevant.

In the 1980s and 1990s, market-based approaches to health gained ground in IOs and healthcare planning, decisively promoted by the World Bank Group's entry into health politics (Ruger 2005; Youde 2012; Mason Meier 2013). These approaches defined health and access to healthcare as global collective goods rather than universal rights. Lending policies linked to structural adjustment programs framed health provision as an investment into realizing economic potential in developing countries. Health sector reform through privatization and 'sustainable' user-fee-financing was promoted as a measure to save costs and relieve state budgets (World Bank 1993); in some cases leading to budget cuts which lowered access and quality of care in rural areas and increased risk of impoverishment (Ruger 2005). The Bank's introduction of population health quantification models further drove health policies away from a holistic definition towards 'absence of illness' within a country's workforce in contrast to the WHO's constitution (Youde 2012).

Nevertheless, the right to health in the 1990s was decisively strengthened through its use by civil society initiatives in the quest for HIV/AIDS awareness, containment and anti-stigmatization (Mason Meier 2013). Governments' denial and refusal to act was countered by civil society putting HIV/AIDS firmly on the agenda, mobilizing Human Rights rhetoric, and opening up the field of legitimate actors in health by putting nongovernmental organizations on the map (Friedman and Mottiar 2005). In South Africa, the right to health was promoted in the early 2000s by the Treatment Action Campaign to secure the right to healthcare providing antiretroviral treatment for HIV-positive mothers (Forman 2010; Heywood 2015). A parallel, civil-society-driven progressive liberalization was achieved in the field of sexual and reproductive health (Baisley 2016; Pizzarossa 2018). Emerging concepts of country ownership and civil society participation can be read as democratizing attempts in development cooperation, and the 2002 appointment of the Special Rapporteur on health underlines ongoing relevance of the right to health.

The post-millennium period can be characterized as one of grand development agendas, fragmentation and organizational proliferation, with direct impact on the state of the right to health (Gostin and Mok 2009). The United Nations (UN) Millennium Development Goals (MDG) featured health in three of eight goals targeting populations (children, mothers), infectious diseases and health-related conditions as hunger or lack of water and sanitation. This galvanized donor attention and increased aid flows (Murray 2015), but long-term impact on policy change remained limited (Buse and Hawkes 2015). New funding mechanisms such as the Global Fund to Fight AIDS, Tuberculosis and Malaria or GAVI (The Vaccine Alliance) and philanthropies like the Bill and Melinda Gates Foundation emerged. These complexified the donor landscape and drove programmes further towards measurable results, value for money and re-verticalization (disease-specificity) – and thereby, as some argue, away from comprehensive HR approaches to health (Storeng, 2014). This dynamic stands in contrast to efforts for sustainable, holistic health understandings (or also the more technical health systems strengthening approaches) tackling infrastructure, access, education and well-being (Biesma et al. 2009).

Human rights are a cross-sectoral issue, meaning that their implementation depends on a number of factors and the successful cooperation of stakeholders. The Sustainable Development Agenda's spin on the MDG health agenda reflects the global acknowledgement of an additional level of complexity. Introduced in 2015, the Sustainable Development Goals (SDGs) specify in Goal 3 that states take on a duty to 'ensure healthy lives and promote well-being for all at all ages'. Rather than focusing on a few selected, vertical health priorities (as in the MDGs), the SDGs shift the focus to horizontal, systemic development goals. As a consequence, universal health coverage enjoys high priority on the agenda of international (development) cooperation. It covers 'financial risk protection, access to quality essential health-care services and access to safe, effective, quality and affordable essential medicines and vaccines for all' (United Nations 2015b). Additionally, non-communicable diseases and sexual and reproductive health care receive attention, but connected determinants outside of health, be it inequality, cultural conflicts, the globalized economy and environmental degradation are not explicitly addressed (Buse and Hawkes 2015). Given the SDG agenda's ambition in considering economic, social and environmental sustainability and the signatory states' freedom to set priorities and a tendency to reach for lower-hanging fruits, its long-term impact remains to be assessed (Yamey et al. 2014).

The previous paragraphs have illustrated that, as much as the right to health has been part and parcel of a broader human rights agenda since World War II, as much its meaning and boundaries have been politically contested. Questions of sustainability and democracy, most notably regarding the shift towards more systemic, durable and accessible health systems as well as regarding the democratization of international institutions governing global health, have had significant influence on re-interpretations of the human right to health and the overall implications of a broad array of human rights in the area of health.

Democracy, sustainability and contemporary debates in health and human rights

As mentioned in the introduction, the themes of this volume, democracy and sustainability, offer numerous entry points to analyzing the health and human rights nexus. For the purpose of this chapter, we refer to sustainability in economic and social terms, rather than ecological ones, emphasizing the link between economically sustainable – i.e., robust, financially stable and accessible – health systems with questions of access and representation, i.e., institutional sustainability. Health is a pillar of the Sustainable Development Goals and it is the question of universal access to healthcare that is central to linking health, human rights and sustainability. Our chapter explores the link between sustainability and democracy by defining democracy primarily in terms of political participation and institutional access. It is, thus, not only the human right to health that is relevant for our discussion but a much broader range of human rights that constitute the fundament of political participation and institutional access in health policymaking. Following these considerations, we decided to zoom in on four pressing aspects of the recent past, all of which exemplify the relevance of sustainability and democracy in health policy but to varying degrees. Two of our four illustrative examples – Universal Health Coverage and One Health – serve to underline the effects of thinking about health policy and health systems in terms of sustainability. The other two examples were chosen because of their suitability for highlighting how issues related to democracy – most notably with regard to a pluralization of the actor landscape and questions of representation and legitimacy – have become more prominent in debates on health policy. We will therefore discuss matters of institutional access to and political representation in global health institutions as well as the contested politics of sexual and reproductive health and rights (SRHR) as being particularly indicative of this trend.

Universal health coverage as right to health?

Arguably, the decade-long efforts towards Universal Health Coverage (UHC) are an obvious starting-point for exploring the interface between sustainability and human rights in contemporary health policymaking. The current debate on the most promising present-day candidate for realizing the human right to health, and its SDG inclusion serve as a suitable starting point for an attempt to take stock. The WHO estimates that 'at least half of the world's population' lacks coverage of essential health services, 100 million people are pushed to poverty by health expenses, and 930 million spend ten percent of their overall household budget on healthcare (World Health Organization 2019). Eight million deaths per year can be traced to poor-quality care in low- and middle-income countries (LMIC; The Lancet Global Health Commission on High Quality Health Systems in the SDG Era 2018). In the same vein, disparities in health linked to income and race prevail (Rasanathan and Diaz 2016). These inequalities are well-reflected by differing disease burdens, higher mortality rates, widespread malnutrition, different life expectancies, financial risks posed by non-communicable diseases and so forth in LMICs *and* poor or marginalized populations worldwide (Niessen et al. 2018).

The idea of UHC has come a long way, from the first approaches to health insurance in the nineteenth century (Abiiro and De Allegri 2015) to an internationally supported concept of health policy with two World Health Assembly Resolutions (2005; 2011) and a UN General Assembly Resolution dedicated to it (United Nations 2012), not to mention the numerous institutional publications (World Health Organization, 2010; 2013). Furthermore, UHC forms a decisive pillar of the Sustainable Development Goal on health (United Nations 2015b).

Central to UHC is maximizing the reach of health care through cost-effective, essential services while minimizing the financial risk posed by medical expenditures. Around these tenets, debates flourish around how to roll out UHC, from financing models to prioritization of quality or coverage, and definitions of essential health care services – so far without agreement on a unitary approach. Discursive boundaries are formed around removing financial barriers and pooling risk by lowering out-of-pocket user payments and introducing prepaid systems and access to promotive, preventive, curative and rehabilitative health interventions. Within this, approaches vary widely (Abiiro and De Allegri 2015).

While the WHO frames UHC as a solution that fulfils its constitutional demands in line with the right to health (Ooms et al. 2014; World Health Organization 2019), critics argue that it is either far from a comprehensive, rights-based healthcare approach, or narrowly skews health towards one-sector health system reform and financing. It lacks both a participatory component in health plan decision-making, and the HR focus on efforts to protect marginalized groups (Ooms et al. 2014). This omission of an outspoken HR framework in the sustainable development agenda fails to protect minorities and enables governments to sideline disadvantaged communities and bypass sensitive issue areas such as SRHR (Chapman 2016). In an attempt to reconcile critical voices, WHO as self-proclaimed authoritative voice now promotes an updated version of Primary Health Care as essential step for achieving (World Health Organization, 2018a).

One major implication of avoiding a human rights commitment in the global goals is its step away from international solidarity and cooperation, which disregards the (negative) health impact of a globalized world on communities and obvious budget constraints of LMICs. While there is substantial evidence on the vast disparities between national health systems and the largely global roots of these disparities (Blouin et al. 2009; Ottersen et al. 2014), UHC achievement is conceptualized as a task for national governments. Human rights as internationalist legal instruments provide normative frameworks for defining health as a global common good, and oblige affluent countries to participate in cost-sharing funding mechanisms instead of driving nationalist understandings of social justice (Ooms et al. 2014; Abiiro and De Allegri 2015; Chapman 2016). Without doubt, thus, the SDGs and its related Agenda 2030 constitute a major turning-point in thinking about global health priorities. Universal access to health systems and medicines is an important component of the right to health. It is to be seen, though, to what extent the vocabulary of 'access' will eventually replace the terminology of human rights or if, indeed, advocacy for HR and access will reinforce each other.

Global health – one health?

The year 2021 turns out to be an exceptionally tragic time to write on the state of sustainability and health, with COVID-19, its catastrophic consequences and humanity's suspected role in its emergence (Jeffries 2020; Randolph 2020). Scholars and practitioners alike observed the rise in animal-to-human infections ranging from Ebola, AIDS, SARS and swine flu to the current global health crisis and relate it to human activities. Humanity's impact on ecosystems and biodiversity through alteration and destructive usage of land, crowding out and locking animals and microorganisms in ever-smaller habitats, increases the probability of spillover effects like zoonoses (Thompson 2013; Kreuder Johnson et al. 2015). This has devastating effects on human lives. Even though the medieval plague shows how these diseases have always existed, modern-day globalization and worldwide travel and trade make containment of emerging infectious diseases especially complex. Promoters of Planetary Health (Whitmee et al. 2015), EcoHealth (Charron 2012) or One Health approaches have for years called for consideration of our surroundings. One Health, as advocated by WHO, the Food and Agriculture Organization (FAO), and the World Organization for Animal Health (OIE), promotes responding to health threats to humans *and* animals through human-animal-plant-environment interfaces and is applied in the programmes of those IOs since 2010 (Bhatia 2019). This holistic understanding of health, including ecosystems, acknowledges that human health is deeply interconnected with the functioning of its environment. It implies overcoming anthropocentrism, radical transformative action and joint risk assessments in health policy and neighboring areas like economy, energy and development cooperation, which are difficult to implement in the context of widely sector-specific policies.

Health and environment bear several more problematic links. The large-scale use of antibiotics in human patients and livestock gives rise to antimicrobial resistances, which is a further issue proving approaches that analyze human action towards its environment in health relevant (e.g. World Health Assembly 2015). Environmental health is an umbrella term for the health consequences of a degraded environment ranging from food security, access to clean water, ambient air quality, temperature and frequency of extreme weather events (droughts, storms, inundations). Vulnerability to changes in climate is predominantly concentrated in LMICs dependent on agricultural production and lacking resilient health systems able to tackle resulting problems (Levy and Patz 2015; World Health Organization 2016; also World Health Organization 2018b). At the same time, the lion's share of greenhouse gas emissions causing global warming emanates from least vulnerable, developed countries (Althor et al. 2016). Disadvantaged populations, women, indigenous communities, elderly people and children are the most directly impacted, calling for a re-framing of the climate debate as one of human rights. According to the WHO, 23 percent of all deaths are attributable to environmental risks and 22 percent of the overall disease-burden in DALYs (World Health Organization 2016). Children under five, especially vulnerable to nutritional, infectious and parasitic diseases, and elderly people prone to NCDs, carry the largest share of these burdens (World Health Organization 2016). This calls for a human rights perspective in designing mitigation and adaptation measures.

The disastrous impact epidemics have implies that democratic and sustainable health policies should prioritize conservation and epidemic preparedness. The SDG agenda is a first step in realizing that creating a humane future is an intersectoral, multi-disciplinary endeavor calling for coordinated efforts in food production, climate change mitigation and change of consumption patterns (SDG 17, United Nations 2015d, Di Marco et al. 2020). Global initiatives for sustainable development need to take into account how, for instance, securing sufficient nutrition (SDG 2; United Nations 2015a) by enhancing cropping and livestock production must align with SDG 15 of conserving ecosystems (SDG 15; United Nations 2015c; Di Marco et al. 2020).

Philanthropy and private sector involvement in global health

When it comes to reflections on democracy, human rights and health, contemporary debates on the democratic quality and legitimacy of public-private global health initiatives spring to mind as an illustrative case. Since the 2000s, new philanthropies such as the Bill and Melinda Gates or Clinton Foundations established themselves as central actors in global health. For instance, the Clinton Foundation played a convening role in fostering partnerships between private and public sectors for providing anti-retroviral drugs in LMICs, while the Gates Foundation funded *inter alia* institutions for the control or eradication of infectious diseases (e.g., Polio eradication, GAVI, Global Fund). Recently, the China-based Jack Ma Foundation positioned itself as distributor of COVID-19 clinical equipment (*The Economist* 2020). While the impact of philanthropies on disease-specific campaigns or access to essential medicines and the size of resource-investment is uncontested (Youde 2012), their overall role in shaping modern health politics remains controversial with critical voices alluding to democratic and sustainability concerns. Philanthropic actors do not face the same scrutiny as government actors in terms of accountability; their decision-making processes remain opaque in comparison to the impacts of their funding streams, which in the case of the Gates couple elaborately shape their public perception (Harman 2016).

They are likewise suspected of upholding ties to corporations, possibly leading to conflicts of interest, and have played a decisive role in reviving 'siloed' approaches, earmarking funds and importing market-prone business approaches to health. Above all the issue of earmarking and concentrating funds is critical in terms of sustainability, leaving recipients of funding with less flexibility to build resilient health systems, while being more or less excluded from priority-setting processes (Biesma et al. 2009). The accountability problems and overly technical understandings of health prevail when analyzing wider private sector involvement, for example consultancies replacing local institutions in public goods provision (Raman and Björkman 2009). This also holds for the later health systems strengthening rhetoric driven by global health initiatives (GHI) such as GAVI, which prioritize technology, value-for-money and measurability of effects – effectively constituting a public relations exercise, far from a holistic effort (Storeng 2014).

None of the above implies that state-centered, multilateral development cooperation does not suffer from limited efficiency, nor that it lives up to democratic ideals of strong accountability mechanisms, empowering recipient states and putting their needs first. Furthermore, pharmaceutical companies should be involved in negotiating access to essential medicines. Indeed, introducing business models and leveraging measurable results where it is adequate can enhance productivity and compliance. Lastly, the public-private collaborations did fill a gap left by market failures, shrinking development assistance and political inertia with governance innovations (Moran and Stevenson 2013). However, in the wider field surrounding the right to health, it does not seem as if these innovations get to the bottom of health inequities – social determinants. They further complexify global health by duplicating structures instead of investing in existing country capacities, thus trading sustainable, inter-sectoral action for quick, disease-specific results that appeal to donors (Ruckert and Labonté 2014; Storeng 2014). It appears, thus, that further scholarly engagement with powerful public-private health initiatives is a crucial field of inquiry when it comes to inquiring about the democratic quality and sustainability of contemporary global health institutions.

The contentious politics of sexual and reproductive health and rights

Sexual and reproductive health and rights are another vital issue within the field of health that demonstrate the tension between the themes of the volume on the one hand and human rights on the other. Freedom from sexual violence and choice over family planning are undoubtedly a basic condition for leading a fulfilled life, but the sensitivity of the topic, most prominently abortion and sexual rights, makes it a subject of harsh contestation. Women's rights activism throughout the 1990s achieved success by mobilizing the normative force of rights-based arguments in several international fora, resulting in several treaties obliging states to introduce measures protecting women's equality and choice (International Conference on Population and Development 1995 United Nations 1995). Along with HIV/AIDS activism, these efforts can be narrated as a success story of civil society engagement in health politics. On the other hand, since the inclusion of SRHR in international treaties, relentless opposition by conservative countries and organized interests prevent any measure going beyond the agreed language on a global scale, even at times risking setbacks. In the 1990s, promotion of traditional family values and resistance to abortion and sexual freedoms was mainly led by a religious, pan-confessional coalition and supporting organizations (Pizzarossa 2018). These movements gained further traction by mobilizing human-rights rhetoric such as 'the right to life,' opposing so-called gender-ideologies. Researchers now speak of a considerably well-organized 'backlash' by Evangelical Christians, authoritarian governments and emergent nationalism across the globe (Paternotte and Kuhar 2018; Sanders 2018).

Despite UN recognition of SRHR being crucial to sustainable development (United Nations 2015b) and efforts to ensure progressive policies in regional agreements (e.g. WHO Regional Committee for Europe 2016), the acceptance of universal SRHR is low and their practical relevance remains limited in large parts of the world. More than half of the world's population lacks access to essential sexual or reproductive health services (Starrs et al. 2018), among them 200 million women without access to contraception, 350 million people in need of sexually transmitted infection treatment and an estimated 25 million unsafe abortions per year (Ghebreyesus and Kanem 2018). The global community's hands are tied in mitigating these humanitarian catastrophes outside of public condemnation, since the existing treaties lack legal 'teeth' to hold governments that do not comply with the negotiated commitments accountable (Nowicka 2011). Major agendas like the MDG and the SDG are limited to provision of (basic) sexual health care such as maternal health, omitting sexual rights altogether (Pizzarossa 2018).

The lack of international consensus on the substance and scope of SRHR and the loss of the progressive momentum during the 1990s is, again, especially harmful for LMIC, minorities and displaced people. With a unified, targeted approach to development cooperation on the subject, focused on human rights and the compelling and well-documented evidence of the health benefits of comprehensive SRHR policies, cultural and religious barriers might be overcome. Investments and progress in SRHR could be framed as measures to better cope with other associated health issues such as maternal deaths and sexually transmitted diseases (Adewole and Gavira 2018), and as affordable, sustainable health politics (Starrs et al. 2018). Yet with a looming re-traditionalization of gender roles due to Covid-19 and conservative, illiberal, authoritarian allies threatening to withhold funds as leverage on developing countries, sustainable provision of SRHR seems rather improbable.

Sexual and reproductive health and rights are, thus, an illustrative example of how human rights, when mobilized in a concerted effort equating sexual and reproductive freedom and choice with a life-negating, family-dissolving, hostile individualist ideology, can effectively be instrumentalized to counter sustainable, democratic health policies.

Conclusion

We have been writing this piece in the midst of a global health emergency that is frequently portrayed as unprecedented and extraordinary in the way it is both caused by and interferes with the countless economic, social and political interdependencies between countries and people worldwide (Faiola 2020). However, comparing the COVID-19 pandemic with previous health crises, in particular the HIV/AIDS epidemic starting in the mid-1980s, there are strong parallels regarding the way international health crises simultaneously expose social and economic inequalities *and* open up new avenues for civic engagement, political activism and demands for human rights, and political representation of marginalized population groups (e.g. USA case, Yong 2020; solidarity in Germany, Kaschel 2020; COVID as catalyst, Bodenheimer and Leidenberger 2020). As exceptional as each of these previous crises may be, they share similarities in terms of their strong effects on institutional transformation in domestic and international polities.

With this chapter, we have carved out how questions of sustainability and democracy are relevant to the nexus between health and human rights at various levels. Exploring the meaning of the 'human right to health', we have pointed out two important implications of incorporating the idea of human rights into health policymaking. First, we have shown how the recognition of the idea of human rights has changed the nature and outreach of health policy making and pushed health policy towards the idea of universal access to health care – the notion of a universal 'human right to health' in fact enabled thinking about health policy in terms of equity and sustainability. Second, we have discussed the relevance of civil and political human rights, most notably the right to participation, on health policymaking and its catalytic effect on rising demands for inclusion, representation, and diversity in the institutions in which health policies are crafted, adopted and implemented. As the composition of expert and review panels, of accredited civil society actors in international negotiations, and of non-state partners in the implementation and assessment of health policies changed, so did, in many cases, the policies adopted and implemented (Holzscheiter 2018). There is thus a clear link between the democratization of health politics on the one hand and the changing meaning of the nexus between human rights and health on the other.

If anything, our contribution has shown that while the terms 'human rights', 'democracy' and 'sustainability' have shaped the debate on and practice of health policy for many decades, their meaning and implications have been and continue to be contested and subject to transformation. The contemporary debate inside the World Health Organization on how to ensure a balanced representation of non-state actors and how to avoid undue influence of (vested) corporate interests on the policies and actions of the single most important multilateral health institution suggests that we have entered a new phase in the politics of health policymaking (Buse and Hawkes 2016) – a phase in which democratization is not so much associated with unprecedented access of non-state actors to international organizations, but rather with "shrinking space" for traditional, nongovernmental organizations and intensifying struggles between civil society actors and other non-state actors, most notably philanthropic foundations and corporations over leverage, resources and legitimacy (van de Pas and van Schaik 2014). More often than not, the financial sustainability of health policies and programs in the twenty-first century depends on partnerships with the private sector, with hybrid public-private partnerships in many areas of global health governance aiming to attract material and immaterial resources from the private sector. In many cases, though, the opaque and exclusive nature of these institutions and their policymaking processes as well as the invisibility of the politics lying behind value choices and policy priorities in these partnerships suggests a trade-off between sustainability and democracy.

Note

1 Writing this chapter would not have been possible without the invaluable research assistance of Martha van Bakel.

References

Abiiro, G.A. and De Allegri, M., 2015. Universal Health Coverage from Multiple Perspectives: A Synthesis of Conceptual Literature and Global Debates. *BMC International Health and Human Rights*, 15, 7.

Adewole, I. and Gavira, A., 2018. Sexual and Reproductive Health and Rights for All: An Urgent Need to Change the Narrative. *The Lancet*, 391, 2585–2587.

Althor, G., Watson, J.E.M. and Fuller, R.A., 2016. Global Mismatch Between Greenhouse Gas Emissions and the Burden of Climate Change. *Scientific Reports*, 6, 20281.

Baisley, E., 2016. Reaching the Tipping Point?: Emerging International Human Rights Norms Pertaining to Sexual Orientation and Gender Identity. *Human Rights Quarterly*, 38, 134–163.

Bhatia, R., 2019. Implementation Framework for One Health Approach. *The Indian Journal of Medical Research*, 149, 329–331.

Bielefeldt, H., Klotz, S., Schmidhuber, M. and Frewer, A., 2017. Healthcare in the Spectrum of Human Rights. An Introduction. In S. Klotz, H. Bielefeldt, M. Schmidhuber and A. Frewer, eds. *Healthcare as a Human Rights Issue: Normative Profile, Conflicts and Implementation*. Bielefeld: Transcript Verlag, 9–19.

Biesma, R.G., Brugha, R., Harmer, A., and Walsh, A et al., 2009. The Effects of Global Health Initiatives on Country Health Systems: A Review of the Evidence from HIV/AIDS Control. *Health Policy and Planning*, 24, 239–252.

Blouin, C., Chopra, M. and Van Der Hoeven, R., 2009. Trade and Social Determinants of Health. *The Lancet*, 373, 502–507.

Bodenheimer, M., and Leidenberger, J., 2020. COVID-19 as a Window of Opportunity for Sustainability Transitions? Narratives and Communication Strategies Beyond the Pandemic. *Sustainability: Science, Practice and Policy*, 16(1), 61–66.

Buse, K. and Hawkes, S., 2016. Sitting on the FENSA: WHO Engagement with Industry. *The Lancet*, 338 (10043), 446–447.

Buse, K. and Hawkes, S., 2015. Health in the Sustainable Development Goals: Ready for a Paradigm Shift? *Globalization and Health*, 11, 13.

Campbell, M., Escobar, O., Fenton, C. and Craig, P., 2018. The Impact of Participatory Budgeting on Health and Wellbeing: a Scoping Review of Evaluations. *BMC Public Health*, 18, 822.

Chapman, A.R., 2016. Assessing the Universal Health Coverage Target in the Sustainable Development Goals from a Human Rights Perspective. *BMC International Health and Human Rights*, 16, 9.

Charron, D.F. eds., 2012. *Ecohealth Research in Practice*. Ottawa: Springer/International Development Research Centre.

Council of Europe, *European Social Charter*, 18 October 1961.

Cueto, M., 2004. The Origins of Primary Health Care and Selective Primary Health Care. *American Journal of Public Health*, 94, 1864–1874.

Di Marco, M., Baker, M.L., Daszak, P., and De Barro, P. et al., 2020. Opinion: Sustainable Development Must Account for Pandemic Risk. *Proceedings of the National Academy of Sciences*, 117, 3888.

European Union, *Charter of Fundamental Rights of the European Union*, 26 October 2012, 2012/C 326/02.

Faiola, A., 2020. The virus that shut down the world [online]. *Washington Post*, 26 June. Available from: www.washingtonpost.com/graphics/2020/world/coronavirus-pandemic-globalization/ [Accessed 1 September 2020].

Forman, L., 2010. What Future for the Minimum Core? Contextualizing the Implications of South African Socioeconomic Rights Jurisprudence for the International Human Right to Health. In J. Harrington and M. Stuttaford, eds. *Global Health and Human Rights: Legal and Philosophical Perspectives*. Abingdon: Routledge, 62–68.

Friedman, S. and Mottiar, S., 2005. A Rewarding Engagement? The Treatment Action Campaign and the Politics of HIV/AIDS. *Politics and Society*, 33, 511–565.

Ghebreyesus, T.A. and Kanem, N., 2018. Defining Sexual and Reproductive Health and Rights for All. *The Lancet*, 391, 2583–2585.

Goldberg, J. and Bryant, M., 2012. Country Ownership and Capacity Building: The Next Buzzwords in Health Systems Strengthening or a Truly New Approach to Development? *BMC Public Health*, 12, 531.

Gostin, L.O. and Mok, E.A., 2009. Grand Challenges in Global Health Governance. *British Medical Bulletin*, 90, 7–18.

Hall, J.J. and Taylor, R., 2003. Health for All Beyond 2000: The Demise of the Alma-Ata Declaration and Primary Health Care in Developing Countries. *Medical Journal of Australia*, 178, 17–20.

Harman, S., 2016. The Bill and Melinda Gates Foundation and Legitimacy in Global Health Governance. *Global Governance*, 22, 349–368.

Heywood, M., 2015. South Africa's Treatment Action Campaign: Combining Law and Social Mobilization to Realize the Right to Health. *Journal of Human Rights*, 1, 14–36.

Holzscheiter, A., 2018. Health. In A. Draude, T. Börzel and T. Risse, eds. *The Oxford Handbook of Governance and Limited Statehood*. Oxford: Oxford University Press.

International Health Conference, *Constitution of the World Health Organization*. 22 July 1946.

Jeffries, B., 2020. *The Loss of Nature and Rise of Pandemics. Protecting Human and Planetary Health* [online]. Gland: World Wildlife Fund. Available from: https://wwf.panda.org/?361716 [Accessed 20 July 2020].

Kaschel, H., 2020. Coronavirus. How Germany Is Showing Solidarity Amid the Outbreak [online]. *Deutsche Welle*, 13 March. Available from: www.dw.com/en/coronavirus-how-germany-is-showing-solidarity-amid-the-outbreak/a-52763215 [Accessed 30 July 2020].

Krennerich, M., 2017. The Human Right to Health. Fundamentals of a Complex Right. In S. Klotz, H. Bielefeldt, M. Schmidhuber and A. Frewer, eds. *Healthcare As A Human Rights Issue. Normative Profile, Conflicts and Implementation*. Bielefeld: Transcript Verlag, 23–54.

Kreuder Johnson, C., Hitchens, P.L., Smiley Evans, T., Goldstein, T., et al., 2015. Spillover and Pandemic Properties of Zoonotic Viruses with High Host Plasticity. *Scientific Reports*, 5, 14830.

Levy, B.S. and Patz, J.A., 2015. Climate Change, Human Rights, and Social Justice. *Annals of Global Health*, 81, 310–322.

Mason Meier, B., 2013. The Political Evolution of Health as Human Right: Conceptualizing Public Health under International Law, 1940s-1990s. In D. Reubi and A. Mold, eds. *Assembling Health Rights in Global Context*. London: Routledge, 73–93.

Moran, M. and Stevenson, M., 2013. Illumination and Innovation: What Philanthropic Foundations Bring to Global Health Governance. *Global Society*, 27, 117–137.

Murray, C.J.L., 2015. Shifting to Sustainable Development Goals – Implications for Global Health. *New England Journal of Medicine*, 373, 1390–1393.

Niessen, L.W., Mohan, D., Akuoku, J.K., Mirelman et al., 2018. Tackling Socioeconomic Inequalities and Non-Communicable Diseases in Low-Income and Middle-Income Countries under the Sustainable Development Agenda. *The Lancet*, 391, 2036–2046.

Nowicka, W., 2011. Sexual and Reproductive Rights and the Human Rights Agenda: Controversial and Contested. *Reproductive Health Matters*, 19, 119–128.

Office of the High Commissioner for Human Rights, n.d., *Ratification Status for CESCR – International Covenant on Economic, Social and Cultural Rights* [online]. Geneva: United Nations. Available from: https://tbinternet.ohchr.org/_layouts/TreatyBodyExternal/Treaty.aspx [Accessed 20 July 2020].

Ooms, G., Latif, L.A., Waris, A., Brolan, C.E., Hammonds, R. et al., 2014. Is Universal Health Coverage the Practical Expression of the Right to Health Care? *BMC International Health and Human Rights*, 14, 3–3.

Organization of African Unity, *African Charter on Human and People's Rights*, Nairobi, 27 June 1981.

Organization of American States, *Additional Protocol to the American Convention on Human Rights in the area of Economic, Social, and Cultural Rights*. 16 November 1999.

Ottersen, O.P., Dasgupta, J., Blouin, C., Buss, P. et al., 2014. The Political Origins of Health Inequity: Prospects for Change. *The Lancet*, 383, 630–67.

Paternotte, D. and Kuhar, R., 2018. Disentangling and Locating the "Global Right": Anti-Gender Campaigns in Europe. *Politics and Governance*, 6, 6–19.

People's Health Movement, n.d., *About the People's Health Movement* [online]. Available from: https://phmovement.org/about/ [Accessed 15 July 2020].

Pizzarossa, L.B., 2018. Here to Stay: The Evolution of Sexual and Reproductive Health and Rights in International Human Rights Law. *Laws*, 7, 1–18.

Raman, V. and Björkman, J.W., 2009. *Public-Private Partnerships in Health Care in India. Lessons for Developing Countries*. Abingdon: Routledge.

Randolph, D.G., 2020. Preventing the Next Pandemic. Zoonotic Diseases and How to Break the Chain of Transmission [online]. Nairobi: United Nations Environment Programme. Available from: www.unenvironment.org/resources/report/preventing-future-zoonotic-disease-outbreaks-protecting-environment-animals-and [Accessed 10 July 2020].

Rasanathan, K. and Diaz, T., 2016. Research on Health Equity in the SDG Era: The Urgent Need For Greater Focus on Implementation. *International Journal for Equity in Health*, 15, 3.

Ruckert, A. and Labonté, R., 2014. Public–Private Partnerships (PPPs) in Global Health: The Good, the Bad and the Ugly. *Third World Quarterly*, 35, 1598–1614.

Ruger, J.P., 2005. The Changing Role of the World Bank in Global Health. *American Journal of Public Health*, 95, 60–70.

Sanders, R., 2018. Norm Spoiling: Undermining the International Women's Rights Agenda. *International Affairs*, 94, 271–291.

Starrs, A.M., Ezeh, A.C., Barker, G., Basu, A. et al., 2018. Accelerate Progress – Sexual and Reproductive Health and Rights for All: Report of the Guttmacher–Lancet Commission. *The Lancet*, 391, 2642–2692.

Storeng, K.T., 2014. The GAVI Alliance and the 'Gates approach' to Health System Strengthening. *Global Public Health*, 9, 865–879.

The Economist, 2020. Thanking Big Brother. China's Post-Covid Propaganda Push [online]. Available from: www.economist.com/china/2020/04/16/chinas-post-covid-propaganda-push [Accessed 12 July 2020].

The Lancet Global Health Commission on High Quality Health Systems in the SDG Era, 2018. High-Quality Health Systems in the Sustainable Development Goals Era: Time for a Revolution. *The Lancet*, e1196–252.

Thompson, R.C.A., 2013. Parasite Zoonoses and Wildlife: One Health, Spillover and Human Activity. *International Journal for Parasitology*, 43, 1079–1088.

Trilsch, M., 2012. *Die Justiziabilität wirtschaftlicher, sozialer und kultureller Rechte im innerstaatlichen Recht*. Heidelberg: Springer.

UNICEF and World Health Organization, *Declaration of Alma-Ata: International Conference on Primary Health Care*, 6–12 September 1978. Alma Ata: UNICEF, World Health Organization.

United Nations General Assembly, 2012. *Resolution 67/81, Global health and Foreign Policy*. A/RES/67/81 (12 December 2012)

United Nations, 2015a. *Sustainable Development Goal 2* [online]. Available from: https://sdgs.un.org/goals/goal2 [Accessed 15 July 2020].

United Nations, 2015b. *Sustainable Development Goal 3* [online]. Available from: https://sdgs.un.org/goals/goal3 [Accessed 15 July 2020].

United Nations, 2015c. *Sustainable Development Goal 15* [online]. Available from: https://sdgs.un.org/goals/goal15 [Accessed 15 July 2020].

United Nations, 2015d. *Sustainable Development Goal 17* [online]. Available from: https://sdgs.un.org/goals/goal17 [Accessed 15 July 2020].

United Nations Committee on Economic Social and Cultural Rights. *General Comment 14: The Right to the Highest Attainable Standard of Health (Art. 12)*. E/C.12/2000/4 (11 August 2000).

United Nations General Assembly. *Universal Declaration of Human Rights*, 10 December 1948, 217 A (III).

United Nations General Assembly. *International Covenant on Economic, Social and Cultural Rights*, 16 December 1966, A/RES/2200A (XXI).

United Nations Population Fund, 1995. *Report of the International Conference on Population and Development, Cairo, 5–13 September 1994*. A/CONF.171/13/Rev.1.

Van de Pas, R. and van Schaik, L.G., 2014. Democratizing the World Health Organization. *Public Health*, 128 (2), 195–201.

Whitmee, S., Haines, A., Beyrer, C., Boltz, F. et al., 2015. Safeguarding Human Health in the Anthropocene Epoch: Report of The Rockefeller Foundation–Lancet Commission on Planetary Health. *The Lancet*, 386, 1973–2028.

WHO Regional Committee for Europe, 2016. *Action Plan for Sexual and Reproductive Health: Towards Achieving the 2030 Agenda for Sustainable Development in Europe – Leaving No One Behind* [online]. Available from: www.euro.who.int/__data/assets/pdf_file/0003/322275/Action-plan-sexual-reproductive-health.pdf [Accessed 14 July 2020].

Wolff, J., 2012. *The Human Right to Health*. New York: W. W. Norton and Company.

World Bank, 1993. *World Development Report. Investing in Health*. New York: Oxford University Press.

World Health Assembly, 2005. *Sustainable Health Financing, Universal Coverage and Social Health Insurance, Resolution 58.33*. Geneva: World Health Organization.

World Health Assembly, 2011. *Sustainable Health Financing Structures and Universal Coverage, Resolution 64.9*. Geneva: World Health Organization.

World Health Assembly, 2015. *Global Action Plan on Antimicrobial Resistance, WHA 68.7*. Geneva: World Health Organization.

World Health Organization, 2008. *Closing the Gap in A Generation: Health Equity Trough Action on the Social Determinants of Health. Final Report of the Commission on Social Determinants of Health* [online]. Geneva: World Health Organization. Available from www.who.int/social_determinants/thecommission/finalreport/en/ [Accessed 17 July 2020].

World Health Organization, 2010. *World Health Report: Health Systems Financing – The Path to Universal Coverage*. Geneva: World Health Organization.

World Health Organization, 2013. *World Health Report: Research for Universal Health Coverage*. Geneva: World Health Organization.

World Health Organization, 2016. *Preventing Disease Through Healthy Environments. A Global Assessment of the Burden of Disease from Environmental Risks* [online]. Geneva: World Health Organization. Available from: www.who.int/quantifying_ehimpacts/publications/preventing-disease/en/ [Accessed 11 July 2020].

World Health Organization and the United Nations Children's Fund, 2018a. *Declaration of Astana, Global Conference on Primary Health Care, 25 – 26 October 2018*. Astana: World Health Organization and the United Nations Children's Fund.

World Health Organization, 2018b. *Fact Sheet – Climate Change and Health* [online]. Geneva: World Health Organization. Available from: www.who.int/news-room/fact-sheets/detail/climate-change-and-health [Accessed 9 July 2020].

World Health Organization, 2019. *Fact Sheet – Universal Health Coverage* (UHC) [online]. Geneva: World Health Organization. Available from: www.who.int/news-room/fact-sheets/detail/universal-health-coverage-(uhc) [Accessed 28 July 2020].

WHO and UNICEF, 1978. *International Conference on Primary Health Care (1978: Alma-Ata, USSR) – Report*. Geneva: World Health Organization.

Yamey, G., Shretta, R. and Binka, F.N., 2014. The 2030 Sustainable Development Goal for Health. *BMJ British Medical Journal*, 349, g5295.

Yong, E., 2020. How the Pandemic Defeated America [online]. *The Atlantic*, 4 August. Available from: www.theatlantic.com/magazine/archive/2020/09/coronavirus-american-failure/614191/ [Accessed 30 July 2020].

Youde, J., 2012. *Global Health Governance*. Cambridge: Polity Press.

PART VI

Innovations and experiments

27
BEHAVIORAL ECONOMICS AND NUDGING

Assessing the democratic quality of sustainable behavior change agendas

Tobias Gumbert

Introduction

Behavioral economics and nudging have become buzzwords in a range of public policy fields since they gained broad recognition in the mid-2000s (Reisch and Thøgersen 2017, 245). Today, they are almost synonymous with innovative tools for steering individual behaviors, promising simple, cost-effective solutions to pressing problems. Nudges are behavioral interventions that influence behavior and decision-making processes through subtle, indirect suggestions and positive reinforcement strategies without directly mandating or limiting particular choices (Thaler and Sunstein 2008). The rationale for these mechanisms is provided by behavioral economics, which studies psychological, emotional, and social factors influencing economic decision-making to make more accurate assumptions about human behavior in various contexts. Behavioral economics has been built on the observation that economic agents have 'bounded rationality,' a concept that describes how rational individual decision-making is continuously limited by cognitive, information, and time constraints that prevent the realization of individuals' 'true' preferences, negatively affecting their well-being (Kahneman 2003). Using these insights from behavioral economics, nudge approaches are designed to counteract, correct, and strategically use behavioral biases by altering the so-called choice environment, simultaneously maximizing individual well-being and social welfare. The authors who popularized the nudge approach, Richard Thaler and Cass Sunstein (Thaler and Sunstein 2008), have also provided a political justification for applying behavioral insights to policy, termed 'libertarian paternalism.' They stress that '[t]o count as a mere nudge, the intervention must be easy and cheap to avoid' (ibid., 6), emphasizing the importance of safeguarding individual freedom of choice. At the same time, public authorities would be obligated to guide people in their decisions to make rational and responsible choices, justifying the paternalistic element of choice editing.

The usefulness of this political tool to influence individual actions to enhance and strengthen sustainability in different areas of everyday life seems obvious: pure market solutions run the risk of being ecologically unsustainable and impair the well-being of present and future generations. Simultaneously, bans and stricter legal regulations not only represent a substantial interference in liberal freedoms but are also said to hinder economic growth (Gumbert 2019a). Framed in this light, nudge strategies seem to be compatible with a range of different environmental management approaches in liberal democracies, which are rooted in the ecological modernization and green growth paradigms, i.e., increasing resource efficiency, expanding 'cradle to cradle' manufacturing, and promoting emissions trading schemes (Hajer 1995; Mol 2001).

However, this alleged win-win-strategy pursued by sustainable behavior change agendas is contested by several environmental studies scholars and political theorists who explicitly draw attention to fundamental political tensions in this debate. It is claimed that nudges may take the form of subliminal marketing, bypassing conscious reflection and autonomous preference transformation (Bovens 2009; Hausmann and Welch 2010; Goodwin 2012). Such tools would run the risk of delegitimizing sustainability agendas and might even depoliticize environmental action by 'overlooking the deeper socio-cultural roots of environmental and social problems' (Heiskanen and Laakso 2019, 160; see also Schubert 2017). Others have voiced concern that by targeting individuals as consumers instead of citizens, more democratic solutions (built on broad participation and deliberation) to the environmental crisis may be undermined, giving way to the power of elites and corporate influence in designing sustainability agendas (Brooks and Bryant 2014; Maniates 2014). The rise of behavior change agendas in sustainability-related policy fields also has more far-reaching consequences on how societies imagine socio-ecological transitions in general. Focusing on simple, cost-efficient solutions in the short-term, transition pathways relying on more comprehensive and progressive environmental policymaking may fade into the background (Fuchs et al. 2016; Gumbert 2019b). Several authors have, therefore, not only begun to discuss behavioral economics in the context of specific sustainability challenges but also increasingly drawn attention to political and democratic values, the role of ethics, and power relations which are often absent in this debate. Nevertheless, despite such efforts, most of the research literature on 'green nudges' to date is concerned with the efficiency and effectiveness of influencing individual behavior through default settings, social norms, or pro-environmental messaging (Reisch and Thøgersen 2017). Without taking the democratic quality of sustainable behavior change agendas into account, effectiveness will remain the only yardstick to judge if this governance approach should be broadly applied, smartly adjusted, or outright rejected.

This chapter makes the central argument that to make a fair and well-balanced assessment, if nudge strategies are a sufficient democratic reaction to the challenges of climate change and sustainability in the twenty-first century, the underlying tensions have to be addressed. In the context of designing interventions to alter people's choice sets, many issues that go far beyond re-arranging food in cafeterias or switching to renewable electricity tariffs have to be evaluated from both a democracy and sustainability perspective. In keeping with the overall focus of this volume, this chapter has three objectives. First, the following section outlines the general debate on behavioral economics and nudging as policy tools to encourage and foster more sustainable societies. It starts with an overview of where behavioral economics has entered sustainability policies, takes a closer look at various types of nudge strategies and the mechanisms by which they operate, and provides a detailed representation of the insights that might be gained by studying them. Second, the subsequent section summarizes a particular part of the debate by drawing on sustainable preference formation and the role of citizens as envisioned by behavior change agendas, commenting on the compatibilities and incompatibilities between behavioral economic approaches and democratic governance. Third, the chapter scrutinizes different explanations for the rise of behavioral economics and nudging on sustainability governance agendas. It argues that this rise can be explained particularly well by its excellent fit with the currently dominant 'techno-economic' and 'ethical-individual' approaches to environmental policymaking (Machin 2013). Lastly, the chapter closes with an outlook on future developments in this area and directions for research.

Behavior change and sustainability governance

While initially applied in the areas of health policy (to promote healthier lifestyles) and economic policy (to promote tax compliance), in recent years, ideas of behavioral economics have increasingly informed policies in many sustainability-related domains. Nudge strategies have become a central part of the policy toolbox, from editing food purchasing behaviors and household waste production habits to energy consumption choices (Ölander and Thøgersen 2014; Sunstein 2014; Lehner et al. 2016). Because of the dominant focus on individual behavior change, questions of sustainable consumption are of particular interest to choice designers. Behavior change strategies 'can be said to represent the current mainstream policy paradigm' (Heiskanen and Laakso 2019, 159) in this field. It has been widely acknowledged that consumer behavior contributes significantly to global CO_2 emissions (Girod et al. 2014; O'Rourke and Lollo 2015). While pro-environmental values have developed and spread globally, behaviors, i.e., practical manifestations of these values, lag behind. (Schor 2010; Krogman 2020). Research has already identified that consumer purchases and actions consistently deviate from their reported sustainability preferences, also known as the 'attitude-behavior gap' or 'value-action gap' (Blake 1999; Kollmuss and Agyeman 2002). Even when targeting specific audiences, the provision of more and 'better' information has not been successful in closing this gap (Ölander and Thøgersen 2014). Therefore, many consumption and sustainability scholars agree that consumer decisions have to be studied in a broader context. Essential factors shaping individual choices include psychological processes, social norms, temporal constraints, and structural conditions (e.g., infrastructural barriers to sustainable consumption) (Defila et al. 2014; O'Rourke and Lollo 2015).

These academic discourses have been transferred to the political arena. The global sustainability architecture, especially the Paris Agreement and the UN Sustainable Development Goals, provides new momentum for sustainable behavior change agendas across countries. The IPCC Fifth Assessment Report states that 'emissions can be substantially lowered through changes in consumption patterns, adoption of energy savings measures [and] dietary change' (IPCC 2014, 28). In 'A Clean Planet for All,' the European Commission's strategic long-term vision for greenhouse gas (GHG) emission reductions (EC COM 2018, 773), the transition to a net-zero GHG economy is increasingly identified with necessary demand-side changes and the need to address 'the way Europeans work, transport themselves and live together' (ibid., 22). In the European Commission's 'Behavioural Insights Applied to Policy' report (EC 2016), the speed by which these logics spread is readily discernible. Behavioral economics is explicitly mentioned in many sustainability-related public policy fields, such as energy, environment, and transport. Nudge strategies (framing, social norms, defaults – see below) are here, by far, the currently most deployed behavior change tools across EU member states (ibid.). The common goal across all of these governance initiatives is to alter how people consume and organize their lives, from energy- and carbon-intensive lifestyles to ecologically responsible consumption practices.

Because behavioral economics and the nudge approach have become so widespread across governance areas and levels, it is crucial to understand how they function and interact with individual behaviors. The basic idea of behavioral economics, as envisioned and developed early on by authors like Daniel Kahneman, Amos Tversky, and Richard Thaler (Tversky and Kahneman 1974; Kahneman and Tversky 1979; Thaler 1980), is to differentiate (economic) behavior according to what is the rational and smart thing do (the focus of neoclassical economics), and what people actually do. The core assumption of economics is that agents will choose behaviors and actions that lead to optimization. They will choose courses of action that ultimately benefit them and make them 'better off.' In the realm of consumption, this logic is probably best described by the notion of consumer sovereignty: individuals will know best which goods and services are suited to increase their own well-being, and their choices are expected to be governed by unbiased beliefs, complete information, and self-interest. Behavioral economics questions this identification of individual consumers with *homines oeconomici* because 'real' people suffer, for example, from loss aversion (they are much stronger affected by potential losses than by potential gains) or exhibit self-control problems (they regularly act against their best interests). In other words, from a rational-economic standpoint, people constantly make errors. The main goal of behavioral economics is, therefore, to supplement the neoclassical model by predicting how peoples' choices deviate from rational behaviors, and in doing so, provide an evidence-based approach to economics.

The so-called nudge approach adds an operational logic to the findings of behavioral economics scholarship. If it is possible to calculate and predict how individuals' choices deviate from rational decisions, it should be possible to devise strategies to correct them (Thaler and Sunstein 2008). The primary function of nudges is to edit particular choice sets by altering the choice environment. Several different operations can achieve this: by removing cues (e.g., removing unhealthy food from eye level in supermarkets), changing default options (e.g., setting renewable energy as the default electricity tariff), implementing heuristics (e.g., triggering mental shortcuts for behaviors, for instance through social comparisons), simplification (e.g., through meta information in the form of labels), or framing particular choices (e.g., through pro-environmental messaging) (see Sunstein 2014 for a list of essential nudges; Bornemann and Burger 2019 for a classification).[1]

Although many different mechanisms have been identified (default nudges, framing nudges, social norm nudges), they often cannot be neatly separated in practice. Jones et al. (2013a) (based on Olivier and Sauneron 2011) provide a pointed example of how green nudges function *in actu*. In the case of promoting energy-saving measures among private households in France, the provision of comparative energy use information on utility bills has two goals: the information is socially meaningful, i.e., households have a better grasp of what high and low energy consumption looks like, and peer-to-peer comparisons have an immediate emotional impact since households are either worse than their peers and over-consumers, or better than their peers and frugal savers (Jones et al. 2013a, xi). This simple behavioral intervention already uses several elements simultaneously: information is reframed, social norms about competitiveness are activated, and pro-environmental values on the virtue of reducing energy demand are implicitly conveyed. The behavior change agenda caters to the calculating rational actor, but it reaches beyond cognition to actors' conscience and emotional apparatus.

Thaler and Sunstein themselves provide another suggestion of how nudges may steer individual behaviors: to improve sustainable mobility, they suggest using fuel economy stickers (as introduced by the US Environmental Protection Agency) on the back of cars (Thaler and Sunstein 2008, 203–205). By translating the information from mileage data into dollars, this nudge would create a standard by which everyone's behavior can be compared and judged. People would signal their green credentials to all around them and interact in a game of 'friendly competition' (ibid., 207). Such a nudge would use simplified 'meta' information (stickers) to increase transparency and combine it with the use of pro-environmental social norms (being an environmentally friendly driver) and triggering heuristics (being better at something than others).

As mentioned in the introduction, the political justification for applying the logic of behavioral economics to sustainable policy agendas rests on the concept of libertarian paternalism. It is libertarian in the sense that it concedes the same freedom of choice to individuals before a behavioral intervention has taken place. Its goal is to be liberty-preserving. The paternalistic element of the concept is concerned with improving individuals' well-being and influencing "the choices of affected parties in a way that will make those parties better off, as judged by themselves" (Thaler and Sunstein 2008, 175). The addition of the 'as judged by themselves' criteria acts as a *de facto* limit to what choice architects can legitimately do, thus combining both libertarian and paternalistic logic (Sunstein 2019, 24–25). Thaler and Sunstein stress that, although nudges change the choice environment, the individual must be fully in control and capable of resisting any nudge with minimal to no effort (Thaler and Sunstein 2008, 6). Therefore, nudges would impose no material burdens and give no material benefits to anyone; they are economically neutral (Sunstein 2019, 17). In theory, nudging puts a premium on human agency and promotes individual well-being and should therefore not be at odds with fundamental principles of democratic governance.

However, hybrid concepts like libertarian paternalism always invite critiques from both ends of the spectrum: for libertarians, nudges undermine the ability of individuals to freely choose for themselves, while paternalists, especially in the context of global sustainability challenges, may argue that strong paternalistic policies are necessary to protect individual and societal well-being. It is, therefore, necessary to take a closer look at such objections.

Sustainable preference transformation and the role of citizens

While politics are regularly concerned with the articulation and aggregation of preferences, it is also concerned with their transformation – especially in sustainability-related matters. For many academics and practitioners alike, it is obvious that in order to advance the sustainability agenda and significantly reduce material throughput in democratic societies, the mindset and everyday routines and habits of individuals will have to change, arguably very drastically, until 2050 (IGES et al. 2019). As Barry explains: 'the normative claims inherent within sustainability require public validation and debate, while the realization of that collectively decided conception of sustainability requires citizen activism premised on the transformation rather than the mere articulation and aggregation of preferences' (1996, 122). In this context, the questions arise who should be allowed to promote and steer preference transformation and in which particular way. Therefore, the debate touches upon the significance of human agency, individual freedom, personal autonomy, rationality, transparency and the legitimacy of the means deployed in transforming sustainable preferences.

Behavioral economics assumes agents' preferences to be generally given and stable. Preferences are not always well-formed, and interventions aim to 'reset' preferences to 'normal,' i.e., their 'true' origin (Thaler and Sunstein 2008). That is why nudges do not alter the preference order of individuals but are rather designed to restore it, and individuals would still be free to make decisions that are either aligned with their own preferences or to act against them. Many authors have been somewhat critical of the notion that nudges would reveal 'true' preferences. Hausmann and Welch argue that nudges may interfere with a person's autonomy if preferences are somehow altered without realization of the nudged agent. If information would be conveyed subliminally (e.g., heuristics based on social norms or moral claims), and agents are restricted in their capacity for rational reflection and processing, this would qualify as diminishing autonomy (Hausmann and Welch 2010, 128; see also Bovens 2009). Here, Mills (2015) suggests being careful and distinguishing between different types of nudges because not all would respect or promote personal autonomy equally. Another objection to 'true' preferences is that, in practice, preferences may not even exist or are simply unknowable (Sugden 2008; Whitman and Rizzo 2015). This raises the issue of what choice architects can legitimately know about individual agents and how they should design choice environments accordingly. Nudges may carry a clear opinion about the acceptability of specific choices and therefore transmit preferences that are defined and framed externally. For some authors, this influence is referred to as manipulation, as a technique that 'perverts the way [a] person reaches decisions, forms preferences or adopts goals' (Wilkinson 2013, 344). In order to safeguard against such manipulative attempts, nudges would have to include a 'genuine escape clause,' 'if the nudger sincerely wants the targets not to act in the nudged way' (Wilkinson 2013, 354). Counter-measures against any 'pre-defined external preferences' include transparency (detailed explanations of the interventions) and open dialogue (communicating about policy goals). Although the nudge approach does not claim to alter preferences, it does promote reasonable choices and aims to rationalize individual conduct. Fateh-Moghadam and Gutmann critically comment that the approach 'presuppose[s] knowledge of what decision is rational for an individual in a concrete situation' (2015, 395) and that it would be able to increase rationality. It remains unclear, though, in what way increased rationality may assist with ethical decisions or be helpful in weighing trade-offs between realizing short-term and long-term preferences (ibid.).

In his recent work, Sunstein counters many of these charges and emphasizes the importance of being clear about who is being assisted by nudges and for what reasons. I will discuss this point at length because it goes to show the inherent complexities and dilemmas of designing choice environments. It is also helpful to reflect on the limits of the approach by closely following the arguments of one of its most prominent proponents. Sunstein makes three important distinctions with reference to the addressees of nudges: individuals who in general do not suffer from (or are not negatively affected by) behavioral biases (whose preference structures are intact), individuals with acute self-control problems (whose preference structures are distorted), and individuals with unclear preference structures (Sunstein 2019). Concerning the first group, even if such individuals can be expected to have clear antecedent preferences, the complexity of everyday life would still create barriers to realizing them. People may want to switch to a green energy tariff, but often they do not know (or overestimate) how simple it is. Here, nudges would increase 'navigability,' i.e., 'making it easier for people to get to their preferred destination' (ibid., 44) without compromising freedom of choice, either by changing the default rule to opting-out or by framing the issue as an important contribution to combat climate change. In this case, choice architects are already faced with the risk of entrenchment, i.e., leading people to specific 'destinations' (although maybe socially desirable) instead of merely providing additional options. Sunstein describes the second group of people as being severely affected by behavioral biases. They may suffer, for example, from present bias (predominantly focusing on today and tomorrow, but not beyond), thereby injuring their long-term selves (ibid., 59; see also Kahneman 2011). The structure of self-control problems can be summarized as having a preference at Time 1, making a choice at Time 2, and regretting the same choice at Time 3. The function of the nudge, in this case, is to help people to either refrain from a choice not aligned with their previous preference or to enable subjectively hard choices. Drug addiction may constitute a case where a nudge is comparatively easy to justify but wanting to adopt a vegetarian or even vegan diet, and failing at it, falls in the same category. Compared to the first group, where the goal of the nudge was to increase navigability, choice architects that design an intervention for overcoming self-control problems are forced to make a range of assumptions: that people are aware of their self-control problem, that, even if they are not aware, they want to be helped, and that the (irrational) choice at Time 2 will inevitably be a choice that decreases their well-being. It is clear that in most cases, choice architects are confronted with 'epistemic deficits' (ibid., 76) and will also have to make moral judgments in designing behavioral options. Lastly, the third group presents an even greater challenge: if people are 'happy either way,' that is before and after a nudge, then what people like may actually be 'a product of the nudge' (ibid., 88). In this context, Sunstein raises the problem of nudges being transformative, similar to the risk of entrenchment discussed earlier, but now, choice architects cannot rely on individual 'true' preferences as a guideline for designing nudges. Instead, they have to either base their assumptions on what makes people 'better off' on the behavior of people who make consistent, informed choices and that are generally able to resist nudges, or to engage with challenging normative issues and make independent judgments about what promotes well-being themselves (ibid., 95–102). In the first instance, choice designers have to generalize from particular cases, and in the second, to universalize their own particular understanding. Both approaches will, however, violate the 'as judged by themselves' rule to a considerable degree. It becomes clear that choice architects face a range of ethical challenges in designing nudges and that these challenges raise further issues in the context of advancing sustainable behavior change agendas in liberal democracies.

The discussion reveals that, although pro-self-nudges may have significant effects on individual well-being, by focusing on 'true' preferences, behavior change agendas at best support incremental changes and small steps to foster sustainable transformations. Bornemann and Burger argue that '[s]ince nudging takes [...] "given" preferences for granted, it comes with a focus on effectiveness and efficiency, leaving considerations of sufficiency (which would imply a reconsideration of preferences) aside' (Bornemann and Burger 2019, 218). I will pick up this point again in the next section.

Before, I want to briefly comment on the role of citizens as imagined by the nudge approach because it ties together the discussion on preference transformation and broader visions of socio-ecological change (see below). Following Barry, citizenship can be understood 'as a mediating practice which connects the individual and the institutional levels of society, as well as a common identity which links otherwise disparate individuals together as a collectivity with common interests' (1996, 123). Being an active citizen means having a political identity and functions as a transmission belt between individuals' everyday lives and political institutions. Taking a closer look at how individuals are addressed through behavioral interventions, it is obvious that the focus is on individual behaviors, individual preferences, and their role and responsibility as consumers. This has been termed the 'consumer-citizen' construct, 'an individual who simultaneously exercises the choices and freedoms bestowed by a neo-liberal economic model, but does so in a way that is socially, economically, and environmentally responsible' (Barr 2015, 93). Behavior change strategies 'hold people responsible for their personal energy use or carbon emissions or consumption of resources with little attention to the larger structures (energy grids, transportation systems, capitalist economies) within which these "individual choices" are made' (Hall 2016, 600). Buying, recycling, or washing are individual instances of responsible action, but demanding free curbside waste collection or pressuring governments to pass anti-packaging laws would rather constitute civic actions (ibid.).

In this sense, uncovering unconscious habits and rationalizing individual behaviors may well contribute to becoming an environmentally responsible consumer. It is, however, safe to assert that nudge approaches are apolitical (not necessarily anti-political) and decontextualize individual behaviors. Arguably, behavioral interventions pay attention to the immediate environment that influences specific behaviors, but the wider context is usually omitted. First, the wider context includes the political arena. Individuals could be encouraged to engage in deliberation with others to discuss their preferences and negotiate them with other stakeholders, which is, from a deliberative democracy perspective, a necessary precondition for preference transformation (John et al. 2009; Olsen and Trenz 2014). Along these lines, Barry argues that 'democracy allows preferences, expectations and behaviour to be altered as a result of debate and persuasion, binding individual behaviour to conform to publicly agreed norms' (1996, 125). In this context, it is also easier to comprehend trade-offs between individual preferences (e.g., a consumerist, energy-intensive lifestyle vs. an intact environment) that have to be compared and subsequently valued and judged. Second, the wider context also includes relations to near, distant, future, and non-human communities. Nudge approaches focus on making individuals better off, and can also be designed as pro-social nudges to produce public welfare effects (Barton and Grüne-Yanoff 2015). But if individual preferences are simply aggregated in order to produce the common good, individuals are not asked what their subjective version of the common good entails, nor if they actually want to contribute. The production of public welfare is in this case not truly 'public,' it is not a 'welfare of the people.' It rather runs the risk of further separating principles of intra-, intergenerational and international justice from achieving sustainability, and it is even less concerned with organizing advocacy for 'those who cannot speak, either because they are yet to be born (future generations), are incapable (non-humans), or are denied citizenship (affected foreigners)' (Barry 1996, 128). From a democratic standpoint, then, sustainable behavior change agendas are always in danger of reducing socio-ecological transformation pathways to the aggregated effects of individual lifestyle changes (substituting carbon-intensive consumer goods and services with 'greener' options), thereby neglecting structural dependencies, relations of power, and justice considerations.

The rise of nudging on sustainability governance agendas

Nudging is seen as a social innovation in sustainability governance because it corresponds to many simultaneous developments in the twenty-first century. Different reasons can be provided that collectively help to explain its rise. These reasons are also important for evaluating the democratic quality of sustainable behavior change agendas in a broader sense.

The first reason should be the most obvious: nudges are relatively low-cost policy tools. They are not subject to lengthy negotiations or party-political cleavages, which means they are usually uncontroversial and do not produce an entitlement mentality among voters or lobby groups. Publics in European countries also broadly tend to support nudges (Reisch and Sunstein 2016). And this is good news: political decision-making has become increasingly complex, and sustainability politics operates under the conditions of uncertainty (regarding time horizons and exact impacts of climate change), and ambiguity (of who should be responsible, of best practices, of most promising solutions) (Maniates 2012). In this age, climate change seems to be an 'agent of metamorphosis' (Beck 2016), altering everyday lives and dissolving safe truths on a global scale. Tensions are inevitable, especially where democratic norms and ideals and the requirements of a sustainability transition collide. Based on the notion of libertarian paternalism, the nudge approach promises to lessen these tensions and avoid conflicts of interest by guaranteeing individuals freedom of choice, supporting market-based behavior change options, and reducing the overall level of resource and energy consumption (Gumbert 2019a). By doing so, sustainable behavior change agendas generally subscribe to a green growth paradigm, taking climate change seriously without compromising economic growth potentials. From a policy implementation perspective, then, the nudge approach is very appealing and convincing.

A second reason for the rise of behavioral economics on public policy agendas has been closely tied to the development of neoliberalism and what Jones et al. (2013a) have termed 'the rise of the psychological state.' Through the advent of neoliberalism throughout the 1980s until today, management and benchmarking tools found their way into public policy (Brown 2015). These microeconomic models were built on the model of *homo oeconomicus* being synonymous with the human condition. Tversky and Kahneman had already deconstructed this idea of rational human decision-making by exposing irrational tendencies in the 1970s, but it was not until much later that these insights sieved through. Behavioral economics now provided the insights and tools to predict actions and behaviors by analyzing biases and using heuristics that could be modeled with the promise to make markets function more efficiently and help people make 'correct' choices (Jones et al. 2013a, 165). At the same time, psychological insights gained broad recognition among public officials for the governance of societies (Jones et al. 2013b). Within neoliberal governance, it is not enough to guide the actions of citizens. Their thoughts and feelings, their 'interior lives' (Rose 1999), must be subjected to political rule as well, and the rationality of behavioral economics justifies this development (see also Jones et al. 2013b). In this regard, behavior change strategies present a novel and allegedly unintrusive way of governing values, emotions, and ethical considerations through policy. Additionally, these strategies introduce corporate techniques into the design of public policy and enable close cooperation between public and private actors (Gumbert 2019b).

Third, the rise of behavior change agendas must also be considered as a successful project of combining the techno-economic approach and the ethical-individual approach to governing climate change.[2] Amanda Machin (2013) argues that the techno-economic approach rests on the believes that technological solutions to global warming will inevitably be found, that opportunities will be spread by market mechanisms, and that, as a consequence, accustomed lifestyles will remain largely the same (ibid., 13). Since the central idea of nudging is to change people's choice environment, choice architects exhibit a general tendency to believe in the power of technological change and planning exercises to shape behavior. On numerous occasions, Cass Sunstein likened the nudge approach to a GPS device because it would tell people how to get in the direction that they want to go. They give guidance and increase 'navigability' but can be easily rejected (Sunstein 2015; Sunstein 2019). Illustrating the nudge approach by drawing on the functionality of GPS devices is hardly accidental: these gadgets are supposed to provide 'neutral' information, without hidden agendas and pre-designed paths to take, they can be easily switched on and off, they produce no lasting negative effects, and people simply have to use a GPS to get from A to B, which means that choice architecture cannot be avoided. The coupling of behavioral interventions with smart metering devices (to encourage energy savings) is one example of how both are directly related in practice. The ethical-individual approach, on the other hand, presupposes that individuals need to develop the 'right' values and act accordingly, that small and simple gestures can amass into a coordinated movement, and that everyone can develop a responsible attitude to the environment if he or she chooses to do so (Machin 2013, 28–29). In other words, although environmental responsibility is mediated by personal conscience, it remains a voluntary choice. Here, the link to sustainable behavior change agendas is notable: individuals are encouraged to behave in environmental-friendly ways without compromising individual freedoms. The ethical-individual approach asserts that there are universally 'right,' i.e., 'rational' and 'good' behaviors, for people to adopt, and therefore supplements the focus on the individual with moral prescriptions that are conveyed by norms, emotions, or other subconscious cues (ibid., 45; see also Reisch and Thogersen 2017; Gumbert 2019a). In addition, the behavior change agenda rests on theories of social change that can be circumscribed with 'aggregation' and 'green purchasing' (Maniates and Princen 2015). Aggregation assumes that change happens when enough individuals change their behavior, and therefore legitimizes a focus on the individual level and indirectly justifies consumption (since individuals have direct access). Green purchasing claims that social change occurs when individuals make financial investments with social and environmental benefits in mind, which justifies reliance on market mechanisms, and again, prioritizing consumption. Although similar to the aggregation argument, it is additionally driven by the moral claim that conscientious consumers make change happen by performing environmental attitudes and values (ibid.). By way of marrying both techno-economic and ethic-individual approaches, behaviorally informed policies create a strong link between sustainable effects on the macro-level (e.g., national GHG emissions) and sustainable actions on the micro-level (individual behaviors).

The combination of these processes – easy implementation, neoliberal governance, and the techno-ethical approach to managing climate change – provides a clearer picture for evaluating the overall contribution of nudge approaches to sustainable transition pathways. While behavior change strategies can be easily modified and tailored to specific contexts, they can also easily be removed. As long as defaults or infrastructural designs are in place, they may be effective in altering individual preferences, but if they are tools to instill an enduring sustainable transformation is a different question. The reliance on micro-level change and operating through the sphere of consumption is in this regard not without its risks. As Maniates points out, 'contemporary environmental action has tilted toward an unpromising politics of guilt focused on the individual behavior of the many, rather than engaging politics of structural transformation that mobilizes the most committed' (Maniates 2012, 122; ct. in Machin 2013, 42). However, it would be wrong to insinuate that nudge approaches would be anti-political or even anti-democratic. Some scholars even emphasize their in-principle compatibility with more democratic elements, such as deliberation (John 2018; Lenzi 2019). Although nudges cannot be said to foreclose attempts to enhance deliberation, social learning, and collective value judgments, it is not something the approach sets out to do. It reproduces and disseminates the belief in technological change, aggregation, and green purchasing, and in this sense, it enhances the risk of suppressing more democratic approaches, e.g., generating public pressure and interest group mobilization. When discussions center on the responsibility of individuals, it is simply more difficult to shift responsibility back to political collectives and institutions (Machin 2013, 40). Behavior change strategies are built on a vision of socio-ecological transformation as incremental change of existing behavioral patterns. They are mainly concerned with governing the present and not oriented towards the future. Policymakers who support the broad application of behavioral insights in public policy at least implicitly subscribe to this underlying vision. Others have also argued that 'nudging seems to lack precisely the kind of transformative impetus that characterizes procedural sustainability conceptions' (Bornemann and Burger 2019, 219).

The future of behavioral economics in sustainability governance – implications for research

In this final section, I want to build on the previous arguments in this chapter and suggest that, in order to enhance the democratic quality of sustainability-oriented nudges, choice architects should pay greater attention to the political and ethical objections that have been put forth by numerous authors, before making some final remarks on the future of nudging in democratic settings.

In the context of democratic sustainability governance, behaviorally informed regulatory options appear to be incredibly modest: their goal is non-forced compliance, they are low-cost, choice-preserving, and aspire to expand the policy toolbox, for example, by adding behavior change instruments to existing policies in order to improve their effectiveness. The simultaneous interrogation of behavioral economics and nudging from the vantage points of democracy and sustainability reveals that there is more to altering the choice environments of individuals than to reduce the size of trays in cafeterias or obtain renewable energy by default option. Nudges have to be evaluated in terms of how they affect individuals, e.g., if the true intent of the nudge is transparent and if it can be easily resisted, but also in terms of their effects on respective fields of sustainability governance as such. Important questions for research are, for example, if specific policy tools have been replaced in the past by behavioral interventions, if the introduction of these approaches has complicated other democratic approaches, or which forces shape the particularities of specific behaviorally informed sustainability policies. As Reisch and Thøgersen remind us, behavior change tools 'have to be accepted and supported by the same democratic processes, public debate, and critical scrutiny of their costs and benefits as other political instruments' (2017, 246). Unfortunately, there is not much empirical research on the democratic quality of behavior change agendas. Democratic ethics are frequently mentioned and drawn upon in debates in political theory and philosophy, but there are hardly systematic analyses that evaluate the design of specific choice environments on the grounds of democratic norms. It is an important task moving forward with research in this area.

In terms of how to generally assess the proliferation of behavioral economic logics across sustainability policy, most commentators neither vote for 'broadly apply' or 'outright reject' nudge approaches. Rather, many opt for 'smart adjustments' of the strategies that have been tested so far. There are numerous reasons for that. First, nudges are broadly described as complements to traditional regulatory tools such as taxing, sanctions, and incentives (Thaler and Sunstein 2008; Sunstein 2014). Reisch and Thøgersen call for treating behaviorally informed policy as a 'flexible, evidence-based, trial-and-error policy approach' (2017, 249), meeting the challenges of case-specific policies (e.g., different consumer groups) through extended field and lab experiments as well as more survey research. This presupposes a rather limited scope for behavioral interventions. For different reasons, others have suggested preventing the overrepresentation of behavioral insights within sustainability governance, for they might potentially detract attention from alternative policy mixes (Schubert 2017; Gumbert 2019b). In the same vein, Bornemann and Burger suggest a policy mix in sustainability-related fields to potentially outbalance possible tensions between nudges and sustainability (2019, 221).

Second, social practice theorists provide a strong reason why behavior change strategies should only be one part of the puzzle. A simplified application of behavioral insights will presuppose that the causes of unsustainable behaviors are the unreflective, intuitive thinking of individuals, which need to be addressed by interventions. Proponents of social practices, by contrast, describe behaviors as 'performances of social practices,' as expressions of socially shared phenomena such as taste, knowledge, skills, infrastructures, etc. (Shove et al. 2012; see also Warde 2005; Keller and Vihalemm 2017) of which behaviors would just make up the tip of the iceberg. In other words, what needs to be addressed by policy is not primarily the intuitive thinking of individuals but rather the 'socially embedded underpinning' (Spurling et al. 2013, 47) of behavior. For example, to get people to eat less meat is not just a matter of more information and pro-environmental heuristics and cues in their choice architecture, but instead influenced by various organizations of the food system, domestic technologies, cultural representations, previous policy interventions, food conventions, everyday resource constraints, food provisioning infrastructure, and so forth (ibid., 17). Here, policy has a range of different options to pursue, for instance, intervening in single practice components (what Spurling et al. call 're-crafting practices') or substituting practices altogether (develop and support alternatives that fulfill the same needs).

Finally, as argued earlier, searching for ways to democratize nudges can redeem part of the critique leveled against the nudge approach. It has been criticized for, inter alia, lack of transparency, threats to individual freedom and autonomy, and manipulation of individual interests. Proponents are certainly right to argue that both the diversity of available nudges and the heterogeneity of individual reactions defy any such generalizing comments (Sunstein 2015; Reisch and Thøgersen 2017). It must be asserted, though, that most practical applications are so far rather bypassing democratic elements instead of incorporating them. Instead of just reflecting on their pro-environmental values and transforming everyday routines and habits, citizens could be nudged to engage in dialogue, to empower them to discuss diverging conceptions of sustainability and their subjective good life within planetary boundaries, and, where value conflicts are unavoidable, to weigh mutually exclusive goals and goods against each other. This would, for example, entail 'navigating' the use of people's time and efforts towards community actions or political forms of consumption (Micheletti and Stolle 2012) instead of focusing on changing singular, carbon-intensive consumption choices. It might also entail reflecting on individual need satisfaction, i.e., what people need in order to live a life they value, as opposed to realizing all of their wants and desires through choosing slightly 'greener' options (see the discussion on needs vs. desires in Fuchs et al. 2021). By doing so, nudging may contribute to 'expanding [citizens'] awareness, experience, and knowledge of the environment in which they live, including their impact on it and its impact on them' (Hall 2016, 604), eventually promoting responsible actions and behaviors beyond the marketplace. If behavior change strategies are understood along these lines as a tool for environmental citizen education, it is apparent that these approaches can only constitute a supplement to existing policy measures. It is therefore advisable, especially since behavior change agendas are expected to continue to spread across sustainability-oriented policy domains globally (Whitehead et al. 2019), to treat them rather as an addendum in the policy mix than as an all-superseding paradigm.

Notes

1 Nudges can further be distinguished into 'pro-self nudges' and 'pro-social nudges' (Barton and Grüne-Yanoff 2015, 344). Whereas the first class of nudges aims to promote private welfare, the second promotes public goods.
2 Others have also highlighted variations of this 'co-dependence' of technological change and behavioral insights. Spurling et al. (2013) describe the three most common problem framings of the sustainability challenge as innovating technology, shifting consumer choices, and changing behavior. These problem framings build on each other since the goal of technical innovation is to reduce the resource intensity of consumption, while 'shifting' and 'change' implies the provision and subsequent behavioral adaptation of more sustainable consumption patterns (ibid. 2013, 5).

References

Barr, S., 2015. Beyond Behaviour Change: Social Practice Theory and the Search for Sustainable Mobility. In E. Huddart Kennedy, M.J. Cohen, and N.T. Krugman, eds. *Putting Sustainability into Practice. Applications and Advances in Research on Sustainable Consumption*. Cheltenham: Edward Elgar, 91–108.
Barry, J., 1996. Sustainability, Political Judgement And Citizenship: Connecting Green Politics and Democracy. In B. Doherty and M. de Geus, eds. *Democracy and Green Political Thought. Sustainability, rights and citizenship*. London and New York: Routledge, 115–131.
Barton, A. and Grüne-Yanoff, T., 2015. From libertarian paternalism to nudging – and beyond. *Review of Philosophy and Psychology*, 6 (3), 341–359.
Beck, U., 2016. *The Metamorphosis of the World*. Cambridge: Polity Press.
Blake, J., 1999. Overcoming the 'value-action gap' in environmental policy: tensions between national policy and local experience. *Local Environment*, 4 (3), 257–278.
Bornemann, B. and Burger, P., 2019. Nudging to Sustainability? Critical Reflections on Nudging from a Theoretically Informed Sustainability Perspective. In H. Straßheim and S. Beck, eds. *Handbook of Behavioural Change and Public Policy*. Cheltenham: Edward Elgar, 209–226.
Bovens, L., 2009. The Ethics of Nudge. In T. Grüne-Yanoff and S. O. Hansson, eds. *Preference Change: Approaches from Philosophy, Economics and Psychology*. Berlin: Springer, 207–220.
Brooks, A. and Bryant, R., 2014. Consumption. In C. Death, eds. *Critical Environmental Politics*. London: Routledge, 72–82.
Brown, W., 2015. *Undoing the Demos: Neoliberalism's Stealth Revolution*. New York: Zone Books.
Defila, R., Di Giulio, A. and Kaufmann-Hayoz, R., 2014. Sustainable Consumption – an Unwieldy Object of Research. *GAIA – Ecological Perspectives for Science and Society*, 23 (Supplement 1), 148–157.

European Commission (EC), 2016. *Behavioural insights applied to policy. European Report 2016 (Joint ResearchCentre Report No. 100146)* [online]. Available from: http://publications.jrc.ec.europa.eu/repository/bitstream/JRC100146/kjna27726enn_new.pdf.

European Commission (EC), 2018. *A Clean Planet for all A European strategic long-term vision for a prosperous, modern, competitive and climate neutral economy* [online]. Available from: https://ec.europa.eu/transparency/regdoc/rep/1/2018/EN/COM-2018-773-F1-EN-MAIN-PART-1.PDF.

Fuchs, D., Di Giulio, A., Glaab, K., Lorek, S., Maniates, M., Princen, T. and Ropke, I., 2016. Power: the missing element in sustainable consumption and absolute reductions research and action. *Journal of Cleaner Production*, 132, 298–307.

Fuchs, D., Sahakian, M., Gumbert, T., Di Giulio, A., Maniates, M., Lorek, S. and Graf, A., 2021. *Consumption Corridors. Living a Good Life within Sustainable Limits*. London: Routledge.

Girod, B., van Vuuren, D. P. and Hertwich, E. G., 2014. Climate policy through changing consumption choices: options and obstacles for reducing greenhouse gas emissions. *Global Environmental Change*, 25 (1), 5–15.

Goodwin, T., 2012. Why we should reject 'nudge'. *Politics*, 32 (2), 85–92.

Gumbert, T., 2019a. Freedom, Autonomy and Sustainable Behaviors: The Politics of Designing Consumer Choice. In C. Isenhour, M. Martiskainen and L. Middlemiss, eds. *Politics, Power & Ideology in Sustainable Consumption*. London and New York: Routledge, 107–123.

Gumbert, T., 2019b. Anti-democratic tenets? Behavioural-economic imaginaries of a future food system. *Politics and Governance*, 7 (4), 94–104.

Hajer, M.A., 1995. *The Politics of Environmental Discourse: Ecological Modernization and the Policy Process*. Oxford: Oxford University Press.

Hall, C., 2016. Framing and Nudging for a Greener Future. In T. Gabrielson, C. Hall, J. M. Meyer and D. Schlosberg, eds. *The Oxford Handbook of Environmental Political Theory*. Oxford: Oxford University Press, 593–607.

Hausman, D. M., and Welch, B., 2010. Debate: to nudge or not to nudge. *Journal of Political Philosophy*, 8 (1), 123–136.

Heiskanen, E. and Laakso, S., 2019. Editing out Unsustainability from Consumption: From Information Provision to Nudging and Social Practice Theory. In O. Mont, eds. *A Research Agenda for Sustainable Consumption Governance*. Cheltenham and Northampton: Edward Elgar, 156–171.

Institute for Global Environmental Strategies (IGES), Aalto University, and D-mat ltd., 2019. *1.5-Degree Lifestyles: Targets and Options for Reducing Lifestyle Carbon Footprints*. Technical Report. Institute for Global Environmental Strategies. Hayama/Japan.

Intergovernmental Panel on Climate Change (IPCC), 2014. *AR5 Synthesis Report: Climate Change 2014*. Contribution of Working Groups I, II and III to the Fifth Assessment Report of the Intergovernmental Panel on Climate Change. IPCC: Geneva.

John, P., 2018. *How Far to Nudge? Assessing Behavioural Public Policy*. Cheltenham: Edward Elgar.

John, P., Smith, G. and Stoker, G., 2009. Nudge nudge, think think. Two strategies for changing civic behaviour. *Political Quarterly*, 80 (3), 361–370.

Jones, R., Pykett, J. and Whitehead, M., 2013a. *Changing Behaviours. On the Rise of the Psychological State*. Cheltenham: Edward Elgar.

Jones, R., Pykett, J., and Whitehead, M., 2013b. Psychological governance and behavior change. *Policy & Politics*, 41 (2), 159–182.

Kahneman, Daniel., 2003. Maps of bounded rationality: psychology for behavioral economics. *The American Economic Review*, 93 (5), 1449–1475.

Kahneman, D., 2011. *Thinking, Fast and Slow*. New York: Farrar, Straus and Giroux.

Kahneman, D. and Tversky, A., 1979. Prospect theory: an analysis of decision under risk. *Econometrica*, 47 (2), 263–291.

Keller, M. and Vihalemm, T., 2017. Practice change and interventions into consumers' everyday life. In M. Keller, B. Halkier, T.A. Wilska and M. Truninger, eds. *Routledge Handbook of Consumption*. London and New York: Routledge, 226–241.

Kollmuss, A. and Agyeman, J., 2002. Mind the gap: why do people act environmentally and what are the barriers to pro-environmental behavior? *Environmental Education Research*, 8 (3), 239–260.

Krogman, N., 2020. Consumer Values and Consumption. In A. Kalfagianni, D. Fuchs and A. Hayden, eds. *Routledge Handbook of Global Sustainability Governance*. London and New York: Routledge, 242–253.

Lehner, M., Mont, O. and Heiskanen, E., 2016. Nudging – a promising tool for sustainable consumption behavior? *Journal of Cleaner Production* 134, 166–177.

Lenzi, D., 2019. Deliberating about climate change: the case for 'thinking and nudging'. *Moral Philosophy and Politics*, 6 (2), 1–22.

Machin, A., 2013. *Negotiating Climate Change: Radical Democracy and the Illusion of Consensus*. London and New York: Zed Books Ltd.

Maniates, M., 2012. Everyday possibilities. *Global Environmental Politics*, 12 (1), 121–125.

Maniates, M., 2014. Sustainable consumption – three paradoxes. *GAIA – Ecological Perspectives for Science and Society*, 23 (3), 201–208.

Maniates, M. and Princen, T., 2015. Fifteen claims: social change and power in environmental studies. *Journal of Environmental Studies and Sciences*, 5, 213–217.

Micheletti, M., and Stolle, D., 2012. Sustainable citizenship and the new politics of consumption. *The Annals of the American Academy of Political and Social Science*, 644, 88–120.

Mills, C., 2015. The heteronomy of choice architecture. *Review of Philosophy and Psychology*, 6, 495–509.

Mol, A.P.J., 2001. *Globalization and Environmental Reform: The Ecological Modernization of the Global Economy*. Cambridge: MIT Press.

O'Rourke, D. and Lollo, N., 2015. Transforming consumption: from decoupling to behavior change, to system changes for sustainable consumption. *Annual Review of Environment and Resources*, 40, 233–259.

Ölander, F. and Thøgersen, J., 2014. Informing versus nudging in environmental policy. *Journal of Consumer Policy*, 37, 341–356.

Olivier, O. and Sauneron, S., 2011. *'Green Nudges': New Incentives for Ecological Behaviour*. Paris: Centre d'analyse stratégique.

Olsen, E.D.H. and Trenz, H.-J., 2014. From citizens' deliberation to popular will formation? Generating democratic legitimacy in transnational deliberative polling. *Political Studies*, 62 (S1), 117–133.

Reisch, L.A. and Thøgersen, J.B., 2017. Behaviorally Informed Consumer Policy. Research and Policy for "Humans". In M. Keller, B. Halkier, T.-A. Wilska and M. Truninger, eds. *Routledge Handbook of Consumption*. London and New York: Routledge, 242–253.

Reisch, L.A. and Sunstein, C.R., 2016. Do Europeans like nudges? *Judgment and Decision Making*, 11 (4), 310–325.

Schor, J., 2010. *Plenitude: The New Economics of True Wealth*. New York: Penguin Press.

Schubert, C., 2017. Green nudges: do they work? are they ethical? *Ecological Economics*, 132, 329–342.

Shove, E., Pantzar, M. and Watson, M., 2012. *The Dynamics of Social Practice: Everyday Life and How it Changes*. London: Sage.

Spurling, N., McMeekin, A., Shove, E., Southerton, D. and Welch, D., 2013. *Interventions in practice: reframing policy approaches to consumer behaviour*. SPRG Report, September 2013.

Sugden, R., 2008. Why incoherent preferences do not justify paternalism. *Constitutional Political Economy*, 19(3), 226–248.

Sunstein, C.R., 2014. Nudging: a very short guide. *Journal of Consumer Policy*, 37, 583–588.

Sunstein, C.R., 2015. Nudges, agency, and abstraction: a reply to critics. *Review of Philosophy and Psychology*, 6, 511–529.

Sunstein, C.R., 2019. *On Freedom*. Princeton: Princeton University Press.

Thaler, R., 1980. Toward a positive theory of consumer choice. *Journal of Economic Behavior & Organization*, 1 (1), 39–60.

Thaler, R. H. and Sunstein, C. R., 2008. *Nudge: Improving Decisions about Health, Wealth and Happiness*. New York: Penguin.

Tversky, A. and Kahneman, D., 1974. Judgement under uncertainty: heuristics and biases. *Science*, 185 (4157), 1124–1131.

Warde, A., 2005. Consumption and theories of practice. *Journal of Consumer Culture*, 5(2), 131–153.

Whitehead, M., Jones, R. and Pykett, J., 2019. Nudging Around the World: A Critical Geography of the Behavior Change Agenda. In H. Straßheim and S. Beck, eds. *Handbook of Behavioural Change and Public Policy*. Cheltenham: Edward Elgar, 90–101.

Whitman, D.G., and Rizzo, M.J., 2015. The problematic welfare standards of behavioral paternalism. *Review of Philosophy and Psychology*, 6, 409–425.

Wilkinson, T.M., 2013. Nudging and manipulation. *Political Studies*, 61 (2), 341–355.

28

COLLABORATIVE CONSUMPTION

A mechanism for sustainability and democracy?

Anna Davies

Introduction

Consumption is a necessary condition of life, but it is widely accepted that current patterns of consumption are not only highly uneven (within and between countries), but also unsustainable when considered at the global scale (Davies et al. 2014). This unsustainability is evidenced by multiple tools from ecological footprinting (Jorgenson 2003) to the transgression of planetary boundaries which identify a safe operating space for humanity on earth (Rockström et al. 2009). Certain drivers of unsustainability relate to the inefficiencies of current consumption practices and this is the issue which many contemporary collaborative consumption activities – particularly those that utilise digital platforms – claim to address by bringing idling resources such as spare bedrooms or car seats into use.

However, unsustainable consumption is also situated within a wider paradigm, which until the twenty-first century generally assumed that more consumption signified 'growth' which would inexorably lead to more development, societal progress and enhanced wellbeing. A series of landmark documents have challenged this assumption, most prominently the work of Tim Jackson and his articulation of strategies for prosperity without growth (Jackson 2009; 2017). These documents confirm that consumption is about much more than meeting essential needs and encompasses a range of contested signifiers relating to status, conceptions of the self in relation to others and 'the good life' (Michaelis 2007). Rather than a neutral practice, consumption has become seen as highly political and it is within this context that the concept of collaborative consumption gained prominence as a subject of analysis in the first decade of the twenty-first century.

The specific links between democracy and consumption have been made more visible by the emergence of ideas around ethical consumption and the reframing of consumers as citizen-consumers (Johnston 2008). Citizen-consumers are seen to 'vote' in order to effect change through their choice of purchases. As Johnston (2008, 229) suggests, this means 'voting with your dollar – that can satisfy competing ideologies of consumerism (an idea rooted in individual self-interest) and citizenship (an ideal rooted in collective responsibility to a social and ecological commons'. In particular arenas such as food, similar concerns have become expressed as

DOI: 10.4324/9780429024085-34

matters of food democracy (Bornemann and Weiland 2019, 1), which fundamentally relates to matters of health, safety, equal rights to culturally-appropriate food, and opportunities to participate in the food system (Davies et al. 2019).

In this Chapter, I will first address the concept of collaborative consumption and its historical roots, before synthesising key dimensions of debates about, within and around collaborative consumption and their intersection with matters of democracy. This is followed by a consideration of the diverse organisational structures that underpin different models of collaborative consumption and an illustration of these with specific reference to collaborative consumption in the arena of social dining, and the relative balance of power and responsibility those models and practices entail. The challenges posed by diverse models of collaborative consumption in relation to matters of democracy and sustainability are then outlined and concluding remarks identify a range of actions needed to address these challenges. Essentially, collaborative consumption is associated with a plethora of promises in relation to sustainability and democracy, amongst other claims, but these claims have little evidence to back them up currently. There are concerns that large-scale commercial platforms claiming to support collaborative consumption are not generating activities which meet these promises and may actually be reinforcing existing inequalities. Alternative models for collaborative consumption – such as platform cooperativism – do exist, but even within these there are a number of outstanding challenges to be addressed.

Definitions and dimensions of collaborative consumption

Precise definitions of collaborative consumption are elusive, although the concept is generally attributed to practices which involve the shared use of a product or service by more than one individual. This contrasts with the individualism that has dominated mainstream consumption where it is typically one person who pays the full cost of acquiring access to and ownership of that which is being consumed. The public profile of collaborative consumption has increased in recent decades as the digital revolution encompassing smart, mobile digital devices, social media apps and web platforms, have offered new ways to connect with others and to share moments of consumption (Davies et al. 2017), but it is by no means a new term. In the 1970s behavioural scientists Marcus Felson and Joe Spaeth (1978) explicitly discussed transactional economic practices, such as eating or drinking together, as moments of collaborative consumption. Its roots can, however, be traced back much further than the last century, to the very foundation of human civilization and in particular hunter-gatherer societies which permitted collaborative food acquisition and consumption (Davies 2019).

Definitional complexities have arisen as advocates, innovators and authors have coined a plethora of umbrella terms to describe elements which overlap with contemporary collaborative consumption, from the 'sharing economy' through to Peer-to-Peer (P2P) platform economies. Key early movers in the resulting definitional debates, Rachel Botsman and Roo Rogers sought to clarify in their book *What's Mine is Yours* (2010) the intersections between these emergent practices, ultimately concluding that collaborative consumption can involve both sharing and peer economies, utilising business-to-business, business-to-charity and peer-to-peer models of exchange. They identify that collaborative consumption activities are particularly activated by product service systems and redistribution marketplaces, as well as in attempts to create more sustainable lifestyles.

Product service systems support individuals or organisations to offer goods as a service which can be shared or rented, as opposed to a product to sell. These systems are often used for durable goods and support those who want the benefits of a product without ownership, for example bike sharing schemes lease bikes and provide an alternative to purchasing one. Redistribution marketplaces, in contrast, offer spaces where used or preowned goods can find new application. The goods may be offered for free, as on Freecycle, or can be swapped (e.g. clothes in thredUP) or sold, as on eBay and craigslist. Collaborative lifestyle ventures, according to Botsman and Rogers (2010), connect people with similar needs or interests to share. Such endeavours may involve the exchange of less tangible assets such as time, space, skills or money. While these exchanges happen predominantly within delimited territorial spaces, exemplified by people sharing working spaces or gardens, they can also occur internationally through activities such as peer-to-peer lending platforms like Zopa.

While collaborative consumption activities are clearly diverse, proponents have suggested that a suite of common characteristics can be discerned: enhanced options for social interaction; increased resource efficiency; a decentralisation of power, flexible work options and a democratisation of entrepreneurship. These characteristics are seen as fuelled by disruptive technological drivers and cumulatively are envisaged as leading to a reconfiguration of consumption relations (Botsman and Rogers 2010). Assertions have been made that through collaborative consumption, power is moving from large, centralised institutions to distributed networks, with individuals and communities reshaping how matters of access and trust in relation to consumption are being approached (Gansky 2010). In particular, the smart digital technologies underpinning platform-based collaborative consumption have permitted more direct exchanges (e.g. P2P), reducing the need for intermediaries and opening up the possibility for people to be both providers and consumers of goods and services. It is the combination of smart digital infrastructure, alongside greater public awareness of environmental pressures and the importance of efficiency in the use of finite resources and assets that has been identified as a key disruptive driver of collaborative consumption. As digital technologies have become more accessible, they have developed the capacity to facilitate mass access to untapped social and economic value, and underutilized assets such as spare bedrooms, empty seats in cars, even idling gardening tools and kitchen utensils, allowing for patterns of ownership and consumption to be reconfigured and claims to environmental resource efficiency to be made.

Early, and broader, understandings of collaborative consumption (Felson and Spaeth 1978) have become supplanted in popular media by definitions of collaborative consumption as primarily an *economic model* based on sharing, swapping, trading or renting products and services facilitated by smart technologies. Much has been made of the fact that contemporary collaborative consumption activities provided opportunities for people to not only obtain products or services, but to become the providers of them. The move away from seeing people as passive consumers only, and recognising their capacity for producing goods and services, was first captured in the 1980s by Alvin Toffler in his term prosumers. However, this emphasis on commercial economic models and the rise of a few large-scale, venture-capitalist-funded, tech-based platforms has been widely criticised, in particular for the limited evidence that the claimed sustainability benefits of these modes of exchange have actually been realised (Davies 2019). Rather than empowering individuals to be active citizen-consumers, enhancing democratic participation in consumption landscapes, some arenas of collaborative consumption have seen the emergence of a few, extremely powerful companies using opaque algorithms to govern the people who work with and for them (Davies et al. 2017).

The following section reviews influential and emergent research examining these claims and concerns.

Collaborative consumption: the state of the art

Following the publication of popular books expounding the transformative potential of collaborative consumption (see Botsman and Rogers 2010; Gansky 2010), more academic scholarship has sought to tease out the complexities and tensions within these arguments. Initial responses focused on identifying the links between contemporary collaborative consumption and past practices (Belk 2014). This work concurs with advocates for tech-supported collaborative consumption that the practices are disrupting established assumptions that 'we are what we own'. However, empirical analyses have also begun to unpick broad statements and test claims about collaborative consumption.

In Möhlmann's (2015) study of a community accommodation marketplace, it was utility, trust, cost savings and familiarity that were identified as essential to users, whereas environmental impact, internet capability and smartphone capability were found to be of less importance. In order to better understand the embryonic landscape of contemporary collaborative consumption as a subject of research and as a practice, Barnes and Mattson (2016), conducted a study with experts in order to identify key drivers and inhibitors as well as the future developments in collaborative consumption they imagine will take place over the next ten years. Like Möhlmann, they also found that while sustainability is often heralded as a key motivator for collaborative consumption, matters of environmental concern and sustainability were considered of minor importance by participants in the research. Going beyond expert perspectives, Hamari et al (2016) surveyed people who were registered on a collaborative consumption site to ascertain why they participated in such activities. They found that participation was motivated by many factors, including enjoyment of the activity as well as economic advantages, but neither empowerment as active citizen-consumers, or enhanced democracy, was mentioned. In contrast to Barnes and Mattson (2016) however, Hamari et al (2016) identified sustainability as one of the motivational factors, but only for those already committed to ecological consumption. In addition, they suggested that participants often assumed that the collaborative consumption they engaged with was more sustainable than other consumption practices, rather than seeing evidence of this.

To date there has been uneven attention by researchers to collaborative consumption practices around the globe. With much of the published work focused on high-income countries, there has been limited examination of collaborative consumption practices elsewhere, despite claims that it offers more sustainable consumption options and therefore is relevant to achieving the global 2030 sustainable development goals (Mi and Coffman 2019). There are a few notable exceptions. Adopting a social practice theory framework and focusing on Bangkok, Metro Manila and Hanoi, Retamal (2019) sets out the prospects for broader uptake of collaborative consumption practices in Southeast Asia and their potential to offer more sustainable consumption options. They found that collaborative consumption services were already established and normalised, indicating good prospects for further participation. However, shared-access collaborative consumption practices also faced significant resistance in all three cities. Whilst Retamal (2019) concludes that this resistance may be reduced through further expansion of the middle classes in these regions, they also recognise the importance of the institutional environment for facilitating greater engagement. Indeed, the governance of collaborative consumption is something that is emerging as a key area of scholarship due to the impacts of large-scale commercial collaborative consumption platforms (Palgan et al. 2017; Winslow and Mont 2019).

Despite the frequent reiteration of the potential for resource efficiencies which can be gained from collaborative consumption, there is limited research detailing the actual impacts in this area. In part, this is because it is a complex task demanding activity data from platforms which could be considered commercially sensitive for an emerging market (Davies et al. 2017a). However, it is also because some of the qualities that collaborative consumption is supposed to support mentioned in the previous section, particularly enhanced community cohesion and the benefits of being able to actively participate in exchange processes, are hard to quantify and speak to different forms of valuation beyond financial profit or loss. Capturing these less tangible benefits is a challenge that is now beginning to be explicitly confronted in relation to social, economic, environmental and governance metrics (Mackensie and Davies 2019). Beyond this, scholars are also beginning to take a critical look at the claims to broader sustainability that have been attributed to collaborative consumption, contrasting the celebrationist perspectives of platform entrepreneurs with those of incumbent industries, governments and grassroots activists. Indeed, rather than a potential pathway to sustainability, critics suggest that collaborative consumption in its commercial forms could actually be a precursor to a nightmarish form of late neoliberalism (Martin 2016). This nightmare would be characterised by precarious work, rising inequalities between those with marketable material goods (e.g. homes, cars, bikes) and skills to share and those without, and even inducing increased demand for goods and services, therefore counteracting any environmental savings from efficiency gains through utilising products idling capacity (Davies et al. 2017). A key concern was the potential for co-option of collaborative consumption by commercial operators focused solely on exploiting its potential as an economic opportunity would not drive the desired sustainability transformation or lead to a deepening of democratic engagement in exchanges.

Diverse activities of collaborative consumption

Despite the prevalence of attention to commercial activities of collaborative consumption, there has been considerable research conducted which focuses on non-commercial and not-for-profit activities. This has become manifest in different ways, through developments relating to platform cooperativism (Martin et al. 2017; Fedosov et al. 2019), which seeks to redistribute benefits of collaborative consumption more equitably, to alignment with broader movements related to commoning and the social economy (Guillemot and Privat 2019). These attempts to expand consideration of what counts as collaborative consumption are driven by a desire to challenge emerging commercial platforms which enact new markets through other people's infrastructure (e.g. care, accommodation, skills etc.). They raise concerns that these commercial processes are effectively creating an on-demand system with the platform companies as a logistical centre point through which all participants must pass and to whom all must pay. Rather than the redistribution of power, flexible work options and democratisation of entrepreneurship which feature heavily in commercially-focused collaborative consumption rhetoric, large-scale, commercial multinational platforms are actually creating a centrally controlled system which relies on opaque algorithms to discipline those who work through them. As a result, there are fears these companies are undermining existing regulations established for public protection, including labour laws; fears which are amplified by the expanding participation in these platforms by citizen-consumers.

In response, platform cooperativism has emerged as a movement and practice which takes the technological heart of commercial platforms and applies it to a cooperative model that seeks to put workers, owners, communities and cities on a more equal footing. A platform cooperative is collectively owned and governed by the people who depend on and participate in it. Whereas commercial platforms extract value from activities and distribute it to the shareholding owners who invest with the goal of attaining a return on their investment, platform cooperatives distribute ownership and management of the enterprise and any value creation amongst its participants (Sandoval 2019). There are many examples of platform cooperativism already in place, not all of which relate to collaborative consumption. Those which are concerned with collaborative consumption often operate in the face of particularly powerful commercial platforms. In the accommodation space this has led to a proliferation of alternatives to Airbnb, from Fairbnb.coop to the city-owned Munibnb. Fairmondo which is a cooperative ebay-like organisation was established in Germany in 2012 as a marketplace selling ethically-sourced products and services. Fairmondo is owned and operated by the buyers, sellers, workers and investors who engage with the platform. It has created a federated model in which an affiliate can launch a co-op in another country using the Fairmondo brand and platform to serve the local market, such as Fairmondo UK. There are plans to create a global network of such country-based cooperative marketplaces. A number of union-backed platforms have also been established, particularly in the mobility sector which has seen powerful ride sharing apps emerge. In other cases, cooperatives have emerged organically, as with Modo.coop, a Vancouver-based carsharing co-operative. It was incorporated in 1997 as a small operation of two cars and 16 members. By 2016 it had more than 16,000 members and a fleet of over 500 sports cars, sedans, trucks, SUVs, vans and hybrids. Modo was the first carshare co-operative established in North America.

While platform cooperativism for collaborative consumption has emerged to directly confront some of the negative impacts of the emergent commercial platform economies, they do not represent a silver bullet for sustainable and democratic collaborative consumption. They do not exist in a vacuum and require resources to establish a more democratic governance architecture, develop legal frameworks and acquire appropriate software systems. This has led to calls for more open-source software to be developed and made accessible. Certainly, there is work to be done around developing greater public literacy about platform cooperativism as an alternative to the incumbent commercial platforms, but as Sandoval (2019) notes, the apparent simplicity of cutting out the corporate intermediaries by setting up cooperative versions is deceiving. While platform cooperativism has the potential to subvert digital capitalism from the inside it is also at risk of being co-opted by it.

Collaborative consumption and food: a case study of social dining

The previous sections have illustrated the diversity of activities which fall under the collaborative consumption banner, addressing the different exchange models (e.g. for profit and cooperative) and the diverse modes of exchange that can operationalise collaborative consumption (e.g. selling, bartering, swapping, gifting etc.). While contemporary ICT (information and communication technology)-mediated collaborative consumption of food has received less attention than some other sectors to date, this belies the many collaborative food-based activities ongoing in this space (Davies 2019). Drilling down into the food sector and focusing on diverse practices of social dining as an archetypal type of collaborative consumption, this section delineates and interrogates their various practices and potential for creating positive sustainability impacts and enhancing food democracy. In particular, commercial social dining platforms are contrasted with those that operate on a not-for-profit basis.

Commercial social dining often involves meal-based experiences advertised through an online platform as a means for hosts and guests to connect and socialize over food and drinks. Such social dining takes place in a range of settings, from the unexpected spaces of pop-up underground supper clubs to the domestic venues offered by hosts through intermediary P2P platforms such as Eatwith or Bookalokal. These social dining platforms promote both the goods that are physically consumed (e.g. the meal) and the experiences of hospitality and conviviality that accompany the meal itself (e.g. the home experience provided by the host). Although the experience of eating is collectively shared, in contrast to more durable goods familiar to other spheres of collaborative consumption – such as cars or houses – the food consumed at the social dining events is a rival good with a limited window of safe edibility.

Research examining social dining has begun to explore the characteristics and motivations of those who seek social dining opportunities (e.g. Privitera 2016; Corigliano and Bricchi 2018; Ketter 2019). The benefits of social dining from a guests' perspective revolve around the authenticity, intimacy and exclusivity of the experience (small numbers in domestic spaces) as well as their interactive and immersive nature, generating conviviality through commensality (Mortara and Fragapane 2018). More than simply providing sustenance, the social dining experience also becomes a 'cultural artefact' (Everett and Aitchison 2008, 151) co-created by hosts and guests and mediated through the influencing framework of the P2P platform. This co-creation process is not entirely seamless. Research has found that in social dining contexts in Athens and Barcelona there were ongoing negotiations between hosts and guests – unsupported by the platform which connects them – regarding matters of authenticity and privacy. This includes hosts wanting to welcome strangers into their home giving them a glimpse of what residing in these cities means (e.g. giving them an authentic experience), but also unsure of where to place the boundaries over which guests should not trespass (Davies et al. 2020). In this research, hosts mentioned guests checking out their fridges and kitchens without asking permission, posting pictures on social media platforms of the dining event including images of their homes without the hosts permission and enquiring about salaries, rents and living costs. The research also uncovered an uneven risk burden between hosts and platforms with regards to liability, with the burden of identifying and complying with local regulations around tax, land use and food safety placed squarely on the shoulders of hosts and scant regard for matters of sustainability (Davies et al. 2020). That said, platform-mediated commercial social dining does provide an additional means for hosts to utilise their culinary skills in exchange for money beyond the mainstream restaurant industry, often within their own living spaces. This has economic benefits for hosts, reducing the need to buy or rent restaurant spaces and kitchens while generating additional income. However, further research is needed in order to fully understand how hosts in commercial P2P social dining settings manage the competing demands of working and living at home, balancing expectations of domestic hospitableness and commercial hospitality (Di Domenico and Lynch 2007). In the absence of leadership from the social dining platforms, participants in commercial social dining are feeling their way through new forms of interaction, exchange and regulation. Essentially, platform-based commercial social dining companies are leaving governance primarily to the morals of the those who dine together (Molz 2013). Certainly, there is scope for commercial social dining platforms to better monitor and measure the impacts of their platforms and the activities they facilitate. At a basic level, sustainability guidelines for hosts and guests could be developed. These guidelines might encourage the use of local organic food produce, support the sustainable use of energy and water in the preparation for, hosting of, and travel to, a social dining event. Commercial social dining companies could also become signatories to global principles for fair work through platform-based economies (Woodcock and Graham 2019).

Beyond straightforward commercial social dining platforms, there are a range of other formats and foci in operation. For example, the app Gnammo, created in Italy, has options for participants to organise or attend home cooking events, to participate in social dinners at specific social restaurants in the city, or simply come together in a mainstream restaurant with strangers to make new social connections. Elsewhere, social dining innovators have embraced collective eating events on a not-for-profit basis, often within community centres or religious spaces. These initiatives may have multiple or overlapping goals, from reducing food waste and fostering greater cohesion between social groups, to providing a food security safety net for vulnerable or disadvantaged communities. These events are called different things depending on the location, from the neighbourhood dinners provided by Open Table in Melbourne, Australia (Edwards and Davies 2018) to the community canteens offered by Be Enriched across locations in London (Marrovelli 2018). Participants in these collaborative consumption events are not passive recipients of free or reduced-price food, rather they are co-creators of social value around the act of creating and eating a meal together with others. Founders of such not-for-profit social dining events seek to meet needs related to both physiological hunger and social inclusion, or what Pfeiffer and colleagues (2015, 485) term 'alimentary participation'. It is the case that people on low incomes are often marginalised from mainstream consumption practices, such as eating out with friends, so these not-for-profit social dining events can provide more accessible opportunities to engage in such commensality.

Adopting a 'more-than-food' (Goodman 2016) approach, non-commercial social dining events aim to build healthier, happier and networked communities. In some cases, as with Be Enriched in London, the dual goals of increasing food security and reducing food waste are operationalised through the use of surplus food at social diners. While an intuitively sensible idea at one level, there are concerns that such redistribution does little to address the root causes of either food waste or food insecurity, with some suggesting it might even go some way to prop up the unsustainable food system (Caraher and Furey 2017). What such activities do address, however, are the immediate needs of those affected by a welfare gap with insufficient income to access to healthy, sustainable and culturally appropriate food. The challenge is to ensure that the root causes of hunger and isolation are also addressed and not obscured by such grassroots innovation. Certainly, more careful sustainability life-cycle analysis, sensitized to include attention to matters of food democracy, is required of all forms of social dining events to fully comprehend the impacts, both positive and negative, that they stimulate.

Collaborative consumption challenges

As this chapter has illustrated, collaborative consumption, for all its promises of sustainable, efficient, connected resource use, also brings a range of challenges. As illustrated in the previous sections, matters of governance in relation to collaborative consumption certainly merit further consideration. In part, this is because of the 'regulatory soup' (Orsi 2010) surrounding platform economies which are mediating elements of collaborative consumption, but it is also because collaborative consumption does not sit easily within a simple private-public action binary. When does a private and personal act of collaborative consumption become a commercial and public one for example? This does not mean that collaborative consumption practices are performed without rules, which can be social and regulatory. Rather, that it is hard to gain clarity regarding the relative rights and responsibilities of those who participate within them, and whether the current burden of responsibility around risks and liabilities is fair and appropriate.

Critics of commercial collaborative consumption platforms have argued that the platforms' claims to be merely logistics intermediaries (match-making those with goods or services to share with those who desire them) ignores the generative nature of the work they do (Davies et al. 2017). It is, of course, practically expedient for commercial collaborative consumption platforms to claim to be mere intermediaries, as it allows them to subvert regulatory frameworks established to govern incumbent industries – such as hotels, taxi services, restaurants – in the mainstream economy. As illustrated by social dining in the previous section, research has shown how the burden of regulatory compliance is shifted to the provider and consumer of the product or service under commercial collaborative models (Davies et al. 2020). Also, the need to already own the physical (e.g. a suitable home to host social dining) and technological (e.g. WiFi, computer etc.) infrastructures and skills rather limits claims for widening democratic participation in these new spaces of exchange. Beyond the social dining sector, mainstream hotels have challenged the legality of short-term rental sites such as Airbnb because those owners typically do not have to adhere to the regulatory requirements of running a hotel. This is seen as unfair competition by the incumbents. The spin-off impacts of commercial collaborative consumption on wider communities – such as the availability of long-term rental accommodation in popular tourist cities – have also stimulated local governments and sometimes national governments to take action to control these negative impacts (Uzunca and Borlenghi 2019). However, it is not only the commercial wing of collaborative consumption that has faced regulatory responses. In the food sector surplus food redistributors have also come into conflict with regulators. As Morrow (2018) found in her analysis of a surplus food redistributing initiative in Berlin (foodsharing.de), which adopts a non-hierarchical, commons-based view of food and attempted to establish a network of community fridges, these activities can also clash with established regulatory frameworks. In this case the initiative's actions brushed up against food safety regulation which requires the identification of a 'responsible individual' to manage risk and assume liability around food. Forming part of an emerging movement around processes of commoning, the stimulus for setting up the fridges was that they would provide open-access, community-managed spaces where food can be freely and anonymously shared, offering a means to reduce food waste and de-stigmatise the consumption of surplus food. Foodsharing. de had already developed a detailed governance strategy to manage food as a commons, but this failed to assuage the concerns of the Berlin Food Safety Authority because of the mismatch between their respective views about the appropriate allocation of risk and responsibility.

Conclusion: collaborative consumption – sustainable and democratic?

Commercial collaborative consumption has been promoted as an instrumental means to generate economic gains and resource efficiencies as part of the mainstream economy by engaging with others socially. However, critics of commercial collaborative consumption have argued that its pro-social claims are a smoke screen to obscure the fundamental profit-motives of the platform 'collaborative consumption' companies that connect people. There are also concerns about the inequitable access to commercial collaborative consumption marketplaces. Participation requires either resources in order to access goods or services or the control of goods and services that others desire access to. A car is required to become an Uber driver and a living space is a pre-requisite to share that space with short-term visitors. Even when access to commercial collaborative consumption marketplaces is secured, the economic benefits are not experienced evenly and for many participants these benefits are precarious and related to the vagaries of reputational rankings and opaque algorithms. Additionally, there are concerns that collaborative consumption may be inducing even more consumption through its multiplication of consumption opportunities, effectively cancelling out any efficiency savings made by reducing idling capacity in goods and services.

Ultimately, mechanisms to conduct sustainability impact assessment of collaborative consumption are needed and not only in relation to the sustainability of the good or service being consumed or matters of democratic participation, but also how they affect wider communities and localities. Data from collaborative consumption activities will be required to do this comprehensively, which might be difficult to access in commercial settings. Nonetheless, recognising the diversity within collaborative consumption, it would be productive to compare the impacts of multinational commercial platforms with those that adopt different not-for-profit or social enterprise models. A global horizon scanning survey could be conducted in order to establish a broader understanding of how goals and exchange models affect the practices and performance of collaborative consumption. These insights could be used to inform the development of a collaborative consumption sustainability impact assessment tool for initiatives, regulators and innovators. The development of the SHARE-IT tool in the food sharing space (Mackensie and Davies 2019) provides one model for this in the food sector which could be extended to incorporate other sectors of collaborative consumption.

In conclusion, collaborative consumption is an umbrella term capturing a range of activities shaped by divergent rules, tools, skills and understandings. Even within the emergent space of ICT-mediated collaborative consumption, which has dominated scholarly attention in the last decade, there are multiple modes of collaboration adopted and diverse organisational forms of initiatives which support it. Without doubt, these different practices are providing new ways to engage with others, new opportunities for accessing goods and services, and additional possibilities for financial and other benefits to accrue to those who have goods and services to spare. However, the sustainability and democratic credentials of collaborative consumption are as yet largely unproven. Indeed, the actual credentials of these initiatives are likely to be as diverse as the modes of exchange and organisational forms that have been adopted to enact collaborative consumption. Improved systems for identifying, monitoring and evaluating sustainability impacts are required and ensuring that such reporting is conducted may well require enhanced regulations to overcome limited access to data within commercial consumption settings. Similarly, while collaborative consumption in its broadest sense provides novel opportunities to engage more people in consumption practices, this does not by extension guarantee that participation becomes more democratic. There are cases where this has occurred – exemplified in this chapter by not-for-profit social dining events and their contribution to greater food democracy – but it cannot be assumed that all collaborative consumption practices will bring similar benefits, particularly in commercial settings. Indeed, there are concerns that digitally enhanced collaborative consumption may serve to entrench rather than resolve inequalities, creating a larger cohort of precarious workers in the collaborative consumption space who carry increased burdens of risk and responsibility while the benefits largely accrue elsewhere. The emergence of more democratic formations – such as platform cooperatives – hold some positive possibilities, but they are by no means a holy grail for sustainable and democratic collaborative consumption.

References

Barnes, S. and Mattson, J., 2016. Understanding current and future issues in collaborative consumption: a four-stage Delphi study. *Technological Forecasting and Social Change*, 104, 200–211.

Belk, R., 2014. You are what you can access: sharing and collaborative consumption online, *Journal of Business Research*, 67(8), 1595–1600.

Bornemann, B. and Weiland, S., 2019. Editorial: new perspectives on food democracy. *Politics and Governance*, 7(4), 1–7.

Botsman, R. and Rogers, R., 2010. *What's Mine is Yours*. New York: Harper Collins.

Caraher, M. and Furey, S., 2017. *Is it Appropriate to use Surplus Food to Feed People in Hunger? Short-term Band-Aid to more Deep Rooted Problems of Poverty*. London: Food Research Collaboration, Centre for Food Policy.

Corigliano, M.A. and Bricchi, S., 2018. Are social eating events a tool to experience the authentic food and wine culture of a place? In N. Bellini, C. Clergeau, O. Etcheverria, eds. *Gastronomy and Local Development: The Quality of Products, Places and Experiences*. Routledge: London.

Davies, A.R., 2019. *Urban Food Sharing*. London: Policy Press.

Davies, A.R., Cretella, A. and Franck, V., 2019. Food sharing initiatives and food democracy: practice and policy in three European cities. *Politics and Governance*, 7(4), 8–20.

Davies, A.R., Cretella, A., Edwards, F. and Marovelli, B., 2020. Motivations, regulations and the boundaries of hospitality for hosts in P2P social dining platforms. *Journal of Sustainable Tourism*. https://doi.org/10.1080/09669582.2020.1838526

Davies, A.R., Edwards, F., Marovelli, B., Morrow, O., Rut, M. and Weymes, M., 2017. Making visible: interrogating the performance of food sharing across 100 urban areas. *Geoforum*, 86, 136–149.

Davies, A.R., Fahy, F. and Rau, H., 2014. *Challenging Consumption: Pathways to a more Sustainable Future*. Routledge: London.

Di Domenico, M. and Lynch, P.A., 2007. Host/guest encounters in the commercial home. *Leisure Studies*, 26(3), 321–338.

Edwards, F. and Davies, A.R., 2018. Connective consumptions: mapping Melbourne's food sharing ecosystem. *Urban Policy and Research*, 36(4), 476–495.

Everett, S. and Aitchison, C., 2008. The role of food tourism in sustaining regional identity: A case study of Cornwall, South West England. *Journal of Sustainable Tourism*, 16(2), 150–167.

Fedosov, A., Lampinen, A., Dillahunt, T., Light, A. and Cheshire, C., 2019. Cooperativism and human-computer interaction. *CHI Conference on Human Factors in Computing Systems* (CHI) May 04–09, 2019.

Felson, M. and Spaeth, J.L., 1978. Community structure and collaborative consumption: a routine activity approach. *American Behavioral Scientist*, 21(4), 61.

Gansky, L., 2010. *The Mesh: Why the Future of Business is Sharing*. London: Penguin.

Goodman, M. K., 2016. Food geographies I: relational foodscapes and the busy-ness of being more-than-food. *Progress in Human Geography*, 40 (2), 257–266.

Guillemot, S. and Privat, H., 2019. The role of technology in collaborative consumer communities. *Journal of Services Marketing*, 31(7), 837–850.

Hamari, J., Sjoklint, M. and Ukkonen, A., 2016. The sharing economy: Why people participate in collaborative consumption. *Journal of the Association for Information Science and Technology*, 67(9), 2047–2059.

Jackson, T., 2017. *Prosperity Without Growth: Foundations for the Economy of Tomorrow*. London: Routledge.

Jackson, T., 2009. *Prosperity Without Growth: The transition to a Sustainable Economy*. Sustainable Development Commission, UK.

Johnston, J., 2008. The citizen-consumer hybrid: ideological tensions and the case of whole foods market. *Theory and Society*, 37(3), 229–270.

Jorgenson, A.K., 2003. Consumption and environmental degradation: a cross-national analysis of the ecological footprint. *Social Problems*, 50(3), 374–394.

Ketter, E., 2019. Eating with EatWith: analysing tourism-sharing economy consumers. *Current Issues in Tourism*, 22(9), 1062–1075.

Martin, C., 2016. The sharing economy: a pathway to sustainability or a nightmarish form of neoliberal capitalism? *Ecological Economics*, 121, 149–159.

Marrovelli, B., 2018. Cooking and eating together in London: food sharing initiatives as collective spaces of encounter. *Geoforum*, 99, 190–201.

Martin, C.J., Upham, P. and Klapper, R., 2017. Democratising platform governance in the sharing economy: An analytical framework and initial empirical insights. *Journal of Cleaner Production*, 166, 1395–1406.

Mi, Z. and Coffman, D., 2019. The sharing economy promotes sustainable societies. *Nature Communications*, 10, 1214.

Michaelis, L., 2007. Consumption behaviour and narratives about the food life. In S.C. Moser, L. Dilling, eds. *Creating a climate for change: Communicating climate change and facilitating social change*. Cambridge: Cambridge University Press, 251–265.

Möhlmann, M., 2015. Collaborative consumption: determinants of satisfaction and the likelihood of using a sharing economy option again. *Journal of Consumer Behaviour*, 14(3), 193–207.

Molz, J.G., 2013. Social networking technologies and the moral economy of alternative tourism: the case of couchsurfing.org. *Annals of Tourism Research*, 43, 210–230.

Morrow, O., 2018. Sharing food and risk in Berlin's urban food commons. *Geoforum*, 99, 202–212.

Orsi, J., 2010. *How to barter, give and get stuff* [online]. Available from: www.shareable.net/blog/how-to-barter-give-and-get-stuff [Accessed 24 June 2015].

Mortara, A. and Fragapane, S., 2018. Vieni a mangiare da me? Un'analisi esplorativa del fenomeno del social eating. *Sociologia Della Comunicazione*, 55(16), 71–86.

Palgan, Y., Zvolska, L. and O Mont, O., 2017. Sustainability framings of accommodation sharing. *Environmental Innovation and Societal Transitions*, 23, 70–83.

Privitera, D., 2016. Describing the collaborative economy: Forms of food sharing initiatives. *Proceedings 2016 International Conference Economic Science for Rural Development, No 43*, Jelgava, LLU ESAF, 21–22 April 2016, 92–98.

Winslow, J., and Mont, O., 2019. Bicycle sharing: Sustainable value creation and institutionalisation strategies in Barcelona. *Sustainability*, 11 (3), 728

Piscicelli, L., Cooper, T. and Fisher, T., 2015. The role of values in collaborative consumption: insights from a product-service system for lending and borrowing in the UK. *Journal of Cleaner Production*, 97, 21–2.

Retamal, M., 2019. Collaborative consumption practices in Southeast Asian cities: prospects for growth and sustainability. *Journal of Cleaner Production*, 22, 143–152.

Rockström, J., Steffen, W. and Noone, K., 2009. A safe operating space for humanity. *Nature*, 461, 472–475.

Sandoval, M., 2019. Entrepreneurial activism? Platform cooperativism between subversion and co-optation. *Critical Sociology*, 46(6), 801–817.

Uzunca, B. and Borlenghi, A., 2019. Regulation strictness and supply in the platform economy: the case of Airbnb and Couchsurfing. *Industry and Innovation*, 26(8), 920–942.

Woodcock, J. and Graham, M., 2019. *The Gig Economy: A Critical Introduction*. Cambridge: Polity.

29
SOCIO-ENVIRONMENTAL MOVEMENTS AS DEMOCRATIZING AGENTS

Viviana Asara

Introduction: social movements and democracy

Social movements have long been the main actors in bringing about the democratisation of modern states, and they have been further favoured by democratisation (Tarrow 1994; Tilly 1995; 2004). The democratic potential of what Della Porta (2020) calls "progressive movements" has occurred at different levels. On the one hand, movements have put forth their critique of conventional politics and established democratic institutions through various forms of action, from protest repertoires to appeals or litigation procedures against companies or government agencies, to lobbying activities. On the other hand, and often in parallel to their vociferous critique, they have also advanced new visions and conceptualisations of democracy as well as experimented with alternative democratic practices and innovations both "within" and "outside" of institutional arenas through various channels. "Within" institutions, they have contributed to the constitution of (deliberative or participatory) arenas for the development of public policies, they have been listened to as (counter-)experts on specific matters, or they have even actively engaged in movement–parties or used their linkages to them to influence policymaking. "Outside" institutions or in any case independently from the action pursued within institutions, they have forged free spaces and other interstitial grassroots experiments, have developed "horizontal" forms of organisation and internal democracy, and have produced alternative imaginaries, forms of knowledge, and subjectivities that have sometimes diffused throughout the social fabric and contaminated the political-institutional field.

Claims around democracy have been pivotal for some of the most important movements of the past and current centuries (Polletta 2013; Della Porta 2015; 2020), from the struggles for civil and social rights typical of the labour movement and the US civil rights movement, to the struggles for reproductive rights, and the politicisation and democratisation of the private sphere and work relations typical of the feminist movement, from the calls for decentralised and participatory forms of democracy typical of new social movements to the development of consensus democracy or "democracy from below" in alternative arenas such as social forums developed by the alterglobalisation movement. More recently, the movement of the squares swept cities' main squares across the globe to protest against the intensification of austerity regimes and to demand "real democracy", while prefiguratively enacting deliberative arenas in the reappropriated urban public spaces (Asara, 2016).

The green movement is no exception. As we will see, a democratic quest has been placed at the core of its very essence. This is especially so for what I will refer to as socio-environmental movements, i.e. those movements whose expression of ecological concerns went hand in hand with broader socio-political claims that are perceived as intimately connected to the ecological issues (see also Asara 2016; 2020). This chapter looks at the way the environmental movement has both envisioned an alternative conceptualisation of democracy and the way this has been (or not) embodied in its form of organisation and practices. The next section will look at how democracy conceptualisations are linked to varieties of environmentalism, while the following section will delve on ecological practices and prefiguration of interstitial urban environmental activism, before conclusions are drawn.

Conceptualisations of democracy and environmentalisms

Environmental movements have been defined as:

> networks of informal interactions that may include, as well as individuals and groups who have no organizational affiliation, organizations of varying degrees of formality (including even political parties, especially Green parties) that are engaged in collective action motivated by shared identity or concern about environmental issues.
>
> Rootes and Brulle 2013

This has also been referred to as a "very broad church" (Berny and Rootes 2018, 947), an "archipelago" (Diani 1987), or a "phenomenon that is highly diverse in its forms of organization and action, from the radical, but sometimes covert direct action of the 'green' movement" (Doherty 2002) through demonstrative public protest, to the often publicly invisible actions of bureaucratised formal organisations that lobby governments or work in concert with governments and/or corporations to achieve desired environmental outcomes" (Rootes and Nulman 2015). This section will delve on the debate on varieties of environmentalism by social movements (§ 2.1) and how these have involved different conceptualisations of democracy as well as degrees of institutionalisation (§ 2.2).

Varieties of environmentalism

According to many authors, the very collective identity of green movements cannot prescind from a grassroots, participatory democracy as well as to a broader link to wider socio-political challenges (Doherty 2002). As put by Eckersley (2020, 217), "the ecopolitical thought that emerged in the 1960s and 1970s alongside environmental movements tended to diagnose the ecological crisis as a crisis of democratic participation". Namely, the environmentalist critique was directed at the role of political and democratic structures – given that the drivers of environmental destruction were supposed to lie in exploitation and alienation – as their redressing was seen as the basis for a radical shift towards an alternative politics and society (Hammond, forthcoming). Environmental movements – and especially so, socio-environmental movements – thus advocated for radical participatory democracy both as their own, prefigurative form of organisation and as their normative model for society (ibid), forging alternative democratic imaginaries embodied also in their practices (Asara 2020). This radical democracy critique was at least in part inherited from the New Left, from whom the environmental movement borrowed several themes from, including the expressive and convivial dimension of politics and the quest for bottom-up change (Doherty 2002).

However, here a "thin" account of environmental democracy can be distinguished from a "thick" account of ecological democracy, a differentiation that is related to the distinction between two main forms of environmentalism identified since the heyday of the green movement, on the one hand (reformist or mainstream) environmentalism, and on the other hand, ecologism or political ecology. André Gorz (1978, 24) was maybe the first to identify these two green varieties: for him while environmentalism only imposes new constraints to capitalist economic rationality without questioning the bottom tendency of the system, ecologism implies a "change of paradigm", questioning the reasoning of techniques, production and consumption, and is aimed at reducing economic rationality and market exchanges for the benefit of societal and cultural goals at the service of individuals' flourishing. A few years later Dobson (2007 [1990]) would similarly argue that while environmentalism argues for a managerial approach to environmental problems without fundamental changes in present values or patterns of production, ecologism holds that a sustainable and fulfilling existence presupposes radical changes both in our relationship to the non-human natural world, and in our mode of social and political life.

Others have however identified a threefold typology, where Gorz' and Dobson's "environmentalism" can be thought of as being differentiated into two further types, i.e. more traditional environmentalists (conservationists) and "new" environmentalists, while the ecologism variety has been variously called "political ecology". In his seminal study on Italian environmental movements in the 1970s and 1980s, Mario Diani (Diani 1987; 1995; Diani and Lodi 1988) elaborated a diachronic typology of ecology movements in Milan based on interpretations of environmental problems as well as on their social and political roots (socio-demographic traits, political background, patterns of recruitment). Diani's typology first pitted the new political ecology groups (similar to Gorz's and Dobson's ecologists) against more traditional conservation groups, which we can think of traditional environmentalists. He later identified a third current to emerge in the late 1970s (Diani 1988), which he calls environmentalists. While conservationists envisaged to defend the environment as understood largely in terms of natural heritage and in aesthetic and ethical terms, attributed the cause of environmental degradation to irrational human behaviour and short-sighted utilitarianism, and sought its remediation through the transformation of individual behaviour, political ecologists were the new movements emerged in the early 1970s following the "Limits to growth" report (Meadows et al. 1972), blamed the capitalist mode of production for the exploitation of both nature and the labour force, and envisioned a change of the goals of social production. Some of the roots of political ecology groups were also located in class conflict forms within (struggles for workers' health and wider control over the production cycle) and outside the factories (struggles against industrial pollution and degraded neighbourhoods) as well as in an environmental counterculture diffused in free spaces and materialised in alternative practices. Political ecology groups mobilised a different notion of environment, which did not simply coincide with natural resources, but also incorporated the social environment and urban areas. Differently from the reactive approach of conservationists, political ecology groups – which held a diverse political activism – sought broader social change, grassroots democracy and the direct control by the citizen over industrial production and over energy and economic policies (Diani and Lodi 1988). It is noteworthy that Diani's words on the political ecology variety resonate with what was contemporaneously happening on the other side of the ocean with the environmental justice movement in the USA from the late 1970s/early 1980s (Agyeman et al. 2016, see below). Finally, Diani and Lodi (1988) also identify a third component of the ecology movement to have emerged later in the 1970s, which resonates with

Dobson's and Gorz's environmentalism not only by its very name but by content, for its pragmatic orientation, weaker ideological coherence and inclusive, more single-issue and short-term patterns of participation (see also Giugni and Grasso 2015, 341).

Similar categories would be found by other authors. A few years later Martinez-Alier (2002) would refer to the conservationists as "cult of wilderness" movement, whose love for pristine nature was however compounded by the non-consideration for the role of local people and their lay knowledge on sustainable natural management. The cult of wilderness would increasingly be allied with the other hegemonic environmentalism, "the gospel of eco-efficiency", concerned with the efficient use of resources by means of, inter alia, their economic valuation (Anguelovski and Martínez Alier 2014). We could think of the gospel of eco-efficiency as the new environmentalists.

More importantly, Martinez-Alier critiqued one of the most important theses on the environmental concerns of "new social movements", the so-called post-materialism thesis. These were an ensemble of movements spanning the student, environmental, peace and second-wave feminism movements which grossly corresponded with Diani's political ecology and environmentalist groups (Diani and Lodi 1988) and which were seen as a product of post-industrial society, focused on cultural and identity issues rather than on class-based, redistributional claims, and displaying decentralised and horizontal forms of democracy (Johnston et al. 1994; Buechler 1995). The post-materialistic thesis by Ronald Inglehart (1977) saw their emergence as linked to the development of so-called "post-material values" following the transition from scarcity to relative affluence of post-industrial societies – thus positing the emergence of higher values only after survival needs had been satisfied. This theory would have a great influence upon New Social Movement theory (e.g. Habermas 1981, 33; Melucci 1989, 177–178; Dalton and Kuechler 1990). However, Martinez-Alier (1995) charged Inglehart of misrepresenting the source of environmental values in Western countries, which according to him were not to be found in an affluence-induced liberation from survival needs, but rather in the environmental consequences produced by affluence, i.e. the increasing environmental pollution and depletion of natural resources in Northern countries. Furthermore, Inglehart's theory was neglecting a third important variety of environmentalism, i.e. the environmentalism of the poor, namely of those who have a material interest in the environment as a source and a requirement for livelihood.

Similarly, environmental sociologists showed that affluence does not make people more concerned about the environment (Brechin and Kempton 1994; Dunlap and York 2008; Givens and Jorgenson 2011; Fairbrother 2013). While New Social Movement Theory saw the environmental movements in Western countries as a predominantly "new middle-class" phenomenon (Offe 1985; Kriesi 1989; Kriesi et al. 1995), this was countered not only by studies on the environmentalism of the poor (Ramachandra and Martinez-Alier 1997) and by a few recent works showing their broader and diverse constituency (Mertig and Dunlap 2001; Norton 2003; Botetzagias and van Schuur 2012), but also by an increasing number of studies emphasising the importance of a labour environmentalism (Stevis et al. 2018) or working class environmentalism (Barca and Leonardi 2018) in the global North during both the first and the second wave of environmentalism (Barca 2012; Ruzzenenti 2020). Furthermore, environmentalism as a middle-class phenomenon was countered by the rise to international visibility of the environmental justice movement, holding a more heterogeneous constituency, including more prominently the poor and marginalised (Sicotte and Brulle 2017), and opposing "what it perceived as the white elite environmental movement" (Doherty and Doyle 2006).

Born in the USA between the late 1970s and early 1980s to struggle against environmental injustice, i.e. the disproportionate burden of environmental harm facing communities of colour, indigenous and working-class communities, it reconceived of the notion of the environment as not simply wilderness, but encompassing the places "where we live, work and play", that is the environmental conditions making up people's everyday lives. This reframing occurred in parallel to a critique of bureaucratic "reform" environmentalism of the institutionalised movement. The environmental justice movement is an exemplary case of what I broadly referred to as a socio-environmental movement, where concerns for the environment are deeply entangled with socio-political claims, seeing social injustice and inequalities as inseparable from environmental degradation. This combination is also reflected into its embedding into other social movements, such as movements for racial equality, the rights of Indigenous people, the poor, workers and movements for occupational health (Sicotte and Brulle 2017). While according to some authors this entanglement can lead to a defuse conceptualisation (Benford 2005) or even diminish a movement's environmentalism (Rootes and Brulle 2013; Diani and Rambaldo 2007; Giugni and Grasso 2015), according to others it can help reach a more heterogeneous constituency (Heaney and Rojas 2014), as well as increase its transformative potential (Asara 2020; Gottlieb 2005). While the term was originally forged in the USA with reference to the inequities in the distribution of environmental bads such as toxic waste facilities, it experienced a substantial expansion at different levels. Content-wise it gradually came to encompass a broader range of issues – encompassing environmental goods, food, water, energy etc – as well as an increasing focus on the demand for participation and democracy in decision-making processes and recognition of diverse categories of differences through an intersectional lens (Schlosberg 2013; Vanderheiden 2016; Pellow 2016). Furthermore, it expanded both geographically – to many other countries and contexts – and in a way to include the transnational and global nature of environmental injustice, as is the case for the climate justice movement (Ciplet et al. 2015). Finally, analysts have increasingly turned their attention to an understanding of the entrenched and embedded character of social inequality (Pellow 2016; Scheidel et al. 2020; Velicu 2020).

The next subsection will delve on the types of democracy conceptualisations associated with varieties of environmentalism and how institutionalisation has also been drawn into the debate on such linkage.

Conceptualisations of democracy and institutionalisation

As previously mentioned, there are different visions of democracy associated with varieties of environmentalism. Eckersley (2020) has distinguished a thin account of environmental democracy – related to Diani's, Gorz's and Dobson's (reformist) environmentalism – from a thick account of (radical) ecological democracy – related to what I referred to here as socio-environmental movements, encompassing what other authors have called ecologism, political ecology, environmentalism of the poor and environmental justice movements. Environmentalists are supporters of environmental democracy as "friendly critics of liberal democracy who seek to work with, and revitalise, the norms and institutions of liberal democracy to bring about environmental change" (ibid, 2). Environmental movements have defended and used the rights, ideals and institutions of liberal democracy to uphold environmental claims. On the one hand, environmental movements have stressed the need for greater citizen participation for example through European Citizens' Initiatives and other procedural democracy initiatives able to improve access to institutions (Bertuzzi 2020; Eckersley 2020). On the other hand, their reformism has encompassed, for instance, "the trust in the possibility of influencing market dynamics" for solving environmental problems (Bertuzzi 2020, 303), e.g. relying on carbon markets solutions as is typical of major Environmental Non-Governmental Organisations (ENGOs) part of the Climate Action network coalition, on forms of corporate social responsibility pressure (Wahlström and Peterson 2006), or on innovative technological devises and changes in individual lifestyles that are "considered the best solutions to the current ecological crisis" (Bertuzzi 2020, 308).

A conspicuous line of research has indissolubly associated reformist environmentalism to the process of institutionalisation of the environmental movement both within the state and in its forms of internal organisation. For example, Bertuzzi (2020) has identified environmental democracy visions in big national and international ENGOs, while grassroots, environmental justice movements espoused ecological democracy visions. A movement's internal organisation is linked to the way its democratic conceptualisations are embodied in its practices and internal democracy. The second wave of environmentalism that coincided with the rise of new social movements has indeed been associated with a process of institutionalisation that occurred both externally – in terms of Environmental Movement Organisations' (EMOs) integration into state and administrative structure, providing services to governments and receiving funding from public and private institutions – and internally through a process of formalisation, bureaucratisation and professionalisation (Berny and Rootes 2017; Kriesi 1996). These trends were heightened by the so-called third wave of environmentalism, where EMOs were seen as protest businesses (Jordan and Maloney 1997), namely centrally managed corporate entities deprived of democratic voice from members, affected by commercialisation, and involved in the competition for membership recruitment and for raising external funding from foundations (Kriesi 1996; Brulle 2000; Dauvergne 2016). According to some, their involvement into the legal and technocratic policy process and related networks of political and economic power contributed not only to fade their internal democratic structures but also to moderate their political goals and repertoires of actions (Brulle 2000), and to bring about forms of cooptation (Douwie 1995; Dauvergne 2016). This especially came to the forefront after the Agenda 21 at the 1992 Rio Earth Summit, which promoted EMOs' role as service providers as well as mediators between the state and the market, from stakeholder participation to eco-labelling and ecocertification initiatives in combination with business (Dauvergne 2016; Doyle 1998; Osti 1998). With neoliberal environmental governance, a new politics of responsibilisation has replaced political obligations with private autonomies (Pellizzoni 2012), turning to "consumers as sources and forces of change, urging them to be 'consumer activists'" (Dauvergne 2016, 14), while EMOs were increasingly involved in political responsibilities previously associated with the state, expanding the public role of private actors and potentially leading to depoliticisation of environmental issues by suppressing social conflict through consensus building (Thörn and Svenberg 2016). However, while some authors have contested that the institutionalisation of environmental movements inevitably leads to bureaucracy, professionalism and the moderation of claims and repertoires of action (Jiménez 2007, 363), others have underlined that grassroots environmental justice movements are not necessarily more democratic (Brulle and Essoka 2005). Through a study on 140 EJ organisations, Brulle and Essoka (2005) depict them as having an oligarchic organisational structure similar to reform and conservationist environmentalism, which weakens the movement's legitimacy as representative of community concerns.

Despite these contradictions, other authors have underlined that socio-environmental movements supporting an ecological democracy model have re-examined the role of founding institutions of liberal democracy such as the capitalist market for their coupling with social and environmental injustices as well as attempted to re-signify the meaning of freedom and equality searching for ways to incorporate the sense of limits in both a social and ecological dimension within democratic institutions (Deriu 2012; Eckersley 2020; Asara 2020; Hammond, forthcoming). On the one hand, ecological democracy implies that socio-environmental movements emphasise "the strong link between social and environmental concerns and frames", for instance by embedding a capitalist critique in their framing of environmental problems (Asara 2020; Bertuzzi 2020, 302). On the other hand, ecological democracy has also involved a rethinking of the idea of Demos in a way to expand it temporally, spatially and substantially, e.g. by including future generations and different forms of life, human and non-human as well as by questioning territorial and electoral boundaries. Socio-environmental movements seek to visibilise a wider range of communities that are systematically unrepresented, such as poor and minority communities or noncitizens outside the polity that are affected by decisions taken within the policy or nonhuman species and broader ecological communities (Centemeri and Asara 2020; Eckersley 2020). This has in some cases led to institutional innovations, such as the provision of environmental rights and norms in constitutions in countries such as Ecuador and Bolivia. Furthermore, similarly to environmental movements, they have also asked for the introduction of new procedural rights, for instance in terms of preventing or controlling large-scale interventions, denouncing the lack of transparency and democracy in decision-making processes and sometimes succeeding in establishing new structures of accountability and the inclusion of participatory procedures and environmental regulations and rights (Barnett and Scott 2007; Urkidi and Walter 2011). However, socio-environmental movements are often conscious that inclusion in formal procedures of consultation and participation "can conceal the ways in which structural inequalities skew deliberative practices in favour of powerful actors" (Barnett and Scott 2007, 2629), which explains why EMOs also employ more contentious forms of mobilisation outside deliberative forums.

While environmental justice movements have often been described as NIMBY, they often oppose a development model that privileges corporate (and colluded state) interests at the expense of territories and communities. EJ movements are often the exercise of active citizenship, visibilising different values and conceptualisations of the common good (Della Porta and Piazza 2007): their democratic potential lies in that "it is through the expression of local concerns that we come to understand the 'common good' for a diverse political community", 288). Furthermore, they can contribute to the politicisation of expertise, opening up a public space of discussion releasing issues from necessity and duty and confronting the different positions in the public arena (Pellizzoni 2011).

Despite the trends towards professionalisation of environmental movements, new cycles of mobilisation have been revamping them, often at the local level, from the British anti-roads protests of the 1990s to the many environmental justice movements of recent years, from the Ende Gelände blockades in Germany against lignite mining to the Notre-dame-des Lands Zad, from the movement against the expansion of the Vienna airport to the NO-TAP movement in the South of Italy against the TAP gas pipeline etc. Some authors have identified their recent increase and radicalisation in the closing of political opportunities especially at the national and supra-national levels due to neoliberal forms of governance, the collusion between state and corporate actors and the weakening of forms of representation such as political parties (Caruso 2015; Della Porta et al. 2019).

However, the recent 2019 environmental cycle – including transnational youth-based movements such as the Fridays for Future (FFF) and Extinction Rebellion (XR), and the more nationally-based Gilets Jaunes in France and the US-based Sunrise movement – has displayed a powerful return to state-addressing forms of political claims, despite the low confidence in governments' ability to address the climate issue (de Moor et al. 2020).

The 2019 environmental cycle,[1] has also foregrounded the return of contentious repertoires of action on the part of environmental movements. Indeed, this new cycle of mobilisation has to some extent represented a counter-tendency to recent trends of urban environmental activism[2] that have prioritised actions focused on prefigurative practices and the creation of interstitial alternatives. Due to a general "bias towards adversarial social movement mobilisation and highly visible social conflict" typical of social movement studies (Yates 2015, 237), previous movement continuity investigations focusing on submerged networks, movement communities or abeyance structures often treated these issues as latency phenomena mostly important for their instrumental role in engendering subsequent cycles of protest. Recently, however, a number of studies (Forno and Graziano 2014; Bosi and Zamponi 2015; Yates 2015; Zamponi and Bosi 2018; Varvarousis et al. 2020) have started to look at these movement alternatives in their own right, testifying to an increasing analytical interest for the understanding of everyday forms of political action and their relationship with socio-environmental movements. The debate on the everyday politics dimension of these new forms of actions will be analysed in the next section.

Movement alternatives, everyday politics and interstitial environmental activism

While "urban" environmental movements from social centres to community gardens date back to a few decades before (Mudu 2004; Cattaneo and Martinez 2014; Bosi and Zamponi 2015), the seemingly increasing focus on "alternatives" on the part of environmental and other social movements in recent years has constituted the object of a blossoming of studies, and a topic of an emerging debate (Bosi and Zamponi 2015; Schlosberg and Coles 2016; Schlosberg 2019). Several authors forged a panoply of different terms to grapple with this novel emphasis on diverse grassroots forms of collective action focused on "alternatives": sustainable community movement (organisations) (Forno and Graziano 2014), alternative action organisations (AAO, see Giugni and Grasso 2018; Zamponi and Bosi 2018), alternative forms of resilience (D'Alisa et al. 2015; Kousis 2017), collective alternative everyday practices (Deflorian 2020), new environmentalism of everyday life (Schlosberg and Coles 2015; Schlosberg 2019), and interstitial environmental activism (MacGregor 2019) are a few of them. While these terms variously refer to different units of analysis, such as organisations (Forno and Graziano 2014; Zamponi and Bosi 2018; Giugni and Grasso 2018), forms of actions (Bosi and Zamponi 2015), practices (Yates 2015; Conill et al. 2012) and movements (Schlosberg 2019), what they have in common is that rather than focusing on state-addressing or contentious repertoires of action, they are centred on the collective organisation and enactment of actions alternative to, and aimed at, transforming dominant socioeconomic and cultural practices and structures through their prefiguration and institutionalisation of different modes of being and relating to the human and non-human world. As put by Naegler (2018, 511), "prefigurative spatial and organizational practices can create the physical and/or conceptual safe spaces in which organizing and processes of imagining alternatives take place". Prefigurative politics, understood as a form of activism that inscribes the goals of the movement into its practices and activities, creating the (vision of) alternative society, both in the present, and through a future-oriented creation of alternatives, thus aims to institutionalise alternative forms of needs satisfaction encompassing collective consumption, production and reproduction, from housing to health, food childcare, education, energy etc. Movements focusing on the implementation or prefiguration of some alternatives see struggle as the incremental modification of the underlying structures of a system and its mechanisms of social reproduction that cumulatively transform the system through an interstitial approach to social change (Wright 2010, 228; Asara 2017).

After discussing the contextual conditions for the emergence of these forms of collective action, this section will analyse whether they hold any political, transformative and democratic potential, by putting into dialogue movement scholars that have discussed this phenomenon from diverse standpoints. As we will see below, behind different evaluations of the political and transformative dimension of this type of activism lie discrepant understandings of what constitutes political action. This chapter contends that beyond a narrower understanding of "the political", this needs to broaden so as to include an ontological politics perspective, attentive to the situatedness of these forms of activism.

Similarly to environmental justice movements, the increase of this type of activism has also been related to the perceived "lack of authentic and efficacious democratic process and output" (Schlosberg 2019, 8) and waning trust in the capacity of representative institutions to mediate citizens' demands for socio-environmental concerns, leading to a withdrawal "from traditional political processes and towards material practice" (Schlosberg 2019, 6). The "failure" of Copenhagen (de Moor and Wahlström, 2019) and the growing climate movement consensus – reinforced with COP21 in Paris – that the UN system was unable to solve the climate crisis, led to an increased role on decentralised actions and organising in the climate movement due to the difficulty to construct alternative "globalities" (de Moor 2018, 2020). This has been related to the birth of "new grassroots climate movements" including Transition Town and Climate Justice Action movement (Kenis 2019).

Furthermore, while the global justice movement since the early 2000s constituted a breeding ground for the spreading of political consumerism (Forno and Graziano 2014; Pleyers 2017), the global economic crisis and escalation of austerity regimes (Hayes 2017), and the ensuing outburst of the movement of the squares have constituted a further spur for these new forms of social and ecological action focused on the enactment of alternatives at different levels (Giugni and Grasso 2018; Schlosberg 2019; Varvarousis et al 2020). Some have seen in these actions a new form of collectivist, rather than an individualistic and private (MacGregor, 2019), political consumerism combining the satisfaction of basic needs with a critique of consumerism, corporate markets and global patterns of unsustainability and exploitation, rather than the expression of postmaterialistic values (Lekakis and Forno 2019; Schlosberg 2019).

A debate has sparkled on the whether these interstitial forms of environmental activism hold transformative potential. Some have underlined that they constitute political action (Forno and Graziano 2014; Zamponi and Bosi 2018; Schlosberg 2019; Varvarousis et al. 2020), and when they confront the basic structural reasons for unsustainability, inequity and injustice, alternatives can constitute a form of resistance (Asara 2017) that prefigures a vision of how sustainable transformative processes could look like (Temper et al. 2018). For example, Schlosberg (2019) highlights their political motivation linked to their concern with the functioning of the non-human realm, their refusal to participate in unjust structures and practices, and their embodiment of resistance to circulatory power through the construction of new systems of material flows. Similarly, Forno and Graziano (2014) read sustainable community movement organisations as a locally-based attempt to re-embed the economic system within social relations.

However, other analysts have underlined that by "focusing on the promotion of alternatives, 'positive solutions' and individual responsibility, and in some cases the rejection of political confrontation" they are the embodiment of the shift towards a post-political consensus (Blühdorn 2017; de Moor et al. 2019, 3). Bluhdorn (2017, 57) for example see them as experiential forms of self-organisation of exclusion by the marginalised afflicted by a self-realisation ultimately based on consumption, and serving to dampen social conflicts. Focusing on the transition town movement and on the climate justice action movement, Kenis (2019) similarly argues that both conceal "the political" though in different forms, which she argues is only located at the discourse level. She defines a discourse post-political when it misrecognises the constructed and contingent nature of the social, conceals that each such construction implies conflicts or antagonisms as well as acts of power (ibid). Others have instead more broadly analysed political subjectivity including the practices followed by participants of grassroots environmental alternatives, finding fluid and volatile participation suffering from the problems of (liquid) identity constructions of late modernity, driving participants to reproduce an unsustainable consumer lifestyle (Deflorian 2020).

Differences here to an important extent revolve around what is meant by political action. De Moor et al (2019) analyse "the political" by breaking it down into three dimension: 1) whether movements advance an idea that challenge the existing order, thus addressing activists' motivation; 2) whether activists embrace or reject agonism; 3) whether activists engage in conflict through contentious action, thus addressing repertoires of action. The authors argue that while Environmental Alternative Action Organisations may be motivated by radical ideas, dissemination of environmental goods can hardly be combined with the expression of agonism through contentious action, thus implying some depoliticisation. However, this is not an iron law, as a few studies focusing on the grassroots spaces and organisations created following the movement of the squares have found a synergistic combination between contentious politics and the development of alternatives (Arampatzi 2017; Blanco and León 2017; Varvarousis et al. 2020). For example, focusing on alternative food economies, Calvário and Kallis (2017) argue that these are central to transformative strategies because they are reciprocal to more classic forms of protest-type politics: politicising the crisis, the economy and the agro-food system, they extend conflict and social struggles, inserting alternatives into oppositional strategies confronting market forces and state power.

Furthermore, while useful, this threefold distinction is however missing the way political meaning and values are (re)produced through the enactment of everyday practices staging alternative ways of being and acting in common, from decommodification of exchanges and consumption, to the sharing of resources and egalitarianism in decision-making and work relations, experimenting with possible economic alternatives and political ideas in everyday life (Yates 2015; Varvarousis et al 2020). From an ontological politics perspective, ecological prefiguration can visibilise a potential ontological alternative by developing alternative value practices – those social actions through which people define what is valuable in a given situation and act accordingly to attain and maintain the condition deemed valuable – opposing neoliberal forms of circulatory power and dominant modes of valuing (Centemeri and Asara 2020). Ecological alternatives can thus potentially embody the "need to transform our attachment [to the territory] as a response to the multiplication and acceleration of processes that damage the environment, experimenting with more just and sustainable modes of ecological, social and economic organisation" (Centemeri 2021, 96, author's translation). A "politics attached to the inhabited territory" takes the "form of a material, technical and affective involvement with territories and their inhabitants", developing new relations of interdependence between them (ibid). According to Pellizzoni (2020) prefiguration can be emancipatory when subtraction or withdrawal – e.g. from circulatory power, the state and capital (Naegler 2018; Schlosberg and Coles 2015) – is not simply instrumental to the affirmation of something else, but becomes form-of-life, where doing coincides with being through an inoperative logic.

Some authors point out that interstitial environmental activism can create counter-flows of democratic power and spaces where resonance with disengaged publics outside of the usual environmentalist suspects might be built, while redrawing the boundaries between the public and the private (Meyer 2015; Eckersley 2020). Eckersley (2020, 223) argues that these movements constitute a new iteration of ecological democracy and an expression of ecological citizenship that "seeks to connect ecology and democracy in everyday life by creating new and more ecologically responsible material practices in collective, embodied and prefigurative ways", thus representing a further shift towards radical and participatory forms of democracy from below. Furthermore, new materialist movements recognise agency in nonhuman nature and the ontological entanglements of humans, nonhumans and ecosystems (ibid; Schlosberg and Coles 2015).

By creating agroecological food networks, collaborative consumption, repair and recycle activities, eco-production and DIY, permaculture experimentation etc they build different society-nature relationships and contribute to "counter-neoliberal urban transformation" through forms of political agency that contest, transform and re-signify "the urban", while often making a difference in the lives of ordinary people (Certomà and Tornaghi 2015, 1123; Macgregor 2019). In any case a nuanced, empirically grounded and situated perspective is necessary when evaluating the transformative potential of these "interstitial environmental activism", that display substantial degrees of diversity (ibid). As pointed out by MacGregor (2019, 14), "strong theorizing" tends to downplay empirical ambiguities inherent in many of these grassroots actions by either too quickly foreclosing their potential or uncritically praising their force to threaten neoliberal consumer capitalism through alternative practices. These ambiguities can span from volatile participation to unreflexive localism, from their failure of targeting environmental problems at their roots to the provisional character of their experiments, from their "potential for 'selling out' by fostering gentrification" (Macgregor 2019, 6) to pragmatic negotiations and contradictions such as paying rent, creating a "sense of living between worlds: the one they are struggling against and the one they are trying to achieve" (Pickerill and Chatterton 2006, 737; MacGregor 2019; Asara and Kallis 2020).

Concluding remarks

Since their birth, socio-environmental movements have represented a key challenge to established democratic norms and institutions, striving for a greater democratisation of society-nature relationships, and more broadly, for a redressing of issues of structural injustice (Young 2011). This chapter has shown how different varieties of environmentalism are linked to different conceptualisations as well as practices of democracy and hinted at some of the contradictions raised by eco-political action by social movements. Of course, there is not always a clear-cut distinction between environmental and ecological democracy and movements, and these should be intended more as heuristic to critically understand a heterogenous social movement field, rather than as rigid categories, and some EMOs or movements may indeed "move" between one and the other.

As the ecological crisis we are living in is acknowledged by more and more people, it seems that the more radical critique made by socio-environmental movements is also gaining ground within the environmental movement broadly conceived, as a radicalisation process has been found in diverse movements such as the climate movement (de Moor 2018) and environmental justice movements (Della Porta et al. 2019). In some countries, a catalytic thrust in this direction was represented by the current coronavirus crisis, which while entailing a stop to street protests of climate and other environmental mobilisations, has also brought with it a cross-fertilisation of movements (such as the feminist and environmental movement, and movements for workers' health) recognising the close coupling of the pandemic with the ecological crisis, itself a result of the undervaluation of the reproductive sphere (FaDA 2020). As one famous meme during the pandemic said, "There is no going back to normal because 'normal' was the problem". However, this shift in movements' critique and imaginaries does not automatically translate in effective socio-environmental change, partly because it is the same systemic and entrenched power inequalities and structural injustices – diffused and reproduced throughout various institutions and cultural meanings – which movements aim to remedy that act to weaken movements' transformative potential.

Notes

1 The term "cycle" here broadly refers to Tarrow's (1998) "protest cycle", meaning a "phase of heightened conflict across the social system, with rapid diffusion of collective action from more mobilized to less mobilized sectors, a rapid pace of innovation in the forms of contention employed, the creation of new or transformed collective action frames, a combination of organized and unorganized participation, and sequences of intensified information flow and interaction between challengers and authorities" (ibid: 199). Waves of environmentalism are instead a broader phenomenon (beyond strictly contentious action, and potentially spanning over a few decades, thus including more cycles of protest), and are often characterised by certain themes.
2 With "urban movements", it is meant all those movements trying to achieve some control over the urban environment, broadly intended. This can be intended as including disparate but connected issues such as the built environment, the social fabric of the city, issues related to collective consumption, urban planning and infrastructural policies, and the local political process (Pruijt, 2007; Andretta et al., 2015)

References

Agyeman, J., Schlosberg, D., Craven, L. and Matthews, C., 2016. Trends and directions in environmental justice: from inequity to everyday life, community, and just sustainabilities. *Annual Review of Environment and Resources*, 41, 321–340.

Andretta, M., Piazza, G. and Subirats, A., 2015. Urban Dynamics and Social Movements. In D. Della Porta and M. Diani, eds. *The Oxford Handbook of Social Movements*. Oxford: Oxford University Press, 200–218.

Anguelovski, I. and Martínez Alier, J., 2014. The "environmentalism of the poor" revisited: territory and place in disconnected glocal struggles. *Ecological Economics*, 102, 167–176.

Arampatzi, A., 2017. The spatiality of counter-austerity politics in Athens, Greece: Emergent 'urban solidarity spaces.' *Urban Studies*, 54(9), 2155–2171.

Asara, V., 2016. The indignados as a socio-environmental movement: framing the crisis and democracy. *Environmental Policy and Governance*, 26(6), 527–542.

Asara, V., 2017. Social Movements and Resistance. In C. L. Spash, eds., *Routledge Handbook of Ecological Economics: Nature and Society*. London: Routledge, 173–182.

Asara, V., 2020. Untangling the radical imaginaries of the Indignados' movement: commons, autonomy and ecologism. *Environmental Politics*, 1–25.

Asara, V. and G. Kallis, G., 2021. Prefigurative territories: the production of space by the Indignados movement. *Environment and Planning C: Politics and Space*. Paper accepted for publication.

Barca, S., 2012. On working-class environmentalism: a historical and transnational overview. *Interface*, 4(November), 61–80.

Barca, S., and Leonardi, E., 2018. Working-class ecology and union politics: a conceptual topology. *Globalizations*, 15(4), 487–503.

Barnett, C. and Scott, D., 2007. Spaces of opposition: activism and deliberation in post-apartheid environmental politics. *Environment and Planning A*, 39(11), 2612–2631.

Benford, R., 2005. The Half-Life of the Environmental Justice Frame: Innovation, Diffusion and Stagnation. In D.N. Pellow and R.J. Brulle, eds. *Power, Justice and the Environment: A Critical Appraisal of the Environmental Justice Movement*. Cambridge: MIT Press, 37–54.

Berny, N. and Rootes, C., 2018. Environmental NGOs at a crossroads? *Environmental Politics*, 27(6), 947–972. doi: 10.1080/09644016.2018.1536293.

Bertuzzi, N., 2020. Normalising the 'alter-Europe' or going beyond this Europe? Italian environmental movements' perspectives on Europe, democracy and the ecological crisis. *European Journal of Cultural and Political Sociology*, 7(3), 291–315.

Blanco, I. and León, M., 2017. Social innovation, reciprocity and contentious politics: facing the socio-urban crisis in Ciutat Meridiana, Barcelona. *Urban Studies*, 54(9), 2172–2188.

Blühdorn, I., 2017. Post-capitalism, post-growth, post-consumerism? Eco-political hopes beyond sustainability. *Global Discourse*, 7(1), 42–61.

Bosi, L., and Zamponi, L., 2015. Direct social actions and economic crises: the relationship between forms of action and socio-economic context in Italy. *Partecipazione e Conflitto*, 8(2), 367–391.

Botetzagias, I. and van Schuur, W., 2012. Active greens: an analysis of the determinants of green party members' activism in environmental movements. *Environmental Behaviour*, 44, 509–544.

Brechin, S.R. and Kempton, W., 1994. Global environmentalism: a challenge to the postmaterialism thesis? *Social Science Quarterly*, 75, 245–269.

Brulle, R. J., 2000. *Agency, Democracy and Nature: The U.S. Environmental Movement from a Critical Theory Perspective*. Cambridge: MIT Press.

Brulle, R. J. and Essoka, J., 2005. Whose Environmental Justice? An Analysis of the Governance Structure of Environmental Justice Organizations in the United States. In D. N. Pellow and R. J. Brulle, eds. *Power, Justice and the Environment. A Critical Appraisal of the Environmental Justice Movement*. Cambridge: MIT Press, 205–218.

Buechler, S.M., 1995. New social movement theories. *The Sociological Quarterly*, 36(3), 441–464.

Calvário, R. and Kallis, G., 2017. Alternative food economies and transformative politics in times of crisis: insights from the Basque Country and Greece. *Antipode*, 49(3), 597–616.

Caruso, L., 2015. Theories of the political process, political opportunities structure and local mobilizations. The case of Italy. *Sociologica*, 9(3). doi: 10.2383/82471.

Cattaneo, C. and Martinez, M.A., eds., 2014. *The Squatters' movement in Europe: Commons and autonomy as alternatives to capitalism*. London: Pluto Press.

Centemeri, L., 2021. Le monde toxique « vu de Seveso »: De la catastrophe à l'alternative écologique. *Monde Commun*, 5(2), 80–97.

Centemeri, L. and Asara, V., 2020. Per un approccio ontologico alla prefigurazione ecologica. *Culture Della Sostenibilità*, 25.

Certomà, C. and Tornaghi, C., 2015. Political gardening. Transforming cities and political agency. *Local Environment*, 20(10), 1123–1131.

Ciplet, D.J., Roberts, T. and Khan, M.R., 2015. *Power in a Warming World : The New Global Politics of Climate Change and the Remaking of Environmental Inequality*. Cambridge: MIT Press.

Conill, J., Cardenas, A., Castells, M., Servon, L. and Hlebik, S., 2012. *Otra vida es possible. Prácticas económicas alternativas durante la crisis*. Barcelona: Editorial UOC.

D'Alisa, G., Forno, F. and Maurano, S., 2015. Grassroots (economic) activism in times of crisis: mapping the redundancy of collective actions. *Partecipazione e Conflitto*, 8(2), 328–342.

Dalton, R. and Kuechler, M. eds., 1990. *Challenging the Political Order: New Social and Political Movements in Western Democracies*. Oxford: Oxford University Press.

Dauvergne, P. 2016. *Environmentalism of the Rich*. London: Massachussetts Institute of Technology.

de Moor, J., 2018. The 'efficacy dilemma' of transnational climate activism: the case of COP21. *Environmental Politics*, 27(6), 1079–1100.

de Moor, J., 2020. Alternative globalities? Climatization processes and the climate movement beyond COPs. *International Politics*, 58, 582–599.

de Moor, J., Catney, P. and Doherty, B., 2019. What hampers 'political' action in environmental alternative action organizations? Exploring the scope for strategic agency under post-political conditions. *Social Movement Studies*, 1–17.

de Moor, J., De Vydt, M., Uba, K. and Wahlström, M., 2020. New kids on the block: taking stock of the recent cycle of climate activism. *Social Movement Studies*, 20(5), 619–625.

de Moor, J. and Wahlström, M., 2019. Narrating political opportunities: explaining strategic adaptation in the climate movement. *Theory and Society*, 48(3), 419–451.

Deflorian, M., 2020. Refigurative politics: understanding the volatile participation of critical creatives in community gardens, repair cafés and clothing swaps. *Social Movement Studies*, 1–18.

Della Porta, D., 2015. Democracy in social movements. In D. Della Porta and M. Diani, eds. *The Oxford Handbook of Social Movements*. Oxford: Oxford University Press.

Della Porta, D., 2020. *How Social Movements can Save Democracy*. Cambridge: Polity Press.

Della Porta, D. and Piazza, G., 2007. Local contention, global framing: the protest campaigns against the TAV in Val Di Susa and the Bridge on the Messina Straits. *Environmental Politics*, 16(5), 864–882. doi: 10.1080/09644010701634257.

Della Porta, D., Piazza, G., Bertuzzi, N. and Sorci, G., 2019. LULUs movements in multilevel struggles: a comparison of four movements in Italy. *Rivista Italiana Di Politiche Pubbliche*, 14(3), 477–513. doi: 10.1483/95213.

Deriu, M., 2012. Democracies with a future: degrowth and the democratic tradition. *Futures*, 44(6), 553–561.

Diani, M., 1988. *Isole Nell'arcipelago. Il Movimento Ecologista in Italia*. Bologna: Il Mulino.

Diani, M., 1995. *[DIANI (1995) Green Networks. A Structural Analysis of the Italian Environmental Movement. pdf*. Edinburgh: Edinburgh University Press.

Diani, M. and Lodi, G., 1988. Three in One-currents in the Milan Ecology Movement. In S. G. Klandermans, B. Kriesi, H, Tarrow, eds. *International Social Movement Research, Vol. I*. Greenwich: JAI Press, 103–124.

Diani, M. and Rambaldo, E., 2007. Still the time of environmental movements? A local perspective. *Environmental Politics*, 16(5), 765–784. doi: 10.1080/09644010701634109.

Dobson, A., 2007 [1990]. *Green Political Thought*. London: Routledge.

Doherty, B., 2002. *Ideas and Actions in the Green Movement*. London: Routledge.

Doherty, B. and Doyle, T., 2006. Beyond borders: transnational politics, social movements and modern environmentalisms. *Environmental Politics*, 15(5), 697–712. doi: 10.1080/09644010600937132.

Doyle, T., 1998. Sustainable Development and Agenda 21: The Secular Bible of Global Free Markets and pluralist democracy. *Third World Quarterly*, 19(4), 771–786.

Dunlap, R.E. and York, R., 2008. The globalization of environmental concern and the limits of the postmaterialist values explanation: evidence from four multinational surveys. *Sociological Quarterly*, 49(3), 529–563. doi:10.1111/j.1533-8525.2008.00127.x.

Eckersley, R., 2020. Ecological democracy and the rise and decline of liberal democracy: looking back, looking forward. *Environmental Politics*, 29(2), 214–234.

FaDA (Feminism and Degrowth Alliance), 2020. *Collaborative Feminist Degrowth: Pandemic as an Opening for a Care-Full Radical Transformation* [online]. Available from: www.degrowth.info/en/feminisms-and-degrowth-alliance-fada/collective-research-notebook/

Fairbrother, M., 2013. Rich people, poor people, and environmental concern: evidence across nations and time. *European Sociological Review*, 29(5), 910–922. doi:10.1093/esr/jcs068.

Forno, F. and Graziano, P. R., 2014. Sustainable community movement organizations. *Journal of Consumer Culture*, 14(2), 139–157.

Giugni, M. and Grasso, M.T., 2015. Environmental movements in advanced industrial democracies: heterogeneity, transformation, and institutionalization. *Annual Review of Environment and Resources*, 40, 337–361.

Giugni, M. and Grasso, M., 2018. Alternative action organizations: social solidarity or political advocacy? *American Behavioral Scientist*, 62(6), 778–795. doi: 10.1177/0002764218768855.

Givens, J.E, and Jorgenson, A.K. 2011. The effects of affluence, economic development, and environmental degradation on environmental concern: a multilevel analysis. *Organization and Environment*, 24(1), 74–91. doi:10.1177/1086026611406030.

Gorz, A., 1978. *Ecologie et politique* [online]. Available from: www.abebooks.it/9782020047715/Ecologie-politique-Gorz-André-2020047713/plp

Gottlieb, R., 2005. *Forcing the Spring. The Transformation of the American Environmental Movement*. Washington: Island Press.

Habermas, J. 1981. New social movements. *Telos*, 49, 33–37. doi:10.3817/0981049033

Hayes, G., 2017. Regimes of austerity. *Social Movement Studies*, 16(1), 21–35.

Heaney, M.T. and Rojas, F., 2014. Hybrid activism: social movement mobilization in a multimovement environment. *American Journal of Sociology*, 119(4), 1047–1103.

Inglehart, R., 1977. *The Silent Revolution: Changing values and political styles among Western publics*. Princeton: Princeton University Press.

Jiménez, M., 2007. The environmental movement in Spain: a growing force of contention. *South European Society and Politics*, 12(3), 359–378.

Johnston, H., Laraña, E. and J. Gusfield, J., 1994. Identities, grievances and new social movements. In D. Laraña, H. Johnston and J. Gusfield, eds. *New Social Movements. From Ideology to Identity*. Philadelphia: Temple University Press.

Jordan, G. and Maloney, W., 1997. *The Protest Business? Mobilizing Campaign Groups*. Manchester: Manchester University Press.

Kenis, A., 2019. Post-politics contested: why multiple voices on climate change do not equal politicisation. *Environment and Planning C: Politics and Space*, 37(5), 831–848.

Kousis, M., 2017. Alternative forms of resilience confronting hard economic times: a South European perspective. *Partecipazione e Conflitto*, 10(1), 119–135.

Kriesi, H., 1989. New social movements and the new class in the Netherlands. *American Journal of Sociology*, 94(5), 1078–1116.

Kriesi, H., 1996. The organizational structure of new social movements in a political context. In *Comparative Perspectives on Social Movements*. Cambridge: Cambridge University Press, 152–184.

Kriesi, H., Koopmans, R., Duyvendak, J. W. and Giugni, M., 1995. *New Social Movements in Western Europe: A Comparative Analysis*. London: UCL Press.

Lekakis, E. J. and Forno, F., 2019. Political consumerism in southern Europe. *The Oxford Handbook of Political Consumerism*, 456–478.

MacGregor, S., 2019. Finding transformative potential in the cracks? The ambiguities of urban environmental activism in a neoliberal city. *Social Movement Studies*, 1–17.

Martínez-Alier J., 1995. The environment as a luxury good or "too poor to be green"? *Ecological Economics*, 13(1), 1–10. doi:10.1016/0921-8009(94)00062-Z.

Martinez-Alier, J., 2002. *The Environmentalism of the Poor: A Study of Ecological Conflicts and Valuation*. Cheltenham: Edward Elgar.

Meadows D.H., Meadows D.L., Randers J. and Berens W.W., 1972. *Limits to Growth*. New York: Universe books.

Melucci, A., 1989. *Nomads of the Present. Social Movements and Individual Needs in Contemporary Society*. London: Hutchinson Radius.

Mertig, A.G. and Dunlap, R.E., 2001. Environmentalism, new social movements, and the new class: a crossnational investigation. *Rural Sociology*, 66, 113–136.

Meyer, J.M., 2015. *Engaging the Everyday*. Cambridge: MIT Press.

Mudu, P., 2004. Resisting and challenging neoliberalism: the development of Italian Social Centers. *Antipode*, 36(5), 917–941.

Naegler, L., 2018. 'Goldman-Sachs doesn't care if you raise chicken': the challenges of resistant prefiguration. *Social Movement Studies*, 17(5), 507–523.

Norton P., 2003. A critique of generative class theories of environmentalism and of the labour environmentalist relationship. *Environmental Politics*, 12, 96–119.

Offe, C., 1985. New social movements: challenging the boundaries of institutional politics. *Social Research*, 52(4), 817–868.

Osti, G., 1998. Quaderni Di Sociologia Dalla Protesta Ai Servizi : Percorsi Del Movimento Ambientalista in Italia. *Quaderni Di Sociologia*, 16, 21–39.

Pellizzoni, L., 2011. The politics of facts: local environmental conflicts and expertise. *Environmental Politics*, 20(6), 765–785.

Pellizzoni, L., 2012. In search of community: political consumerism, governmentality and immunization. *European Journal of Social Theory*, 15(2), 221–241.

Pellizzoni, L., 2020. Prefiguration, subtraction and emancipation. *Social Movement Studies*, 1–16.

Pellow, D., 2016. Toward a critical environmental justice studies: Black Lives Matter as an environmental justice challenge. *Du Bois Review: Social Science Research on Race*, 13(2), 221–236. doi:10.1017/S1742058X1600014X.

Pickerill, J. and Chatterton, P., 2006. Notes towards autonomous geographies: creation, resistance and self-management as survival tactics. *Progress in Human Geography*, 30(6), 730–746.

Pleyers, G., 2017. Local food movements: from prefigurative activism to social innovations. *Interface: A Journal for and about Social Movements*, 9(1), 123–139.

Polletta, F., 2013. Participatory democracy in social movements. In D.A. Snow, D. Della Porta, B. Klandermans and D. McAdam, eds. *The Wiley Blackwell Encyclopedia of Social and Political Movements*. Chicheste: John Wiley & Sons, Ltd, 907–910.

Pruijt, H. 2007. Urban movements. In G. Ritzer, ed. *Blackwell Encyclopaedia of Sociology*. Malden: Blackwell, 5115–5119.

Ramachandra, G., and Martinez-Alier, J., 1997. *Varieties of Environmentalism: Essays North and South*. London: Earthscan.

Rootes, C. and Brulle, R., 2013. Environmental movements. In D. A. Snow, D. della Porta, B. Klandermans, and D. McAdam, eds. *The Wliley-Blackwell Encyclopedia of Social and Political Movements*. John Wiley and Sons, Ltd, 413–419.

Rootes, C. and Nulman, E., 2015. The Impacts of Environmental Movements. In D. Della Porta and M. Diani, eds. *The Oxford Handbook of Social Movements* (Issue May). Oxford: Oxford University Press, 729–742.

Ruzzenenti, M., 2020. Dossier '1970' — Le Radici Operaie Dell'ambientalismo Italiano. *Altronovecento*, 43(Dicembre). Available at www.fondazionemicheletti.it/altronovecento/articolo.aspx?id_articolo=43&tipo_articolo=d_saggi&id=422.

Scheidel, A., et al., 2020. Environmental conflicts and defenders: a global overview. *Global Environmental Change*, 63(May). doi: 10.1016/j.gloenvcha.2020.102104.

Schlosberg, D., 2013. Theorising environmental justice: the expanding sphere of a discourse. *Environmental Politics*, 22(1), 37–55. doi: 10.1080/09644016.2013.755387.

Schlosberg, D., 2019. From postmaterialism to sustainable materialism: the environmental politics of practice-based movements. *Environmental Politics*. https://doi.org/10.1080/09644016.2019.1587215

Schlosberg, D., and Coles, R., 2016. The new environmentalism of everyday life: sustainability, material flows and movements. *Contemporary Political Theory*, 15(2), 160–181. doi: 10.1057/cpt.2015.34.

Sicotte, D.M. and Brulle, R.J., 2017. Social movements for environmental justice through the lens of social movement theory. In R. Holifield, J. Chakraborty, and G. Walker, eds. *The Routledge Handbook of Environmental Justice*. London: Routledge.

Stevis, D., Uzzell, D. and Räthzel, N., 2018. The labour–nature relationship: varieties of labour environmentalism. *Globalizations*, 15(4), 439–453.

Tarrow, S. G., 1998. *Power in Movements: Social Movements and Contentious Politics* (Third Edit). Cambridge: Cambridge University Press.

Temper, L., Walter, M., Rodriguez, I., Kothari, A. and Turhan, E.. 2018. A perspective on radical transformations to sustainability: resistances, movements and alternatives. *Sustainability Science*, 13(3), 747–764.

Thörn, H., and Svenberg, S., 2016. We feel the responsibility that you shirk': movement institutionalization, the politics of responsibility and the case of the Swedish environmental movement. *Social Movement Studies*, 15(6), 593–609.

Tilly, C., 1995. *Popular Contention in Great Britain, 1758–1834*. Cambridge: Harvard University Press.

Tilly, C., 2004. *Social Movements: 1768–2004*. Boulder: Paradigm.

Urkidi, L. and Walter, M., 2011. Dimensions of environmental justice in anti-gold mining movements in Latin America. *Geoforum*, 42(6), 683–695. doi: 10.1016/j.geoforum.2011.06.003.

Vanderheiden, S. 2016. Oxford handbooks online environmental and climate justice. In T. Gabrielson, C. Hall, J. M. Meyer, and D. Schlosberg, eds. *The Oxford Handbook of Environmental Political Theory*. Oxford: Oxford University Press.

Varvarousis, A., Asara, V. and Akbulut, B., 2021. Commons: a social outcome of the movement of the squares. *Social Movement Studies*, 20(3), 292–311. doi: 10.1080/14742837.2020.1793753.

Velicu, I., 2020. Prospective environmental injustice: insights from anti-mining struggles in Romania and Bulgaria. *Environmental Politics*, 29(3), 414–434.

Wahlström, M. and Peterson, A., 2006. Between the state and the market: expanding the concept of "political opportunity structure." *Acta Sociologica*, 49(4), 363–377.

Wright, E. O., 2010. *Envisioning Real Utopias*. London: Verso Books.

Yates, L.,2015. Everyday politics, social practices and movement networks: daily life in Barcelona's social centres. *British Journal of Sociology*, 66(2), 236–258.

Young, I.M., 2011. *Responsibility for Justice*. Oxford: Oxford University Press.

Zamponi, L. and Bosi, L., 2018. Politicizing solidarity in times of crisis: the politics of alternative action organizations in Greece, Italy, and Spain. *American Behavioral Scientist*, 62(6), 796–815.

PART VII

Challenges and perspectives

30
SUSTAINABLE DEVELOPMENT AND REGIME TYPE
What can we learn from a comparison of democracies and autocracies?

Stefan Wurster

Introduction

In the context of major global challenges, sustainability targets – encompassing economic, social and ecological aspects of long-term responsibility – have gained importance at both national and international levels. To achieve high sustainability performance, a country must tackle diverse tasks, including inter alia the protection of natural resources, the preservation of social cohesion today and in the long run, as well as financial stability (for instance reduction of public debt). Different policy tools are available to cope with the complex cross-sectional issue of sustainable development, especially in democracies. However, looking at the sustainability performance of countries with different regime types, a general democracy advantage identified in specific policy areas (see for instance Halperin et al. 2009) seems to be hard to find. Many democracies have serious sustainability deficits especially in the area of environmental and climate protection (Weidner and Jänicke, 2002; Scruggs 2003; Jahn 2016), while at least some autocracies have realized notable achievements in certain areas (Besley and Kudamatsu 2007; Beeson 2009). Examples include the rapid expansion of renewable energies in China (Harris 2019), long-term civil protection measures in Cuba (Kirk 2017), or innovation- and sustainability-oriented administrative management in Singapore (Dale 2008). This could lead to the assumption that contrary to the "Churchill hypothesis", which describes democracy as the best regime type compared to all others (Churchill and James 1974, 7566), autocracies have an advantage in overcoming future challenges, which could also shed a different light on the worldwide strengthening of autocratic tendencies in our days. Even if this assumption is denied, why so many democracies are struggling to take the interests of future generations into account remains an open question. Besides exploring if we can see a strong link between democracy and sustainable development, this chapter specifically asks about what specific strengths and weaknesses democratic (and autocratic) states have in implementing sustainable policies: Under what conditions can democracy and sustainable development go together and what policy instruments might help to find democratic pathways to more sustainability? To answer these questions, the chapter is structured as follows: The second and third sections provide a critical overview of the theoretical considerations underlying sustainable policy as a difficult political task and of the theoretical relationship between regime type and sustainable development. In the fourth section, empirical findings on different policy fields from an international comparative perspective are presented. The fifth section, besides focusing on specific challenges in democracies, elaborates on (new) sustainability instruments that could help to promote sustainable decision-making. The sixth section concludes with a discussion of the policy recommendations and suggestions for future research.

Sustainability policy: a difficult task

One should note that sustainability policy is a very complex task (see other contributions in this volume). To meet "the needs of the present without compromising the ability of future generations to meet their own needs" (Brundtland Commission 1987) means to expand political responsibility from "here and now" to "there and later" adapting and balancing current and future interests. This normative task poses challenges for politicians in at least three ways (Wurster 2021):

> First of all it is a multi-dimensional, cross-policy, cross-sectional mission that has to take into account very different policy objectives ("sustainability triangle" of economic, social and environmental tasks) in parallel. In addition to the optimization of individual sustainability goals in different policy fields, balancing of diverse needs and overcoming conflicting goals places high demands on political decisions, making a systematic, holistic approach necessary. It is not enough just to pursue one single sustainability goal. Instead, all goals must be realized in a balanced manner. In addition to a high level of political assertiveness and steering capacity, the integration of different perspectives and expertise in sustainability-oriented decision-making is of importance.
>
> Bornemann 2014; Tosun and Lang 2017

In addition to that addressing problems of current and future generations does not only increase the complexity of political decisions, it also forces politicians to take action under the conditions of fundamental uncertainty (Klinke and Renn 2012). Every decision we make today has an impact on future generations. The further we look into the future, the more unclear however the effects of current decisions become, as unintended consequences and reflexive social behavior makes foreseeing possible effects harder. Long-term political planning capacity is therefore of central importance (Bornemann and Strassheim 2019).

Finally, as a normative concept, sustainable development claims to create intergenerational and intragenerational justice (Law 2019; Clark 2020). Intergenerational justice requires taking the interests of future generations into account and to overcome discounting incentives of current generations, while intragenerational justice requires to consider the needs of distant people and to overcome international cross border problems like climate change, invasive species, etc. Besides corresponding skills, the willingness to take responsibility is crucial. Hence, we should take all these aspects and their interplay into consideration to answer the question of how best to accomplish sustainable development.

A look into theory: what relationship between regime type and sustainability can we expect?

Following Robert Dahl (1971), we can define a democracy as a political system characterized by the existence of "contested elections" that are meaningful for the functioning of the political system as a whole. As a rule changer, public contestation and the right to participate guaranteed by free and fair elections implies popular government and builds the foundation of three key pillars of democracy: freedom and equality for voters living in a country today as well as control of government to ensure that the interests of the majority of voters are represented. In an embedded democracy, a system of checks and balances as well as political and civil rights also protects the rights of minorities (Merkel 2004). In contrast, autocracy implies more or less unrestricted rule of an autocratic body (a person or a group of persons) without meaningful participation, consent or control of the ruled (Schmidt 2010, 72). The political and civil rights of the subservient are not effectively protected, while the government can neglect the interests of a majority of the people, as long as central pillars of the regime remain loyal. Keeping these differences between democracies and autocracies in mind, the following discusses the interplay between the three key challenges of sustainable policymaking (see above) and regime type.

Sustainability policy as a holistic approach

Sustainability as a holistic approach requires overcoming manifest conflicts of objectives (inter alia economic and ecological goals) and enforcing reforms that are very unpopular among today's citizens -- at least in some respect. For a democratic government, enforcement against strong opposition from powerful "distributional coalitions" (Olson 1982), focusing on current interest, is difficult. A high number of veto players (Tsebelis 2002), as a result of institutional checks and balances, makes unrestricted governance, which seems possible in autocracies, very unlikely in democracies. At first glance, this appears to be a disadvantage of democracies considering the impressive success stories of some autocracies, pursuing specific sustainability tasks in a very short time. In China, for example, it was possible to promote the rapid expansion of renewable energies even against local resistance (Chen and Lees 2016). However, besides the fact that the use of force produces numerous negative side effects,[1] the lengthy decision-making and negotiation processes that are necessary to overcome veto players in democracies, frequently leading to results on the level of the lowest common denominator (Scharpf 1997), have also some positive effects. Participation of different social and political actors that flourish in democracies[2] means that additional expertise is taken into account and that there can be a balanced consideration of different interests. This facilitates holistic approaches and policy implementation, since pluralistic decisions can rely on a strong input capacity and legitimation. Comparative studies on the ecological performance of democracies show that a combination of strong interest groups and consensual policymaking style can result in better results (Scruggs 2003; Jahn 2016). The problem of a one-sided focus on one sustainability goal can be illustrated using the example of the China Three Gorges Dam. Here, the focus was unilaterally on the expansion of renewable energy capacities, and the considerable ecological, social and economic side effects were not taken into account because no critical actors fed them into the political decision-making process (Gilley 2012).

Handling uncertainty

In order to deal with uncertainties about long-term economic, social and environmental developments, two things are necessary: long-term planning capacities and the ability to react on new findings and to consider them when making political decisions. Besides high state capacity (Norris 2012), stable and predictable institutional arrangements are important for the first point. Democracies as systems "of ruled open-endedness, or organized uncertainty" (Przeworski 1991, 13) provide this. This is true since the institutionalization of regular elections path the ways to regulated transition of the rulers, while in most autocracies no institutionalized ways to change the government are in place (unregulated transitions, Wurster 2011; Kailitz and Wurster 2017). Here, changes in government regularly lead to a systemic crisis and periods of extreme political instability (fundamental regime upheavals, I Miquel 2007). Under these conditions of instability and rupture, sustainable policy is difficult, if not impossible. The specific transition problem in autocracies[3] arises even if one follows the so-called "stationary-bandit thesis" by Olson (1993), stating that the expectation of a long reign period of an autocratic ruler may lead to long-term oriented policy.[4] The lack of government control provided by regular elections and a system of checks and balances impedes however sustainable policies in an autocracy over time, since the danger of degeneration of authoritarian rule stays always latent. Even autocracies that started with altruistic goals (such as the communist regimes of the twentieth century) with a few exceptions made the experience that abuse of power (corruption) ultimately leads to unsustainable practices.

Competitive and transparent decision-making processes in democracies do not only prevent power abuse by the government, but they also help to identify negative developments and unintended side effects of policy measures. Tocqueville (1835/1840) already pointed out the high learning and error correction capability resulting from democratic competition. It facilitates rapid adaptation of new insights since deficiencies become rather known (early warning system), and the rulers have a permanent incentive to seek for better policy solutions. Additional expertise is taken into the political decision-making process providing an early warning system for problematic developments. Governments are confronted with differentiated ideas, opinions and interests in the public debate, so they have to reconcile in order to gain a majority in the next elections. Balanced consideration of different interests might facilitate to find holistic solutions that also include the interests of poor and vulnerable parts of the population. Even though there are also examples of authoritarian learning (Hall and Ambrosio 2017), in a monolithic autocratic system such incentives are weaker, reducing its ability to innovate in the medium- to long-term.

Intra- and intergenerational justice

Finally, the question arises whether there are systematic regime differences with regard to common good orientation, as a basis for sustainable development, and the willingness to take over intra- and intergenerational responsibility. According to the supporters of the so-called "selectorate theory" (Bueno de Mesquita et al. 2002), there might be strong incentive towards such an orientation in democracies. Since the "selectorate", i.e. the persons who have a say in choosing the political leader, in a democratic country consists of all voting citizens living today, a democratic government must satisfy the interests of broad segments of the population as also in line with the median voter theory (Downs 1957). The "winning-coalition", i.e. those whose support translates into victory, consists of a majority of today's voters. In autocracies, where rulers are not chosen through free and fair elections, it comprises much smaller groups, such as senior figures in the security forces, party delegates or business oligarchs (Bueno de Mesquita and Smith 2012). In case the winning coalition is large, as in democracies, the leaders will tend to use public goods to satisfy "its winning-coalition",[5] what might also have positive effects for other groups in society and future generations.[6] In autocracies with small winning coalitions, leaders will provide private goods for their supporters only, neglecting public goods. Even if democracy can be understood as a system to meet the current needs of a majority of the population in a country, with regard to the sustainability impact, however, the question arises to what extent inter- and intra-generational interests (future generations and interests abroad) are also taken into account. Such an interest consideration for future generations seems all the more likely, the more one can expect also advantages for citizens living today (Wurster 2013). Limited spatial solidarity by focusing on close reference groups such as one's own family, local communities, and one's own nation as a general human phenomenon plays a role here, as well as the problem of discounting by valuing goods in the future less than goods now (Jacobs and Matthews 2012). While these effects apply to democracies and autocracies, democracies pose an additional problem: its short-lived political time timeframe. Under the sword of Damocles of short-term deselection and a permanent election atmosphere, governments in democracies tend to focus on the management of upcoming challenges and the short-term satisfaction of current political majorities. This excessive weighting of present interests hampers long-term planning processes and seduces decision-makers to shift the solution of long-term problems into the future (Kielmansegg 2003). The institutional stability of democracies does not guarantee that political processes are geared to a long time horizon (Wurster 2011).

Concluding the theoretical discussion, we see contradictory arguments regarding a positive relationship between democracy and sustainable development. On the one hand, institutional stability, power control, broad interest orientation and political competition (high learning and error correction capability) speak for democracies. On the other hand, a short-lived political timeframe, excessive weighting of current majority interests and inadequate enforcement instruments might be their specific Achilles' heels.

A look into the real world: results from different policy fields

If we compare the sustainability performance of democracies and autocracies in different policy fields, we can see patterns that are in line with at least some of the theoretical considerations presented above. In the following, I look into one policy area for each dimension of sustainability (economic, social and ecological).

Public debt

Fiscal solidity and preventing public over-indebtedness play an important role in economic sustainability. Intergenerational sustainability can only be ensured if the state is able to finance its tasks in the long run while not burden future generations with excessive financial deficits. Fiscal solidity of the state includes hereby to secure public financial capacity, avoid defaults, reduce long term indebtedness, and as a "gold standard" even increase the common capital stock of future generations (Wurster 2012; 2015). As the sovereign debt crisis at the beginning of the 2000s has shown, excessive public debt is not only a problem for future generations, but it can also have massive negative effects here and now (state bankruptcy, followed by economic collapse and impoverishment of the population, see for example Greece, Frangakis 2015). The specific problem of democracy that shows up here is its permanent tendency to shift fiscal burdens into the future. Doing so, democratically elected politicians react on incentives from their electorate. Even if citizens in a democracy want to avoid public indebtedness, there is always the urge of large parts of the electorate to pursue a strategy of maximizing expenditures now and ignore the negative long-term consequences (Posner and Blöndal 2011, 28). For politicians, to go into public debt is a very attractive way to spend now without to tax (perceptible expenditures with imperceptible revenues, Wenzelburger 2010, 58). This is possible due to the fiscal illusion among the electorate (Jacobs and Matthews 2012). Voters

> ignore the government's intertemporal budget restriction and do not realize that additional expenditures today are connected with a greater tax burden tomorrow, or they underestimate the "tax cost" of providing more public goods. Opportunistic politicians are exploiting this situation and increase government spending to gain votes.
>
> *Wenzelburger 2010, 51 translation by the author*[7]

As a result, we see no democracy advantage when we compare national and foreign debt performance of democracies and autocracies with each other (Wurster 2012, 2015). Rather, some of the most domestically indebted countries (Japan, USA) and, even more problematic in terms of repayment possibilities, countries in debt abroad (Greece, Argentina) are democracies. In contrast, at least some stable autocratic regimes (stationary bandits) had been more successful in decoupling from short-term spending incentives promoted by large segments of their population. Some (resource-rich) autocracies had even been able to accumulate considerable foreign assets, although it is questionable whether they will be used in the interest of future generations or exclusively in the interests of the current rulers. We see a clear problem of over-indebtedness in democracies; however, there are also examples of governments in democracies pushing through spending cuts punishing current voters (Zohlnhöfer 2009). This becomes likely in democracies, if the consequences of excessive indebtedness, usually perceived only as diffuse future costs, become manifest for the current population (Posner and Blöndal 2011, 20). If financial crisis or state bankruptcy, with its large negative economic and social impacts (Reinhart and Rogoff 2009), becomes an acute threat, prevention of payment defaults becomes a public good that democratic governments, for the sake of regime stability, have to take care of. This yet presents an important difference in comparison with autocracies. Autocracies may not only harm future generations by excessive indebtedness (problem of future discounting) but also their present subjects. As long as the small winning coalition the autocratic ruler leans on is not negatively affected by state bankruptcy, the regime may continue with an indebtedness strategy even though large parts of the population are suffering under its negative economic consequences (Oatley 2010, 180). Zimbabwe's autocratic regime under Mugabe, which had been stuck in state bankruptcy for decades, shows this impressively. The empirical comparison shows that democracies on average have been better able to avoid state bankruptcy in the past (Wurster 2012; 2015).[8] We can learn from this example that the tendency in democracies to avoid burdens for today's voters can lead to major long-term problems, while a "stationary bandit effect" in autocracies may help to overcome such problems. In case of an acute financial crisis, democracies do more to protect today's population.

Life expectancy and infant mortality

Increasing life expectancy in a country is a social target for both present and future generations. Since the increase in average life expectancy depends on numerous social, economic, nutritional, ecological, health and hygiene factors, this is a complex and holistic goal that cannot be achieved with a single measure alone. Even if states at different economic development levels face different challenges, providing substantial medical care and adequate food, water, shelter, sanitation and hygienic conditions for broad sections of the population are central for all countries. People today as well as future generations may benefit from them. While combating child mortality is a key sustainability challenge for many developing countries,[9] the focus in developed countries is more on expanding long-term health infrastructure, promoting favorable living conditions and healthy lifestyles as well as combating chronic illnesses. There are three main reasons to expect that democracies are doing better in increasing live expectancy by delivering public goods, including basic social services: its focus on meeting the needs of a majority of today's population, its participation based capacity to handle complex issues in a balanced and holistic way and its institutionalized protection of human rights (see section 3 for the general discussion).

The first argument is based on the assumption that democracies tend to adopt policies for the poor and the middle class, thus for a majority of the population.[10] This should have a positive impact on the provision of basic social and health services. Democratic participation rights "enfranchise more people inadequately served by health care, water and sanitation, education or family planning, [to push] vote-maximising politicians [...] to improve the quality, quantity and accessibility of such services" (McGuire 2013, 57, square brackets inserted by the author).[11] With regard to the provision of basic social and health infrastructure, not only current but also future generations might benefit from this since intergenerational distribution conflicts are not dominant here.

Electoral incentives might be one mechanism in democracies affecting health care policy, having long-term effects on average life expectancy. Strong participation of different social and political actors and free media that flourish in democracies might be another. Community activists, interest groups and issue networks (informal groups of experts in a particular area of public policy) have leeway in democracies to press for policies that improve social services, while freedom of media and speech enables journalists and others to call attention to problems in the healthcare system (McGuire 2013, 57).

Finally, apart from the broader competence of considering interests across numerous social groups little inclination to repression, higher institutional stability (rule of law) and strong guarantees of human rights might be further arguments in favor of democratic countries when it comes to ensuring favorable living conditions for large sections of the population. Stable institutions and rule of law are crucial for a long term provision of basic social needs, since ratcheting up legal social rights (right to health, medical care, education etc.) leads at least in the longer term to an evolution of expectations about who should be eligible for state services, subsidies and social assistance (Wurster 2011; McGuire 2013, 57).[12]

Rule of law is also a barrier of power abuse by the government and it prevents rulers from withholding basic social infrastructure from groups that are in opposition to them. In autocracies however, repression against opponents of the regime is frequently used as an instrument to maintain power, and in extreme cases to cut certain sections of the population off from basic social services and starving them to death.[13]

In line with these theoretical arguments, most of the empirical studies find a significant positive relationship between democracy, high life expectancy (Wigley and Akkoyunlu-Wigley 2011; Mackenbach et al. 2013; Bollyky et al. 2019) and low infant mortality (Zweifel and Navia 2003; Mc Guire 2013). This holds true even when controlling for potential effects of other economic and social factors. In addition to that, we see interesting patterns when looking at the performance of different autocratic subtypes. While military, one-party and personalist autocracies tend to have very high infant mortality rates, electoral autocracies, communist ideocracies and monarchies perform far better (some even better than the bulk of democracies, Kailitz, Wurster and Tanneberg 2017).[14] In line with the expectations of the "selectorate theory" (Bueno de Mesquita et al. 2002), electoral autocracies show reasonable results. By at least simulating democratic elections, electoral autocracies are under considerable pressure to meet at least to some extent the needs of a larger amount of its citizens. Solid performance of communist ideocracies and monarchies does however not fit well into their small selectorate and winning coalition. This shows that other factors besides voter orientation such as institutional stability, inclination to repression and concepts of regime legitimation are also important (Kailitz, Wurster and Tanneberg 2017, 294). While military dictatorships (high inclination to repression) on average perform very poorly in relation to other autocracies, monarchies (institutionally controlled transition rule) seem to care a little more about the long-term well-being of their subjects (Wurster 2011). In communist ideocracies, social welfare and worker protection are at the core of the regime ideology and legitimation (Kailitz, Wurster and Tanneberg 2017) providing a better chance to reduce infant mortality and expand life expectancy.

Overall, democracies are doing a better job than their autocratic counterparts since they have to take the long-term interests of large (also poor) segments of today's population into account, which are in this case highly congruent with the interests of future generations. Democratic participation processes may also form a building block to handle the high complexity of this issue (multiple dimensions of medical care, nutrition, etc.). Even if some autocracies with a high state capacity have made remarkable progress, especially in reducing infant mortality, systemic repression orientation in autocracies creates a permanent threat that the provision of basic needs is subordinated to regime survival which can result in the persecution and punishment of opposition groups.

Environmental and climate protection

Since the beginning of the debate about sustainability, environmental and climate protection has been one of its core components.[15] For the extent of ecological sustainability orientation, the differentiation between weak and strong sustainability measures plays an important role (Wurster 2013, 77–78). Following the "capital approach", it is crucial whether we allow measures that give leeway to substitute natural capital at least to some extent by artificial (financial, produced, human or social) capital. For representatives of "weak sustainability" a substitution of natural resources is acceptable as long as the total capital does not decrease. For supporters of "strong sustainability", this is not acceptable, since they try to guarantee that natural capital is preserved absolutely intact (Strange and Bayley 2009, 105). For the former, short-term (technical) adaptation measures that help to overcome acute (regional) sustainability problems in an efficient way might be sufficient, while the latter implies that measures initiating fundamental behavioral, economic and lifestyle changes are implemented.[16] With regard to environmental and climate protection, "strong sustainability" means that non-renewable environmental goods (biodiversity, natural habitats, etc.) are protected without allowing compensation measures and climate emissions are reduced in absolute numbers. Only efficiency (efficient use of energy) and consistency measures, (expansion of renewable energies, Huber (2000)), especially if they do not reduce the total consumption but rather trigger rebound effects and a focus on resolving sectoral (highly visible) environmental problems without tackling the creeping accumulation of cross-sectoral environmental and climate impacts, which often run unnoticed by the public up to a tipping point, are not sufficient. This differentiation between weak and strong sustainability measures helps to explain regime effects with regard to environmental and climate protection since performance of political regimes varies depending on the field and indicator of environmental protection. Most democracies are doing better than their autocratic counterparts in overcoming sectoral, highly visible environmental problems with direct health effects on today's population (e.g. avoidance of damages related to lead exposure) and in realizing easy-to-implement environmental protection measures (expansion of protected land area, Eichhorn and Linhart 2019, 12). In open democratic societies with a free press and active civil society it seems harder to cover up current environmental problems and suppress feedback loops from environmental groups and movements. It is easier for them in democracies to rise and to put pressure on governments to handle acute environmental problems and to take sector specific action.[17] The more inclusive and deliberative the processes in democracies are, the more likely it is that environmental interests will be taken into account.[18] Democracies are doing more for environment and climate protection if adaption measures are technically feasible and if implementation causes (economic) win-win effects (for current generations). This is the case when it comes to energy efficiency measures or the expansion of renewable energies (Wurster 2011; 2013; Eichhorn and Linhart 2019) that have a positive impact on economic development. Strong political competition in democracies puts permanent pressure on governments to search for innovative win-win solutions. This makes it easier to promote such innovative, efficiency-oriented instruments and policy solutions.[19] However we see that political competitiveness is not the only relevant factor to explain environmental performance.[20] For the implementation of complex and technically demanding environmental protection measures, a certain economic development level and high state capacity are also important. This explains why some economically developed autocracies with high state capacity (China, Singapore) outperform democracies when it comes to expanding renewable energies, yet this is not the case for most of the other autocratic regimes (large autocratic heterogeneity, Eichhorn and Linhart 2019, 12).

If we look at the handling of long-term environmental problems that accumulate in intensity over time (energy consumption and CO_2 emissions), we see no clear democracy advantage (Wurster 2013; Eichhorn and Linhart 2019, 12). Rather democracies display significant deficits in overcoming such creeping and global environmental problems for which there are no cheap technical solutions. They must be rectified by means of fundamental changes in lifestyles and the economy. Despite their high inclusiveness for present interests, democratic regimes have specific problems to enforce future interests against resistance of powerful stakeholders (Wurster 2013), as long as there is not also a positive impact for today's voters. This is the key problem regarding creeping threats, since democracy seems "not adequate to the type of socio-economic transition deemed necessary to rectify major environmental and ecological challenges" (Lafferty 2004, 2).

Summing up we can conclude "Democracies adapt but do not really solve major environmental problems" (Wurster 2013, 89). In most democracies we see no problem of perception, but of implementation, since political will to overcome discounting incentives that spare today's voters from fundamental changes in lifestyles and economies is still missing. Focusing on a "weak sustainability" strategy might however not be enough to really overcome the major ecological challenges in the future.

A toolbox of (new) sustainability instruments in democracies

Against the background of the significant sustainability deficits shown in different policy fields, it seems necessary to think about new instruments and institutional reforms that can help to make democracies more sensible for the interest of future generations. Besides strengthening the already high competence of information processing, networking and handling cross-cutting issues, public deliberation should be improved so that interests of future generations are continuously fed into the decision-making processes. Instruments of (self-)commitment of today's majorities are conceivable in order to promote intergenerational sustainability. In addition to that, participation rights of younger generations can be strengthened. Against this background, we see a wide arsenal of possible sustainability instruments. We can arrange them according to the level of intervention into the democratic process. For low level of intervention, one can implement process hurdles, like mandatory sustainable impact assessment, information requirements, like consultative expert panels without veto, as well as participation or competition-oriented instruments, like ombudsman systems (Lou Mathis, Rose and Newig 2020) or sustainability strategies with a benchmarking system (see Figure 30.1). Self-limitations of the sovereign, be it constitutional requirements, such as debt brakes, are cutting much deeper into the democratic process. While lowering the voting age for young citizens to give them more weight in elections or limiting the terms in office of politicians to reduce incrustation could moderately intervene into the democratic process, expert panels with suspensive or even absolute veto rights to block unsustainable decisions or extra voting right for parents, assuming that they would better protect the interests of their children, would fundamentally question basic democratic principles like equality and majority rule and are therefore highly controversial. However they could have the potential to counteract short-term orientation in democracies.

It turns out that at least some of these instruments are already used by states as demonstrated by the *Index of Sustainability Instruments*. This index shows for 50 industrialized and emerging countries how many sustainability instruments are already in place. In doing so, it divides sustainability instruments into four groups: 1) Legal instruments like constitutional obligations, criminal law, integration into international sustainability regimes; 2) Institutionalization like sustainability under the responsibility of the head of government, sustainability institution, sustainability coordination committee; 3) Planning and financial instruments like sustainability

Processional hurdles and information requirements	Self-limitation of the sovereign	Substantial chance of the democratic process
• Sustainable impact assessment • Expert panels (with suspensive veto) • Ombudsman system • Benchmarking systems (blaming and shaming) • ...	• Constitutional obligations • Intertemporal budgeting • Institutional debt brakes • Sustainability funds • ...	• Reduction of voting age • Extra voting right for parents • Limitation of terms in office • Expert panels (with absolute veto) • ...

→ More serious interference into democracy

Figure 30.1 Sustainability Instruments in Democracies
Source: Author's own considerations.

strategy, sustainable impact assessment, sustainability fund; 4) Participation-based instruments like Ombudsman for sustainable development, external advisory board, Agenda 21 processes (Wurster et al. 2015, 187). A comparison of the utilization of these sustainability instruments in democracies and autocracies shows that democracies use more and a wider repertoire, in particular participation-based and cross-sectional coordination-oriented ones.[21] High state capacity is an essential ingredient for the implementation of planning measures, which some autocracies also have in their repertoire (Wurster et al. 2015, 195). For the use of complex sustainability instruments, both high state capacity (skill) and democratic participation (political will, see for the importance of this combination Norris 2012) seem necessary. Even so democracies use more sustainability instruments, we see a high variance within democracies. In other words, a remarkable number of democracies have not yet tapped the full spectrum (Wurster et al. 2015).

Conclusion

In accordance with our theoretical expectations, we can see clear patterns of sustainability-regime type linkages in different policy fields. What we cannot see however is a general democracy advantage. Rather, when comparing democracies and autocracies, we can identify differentiated results depending on the specific policy area. We can explain this with the specific Achilles' heels of democracy, which are more meaningful in some policy areas than in others. Under specific conditions, this can mask the general advantages of democracy. While democracies have an advantage when it comes to identifying sustainability problems and developing holistic solutions, the main problems of democracy lies in the consistent implementation of measures that were recognized as actually necessary and in the willingness to overcome short-term orientations and take responsibility for future generations seriously, even if it means high costs for today's voters.[22]

If democracies want to overcome their sustainability problems, they have to reduce these weaknesses without violating the core of democratic decision-making. Some instruments for doing so were presented here. Whether these instruments are really suitable for achieving the desired sustainability should be the subject of further comparative studies. Beside this analysis, analyses across a wider array of policy fields are needed to learn more about the specific system logic of democracies and autocracies regarding different aspects of sustainable policy making and to promote better handling of sustainability problems in the future.

Notes

1 In addition to the fact that repression is very often used by autocratic government to promote very unsustainable practices, it leads to a distorted perception of reality by political leaders over time. Citizens and subordinate institutions are not willing to pass on information to the political leadership, in particular about the true extent of problems. This causes an insufficient political feedback loop, which leads to a distorted perception of reality by the political leadership, making informed decision-making difficult (so called dictator's dilemma, see Wintrobe 1998; 2009).
2 Political freedom, the right to participate and political competition pave the way for (new) interest groups (for instance climate protection initiatives, Fredriksson et al. 2005, such as the "Fridays for Future" movement) that are oriented towards sustainability goals. In contrast, autocracies have a structural deficit in initiating such movements and initiatives (Wintrobe 2009, 388; Böhmelt 2015).
3 Dynastic ruler change in monarchies and the regulated transition of power practiced in China's one-party dictatorship in the past decades may be a functional equivalent to clear transition rules in democracies.
4 In theory one could expect that a benevolent dictator, who expects a long reign and therefore pursues long-term-oriented politics out of self-interest, behaves "not like the wolf that preys on the elk, but more like the rancher who makes sure his cattle are protected and are given water" (Olson 1993, 569).

5 In line with the median voter theory, income under majority rule should be redistributed downward since democratization (e.g. the extension of the franchise) might pull the income of the median voter below the mean income of all voters (Meltzer and Richard 1981).
6 So Bernauer and Koubi (2009) as well as Cao and Ward (2015) can show that larger winning coalitions are related to higher levels of environmental protection.
7 This is also one reason why deficit spending as a countercyclical fiscal answer promoted by Keynesian economics to overcome economic recessions is critically discussed. There is always the risk that debts incurred in the recession will not be repaid in good economic times because this would mean unpopular cuts (only run cyclical deficits and not structural deficits).
8 The higher democratic solvency is also based on more reliable institutional arrangements and a stronger rule of law, which increases its creditworthiness. An easy access to the credit market is, however, with regard to long-term debt, a double-edged sword (Wurster 2015, 11).
9 Infant mortality is a telling indicator of social sustainability performance of governments, especially in developing countries, since it results, unlike adult mortality, from a manageable number of preventable causes and thus to be reducible in a relatively short time by a coordinated regime policy (McGuire 2013, 55). Success here can also solve another sustainability problem in developing countries, that of overpopulation. Low infant mortality can lead to a decline in births in the medium term (Bongaarts 2008), since it reduces the demand for children by improving the chances of survival to adulthood.
10 There is however also a debate, whether democracies spend more for poor sections of the population, who make a large part of the potential electorate, or whether middle- and upper-income groups benefit the most form public spending (see Ross 2006).
11 In line with this argumentation and the "selectorate theory" studies show, that the size and composition of the actor coalition that hold an autocratic ruler in power is also decisive for the variance of its social policy profile (Knutsen and Rasmussen 2014).
12 "The principle that citizens have equal rights – one person, one vote – sets in motion a gradual evolution toward a belief that the state is obliged to provide social services that are sufficient to enable every citizen, no matter how poor, to survive and to live with dignity. The diffusion throughout society, including among the poor, of an expectation that the state will attend to basic social needs is another mechanism by which democracy can promote the extension of social services to those who had previously lacked them, as well as create a perception among the previously underserved that they, too, are entitled to utilise state-provided or subsidized services and social assistance. The evolution of expectations about state obligations to impoverished (as well as other) citizens should encourage not only the provision but also the utilisation of mortality-reducing social services" (McGuire 2013, 57).
13 In contrast, democracy makes mass killings and neglecting of basic needs of the population, as for example in case of famines, much more expensive for the government, since it can be criticized by opposition parties and by the media, reducing its chances to be reelected tremendously, aside from a likely later prosecution (Sen et al. 1990; Zweifel and Navia 2003, 101).
14 Autocratic monarchies legitimize their rule by claiming that the ruler was chosen by God, while the preservation of internal or external security plays an important role for military dictatorships to justify their claim to power. Communist ideocracies are characterized by a closed ideology, while this is not the case for all one-party regimes. Personalist autocracies rely on the charisma of the ruler, while electoral autocracies, similar to democracies, legitimize themselves through popular elections, although the rulers are not willing to jeopardize their political power in free and fair elections (Kailitz, Wurster and Tanneberg 2017).
15 As political milestones see the Club of Rome's Limits to growth report (Meadows et al. 1972), Brundtland Commission's report (Brundtland Commission 1987), and the documents of the major international climate and environmental conferences, Rio 1992, Kyoto 1997 and Paris 2015.
16 "Strong sustainable development is more demanding, both ethically and substantively, than simply eco-modernising the existing economy" (Lafferty 2004, 15).
17 A good example of this is the role of anti-nuclear movements, which were more pronounced in democracies than in autocracies. This may have promoted the stronger retrenchment of nuclear power after Chernobyl accident in democracies than in autocracies (Richter and Wurster 2016).
18 The importance of public deliberation processes for sustainability decisions can be demonstrated using the example of the Swiss semi-direct democracy. Rohm and Wurster (2016) tested, while looking at sustainability-related proposals, which were presented both to Swiss voters and Swiss National Council, to what extent Swiss voters and the Swiss parliament tends to vote in favor of inter- and intragenerational sustainable issues. The Swiss parliament voted particularly with regard to

19 intragenerational sustainable issues in favor of the more sustainable option. In contrast to the public voting processes in parliament, the possibility of a secret vote in referendums may facilitate selfish motives (here and now interests) come to the fore and voting results in terms of sustainable responsibility in referendums are therefore less likely. While the repetitive negotiation situations in parliamentary committees and the principle of representation facilitate a broad consideration of different present interests (advantage in terms of intragenerational sustainability), the short-term re-election interest of the parliamentarians also leads to a neglect of intergenerational sustainability aspects (as it also takes place in plebiscites, Rohm and Wurster 2016, 196).
19 Fredriksson et al. (2005) argues that the effect of participatory rights on environmental policy stringency is dependent on political competition.
20 Eichhorn and Linhart (2019) can show for some indicators of environmental protection like the Environmental Performance Index (EPI) or Ecological Footprint a u-shaped relationship between regime types ordered by competitiveness and environmental protection. Intermediate regimes perform worse than monarchies (low competitiveness) and democracies (high competitiveness). In addition to that, competitive authoritarian regimes do not necessarily outperform other autocratic subtypes with a lower degree of political competitiveness.
21 By contrast, the use of legal instruments shows no systematic pattern when we compare political regimes with each other.
22 A similar pattern appears to be evident when comparing the reaction of autocracies and democracies in acute crises, such as Coronavirus disease (COVID-19). While China wasted a lot of time at the beginning of the virus spread due to insufficient information processing and local cover-up attempts, the regime was subsequently able to contain the epidemic through consistent measures. While democracies found it difficult to implement such tough measures (curfews), they tried to develop more holistic approaches to combat the pandemic (Tisdall 2020).

References

Beeson, M., 2009. The coming of environmental authoritarianism. *Environmental Politics*, 19 (2), 276–294.
Bernauer, T. and Koubi, V., 2009. Effects of political institutions on air quality. *Ecological Economics*, 68 (5), 1355–1365.
Besley, T. and Kudamatsu, M., 2007. *Making Autocracy Work*. London: Centre for Economic Policy Research.
Böhmelt, T., 2015. Environmental interest groups and authoritarian regime diversity. *VOLUNTAS: International Journal of Voluntary and Nonprofit Organizations*, 26 (1), 315–335.
Bollyky, T.J., et al., 2019. The relationships between democratic experience, adult health, and cause-specific mortality in 170 countries between 1980 and 2016: an observational analysis. *The Lancet*, 393 (10181), 1628–1640.
Bongaarts, J., 2008. Fertility transitions in developing countries: progress or stagnation? *Studies in Family Planning*, 39 (2), 105–110.
Bornemann, B. (ed.), 2014. *Policy-Integration und Nachhaltigkeit: Integrative Politik in der Nachhaltigkeitsstrategie der deutschen Bundesregierung*. Wiesbaden: Springer.
Bornemann, B. and Strassheim, H., 2019. Governing time for sustainability: analyzing the temporal implications of sustainability governance. *Sustainability Science*, 14, 1001–1013.
Brundtland Commission, 1987. *Our Common Future*. Oxford: Oxford University Press.
Bueno de Mesquita, et al., 2002. Political institutions, policy choice and the survival of leaders. *British Journal of Political Science*, 32 (4), 559–590.
Bueno de Mesquita, B. and Smith, A., 2012. *The Dictator's Handbook: Why Bad Behavior is Almost Always Good Politics*. New York: PublicAffairs.
Cao, X. and Ward, H., 2015. Winning coalition size, state capacity, and time horizons: an application of modified selectorate theory to environmental public goods provision. *International Studies Quarterly*, 59 (2), 264–279.
Chen, G.C. and Lees, C., 2016. Growing China's renewables sector: a developmental state approach. *New Political Economy*, 21(6), 574–586.
Churchill, W. and James, R.R., 1974. *Winston S. Churchill: His Complete Speeches, 1897–1963, Vol. VII 1943–1949*. New York: Chelsea House Publishers.

Clark, B., 2020. Neutrality, nature, and intergenerational justice. *Environmental Politics*, www.tandfonline.com/doi/full/10.1080/09644016.2020.1779564

Dahl, R.A., 1971. *Polyarchy: Participation and Opposition*. New Haven: Yale University Press.

Dale O.J., 2008. Sustainable City Centre Development: The Singapore City Centre in the Context of Sustainable Development. In T.-C. Wong, B. Yuen and C. Goldblum, eds. *Spatial Planning for a Sustainable Singapore*. Dordrecht: Springer, 31–57.

Downs, A., 1957. An economic theory of political action in a democracy. *Journal of Political Economy*, 65 (2), 135–150.

Eichhorn, K. and Linhart, E., 2019. *Environmental Protection as a Public Good in Autocratic Regimes*. Political Studies Association Annual Conference 2019, Nottingham, 15/04/19 – 17/04/19.

Frangakis, M., 2015. Public debt crisis, austerity and deflation: the case of Greece. *Review of Keynesian Economics*, 3 (3), 295–313.

Fredriksson, P.G., et al., 2005. Environmentalism, democracy, and pollution control. *Journal of Environmental Economics and Management*, 49 (2), 343–365.

Gilley, B., 2012. Authoritarian environmentalism and China's response to climate change. *Environmental Politics*, 21(2), 287–307.

Hall, S.G.F. and Ambrosio, T., 2017. Authoritarian learning: a conceptual overview. *East European Politics*, 33 (2), 143–161.

Halperin, M.H., Siegle, J.T., and Weinstein, M.M., 2009. *The Democracy Advantage: How Democracies Promote Prosperity and Peace*. New York: Routledge.

Harris, J., 2019. Can China's Green Socialism transform global capitalism? *Civitas – Revista de Ciências Sociais*, 19 (2), 354–373.

Huber, J., 2000. Towards industrial ecology –sustainable development as a concept of ecological modernization. *Journal of Environmental Policy and Planning*, 2(4), 269–285.

I Miquel, G.P., 2007. The control of politicians in divided societies: the politics of fear. *Review of Economic Studies*, 74 (4), 1259–1274.

Jacobs, A. and Matthews, J.S., 2012. Why do citizens discount the future? Public opinion and the timing of policy consequences. *British Journal of Political Science*, 42 (4), 903–935.

Jahn, D., 2016. *The Politics of Environmental Performance: Institutions and Preferences in Industrialized Democracies*. Cambridge: Cambridge University Press

Kailitz, S. and Wurster, S., 2017. Legitimationsstrategien von Autokratien: Eine Einführung. *Special Issue: Legitimationsstrategien von Autokratien, Zeitschrift für Vergleichende Politikwissenschaft*, 11 (2), 141–151.

Kailitz, S., Wurster, S., and Tanneberg, D., 2017. Autokratische Regimelegitimation und soziale Entwicklung. *Special Issue: Legitimationsstrategien von Autokratien, Zeitschrift für Vergleichende Politikwissenschaft*, 11 (2), 275–299.

Kielmansegg, P., 2003. Können Demokratien zukunftsverantwortlich handeln? *Merkur – Deutsche Zeitschrift für europäisches Denken*, 57 (7), 583–594.

Kirk, E.J., 2017. Alternatives – dealing with the perfect storm: Cuban disaster management. *Studies in Political Economy*, 98 (1), 93–103.

Klinke, A and Renn, O., 2012. Adaptive and integrative governance on risk and uncertainty. *Journal of Risk Research*, 15(3), 273–292.

Knutsen, C.H. and Rasmussen, M.B., 2014. *The Autocratic Welfare State: Resource Distribution, Credible Commitments and Political Survival*. University of Oslo, University of Aarhus.

Lafferty, W.M., 2004. Introduction: Form and Function in Governance for Sustainable Development. In W.M. Lafferty, ed. *Governance for Sustainable Development: the challenge of adapting form to function*. Cheltenham: Edward Elgar, 1–31.

Law V.T., 2019. Intergenerational and Sustainable Development. In Leal Filho W. (eds) *Encyclopedia of Sustainability in Higher Education*. Cham: Springer.

Lou Mathis, O., Rose, M., Newig, J., 2020. *Sustainability Governance Via Institutional Design? Conceptualizing National Sustainability Institutions*. Presentation at the ECPR Conference 2020. https://ecpr.eu/Events/Event/PaperDetails/53721

Mackenbach, J.P., Hu, Y., and Looman, C.W., 2013. Democratization and life expectancy in Europe, 1960–2008. *Social Science & Medicine*, 93, 166–175.

McGuire, J.W., 2013. Political regime and social performance. *Contemporary Politics*, 19 (1), 55–75.

Meadows, D.H., et al., 1972. *The Limits to Growth*. New York: Universe Books.

Meltzer, A.H. and Richard, S.F., 1981. A rational theory of the size of government. *Journal of Political Economy*, 89 (5), 914–927.

Merkel, W., 2004. Embedded and defective democracies. *Democratization*, 11 (5), 33–58.

Norris, P., 2012. *Making Democratic Governance Work: The Impact of Regimes on Prosperity, Welfare and Peace*. New York: Cambridge University Press.

Oatley, T., 2010. Political institutions and foreign debt in the developing world. *International Studies Quarterly*, 54, 175–197.

Olson, M., 1982. *The Rise and Decline of Nations: Economic Growth, Stagflation, and Social Rigidities*. New Haven: Yale University Press.

Olson, M., 1993. Dictatorship, democracy and development. *American Political Science Review*, 87, 567–576.

Posner, P. and Blöndal, J., 2011. Democracies and deficits: prospects of fiscal responsibility in democratic nations. *Governance: An International Journal of Policy, Administration, and Institutions*, 25 (1), 11–34.

Przeworski, A., 1991. *Democracy and the market: Political and economic reforms in Eastern Europe and Latin America*. Cambridge: Cambridge University Press.

Reinhart, C.M. and Rogoff, K.S., 2009. *This Time Is Different: Eight Centuries of Financial Folly*. Princeton: Princeton University Press.

Richter, T. and Wurster, S., 2016. Policy diffusion among democracies and autocracies: a comparison of trade reforms and nuclear energy policy. *Global Policy*, 7 (4), 541–547.

Rohm, C. and Wurster, S., 2016. Volk oder Parlament: Wer entscheidet nachhaltiger? Eine vergleichende Untersuchung von Nachhaltigkeitsabstimmungen in der Schweiz. *Swiss Political Science Review*, 22 (2), 185–212.

Ross, M., 2006. Is democracy good for the poor? *American Journal of Political Science*, 50 (4), 860–874.

Scharpf, F.W., 1997. *Games Real Actors Play: Actor-Centered Institutionalism in Policy Research*. Boulder: Westview Press.

Schmidt, M.G. 2010. *Wörterbuch zur Politik*, Stuttgart: Kröner.

Scruggs, L. A., 2003. *Sustaining Abundance Environmental Performance in Industrial Democracies*. New York: Cambridge University Press.

Sen, A., Stern, N., and Stiglitz, J., 1990. *Roundtable Discussion – Development Strategies: The Roles of the State and the Private Sector (English)*. Washington: The World Bank.

Strange, T. and Bayley, A., 2009. Measuring Sustainability. In OECD, ed. *Sustainable Development: Linking Economy, Society, Environment*. Paris: OECD Publishing, 99–113.

Tisdall, S., 2020. COVID-19 is exposing the frailty in autocrats and democrats alike. *The Guardian*, 15 March. Available from: www.theguardian.com/commentisfree/2020/mar/15/covid-19-exposing-frailties-autocrats-democrats-alike-trump-xi-eu-un [Accessed 23 March 2020].

Tocqueville, A., 1835/1840. *De la Démocratie en Amérique*. Paris: Springer.

Tsebelis, G., 2002. *Veto Players: How Political Institutions Work*. Princeton: Princeton University Press.

Tosun, J. and Lang, A., 2017. Policy integration: mapping the different concepts. *Policy Studies*, 38(6), 553–570.

Weidner, H. and Jänicke, M. (eds.), 2002. *Capacity Building in National Environmental Policy. A Comparative Study of 17 Countries*, Berlin, Heidelberg and New York: Springer.

Wenzelburger, G., 2010. *Haushaltskonsolidierungen und Reformprozesse: Determinanten, Konsolidierungsprofile und Reformstrategien in der Analyse*. Münster: LIT Verlag.

Wigley, S. and Akkoyunlu-Wigley, A., 2011. The impact of regime type on health: does redistribution explain everything? *World Politics*, 63 (4), 647–677.

Wintrobe, R., 1998. *The Political Economy of Dictatorship*. Cambridge: Cambridge University Press.

Wintrobe, R., 2009. Dictatorship: Analytical Approaches. In C. Boix and S. C. Stokes, eds. *The Oxford Handbook of Comparative Politics*. Oxford: Oxford University Press, 363–394.

Wurster, S., 2011. Sustainability and regime type: do democracies perform better in promoting sustainable development than autocracies? *Zeitschrift für Staats- und Europawissenschaften*, 9 (4), 538–559.

Wurster, S., 2012. Sparen Demokratien leichter? – Die Nachhaltigkeit der Finanzpolitik von Demokratien und Autokratien im Vergleich. *dms – der moderne staat – Zeitschrift für Public Policy, Recht und Management*, 5 (2), 269–290.

Wurster, S., 2013. Comparing ecological sustainability in autocracies and democracies. *Contemporary Politics*, 19 (1), 76–93.

Wurster, S., 2015. Sustainability of fiscal policy in democracies and autocracies. *Challenges in Sustainability*, 3 (1), 1–15.

Wurster S., 2021. Können Demokratien Nachhaltigkeit? In H. Prütting, ed. *100 Jahre Rechtswissenschaftliche Fakultät der Universität zu Köln*. Köln: Dr.-Otto-Schmidt Verlag, 179–190.

Wurster, S., et al., 2015. Institutionelle Voraussetzungen nachhaltiger Politikgestaltung. *Zeitschrift für Politik*, 62 (2), 177–196.

Zohlnhöfer, R., 2009. *Globalisierung der Wirtschaft und finanzpolitische Anpassungsreaktionen in Westeuropa*. Baden-Baden: Nomos.

Zweifel, T.D. and Navia, P., 2003. Democracy, dictatorship, and infant mortality revisited. *Journal of Democracy*, 14 (3), 90–103.

31
DEMOCRATIC GOVERNANCE AND ENVIRONMENTAL SUSTAINABILITY
Engaging the technocratic challenge deliberatively

Frank Fischer

The ecological promise of democracy[1]

Democracy has been associated with environmentalism and sustainability from the outset (Fischer 2000). Emerging as a grassroots movement in the 1960s, the call for democracy largely came from protests undertaken by ordinary citizens, young and old. The struggle for democratic environmental politics is in its various forms the product of a mix of environmental reform efforts and environmental political thought. Therefore, it is important to recognize the long and ongoing connection between environmentalism and environmental democratic politics of which the concept is a part.

At the outset of the environmental movement, the political debates were often focused on the perceived need for radical transformation to avert ecological tragedy (Dryzek 1997). Limiting economic growth to save the planet was generally an organizing theme of ongoing political demonstrations. Some called for getting rid of the capitalist system, seen to be the engine of degradation, and for a return to simpler ways of life (Bookchin 1996; Klein 2014). The basic political mechanism for achieving these goals involved incorporating a wider range of interests and views. This could only be accomplished, it was argued, through the democratization of environmental governance processes and a return to local production (Morrison 1995).

In reaction to this environmental activism, much of the initial legislation, such as the National Environmental Policy Act of 1970 in the United States, stressed the role of citizen involvement and provided institutional procedures to guarantee a wider range of views in dealing with the many consequences of environmental destruction. The legislation mandated that environmental impact assessments (EIAs) with citizen participation be carried out for major technological projects that potentially endangered the environment. These measures were first introduced in the United States, but instituted in various European countries years later (Staeck et al. 2001, 33–42). As a participatory mechanism, the environmental impact assessment required that both citizens and stakeholders be consulted in the inquiry process. Through citizen engagement,

EIAs have been meant to increase the public's environmental awareness to balance contending interests and resist politically biased decision-making by governmental officials (Fischer 2017).

Another initiative came in the form of citizens' "Right-to-Know" laws, which provide information to assist the public with environmental decisions. Basic to the right-to-know-movement was an acknowledgement that participatory practices were only successful when citizens were provided with the information and knowledge needed to render intelligent decisions (Fischer 2018b).

In practical terms, the struggle to pass "Right-to-Know" laws is viewed as a significant achievement in democratic environmental politics (Fischer 2017). This legislation, for instance, provides participants with means of obtaining information about toxic chemical spills in their neighborhoods, what types of chemical particles are being breathed in, and more. As Hazen (1997) has explained: Right-to-Know legislation provides both a chance to engage in environmental matters and a civic responsibility to grasp and assess the meaning of the available data. Even though the practice has its limitations, it can nonetheless be employed to empower local areas to take on their own environmental investigations.

Since the beginning of EIA practices and Right-to-Know legislation, citizen participation has been extended over a large range of environmental decision-making processes (Beierle and Cayford 2002). No call for citizen participation, however, has been more influential and extensively circulated than *Our Common Future* by the World Commission on Environmental Development, put forward by the United Nations (Fischer 2017). Also known as the Brundtland Report and sparking the process leading up to the Rio Earth Summit in 1992, the report states that access in achieving sustainability "will depend on widespread support and involvement of an informed public" (WCED 1987, 21). As the report puts it, sustainable development requires "a political system that secures effective citizen participation in decision-making" (WCED 1987, 65). The document calls for a greater role for public participation in the planning, development, decision-making, and implementation of environmental programs (Stirling 2009).

Recognizing that effective policies and programs need to be designed around everyday life, the Rio summit put forward measures for the support and promotion of sustainable development in the local sphere – namely the Local Agenda 21 Action Program. As a result, public participation emerged as a "best practice" in environmental policy formation and implementation. Supporting these practices has been a variety of studies that have examined how and when environmental participation works (Beierle and Cayford 2002; Eckersley 2004; Newig and Fritsch 2009).

These efforts, theoretical and practical, stress the role of citizens and the opportunities to engage in environmental governance in ways that can influence environmental debates and, as such, have significantly influenced public environmental discourse. In the domain of environmental theory, scholars have devoted considerable attention to the concept of environmental citizenship, the role of citizen deliberation in environmental policymaking, and the democratization of the green state (Smith 2003; Eckersley 2004; Fischer 2017).

Fundamental here is the view that citizen participation in environmental decisions is not only a political expression of the citizen's agency, but also his or her right to shape the conditions that determine their ways of life. In this understanding, a clean environment is taken to be one of those basic conditions (Gould 2013, 2). The literature on the environment and democracy includes a significant list of prominent scholars in the field.[2] Numerous scholars, moreover, have extended the call for participation to include a more fully developed concept of environmental democracy.

According to Worker and Ratté (2014) at the World Resources Institute, "environmental democracy can be defined in somewhat different ways, but all of them involve the belief that citizens affected by environmental concerns should have equal rights in participating in the environmental policy decision-processes." It refers to a democratic alternative that seeks to include the full range of interested or concerned publics into environmental policymaking processes. In doing so, it rejects political structures and processes that extend amenities to some while leaving others to deal with environmental risk and degradation. As Hazen (1997) has written, environmental democracy recognizes

> that environmental issues must be addressed by all those affected by their outcome, not just by governments and industrial sectors. It captures the principle of equal rights for all those in the environment debate – including the public, community groups, advocates, industrial leaders, workers, governments, academics, and health care professionals.

For those whose lives depend on the quality the environment, participation in decisions about ecological issues is as important and urgent as it is in matters related to heath, education, and finance.

These ideas came together in the 1990s in both the theory and practices of environmental movements and green political parties (Fischer 2017; 2018). Although citizen participation does not necessarily require deliberation (e.g., protesting, voting, or distributing pamphlets), the emphasis on participation in the early 2000s came together around concepts such as deliberative democracy and participatory governance (De-Shalit 2000, 135–145). Democratic participation and citizen deliberation are now taken to be essential requirements for resolving environmental conflicts and creating of a sustainable society, a point that is now enshrined in official environmental documents.

The argument has also been carried into the politics of global climate change. Theorists such as Welzer and Leggewie (2009), for instance, maintain that citizen participation needs to be a major component of climate change policy, asserting that the redesign of the industrial society can only be effective when citizens can comprehend and identify with it. Siller (2010) argues that the destruction of the climate can only be reversed through thorough democratic processes. Stehr (2016) asserts that the solution to the climate crisis involves more rather than less democracy.

Technocratic expertise and post-politics

At the same time, attention in other quarters shifted to the technical complexities and uncertainties of the issues (Fischer 2018b). In this turn, environmental participation was often portrayed as "ill-advised." Pointing to what they have described as far-fetched fantasies about a coming tragedy, these writers reflected in part a backlash by those running the institutions fundamental to the technologically driven capitalist system, institutions that were heavily criticized by those calling for a democratically-oriented ecological transformation. Stressing the complexity of the challenge, they have called for additional research into the nature and causes of the problem and the need to develop technological solutions. In this view, environmental dangers need to be converted into the language of risks and approached with methods such as risk-benefit analysis (Lomborg 2001). If technology had gotten us into this situation, the technical community should also be able to innovate a way out of the dangers ahead. This involved, in short, a revival of technocratic politics, described by a number of theorists as a new "post-political" era of environmental politics (Blühdorn 2007; Swyngedouw 2009).

The call for technocratic governance is certainly not new. It rests, in fact, on a social theory put forward by Saint-Simon and August Comte in the nineteenth century. Since that time, it has experienced numerous periods of ascendancy, particularly in times of social and political crisis. Although it has featured different contours, the various forms have tended to share a set of underlying principles. Perhaps foremost, technocracy takes decision-making by experts to be a mode of governing superior to democratic forms of governance. Toward this end, it is depicted as an "apolitical" mode that transcends party politics. Compromise and "muddling through" are portrayed as irrational approaches for decision-making concerning complex matters (Fischer 1980).

For technocrats, the solution is to replace the "irrational" decision processes of democratic governance (geared to group competition, bargaining, and compromise) with empirical methodologies of scientific decision-making, referred to as "methodological decision-making." No practice is seen to be more irrational to technocrats than the "disjointed, incremental forms of decision making" that result from a commitment to pluralist competition and political compromise. Even though many political thinkers have long praised these commitments as the hallmarks of a politically legitimate, well-functioning government, technocratic theorists see these practices as a paragon of irrationality – a form of governance that regularly delivers inferior policies that mainly exasperate the problems they attempt to solve. Such an approach, in their view, has no role in a complex technological societal system (Fischer 1990, 22).

Technocrats, in short, see political decision-making as a *problem* rather than an acceptable approach to developing solutions (Fischer 1980). Social and political problems – coronavirus pandemic, pollution, budgetary crises, inflation, poverty, educational decline, energy shortages, crime, and so on – are seen to be attributable to the failures of democratic decision-making. To ask the political representative and their citizen constituents is outmoded. None of them have the intellectual sophistication and information to effectively deal with these decisions. The job, as they see it, needs to be handed over to qualified experts.

Even though the politics of technocracy was denigrated by most during much of the past century, it has managed to reassert itself in more recent years (Fischer 2017). Contemporary illustrations are found in Italy, Greece, Spain, and Portugal, especially after the onslaught of the finance crisis in 2008. In view of the failures of these democratic countries to bring their expenditures under control, eliminate corruption and to restart the economic growth, a growing number of commentators, including public officials, called for a greater role for technical experts – especially economists – as a way to eliminate incompetent, often corrupt practices of the ruling political elites (Müller 2016). The most widely discussed case has been the technocratic role of Mario Monti in Italy, an economist by training. Monti was extensively praised for seemingly applying professional reason to the many problems plaguing the country. Numerous influential publications such as the *Wall Street Journal* and *The Economist* readily supported such measures (Fischer 2017). The implication of this support was clear enough: democratic politicians need to take a back seat, at least until the financial crisis has been resolved.

This has led many to find the idea of turning to the experts appealing, even if awkward to admit, doing so in the name of knowledge and competence. In environmental theory, this position has been supported by an increasing number of thinkers, including an assortment of environmental groups. Wissenburg (2019), for example, shows how even organizations such as the IPCC and Earth Systems Science are, despite objections to the contrary, grounded in technocratic assumptions. Others such as Nordhaus and Schnellenberger (2014) have unapologetically advocated a form of techno-environmentalism. It would, however, be difficult to find a stronger statement of this position than the view put advanced by the celebrated British scientist, James Lovelock, who has asserted that human beings are not intelligent enough to come to terms with global warming. As he has stated, "I don't think we are yet evolved enough to the point where we're clever enough to handle a situation as complex as climate change. The inertia of humans is so huge that you can't really do anything meaningful" (quoted in Hickman 2010). Further, he argued that government by the people would need to be reconsidered and put on the shelf for the time being. In his words, "Even the best democracies agree that when a major war approaches, democracies must be put on hold for the time being," adding that "I have a feeling that climate change may be an issues *as* severe as war" (Ibid). Somewhat similarly, leading sociologist Anthony Giddens (2009 has called for taking climate change policy out of politics and giving it over to a more expert-based mode of centralized planning oriented on the achievement of specific environmental goals.

A number of theorists seek to offer a theoretical grounding for the position. For example, Goodin (1992), a political theorist, has argued that ecological solutions are not amenable to democratic decision-making, pointing to a sharp distinction between the procedural nature of democracy and the substantive requirements of environmentalism. As Goodin (1992, 168) has written, "To advocate democracy is to advocate procedures, to advocate environmentalism is to advocate substantive outcomes: What guarantee can we have that the former procedures will yield the latter sorts of outcomes?" Substantive outcomes were issues for experts with reliable empirical knowledge (Fischer 2017).

Goodin has argued that there is a conflict between process and substance that is not widely understood. Environmentalists advocate a green theory of value but fail to recognize that it conflicts with their emphasis on democratic political institutions. In short, there is no guarantee that procedural democracy, deliberative or otherwise, will ensure substantive environmental norms and values. A green theory of political agency, it is argued, cannot thus be derived from a green theory of value. From this perspective, the main objective of green politics should be the advance of basic green values and the protection of the ecological system, as a form of democratic governance cannot be compatible with these green values. It is therefore needed to be a secondary consideration.

We can recognize this conflict in a much-cited paper on "ecological rationality" by Dryzek (1987). He defines ecological rationality as "the capacity of ecosystems consistently and effectively to provide the good of *human life* support." From this view of ecological rationality, "what one is interested in is the capacity of human systems and natural systems in combination to cope with human-induced problems" (1987, 36). Such an understanding presents problems for environmental democracy as it only pertains to the support of human life without concerns for values such as social justice or democracy. Even though Dryzek has regularly advocated environmental democracy, his definition illustrates the functional nature of ecological systems and thus the potential conflicts with public deliberation. If ecology has its own imperatives, these functional requirements have to be considered on their own terms, exempting many concerns from discussion. It could be argued from the perspective that human beings only need to adapt. Later, we shall discuss, such adaptation is itself not as straightforward as it might first appear; a closer look shows that it too requires political decisions.

For Torgerson (1999, 126), there is within green political theory a "latent authoritarian tendency," even when subtle. For numerous environmental political theorists, it is impermissible to set aside rein priorities and principles. Or as Smith (2003, 67) explains, "the contingency and uncertainty inherent in decision making within democratic institutions becomes unacceptable to more fundamentalist greens." It is here that we can find convergence with both the technocratic mentality and post-political demands for a techno-environmental elite to direct economic and social affairs. Some writers have taken the issue further, openly calling for a more authoritarian turn to the technological elites (Fischer 2017). Sherman and Smith (2007), for example, argue that an enlightened technocracy would be the best choice. Such technical authorities would not only wisely innovate the sorts of technological choices required, but they would also provide the kinds of informed governance that environmental survival will require. Although Sherman and Smith acknowledge various merits to democracy, they see the system as a whole to be unsustainable, particularly in the longer perspective. In their view, the country of Singapore, governed by authoritarian leaders, provides a method of governance more suited to the future of environmental crisis. For them, Singapore is an example of benevolent techno-managerial governance.

This view reflects a running loss of patience with democratic politics by the supporters of technocracy. Disturbed by the failures of politicians to make the necessary decisions, such thinkers see technological expertise as the most promising hope for a sustainable transition – or what is often called a "technological fix" (Huesemann and Huesemann 2011). This would involve new technologies, especially a transition to a low-carbon way of life. Technical innovation is seen to offer a way to avoid the limitations and failures of democratic decision-making. Toward this end, they make a case for the geoengineering of the climate, nuclear power, and carbon capture, and more.

To be sure, the development of new technologies will become more and more pressing. For this reason, many have called for something similar to an Apollo or Manhattan Project to meet the challenges posed by the environmental crisis, challenges that may well bring forward fundamental concerns related to survival (Gore 1992). In fact, technological innovation was one of the most important themes at the Paris COP21 summit. Movement in this direction, however, remains seriously wanting. There are surely important technological innovations. At the same time, however, the emphasis has been on identifying a technical fix that can avoid the need to deal with underlying social-ecological issues – especially the issues pertinent to societal transformation – that undergird the crisis, geoengineering serving as an extreme illustration.

Environmental critique of technocratic governance

The turn to technical experts has its critics. Many environmentalists view this effort to take technical control of the problem as a way to circumvent the larger changes in the economy and society generally that have given rise to the problem. For these environmental critics, reliance on technical experts and technologies can only achieve a "technological fix" that fails to attack the problems at their roots (Rosner 2004; Huesemann and Huesemann 2011). Such technological changes are intended to avoid disrupting established economic and social arrangements, including the practices of the capitalist economy. It can be equivalent to outfitting the automobile with a new exhaust pipe while neglecting the more fundamental problems posed by the engine.

Redesigning the engine is, to be sure, a technical task. The technical process, however, is not as straightforward as one might think. Technological change under capitalism is influenced by the profit motive. By and large, the technological community is financed by the corporate world, its political representatives, and the military. Technological advances, as such, are largely motivated by economic concerns rather than the interests of the public per se. The work of engineers and scientists is thus mainly geared to the imperatives of the industrial capitalist system, largely focused on short-term financial gains (Fischer 2017). New technological developments are taken into and marketed by the economic system. In this way, as environmental critics argue, advanced industrial systems can continue to create material goods and services, while technologists can "geo-engineer" the climate (Kreuter 2015). Advanced as "ecological modernization," the market-oriented process can fix in a piecemeal fashion the climate while the economic system continues to produce the goods for high consumption societies. In other words, an unsustainable economy is perpetuated (Blühdorn 2007).

Environmental democrats, alternatively, maintain that sustainability requires more than the application of new technologies. In addition, it means changing our societal systems and the ways of life associated with them (Princen 2005). This requires deliberation about fundamental values, goals, and new forms of social and political coordination across the various levels of the societal systems. In addition, innovative practices in business firms need new modes of participatory management, even economic democracy. Further, different realms of government will have to deliberatively develop and coordinate sustainable policy systems. Democratic policy-making would be required to shape legitimate decisions that can motivate the public to assist in the implementation of processes, especially at the local and community levels where the problems have to be solved.

Can environmental expertise be democratic?

During more recent decades, there have been various attempts to make technological decisions both more democratic and socially just. The role of citizen participation in matters pertaining to scientific and technological expertise is one of the most important issues for democratic governance. Insofar as environmentally sound technological innovations are essential components of a sustainable socio-ecological transition, the concern is highly important (Stevenson 2013).

Among the various effort to address this question has been methods such as participatory technology assessment, popular epidemiology, analytical-deliberation, democratic participatory expertise, and deliberative policy analysis (Fischer 2000). These approaches attempt epistemologically to integrate the political logic of democratic compromise with the technical logic of efficiency (Fischer 2009). And if so, how? In this chapter, we emphasize deliberative policy analysis as it in various ways underlies the others.

From a deliberative perspective, the technocratic orientation misses or neglects the fact that both the political legitimacy and administrative implementation of technological measures depend on political and social questions. Technology, impacting societies differently, is never fully neutral in its societal effects. In bringing together citizens and technical experts in policy deliberations concerning eco-technologies deliberative policy analysis puts the emphasis on public inputs, both political and social (Fischer 2000). Even though such deliberation does not deal with the nuts and bolts of the technical issues, the resulting consequences can be related back to the technical design processes. In the pursuit of effective decision-making, the task of deliberative expertise is to integrate these two different normative and empirical assignments in mutually beneficial exchanges.

For deliberative policy analysis, the task is thus addressing the fact that policy-related decisions in the political realm are about how to orient ourselves to the outcomes of both ecological science and technological processes. With regard to such questions, then, it involves more than a focus on the issues posed by technical science; they also involve the need to discuss how we wish to live together in face pressing challenges.

It is at this point that one can meaningfully speak of democratic participatory expertise (Fischer 2009). In this practice, the social and political issues involved are recognized, not just the concerns of the environmental experts. Although the development of eco-technological solutions is the engineers' task, they have no privileged position in concerns pertinent societal values and goals. They are themselves, in this respect, only citizens among fellow citizens. To proceed without the citizens' political and social judgments is to risk failure, whether it arrives earlier or later.

Citizens and experts in deliberative policy analysis

Bringing democracy and sustainability together in a mutually beneficial way requires breaking down the epistemic division between empirical and normative inquiry. From a postpositivist perspective, we can recognize that "the normative elements lodged in the construction of empirical policy research rest on interpretive judgments that also need to be made accessible for examination and discussion" (Fischer 2009). In this view, "the social meanings underlying policy research are always interpreted in a particular sociopolitical context – whether the context of an expert community, a particular social group or society more generally." A postpositivist deliberative approach "thus focuses on the ways such research and its findings are themselves built upon normative assumptions that, in turn, have implications for political decision-making." That is, they are lodged in the understandings of the relationships and objects that technocratic experts analyze. In fact, the very social construction of the object to be assessed is sometimes at issue.

Beyond understanding normative and empirical environmental investigation to be altogether different activities, they should be seen as components of a process of deliberation running along an interpretive spectrum ranging from the normative the techno-empirical to the normative (Fischer 2009). As these assessments occur in both empirical and normative inquiry, they can be understood as two dimensions on continuum in a process knowledge co-production (Jasanoff 2004).

The effort to better understand this process of co-production is central to the goal of deliberative policy analysis. With origins in the "argumentative turn," the method brings together empirical and normative considerations in a communicative exchange with the relevant participants (Fischer and Forester 1993; Fischer 1995; Fischer and Gottweis 2012). Taking direct aim at technocratic policy analysis, such a deliberative approach is designed to facilitate the democratization of the policy process.

This does not make science useless, as some might fear. But it does mean that its expert evaluations have to be understood as factors for consideration rather than as final answers. Those involved in decision-making need to weigh the technical results against the social and pragmatic considerations. Such judgments necessitate a multi-disciplinary deliberative approach. Under such circumstances decisions are best taken after discussing the situation from various points of view, both normative and scientific. It is necessary to examine the various perspectives that can legitimately assess the implications of the different options and evaluate them against the values and goals of the communities involved. Scientific and technical communities are thus only one of the groups that can make judgments about social and physical realities. Other groups grounded in different modes of rationality can as well make relevant assessments about the same realities (Fischer 2000). At various points, this can also include lay citizens with important empirical and social and empirical experiences (Stillitoe 2007). Not only do laypersons frequently possess specific knowledge about the local situation needed by policy decision-makers, but their motivation and legitimation are often essential as well for the successful implementation of regulations and policies.

The integration of empirical and normative inquiry, for these reasons, needs a method for organizing and guiding such deliberation. The development of such a framework has been a primary mission of deliberative policy analysis. The task is to include technical knowledge but to locate it within the situational, societal, and ideological contexts in which give problems their social meaning (Fischer 2003). As such, the goal is to organize a dialectical interaction between the knowledge of the expert and the ordinary practical knowledge of policymakers and citizens. The has led to an emphasis on participatory or collaborative investigation.

This need not involve political advocacy for particular views. Instead of advocating social or political judgments, experts can follow a proposal initially put forth by Dewey (1927) and lay out the implications of various positions, normative and empirical. The task of the participatory policy expert, as deliberative policy analysis understands it, should be to bring the facts and values together in ways that illustrate what different configurations of the two would mean for particular policy decisions pertaining to specific situations (Hajer and Wagenaar 2003; Fischer 2006, 223; Fischer and Boossabong 2018).

It also resonates with Burawoy's (2005) concept of a "public social science," in which the empirical findings and theoretical perspectives of social science could be brought to bear on important public issues. Instead of just engaging other social scientists in academic discussions, social scientists could rigorously inform public debates about the facts related to a problem but also about what they mean in terms of current political judgments, alternative policy possibilities, and normative judgments generally.

Other work on deliberative policy analysis seeks to elaborate on this public role. Drawing on theorists such as Freire and Mezirow, it focuses on the expert as a facilitator of citizen learning (Fischer 2009). This involves a pedagogical understanding of genuine learning conditions and in particular the design and facilitation of a learning environment for politicians, policymakers, and citizens. In brief, experts would have to assume the extra task of becoming experts on how social actors – citizens, politicians, and experts – learn, clarify, and make decisions. The emphasis is on establishing the institutional conditions within which people can draw on their own individual and collective agencies to solve their problems. Much like the critical educator or mentor, experts could act as educational programmers, mobilizers of resources, and consultants to a self-exploration and learning process of the part of group members.

While deliberative policy analysis is seldom formally practiced on the main political stage, there are numerous experiences in smaller contexts. One major exception to this, however, has been the Danish consensus conference, which took place in parliament and was broadcast on national television (Durant and Joss 1995). Others include participatory budgeting in Brazil, described by Carole Pateman (2012) as the example of participatory democracy par excellence; people planning in Kerala, India; community forestry in Nepal and participatory governance and deliberative policy analysis in Khon Kaen, Thailand (Fischer and Boossabong 2018). In the next and concluding section, we briefly outline deliberative policy analysis in Khon Kaen as a concrete illustration.

Deliberative policy analysis in Khon Kaen, Thailand

Taking advantage of a Constitutional provision calling for decentralized governmental structures, the City Municipality of Khon Kaen initiated a well-developed process of local participatory, deliberative governance (Teekayapan 2014).[3] The approach was presented by the mayor as one that shifts the focus from "working for" the local communities to "working with" them by allowing communities to play a role as a "sub-municipalities" with their own autonomy. In the process, the relations between the municipality and the communities turned from an earlier patron–client system to a participatory governmental network that permitted local residents and administrators to democratically collaborate in formulating and guiding their own governance activities (Boossabong and Chamchong 2019; Fischer and Boossabong 2018).

Organized around town meetings, the City's Division of Participation Promotion developed a deliberative process that brought the mayor, the local citizens, businesses, and relevant interest groups together in a participatory effort to deliberatively formulate the city's policy decisions. In addition to setting out a deliberative process, the Department of Participation selected a relatively random group of citizens to engage in the deliberative process and prepared an agenda geared to the problems and demands that local citizens collected and put forward.

The deliberative process began with working groups made up of the participating citizens who developed scenarios and plans for dealing with the specific problems. The groups then examined and compared their plans with those of the other groups and sought to forge a degree of agreement among them before turning to a more general town meeting deliberation with a larger a significant segment of the local citizenry (Fischer and Boossabong 2018).

At the end of the group discussions, the participants reassembled in larger groups, including now interested members of the public, to present their proposals for further deliberation at the "open for all" town hall gathering. In this setting, Khon Kaen's mayor and his top civil servants were also in attendance. If there were workable agreements at the end of these exchanges, the municipality agreed, with the consent of the mayor, to adopt the plan and give it over to the appropriate ministry for implementation.

Throughout these deliberative phases, the focus was on the collection, presentation and examination of findings pertaining to the policy or planning problems at hand. Of particular importance for the success of these deliberations was the role of collaborative expertise that supported the deliberations of the working groups. This was the contribution of a group of academics, mainly urban planners, from the local universities – who constituted themselves as a think tank – to facilitate the group deliberations with information and analysis, drawing on ideas and practices learned from academic studies abroad, especially studies in Europe and the United States. These ideas related in particular to theories and practices of collaborative planning, deliberative policy analysis, and deliberative democracy. Included here were the ideas of academics such as Patsy Healey (2006), Maarten Hajer and Hendrik Wagenaar (2003), John Dryzek (2020), Judith Innes and David Booher (2004), Frank Fischer and John Forester (1993), all theorists of participatory and deliberative-oriented collaborative planning and postpositivist policy analysis. As such, the projects serve as an excellent example of knowledge transfer.

As a first step based on these theoretical contributions, the think tank members established the discursive standards designed to guide the participatory deliberations. The emphasis was on ensuring that each participant would have full rights to offer their views, to learn the ideas of their fellow citizens, have a chance to shape discussions with other members of the community, and an opportunity to influence the final decisions. They also devoted particular attention to the value conflicts associated with the various policy problems that could interrupt the deliberative process, including issues related to authoritarian practices common in the country's political culture, especially in view of the military government in charge of the country as a whole (Fischer and Boossabong 2018).

The second step focused on facilitating the discursive interactions among the citizen participants. Toward this end, the planners assembled the relevant objective information needed for effective policy decisions, at times engaging in original research to better understand or clarify aspects of issues pertaining to the municipality and its communities. In particular, they explored the relation of the empirical dimensions of the problem to the normative implications of competing decisions. For this, they diagrammed the decision processes and mapped out the likely consequences of each decision.

The ongoing processes have already illustrated important successes that permitted the participants to transcend the political gridlock that had often griped the decision processes of municipal governance. Among the more important examples have been the establishment of disaster and emergence warning systems designed to improve flooding and water drainage control, especially important for a country that lives with monsoon seasons. Another illustration was the development of a public transport system with serious traffic problems. And yet another has been the development of a range of cultural projects.

We can conclude this section by noting that the development of the argumentative perspective and deliberative policy analysis has occurred in the academy as alternative to technocratic policy analysis. To the degree that technocrats are willing to engage in methodological discussions, the issue of criteria opens the door to a "politics of methodology." Such politics can assume particular significance in the university. Given that the professional schools of the university are the primary sites for technocratic training, such strife is at times a source of concern for those charged with advancing professional ideologies and their technocratic models of governance. Part of the strategy of deliberative policy analysts, then, is to cultivate and train a cadre of alternative experts that can both battle with technocratic policymakers but also assist citizens in putting forward their own arguments in the context of political struggles.

Conclusion

Democracy, as we saw, was from the outset closely associated with the environmental movement and it remains still widely seen today by environmentalists as a necessary foundation for a sustainable transformation. However, it was not long after the outset of the movement that the complexities of environmental problems became clearer and paved the way for technical experts to move to the forefront of environmental decision-making in the corridors of governments worldwide. Indeed, it led over time to a counter-movement that continues to directly challenge the environmental movement (Nordhaus and Shellenberger 2014). How can ordinary citizens meaningfully participate in such discussions, as techno-managerialists typically ask. Rather than citizen participation, the solution for them is to be found in new and innovative technologies that could resolve pressing environmental problems, from carbon capture techniques, geoengineering, and advanced nuclear energy technologies, among others.

Whereas environmental theorists have called for new forms of democratic environmental citizenship, scientific and technical experts and their supporters see the possibility of technological fixes that might sidestep the complicated social and political issues that many or most environmentalists emphasize, environmental justice in particular. This became especially clear with the call for the transformation to a sustainable society, raising questions about the relation of the social considerations to the ecological dimensions of the emerging crisis.

Environmentalists point to the way that both the solutions and their implementation bring the social and ecological together. Participation is seen to play an important role in the search for solutions, especially at the local level, where citizens often have first-hand knowledge of the problems. Citizen involvement can also play an important role in politically legitimating environmental policies and motivating citizens to help implement them.

This has posed the challenging question of how to bring citizens and experts together to work more productively on finding problem solutions. That is, how can the empirical and normative dimensions of environmental problems be brought together in meaningful communicative exchanges that can coordinate the relationship between these otherwise clashing forces.

The answer proposed here involves a turn to the democratic practices of deliberative policy analysis, designed to bring together the various technical and social voices. For many, this sounds idealistic. But emerging experiences suggest otherwise. To illustrate the point, we have presented here the case of deliberative policy analysis as practiced in the city of Khon Kean in Thailand. The experience not only shows that the citizens can participate, but also that such a procedure can lead to effective solutions to complicated problems. While this cannot be the end of the story, the case offers fruitful material to further investigate a democratic way forward towards a more sustainable society.

Notes

1. This chapter draws on contributions published elsewhere, in particular Frank Fischer, "Environmental Democracy: Participation, Deliberation and Citizenship," in M. Boström and D. J. Davidson, eds. *Environmental and Society: Concepts and Challenges.* Cham: Palgrave Macmillan; Frank Fischer, Citizens, Experts and the Environment, Duke University Press. 2000, Frank Fischer. 2009. *Democracy and Expertise*, and Frank Fischer, 2017. *Climate Crisis and the Democratic Prospect: Participatory Governance in Sustainable Communities.* Oxford University Press. and Frank Fischer and Piyapong Boossabong. 2018. "Deliberative Policy Analysis" in the *Handbook of Deliberative Democracy*, ed. by J. Dryzek, et. al, Oxford: Oxford University Press.
2. See, for example, Eckersley (2004), Smith (2003), Dryzek (2000), Shiva (2005), Baber and Bartlett (2005), Mason (1999), Bäckstrand et al. (2010), Barry (2001), Christoff (1996), and Paehlke (1995), among numerous others.
3. This section is based on research conducted with Piyapong Boossabong. A more detailed version of the case has appeared in Fischer and Boossabong (2018).

References

Baber, W.F. and Bartlett, R.V., 2005. *Deliberative Environmental Politics: Democracy and Ecological Rationality.* Cambridge: MIT Press.
Bäckstrand, K., Kahn, J., Kronsell, A. and Loevbrand, E., eds., 2010. *Environmental Politics and Deliberative Democracy: Examining the Promise of New Modes of Governance.* Cheltenham: Edward. Edward Elgar.
Barry, J., 2001. Greening Liberal Democracy: Theory, Practice and Political Economy. In J. Barry and M. Wissenburg, eds. *Sustaining Liberal Democracy: Ecological Challenges and Opportunities.* London: Palgrave, 59–81.
Beierle, T. C., and Cayford, J., 2002. *Democracy in Practice: Public Participation in Environmental Decisions.* Washington: Resources for the Future.
Blühdorn, I., 2007. Sustaining the Unsustainable: Symbolic Politics and the Politics of Simulation. *Environmental Politics*, 16 (2), 251–275.
Bookchin, M., 1996. *Toward and Ecological Society.* Montreal: Black Rose Books.
Boossabong, P. and Chamchong, P., 2019. The Practice of Deliberative Policy Analysis in the Context of Political and Cultural Challenges: Lessons from Thailand. *Policy Studies*, 40(5), 476–491.
Burawoy, M., 2005. For public sociology. *American Sociological Review*, 70(1), 4–28. https://doi.org/10.1177/000312240507000102
Christoff, P.,1996. Ecological Citizens and Ecologically Guided Democracy. In B. Barry and M. de Gues, eds. *Democracy and Green Political Thought: Sustainability, Rights, and Citizenship.* London: Routledge, 151–169.
De-Shalit, A., 2000. *The Environment: Between Theory and Practice.* Oxford: Oxford University Press.
Dewey, J., 1927. *The Public and its Problems.* New York: Holt.
Dryzek, J., 1997. *The Politics of the Earth: Environmental discourses.* Oxford: Oxford University Press.
Dryzek, J.S., 1987. *Rational Ecology: Environment and Political Economy.* Oxford and New York: Basil Blackwell.
Dryzek, J.S., 2000. *Deliberative Democracy and Beyond: Liberals, Critics, Contestations.* Oxford: Oxford University Press.
Eckersley, R., 2004. *The Green State: Rethinking Democracy and Sovereignty.* Cambridge: MIT Press.
Fischer, F., 1980. *Politics, Values and Public Policy: The Problem of Methodology.* Boulder: Westview.
Fischer, F., 1990. *Technocracy and the Politics of Expertise.* Newbury Park: Sage.
Fischer, F., 1995. *Evaluating Public Policy.* Chicago: Nelson-Hall Publishers.
Fischer, F., 2000. *Citizens, Experts, and the Environment: The Politics of Local Knowledge.* Durham: Duke University Press.
Fischer, F., 2003. *Reframing Public Policy: Discursive Politics and Deliberative Practices.* Oxford: Oxford University Press.

Fischer, F., 2006. Deliberative Policy Analysis as Practical Reason: Integrating Empirical and Normative Arguments. In Fischer, F. Miller, G. and Sidney, M. eds. *Handbook of Public Policy Analysis: Theory, Politics and Methods*. New York: Taylor and Francis, 223–236.

Fischer, F., 2009. *Democracy and Expertise*. Oxford: Oxford University Press.

Fischer, F., 2017. *Climate Crisis and the Democratic Prospect: Participatory governance in Sustainable Communities*. Oxford: Oxford University Press.

Fischer, F. 2018. Environmental Democracy: Participation, Deliberation and Citizenship. In M. Bostrom and D.J. Davidson, eds. *Environment and Society: Concepts and Challenges*. London: Palgrave, 257–280.

Fischer, F. and Boossabong, P., 2018. Deliberative Policy Analysis. In A. Bächtiger, J.S. Dryzek, J.J. Mansbridge and M. Warren, eds. *The Oxford Handbook of Deliberative Democracy*. Oxford: Oxford University Press, 584–594.

Fischer, F. and Forester, J., eds., 1993. *The Argumentative Turn in Policy Analysis and Planning*. Durham: Duke University Press.

Fischer, F. and Gottweis, H., eds., 2012. *The Argumentative Turn Revisited: Public Policy as Communicative Practice*. Durham: Duke University Press.

Giddens, A., 2009. *The Politics of Climate Change*. London: Polity Press.

Goodin, R., 1992. *Green Political Theory*. Cambridge: Polity Press.

Gore, A., 1992. *Earth in the Balance: Ecology and the Human Spirit*. New York:

Gould, C., 2013. *Beyond the Dual Crisis: From Climate Change to Democratic Change*. www.humansandnature.org/democracy-carol-gould

Hajer, M.A. and Wagenaar, H., eds. 2003. *Theories of Institutional Design. Deliberative Policy Analysis: Understanding Governance in the Network Society*. Cambridge: Cambridge University Press.

Hazen, S., 1997. Environmental Democracy. Our Planet: The magazine of the United Nations Environment Programme, 8 (March 1997), Nairobi, Kenya: UNEP Information and Public Affairs.

Healey, P., 1997. *Collaborative Planning: Shaping Places in Fragmented Societies*. Basingstoke: Palgrave Macmillan.

Hickman, L., 2010. James Lovelock: Humans are too Stupid to Prevent Climate Change. *The Guardian*. www.theguardian.com/science/2010/mar/29/james-lovelock-climate-change

Innes, J.E. and Booher, D.E., 2004. Reframing Public Participation: Strategies for the 21st Century. *Planning Theory & Practice*, 5(4), 419–436. https://doi.org/10.1080/1464935042000293170

Jasanoff, S., ed., 2004. *States of Knowledge: The Co-production of Science and Social Order*. London and New York: Routledge.

Joss, S. and Durant, J., eds., 1995. *Public Participation in Science: The Role of Consensus Conferences in Europe*. London: Science Museum.

Klein, N., 2014. *This Changes Everything: Capitalism and Climate*. New York: Simon and Schuster.

Kreuter, J., 2015. "Climate Engineering – A Technofix to Solve the Problem of Climate Change?" *KIB*. www.kib.be/articles/1103/climate-engineering-a-technofix-to-solve-the-problem-of-climate-change.

Lomborg, B., 2001. *The Skeptical Environmentalist*. Cambridge: Cambridge University Press.

Mason, M, 1999. *Environmental Democracy*. London: Earthscan.

Morrison R., 1995. *Ecological Democracy*. Boston: South End Press.

Müller, J., 2016. The EU's Democratic Deficit and the Public Sphere. *Current History*, 115 (79): 83–88.

Newig, J. and Fritsch, O., 2009. Environmental Governance: Participatory, Multi-level and Effective? *Environmental Policy and Governance*, 19, 197–214.

Nordhaus, T. and Shellenberger, M., 2014. *Breakthrough: From the Death of Environmentalism to the Politics of Possibility*. New York: Houghton Mifflin.

Paehlke, R., 1995. Environmental Values for a Sustainable Society: The Democratic Challenge: In F. Fischer and M. Black. eds., *Greening Environmental Policy: The Politics of a Sustainable Future*. New York: St. Martins, 129–144.

Pateman, C. 2012. Participatory Democracy Revisited. *Perspectives on Politics*, 10 (1), 7–19.

Princen, T., 2005. *The Logic of Sufficiency*. Cambridge: MIT Press.

Rosner, L., eds., 2004. *Technological Fix: How People Use Technology to Create and Solve Problems*. New York: Routledge.

Shearman, D. and Smith, J. W., 2007. *The Climate Change Challenge and the Failure of Democracy*. Westport: Greenwood Publishing.

Shiva, V., 2005. *Earth Democracy: Justice, Sustainability and Peace*. London: Zed Books.

Siller, P., 2010. *Demokratie und Klimawandel: Ökologen als Vordenker einer Expertokratie?* Heinrich Böll Stiftung. www.boell.de/de/demokratie/akademie-postdemokratie-expertokratie-8729.html

Sillitoe, P., ed., 2007. *Local Science vs. Global Science: Approaches to Indigenous Knowledge in International Development*. New York: Berghahn Books.

Smith, G., 2003. *Deliberative Democracy and the Environment*. London: Routledge.

Staeck, N., Malek, T. and Heinelt, H., 2001. The Environmental Impact Assessment Directive. In H. Heinelt, T., Malek, R., Smith, R. and A.E. Töller, eds., *European Union Environment Policy and New Norms of Governance*. Aldershot: Ashgate, 33–42.

Stehr, N., 2016. Exceptional Circumstances: Does Climate Change Trump Democracy. *Issues in Science and Technology*, Winter. www.academia.edu/20201986/Exceptional_circumstances_Does_climatechange_trump_democracy.

Stevenson, H., 2013. Governing Climate Change Technologies: Is There Room for Democracy? *Environmental Values*, 22 (59), 567–587.

Stirling, A., 2009. Participation, Precaution and Reflexive Governance for Sustainable Development. In W.N. Adger and A. Jordan, eds., *Governing Sustainability*. Cambridge: Cambridge University Press, 193–225.

Swyngedouw, E., 2009. The Antinomies Of The Postpolitical: In Search of a Democratic Politics Of Environmental Protection. *International Journal of Urban and Regional Research*, 33 (3), 601–620.

Teekayapan, T., 2014. *Khon-Kaen City and Developmental Innovation*. Bangkok: Thailand Research Fund.

WCED (World Commission on Environment and Development), 1987. *Our Common Future* (The Brundtland Report). Oxford: Oxford University Press.

Wissenburg, M., 2019. The Anthropocene and the Republic. *Critical Review of International Social and Political Philosophy*. doi: 10.1080/13698230.2019.1698152.

Welzer, H. and Leggewie, C., 2009. *Das Ende der Welt, Wie Wir Sie Kannten: Klima, Zukunft und die Chancen der Demokratie*. Frankfurt am Main: S. Fischer Verlag.

Worker, J. and Ratté, S., 2014. *What Does Environmental Democracy look Like?* World Resources Institute. www.wri.org/insights/what-does-environmental-democracy-look.

32
REFRAMING THE ANTHROPOCENE
Democratic challenges and openings for sustainability

Ayşem Mert and Jens Marquardt

Acknowledgments

This work has been partially funded by FORMAS (Swedish Research Council for Sustainable Development).

Introduction

The Anthropocene was first proposed as a geological era, as a plausible successor to the Holocene (Crutzen, 2002). The idea has gained traction in other disciplines of academia as well as in politics, culture, art, and media, and the term has seen a stellar career over the last two decades. The proponents of the Anthropocene argue that humans have become the primary geological force on Earth. This gives humans the responsibility towards the biogeochemical cycles of the planet, on which all life depends. Since its conception, the term arguably lost its geological connotation at least to some degree; and environmental, ethical, political, and philosophical debates emerged around the Anthropocene. These debates on the political implications of the Anthropocene and the assumptions underlying different definitions of it, are central to understanding sustainability politics in the twenty-first century. An important dimension of how the concept of the Anthropocene influences sustainability politics is the question of democracy, if and how this new era can be addressed by the current global environmental governance institutions and concepts. Accordingly, in this chapter, we focus on the questions of democracy in the Anthropocene. We argue that answers to them depend on the concept's framing, and the meanings attached to it.

We understand frames and framing as central to studying emergent contested concepts like the Anthropocene since they establish the relationship between various contexts and semiotic networks in which a concept, a narrative, or discourse is embedded, and "makes sense" accordingly (Bateson, 1972; Goffman, 1974). We do not assume that the Anthropocene has been strategically framed with a political end goal in mind by those involved in the debate. Yet, the contexts in which a concept is introduced, celebrated and taken forward have ideological and sociopolitical implications. The Anthropocene's widespread perception captures fundamental debates on our relation to the planet we inhabit, and how societies should transition into sustainability. These assumptions and debates in turn, have impacts on our democratic imaginary. While a science-driven, eco-modernist, and techno-deterministic framing of the Anthropocene is likely to narrow down the room for democratic interventions, a more open, inclusive and reflexive use of the concept could enhance democratic debates around sustainability.

Initial contestations

The initial contestation about the Anthropocene has taken place between geologists. In 2018, the International Commission on Stratigraphy (ICS) refused to formally approve the Anthropocene as a geological epoche (Meyer, 2018). Instead, the ICS announced in August 2018 to split the current geological time of the Holocene into three subdivisions, making another decision on the Anthropocene in the near future less likely. Yet, the 34-member Anthropocene Working Group voted to recognize the Anthropocene as a new ecological epoch in 2019 and revealed their plans to submit another formal proposal for the new epoch to the ICS by 2021 (Subramanian, 2019). Despite the lack of scientific consensus about its relevance to geological timelines, the term was still celebrated, investigated, and problematized across disciplines, as it came to represent the detrimental influence of human economic and industrial activity on the large-scale planetary ecosystems.

The notion of a human-made era and the idea of humanity as the "most significant global geomorphological driving force" (Cooper et al., 2018) on Earth has created both excitement and skepticism. Excitement arose from the perceived opportunities of this new era of modernity, and a paradigmatic shift in human-nature relations. In its prominent cover story, *The Economist* (2011) welcomed the Anthropocene and embraced "geology's new age" as a chance for crafting a great new world through piecemeal actions. At the same time, the Anthropocene was being linked to concepts pointing at the limits of the Earth's carrying capacity, such as *planetary boundaries* and *limits to growth* both theoretically (e.g. Rockström et al., 2009; Semal, 2015) and conceptually in popular science, blogs and discussions (e.g. see the *Anthropocene Blog*, and the *Anthropocene Curriculum* websites). This instigated arguments in support of the Anthropocene, as it could eventually become a strong driver for action to achieve a transformation towards sustainability. Along these lines, embracing the Anthropocene means to mobilize human capacity, technology, and cutting-edge knowledge to solve the environmental crises of our time, such as the climate crisis or large-scale biodiversity loss. It also assumes the possibility that human societies have or can develop the technological capacities to control and transform nature to ensure human survival. Large-scale technological endeavors such as solar geoengineering are seen as legitimate (if not unavoidable) solutions to combat global threats like anthropogenic climate change (Baskin, 2019).

Skepticism results from the lack of public debate and democratic intervention in this science- and technology-dominated discourse. Critics argue that a techno-deterministic approach to the Anthropocene leaves little room for alternative modes of transformation (Schwindenhammer, 2019). By placing humanity in the center stage, as an undifferentiated whole, the Anthropocene makes a critical reflection on power relations, historical and ongoing injustices, or the inequalities resulting from the capitalist system difficult (Moore, 2016). Voices from social sciences, as well as people from the Global South, are inadequately represented in defining, further developing, and making sense of the Anthropocene (Lövbrand et al., 2015; Marquardt, 2018). The skeptics note that if science is expected to "guide humanity's path towards plausible, desirable and novel futures in the Anthropocene" (Bai et al., 2016, 358), which defines planetary threats and leads the way to sustainability, democratic decision-making seems of little reference. Furthermore, the Anthropocene can even be perceived as a threat to democracy, when it is used to justify eco-authoritarian policies which are presumably required due to the seriousness of the ecological crises (Stevenson and Dryzek, 2014; Purdy, 2015; Mert, 2019).

These tensions show that the Anthropocene is much more than a scientifically grounded, neutral, and apolitical label for a geological epoch. It is an essentially contested concept which encapsulates divergent worldviews, beliefs, ideas of social and political order, and fundamental understandings of human activity and society at large. Hence, the democratic implications of the Anthropocene largely depend on how we frame the concept and which meanings we attach to it. In what follows, we discuss how different framings of the Anthropocene can lead to more or less inclusive and democratic debates around sustainability. To do this, we ask: what are the different framings of the Anthropocene? What kind of democratic challenges do they pose? And how can its different readings affect the democratic underpinning of debates around sustainability?

Framing the Anthropocene

In its narrow sense, the Anthropocene reflects a highly complex debate about an ecological epoch based on measurable indicators, golden spikes, and geological layers. At the same time, normative arguments, political programs, and calls for action are derived from such ecological evidence. For example, Crutzen and Schwägerl (2011) advocate for advanced technologies and innovations from the industrialized world as the primary solution to the environmental problems that are characteristic of the Anthropocene. On a prominent blog post for *Yale Environment 360*, they argue that

> [t]o accommodate the current Western lifestyle for 9 billion people, we'd need several more planets. With countries worldwide striving to attain the "American Way of Life," citizens of the West should redefine it – and pioneer a modest, renewable, mindful, and less material lifestyle.
>
> *Ibid*

Taking a Western-centered view, and presuming that the American lifestyle is desirable (if not the most desirable), they suggest a reduction in meat consumption and using public transport, high-tech global agriculture, and carbon capture and storage. But most importantly, they note that our cultures should adapt to sustaining the "world organism", a term "not coined by an esoteric Gaia guru, but by eminent German scientist Alexander von Humboldt" (ibid) using a sardonic tone for non-Western approaches, and placing the Western Enlightenment scientist on top of their presumed hierarchy.

Solutions to global ecological threats are often considered universal as they shape all aspects of society in all areas of the world. Thus, a grand transformation towards global sustainability becomes imperative for all nations based on the highly normative Anthropocene narrative (Weißpflug, 2019). Many different types of normative underpinnings can be found across the depictions of the Anthropocene, and the framing of the concept plays an important role in these different convictions. Furthermore, this results in a lack of coherent definitions for the Anthropocene, an issue that, as Dryzek and Pickering (2019, 135–136) note, impedes political debate by informed and empowered citizens.

Also in academic literature, the term gives room to different interpretations and various forms of contestation concerning its meanings and implications. In a comprehensive literature review, Brondizio and colleagues (2016) suggest that on the one hand, the term is widely accepted and used. On the other hand, they present its interpretive flexibility and show how varied the emerging narratives are, and how deep contestations and debates it has instigated. When understood as a multi-layered "narrative in the making" (Lidskog and Waterton, 2015), the Anthropocene reshapes fundamental concepts of politics, ideas of social life, and human-nature relations. It is critical to note that there is not a single political rationale behind the Anthropocene concept. In contrast, the ambiguity of the Anthropocene imagery allows for several governmental and international policy programs on sustainability (Lövbrand et al., 2009, 11), and corporate strategies.

The two ideal-type Anthropocene framings we identify and discuss here serve as two poles on a spectrum that reflects a diversity of narratives and meanings attached to the Anthropocene. Both frames outlined here coexist, and yet are largely in opposition to one another (see also Mert, 2019). Their juxtaposition reveals how the concept has captured the imaginations of scientists and society at large but also summarizes how different frames depict opposing solutions to environmental crises, and decision-making processes in the Anthropocene.

The positivist frame of the Anthropocene

The first frame of the Anthropocene follows the perspective we described above: It understands the concept as an indicator of humanity's detrimental influence and as a warning. If humans, as a species, want to survive, they should act rationally and invest in technological and institutional solutions to ensure existence in a different (definitely hotter, but still survivable) ecological state. We call this frame, which largely dominates the perceptions about the Anthropocene, the *positivist frame,* since it is in line with techno-corporate eco-modernism (Hajer, 1995), and the rationalist, post-/positivist epistemic traditions.

The positive Anthropocene frame focuses on humanity's capacity to destroy and transform, but also protect the planet. In this imaginary, all humans share some responsibility in addressing the ecological crises through historically aggregated industrial and economic activities. Following a managerial approach, human control and self-determination are understood as the key to solving ecological crises. Technological fixes like geoengineering, expert management, and manipulation of the atmosphere are recognized as the preferred policy option. Thus, it is argued, that various policy responses are on the table, but the focus should be on efficiency: Stakeholder involvement through limited democratic means could be one option, but large-scale interventions that would "hack the planet" to address climate change (Kintisch, 2010), or geoengineering approaches, in general, are likely to be increasingly normalized (cf. Crutzen, 2006 on stratospheric sulfur). Time-consuming democratic processes can be circumvented to ensure convenient solutions to global environmental threats if authoritative experts guide decision-making based on available scientific knowledge. This would be more feasible and efficient, in the face of approaching doom, compared to a deep social, economic, and political change bordering an ecological revolution, on which millions of individuals and hundreds of states are unlikely to agree and act.

While it remains to be the dominant framing of the Anthropocene, there are important incongruences in its logic. The technoscientific solutions proposed in the context of the Anthropocene, such as planet-scale geoengineering to tackle climate change, reify the dominant economic paradigm in the world, and avoids a radical alteration of socio-economic structures, especially those of production and consumption. While the recommended policies seem more manageable, in the sense that they require less radical action from the current generations it conceals the conflicts and antagonisms underlying the Anthropocene. Efforts to de-politicize, economize, technocratize, and securitize environmental politics in general, and climate politics, in particular, have been an on-going part of the liberal (Bernstein, 2001) and neo-liberal (Methmann et al., 2013; Büscher et al., 2014; Lawrence, 2017; Swyngedouw and Ernstson, 2018), agendas for several decades. Each one of these techniques aims to circumvent the emerging ideological contestation by representing the conflict in other (economic, technical, etc.) terms, and politics is replaced by another type of hegemonic struggle. In the imaginaries around the positivist framing of the Anthropocene, such hegemonic struggles are necessarily over techno-managerial planning (Swyngedouw, 2013).

Accordingly, the political implications of the Anthropocene's positivist framing generate further problems for the democratic imaginary. Some of the suggestions, such as suspending democracy, or limiting it to a nominal condition will be discussed in the subsequent section.

The deconstructivist frame of the Anthropocene

While the positivist frame of the Anthropocene reduces human-nature interactions to spheres of science and technology that need to be managed and administered, there is another frame that has emerged in response, which we will call the *deconstructivist* frame of the Anthropocene. This second frame raises questions about legitimate knowledge claims and the authority assumed by the experts, points at alternative ways of knowing nature, and reveals competing understandings of human-nature relations which lead to aspects of societal and political contestation. As David Chandler (2018, 3) aptly puts, the undeniable conclusion of the debates and discussions about when the Anthropocene began is the shared conviction "that today human history cannot be understood as separate to geological history." This "deep intertwining of natural and human systems" (Lövbrand et al., 2015, 212) is a different way of looking at history, society, humanity, and nature than that of the positivist frame, with its focus on human control and domination of nature. Surely, in the positivist framing of the Anthropocene, a post-natural ontology is often employed, and it is argued that humankind's influence on Earth reshapes the planet and thus nature fundamentally. Transformed landscapes, industrial agriculture, megacities, and geoengineering are just a few examples of humans' observed or envisioned ability to shape planet Earth. "Natural forces and human forces," Zalasiewic and colleagues (2010, 2231) argue, "are so intertwined that the fate of one determines the fate of the other." The difference between the two narratives is not in the recognition of the intertwining of the human and natural forces, but in the direction, determinism and causality assumed in it. While the positivist framing understands the intertwining as a reason to start acting more responsibly and managing the earth's systems more carefully, it gives humans a lot of agency and assumes we have ways of controlling nature more perfectly. The deconstructivist frame on the other hand, challenges these ways of knowing nature and acting on it:

> The absence of a reflection on revolutionary practices and subjects is the main weakness of the radical critique of the Anthropocene. The risk is to envision the Anthropocene as a space for villains and victims but not for revolutionaries. It is crucial to challenge the (in)visibility and (un)knowability of the Anthropocene beyond geological strata and planetary boundaries.
>
> *Armiero and De Angelis, 2017, 345*

The deconstructivist frame regards the Anthropocene as an imaginary of the future with several possible trajectories. Learning from the constructivist, post-colonial, post-human, and post-structuralist traditions, these critical interpretations aim to cultivate "multiple interpretations of the Anthropocene [so that] the social sciences can help to extend the realm of the possible for environmental politics" (Lövbrand et al., 2015, 211; see Castree 2015 for how conservatively this potential may be being used in the Anthropocene debates). The Anthropocene is welcomed as an opportunity to engage with questions about ethics and politics in a time of rapid biophysical change (Rose et al., 2012, 1), and to rethink modernist ontologies to end the separation between Nature and Human (Haraway, 2015; Latour, 2015).

The deconstructivist frame focuses on the ontological novelty that the Anthropocene represents, introducing a continuum of co-existing rationales, and bringing an end to the modernist dichotomies such as nature/society, (hu)man/non-human, rational/irrational, agency/structure, being/becoming, and so forth. This multiplicity of emergent narratives allows multiple subjectivities to be expressed at the center of these concepts. This stands in contrast to the positivist frame of the Anthropocene, which has been criticized for overlooking the qualitative questions of meaning, value, responsibility, and purpose (Lövbrand et al., 2015). The deconstructivist frame contains various approaches that have different answers to how universal our policies and goals can be. On the one hand, they share a common understanding in that:

- Human beings share a complex, entangled, and unpredictable world with each other and all other species with different and at times competing histories, requirements, and conditions for survival.
- There is no technological solution or a singular path to a greener, more sustainable steady state for all societies.
- The solutions that might address some of the problems in the Anthropocene will be diverse and bottom-up, radical, and place-based; and affected by historical and geographical experiences;
- Nation-states are unlikely loci for progressive and radical change, which can save some of the species and communities that share the earth. In fact, a policy to save most would require overcoming deadlocks caused by the current world order which uses state-level decision-making processes to address global crises.

Against these loosely shared principles, some thinkers focus on the necessity of diverse and diffused solutions (e.g. Bulkeley forthcoming) whereas others seek a more unified guiding principle. Here, the scale and complexity of ecological crises like climate change are understood to require a new ethical framework for Earth stewardship. For instance, Karen Litfin (2005) takes the first step towards an ethical framework when aligning human purposes with the "function of Gaia." Her vision of "Gaian democracies" on global scales implies a clear break with modern institutions such as the sovereign state and the autonomous and free individual. In Litfin's (2005, 514) framework, "hierarchical structures of domination would give way to participatory networks, and symbiosis would displace competition as the defining modality in economic exchange."

Outside academic debates, popular representations of the Anthropocene in media, art, politics, and culture "give more space to the alternative interpretations and narratives of the Anthropocene and often focus on its underlying dilemmas and contradictions" (Mert, 2019, 132). Accordingly, the deconstructivist framing can be traced in such work, revealing the underlying logics, promises, fantasies, problems, and dilemmas of the Anthropocene. It links the Anthropocene to contemporary and future-related questions of meaning, values, responsibility, and ultimately of decision-making. A central role is given to deliberation, reflexivity, and institutional flexibility (Niemeyer, 2014; Dryzek and Pickering, 2017), which allows for knowledge pluralism that comprises of "multiple forms of human and non-human expertise"

(Lorimer, 2012). The non-human environment and the most vulnerable citizens of the world are given "formative agency" (Dryzek and Pickering, 2019) connecting the debates to earlier Science and Technology Studies (e.g. Latour, 1993), and eco-political thought (Stone, 1974).

Taking into account the questions the deconstructivist framing poses to the Anthropocene debate allows us to think further about possible democratic openings in sustainability governance. At the same time, a positivist reading of the Anthropocene manifests the democratic shortcomings emerging from global sustainability politics.

Democratic challenges in sustainability politics

Global sustainability politics and international environmental governance in the last 30 years have largely reflected a modernist, developmentalist approach that tries to reconcile economic growth with a relative reduction in the damages to the Earth's ecosystems. In many ways, it shares the anthropocentric approach of the positivist framing of the Anthropocene discussed above. An important milestone in this narrative has been set in 1987 when the United Nations sketched out the future of environmental politics. The World Commission on Environment and Development (WCED, or the Brundtland Commission) published "Our Common Future," fostering an internationalization of environmental politics. With the mission of writing down the international political strategies for environmental protection, the Brundtland Commission fused the need for environmental protection with the desire for industrial development, defining sustainable development as "development which meets the needs of the present without compromising the ability of future generations to meet their own needs" (WCED, 1987). This has placed environmental politics into the domain of nation-states and international institutions (with the UN in the center of global environmental governance). It has arguably equated the need for development to the need to industrialize, making development infinitely possible and desirable rather than meaningful only within reasonable and human-scale limits (Mert, 2015, 155–159). It also popularised ethical narratives of future generations, unifying humanity across time. Promoting sustainable growth, the UN Sustainable Development Goals (SDGs) are a direct response to the environmental crises in the Anthropocene (Haines, 2017).

The Anthropocene has become the underlying rationale for sustainability and the compass for sustainable development. Griggs and colleagues (2013) even adapt the Brundtland definition of sustainable development to the Anthropocene as "development that meets the needs of the present while safeguarding Earth's life-support system, on which the welfare of current and future generations depends." Along these lines, Olsson and colleagues (2017) celebrate the Anthropocene as "a game-changer" for achieving the SDGs through social innovation and sustainability transformations. The human age acts as a moral obligation, a motivation, and a justification for action towards sustainability as it predefines the room for policy action in fields like climate change, biodiversity protection, or oceans. The Anthropocene is used to legitimize implementing (large-scale) technical solutions to these global environmental threats to keep humanity within the planet's "safe operating system" (Rockström et al. 2009). Lim and colleagues (2018) even suggest reframing the SDGs towards an explicit "end goal" in light of the Anthropocene and planetary boundaries.

These technocentric, apolitical, and science-driven narratives can turn into technocratic and undemocratic policymaking in environments like the UN, as experienced by Melissa Leach, a social anthropologist and geographer. As part of a group of 28 academics, Leach was invited by the UN Department of Economic and Social Affairs to discuss science and global sustainability goals in the run-up to the creation of the SDGs. Her reflections on a "dangerous new world of undisputed scientific authority and anti-democratic politics" (Leach,

2013) in the Anthropocene triggered a lively debate about the tensions between sustainability, the Anthropocene, and democracy. Leach criticized the portrayal of the Anthropocene as an age defined by natural limits and planetary boundaries which leads to clear and measurable goals and solutions. "It is co-constructed with ideas of scientific authority and incontrovertible evidence; with the closing down of uncertainty or at least its reduction into clear, manageable risks and consensual messages" (Leach, 2013). An observation that Roger Pielke Jr. (2013), a professor of environmental studies, later described as a "power grab by the experts." Such a characterization of the Anthropocene makes it seem incompatible with an open, reflexive, and democratic decision-making process. If democratic governance is a goal for the UN, then it is important that the framing of the Anthropocene does not reproduce the Enlightenment in its positivist sense and set expertise and science above democratic choices. Nor should it narrate nature in rationalist, eco-modernist and positivist accounts as an object to be quantified and even more precisely managed through science, since such narratives give little agency to humans in choosing the exact direction or content of the socio-ecological changes taking place in their lives.

A positivist framing of the Anthropocene already predefines the room for debate and competing arguments by the idea of "settled" scientific evidence and "natural" limits like the often unquestioned planetary boundaries. Such a notion runs the risk of promoting pseudo-democratic activities where people's freedom of expression encounters limitations. For example, public participation (e.g. for the design and the scale of a renewable energy project or concerning the question of whether there is a need to transition to electric vehicles) seems obsolete or at least of little value if critical debates around the underlying worldviews and assumptions are not encouraged or even get silenced. Civil society can play a crucial role in fostering public deliberation, translating concepts, ideas, and messages across various platforms and worldviews, and promoting and facilitating deliberative accountability (Stevenson, 2013). This would generate democratic legitimacy even within the confines of the UN system.

Imagining democracy based on the post-social and/or post-political ontologies of the Anthropocene also precludes the possibility of epistemic pluralism. Such a reading provides little room for the plurality of knowledge, cultures, and conceptions of the less industrialized, modernized, Westernized. At the same time, it universalizes the hegemonic knowledge of those who benefit(ed) disproportionately from the past and present power structures. In a detailed account of democratic decision-making in global governance, Hayley Stevenson (2013, 400) argues that there is not only an intrinsic value to democracy but also an instrumental value to it, which she expresses as "the rule of the many is epistemically superior to the rule of one or the rule of the few." Such an approach dislocates the belief that technoscientific solutions can (best) address the questions the Anthropocene poses. Even if technoscience can provide some solutions to a limited set of these problems, with varying degrees of certainty, it is possible to devise a democratic model that would potentially allow choosing one of these options over the others. However, it is also important to note that many Anthropocene narratives frame the concept in this positivist sense, without being anti-democratic or even undemocratic. Many proponents of a science- and technology-driven understanding of the Anthropocene highlight the importance of democratic decision-making, albeit informed through science. From this viewpoint, scientists should not have per se a stronger voice than others, as Schellnhuber and colleagues (2005, 18) argue, "yet they should have a dominant role in determining the likelihood of various future scenarios and their courses and impacts."

The concept of the Anthropocene refers to the influence of our whole species on the planet, which makes it necessary to think about a *global demos* constituted by the whole world population. However, International Relations scholars generally assume that states have a high threshold of democracy, while at larger scales, "the threshold of acceptability should not be as high as a well-ordered society" (Keohane, 2011, 100). Scholars tend to apply nation-level democratic principles to the international level, mainly because states are the main agents in today's world order. Such a nation-level bias structures and limits the democratic imaginary. For instance, Robert Keohane (2016, 938) notes that "no global government could harness the emotional support of nationalism." He argues that the necessary infrastructure for democracy is absent at the global level. Therefore, the best possibility is maintaining some key features of democracy, such as accountability of elites to publics, widespread participation, protection of minority rights, and deliberation within civil society. Paradoxically, he also warns against hypocritical nominal democratization that is void of substance.

Sofia Näsström (2010) accuses democratic theorists to "speak for the people by constructing a theory without the people" due to the lack of a global demos. This can be a misleading argument, however, if historicity is not taken into account: The construction of a demos has always required a presupposition that some historical principle united "a people" (Dahl, 1989, 3). It has always involved a biased selection and exclusion. Democracy has been made possible for larger and larger numbers of people in history, through various means that are not limited to representation. If there is any way of describing "a people" without bias and exclusion, this would include all of the planet's population, which the Anthropocene imaginary makes possible. Although the habitual questions and solutions of democratic theory are less pertinent at the global level due to blurry definitions of demos, territoriality, and representation, a loosely connected albeit largely unorganized demos already exists for a discourse on the democratization of planetary governance, that also takes action in various ways (e.g., in mass protests and petitions to international organizations).

These questions about participation and democratization are intrinsically linked to questions of who gets represented by what means in global discourses. Following its positivist understanding, the Anthropocene is often used as a framework to talk about the role of "others" in a human-made world instead of having an open conversation with them. For example, large-scale geoengineering projects in MIT laboratories and elsewhere take little notice of farmers, fishers, or other marginalized groups, except when their increased vulnerability legitimizes their research. Their under- or misrepresentation translates into the challenge to imagine social and political order beyond technological fixes (Garrard et al., 2014) in the absence of inclusive, truly deliberative participatory processes. After drawing such a bleak picture for inclusive, participatory, and democratic decision-making in the Anthropocene, we show how the concept also offers a variety of democratic openings in the next section.

Democratic openings in the Anthropocene

To place the Anthropocene in its political context, Jedediah Purdy (2015, 257) notes that "in the past decade [...] democratic citizens' capacity to rework their own common lives has been hollowed out in overt and explicit ways, and eroded by a decline in political imagination." He argues against "calling for more democracy when democracy seems a formula for failure," which would further alienate and frustrate the citizens. Instead, he suggests taking *the Anthropocene question* as a challenge to democracy: If the Anthropocene is a question about what kind of world to make together, the democracy that can address this question cannot be more of the same (Purdy, 2015, 267). Such a reading of the Anthropocene links social and political issues like wealth distribution, justice, or equity to how we solve sustainability concerns. It also invites reflections on what changes in a democracy are needed to address them, especially when it comes to the existing environmental governance institutions.

To construct a democratic imagery wherein political agency is possible for citizens, institutions, and civil society, as well as the non-human environment and future generations, the Anthropocene has to be reconstructed not only as an epoch but also as a new democratic scale (Mert, 2019). A deconstructivist approach towards the Anthropocene asks which part of the decision-making process is up for democratic interventions and who is being included or excluded from that debate. Furthermore, it asks how the idea of the Anthropocene could help societies overcome the limitations of democracy, and radicalize the debate on responding to global ecological challenges. Robyn Eckersley (2015) notes that this puts liberal democracy under great stress, revealing its limitations in serving the long-term public good of environmental protection. Overcoming these limitations, she argues, depends on detaching political processes from the outdated narrative of human progress. A deconstructivist framing of the Anthropocene can provide various democratic openings and challenge "the global democratic deficit" (Dingwerth, 2007). It can substantiate core values that constitute democracy at a global scale such as participation and representation (Bäckstrand and Kuyper, 2017) but also create openings for reflections about issues of political contestation and the role of science and knowledge claims (Jasanoff, 2004).

To begin with, let us consider how the deconstructive framing relies on different constructions of nature and science. Nature becomes knowable through the intermediate system of science, which is shaped by cultural contexts, histories, and normative ideas of society. Science and its underlying processes and practices are "interwoven with issues of meaning, values, and power in ways that demand sustained critical inquiry" (Jasanoff, 2004, 15). Opening up the democratic underpinning of science in society – or the lack thereof – a deconstructivist framing of the Anthropocene can bring scientific pluralism and inclusiveness to the debate. It allows us to bridge the distinction "between the laws of external nature and the conventions of society" (Latour, 1993, 130) to foster more inclusive and democratic interactions between different sorts of expertise and knowledge. Such a perspective refuses the purification of science and acknowledges its performative dimension within cultural and historical contexts. In a world facing "the unintended consequences of scientific progress, participatory procedures involving scientists, stakeholders, advocates, active citizens, and users of knowledge are critically needed" (see also Norris, 1999; Kates, 2001, 641). The Anthropocene can function as a "bridging concept" (Brondizio et al., 2016, 320) to overcome epistemological divides between and within the natural and social sciences and the humanities. At least the academic debate about the Anthropocene includes a wide range of scientific disciplines such as geology, ecology, philosophy, history of sociology, environmental science, anthropology, economy, psychology, and gender studies, according to a broad literature review (Correia et al., 2018, 1873). These findings support the idea that the representation of the Anthropocene in scientific debates has been shaped by an increasingly interdisciplinary understanding of Earth systems (e.g. as often found in the works of the *Earth System Governance Network*). Besides, a deconstructivist framing of the Anthropocene invites different communities to engage in making sense of our planet and its future as it acknowledges the plurality of knowledge-making traditions (Mert, 2019).

Who gets to speak and what gets represented in the Anthropocene is thus very much intertwined with the legitimacy of knowledge claims. A deconstructivist framing of the Anthropocene challenges the science- and techno-centric idea of sustainable development based on a largely Western discourse led by white, male scholars with a background in natural science. Instead, voices from the Global South, for example, are brought to the forefront of debate, and so are their (alternative) ideas of social life and political order (Marquardt, 2018). Such an understanding of the Anthropocene gives room to "radical alternatives to sustainable development" (Kothari, 2015) such as Buen Vivir or Radical Ecological Democracy, which seem otherwise incompatible with the positivist framing of the Anthropocene. Briggs and Sharp (2004) argue that instead of being integrated into a positivist Anthropocene discourse and universalistic approaches like a global governance architecture for the Anthropocene (Biermann et al., 2012), non-Western voices, ideas, and knowledge claims should be acknowledged to allow for critical reflections. These voices "must be allowed to criticize dominant worldviews, challenge terms of debate and propose alternative agendas, rather than simply being added into an existing way of doing things" (Briggs and Sharp, 2004, 668).

While the 2030 Agenda for Sustainable Development aims to take "bold and transformative steps" (UN DESA, 2015) towards sustainable and resilient development, achieving societal change goes far beyond technological shifts (Smith et al., 2005, 1493). Because sustainability transformations encapsulate different worldviews and normative ideas of society at large, we need to acknowledge the embedded or "situated" (Haraway, 1989) nature of these transformations into broader socio-political environments, institutions, and knowledge infrastructures for which a deconstructivist framing of the Anthropocene provides helpful openings for reflection. It brings back contested ideas of societal and political change, such as alternative lifestyles, behavioral changes, or forms of democratization. Some examples of these are recently revived or radicalized concepts of conviviality, degrowth, Buen Vivir, Ubuntu, etc. Sustainability transformations in times of global threats such as climate change reflect deep societal struggles over power, knowledge, technology, economy and the future of society at large.

"Navigating the Anthropocene" with its implications for deep societal change requires more than improved, effective, and reformed governance structures (Biermann et al., 2012, 1306). Instead, the Anthropocene could allow us to break out of the "pathological path dependencies" that are inherent to established institutions and prevent transformative change (Dryzek and Pickering, 2018). The concept has the potential to help us rethink sustainability governance as a highly political and complex process of policymaking while acknowledging the co-productionist nature of science and social order (Jasanoff, 2004) and recognizing non-Western knowledge claims in complex human-nature relations. The Anthropocene can act as an opportunity to rethink sustainability governance as well as democratic scale pushing it in two directions. It can be understood to require more democratic decision-making at the global level, therefore planet scale environmental issues are not addressed in a top-down, exclusive fashion. Otherwise, it can be understood as a call for diffused, deliberative, experimental, and local models and practices of democracy that allow for connectivity between the individual subject, the socio-ecological systems in question, and the decisions made.

Finally, a deconstructive framing of the Anthropocene reconstructs sustainability by highlighting complex power dynamics, and related hegemonic contestations. This gives the Anthropocene the potential to re-politicize environmental action by highlighting the broader political and societal implications of over 30 years of sustainable *development*. Pointing at issues like marginalization, participation, and inclusion, the concept can redirect our attention to what needs to be sustained and how long. While a positivist framing of the Anthropocene can be criticized for narrowing down democratic interventions, a more optimistic reading can thus foster and enable democratic debates in and for sustainability.

Conclusion

Globalization has changed our understanding of democracy. Nation-states are no longer the only locus of politics; and large-scale transformations (e.g. the digital revolution, or global ecological, financial, and health crises) influence all humanity. Various social, ethical, and economic challenges are regarded as global issues that require international and transnational policy responses. However, the "democratic deficit" in global governance and the inequalities resulting from this deficit cause governance failures in coping with global crises (Mouffe, 2000; Haas, 2004; Bäckstrand, 2006).

The Anthropocene opens up opportunities to critically reflect on humanity's responsibilities on the planet we live on. For this to happen, we have identified the necessity of addressing the current problems with representation, participation, power dynamics, and knowledge-making. We need to open up the debate especially to local knowledge claims, non-Western/Global North perspectives, and the social sciences to unpack the Anthropocene and derive the concept's underlying meanings and understandings of the world.

While a positivist framing of the Anthropocene restricts (global) democracy, a deconstructivist framing could do the opposite: shedding light on the intertwined nature of knowledge and social order, linking existing political orders to the contested visions of societies different communities want to live in, and eventually enhancing (global) democracy through localized and diffused democratic action and practices. Modern democratic imaginaries seem limited in their ability to inclusion and scale, but we can mobilize the Anthropocene to construct a global, yet locally embedded demos responsive to the social and political changes needed to address global environmental problems.

References

Armiero, M. and De Angelis, M., 2017. Anthropocene: victims, narrators, and revolutionaries, *South Atlantic Quarterly*, 116(2), 345–362.
Bäckstrand, K., 2006. Democratizing global environmental governance? Stakeholder democracy after the World Summit on Sustainable Development, *European Journal of International Relations*, 12(4), 467–498.
Bäckstrand, K. and Kuyper, J. W., 2017. The democratic legitimacy of orchestration: the UNFCCC, non-state actors, and transnational climate governance, *Environmental Politics*, 26(4), 764–788.
Bai, X. et al., 2016. Plausible and desirable futures in the Anthropocene: a new research agenda, *Global Environmental Change*, 39, 351–362.
Baskin, J., 2019. *Geoengineering, the Anthropocene and the End of Nature*. London: Palgrave Macmillan.
Bateson, G., 1972. *Steps to an Ecology of Mind*. Northvale: Jason Aronson Inc.
Bernstein, S., 2001. *The Compromise of Liberal Environmentalism*. New York: Columbia University Press.
Biermann, F. et al., 2012. Navigating the Anthropocene: improving earth system governance, *Science*, 335(6074), 1306–1307.
Briggs, J. and Sharp, J., 2004. Indigenous knowledges and development: a postcolonial caution, *Third World Quarterly*, 25(4), 661–676.
Brondizio, E. S. et al., 2016. Re-conceptualizing the Anthropocene: a call for collaboration, *Global Environmental Change*, 39, 318–327.
Bulkeley, H., (forthcoming). Climate Changed urban futures: environmental politics in the Anthropocene city, *Environmental Politics*.
Büscher, B., Dressler, W. and Fletcher, R., 2014. *Nature^{TM} Inc: Environmental Conservation in the Neoliberal Age*. Tuscon: University of Arizona Press.
Castree, N., 2015. Geographers and the discourse of an earth transformed: influencing the intellectual weather or changing the intellectual climate?, *Geographical Research*, 53(3), 244–254.
Chandler, D., 2018. *Ontopolitics in the Anthropocene: An Introduction to Mapping, Sensing and Hacking*. London and New York: Routledge.
Cooper, A. H. et al., 2018. Humans are the most significant global geomorphological driving force of the 21st century, 1–8. *The Anthropocene Review*, 5(3).
Correia, R. A. et al., 2018. Pivotal 20th century contributions to the development of the Anthropocene concept: overview and implications, *Current Science*, 115(10), 1871–1875.
Crutzen, P., 2002. Geology of mankind, *Nature*, 415(6867), 23–23.
Crutzen, P., 2006. Albedo enhancement by stratospheric sulfur injections: a contribution to resolve a policy dilemma?, *Climatic Change*, 77(3–4), 211–220.

Crutzen, P. and Schwägerl, C. (2011) *Living in the Anthropocene: Toward a New Global Ethos*, Yale Environment 360 [online]. Available from: http://e360.yale.edu/features/living_in_the_anthropocene_toward_a_new_global_ethos [Accessed: 1 April 2017].

Dahl, R. A., 1989. *Democracy and Its Critics*. New Haven: Yale University Press.

Dingwerth, K., 2007. *The new transnationalism. Transnational governance and Legitimacy*. London: Palgrave MacMillan.

Dryzek, J. S. and Pickering, J., 2017. Deliberation as a catalyst for reflexive environmental governance, *Ecological Economics*, 131, 353–360.

Dryzek, J. S. and Pickering, J., 2018. *The Politics of the Anthropocene*. Oxford: Oxford University Press.

Dryzek, J. S. and Pickering, J., 2019. *The Politics of the Anthropocene*. New York: Oxford University Press.

Eckersley, R., 2015. *Anthropocene raises risks of Earth without democracy and without us*, The Conversation [online]. Available from: https://theconversation.com/anthropocene-raises-risks-of-earth-without-democracy-and-without-us-38911 [Accessed: 2 August 2019].

Economist, 2011. *The geology of the planet. Welcome to the Anthropocene*, The Economist [online]. Available from: www.economist.com/leaders/2011/05/26/welcome-to-the-anthropocene [Accessed: 2 August 2019].

Garrard, G., Handwerk, G. and Wilke, S., 2014. Introduction: "Imagining Anew", *Challenges of Representing the Anthropocene*, 5, 149–153.

Goffman, E., 1974. *Frame Analysis: An Essay on the Organization of Experience*. Cambridge: Harvard University Press.

Griggs, D. et al., 2013. Policy: Sustainable development goals for people and planet., *Nature*, 495(7441), 305–7.

Haas, P. M., 2004. Addressing the global governance deficit, *Global Environmental Politics*, 4(4), 1–15.

Haines, A., 2017. *How Can The SDGs Help Us Survive The Anthropocene Epoch?*, Huffington Post [online]. Available from: www.huffingtonpost.com/sir-andy-haines/how-can-the-sdgs-help-us-_b_12118778.html?guccounter=1 [Accessed: 24 January 2019].

Hajer, M. A., 1995. *The Politics of Environmental Discourse. Ecological Modernisation and the Policy Process*. Oxford: Clarendon Press.

Haraway, D. J., 1989. *Primate Visions: Gender, Race, and Nature in the World of Modern Science*. New York: Routledge.

Haraway, D. J., 2015. Anthropocene, Capitalocene, Plantationocene, Chthulucene: making kin, *Environmental Humanities*, 6(1), 159–165.

Jasanoff, S., 2004. Ordering Knowledge, Ordering Society, In S. Jasanoff, eds. *States of Knowledge. The Co-production of Science and Social Order*. London: Routledge, 13–45.

Kates, R. W., 2001. Sustainability science, *Science*, 292(5517), 641–642.

Keohane, R. O., 2011. Global governance and legitimacy, *Review of International Political Economy*, 18(1), 99–109.

Keohane, R. O., 2016. Nominal democracy?: A rejoinder to Gráinne de Búrca and Jonathan Kuyper and John Dryzek, *International Journal of Constitutional Law*, 14(4), 938–940.

Kintisch, E., 2010. *Hack the Planet: Sciences Best Hope – or Worst Nightmare – for Averting Climate Catastrophe*. New Jersey: John Wiley & Sons.

Kothari, A., 2015. *Why Sustainable Development and Radical Alternatives are not Compatible*, degrowth [online]. Available from: www.degrowth.info/en/2015/12/why-sustainable-development-and-radical-alternatives-are-not-compatible/ [Accessed: 2 August 2019].

Latour, B., 1993. *We Have Never Been Modern*. Cambridge: Harvard University Press.

Latour, B., 2015. Telling Friends from Foes in the Time of the Anthropocene. In C. Hamilton, C. Bonneuil, and F. Gemenne, eds. *The Anthropocene and the Global Environment Crisis – Rethinking Modernity in a New Epoch*. London: Routledge, 145–155.

Lawrence, J. C., 2017. Managing the Environment: Neoliberal Governmentality in the Anthropocene. In P. Heikkurinen, eds. *Sustainability and Peaceful Coexistence for the Anthropocene*. London: Routledge, 88–104.

Leach, M., 2013. *Democracy in the Anthropocene?*, Huffington Post [online]. Available from: www.huffingtonpost.co.uk/Melissa-Leach/democracy-in-the-anthropocene_b_2966341.html [Accessed: 2 August 2019].

Lidskog, R. and Waterton, C., 2015. The Anthropocene: A Narrative in the Making. In M. Boström, and D.J. Davidson, eds. *Environment and Society. Concepts and Challenges*. Cham: Palgrave Macmillan.

Lim, M. M. L., Jørgensen, P. S. and Wyborn, C. A., 2018. Reframing the sustainable development goals to achieve sustainable development in the Anthropocene – a systems approach, *Ecology and Society*, 23(3).

Litfin, K., 2005. Gaia Theory: Intimations for Global Environmental Politics. In P. Dauvergne, eds. *Handbook of Global Environmental Politics*. Northampton: Edward Elgar Publishing, ch 30.

Lorimer, J., 2012. Multinatural geographies for the Anthropocene, *Progress in Human Geography*, 36(5), 593–612.

Lövbrand, E. et al., 2015. Who speaks for the future of Earth? How critical social science can extend the conversation on the Anthropocene, *Global Environmental Change*, 32, 211–218.

Lövbrand, E., Stripple, J. and Wiman, B., 2009. Earth system governmentality. Reflections on science in the Anthropocene, *Global Environmental Change*, 19(1), 7–13.

Marquardt, J., 2018. Worlds apart? The Global South and the Anthropocene. In T. Hickmann, et al., eds. *The Anthropocene Debate and Political Science*. London: Routledge, 200–218.

Mert, A., 2015. *Environmental Governance through Partnerships: A Discourse Theoretical Study*. Cheltenham: Edward Elgar.

Mert, A., 2019. Democracy in the Anthropocene: A New Scale. In F. Biermann and E. Lövbrand, eds *Anthropocene Encounters. New Directions in Green Political Thinking*. Cambridge: Cambridge University Press, 128–149.

Methmann, C., Rothe, D. and Stephan, B. eds., 2013. *Interpretive Approaches to Global Climate Governance: (De)constructing the Greenhouse*. London: Routledge.

Meyer, R., 2018. Geologys Timekeepers Are Feuding, *The Atlantic* [online]. Available from: www.theatlantic.com/science/archive/2018/07/anthropocene-holocene-geology-drama/565628/ [Accessed: 25 February 2019].

Moore, J. W., 2016. The Rise of Cheap Nature. In J. Moore, eds. *Anthropocene or Capitalocene? Nature, History, and the Crisis of Capitalism*. Oakland: PM Press, 78–115.

Mouffe, C., 2000. *The Democratic Paradox*. London: Verso.

Näsström, S., 2010. Democracy Counts: Problems of Equality in Transnational Democracy. In C. Jönsson and J. Tallberg, eds. *Transnational Actors in Global Governance*. London: Palgrave Macmillan, 197–217.

Niemeyer, S., 2014. A defence of (deliberative) democracy in the Anthropocene, *Ethical Perspectives*, 21(1), 15–45.

Norris, P. eds., 1999. *Critical Citizens: Global Support for Democratic Government*. Oxford: Oxford University Press.

Olsson, P. et al., 2017. The concept of the Anthropocene as a game-changer: a new context for social innovation and transformations to sustainability, *Ecology and Society*, 22(2).

Pielke, R., 2013. Planetary Boundaries as Power Grab, *Roger Pielke Jr.s Blog* [online]. Available from: https://rogerpielkejr.blogspot.com/2013/04/planetary-boundries-as-power-grab.html [Accessed: 25 August 2020].

Purdy, J., 2015. *After Nature: A Politics for the Anthropocene*. Cambridge: Harvard University Press.

Rockström, J. et al., 2009. A safe operating space for humanity, *Nature*, 461(7263), 472–475.

Rose, D. B. et al., 2012. Thinking through the environment, unsettling the humanities, *Environmental Humanities*, 1(1), 1–5.

Schellnhuber, H. J. et al., 2005. Earth system analysis for sustainability, *Environment*, 47(8), 10–25.

Schwindenhammer, S., 2019. Agricultural Governance in the Anthropocene: A Research Agenda. In T. Hickmann et al., eds. *The Anthropocene Debate and Political Science*. Abingdon: Routledge, 146–163.

Semal, L., 2015. Anthropocene, Catastrophism and Green Political Theory. In C. Hamilton, F. Gemenne and C. Bonneuil, eds. *The Anthropocene and the Global Environmental Crisis: Rethinking Modernity in a new Epoch*. London and New York: Routledge, 87–99.

Smith, A., Stirling, A. and Berkhout, F., 2005. The governance of sustainable socio-technical transitions, *Research Policy*, 34(10), 1491–1510.

Stevenson, H., 2013. Governing climate technologies: is there room for democracy?, *Environmental Values*, 22(5), 567–587.

Stevenson, H. and Dryzek, J. S., 2014. *Democratizing Global Climate Governance*. Cambridge: Cambridge University Press.

Stone, C., 1974. *Should Trees Have Standing? Toward Legal Rights for Natural Objects*. Los Altos: Fla. St. U. L. Rev.

Subramanian, M., 2019. Anthropocene now: influential panel votes to recognize Earths new epoch, *nature.com* [online]. Available from: www.nature.com/articles/d41586-019-01641-5 [Accessed: 25 February 2020].

Swyngedouw, E., 2013. The non-political politics of climate change, *ACME: An International Journal for Critical Geographies*, 12(1), 1–8.

Swyngedouw, E. and Ernstson, H., 2018. Interrupting the Anthropo-obScene: immuno-biopolitics and depoliticizing ontologies in the Anthropocene, *Theory, Culture and Society*, 35(6), 3–30.

UN DESA, 2015. *Transforming our world: the 2030 Agenda for Sustainable Development*, Sustainable Development Knowledge Platform [online]. Available from: https://sdgs.un.org/2030agenda [Accessed: 2 November 2021].

WCED, 1987. *Our Common Future* [online]. Available from: www.un-documents.net/wced-ocf.htm [Accessed: 11 September 2017].

Weißpflug, M., 2019. A Natural History for the 21st century Rethinking the Anthropocene Narrative with Arendt and Adorno. In T. Hickmann et al., eds. *The Anthropocene Debate and Political Science*. London: Routledge.

Zalasiewicz, J. A. N. et al., 2010. The new world of the Anthropocene, *Environmental Science and Technology*, 44(7), 2228–2231.

33
POST-DEMOCRACY AND POST-SUSTAINABILITY

Ingolfur Blühdorn

Introduction

The belief that democracy and sustainability are not simply mutually compatible but indeed inseparably connected to and dependent on each other belongs to the well-established orthodoxies of eco-political movements, thinking and policy. Since the emancipatory *new social movements* of the 1970s, in particular, the democratic empowerment of citizens is widely considered an essential precondition for the achievement of environmental objectives, and there is a consensus that any societal transformation towards sustainability can only be a democratic transformation. After the collapse of the bipolar world order of the Cold War, the state of the biophysical environment in many countries of the former Soviet Union seemed to confirm that democratic systems are much better positioned to take care of the natural environment than their non-democratic competitors. More recently, however, further changes in the socio-economic structure and political culture of capitalist consumer societies have shed doubt on these beliefs. Empirically oriented researchers as well as democratic theorists have diagnosed a *recession of democracy* (Diamond 2015; 2021), a *post-democratic turn* (Crouch 2004; Blühdorn 2013) and the rise of new, autocratic-authoritarian forms of politics (Lührmann and Lindberg 2019; Maerz et al. 2020; Blühdorn 2021) – also in the field of eco- and climate policy (Beeson 2010). Eco-sociological observers, in turn, have drawn attention to a *post-ecologist turn* (Blühdorn 2000), the *end of sustainability* (Foster 2015; Benson and Craig 2017) and the rise of a *politics of unsustainability* (Blühdorn 2007; 2011; 2013). These concepts are trying to capture substantial changes in the condition and prevailing understandings of democracy and no less significant changes in the condition of the biophysical environment and prevailing framings of *the ecological problem* and *the ecological question*. The changes which these concepts are concerned with challenge established beliefs about the democracy/sustainability relationship, and they profoundly reconfigure their interconnection.

Despite the prevailing views of this relationship, doubts about the suitability of democratic approaches to achieving environmental goals are, of course, by no means new. Already in the 1970s eco-political thinkers such as Paul Ehrlich (1971), Robert Heilbroner (1974) or William Ophuls had argued that the ecological crisis 'may require the sacrifice of equality and majority rule' and that to secure the survival of the human species 'democracy *must* give way to elite rule' (Ophuls 1977, 159). Yet, in the 1980s these *survivalist* arguments subsided and democratic approaches prevailed, not least because the new social movements were *emancipatory* movements which conceived of, and framed, environmental issues from a specifically emancipatory – rather than survivalist – point of view. For them, the democratisation and the ecologisation of modern societies were two dimensions of the same *progressive* project, inseparably connected to each other as two sides of the same coin. When in the 1980s issues of environmental protection became fully mainstreamed and increasingly institutionalised – first at the level of national governments and then at the international and global levels, too – the participation and engagement of citizens incrementally became an uncontested core principle of environmental *good governance* (Bäckstrand et al. 2010; Fischer 2017). Although many environmentalists had, early on, regarded 'standard *liberal democratic* institutions and practices', in particular, as 'ill-suited to managing the [increasingly] boundless character of world risks' (Eckersley 2017, 9; my emphasis), they were convinced that new *grass-roots*, *participatory* and *deliberative* forms of democracy will much improve the quality, legitimacy and implementation of environmental policy (Newig 2007; Blühdorn and Deflorian 2019) and, at the same time, remedy existing democratic deficits and truly democratise liberal representative democracy (Dryzek 2000).

Yet, despite all agendas of democratising democracy, the multiple sustainability crisis continued to tighten. Adding to older topics such as species decline and the depletion of finite natural resources, global warming, in particular, became an increasingly prominent issue. And leading democratic polities such as the USA, Canada and Australia consistently appeared as eco-political laggards, while market-liberal as well as right-wing populist actors invoked democratic values to legitimate explicitly anti-environmental and socially destructive agendas. Hence, the earlier eco-political confidence in democracy began to turn into disillusionment. New demands came up that environmentalists end their 'love affair with democracy' (Shearman and Smith 2008, 121). In view of the continuing accumulation of economic and political power in the hands of a small global elite, many eco-emancipatory movements and critical environmental sociologists are holding on to their critique of capitalist power-relations and their agendas of democratic empowerment. But evidence is mounting that, in a number of respects democracies are actually not well equipped for effective environmental policy making. Their fixation on the present, their short electoral cycles, their territorial boundaries or their principle of compromise are just some prominent weaknesses (Blühdorn 2013; 2020a; 2021b). Also, for their own stabilisation and reproduction, democratic polities seem to be inherently reliant on economic growth and environmental exploitation (Mitchell 2011; Pichler et al. 2020). And for the modern environmental state, dependence on democratic legitimacy, increasingly, appears to be a major obstacle to ambitious climate and sustainability policy. In fact, this dependence on democratic legitimacy has been portrayed as the *glass ceiling* to the environmental state's efforts to achieve a socio-ecological transformation (Hausknost 2020).

Perhaps unsurprisingly, therefore, academic observers note a new surge of 'interest in non-democratic approaches to environmentalism as an alternative environmental policy model' (Beeson 2010; Chen and Lees 2018, 2). The strong, autocratic state is, by some, once again ascribed the potential to 'achieve [eco-]political feats unimaginable in liberal democracy' (Wainwright and Mann 2013, 10). In fact, in the wake of the COVID-19 pandemic, this argument gained considerable prominence. Environmental activists demanded the state to address the climate- and sustainability crisis with the same determination as – some governments – tackled the COVID-pandemic. And more openly than ever, commentators pondered whether centralist and authoritarian systems such as China may, after all, be better positioned for coping with the threats and catastrophes which in the Anthropocene are, increasingly, part of the normality that contemporary societies have to confront. At the same time, the COVID-pandemic also provided further evidence of emancipatory-democratic values being appropriated by movements rallying against government restrictions devised to contain the virus and protect public health (Lütjen 2021). Compared to the changes in behaviour, lifestyles and social relations which any serious sustainability transformation would require, these restrictions were, undoubtedly, modest, and they were only temporary. Yet, the resistance they triggered in some parts of society – in the name of freedom, citizen rights and authentic democracy – and the desire to *return to normality* which was powerfully articulated by others, signalled more clearly than ever what kind of protests any serious attempt to overcome the established order of unsustainability would have to confront. Thus, with democratic values being appropriated by anti-environmental and anti-egalitarian actors; with eco-political movements such as *Extinction Rebellion* or *Fridays for Future* framing their concerns and agendas in neo-survivalist manners, and with the urgency of a socio-ecological transformation apparently necessitating autocratic-authoritarian approaches, established beliefs about the democracy/sustainability relationship have become very uncertain again.

To explore the ongoing reconfiguration of this relationship is the objective of this contribution. For this endeavour, the dual starting point is, firstly, that the notions of *sustainability* and sustainable development are just one particular framing of *the ecological problem* or *the ecological issue* that competes with other such framings, e.g. the thinking of *radical ecology* or of *degrowth*. Secondly, and related to this, I proceed from the insight that both, *sustainability* as well as *democracy* are what Gallie (1956) once called *essentially contested concepts*: The meaning of these concepts is not fixed but constantly being renegotiated – whereby the understandings of autonomy, subjectivity, identity and a good life prevailing in a particular community at a particular point in time are the crucial point of reference. Thus, these changing ideals of subjectivity, the ongoing reinterpretation of democracy and democratisation, and the continuous reframing of ecological concerns and objectives are three constitutive dimensions of this exploration of the democracy/sustainability nexus. To begin with, the focus is on the democratic dimension. Under the heading of the *dialectic of democracy* (Blühdorn 2020b), I will explore how changes in prevailing understandings of freedom, self-determination and a good life have nurtured increasingly ambivalent attitudes towards democracy, and are an important parameter in explaining the much-debated *crisis of democracy* and the *autocratic-authoritarian turn*. Section 3 addresses the ecological dimension. It investigates how changing notions of autonomy, subjectivity and identity impact on the ways in which eco-political issues are being framed and addressed – taking eco-political discourse in contemporary consumer societies not only beyond the thinking of *political ecology* (Gorz 1987; Lipietz 1995) but also beyond the paradigm of *sustainability* (Foster 2015; Benson and Craig 2017). Section 4 then explores how in capitalist consumer societies of the global North, the change in prevailing notions of freedom, self-realisation and a good life give rise to forms of democracy which are conducive to the *politics of unsustainability*. The conclusion considers the normative dilemmas which analysis in terms of post-democracy and post-sustainability implies for critical environmental sociology.

The dialectic of democracy

Today's concerns about a crisis and *recession of democracy* (Diamond 2015; 2021), a *democratic fatigue syndrome* (Appadurai 2017) and an *autocratic-authoritarian turn* (Lührmann 1989; Blühdorn 2021a) may actually be traced back over several decades. Already in the 1960s, when Almond and Verba first diagnosed what they called a *participation explosion*, they were concerned that this new emancipatory impulse may actually destabilise rather than improve liberal democracy (Almond and Verba 1963). In the mid-1970s, Huntington, Crozier, King and others raised concerns that the *democratic distemper*, energised by the value and culture change which

Inglehart shortly after conceptualised as the *silent revolution* (Inglehart 1977) might lead to *state overload* and a condition of *ungovernability* (Crozier et al. 1975). In the 1980s and 1990s there was much debate about the decline of traditional political parties and political organisations such as trade unions, and about the growing number of voters who no longer participated in electoral politics (Dalton and Wattenberg 2000; Dalton 2004; Mair 2013). Around the turn to the new millennium these debates then culminated in the diagnosis of a condition of *post-democracy* (Rancière 1999; Crouch 2004) and *post-politics* (Boggs 2000; Wilson and Swyngedouw 2014) – terms which swiftly gained popularity well beyond the academic realm. They are being used to describe a variety of phenomena and may articulate a range of concerns, normally implying a critique of some kind of deviation from established democratic norms or expectations. Indeed, these concepts may carry diagnoses and agendas to which authoritarian right-wing populists subscribe, just as much as they may be mobilised for the political narratives promoted by liberals or by egalitarian radical democrats.

The best-known account of *post-democracy* is undoubtedly the one provided by Colin Crouch (2004). Crouch suggests that in contemporary Western democracies citizens just play 'a passive, quiescent, even apathetic part, responding only to the signals given them' (Crouch 2004, 4). His understanding of post-democracy as a kind of democratic theatre disguising that, factually, 'politics and government are increasingly slipping back into the control of privileged elites' (p. 6) resembles the much older critique of *symbolic politics* (Edelman 1964). Crouch points to a number of reasons for the emergence of the post-democratic state of politics. *Inter alia*, he refers to a modernisation-induced and supposedly irreversible 'entropy of democracy' (Crouch 2004, 11f, 29). Ultimately, however, he locates the 'true causes of the problems' in 'the profit-seeking behaviour of the large corporations' which 'are destroying communities and creating instability the world over', and in 'a political class which has become cynical, amoral and cut off from scrutiny and from the public' (p. 10, 119). Constructing a clear cut opposition between, on the one hand, 'small circles of overlapping business lobbyists and a politico-economic elite' (Crouch 2016, 71) who are 'reducing' citizens 'to the role of passive, rare participants' (2004, 21) and, on the other, those 'who were cowed by the apparent superiority' (p. 107) of neoliberal ideology, but whose 'massive escalation of truly disruptive actions' (p. 123) will, at some stage, launch 'a counter-attack on the Anglo-American model' (p. 107), Crouch offers a narrative that talks to popular sentiments well beyond the post-Marxist critical left.

Sociologically, however, neither the assertion that the decline of democratic processes and institutions has been induced primarily by corrupt elites is satisfactory, nor the narrative of an egalitarian counter-attack on the prevailing order of socio-ecological exclusion and destruction. In fact, both suggestions directly contradict Crouch's own hypothesis of an *irreversible entropy* of democracy. And empirically, despite all debates about the multiple unsustainability of the established socio-economic order; despite the impressive mobilisation of movements such as *Fridays for Future* or *Black Lives Matter*, there is not much evidence of any promising eco-egalitarian 'counter-attack on the Anglo-American model'. Quite the contrary, when in 2020 and 2021 the COVID-19 pandemic, more dramatically than ever, exposed and exacerbated the weaknesses and injustice of the established socio-economic order, the governance of the pandemic was not guided by any logic of radical transformation, but by the desire to *return to normality* as swiftly as possible. Indeed, governments invested unprecedented resources into re-stabilising an economic system that is very well known to be not only unsustainable but highly destructive both socially and ecologically.

Therefore, taking a modernisation- and subject-theoretical approach, the diverse phenomena widely discussed as the *crisis of democracy* have also been conceptualised as a *post-democratic turn* (Blühdorn 2000; 2007; 2013) – a concept that facilitates a more nuanced understanding than Crouch's rather one-dimensional notion of post-democracy. It suggests that in advanced modern societies, democratic norms, as understood in the Fordist and post-Fordist era, are becoming exhausted – or at least highly ambivalent and are now perceived as a threat at least as much as a promise. Rather than putting the blame, one-dimensionally, on corrupt economic and political elites, this approach explains the new democratic ambivalence also in terms of a modernisation-induced *triple dysfunctionality* and *legitimation crisis* of democracy (Blühdorn 2020a; 2020b). Adapting and expanding the established distinction between the *systemic* performance (problem solving capacity) and the *democratic* performance (ability to deliver to specifically democratic expectations) of political systems (Fuchs 1998; Roller 2005), this new democratic ambivalence may be said to derive from (a) democracy's *systemic dysfunctionality*, i.e. its insufficient problem-solving capacities; (b) its *emancipatory dysfunctionality*, i.e. its unsuitability as a political tool for the realisation of today's understandings of autonomy and self-realisation; and (c) what might be described as *mechanical dysfunctionality*, i.e. its break down due to the corrosion of structural parts on which democratic politics vitally depends.

Of these three dimensions, the first one, i.e. the limited problem-solving capacity of democracy is best researched and the most widely debated. Already in the 1990s, reform governments set out to modernise democratic politics, seeking to increase its efficiency and effectiveness in societies which are becoming ever more complex, internationalised and innovation-oriented. The devolution of responsibilities which the state had once adopted, the depoliticisation of public policy by means of delegation to expert committees, and the streamlining of participation, consultation and decision-making processes were supposed to restore the responsiveness and quality of democratic policy making (Wood and Flinders 2014). Improved *output-legitimacy* was supposed to compensate for the reduction of traditional-style democratic *input-legitimacy* (Scharpf 1999). Yet, given the dynamic of modernisation, these strategies did little to overcome the structural problems of democracy. Whilst challenges such as social inequality, global warming, migration or demographic change are becoming ever more complex and urgent, democratic institutions retain little ability to plan, direct, regulate and coordinate societal development – least of all a socio-ecological transformation towards sustainability. The challenges of the COVID-19 pandemic powerfully illustrated the problems democratic governments have to confront.

The *emancipatory dysfunctionality* of democracy, i.e. its increasing unsuitability as a tool for goals of self-determination and self-realisation, derives from the modernisation-induced shift in prevalent understandings of freedom, subjectivity and identity. This shift may be conceptualised as a process of *second-order emancipation* (Blühdorn 2013; 2014; 2017) in which *progressive* and *competitive* individuals (Bröckling 2015; Boltanski and Chiapello 2017) liberate themselves from established emancipatory norms, ideals and assumptions which in advanced modern societies appear unduly restrictive. These include, for example, the protestant, bourgeois and (post-)Marxist assertion that the truly autonomous self can be realised only beyond – and by resisting – the *false promises* and *superficiality* of the *alienating* consumer culture (e.g. Marcuse 1972); the expectation that the fully emancipated subject will develop a consistent, principled and stable identity, thereby achieving personal and political *maturity*, or the commitment to social ties, obligations, responsibilities and solidarities which appear to stand in the way of the full realization of the individuals potentials and opportunities. The suspension of these older notions of subjectivity and identity and the related change in prevailing patterns of self-realisation have been theorized by Sennett (1999), Beck and Beck-Gernsheim (2002), Bauman (2000; 2001), Boltanski and Chiapello (2017), Reckwitz (2020) and many others. It implies, *inter alia*, that for *progressive* individuals democracy and democratisation, which had once been the most important tool for the emancipatory project, increasingly turn into a burden and obstacle: They can neither articulate nor represent the complexity and flexibility of modern individuals and their identity needs, nor can they respond to the dynamics of modern lifestyles and the reality of the competitive struggle for social opportunities. And most importantly: In a societal constellation where the new understandings of autonomy, subjectivity and identity clash, ever more openly, with biophysical limits and persistently low economic growth, the democratic principles of egalitarianism, social justice and social inclusion become a major obstacle to individual freedom and self-realisation.

Hence, from the perspective of contemporary ideals of self-realisation and a good life, egalitarian, participatory and deliberative understandings of democracy, in particular, appear increasingly dysfunctional. Emancipatory movements do, of course, continue to campaign for their respective ideals of a *more authentically democratic* and *more ecologically effective* democracy. But this does not unhinge the progressive liberation from established normative commitments and socio-ecological responsibilities, i.e. the dynamics of *second-order emancipation*. Zygmunt Bauman conceptualised this liberation as the *secession of the successful* (Bauman 2001, 50–57) which he describes as a 'declared war on the community', 'waged in the name of freeing the individual from the inertia of the mass' (Bauman 2001, 27). Whilst 'received notions of communal duty' are being 'dismissed as outmoded tradition', Bauman notes, those endowed with the required forms of capital regard 'the sky' as 'the sole limit' of their ambition (Bauman 2001, 30). Again, the COVID-19 pandemic powerfully illustrated that prevailing understandings of individual rights, freedoms and lifestyles may be suspended, if at all, only briefly and exceptionally. They are perceived as emancipatory achievements which are non-negotiable, and political attempts to restrict or renegotiate these freedoms have to confront insurmountable resistance.

The third dimension of democratic dysfunctionality, described here as *mechanical dysfunctionality*, is directly related to this transformation of prevailing understandings of autonomy, subjectivity and identity. Yet, while the previous two forms of dysfunctionality consider the usefulness of democracy as a tool for a particular purpose (problem-solving, emancipatory self-realisation), this third dimension concerns the functioning of democracy itself. This functioning depends on *material* resources which democracy depletes but does not reproduce (Pichler et al. 2020) but, at least as importantly, on non-material, *ideational* resources which it also depletes without being able to reproduce them. These include, in particular, the Enlightenment idea of the *autonomous subject*. Had it not been for this ideal, neither the emancipatory nor the democratic project would ever have evolved. And one of the fundamental assumptions underpinning both these projects was, from the very outset, that autonomy and subjectivity, liberty and self-determination, were conceived of as being restricted in multiple respects. For, Kant's famous *emergence of mankind from its self-imposed immaturity* was never supposed to imply the complete removal of all restrictions and restraints, but the achievement of *maturity* – which from Kant to the political ecologists of the 1980s always denoted a synthesis of freedom and the subordination to imperatives of reason as two equally constitutive principles of a self-determined and socially just and ecologically responsible society. These bounded notions of freedom and self-determination became democracy's normative point of reference. Indeed, democracy can only function, if the autonomy and subject-status that it is intended to deliver and guarantee are defined and limited in this way.

Yet, by its very nature, by virtue of being emancipatory, the emancipatory project persistently challenged all limitations, including those delimiting its own objectives. Untiringly, progressive movements fought for the flexibilisation of values, of established truth, of morals, of identity, of subjectivity, of nature, of reason, etc. And in the wake of this struggle, the Kantian emergence from self-imposed immaturity seamlessly merged into the disposal of the duty to *mature*, i.e., the commitment to the principles of reason and its constraints on freedom. In fact, this is what *second-order emancipation* is all about. Incrementally, emancipatory movements thus undermined the ideational foundations on which democracy rests and depleted the normative resources without which it cannot survive. By removing the boundaries of freedom; by suspending the Enlightenment notion of the *subject*, it renders democracy – liberal, egalitarian, representative, participatory or deliberative – dysfunctional in a quite literal, mechanical sense.

To a significant extent – but by no means exclusively, of course – the phenomena that have been conceptualized as a *crisis of democracy* (Crozier et al. 1975), a *recession of democracy* (Diamond 2015; 2021), the *democratic fatigue syndrome* (Appadurai 2017) or even the *hatred of democracy* (Ranciere 2006) may, therefore, be traced back to a *dialectic of emancipation* (Blühdorn 2021a) that, by hollowing out democracy's normative core and point of reference, propels a *dialectic of democracy* and causes a genuine *legitimation crisis* of democracy (Blühdorn 2020a). Incrementally, it renders democracy not only structurally inadequate for contemporary consumer societies, but also normatively questionable: From the perspective of second-order emancipation, democracy no longer delivers – and in fact *obstructs* – what contemporary individuals regard as their inalienable rights. Hence, the development of democracy can, taking up the concepts suggested by Crouch (2004), indeed, be described in terms of a *parabola* and an *irreversible entropy*. But while Crouch – contradicting his own concepts – remains confident that the emancipatory-democratic project can somehow be revived and the direction of the democratic parabola reversed, the notions of *second-order emancipation* and the *post-democratic turn* suggest – in line with empirical experience – that the democratic project, as the new social movements of the 1970s and 1980s had emphatically rearticulated it, can most probably not be resuscitated. This does not necessarily signal the *end* or *death* of democracy (Keane 2009; Bouffin de Chosal 2017), nor does it imply that the struggle for emancipation is over. As Bauman put it, it is: 'only the meaning assigned to emancipation' – and democracy – 'under past but no more present conditions that has become obsolete' (Bauman 2000: 48). Indeed, given that citizen claims for participation and expectations for better representation continue to rise, a *transformation* of democracy into a new form of appearance that reflects the notions of freedom, subjectivity and self-realisation now prevailing in contemporary consumer societies is the more likely scenario. Exactly this is what the term *dialectic of democracy* aims to capture.

Ecology beyond the transformative project

The societal value- and culture shift conceptualised here as second-order emancipation impacts on eco-political debates and agendas no less than on the project of democracy and democratisation; in fact, it is a key parameter in explaining the condition of *sustained unsustainability* (Blühdorn 2007; 2011). For an adequate understanding of this impact, it is essential to call to mind that eco-political discourse, struggles and policymaking are – contrary to common intuition and the narratives offered by eco-political activists – never primarily about *extra-societal* facts, *environmental* problems and *bio-physical* conditions or changes but, first and foremost, about *societal* perceptions of these conditions and changes, their *social framing* as problematic and about grievances about the violation of *social* norms and expectations (e.g. Luhmann 1989; Eder 1996; Latour 2004). Bio-physical conditions and changes do play a significant role, of course, but ultimately, eco-political discourses, concerns and struggles are, and have always been, primarily about the perceived violation of social norms. When environmental movements first emerged, towards the end of the nineteenth century, they were triggered by the critique of modernity, modernisation and industrialisation. This was a conservative as well as an emancipatory-progressive critique, and it related to both, perceived changes in the bio-physical environment and changes in everyday life and social relations. Conservatives were worried about the loss of tradition, of established privileges, sources of orientation and meaning, and they criticised human hubris and the belief that humans have the right and ability to unhinge, reorganise and master what they perceived as the intangible, *natural* order. Progressive, emancipatory movements, in turn, were not so much concerned about the loss of traditions – which they perceived not as *natural* but as unduly restrictive and anti-emancipatory – but they shared the concern about the loss of meaning and the perception of dis-embedding. Furthermore, they also shared the critique of industrialisation and human hubris. For them, the main critique was, that the logic and rationality of capitalism, i.e. a logic of exploitation, inequality and domination was being installed in the place of tradition. Put differently, the replacement of tradition was not emancipatory and progressive, but brought just another form of domination, alienation and control. But despite these differences, both the conservative and the progressive critique – this is the key point here – were underpinned by *cultural* norms and ideals about the good, natural and moral (Dominick 1992; Dobson and Eckersley 2006). From the very beginning, such *cultural* norms have always been the crucial driver of *environmental* movements (Guha 2000; Radkau 2014). Hence such norms, their ongoing change and their competitive struggle for hegemony are a centrally important parameter in the investigation of environmental movements and eco-political discourse.

When in the 1970s – long before the concept of *sustainability* became hegemonic – environmental movements rapidly gained mass support, this was partially, of course, a response to the environmental side-effects of rapid industrial development and the consumer economy becoming increasingly visible. At least as importantly, however, the tide of these movements signalled the rise of what Inglehart first called *post-materialist* values and later values of *self-expression* and *self-experience* (Inglehart 1977; 1997). Increasingly educated, informed, articulate and self-confident citizens placed ever more emphasis on self-determination and *quality of life* issues, including matters of identity, health and environmental pollution. At the time, public authorities addressed environmental concerns primarily by implementing *add-on* or *end-of-pipe* solutions. Such technological fixes contributed a lot to cleaning the emissions from industry chimneys or waste water pipes. Yet, they left the underlying causes of environmental problems in place, i.e. they were unable to address, for example, that the capitalist economy is inherently based on the principle of continuous growth, on the exploitation of resources and the externalisation of social and ecological costs. And they also failed to address the emancipatory claims of the citizenry, who now asserted their right to self-determination and autonomous self-realisation, and who self-confidently insisted on their political competence and maturity.

Reflecting and articulating these more encompassing concerns, a different, emancipatory-progressive strand of eco-political thinking gained in significance that was much more ambitious than technology-oriented environmental protection. In the course of the 1970s, it gradually evolved into what some observers later conceptualised as a political ideology in its own right – *ecologism* (Dobson 1990). *Ecologist* thinking shifted the emancipatory agenda and the claim to autonomy – also for nature – centre stage. It entailed a radical critique of modern society and industrial capitalism. It drew attention to the re-emergence of mass-unemployment in the industrialised North, the persistence of deep poverty in the global South, capitalist power relations and the ways in which the consumer culture systematically alienated modern citizens, obstructed their true self-realisation and enslaved nature, too (Marcuse 1972; Gorz 1987). In other words, *ecologist* thinking raised a range of concerns which the technology-oriented *environmental protection* programmes which some progressive national governments were implementing at the time did not address. It diagnosed a profound crisis not only in ecological terms, but in the social, economic and cultural dimensions of modern societies, too. Radically challenging the established socio-economic as well as political order of the industrialised countries, including their relationship to the developing world, ecologists demanded a comprehensive transformation of the established economic structures, the political system, personal lifestyles as well as cultural values and notions of identity. In fact, ecologism envisaged a radically different society in which the tensions between economic, social and ecological concerns would be fully overcome and established socio-ecological relations fundamentally reorganised. In this sense, ecologism was profoundly *political* and is, therefore, often also referred to as *political ecology* (Gorz 1987; Lipietz 1995).

Yet, although its demands for comprehensive socio-cultural change – and in particular its emancipatory agenda of self-determination and democratic empowerment – echoed many concerns of the new educated and politically articulate middle classes, in particular, radical ecologism also triggered substantial resistance: By the less privileged parts of society, it was perceived as an elite agenda and a threat to their own aspirations for further development, social equality and inclusion. And even to many privileged and environmentally aware citizens, the anti-capitalist and anti-consumerist critique of political ecology appeared as a threat to their achievements and the pleasures and conveniences of their established lifestyles. Unsurprisingly, therefore, the ecologist belief that the protection of the natural environment, the realisation of human autonomy and the achievement of social and ecological peace necessarily demand that the capitalist consumer economy be abandoned, triggered deep ideological divisions and gave rise to an eco-political deadlock in which ecological and economic interests seemed mutually incompatible.

In the second half of the 1980s, a further reframing of environmental concerns and policy approaches appeared as the magic solution to this eco-political impasse. The new paradigm of *sustainability* and *sustainable development*, first introduced by the UN Brundtland Report (WCED 1987) and then fully mainstreamed at the UN's 1992 Earth Summit in Rio, emerged as a new eco-political master-frame that soon became hegemonic in mainstream institutionalised eco-policy. It recognised the concerns articulated, in particular, by the younger, materially secure cohorts in Western, post-industrial societies. But at the same time, it also accommodated the interests of those – in the industrialised countries as well as the global South – who were desperately hoping for further economic development and the improvement of their material situation. The Brundtland Report explicitly acknowledged the problems of international inequality and poverty in the global South, as well as the unsuitability of the industrial countries' model of development as an example to be emulated in other parts of the world. It emphasised that the protection of the natural environment would, henceforth, have to be a priority concern in all policymaking and confirmed that there are bio-physical limits which must be respected. In line with *ecologist* thinking, the report also stipulated that the industrial countries would need to undergo a structural transformation so as to make sure that their development remains within 'the bounds of the ecologically possible' (WCED 1987, 55). At the same time, however, the Brundtland Commission also suggested that there is no need for any radical departure from the established trajectory of modernisation, for the abandonment of consumer capitalism or for 'the cessation of economic growth' (p. 40). Quite the contrary, the report explicitly underlined that the international economy 'must speed up world growth' (p. 89). The development of new resource-efficient technologies, improved management and monitoring schemes, and the internalisation of social and ecological costs which had so far been discounted were presented as suitable means allowing to hold on to the capitalist economy and the principle of economic growth, but still 'avert economic, social and environmental catastrophes' (ibid.). Thus, the paradigm of sustainability bridged the abyss between ecology and economy. Yet, in the sense that it fully relied on technological innovation and market instruments; in as much as it dismissed the agenda of anti-capitalism and reframed emancipation as a project to be achieved *within* rather than *beyond* the established socio-economic order, the sustainability frame was clearly *post-ecologist* (Blühdorn 2000; 2011).

From today's perspective, the sustainability paradigm itself seems exhausted (Blühdorn and Welsh 2007). Already the UN Rio+10 Summit in Johannesburg (2002) had signalled a cooling of the optimism and dynamic of the early 1990s, yet, by the end of the decade, the notion of sustainability had been appropriated by a diverse range of actors for an equally diverse range of purposes and had visibly lost its ability to energise and guide an integrated global transformation (Blühdorn 2011; 2021b). At the time, the collapse of the American investment bank Leeman Brothers and the subsequent crisis of the global banking and financial system triggered a global economic downturn. Governments imposed draconian austerity programmes on their countries, whilst sustainability and sustainable development had degenerated into fuzzy concepts unable to guide any structural transformation of liberal consumer capitalism or give orientation for a socially and ecologically benign development of the Global South. At the Rio+20 Summit of 2012, again held in Rio de Janeiro, national leaders signalled 'little political appetite for anything but very modest change' (Linnér and Selin 2013, 983). Yet, global warming, resource extraction, biodiversity loss and social inequality continued to worsen in an essentially unabated manner, which put 'both sustainability governance and the sustainable development concept under growing pressure' (Bulkeley et al. 2013, 958). 'Mainstreamed as sustainability or sustainable development', John Foster noted, 'environmentalism has failed to reduce, even remotely adequately, the impact of humans on the biosphere' (Foster 2015, 2). Hence, the paradigm that had once been invested with so much hope was increasingly regarded as 'an irretrievably misconceived framework and a delusive policy goal' (Foster 2015, Preface). A world characterised by unprecedented 'complexity, radical uncertainty and [a] lack of stationarity', Benson and Craig argued, 'must face the impossibility of defining – let alone pursuing – a goal of *sustainability*' (Benson and Craig 2014, 777). With the notion of sustainability being little more today than an *empty signifier* in the sense of Laclau (Brown 2016), it 'isn't actually part of the solution' to the socio-ecological crisis, but a 'deeply embedded part of the problem' (Foster 2015, 35).

In public discourse, the concept of sustainability, nevertheless, remains very prominent, not least because in 2015, the United Nations undertook a new attempt to update and revitalise its sustainability agenda. The document *Transforming our world: The 2030 Agenda for Sustainable Development* (2015) restated the commitment to achieving a genuine transformation rather than just marginal reforms, and to achieving it at a global scale. Yet, the prospects for this agenda to be implemented do not look favourable. Not only does the logic of capitalism, i.e. the logic of growth, inequality, exploitation, etc, remain unchanged, but the prevailing notions of subjectivity, autonomy and a good life seem to have largely aligned with this logic (Bauman 2000; Boltanski and Chiapello 2017; Reckwitz 2020), and in the affluent consumer societies of the global North, an order and politics of *unsustainability* (Blühdorn 2007; 2011; 2017; Blühdorn and Deflorian 2019) now actually seems more entrenched than ever before: Empirical data on the state of biophysical environment and the impact of human civilisation on eco-systems are more abundant and publicly accessible than ever before. Scientific knowledge on anthropogenic environmental and climate change is more comprehensive and detailed than it has ever been. Still, the established economic order and prevailing understandings of autonomy and self-realisation seem non-negotiable. Despite all declaratory commitment to ecological goals and the urgency of a socio-ecological transformation, the resolve to sustain established values, lifestyles and visions of progress, success and a good life seem adamant.

In fact, the COVID-19 pandemic may have delivered the final blow to the project of an international sustainability transformation: It has triggered unprecedented new investment in the further stabilisation of a socio-economic order of growth, resource exploitation and consumerism. During the COVID-19 pandemic, the public desire to *return to normality*, the adamant determination to re-stabilise the established order, *whatever the cost*, provided clear evidence of the extent to which the culture- and value shift conceptualised above, that is, the ongoing *modernisation* of prevailing understandings of autonomy, subjectivity and identity, has eroded the political resonance and transformative potential of the eco-emancipatory imperatives political ecologists had once articulated. In the wake of the pandemic, *resilience* seems to be firmly establishing itself as the new eco-political lead concept and master-frame (Benson and Craig 2017). Essentially, it suspends the emancipatory and transformative project and focuses, instead, on the individual and societal ability to absorb and cope with the social and environmental catastrophes which in the new geological epoch, the Anthropocene, are, increasingly, perceived as normal and unavoidable. Whilst *post-ecologism* and *post-sustainability* are, more than anything, negative concepts which signal what today's eco-politics – in terms of its values and visions – has left behind, the notion of *resilience* may capture in more positive terms what the eco-politics beyond the frames of ecologism and sustainability is aiming for.

Democratised exclusion and authoritarian governance

This brief and deliberately simplifying sketch of how changes in the prevailing notions of autonomy, identity and a good life have impacted on perceptions and understandings of both democracy and sustainability offers a nuanced explanation for the *postdemocratic turn* and the strikingly stable condition of *sustained unsustainability*. It sheds light on the rise of a *politics of post-* or *unsustainability*. Indeed, the value and culture shift underpinning the phenomena of post-democracy and post-sustainability is no less significant than the *silent revolution* that Inglehart had diagnosed when the societies to which this cultural shift pertains were moving from their industrial to the post-industrial stage of development (Inglehart 1977; 1997). In a curious manner, this further silent revolution delivers exactly what sustainable development and the proponents of *ecological modernization* approaches (Mol and Sonnenfeld 2000) had always aimed for and promised: *modern societies are modernizing themselves out of their sustainability crisis* (Mol 1995, 42). Yet, going beyond what ecological modernization theorists had proposed, they are doing so not only by developing techno-managerial solutions to supposedly objective environmental problems but, no less importantly, by adapting their normative yardstick und societal modes of problem perception (framing). They are redefining what is regarded as categorically necessary and shifting the boundaries of the socially palatable, so as to accommodate the unavoidable implications of the particular ways in which contemporary individuals are interpreting their essential needs, inalienable rights and non-negotiable freedoms. Indeed, this adaptation of norms and perceptions may be understood as an indispensable strategy of resilience; for, these supposedly inalienable rights and non-negotiable freedoms are based on the premise that those providing the goods and services required for their fulfilment must not claim – or be granted – the same rights and freedoms. Put differently, the realisation and maintenance of the freedom, rights, lifestyles and patterns of self-realisation which majorities in the affluent societies of the Global North are determined to sustain – or to which they aspire – explicitly demand that these rights and freedoms must not be generalised. They are inherently based on the principle of exclusion. The enjoyment of these rights, freedoms and lifestyles by some is being paid for by the exclusion of others – within national societies, and internationally. And in as much as this principle of exclusion is incompatible with the declared commitment to equality, justice, democracy, the rule of law, universal human rights, and so forth, this *imperial mode of living* (Brand and Wissen 2018) in modern *externalisation societies* (Lessenich 2019) necessitates not only a 'new politics of exclusion' (Appadurai 2017, 8), but new strategies of resilience, too, which render the unavoidable implications of the latter more palatable.

In fact, as economic growth rates are set to remain low, *planetary boundaries* (Rockström et al. 2009; Biermann 2012) are becoming ever more visible, and the social implications of global warming and bio-physical system collapse are increasingly tangible, this politics of exclusion becomes ever more urgent, and it has to be ever more effective. Reversely, a re-invigoration of the ecologist-transformative agenda and egalitarian democracy seems ever less likely. Although environmental activists continue to campaign for a *degrowth* society, against endemic injustice and racism and for a *new social contract for sustainability* (WBGU 2011), the reality of eco-politics in modern consumer societies is shaped – as the governance of the COVID-19 pandemic powerfully illustrated – by a stronger than ever *social contract for sustaining the unsustainable*. Indeed, rather than reinforcing the transformative impetus which many believed the *Fridays for Future* movement had delivered, the COVID-19 pandemic dramatically reinforced social inequalities, the *secession of the successful* (Bauman 2001, 50–57) and their retreat into exclusive escape properties. In order to re-stabilise and sustain the established order, governments have accumulated unprecedented public debt which will weigh heavily for decades. And the *competition of systems* between the US and China that US President Joe Biden officially declared seems set to further cement the politics of unsustainability.

This politics of unsustainability does not preclude, for example, efforts to develop innovative, resource-saving technologies, to reduce CO_2 emissions, or to stimulate *green growth* and *responsible consumption*. But it precludes that the underlying logic of inequality, exploitation, acceleration, expansion and growth and the underlying socio-ecological power-relations are unhinged. It is a politics of unsustainability exactly in the sense that this underlying logic is being defended and sustained at any cost. And one of its distinctive features is that this politics of *sustaining the unsustainable* (Blühdorn 2007; 2013; 2014) still has to take the form of a democratic politics. For, despite the multiple dysfunctionality and the legitimation crisis of democracy; despite the proliferation of *anti-democratic feelings* (Rancière 2006) and *anti-political sentiments* (Mair 2006); and although contemporary consumer societies show clear symptoms of 'democratic fatigue syndrome' (van Reybrouck 2016; Appadurai 2017), citizens in these societies are making ever more vociferous claims for democratic participation, representation, self-determination and self-realisation. Hence, although this may appear as a contradiction in terms, the new politics of exclusion must be organised in a *democratic* way. Put differently, democracy has to evolve in a way that accommodates this requirement of exclusion. And there is plenty of evidence that it is actually doing so. This is what the seemingly self-contradictory terms *democratised exclusion* and *authoritarian governance* aim to capture.

This transformation of democracy is facilitated, first, by the fact that democracy has always been highly adaptable and that, second, it has always been not only 'a mechanism of inclusion but also of exclusion' (Krastev 2017, 74; Mouffe 2018). It does not come as a surprise, therefore, that it is explicitly in the name of the people's democratic self-determination and desire to *take back control*, that right-wing populist movements and governments – witness the Trump-government in the US or the Johnson-government in the UK – back out of international agreements and structures of governance, challenge what has been achieved in terms of a societal consensus that a socio-ecological transformation is necessary and urgent, relax existing environmental legislation, cut welfare provision for those deemed *undeserving*, pursue illiberal and xenophobic agendas, and vow to always put their respective country first. In fact, popular pressure for more direct democracy is an important driver of the transformation of 'democracy as a regime favouring the emancipation of minorities' into 'democracy as a political regime that secures the power of majorities' (Krastev 2017, 69), in particular, when these majorities are experiencing some kind of threat. In the affluent societies of the global North which conceive of themselves as the most *advanced* and *progressive*, these 'threatened majorities' (Krastev 2017: 67) are a most powerful and agenda-setting political force (Inglehart und Norris 2017; Lilla 2017; Norris and Inglehart 2019). They are not just the often-cited *losers of modernisation* (Blühdorn and Butzlaff 2019), nor is their political agenda well described as 'a reversal' of the 'progressive development' of earlier decades (Geiselberger 2017; Krastev 2017; Inglehart and Norris 2017; Norris and Inglehart 2019). Instead, this threatened majority is, as explicated below, a broad, inclusive – and not necessarily openly declared, or even conscious – discursive alliance of diverse societal groups all sharing the concern that in view of low economic growth rates, clearly visible bio-physical limits, ever increasing global competition for resources and steadily rising social inequality, nationally and internationally, their particular understandings of freedom, self-determination and self-realisation, and the lifestyles and notions of fulfilment which they entertain, or are aspiring to, are under severe threat. Yet, these majorities are determined to defend the achievements and promises of *their* emancipatory project. For exactly this reason they are neither well described in terms of a *backlash* (Inglehart), *regression* (Geiselberger) or *retrotopia* (Bauman), nor are they well understood as a *counter*-movement launching an 'attack on the Anglo-American model' of market-liberalism (Crouch 2004: 107).

The empowerment of this threatened majority is a key tool in the new politics of unsustainability. It effectively obstructs political intervention into what these majorities regard as their private sphere, the regulation of what they see as their personal choices, and the restriction of the rights and freedoms which they consider as non-negotiable. Furthermore, the empowerment of this threatened majority organises the democratic definition and implementation of new lines of demarcation and exclusion both within the respective polities and beyond. Its objective is to collectively – and democratically – offload established egalitarian obligations and ecological commitments so as to secure the continuation of the established socio-economic order and socio-ecological relations. This implies, not least, the *democratic* suspension of *universal* human rights and the *inviolable* dignity of (wo)man which are being subordinated – as prominently evidenced, for example, by the EU's migration policy or its economic policy towards China – to the defence of established privileges, freedoms and lifestyles.

Thus, contemporary consumer societies are witnessing *the people's inclusion into the politics of exclusion*. This *democratisation of exclusion* executes the (ever less) tacit social contract for unsustainability. It co-opts even societal groups into the politics of exclusion, and instrumentalises them for the *governance* of unsustainability (Blühdorn 2013; 2014), who are themselves unlikely to benefit from it, but who are required so as to endow this politics with democratic legitimacy (Davies 2011; Boezeman et al. 2014). For this governance of unsustainability, the flexible, decentralised, participative and consensus-oriented practices of stakeholder governance, which are increasingly replacing centralised, interventionist environmental government, are proving particularly helpful (Blühdorn and Deflorian 2019). But the threatened majority has also 'turned the state into its own private possession' (Krastev 2017, 74), instrumentalising it for the provision and enforcement of the institutional framework required for the politics of exclusion. Unsurprisingly, therefore, the democratically legitimated environmental state is structurally unable to organise any socio-ecological transformation of capitalist consumer societies that really suspends their underlying logic of unsustainability (Hausknost 2020).

At the same time, the interplay of: (a) the ongoing reframing of notions of autonomy and emancipation; (b) the ever-widening abyss between claims to autonomy and self-realisation, on the one hand, and practical experiences of increasing disempowerment, inequality and exclusion, on the other; and (c) the increasing visibility of planetary boundaries which render prevailing notions of autonomy and emancipation ever more directly dependent on rising levels of social inequality and exclusion not only triggers – as outlined above – a dramatic erosion of confidence in democratic procedures and institutions (e.g. Mair 2013; Blühdorn, 2020a; 2020b), but it gives rise to explicit demands for autocratic-authoritarian rule. It triggers a dynamic of autocratisation that is propelled by rather diverse actors and agendas:

- The much-cited *losers of modernisation* who in search of orientation and protection turn towards illiberal, anti-pluralist and authoritarian leaders.
- The *politically disillusioned* who are deeply disappointed by established politics, experience a profound crisis of political representation, no longer believe that political institutions may be reformed and have adopted a mode of permanent rebellion against the established order and its rationality.
- Those looking for narratives helping them to make sense of and navigate conditions of high complexity, and allowing them to *take back control* and reinstate a sense of self-efficacy.
- Those entertaining understandings of autonomy, self-determination and a good life whose viability demands effective policies of social exclusion.
- Those who believe that the societal issues that need to be dealt with swiftly and efficiently – ranging from the containment of COVID-19 to the new system-competition with China – are best managed by non-majoritarian modes of expert governance.
- Those who in view of the *liberation from maturity* visible in virtually all sectors of society have lost confidence in the political competence and responsibility of major parts of the citizenry (e.g. Brennan, 2016; van Reybrouck, 2016).
- Those demanding rigorous government action to enforce restrictions which may stave off ecological collapse, catastrophic global warming and the extinction of the human species.

This enumeration is not meant to be exhaustive, and the diverse motivations for autocratic-authoritarian inclinations distinguished here empirically blend in a variety of ways, giving rise to heterogeneous ideological orientations and forms of political practice. These diverse actors may well conceive of each other as political enemies – the radical opposition between American Trumpism and the *Fridays for Future* movement being a prominent case in point. Indeed, the deepening division and polarisation within national societies, transnational communities such as the EU and the global community seem to be a distinctive feature of the new socio-political constellation. Yet, collectively – even if against each other – these diverse actors propel the autocratic-authoritarian turn and are in this sense partners on the road towards new forms of *authoritarian governance* (Swyngedouw 2000; Blühdorn 2021a). In the politics of unsustainability, this authoritarian governance is no less important a parameter than the democratisation of exclusion. Both appear to be contradictions in term, and in exactly that they both signal the emergence of something fundamentally new beyond the binary distinction between democracy and authoritarianism.

Conclusion

Thus, in the wake of the post-democratic turn and the rise of the politics of unsustainability – both of which have been induced, not least, by the value- and culture shift conceptualised here as a *second silent revolution* and as *second-order emancipation* – the relationship between democracy and ecology has profoundly changed. Democracy and democratisation which the emancipatory new social movements had once regarded as the most important tool for forcing environmental issues onto the political agenda and for empowering ecological reason and responsibility vis-à-vis the destructive logic of the capitalist economy, modern technology and the bureaucratic state, seem to be metamorphosing into a tool for organising and legitimating the politics of unsustainability, of exclusion and of defending this very logic they were supposed to unhinge. This metamorphosis does not come entirely unexpected, of course: For most of its history, democracy has had a rather negative reputation. Concerned that popular demands for freedom would invariably become excessive, Plato had famously described democracy as the precursor to tyranny (Plato 1955). When Almond and Verba published their seminal work on the *civic culture* (1963), they still highlighted that what they called the *participatory explosion* would be beneficial to modern societies, only if the new participatory impulses are effectively tamed and moderated. At the threshold to post-industrial society, Inglehart and many others then believed, economic development and the expansion of mass education had finally given citizens the competence and self-confidence to take societal affairs into their own hands – and achieve political maturity. Social movements now portrayed themselves as the avantgarde of a truly democratic and ecologically responsible society. They promised to give a voice to concerns – social and ecological – which had so far been muted and secure equal recognition for subjectivities which had so far been oppressed. Civil society was now widely regarded as the subject and voice of authentic reason and responsibility; and, accordingly, the empowerment of civil society appeared as the most – indeed, the only – promising strategy in the struggle against the immoral, instrumental and destructive interests of elites, and the alienating logic of *the system* comprising the capitalist economy, industrial technology and the bureaucratic state.

In contemporary societies, however, a range of political actors are, for a variety of reasons, increasingly ambivalent about democratic procedures and the prospect of a further democratisation of institutions and policy making. Processes of *second-order emancipation* seem to be effecting a *liberation from maturity* across different sections of the ideological spectrum, giving rise to an increasingly *uncivil society*. As popular movements are appropriating democratic values to legitimise agendas which are explicitly directed against goals of social justice and ecological integrity, and which are *emancipatory* in a radically redefined, exclusive sense, civil society can no longer easily be regarded as the avantgarde prefiguring a socially just and ecologically benign society, nor do democracy and democratisation necessarily appear as a promising tool for achieving it.

For critical environmental sociology, the very idea that emancipation and democratisation might – in the wake of a dialectic transformation – themselves metamorphose into drivers for a politics of unsustainability is extremely challenging. For, not only is there no reason to assume that non-democratic approaches might be more effective in protecting the bio-physical environment, let alone for achieving the emancipatory objectives which *progressive* movements, in the established sense, have sought to promote; but the *dialectic of emancipation* also destroys the normative foundations of the critical project at large (Blühdorn 2021a). Critical environmental sociology has always had a dual commitment: It wanted to provide a societal diagnosis and analysis, and it wanted to change modern societies towards the full realisation of progressive, emancipatory ideals. Yet, if in its diagnostic dimension it finds evidence of, and theorises, what has been described here as a dialectic of emancipation and democracy, critical sociology undermines its own transformative agenda. Still, refusing to diagnose and theorise these phenomena would amount to a 'refusal to see' (Foster 2015, 7) and only reproduce the 'pervasive culture of denial' (Foster 2015, 35) that social movements and critical sociologists have always campaigned against. This is a dilemma which cannot easily be resolved.

In a sense, calling to mind that the key concepts investigated here – ecology, emancipation, democracy – are all *essentially contested concepts* which cannot be monopolised for any particular strands of thinking; and stating unequivocally that the terms *second-order emancipation* and *dysfunctionality of democracy*, in particular, neither imply any normative approval of the value and culture shift they conceptualise, nor describe any end point of the struggle between ever-evolving notions of freedom, justice and self-determination may render the outcomes of the above analysis more palatable. At this particular point in time, the objective of this chapter has been to shed light on the reconfiguration of the democracy/ecology nexus as it currently appears. In doing so, the particular focus has been on the understandings of freedom, self-determination and self-realisation which, according to Inglehart, Bauman, Reckwitz and many others, have become prevalent in contemporary consumer societies. Undeniably, this analysis raises fundamental problems and leaves critical environmental sociology with fundamental dilemmas. Yet, for critical environmental sociology analysis in terms of the dialectic of democracy, the dialectic of emancipation and the metamorphosis of the democracy/sustainability relationship might also bear considerable potentials: Not only does it help critical sociology to keep its diagnostic commitment but, more importantly, a more differentiated understanding the politics of unsustainability is, undoubtedly, a necessary precondition for any promising attempt at overcoming it.

References

Almond, G. and Verba, S., 1963. *The Civic Culture. Political Attitudes and Democracy in Five Nations*. Princeton, NJ: Princeton University Press.

Appadurai, A., 2017. Democracy Fatigue. In H. Geiselberger, ed. *The Great Regression*. Cambridge, UK; Malden, MA: Polity Press, 1–12.

Bäckstrand, K., Jamil Khan, J. and Kronsell, A., 2010. *Environmental Politics and Deliberative Democracy. Examining the Promise of New Modes of Governance*. Cheltenham: Edward Elgar.

Bauman, Z., 2000. *Liquid Modernity*. Cambridge: Polity.

Bauman, Z., 2001. *Community. Seeking Safety in an Insecure World*. Cambridge: Polity.

Beck, U. and Beck-Gernsheim, E., 2002. *Individualization: Institutionalized Individualism and its Social and Political Consequences*. London: Sage.

Beeson, M., 2010. The coming of environmental authoritarianism. *Environmental Politics*, 19 (2), 276–294.

Benson, M.H. and Craig, R.K., 2014. The end of sustainability. *Society & Natural Resources*, 27 (7), 777–782.

Benson, M.H. and Craig, R.K., 2017. *The End of Sustainability. Resilience and the Future of Environmental Governance in the Anthropocene*. Lawrence, Kansas: University Press of Kansas.

Biermann, F., 2012. Planetary boundaries and earth system governance: exploring the links. *Ecological Economics*, 81, 4–9.

Blühdorn, I., 2000. *Post-ecologist Politics. Social Theory and the Abdication of the Ecologist Paradigm*. London: Routledge.

Blühdorn, I., 2007. Sustaining the unsustainable: symbolic politics and the politics of simulation. *Environmental Politics*, 16 (2), 251–275.

Blühdorn, I., 2011. The politics of unsustainability: COP15, post-ecologism and the ecological paradox. *Organization & Environment*, 24 (1), 34–53.

Blühdorn, I., 2013. The governance of unsustainability: ecology and democracy after the post-democratic turn. *Environmental Politics*, 22 (1), 16–36.

Blühdorn, I., 2014. Post-ecologist Governmentality: Post-democracy, Post-politics and the Politics of Unsustainability. In J. Wilson and E. Swyngedouw, eds. *The Post-Political and Its Discontents. Spaces of Depoliticisation, Spectres of Radical Politics*. Edinburgh: Edinburgh University Press, 146–166.

Blühdorn, I., 2017. Post-capitalism, post-growth, post-consumerism? Eco-political hopes beyond sustainability. *Global Discourse*, 7 (1), 42–61.

Blühdorn, I., 2020a. The legitimation crisis of democracy: emancipatory politics, the environmental state and the glass ceiling to socio-ecological transformation. *Environmental Politics*, 29 (1), 38–57.

Blühdorn, I., 2020b. The dialectic of democracy: modernization, emancipation and the great regression. *Democratization*, 27 (3), 389–407.

Blühdorn, I., 2021a. Liberation and limitation: the emancipatory project and the grammar of the autocratic-authoritarian turn. *European Journal of Social Theory*.

Blühdorn, I., 2021b. Sustainability. Buying time for consumer capitalism and European Modernity. In Asara, V., Leonardi, E., Pellizzoni, L. (eds) *Elgar Handbook of Critical Environmental Politics*. Cheltenham: Elgar (forthcoming).

Blühdorn, I. and Butzlaff F., 2019. Rethinking populism: peak democracy, liquid identity and the performance of sovereignty. *European Journal of Social Theory*, 22 (2), 191–211.

Blühdorn, I. and Deflorian M., 2019. The collaborative management of sustained unsustainability: on the performance of participatory forms of environmental governance. *Sustainability*, 11 (4), 1189.

Blühdorn, I. and Deflorian M., 2021. Politicisation beyond post-politics: new social activism and the reconfiguration of political discourse. *Social Movement Studies*, 20 (3), 259–275.

Blühdorn, I. and Welsh I., 2007. Eco-politics beyond the paradigm of sustainability: a conceptual framework and research agenda. *Environmental Politics*, 16 (2), 185–205.

Boezeman, D., Vink, M., Leroy, P. and Halffman W., 2014. Participation under a spell of instrumentalization? Reflections on action research in an entrenched climate adaptation policy process. *Critical Policy Studies*, 8 (4), 407–426.

Boltanski, L. and Chiapello, È., 2017. *The New Spirit of Capitalism*. London: Verso.

Boggs, C., 2000. *The End of Politics. Corporate Power and the Decline of the Public Sphere*. New York and London: The Guilford Press.

Bouffin de Chosal, C., 2017. *The End of Democracy*. Arcadia: Tumblar House.

Brand, U. and Wissen M., 2018. *Limits to Capitalist Nature. Theorizing and Overcoming the Imperial Mode of Living*. London and New York: Rowman & Littlefield.

Brennan, J., 2016. *Against Democracy*. Princeton, NJ: Princeton University Press.

Bröckling, U., 2015. *The Entrepreneurial Self. Fabricating a New Type of Subject*. London: Sage.

Brown, T., 2016. Sustainability as empty signifier: its rise, fall, and radical potential. *Antipode*, 48 (1), 115–133.

Bulkeley, H., Jordan, A., Perkins, P. and Selin, H., 2013. Governing sustainability: Rio+20 and the road beyond. *Environment and Planning C: Government and Policy*, 31 (6), 958–970.

Chen, G.C. and Lees, C., 2018. The new, green, urbanization in China: between authoritarian environmentalism and decentralization. *Chinese Political Science Review*, 3 (2), 212–231.

Crouch, C., 2004. *Post-democracy*. Cambridge: Polity.

Crouch, C., 2016. The march towards post-democracy: ten years on. *The Political Quarterly*, 87 (1), 71–75.

Crozier, M., Huntington, S.P. and Watanuki, J., 1975. *The Crisis of Democracy: Report on the Governability of Democracies to the Trilateral Commission*. New York: New York University Press.

Dalton, R.J., 2004. *Democratic Challenges – Democratic Choices. The Erosion of Political Support in Advanced Industrial Democracies*. Oxford: Oxford University Press.

Dalton, R.J. and Wattenberg, M.P., 2000. *Parties without Partisans. Political Change in Advanced Industrial Democracies*. Oxford: Oxford University Press.

Davies, J., 2011. *Challenging Governance Theory. From Networks to Hegemony*. Bristol: Policy Press.

Diamond, L., 2015. Facing up to the democratic recession. *Journal of Democracy*, 26 (1), 141–155.

Diamond, L., 2021. Democratic regression in comparative perspective: scope, methods, and causes. *Democratization*, 28 (1), 22–42.

Dobson, A., 1990. *Green Political Thought*. London and New York: Routledge.

Dobson, A. and R. Eckersley, eds., 2006. *Political Theory and the Ecological Challenge*. Cambridge: Cambridge University Press.

Dominick, R.H., 1992. *The Environmental Movement in Germany: Prophets & Pioneers 1871–1971*. Bloomington, IN: Indiana University Press.

Dryzek, J., 2000. *Deliberative Democracy and Beyond. Liberals, Critics, Contestations*. Oxford: Oxford University Press.

Eckersley, R., 2017. Geopolitan DEMOCRACY in the Anthropocene. *Political Studies*, 65 (4), 983–999.

Edelman, M., 1964. *The Symbolic Uses of Politics*. Champaign: University of Illinois Press.

Eder, K., 1996. *The Social Construction of Nature*. London: Sage.

Ehrlich, P., 1971. *The Population Bomb*. Cutchogue; NY: Buccaneer Books.

Fischer, F., 2017. *Climate Crisis and the Democratic Prospect. Participatory Governance in Sustainable Communities*. Oxford: Oxford University Press.

Foster, J., 2015. *After Sustainability. Denial, Hope, Retrieval*. London: Routledge.

Fuchs, D., 1998. Kriterien demokratischer Performanz in Liberalen Demokratien. In M.T. Greven, ed. *Demokratie – eine Kultur des Westens?* Bamberg, Opladen: Leske + Budrich, 151–179.

Gallie, W.B., 1956. Essentially contested concepts. *Proceedings of the Aristotelian Society*, 56, 167–198.

Geiselberger, H., 2017. *The Great Regression*. Cambridge: Polity Press.

Gorz, A., 1987. *Ecology as Politics*. London: Pluto Press.

Guha, R., 2000. *Environmentalism: a Global History*. New York: Longman.

Hausknost, D., 2020. The environmental state and the glass ceiling of transformation. *Environmental Politics*, 29, 17–37.

Heilbroner, R.L., 1974. *An Inquiry into the Human Prospect*. New York: W.W. Norton & Co.

Inglehart, R., 1977. *The Silent Revolution: Changing Values and Political Styles among Western Publics*. Princeton, NJ: Princeton University Press.

Inglehart, R., 1997. *Modernization and Postmodernization: Cultural, Economic, and Political Change in 43 Societies*. Princeton, NJ: Princeton University Press.

Inglehart, R. and Norris, P., 2017. Trump and the populist authoritarian parties: the silent revolution in reverse. *Perspectives on Politics*, 15 (2), 443–454.

Krastev, I., 2017. Majoritarian Futures. In H. Geiselberger, ed. *The Great Regression*. Cambridge: Polity, 65–77.

Keane, J., 2009. *The Life and Death of Democracy*. London: Pocket Books.

Latour, B., 2004. Why has critique run out of steam? From matters of fact to matters of concern. *Critical Inquiry*, 30 (2), 225–248.

Lessenich, S., 2019. *Living Well at Others' expense. The Hidden Cost of Western Prosperity*. Chichester: Wiley.

Lilla, M., 2017. *The Once and Future Liberal: After Identity Politics*. New York: Harper Collins.

Linnér, B.-O. and Selin, H., 2013. The United Nations Conference on Sustainable Development: forty years in the making. *Environment and Planning C: Government and Policy*, 31 (6), 971–987.

Lipietz, A., 1995. *Green hopes. The Future of Political Ecology*. Cambridge: Polity.

Lühmann, N., 1989. *Ecological Communication*. Cambridge: Polity.

Lütjen, T., 2021. The anti-authoritarian revolt: right-wing populism as self-empowerment? *European Journal of Social Theory* (forthcoming).

Lührmann, A. and Lindberg, S.I., 2019. A third wave of autocratization is here: what is new about it? *Democratization*, 26 (7), 1095–1113.

Maerz, S.F., Lührmann, A., Hellmeier, S., Grahn, S. and Lindberg, S.I., 2020. State of the World 2019: autocratization surges – resistance grows. *Democratization*, 27 (6), 909–927.

Mair, P., 2006. Ruling the void. *New Left Review*, 42, 25–51.

Mair, P., 2013. *Ruling the Void: The Hollowing of Western Democracy*. London: Verso.

Marcuse, H., 1972. *Counterrevolution and Revolt*. Boston: Beacon Press.

Mitchell, T., 2011. *Carbon democracy. Political Power in the Age of Oil*. London: Verso.

Mol, A., 1995. *The Refinement of Production: Ecological Modernisation Theory and the Chemical Industry*. Utrecht: van Arkel.

Mol, A. and Sonnenfeld, D., 2000. *Ecological modernisation around the world. Perspectives and critical debates*. London: Routledge.

Mouffe, C., 2018. *For a Left Populism*. London: Verso.

Newig, J., 2007. Does public participation in environmental decisions lead to improved environmental quality? Towards an analytical framework. *Communication, Cooperation, Participation (International Journal of Sustainability Communication)*, 1 (1), 51–71.

Norris, P. and Inglehart, R., 2019. *Cultural Backlash. Trump, Brexit, and authoritarian populism*. Cambridge: Cambridge University Press.

Ophuls, W., 1977. *Ecology and the Politics of Scarcity*. San Francisco, CA: W.H. Freeman.

Pichler, M., Brand, U. and Görg, C., 2020. The double materiality of democracy in capitalist societies: challenges for social-ecological transformations. *Environmental Politics*, 29 (2), 193–213.

Plato, 1955. *The Republic*. Baltimore, MD: Penguin Books.

Radkau, J., 2014. *The Age of Ecology*. Cambridge: Polity Press.

Rancière, J., 1999. *Disagreement: Politics and Philosophy*. Minneapolis, MN: University of Minnesota Press.

Rockström, J., Steffen, W., Noone, K. et al., 2009. Planetary Boundaries: exploring the safe operating space for humanity. *Ecology and Society*, 14 (2), 32.

Roller, E., 2005. *The Performance of Democracies. Political Institutions and Public Policies*. Oxford: Oxford University Press.

Reckwitz, A., 2020. *The Society of Singularities*. Cambridge: Polity.

Scharpf, F.W., 1999. *Governing in Europe. Effective and democratic?* Oxford: Oxford University Press.

Sennett, R., 1999. *The Corrosion of Character: The Personal Consequences of Work in the New Capitalism*. London and New York: W. W. Norton.

Shearman, D. and Smith, J. W., 2008. *The Climate Change Challenge and the Failure of Democracy*. Westport, CT: Praeger.

Swyngedouw, E., 2000. Authoritarian governance, power, and the politics of rescaling. *Environment and Planning D: Society and Space*, 18, 63–76.

van Reybrouck, D., 2016. *Against Elections: The Case for Democracy*. London: The Bodley Head.
Wainwright, J. and Mann, G., 2013. Climate Leviathan. *Antipode*, 45 (1), 1–22.
WBGU, 2011. *World in Transition. A Social Contract for Sustainability*. German Advisory Council on Global Change, Berlin.
WCED, 1987. *Our Common Future*. Oxford: Oxford University Press.
Wilson, J. and Swyngedouw, E., 2014. *The Post-political and its Discontents. Spaces of Depoliticisation, Spectres of Radical Politics*. Edinburgh: Edinburgh University Press.
Wood, M. and Flinders, M., 2014. Rethinking depoliticisation: beyond the governmental. *Policy & Politics*, 42 (2), 151–170.

34
STRUCTURAL IRRESPONSIBILITY
Politics of an imperfect future

Barbara Adam

Acknowledgements

The arguments presented in this paper are based on research conducted during an ESRC funded Professorial Fellowship (2003–2007) entitled *In Pursuit of the Future*.

Introduction

Successive technological developments have hastened the pace of social life and, in conjunction with economic pressures, have dramatically reduced the futures horizon to a point where the present becomes the primary focus for decisions and policies.[1] This acceleration has a number of interdependent consequences for both knowledge and action. First, the increased pace and scale of change mean that the past becomes an ever less reliable guide to the future. Second, the faster the pace, the more our energies and attention are focused on the present. At the same time, however, the effects of our technologies tend to extend ever further into the long-term future: products of nuclear power will stay radioactive for an estimated one hundred thousand years; synthetic chemicals move through the food chain affecting beings for an unlimited period; carbon dioxide emissions contribute to climate change for an un-specifiable period and genetically modified organisms have the potential to mutate until the end of time. The associated uncertainty of long-term outcomes and the extensive drifting apart of actions and their effects pose significant problems for political democracies today. To address these necessitates a prior engagement with some implicit assumptions of the knowledge practices[2] involved, which I seek to explicate in this chapter. This involves making visible what previously had been taken for granted and was thus hidden from view.

At the political level, contemporary debates have entered the future worlds of tens, hundreds and even thousands of generations hence. Such extended timescales apply, for example, to appropriate responses to climate change, the management of nuclear power and its waste products, strategies about genetic engineering and the regulation of chemicals together with their globally dispersed pollutants. Such debates arise because environmental impacts reach deep into matter and across all of space and time, affecting an open future not just of human societies but also the earth's flora, fauna and even our climate. It means that decisions made, and policies established, by todays Liberal Democracies extend far beyond the period for which their representative governments are elected. Of course, potentially the impact of all political action extends beyond a government's period of office. For actions that affect us and our children in the near future, there is an implicit understanding that the public have given a mandate to the government of the day to act not just on behalf of their future, but also their children's future. However, with today's political decisions, which affect the very long-term future, this is no longer the case. The implicit contract is breached. Furthermore, in political contexts where impacts of present politics extend into open futures, the interdependent domains of action, knowledge and ethics have come adrift and, thus far, liberal democracies seem to lack institutional structures to compensate for this situation.

I begin this chapter by exploring how and why the elements of this interdependence have come adrift – how and why decisions and policies, knowledge of outcomes and responsibility structures are no longer compatible – and I consider the impacts of this mismatch on the capacity of liberal democracies to conduct themselves responsibly where they lack operational mandates. In the course of the exploration, I briefly investigate the temporal orientations of some of the key institutional guides for contemporary politics of the future, such as science, economics and law, as well as conventional moral codes that are drawn upon to establish what is right, good and just. The point is to try and re-establish some of the connections between action, knowledge and ethics, which are largely disconnected in todays Liberal Democracies and bring them back into a meaningful relation. The extensive powers of humans to not just change but also create nature have been recognized by Paul Crutzen, atmospheric chemist and Nobel laureate, who concluded that the world has entered a new geological age, which he called the Anthropocene.[3] The expansion of human influence – with nuclear, chemical and genetic technologies, for example – requires changes to politics and conventional institutional responsibility structures so that they may become adequate to their contemporary conditions.

Politics of the future

The political vacuum

Looking at the system of liberal democratic politics from a time perspective, it becomes quickly apparent that it has developed historically as a politics of space and matter, with its sphere of responsibility extending to a nation's territory, its resources and its wealth distribution. It is in charge of things that can be measured and counted, ranging from territories and people to institutions, traffic, crime, budgets and Gross National Products. However, much of today's politics operates not just in space but also in and over time for which, thus far, no appropriate institutional frameworks seem to have been established. With many of today's long-term policies, effects are stretched across vast periods of time and the processes involved marked by contingency, time lags and periods of invisibility where beginnings and ends, inception and impacts can no longer be held together in either theory of practice. In such contexts the politics of space and matter is out of its depths and no longer appropriate to the contemporary conditions of its making.

When risks and hazards, created within the jurisdictional time-space of a particular liberal democracy transcend their electoral boundaries, associated impacts are in effect externalised: to other nations and/or to successor generations. The problems are shunted along, moved outside the sphere of responsibility. This means the effects of policies are not just experienced by their voters, their children and their children's children, but by an open-ended chain of generations without vote, voice or advocates to speak for them. In the absence of any higher time-space authority, hazards externalised in time and space tend to be moved outside the horizon of concern of the acting nation's representative government in office. The long-term policies routinely pursued by contemporary liberal democracies, therefore, transgress not only the spatial but also the temporal boundaries of their political mandates and realms of jurisdiction. Moreover, since elected representatives are responsible to their electorate only, and since it is this electorate that bestows legitimacy on a government, the rights of future and distant people, who cannot enact that power relation, tend to be 'discounted' in a way that is analogous to the discounting of the future in economic processes. As such, politicians find themselves in a temporal context of structural irresponsibility.[4]

Importantly, for the production of long-term futures, today's politics draw on three dominant institutions: Science, economics and law. All three social institutions, however, have time-space characteristics that make them eminently unsuitable for the task of guiding future-creating policies. Science draws its evidence from accumulated knowledge of the past. Economics operates from the present for the present, that is, all its forays into the future are parasitical on successor generations of humans and fellow beings. Law is guided by precedent, insists on past-based causality for evidence and arbitrates future operations on the basis of tradition in a spatially anchored jurisdictional realm. All have their competencies rooted in space and matter and most depend for their functioning on bracketing all things temporal beyond the time of calendars and clocks. In light of this, I want to propose that the conventional guidance structure leaves Liberal Democracies ill-equipped to deal with long-term futures of their making. Without institutional structures for the operational realm of the future, therefore, today's future-creating actions are conducted in a political vacuum. To elaborate on this assertion, it is necessary to look in a bit more detail at the implicit assumptions that underpin the knowledge practices associated with these key institutions.

Knowledge vacuum

All three guiding institutions understand the future in contrast to the world of facts, that is, as the not-yet, thus mostly as empty realm of potential and choice, which becomes real only after it is activated into present existence. Bertrand de Jouvenel (1967) explains the distinction through the Latin *facta* and *futura*. *Facta* refer to past events, done, achieved, completed and thus empirically accessible as facts. *Futura,* in contrast, encompass that which has not yet come about, something non-factual, which will become a *factum* only after it has occurred. While the one has already taken (unalterable) form the other is still open to influence and thus 'capable of ending or being completed in various ways' (1967, 3). In other words, there can be no past possibilities and no future facts (Bell and Mau 1971, 9). It means that the past is closed to influence, thus open to factual knowledge while the future is open to choice and efforts to colonize and control, thus closed to factual inquiry. The distinction underpins the logic of scientific inquiry, economics and law, the very institutions, which are so centrally implicated in the creation and adjudication of contemporary techno-futures in progress. This dualistic distinction between *facta* and *futura* is difficult to uphold today.

Scientific laws are established on the basis that events, which have recurred reliably in the past, are expected to continue to do so in the future. If one has full and extensive knowledge of such recurring processes one can predict that, in the same circumstances, the same conjunctures will occur in the same way in the future. The source of knowledge for such predictions is thus a collection of past observations, projected into the future. This means that the past is the basis on which it is possible to know, for example, the next eclipse of the moon or that water will freeze at zero degrees centigrade. The socio-historical and economic world, however, does not provide us with equivalent past-based social laws. That is to say, the social past does not determine the social future in the same reliable way. History, therefore, is clearly not an infallible guide to what is to come. Despite this general difficulty, however, during the late sixteenth and early seventeenth centuries first attempts were made to tell the social future scientifically on the basis of aggregates of past and present facts. Rates of change rather than individual or unique change became the focus of predictive attention. This was the beginning of probability calculations. Church records, for example, showed that death rates were reasonably constant over time, as were the average life expectancy, the annual baptisms and the marriages. Even the causes of death seemed to follow identifiable patterns. With the application of statistical methods, it was possible to project those aggregated known figures into the future and predict such social patterns with surprising accuracy.

However, the accuracy of past-based predictions deteriorated with the pursuit of progress and innovative technology. In cases where there are no, or very few, past and existing aggregates of assembled facts, therefore, the future cannot be reliably predicted. This means that the more novel the situation to be projected is, the less scientific prediction will be appropriate as a tool for telling the probabilistic future. For UK citizens, for example, the BSE (Bovine Spongiform Encephalopathy) crisis during the late 1980s was a prime case in point. When cattle were afflicted by an unknown *prion* disease, which seemed capable of being transferred to humans, scientists had no prior knowledge upon which to predict future deaths of animals and humans. This drama of uncertainty, rooted in the lack of past knowledge and inadequacy of established tools, was played out daily on television and in the newspapers. Politicians and journalists were demanding predictions and prognoses about the progression of this disease in order to be able to act appropriately, while scientists desperately sought to explain that this was a situation where science was unable to provide the required knowledge. Without certainty of past facts, scientists were insisting, they had no basis upon which to calculate the probable future. Many years of research would be needed to accumulate and collate data to provide a secure base from which to make predictions about the progression of this unknown disease (Adam 2000).[5] To recap, science predicts the probable future based on known aggregates of causally connected past facts. This applies to knowledge about the cosmos, nature and the social realm. In cases of intense newness or innovation, where there are few or no past records, no relevant causal chains and/or no available accumulated data, there simply is no future to foretell. Thankfully, such cases are rare, and science tends to find enough existing evidence on which to build models of probable future occurrences.

A very different situation arises where futures are projected on the basis of *promised* outcomes. Not just economists and politicians make their intended actions public, today science too engages in projected, expected outcomes of chosen actions in the present. Such promised futures emanate regularly from the laboratories of science, medical research centres, pharmaceutical companies and many more institutions where science finds application. Thus, for example, with nuclear power the public was promised electricity too cheap to meter, with geno-technology cheap, nutritious food to feed the starving, as well as wholesale modernisation of agriculture and cures for numerous genetic diseases. The promises, projections and visions of potential issuing from the various branches of applied science are no more certain of their predicted outcome than those made by economists or politicians. They are subject to the same limitations and thus equally vulnerable to disappointment. Here, as everywhere else, conditions and interdependencies influence projected outcomes: The more innovative the practice, the less secure will be the basis from which to make accurate projections. Equally, the more socially interconnected the activity, the more chance there is for interference and derailment of the plans. Importantly, the more extensive the reach of actions into the future and the more interdependent and interconnected the processes involved, the more likely it is that unexpected mutations and tipping points will occur, derailing otherwise well calculated models of future occurrences. Thus, innovation, networked interdependency and temporal reach have inevitable knock-on effects for bringing promises to fruition, irrespective of whether the purveyors are economists, politicians or scientists. In the case of projected outcomes of planned actions, therefore, experts lack a privileged position with respect to the accuracy of their promised results. More importantly still, with predictions based on projected promises, these experts have abandoned the territory upon which the logic of their investigation of the future is founded and consequently operate like everyone else in the realm of speculation.

When politicians turn to science for guiding predictions about the future, therefore, they need to be aware what science can offer and where its boundaries to secure calculation are drawn. Furthermore, with respect to innovative technology, politicians need to recognize what precisely lies within and what outside the scientific sphere of competence. Importantly, they need to appreciate that knowledge systems rooted in space and matter bracket the temporal realm and with it much of the socio-scientifically created, time-space distantiated future, that is, the long-term impacts of many of today's scientific inventions and their applications in innovative technologies.

Similar contradictions are to be found with economic approaches to the future. Here too, evidence is rooted in factual data built up over time and predictions are established on similar foundations to those of science, that is, on the basis of knowledge rooted in the past. When probability theory is applied in economic contexts, for example, it is again aggregate phenomena that are being calculated and projected, such as the distribution of income and expenditure. In addition to these and other key features that allow for past-based prediction, economists have noted regularly recurring cycles of crisis, recovery and growth. Such patterns were observed within the retail price index, mortgage rates, bank base rates and many more economic variables. These proved strong predictors as long as no extra-ordinary circumstances arose. For example, the great depression of the late twentieth century, just like the banking crisis of the early twenty-first century, did not fit any of the mapped and projected cycles and consequently caught most economic forecasters by surprise. Since the economy is sensitive to socio-political events there is much that can and will interfere with even the most stable and established patterns of economic activity and thus thwart economists' calculations of future effects.

It is important to note that, analogous to scientific causal analyses and predictions, the foci of economic predictions are on past and present futures, the latter being ones that are imagined, planned, projected, and produced in and for the present. Moreover, the economic future is conceived as a (free) resource that equals money. As such it is traded, managed and controlled like any other resource. Costs and benefits of specific futures are calculated with reference to their exclusive utility for the present. To establish the present value of the future, finally, the future is discounted with the following effect: The further in the future the value to be calculated is, the less it counts from the position of the present. Thus, for example, serious trouble in a hundred years hence is considered negligible when discounted with reference to and for the present. The economic future is thus firmly tied to both the past and present. Given this orientation, economics is a poor knowledge base upon which to build and establish a responsible politics of the future.

The situation is equally problematic for liberal democracies' legal systems' engagement with the long-term future. Law is strongly oriented towards the past through 'precedence', 'grandfathering' and many other legal tools and strategies, whilst simultaneously creating and managing futures through its laws as guides to appropriate action. Tradition and institutional logic act as barriers to effective engagements with socio-environmental processes, which involve effects that are dispersed into the long-term futures. Law is generally considered to be conservative and oriented to the past, given that the purpose of law is to act as stabilising force in society, which makes it a powerful force to uphold the status quo. This is reflected in the pervasive practice of 'grand fathering' existing economic activities, which legally shields activities from compliance with stricter legal standards that might become necessary in light of new knowledge or changing social values. Similarly, the 'precedence principle' makes it difficult for law to deal with innovative technologies and time-space distanciated problems marked by substantial uncertainty. A third example would be the principle of path-dependence, which tends to accompany and shape legal reform with the result of biasing options towards existing institutional regimes, ideologies and precedents. Yet, of course, all these practices bleed into the future, setting conditions for and delimiting future actions.

Some of the key temporal assumptions, associated with the troubling *knowledge vacuum*, which underpin dominant knowledge practices informing Liberal Demcoracies' future-creating decisions and actions, are worth summarising at this point. First to note are the exclusively space- and matter-based knowledge practices, which are inappropriately adopted for a time politics of the future where effects outlast their creators and regulators by hundreds and even thousands of years. Second, reliance on the past tends to be largely inadequate for contexts where the complexity of potential outcomes is set in motion with uncertain outcomes. Third, economic futures tend to be approached from the position of and for the present, treated as a resource available for use as needed and discounted as deemed appropriate for present requirements. Yet, clearly, the *present future* today is the *future present*[6] of successors and it is they who have to deal with the consequences of the imposed colonisation and misappropriation of their rightful domain. Fourth, law's temporal logic and reach tend to be woefully inadequate for contemporary actions whose impacts extend to centuries and millennia. Finally, there is a need to acknowledge that the politics of space and matter operate without a mandate in the future-present of successors. This means that citizens of liberal democracies, their chosen representatives and their products with time-space distanciated impacts should be recognized as illegal colonizers. Together, these points indicate that liberal democracies operate in a *knowledge vacuum* as long as they do not adapt their knowledge practices to the temporal domains of their influence and making.

The moral vacuum

The situation does not improve when one scrutinizes either the ethical context or the moral assumptions that are brought to bear on what is considered to be right and just in the politics of the future. That is to say, politics marked by a double vacuum of practice and knowledge tends to bracket thoughts of accountability and responsibility for actions extending into the long-term future. Where neither outcomes could be foreseen nor causal links established, everyone is able to act with impunity: politicians, their expert guides and citizens.

The first thing to note is that members of contemporary liberal democracies tend to feel both legally and morally exonerated from responsibility when effects could not be foreseen at the time of action. Thus, for example, the people who counselled governments on whether or not to establish a nuclear capability, and who happened not to take account of the wide-ranging associated problems of safety, decommissioning and waste management, were and are not being held responsible for either the resulting health hazards or massive economic burdens. Non-knowledge and unintended or unforeseen consequences all tend to absolve actors from personal and public responsibility. The tide, however, is turning. Thalidomide, Asbestosis, smoking-related diseases and similar technologically produced hazards are cases in point where companies are being held responsible for the harm produced by their products. Thus far, however, such apportioning of responsibility for time-space distantiated effects is applied predominantly to cases where causal chains can be established over the lifetimes of individuals and companies. But what happens to responsibility in situations where effects do not materialise as symptoms for hundreds and even thousands of years? This clearly constitutes a problem because responsibility – be this of a political, scientific, economic, legal or personal kind – is tied to knowledge in contexts where lack of secure knowledge of outcomes is increasingly becoming a dominant feature.

This approach to responsibility appears to be deeply rooted in western cultural history. According to Hans Jonas (1984), contemporary ideas about moral conduct are predominantly rooted in the *polis*, the realm of social relations and human debate of Greek antiquity, which entailed a number of key assumptions that still resonate strongly with moral sentiments today. In the *polis*, responsibility was held to pertain between known individuals and excluded actions involving non-human things, created in the sphere of *techne* as well as those entailing physical toil in the sphere of work. Virtuous moral action was to be achieved in the here and now of political debate. This meant that moral action and matters of ethics were defined by close proximity, by effects of actions that were limited in time and space. The long-term future, in contrast, was associated with fate, providence and destiny, which was considered the realm of gods, thus outside the sphere of moral action and human responsibility. Third, this present-based, delimited morality was counterbalanced by an ethical orientation focused on the good and the beautiful, truth and virtue, ideas and ideals. Responsibility of individuals and political leaders was consequently defined by eternal values, to be enacted in the present by members of particular communities.

Obligation towards a technologically produced, open future is a much later development that arose with the age of science. It emerged with the capacity to create futures that outlast their originators and with it the human potential to threaten not just individual existences but the continuity of the species and life as we know it. The associated pursuit of progress destabilised eternal values and rendered them historical. Nothing in the western moral tradition was able to provide a base for the development of tools that could deal with this shift from an individual to a collective base, from local to global effects and from present impacts of actions that may not materialise as symptom for a very long time in some distant future. Today's common-sense ethical assumptions, inherited from the Greeks, therefore, are no longer adequate for the contemporary condition.

Effects of today's socio-technical, socio-economic and political processes are no longer spatially or temporally bounded. They are tied to systemic processes that ripple outwards in chain reactions of interdependence. For example, nuclear radiation, although most dangerous in the immediate vicinity of any leakage or accident, spreads inwards in matter and organisms, leaches outwards permeating space and extends temporally into the long-term future. Moral principles grounded in the immediacy of the here and now, therefore, are in urgent need of adjustment to fit the *un*bounded potential of outcomes. Expansion of responsibility to the potential reach of actions, however, places politics in a new and untested territory with respect to what can and can't be known, done and controlled. While responsibility associated with individuals and their deeds still holds good today, especially in the eyes of the law, for example, technological activity in general and the policies associated with innovative technologies in particular have the potential to affect the living conditions of all people now and in the future. This is not to suggest that the impact of decisions regarding such long-term effects as radioactive waste management, for example, will be equal across time and space, but simply to point out that the time-space dispersal of effects is no longer encompassed by a moral code focused on the actions of individuals. The changed context means that the moral project of modernity has become not just an individual but also a collective, international and cosmopolitan endeavour. National policies have to be enacted with an eye to actions and policies of other countries and with recognition of the temporally open, trans-boundary nature of potential disasters arising from present policy decisions.

Clearly, the transformative power of humans has always been extensive. In the industrial age, however, this capacity has reached undreamt of heights. In the process it has changed our relationship to nature. Today, nature is no longer the mere backdrop to human action but subject to human intervention and scientific invention. Flora and fauna, mountains and valleys, riverbeds and oceans, the biosphere and stratosphere – all are influenced, (re)created and produced by contemporary actions. Scientists have argued that this shift has ushered in a new age of Anthropocene. This implies that nature too has become ethically significant. Importantly, none of the future recipients of technological impact have their 'interests' represented in the socio-environmental polity of today.[7] Instead, human interests grounded in the short-term politics of the here-and-now are arbitrated by science, justified on the basis of economic arguments and legitimated by a legal logic that does not extend to the reach of human action.

Taken together, the points raised with respect to political, knowledge and moral vacuum bring us to the inevitable conclusion that despite the extensive scales involved, responsibility extends to the reach of our actions. This principle applies irrespective of whether or not the affected and afflicted are able to hold us to account. Moreover, our collusion with the policies produced by our political representatives makes each one of us individually and collectively responsible for the techno-futures set in motion; yesterday, today and tomorrow. We are charged therefore as individuals, experts and politicians not just to understand the contemporary drifting apart of action, knowledge and ethics[8] but also to seek openings for change that help bring back into touch those three spheres of social action which have come adrift during the scientific age. This, however, is significantly more difficult than it sounds and involves changes not just at the level of political structure and practice but also at a deep level of taken-for-granted assumptions.

Openings for change

The future as operational domain of science, economics and law is delimited by the respective logics of the policy-guiding institutions and their implicit assumptions about the reality status of the future. This, in turn, impacts on both the organisational structure and the temporal reach of contemporary liberal democratic politics. Openings for change, therefore, have to be explored and sought at all these levels.

At a conceptual level, there is an urgent need to move away from prediction and foresight exercises for decisions implicating the long-term future, where these methods have little purchase, to an acknowledgement of the limitations of science, economics and law with respect to long-term futures. Conventional expertise thus needs to be supplemented and it will be up to social debate to establish who might be best placed to take on the role of guardian of the future. Some of this debate is well established since the publication of the Brundtland Report (WCED 1987), which acknowledged sustainability as a futures issue and subtly challenged the taken-for-granted status quo of economic, scientific and socio-political approaches to the future. With its triple location in the environment, economy and society, sustainability was conceived inclusively and demanded approaches that could make common cause in contexts of differences and opposing tendencies.

Members of the German network *Netzwerk Vorsorgendes Wirtschaften*[9] proffer such a sustainability perspectives by thinking the triple relation as one and, through the concept of '*Vorsorge*' (literally translated: care for what lies ahead, care for the future), provide for sustainability this elusive extension into the future. Emphasis on *Vorsorge*, rather than scientific and economic concern with knowledge, prediction and foresight, shifts attention from the goal of certainty and control to moral engagements with an indeterminate future present that results from determining present actions. This is an important corrective to the conventional way of approaching the future as *present future*. In contrast to this convention, the *future present* is the primary domain of *Vorsorge*. In the spirit of the Brundtland Commission, it entails extension of both knowledge and concern to encompass present implication in potential outcomes, as they are stretched across space and time.

Importantly, it allows concerns about what is right and just, rather than only cost effectiveness, to enter considerations. Taking the standpoint of the future present means being mindful of the way current resource use affects the resource base of successors. *Vorsorge*, with its caring concern for what lies ahead, thus seeks to accompany present decisions and actions through their latent and invisible phases to their potential time-space distantiated impacts. This means that the responsibility involved is not imputed because we are held liable. Rather, it is a responsibility that is actively taken because we relate potential outcomes at some time and somewhere to present decisions and actions (Adam and Groves 2011). It thus encompasses responsibility in a context where reciprocity no longer applies, given that contemporaries and their successors are not co-present. Through *Vorsorge*, therefore, the needs of future generations can be related to present needs with the explicit aim of not compromising the capacity of the former to meet their needs, just as the Brundtland definition demanded. As such, *Vorsorge* implies engagement with a lived and living future present of successors that opens out the temporal scope to encompass the reach of our actions. This means, acknowledging our implication not just in spatially constituted ecological footprints but also in 'timeprints',[10] their temporal counterpart.

To operationalize *Vorsorge*, however, requires that futures in the making are understood as *fact* and thereby accorded reality status, a status rooted in intangible processes rather than merely their tangible outcomes. This cannot be achieved as long as we continue to hold on to the (implicit) distinction between *facta* and *futura*. It requires an understanding of the future as process in progress: on-going, open-ended and including the past. Thus, to appreciate the future as fact needs the temporal perspective to be opened up to encompass both past and future. The current context of debates about climate change, environmental degradation and pollution, helps us to recognise that our own present was our predecessors' empty and open future of fortune: their dreams, desires and discoveries, their imaginations, innovations and impositions, their hopes and fears, their creations. Our progress as well as our changing climate change, our colonial and contractual responsibilities as well as our global institutions, markets and financial systems were their empty, open futures in progress. Our contemporary condition is predecessors' creative imaginations working themselves out in and as our embodied, embedded and extended present as on-going, time-space-matter distantiating process that constitutes future presents of successors.

At the institutional level, openings for change need to be sought at the level of institutional structure, knowledge and ethics. To begin to envisage a politics appropriate to the anthropocene, and realize a politics of the long-term future, would need the politics of space and matter to be expanded to encompass the temporal reach of today's knowledge practices.

That is to say, it would require the creation of political structures suited to the future-creating contemporary condition. Since the techno-futures, which are created today, affect not just the societies who produced them, those others in time and space who are implicated through the time-space distantiated effects have a right to political representation. This would involve political structures that extend in time, thus beyond the United Nations and similar trans-national, space-based, political organisations. Moreover, it would entail that current governmental structures of 4 – 5 year periods of office be extended for political representatives whose remit and responsibility would be the long-term future. This would entail establishing institutional structures that encompass future generations who currently have no voice or vote, who therefore cannot hold us to account, but for whose livelihood we are *de facto* responsible as soon as currently produced techno-futures impact on their general wellbeing, their environments and their livelihoods. It means further that dominant knowledge institutions, which currently guide political decision-making, need to be opened up to include who-ever we might collectively declare to be experts on the future. This is a socio-political debate that has yet to get off the ground. Serious attention thus needs to be given not just to political but also social institutional structures, taken-for-granted assumptions and the implicit moral codes that guide considerations of what might be right and just.

Present political structures with their division into the legislative, executive and judiciary powers, need to be extended by a consultative power drawn from citizens. In contrast to the 'Konsultative' proposed by Patrizia Nanz and Claus Leggewie (2019), the explicit task of such a consultative arm of politics would include speaking for those not yet existing beings who are affected by current actions, which include not just humans but fellow beings with whom we share this earth. To take account of the future is already part a numerous political arrangements such as, for example, in Wales where concern for the wellbeing of future generations is constitutionally enshrined in the Wellbeing of Future Generations Act (2015), and operationalized with the appointment of a permanent commissioner. Despite the commissioner's remit being the wellbeing of future generations, the Act is conceived from within the politics of space and matter, with the future as an after-thought. Importantly, the task to consider wellbeing is not defined with respect to the reach of past and present actions but is focused instead on the exclusive wellbeing of future people. Thus, while such attempts are laudable steps towards a politics that extends to future generations, it does not yet deal with the issues I have addressed in this contribution. In this chapter I am suggesting more than a future of decades, which is already enshrined in numerous current inter/national agreements and acts. Rather, I am focused on the *timeprints* of actions and appropriate political horizons of concern. With the argument presented here, I do not want downplay the importance of current efforts to extend politics into the future: they are crucial. What I have been addressing, however, goes deeper and further than any already existing efforts of instituting generational justice. To avoid continued operations in the three-fold vacuum of political action, knowledge and ethics for long-term socio-political futures in the making, I have argued that there is a need to change not only political structure but also some of the associated, deeply embedded assumptions discussed above.

Coda

While the future has always been uncertain, humans were not called upon to take responsibility for what was outside their control and jurisdiction. They were merely required to act responsibly in and towards the realm that did not belong to them. In a world that is understood to be largely the outcome of human action, as encompassed in the newly defined age of the Anthropocene, these assumptions no longer apply. Crucially, futures emerging from those actions cannot be predicted with certainty on the basis of a known past. Past bonds of reliance on knowledge of outcomes, therefore, have to be broken and the uncertain, indeterminate, open-ended and largely unknown futures created by human action encompassed in socio-political responsibility structures. Uncertainty of potential outcomes can no longer absolve social producers of long-term, open-ended impacts from responsibility to those affected in remote futures and places. This requires a shift in standpoint and perspective. Thus, when actions are viewed from the position of potentially affected others, it becomes more likely that decisions are reached, which take account of their and not just our interests. Therefore, when quests for control and certainty, in contexts of uncertainty, are accompanied by genuine care and concern for future presents – both latent and potential – openings for change begin to emerge. The embedded structures of irresponsibility become visible and can begin to be addressed. Importantly, expectations of mastery are tempered and responsibilities to others (humans and fellow species), distant in time and space can be taken seriously.

Notes

1 For detailed work on those processes, see Adam (1998 and 2004) as well as Adam and Groves (2007).
2 'Knowledge practices' as shorthand for the combination of assumptions, concepts, approaches and (inter/trans)actions.
3 The much debated Anthropocene has become an environmental buzzword ever since it was proposed by Paul Crutzen (Crutzen, P.J. & Stoermer, E.F. 2000).
4 On time-based structural irresponsibility see Adam and Groves (2007); see also Beck (1992/1986 and 1999) who first raised the issue of structural irresponsibility, if on the basis of a different analytical path.
5 Medical physicians, who are regularly expected to make prognoses about the progression of their patients' recoveries from illness, for example, would be in a similar predicament when confronted with an unknown disease.
6 Niklas Luhmann (1982: 281) introduced the distinction between 'present future' and 'future present' for the social sciences. He suggested that 'present future' is a utopian perspective that enables prediction whilst 'future present' is technologically constituted and as such allows transformation of future presents into present presents. Chris Groves and I have developed the distinction further (Adam and Groves 2007) and, as I show in this paper, taken it into a different conceptual direction with significant consequences for sustainable praxis.
7 Where future generations play a role, as for example in the Welsh *Wellbeing of Future Generations Act* (2015), the future involved is not explicated, implies a few generations of humans only and does not include reach of actions.
8 For an extended thesis on this subject see Adam and Groves (2007).
9 www.vorsorgendeswirtschaften.de see also Netzwerk Vorsorgendes Wirtschaften (2013).
10 This concept was first developed and theorized in Adam and Groves (2007). It emphasizes the temporal reach of actions without neglecting space and matter, draws attention to the tendency to consume future potential and appropriate successors' futures, and points to a time-based mismatch between the consumption of natural resources and the earth's ecological capacity to regenerate them over time.

References

Adam, B., 1998. *Timescapes of Modernity. The Environment and Invisible Hazards*. London and New York: Routledge.
Adam, B., 2000. Mediated Risk: BSE in the Broadsheets. In S. Allan, B. Adam, and C. Carter, eds. *Environmental Risks and the Media*. London and New York: Routledge, 117–129.
Adam, B., 2004. *Time*. Cambridge, UK and Malden, MA: Polity.
Adam, B. and Groves, C., 2007. *Future Matters. Action, Knowledge, Ethics*. Leiden: Brill.
Adam, B. and Groves, C., 2011. Futures Tended: Care and Future-Oriented Responsibility. *Bulletin of Science, Technology & Society*, 3(1), 17–27.
Beck, U., 1992/1986. *Risk Society. Towards a New Modernity*. London: Sage.

Beck, U., 1999. *World Risk Society*. Cambridge: Polity.
Bell, W. and Mau, J., eds., 1971. *The Sociology of the Future. Theory, Cases, and Annotated Bibliography*. New York: Russell Sage Foundation.
Crutzen, P.J. and Stoermer, E.F., 2000. The 'Anthropocene'. *Global Change Newsletter*, 41, 17–18.
Jonas, H., 1984. *The Imperative of Responsibility. In Search of an Ethics for the Technological Age*. Chicago: Chicago University Press.
De Jouvenel, B., 1967. *The Art of Conjecture*, transl. from French by N. Lary, London: Weidenfeld and Nicolson.
Luhmann, N., 1982. *The Differentiation of Society*. New York: Columbia UP.
Nanz, P. and Leggewie, C., 2019. *No Representation Without Consultation: A Citizen's Guide to Participatory Democracy*. Translated by Damian Harrison with Stephen Roche. Toronto: Between the Lines.
Netzwerk Vorsorgendes Wirtschaften, eds., 2013. *Wege Vorsorgenden Wirtschaftens*. Marburg: Metropolis Verlag.
WCED (World Commission on Environment and Development), 1987. *Our Common Future* (The Brundtland Report). Oxford: Oxford UP.
Welsh Assembly Government. (2015). Well-being of future generations (Wales) act (2015 anaw 2).

INDEX

Abbott, T. 196
acceleration 153–5, 159–61
accountability 248, 255–60, 377
actor–network theory (ANT) 157–8
Adam, B. 495–505
adaptability 60
advertising 227, 231, 233
affirmative action 330
Africa Climate Week 245–6
agency 178, 182–5; *see also* consumerism; nudge strategies; representation
Agenda 21 40–1, 165, 418
2030 Agenda for Sustainable Development 6, 43–4, 258, 485
aggregation 395–6
agonistic democracy 309
agriculture: biodiversity 321–2; food democracy 356–7; food sustainability 352–5
Alaimo, S. 45
all-affected principle 71–2, 256–7, 261
Almond, G. 478, 490
Anand, S. 143
Andersson, K. 333
Angelo, H. 267
Angermeier, P. 319
Anthropocene 7, 44, 61–2, 83–4, 461–2, 471–2, 502; contested concept 462–4; deconstructivist frame 465–7, 470–1; democratic changes 469–71; futures 86–7; geological definition 462; positivist frame 462, 464–5; skepticism 462–3; sustainability politics 467–9; temporality 117–18; uneven impacts 88, 110, 112–13; *see also* climate change
anti-capitalist movements *see* emancipatory movements
Arendt, H. 32, 109, 115–16, 184–5
Arias-Maldonado, M. 51–62

Arikan, G. 192
Aristotle 22–3, 185
Arrighi, G. 156
Asara, V. 413–24
attitude-behaviour gap 230, 389
Austria 175
authoritarianism 4, 21, 489; eco-authoritarianism 7, 55–7, 212–14, 451–2, 477–8; *see also* populism
autocratic states 431, 433, 441; environmental and climate protection 438–9; holistic sustainability policy 433; intergenerational justice 434–5; life expectancy and infant mortality 437–8; public debt 436; uncertainty handling 434
autonomy 125, 480–2, 488–9; *see also* agency; freedom
Axelsson, S. 247

Baber, W.F. 261
Bachrach, P. 180
Bäckstrand, K. 5, 237–48, 256–7, 287
Bahr, T. 368–79
Baker, S. 35–47
Ball, T. 303
Balvanera, P. 293
Bansard, J.S. 283–93
Baptiste, B. 293
Baratz, M.S. 180
Barnes, S. 404
Barnett, J. 306
Barnett, M. 183
Barry, J. 391, 393–4
Bartlett, R.V. 261
Bauman, Z. 480–2
Bawa, K.S. 317
Béal, V. 267–76
Beck, S. 286

Index

Beck, U. 153–61, 480
Beck-Gernsheim, E. 480
Beckman, L. 73, 214
Bedall, P. 181
behavioural economics 387–91, 394–7; *see also* nudge strategies
behaviour-impact gap 230–1
Beinlich, A.-K. 191
Ben-Nun Bloom, P. 192
Benjamin, W. 113–14
Benson, M.H. 485
Bentham, J. 140
Berlin, I. 125
Bertelsmann Transformation Index 28–9
Bertuzzi, N. 418
Betts, A. 344
Bexell, M. 254–64
bias 77
Biermann, F. 342
biodiversity 313–14, 322–3; agriculture 321–2, 352; Biosphere Reserves 320–1; conservation 314–15; democracy 315–17; democratic legitimacy 317–19; environmental health 375–6; protected areas 319–20; science 315–16
Biosphere Reserves 320–1
Black Lives Matter 4
Black, R. 341
Blair, T. 270
Blatter, J. 345
Blättler, A. 345
Blühdorn, I. 57, 61, 171, 248, 421, 476–91
Boas, I. 342
Bolsonaro, J. 283
Boltanski, L. 480
Booher, D. 456
Born, B. 274
Bornemann, B. 1–15, 350–64, 393, 397
Bos, A.L. 330
Boström, M. 173
Botsman, R. 402–3
bottom-up democratization 14, 172–4, 307–8; biodiversity 317; urban sustainability 268–9, 271–3; *see also* emancipatory movements; environmental movements
Bourdieu, P. 164
Bowman, S. 228
Brand, U. 166, 181, 223
Braungart, C. 191
Brenner, N. 267
Briggs, J. 471
Brondizio, E.S. 46
Brulle, R. 226, 418
Brundtland Report 5, 37–41, 136–7, 207, 448, 467, 484, 502–3
Brunner, K.-M. 163–75
Burawoy, M. 455

Burger, P. 135–47, 393, 397
Burke, E. 85
business actors *see* non-state actors; private sector; transnational corporations (TNCs)

Calvário, R. 422
Campbell, J. 306
Canada 275
Caney, S. 73
Canney, S.M. 314
Capability Approach (CA) 140–6
capitalism 163–4, 166, 168–71, 173–4; global risk 154–7, 160; green economy 42–3, 165–6, 172–5, 229–31; Marxist critiques 31, 479–80; political ecology critique 334–5, 415–17, 483–6, 490–1; technological change 452–3; transnational corporations 180–1; *see also* consumerism; neoliberalism; transnational corporations (TNCs)
Carlone, H.B. 289
Carolan, M.S. 287
Carroll, C. 315–16
carrying capacities 135–7
Carson, R. 36
Carter, A. 308
Castells, M. 157
Chakrabarty, D. 89, 109
Chandler, D. 465
change *see* transformation
Chaplin, J. 194
Chernobyl 115–16
Chiapello, È. 480
China 218
choice *see* consumerism; nudge strategies
Christen, M. 135–47
Christianity 193–6; *see also* religion
Christoff, P. 5
cities *see* urban sustainability
citizen's assemblies 76–9, 98, 100–1
citizenship 61, 345–6, 393–4, 447–9
Clarck, W.C. 333
classical antiquity 22–3, 124, 185, 501
classical political economy 36
climate change 115, 301–2, 310, 421; agonistic democracy 309; cosmopolitan democracy 306–7; court cases 85–6; deliberative democracy 304–7, 449; food production 352; health 376; local democracy 307–8; migration 341–3; representative democracy 302–4; *see also* Anthropocene
climate denialism 6, 32–3, 193–4, 227, 275–6, 283
climate governance 216–17, 237–8, 248–9; democratic legitimacy 239–41; non-state actors 239–45; regime types 438–9; regional climate weeks 245–6; Sweden 246–8; techno-ethical approach 395–6; UNFCCC 242–5

climate movement 4, 59, 84–6, 166, 182–3, 275, 487
closed sustainability 59–60
Coetzer, K.L. 320
collaborative consumption 401–2, 409–10; challenges 408–9; definitions 402–3; digitalization 403, 406–8, 410; empirical research 404–5; platform cooperativism 405–6; social dining 406–8
collective action *see* climate governance; global governance
Collier, P. 344
colonialism 111–13, 167–8
commercial advertising *see* advertising
Committee of Economic, Social and Cultural Rights (CESCR) 370–2
competitive elitism 99–100
complex democracy 359
complexity theory 158–9
Conference of Parties (COP) *see* United Nations Framework Convention for Climate Change (UNFCCC)
Conroy-Ben, O. 293
consensus model 29–30, 32
consequentialism 56
conservation *see* biodiversity; environmental movements
conspiracy theories 32–3
Constant, B. 124
constitutionalism 24–5
constructivist representation 87, 93; constitutive 90; creative act 87–9; partial nature 89–90; performative practices 90–2
consumerism 174–5; consumer sovereignty 229–32, 390; democracy 170–4, 487–8; development of 163–5; digitalization 164–5; Fordism 168–9; green economy 165–6, 172–3; historical roots 167–8; limits 231; neoclassical economics 164; post-Fordism 169–71; social sciences 164; societal lock-in 170–2, 485; *see also* collaborative consumption; nudge strategies
consumption corridors 231, 233
Contarini, G. 24
contingency 114–17
Convention on Biological Diversity (CBD) 314, 316
Corbera, E. 288–9
Corporate Social Responsibility 228
corporations *see* non-state actors; private sector; transnational corporations (TNCs)
cosmopolitanism 262–3, 306–7
cosmopolitanization 153–5, 157, 159–61
COVID-19 378, 485–7
Craig, R.K. 485
Crawford, N.C. 92
crises 114–16, 160; democracy 478–82; food 352–3
Crouch, C. 479, 482
Crutzen, P. 463

Dachner, N. 274
Dahl, R. 29, 70–1, 79, 180, 433
Daly, H. 36, 39
Danish Board of Technology (DBT) 98
Dauvergne, P. 62
Davies, A. 401–10
de Jouvenel, B. 497
de Moor, J. 422
DeCaro, D. 315
decentralization *see* bottom-up democratization; deliberative democracy
decision-making *see* deliberative democracy; nudge strategies
Declaration of Alma Ata 372
Deflorian, M. 248
degrowth 39, 320, 487; *see also* environmental movements; political ecology
Deitz, S. 289
Delgado, R. 291
deliberative democracy 30–2, 60, 70–1, 96–7, 129–30, 184, 233; Anthropocene 468–9, 471; biodiversity 318–19; climate change 304–7; as critical social theory 99–100, 448–9; deliberative culture 103; economic practices 103; food 356; gender 331; global governance 256–8; institutional turn 100–1; mini-publics 76–9, 98, 100–1; nudge strategies 396; as policy instrument 97–9, 224, 439; science 285–7; systems thinking 101–3; theoretical history 99–101; *see also* participatory democracy
deliberative mini-publics 76–9, 98, 100–1
deliberative policy analysis 453–7
Della Porta, D. 413
democracy 1–2, 107–8; biodiversity compatibility 315–17; consumerism 170–4; freedom 121–2, 124; material dimension 25–6; post-democratic turn 21, 57, 479–82; proceduralism 51–3, 71, 260–3; recent transformations 3–5; religion 192–3, 195–8; rhetorical ubiquity 21; sustainability compatibility 2–3, 7, 51–5, 57–61, 146–7, 213–15, 476–8, 489–91
democratic food *see* food democracy
democratic inclusion 24–5, 28–9, 32–3, 69–73, 80; all-affected principle 71–2; deliberative mini-publics 76–9; future-generations 73–4; gender 330; incongruence problems 71–3; science 287–91; *see also* exclusion; participatory democracy; representation
democratic legitimacy 216, 239–41, 259–62, 318–19, 477; crisis of 480, 482, 487–8
democratic pathways 301–2; green agonistic 309; green cosmopolitan democracy 306–7; green deliberative democracy 304–6; green local democracy 307–8; green representative democracy 302–4
democratic representation *see* representation

democratic states 433, 441; environmental and climate protection 438–9; holistic sustainability policy 433; intergenerational justice 434–5; life expectancy and infant mortality 437–8; public debt 435–6; uncertainty handling 434
democratic theory 33; Age of Revolution 24–5; classical antiquity 22–3; competitive model 31; consensus and majoritarian models 29–30; definitions 26–9, 145–6; early-modern 23–4; empirical indicators 28–9; global governance 255–7; inclusion 70–3; Marxism 31; material and symbolic equality 28; normative models 30–1; pluralism 32–3; realist (minimal) definition 26–7; Rule of Law definition 27–8; toolbox approach 32; *see also* representation
democratic values *see* accountability; representation; transparency
democratization *see* bottom-up democratization
demos see democratic inclusion; exclusion
dependency theory 36, 156–7, 166
depoliticisation *see* post-democratic turn; technocratic governance
descriptive representation 86
development *see* sustainable development
Dewey, J. 455
Di Chiro, G. 335
Diani, M. 415–16
Díaz-Reviriego, I. 289
digitalization 164–5, 173, 403, 406–8, 410
Dingwerth, K. 260
direct democracy *see* bottom-up democratization; deliberative democracy; participatory democracy
Disch, L. 88, 93
discursive power 225, 227–8
disinformation campaigns 4
distributive justice 142–3
diversity *see* deliberative democracy; inclusion; plurality
Dobson, A. 74, 85, 123–4, 302, 415
Dolinga, S. 222–33
Doneys, P. 328–36
Dovers, S.R. 209, 215
Driessen, M.D. 193
Dryzek, J. 55, 100, 256–7, 305, 307, 451, 456, 463
Dutch Republic 23
Duvall, R. 183
dynamization 159–61

Eckersley, R. 5, 87, 110, 183–5, 263, 303–4, 414, 417, 470
eco-authoritarianism 7, 55–7, 212–14, 451–2, 477–8
ecological governance 209–10, 212–15, 217–18, 438–9; *see also* sustainability governance
ecological modernisation 42–3, 270, 486
ecological rationality 451

ecologism *see* environmental movements; political ecology
ecomodernism 57, 130, 464–5
economic development *see* sustainable development
economic growth 36, 38, 110, 154, 159–61, 165–74, 211, 229, 232, 401; *see also* capitalism; consumerism; sustainable development
economic inequality 28, 75–6, 89, 171–2; colonialism 111–13, 167–8; consumerism 164, 166; distributive justice 142–3; food 352–4; gender 333–4; geographical bias 88, 166, 239, 244, 270, 290–1, 302–3, 341, 352–3; health 374–6; sustainable development 38–40, 275–6; *see also* emancipatory movements; political ecology
economics: behavioural economics 387–91, 394–7; classical political economy 36; future valuation 499; neoclassical economics 164
ecovillages 308
Edkins, J. 113
Ehrlich, P. 36, 55, 476
Ekeli, K.S. 74
elections 25–6, 345–6
electromobility 166
Elliott, K. 59–60
Elster, J. 304
emancipatory dysfunctionality 480–1
emancipatory movements 4, 172–4, 182–3, 413–14, 480–2, 489–90; *see also* bottom-up democratization; environmental movements
Engelen, E. 316
Engels, F. 156
environmental health 375–6
environmental impact assessments (EIAs) 447–8
Environmental Kuznets Curve (EKC) 215, 218, 313–14
Environmental Movement Organisations (EMOs) 418–19
environmental movements 414, 423–4, 447–9, 477–8, 482–3, 489–90; climate movement 4, 59, 84–6, 166, 182–3, 275, 487; conservationists 415–18; democracy 417–20; environmental justice 417; Extinction Rebellion (XR) 101; food movements 273–5, 353, 357–8, 408–9, 422–3; Fridays for Future 4, 84–6, 166, 182, 487; institutionalisation 418; interstitial activism 420–3; labour and class 416–17; March for Science 283–4, 292; political ecology 415–17, 483–6; socio-environmental movements 416–20, 489–90; *see also* bottom-up democratization; emancipatory movements
Environmental Non-Governmental Organisations (ENGOs) 417–18
Environmental Performance Index (EPI) 213, 218
epidemics 371, 375–6; COVID-19 378, 485–7
Erdal, M.B. 344–5

Index

escalation 154–5, 159–61
Essoka, J. 418
ethical responsibility 500–5
Eudaemonism 140–1
European Commission 165–6
European Union (EU): biodiversity 316–17; migration 343–6; right to health 370; technocratic governance 450; voting rights 345–6
Ewert, S. 313–23
exclusion 70, 72–3, 90, 244, 303, 486–9; consumerism 170–1; gender 329–31; local food systems 274; temporality 110–11; *see also* inclusion
experts *see* technocratic governance
extinction 314–15
Extinction Rebellion (XR) 101

Faets, S. 108
Fairmondo 406
Felson, M. 402
feminism 92, 165, 329; political ecology 334–5; *see also* gender
Fiorino, D. 207–18
Fischer, F. 302, 308, 447–58
food democracy 350–1, 356, 363–4; critical perspectives 358–9; food sustainability 359–63; problems 356–7; social dining 406–8
food movements 273–5, 353, 357–8, 408–9, 422–3
Food Policy Councils (FPCs) 274–5
food sustainability 350–6, 363–4; food democracy 359–63; politics and policy 353–4; problems 352–3
Fordism 168–9
Forester, J. 456
Forno, F. 421
Fossil Free Sweden (FFS) 246–8
Foster, J. 485
France 269, 271–2, 276
franchise 25–6, 345–6
Fraser, N. 333
freedom 121–3, 131; ancient and modern democracy 124; autonomy 125, 480–2, 488–9; conceptual distinctions 125–6; exceptions 130; nature's value 126–8; reflective rationality 129–30; sustainabilities 123–4; value of 125–6, 128
Freedom House Index 28–9
Frenken, K. 173
Fridays for Future 4, 84–6, 166, 182, 487
Friedmann, H. 273
Fuchs, D. 222–33
functional differentiation 155–6
future design model 78
future generations 73–4, 102, 333, 504; deliberative mini-publics 76–9; participation on behalf of 74–6; representation 76–9, 84–7, 303–4

futures 86–7, 107–8, 495–6, 504–5; intergenerational justice 71–2, 76–9, 108, 113, 144–5, 432, 434–5; knowledge 497–500; law 499–500; moral responsibility 500–5; openings for change 114–17, 502–4; political 496–7, 503–4; predictability 497–8; promises and projections 498–9; science 497–9, 501–3; *see also* temporality

Gallie, W.B. 478
Garner, R. 306
Gastil, J. 79
Gates Foundation 376–7
gender 4, 165, 328–9, 336; political representation 329–31; sexual and reproductive health and rights 377–8; sustainable development 332–6; *see also* feminism
geoengineering 462, 464
geographical bias 88, 166, 239, 244, 270, 290–1, 302–3, 341, 352–3; *see also* exclusion
Germany 168–9, 175; food redistribution initiative 409; non-state actors 244; urban sustainability 269, 274–5
Giddens, A. 451
Gilley, B. 55–6
Global Climate Action Summit (2018) 244–5
global climate justice movement *see* climate movement
global governance 254–5, 263–4, 468–71; deliberative democracy 256–8; empirical models 257–60; futures 504; normative debates 255–7; procedural concerns 260–3; stakeholder democracy 256–60; *see also* climate governance; United Nations
Global North/South bias *see* geographical bias
globalization *see* cosmopolitanization; neoliberalism; transnational corporations (TNCs)
goal-setting 43–4; Sustainable Development Goals (SDGs) 2, 6, 43, 99, 165–6, 229, 258, 328, 354, 373–6
Goodin, R. 51, 126, 451
Gore, A. 217
Görg, C. 181
Gorz, A. 415
Gould, C. 261
governance 207–8; collaborative consumption 404, 406–9; ecological governance 209–10, 212–15, 217–18, 438–9; futures 504; multi-level governance 71, 241–9, 262–3; short-termism 73–4, 84–5, 209, 217, 435, 496–7, 504; through goals 43–4; *see also* climate governance; global governance; technocratic governance
Gramsci, A. 171
grassroots movements *see* bottom-up democratization; emancipatory movements; environmental movements

Graziano, P.R. 421
green cities *see* urban sustainability
green democratic pathways: agonistic 309; cosmopolitan 306–7; deliberative 304–7; local 307–8; representative 302–4
green economy 42–3, 165–6, 172–5, 229–31
green republicanism 129, 184–5
greening of religion 194–5
Griggs, D. 467
Grosz, E. 114
growth *see* economic growth
Guenther, L. 289–90
Gumbert, T. 387–98
Guterres, A. 244–5
Gutmann, A. 100

Habermas, J. 27, 30–1, 76–7, 100, 129–30, 184, 190, 304
Hailwood, S. 127
Hajer, M.A. 86–7, 90–1, 456
Hamari, J. 404
Hambler, C. 314
Hammond, M. 96–103, 306
handbook: concept 8; future outlook 14–15; overview 8–14
Hanusch, F. 58
Hara, K. 78
Haraway, D. 333
Hardin, G. 36, 55
Hardt, M. 115
Harvey, D. 156
Hassanein, N. 274, 358–9
Hausmann, D.M. 391
Haynes, J. 191–2
Hayward, B. 304
Hazen, S. 448–9
Healey, P. 456
health 368–9, 378–9; environmental health 375–6; global health policy 371–3, 375–6; philanthropy 376–7; private sector 376–7; regime types 436–8; sexual and reproductive 377–8; social determinants 371; universal health coverage (UHC) 374–5; *see also* human right to health
Hedonism 140
Heidenreich, F. 21–33, 183–4
Heilbroner, R. 55, 212, 476
Held, D. 244, 306
Hervey, A. 306
Heyward, C. 77–8
historical time 109–14
HIV-AIDS 372
Hobbes, T. 23, 55
Hochstetler, K. 213
Holden, B. 307
Holzscheiter, A. 91, 368–79
Honig, B. 32
Hsu, A. 238

Human Development Index (HDI) 141
human right to health 368–9, 378–9; climate change 376; codification 369–71; political contestation 371–3; universal health coverage UHC) 374–5
human rights 261, 368–70, 488; sexual and reproductive 377–8; social and economic 375
hybrid governance *see* global governance; governance

identity politics 28
imperial mode of living 166, 171–2, 174
inclusion 24–5, 28–9, 32–3, 69–73, 80; all-affected principle 71–2; deliberative mini-publics 76–9; future-generations 73–4; gender 330; incongruence problems 71–3; science 287–91; social inclusion 343–5; *see also* exclusion; participatory democracy; representation
incongruence problems 71–3
India 167–8
individual choice *see* consumerism; nudge strategies
individual rights 27–8, 33, 262–3; democratised exclusion 486–8; migrants 345–6; *see also* freedom; human rights
Indonesia 195–6
industrial pollution 112, 209–10, 483
industrialization 167–8
inequality *see* economic inequality; exclusion; geographical bias
infant mortality 437–8
Inglehart, R. 415, 478–9, 483, 490
Innes, J. 456
instrumental power 224–6
instrumental rationality 100
intergenerational justice 71–2, 76–9, 108, 113, 144–5, 432, 434–5
Intergovernmental Panel on Climate Change (IPCC) 286–9
Intergovernmental Science- Policy Platform on Biodiversity and Ecosystem Services (IPBES) 211
international governance *see* climate governance; global governance
international relations (IR) 5; global governance 255–7, 468–9; performativity 91–2; power dynamics 180–1; university curricula 289
intersectionality 4–5, 292–3, 334–5
interstitial activism 420–3
Islam 193, 195–6; *see also* religion

Jacobs, A.M. 73
Jaeger-Erben, M. 173
Jamieson, D. 301
Jevons, W.S. 36
Johannesburg Summit *see* World Summit on Sustainable Development (WSSD)

Index

Johnson, A. 289
Jonas, H. 501
Jonas, M. 163–75
Jones, R. 390
Joubert, M. 289–90
justice 137, 142–7; distributive justice 142–3; food 355; gender 333–6; intergenerational justice 71–2, 76–9, 108, 113, 144–5, 432, 434–5; metric 143–4; non-ideal 145

Kahneman, D. 389, 394
Kairós-Theory 114–17
Kalfagianni, A. 227
Kallis, G. 422
Kant, I. 481–2
Karlsson, R. 131
Karlsson, S. 290
Karnein, A. 92, 303
Kelz, R. 107–18
Kenis, A. 308, 421
Keutsch, F. 286
King, A. 227
Klintman, M. 173
Knappe, H. 1–15, 83–93, 107–18
Köhrsen, J. 189–98
Kuyper, J.W. 5

Lang, S. 274
Lang, T. 356
Langhelle, O. 216
Latouche, S. 42
Latour, B. 157–8
law 499–500
Leach, M. 302, 467–8
Leach, W.D. 318
Leggewie, C. 449, 504
legitimacy *see* democratic legitimacy
Leimgruber, W. 345–6
Lenox, M. 227
Levkoe, C.Z. 274
liberal democracy 30–3, 44–6, 52–3, 56–61, 121–2, 131; cosmopolitanism 262–3; ecological governance 212–16; Environmental Performance Index (EPI) 213; environmentalist critiques 126–30, 172; freedom 122–6; futures 496–504; liberal societies 60–2, 183; *see also* democratic states; representation
libertarian paternalism 390–1
life expectancy 436–8
Lijphart, A. 29–30
limits to growth discourse 36–9, 45–6, 462; *see also* planetary boundaries
linear time 109–11, 113–14
Litfin, K. 308, 466
Littig, B. 163–75
lobbying 225–6
local democracy *see* bottom-up democratization
local food systems 274, 360–1

Locke, J. 23
Lodi, G. 415–16
Lövbrand, E. 83–4, 86, 108
Lovelock, J. 212–13, 450–1
Lovrich, N.P. 333
Luhmann, N. 115, 155–6
Lukes, S. 183
Lundegård, I. 289

Macdonald, K. 258
Macdonald, T. 258
MacGregor, S. 423
Machin, A. 301–10, 395
MacKenzie, M. 79
Mackinnon, C. 329
Mahony, M. 286
majority rule 2, 29–30, 53, 487–8
Malthus, T. 36, 55
Maniates, M. 232, 396
Mansbridge, J. 73–4, 91
March for Science 283–4, 292
Marquardt, J. 237–48, 461–72
Marrakech Partnership for Global Climate Action 243–4, 246
Marshall, T.H. 345
Martinez-Alier, J. 416
Marx, K. 156
Marxism 31, 156–7
Mascia, M.B. 320
Mateo, M.M. 92
Mathijs, E. 308
Matson, P. 333
Mattson, J. 404
Mayer, M. 269
Meadowcroft, J. 209
mechanical dysfunctionality 481
Meehan, K. 289
Mert, A. 461–72
methodological nationalism 155–7, 159, 340
migration 339–40, 346–7; climate change 341–3; mobility 340–1; participation 345–6; remittances 342; social inclusion 343–5
Milkman, K.L. 290
Mill, J.S. 36
Miller, D. 255–6, 305
Miller, M.K. 346
Mills, C. 391
mini-publics 76–9, 98, 100–1
Minkenberg, M. 192
Mitchell, R.E. 316
Mitchell, T. 170
mixed government 23–4
mobility 340–1
Möhlmann, M. 404
Montesquieu 23
Monti, M. 450
Moore, G.E. 140
moral consequentialism 56

moral responsibility 500–5
Moran-Taylor, M.J. 342
Morrow, O. 409
Mouff, C. 31, 309
multi-level governance 71, 241–9, 262–3
multilateral action *see* climate governance; global governance
myopia *see* short-termism

Naegler, L. 420
Naess, A. 38
Nagendra, H. 291
Nagle, M.K. 111
Nanz, P. 1–15, 504
Narain, S. 180
Narveson, J. 127
Näsström, S. 72, 469
nationalism: methodological 155–7, 159, 340; populism 3–4, 6, 27–8, 58, 216, 283, 487
Nationally Determined Contributions (NDCs) 237–8, 248; democratic legitimacy 239–41; multi-level governance 241–6; Sweden 246–8
Natura 2000 framework 316–17
nature: human relation to 293, 332–3, 502; intrinsic value 126–8; political representation 303; *see also* Anthropocene; biodiversity
needs 138, 143–4
negative emission technologies (NETs) 286–7
negative liberty 125
Negri, A. 115
neoclassical economics 164
neoliberalism 110; behavioural economics 394–5; consumerism 164, 170–3, 405; health policy 372; power 180–1, 225–30; sustainable development 38–41, 485; urban sustainability 269–71; *see also* consumerism; ecomodernism; transnational corporations (TNCs)
Network of Regional Governments for Sustainable Development (2019) 246
network theories 157–8
Netzwerk Vorsorgendes Wirtschaften 503
Neupert-Doppler, A. 107
New Social Movement Theory 416
Newell, P. 289
Niemeyer, S. 305
Nita, M. 196
non-governmental organizations (NGOs) *see* non-state actors
Non-State Actor Zone for Climate Action (NAZCA) 238, 242, 244–5, 247
non-state actors 5, 237–8, 248–9; climate governance 239–42; democratic legitimacy 239–41; global climate regime 242–5; public-private partnerships 180, 257, 376–7; regional level 245–6; Sweden 246–8; *see also* emancipatory movements; environmental movements; transnational corporations (TNCs)

Nordhaus, T. 450
Norton, B. 54, 59–60
nudge strategies 387–8; assessment 396–7; citizenship 393–4, 397–8; climate governance 395–6; ease of implementation 394; governance agendas 394–6; individual behaviour 389–90; libertarian paternalism 390–1; neoliberal governance 394–5; preference transformation 391–4; social practice theory 397
Nussbaum, M. 28, 128, 140–1, 143

Offe, C. 97
Olson, M. 434
Olsson, P. 467
open sustainability 59–60
Ophuls, W. 55, 212, 476
opportunity *see* futures
opposition 26
Ordway, S. 36
Osborn, F. 36
Our Common Future see Brundtland Report

paludiculture 322
Paris Agreement 237–9, 241–4, 247–9
Parsons, T. 182
participatory democracy 60, 70–1, 223–4, 259, 447–9, 490; Anthropocene 468–71; biodiversity 318–19; corporate power 231–3; deliberative policy analysis 453–7; food 358–9, 361; future generations 74–6; gender 330–1; migration 345–6; science 287–91; *see also* deliberative democracy; inclusion; representation
Partzsch, L. 178–85
Pasgaard, M. 290
past injustice 111–14
Pateman, C. 455
Pellizzoni, L. 422
performativity 91–2; *see also* constructivist representation
Persson, Å. 287
Peters, M.E. 346
philanthropy 376–7
Pickering, J. 287, 463
Pielke, R. 468
Pitkin, H. 85–6, 182–3
planetary boundaries 27–8, 38–9, 60, 131, 135–6, 210–11, 286–7, 462, 487; *see also* limits to growth discourse
platform cooperativism 405–6
Plato 22–3, 490
plurality 32–3, 57, 60, 129, 257, 433
Poland 98–9
the political 31, 421–2
political ecology 334–5, 415–17, 483–6, 490–1; ecological governance 209–10, 212–15, 217–18, 438–9; *see also* emancipatory movements; environmental movements

514

political franchise 25–6, 345–6
political representation *see* representation
pollution 112, 209–10, 483
Polybius 23
Pope Francis 196
populism 3–4, 6, 27–8, 58, 216, 283, 487
positive liberty 125
post-democracy 479
post-democratic turn 57, 479–82
post-Fordism 169–71
post-materialism 415, 483
post-political *see* technocratic governance
post-secularity 190–2, 197–8; *see also* religion
power relations 178, 185; definitions 179–80; discursive 225, 227–8; gender 331–6; global governance 257; instrumental 224–6; power over 179–82; power to 179; power with 179; structural 225–7
practice theory 5
preference transformation 391–4
prefigurative politics 116–17, 420–3
Prescod-Weinstein, C. 284
presentism *see* short-termism
Preuss, U.K. 97
Primary Health Care (PHC) 372, 375
private sector 212, 227–8, 376–7, 405–6; *see also* non-state actors; transnational corporations (TNCs)
proceduralism 51–3, 71, 260–3; *see also* participatory democracy
product service systems 402–3
progress 109–10, 160
progressive movements *see* emancipatory movements; environmental movements
protected areas 319–20
proxy representation 76, 79, 85–6; *see also* mini-publics; representation
public campaigning, religion 195–7
public debt 435–6
public image 227–8
public sphere *see* deliberative democracy; participatory democracy
Purcell, M. 274

Qureshi, S. 289

radical democracy *see* emancipatory movements
Ranger, S. 317–19
Rask, M. 316
rationality 100, 391–2; ecological 451; reflective 129–30; *see also* deliberative democracy; technocratic governance
Ratté, S. 449
Rawls, J. 123, 126–30, 142–6, 304
Raynor, S. 286
Raz, J. 128
realism 255

Reckwitz, A. 480
recognition 28, 289–90
redistribution marketplaces 403
Redpath, S.M. 318
reflexivity 60, 129–30, 159–61
refugee 342
regime type 431–3, 441; environmental and climate protection 438–9; holistic sustainability policy 433; intergenerational justice 434–5; life expectancy and infant mortality 436–8; public debt 435–6; uncertainty handling 434
Regional Climate Weeks 245–6
regional platforms 245–6
regulation *see* climate governance; governance; sustainability governance
regulatory failure 83–4, 86
Reisch, L.A. 397
religion 189–90, 197–8; democracy 192–3, 195–8; greening of religion 194–5; post-secularity 190–2, 197; public campaigning 195–7; self-secularization 196–8; sustainable development 191–8; United Nations 191–2, 196
representation 25, 70, 83–4, 93, 256–8; Anthropocene 469–71; climate change 302–4; constitutive 90; constructivist representation 87–93; as creative act 87–9; future generations 76–9, 84–7; gender 329–31; partial 89–90; performative practices 90–2; science 287–90; temporality 110; *see also* exclusion; inclusion; participatory democracy
Republic of Venice 24, 30
republicanism 30, 32–3; early-modern 23–4; freedom 122–6, 129–30; green republicanism 129, 184–5; power 179
resilience 61, 136–7, 355, 486–7
responsibility 500–5
Resurrección, B.P. 328–36
Retamal, M. 404
Ricardo, D. 36
Right-to-Know legislation 448
right-wing populism 3–4, 6, 27–8, 58, 216, 283, 487
rights *see* human rights; individual rights; liberal democracy
Rio Earth Summit (1992) 5, 40–1, 165–6, 448, 484
Rockström, J. 60, 286, 315
Roger, C. 244
Rogers, R 402–3
Rosa, H. 153–61
Rosanvallon, P. 32
Rosol, M. 267–76
Rousseau, J.J. 25
Rückert-John, J. 173
rule of law 27–8
Ruser, A. 306–7
Rydén, O. 316

Sandoval, M. 406
Sarkozy, N. 271
satisfaction of needs 138, 143–4
Sauer, B. 92
Saward, M. 87–9, 91
scarcity 56
Schäfer, M. 173
Schellenberger, M. 450
Schlosberg, D. 127, 421
Schmid, C. 267
Schmid, S. 345
Schmitt, C. 31
Schor, J. 164, 173
Schumpeter, J.A. 26
Schwägerl, C. 463
science 283–5, 291–3; biodiversity 315–16; decision-making 285–7; deliberative policy analysis 454; futures 497–9, 501–3; local and Indigenous knowledge 293; opening up 292–3; participation 288–91; recognition 289–90; representation 287–90; teaching 289; *see also* Anthropocene
Scoones, I. 302, 332
Scriven, T. 127–8
Scruggs, L. 214–15
Sealey-Huggins, L. 112
secularization thesis 189–90; *see also* religion
selectorate theory 434
self-regulation 226–7
Sen, A. 140, 143
Sennett, R. 480
separation of powers 23–4
Setälä, M. 69–80
sexual and reproductive health and rights 377–8
Shahar, D. 56
sharing economy *see* collaborative consumption
Sharp, J. 471
short-termism 73–4, 84–5, 209, 217, 435, 496–7, 504
side effects *see* escalation
Siller, P. 449
Simon, C.A. 333
Smith, A. 36
Smith, G. 74, 96–103
social acceleration 153–5, 159–61
social capital 183
social dining 406–8
social inclusion 343–5
social media 165
social movements *see* bottom-up democratisation; emancipatory movements; environmental movements
social nature 332–3
social practice theory 397, 404
sociology 155; Anthropocene 465–7; complexity theory 158–9; consumerism 164; functional differentiation 155–6; futures 498–9; methodological nationalism 155–7, 159; network theories 157–8; reflexive dynamization 159–61; religion 189–98; systems theory 155–7; *see also* economics; international relations (IR); political ecology
Sontag, K. 339–47
sortition 101
South Africa 371–2
sovereignty 27–8
Spaeth, J. 402
Sperl, M. 368–79
Spivak, G.C. 88, 336
stakeholder democracy 256–60, 318
state 217–18; democratic exclusion 488; democratic viability 212–15; ecological governance 209–11, 214–15; legitimacy 216; migration 340; planetary boundaries 211; role in sustainability 211; *see also* autocratic states; democratic states
steady state economy 36
Steel, B.S. 333
Steffek, J. 261–2
Stephens, P. 12
Stevenson, H. 256–7, 307
Stirling, A. 302, 310
Stockholm Resilience Centre 39
Stokes, M. 315
Stoll-Kleemann, S. 313–23
Streeck, W. 171
structural power 225–7
structure-agency debate *see* power
subjectivity 480–2
substantive representation 85
sufficiency 231, 233
suffrage 25–6, 345–6; *see also* representation
Sunstein, C.R. 387, 390, 392–3, 395
supranational governance *see* climate governance; global governance
sustainability governance 5–6, 212, 222–4, 487; Brundtland Report 5, 37–41, 136–7, 207, 448, 467, 484, 502–3; corporate power 225–33; deliberation 97; ecological governance 209–10, 212–15, 217–18, 438–9; instruments 439–41; nudge strategies 389–91, 394–8; planetary boundaries 27–8, 38–9, 60, 131, 135–6, 210–11, 286–7, 462, 487; self-regulation 226–7; *see also* climate governance; global governance; governance; technocratic governance
sustainability transformation 14–15, 116–17, 471, 484–6; consumerist democracy 170–4; escalation 153–5; futures 502–5; power 182–5; private sector 212, 230–1; reflexive dynamization 159–61; requirements 223–4; sociological theories 155–9; sustainable preferences 391–4; *see also* democratic pathways
sustainable cities *see* urban sustainability

Index

sustainable consumption *see* collaborative consumption
sustainable development 35–6, 44–7, 54, 107–8, 207–8, 432, 484–6; Anthropocene 467–9; consumerism 170–4; democratic compatibility 1–3, 5–7, 51–5, 57–61, 146–7, 476–8, 489–91; freedom 121–4; gender 332–6; green economy model 165–6; health 374–6; historical context 36; institutionalisation 40–4; justice 142–7, 275–6; limits to growth discourse 36–9, 45–6, 462; migration 343–5; normativity 135–9, 141–2, 145–7; production and consumption 42; regime type 433–41; religion 191–8; strong and weak forms 37–9, 42–3, 45–6, 54–5; well-being 138–42, 145–7
Sustainable Development Goals (SDGs) 2, 6, 43, 99, 165–6, 229, 258, 328, 354, 373–6
sustainable food *see* food sustainability
sustainable migration 344–5
sustainable preference transformation 391–4
Sweden 246–8, 270–1
Switzerland 25, 29, 344–6
systemic dysfunctionality 480
systems theory 155–7, 208
Sze, J. 335

Tarasuk, V. 274
Taylor, M.J. 342
techno-ethical governance 395–6
technocratic governance 449–52, 457–8; Anthropocene 462, 464–5, 467–8; deliberative policy analysis 453–7; environmental critique 452–3
teleological history 109–10
temporality 107–9, 117–18, 495; colonialism 111–13; contingency and opportunity 114–17; historical time 109–11; knowledge vacuum 497–500; moral responsibility 500–5; past injustice 112–14; political vacuum 496–7, 503–4; *see also* acceleration; futures; short-termism
Thailand 455–7
Thaler, R. 387, 389–90
Thatcher, M. 110
Thøgersen, J.B. 397
Thomas, P. 289
Thompson, D.F. 85–6
threshold approach 143–5
Thunberg, G. 4, 84, 245
time *see* acceleration; futures; temporality
Tocqueville, A. 434
Toffler, A. 403
toolbox approach 32
transformation 14–15, 116–17, 471, 484–6; consumerist democracy 170–4; escalation 153–5; futures 502–5; power 182–5; private sector 212, 230–1; reflexive dynamization 159–61; requirements 223–4; sociological theories 155–9; sustainable preferences 391–4; *see also* democratic pathways
Transition Towns 308, 421
transnational corporations (TNCs) 5, 7, 222; discursive power 225, 227–8; instrumental power 224–6; power over 180–1; rise of 228–9; strategies to limit 232–3; structural power 225–7; undermining democracy and sustainability 230–3, 479; *see also* non-state actors; private sector
transnational governance *see* climate governance; global governance
transparency 245, 248
Trump, D. 3–4, 283
trusteeship 85–6
Tully, J. 309
Tversky, A. 389, 394

UK 167–8, 270; Citizens' Assemblies 78, 98, 101
uncertainty 434
uncertainty *see* futures
United Nations: 2030 Agenda for Sustainable Development 6, 43–4, 258, 485; Biodiversity Conference (COP15) 112; Brundtland Report 5, 37–41, 136–7, 207, 448, 467, 484, 502–3; Conference on Environment and Development (Rio Earth Summit) 5, 40–1, 165–6, 448, 484; Conference on Sustainable Development (Rio+20) 5, 42, 165; Development Program (UNDP) 245–6; Framework Convention on Climate Change (UNFCCC) 196, 237–8, 241–6, 248, 257; Green Economy model 42–3; Intergovernmental Panel on Climate Change (IPCC) 286–9; Millennium Development Goals (MDGs) 42, 373; religion 191–2, 196; right to health 370–3; Sustainable Development Goals (SDGs) 2, 6, 43, 99, 165–6, 229, 258, 328, 354, 373–6; UNESCO Declaration on Science 288, 290; World Summit on Sustainable Development (WSSD) 41–2; *see also* global governance
United States 167–9, 214, 217, 447–8; lobbying 226–7; migration 344; urban sustainability 272–3
universal health coverage (UHC) 374–5
urban sustainability 267–8, 275–6; contesting 271–3; food movements 273–5; geographical bias 291; grassroots movements 268–9, 271–3, 420–3; neoliberalism 269–71
Urry, J. 158
utopianism 57–8

values *see* accountability; inclusion; representation; transparency
van der Hel, S. 283–93
Veblen, T. 164
Venice 24, 30
Verba, S. 478, 490

veto players 433
Victor, D. 217
Vorsorge 503

Wachsmuth, D. 267
Wagenaar, H. 456
Wallerstein, I. 115, 156–7
Warre, M.E. 32
Warren, M.E. 79
Watson, J.E.M. 319
Weber, E. 75
Weber, M. 180
Welch, B. 391
well-being 137–42, 145–7, 211, 333, 504; *see also* human right to health
Welzer, H. 449
White, L. 193–4
Wilhite, H. 173
Wilson, E.O. 314
Wissen, M. 166
Wissenburg, M. 121–31, 450
women's rights *see* feminism; gender
Wood, A. 313–14

Worker, J. 449
World Bank 372
World Commission on Environment and Development (WCED) *see* Brundtland Report
World Conservation Strategy – Living Resource Conservation for Sustainable Development (1980) 36
World Health Organization (WHO) 369, 372, 374–6
World Summit on Sustainable Development (WSSD) 41–2
Worthington, R. 316
Wright, E.O. 102
Wurster, S. 431–41

Yellow Vest movement 276
Young, I. 70
Young, R.S. 284

Zalasiewic, J.A.N. 465
Zerzan, J. 130
Zevallos, Z. 284
Zürn, M. 71

Printed in the United States
by Baker & Taylor Publisher Services